Up Against the Law

Justice, Power, and Politics

COEDITORS
Heather Ann Thompson
Rhonda Y. Williams

EDITORIAL ADVISORY BOARD
Peniel E. Joseph
Daryl Maeda
Barbara Ransby
Vicki L. Ruiz
Marc Stein

The Justice, Power, and Politics series publishes new works in history that explore the myriad struggles for justice, battles for power, and shifts in politics that have shaped the United States over time. Through the lenses of justice, power, and politics, the series seeks to broaden scholarly debates about America's past as well as to inform public discussions about its future.

More information on the series, including a complete list of books published, is available at http://justicepowerandpolitics.com/.

Up Against the Law

Radical Lawyers and Social Movements, 1960s–1970s

. . . .

LUCA FALCIOLA

The University of North Carolina Press Chapel Hill

© 2022 Luca Falciola

All rights reserved

Set in Charis by Westchester Publishing Services

Manufactured in the United States of America

The University of North Carolina Press has been a member
of the Green Press Initiative since 2003.

Complete Library of Congress Cataloging-in-Publication Data for this title
is available at https://lccn.loc.gov/2022015994.

ISBN 978-1-4696-7028-7 (cloth: alk. paper)

ISBN 978-1-4696-7029-4 (pbk.: alk. paper)

ISBN 978-1-4696-7030-0 (ebook)

Cover illustration: William Kunstler at the University of Cincinnati, 1969
(Ken Hawkins/Alamy Stock Photo).

To Silvia and her radical joy of living

Contents

Up Against the Law

Introduction

· ·

A press photo, May 1968: A young law school graduate has been severely clubbed by police during a student demonstration at San Francisco State College. Blood leaks from the wounds onto his clean-shaven face and his newly purchased professional suit. Through the gore he yells at police.

A video recording, circa 1969: After addressing a theater full of radical students with an inflammatory speech, a long-haired, scruffy lawyer salutes the crowd. Clenching his fist, he shouts, "All power to the people. Right on!" He receives a thunderous standing ovation.

An intelligence dispatch, 1970: FBI director J. Edgar Hoover informs a special agent that a lawyer "is in reality the leader of the Black Panther Party although he does not identify himself as such." Hoover also requests that this person be placed on the list of the most dangerous subversive individuals.

A best-selling book—*Soledad Brother*—1970: George Jackson, a Black Panther icon and the author of the book, makes multiple references to his "favorite person." This person is actually his lawyer, who has fallen in love with him, worked tirelessly for his release, arranged for the publication of his famous epistolary, and organized one of the most vocal defense committees ever seen.

A California newspaper, August 1971: A young lawyer faces charges of smuggling a gun into San Quentin prison just before George Jackson's ill-fated jailbreak. Hounded by the FBI and fearing for his life, he would go into hiding, leave the country, and remain underground for thirteen years.

A lawyer's memoir, 1994: "I felt that these men, society's outcasts, were my people, my constituents. . . . I wanted to demonstrate that I was with them completely and that I recognized the significance of this moment. I wanted them to know I was not just another lawyer with a briefcase saying, 'I'll do the best I can.' I wanted them to know that I was willing to go to the wire for them."

· · · · · ·

Fragmentary sources such as these are enough to give a glimpse of a phenomenon as much significant as overlooked: during the 1960s and 1970s, lawyers and social movements wove profound, intricate, and multifaceted relationships. While a generation of Americans were exploring the outer reaches of protest, scores of lawyers put their hearts and souls into radical causes. They made themselves and their skills available to activists and militants of any kind, in the most diverse circumstances, not only in the courtrooms but also in the streets, behind prison walls, around military bases, on picket lines at work sites, on university campuses, across destitute neighborhoods, and within Indian reservations.

And yet the observers and scholars who have examined those two decades of widespread political mobilization have generally focused on other social actors, such as students, racial and sexual minorities, workers, and soldiers. When lawyers enter the picture, they are often granted only a secondary part, hovering in the background, filing lawsuits from their downtown offices, or escorting their clients to arraignments in their formal attire.

To be sure, some studies have maintained that lawyers play a crucial role in social movements and have connected this phenomenon to both the legalistic spirit of the American people and the structural design of the common-law system. Following Alexis de Tocqueville, many commentators have stressed the salience of law and the centrality of attorneys in U.S. culture.[1] Litigation, indeed, has always been considered a valuable form of political action in the United States. The government can be questioned through lawsuits and before courts, where the neglect of constitutional values can be redressed.[2] As historian Lawrence Friedman put it, legal initiatives provide "nonstatist mechanisms through which individuals and groups can demand high standards of justice from government."[3] Civil liberties litigation before the Supreme Court, as everyone knows, has shaped national policy in areas of intense social and political concern. In particular, the use of lawsuits as a device of social transformation has dramatically increased since the 1950s, opening the door to the claims of disenfranchised people.[4] The extraordinary success of legal liberalism in the 1960s rested on the faith that courts, notably the Supreme Court, were powerful engines of change and could correct most of the flaws in American society.[5]

From a different perspective, critics of legalism have argued that social change in the United States is primarily—and almost exclusively—conceived within institutional and conventional channels. Political scientist Stuart Scheingold identified the existence of a "myth of rights," wherein citizens associate moral conduct with rule following, cherish the idea of "freedom under the law," and constantly overrate the progressive capacity of the law. As politics must be conducted in accordance with the law, every political issue tends to become a legal issue.[6] According to this line of reasoning, too, the widespread presence and engagement of lawyers in social movements would be an ordinary and recurring feature of the U.S. system.[7] Once again, building on Tocqueville's early intuitions, it is predictable that Americans would see legal practitioners as prominent actors in molding public life and democratic institutions.[8]

Certainly, such an underlying nexus between law and society helps to explain why lawyers and movements have been so deeply interwoven, especially in periods of sweeping reformism. And yet many of the lawyers who participated in the social struggles of the 1960s and 1970s rarely saw the law as a means to redress social issues and strove for a fundamental change of power relationships. While offering representation to activists and insurgents, they identified with their clients, including the most controversial ones, and they challenged their professional standards, including the most revered ones. In the process, these lawyers altered their priorities and transformed their habits. They used the courtrooms as political arenas and developed new strategies of litigation. Their presence alongside activists and militants was pervasive not only—and quite predictably—in court but also out of court. Many of them became deeply involved with the organization of dissent, taking personal risks and endangering their own careers. By virtue of their embrace of radicalism, they also formulated a far-reaching critique of the legal system: they ended up questioning the neutrality, the color blindness, the transformative power, and, in some instances, even the intrinsic value of the law. As a result, they shook up the legal arena and simultaneously afforded social movements invaluable energies.

Since the 1970s, legal scholars and sociologists have adopted the category of "cause lawyers" to designate the attorneys who operated outside the mainstream practice, dedicating their efforts to the pursuit of specific political or moral commitments. However, this definition looks intrinsically loose, as it conflates lawyers who retained a strong faith in court-based reform and lawyers who were highly skeptical of litigation-centered approaches to social change. Indeed, cause lawyers could be on the Left, on the Right, or simply devoted to public interest issues that cut across political lines.[9] By contrast, this book emphasizes the agency and reconstructs the history of "radical lawyers"—namely, partisan lawyers who stood unmistakably on the Left, joined the most combative social movements, shared their clients' substantive political claims, sought to transform legal questions into political issues, and criticized the law as an instrument perpetuating systemic injustice.[10]

Without a doubt, the phenomenon of radical lawyers blossomed in the wake of the social mobilization of the 1960s. The cycle of protest of the "long sixties" provided lawyers with exceptional revolutionary perspectives, a huge groundswell of antigovernment sentiment, extraordinary organizing resources, iconic clients with global resonance, and new platforms to make their voices heard.[11] Those seismic years substantially redefined the meaning of legal-political engagement and represented the zenith of that experience.[12]

However, the modern notions of radical lawyer and legal militancy first emerged in the late nineteenth century, and most notably in 1886–87, during the campaign to defend the eight anarchists charged with the bombing at Chicago's Haymarket Square. While sympathetic lawyers battled in the courtroom, the trial created an opportunity to publicly argue for the right to insurrection and against the injustice of the capitalist system. The labor slogan "An injury to one is an injury to all" translated into reality with a broad mobilization to free the defendants. Following this campaign, which could not prevent the execution of the anarchists, the first legal defense organizations that would assist agitators on a consistent basis were created.[13]

In fact, a more codified practice known as "radical labor defense" took shape later, in response to the struggles of the Industrial Workers of the World—a confrontational labor union founded in 1905, which became the victim of mob attacks and state repression. The Wobblies, as its members were known, hired specialized lawyers and rallied masses of supporters through defense committees on behalf of dissenters who were in trouble with the law, and they did so by championing direct action and castigating the legal system. In 1925, the Communist Party's International Labor Defense (ILD) inherited this tradition, taking center stage as the most prominent radical defense organization in the country. Known as the Red Cross of the labor movement, the ILD supported renowned defendants, such as the two Italian anarchists Nicola Sacco and Bartolomeo Vanzetti, but also unknown immigrants who were singled out as subversive and threatened with prosecution and deportation.

The ILD's lawyers and activists also defended those who were discriminated against because of the color of their skin. In doing so, the ILD orchestrated a number of legal-political campaigns, including the one to stop the executions of the Scottsboro Nine, a group of Black young people who were unjustly charged with raping two women on a train in 1931.[14] The ILD also served as the North American section of the International Red Aid, a network of committees established by the Soviets to provide legal, material, political, and moral support to the international proletariat, allegedly the victim of bourgeois and fascist repression. Therefore, the ILD's intervention crossed borders and extended to other continents. But such a tight relationship with the Soviet Union made its provision of help increasingly selective and controversial, especially when Stalinism imposed the Red Aid sections to disregard non-communists and critics of Soviet repression.[15]

In the meantime, another organization, the National Lawyers Guild (NLG), was born and gradually emerged as the main beacon of radical legal defense in the twentieth century. Established in February 1937 as the first integrated and progressive bar association of America, the Guild set out to fight in the name of free speech, for the rights of workers, and against the prosecution of leftist militants. As its constitution read, the NLG aimed "to unite the lawyers of America in a professional organization which shall function as an effective social force in the service of the people to the end that human rights shall be regarded as more sacred than property rights."[16]

Quite paradoxically, the NLG was born as an ally of the government, as it supported President Roosevelt's New Deal, which then faced staunch opposition from the all-white and mainly conservative American Bar Association. Frank P. Walsh, a progressive lawyer and a labor advocate close to the Democratic administration, served as the first president of the NLG, while sitting or retired judges featured among its early national officials. Guild members, who totaled two thousand by the end of the organization's first year of activity, ranged from progressives to liberals, from communists to civil libertarians.[17] In April 1945, the NLG was one of the forty-two consultant organizations selected by the U.S. government to participate in the San Francisco Conference, which resulted in the creation of the United Nations Charter. After the war, the Guild also sent observers to the Nuremberg trials, and two of its affiliates were part of the U.S. prosecution team.[18]

While the Cold War unfolded, the NLG naturally morphed into a force of political opposition that made common cause with but was never controlled by the Communist Party USA. Guild lawyers pledged to assist political undesirables who were not only targeted by the red scare but also frequently denied counsel by mainstream professionals. Guild attorneys represented Communist Party members, alleged communists, and many of the people who were pursued by the FBI and subpoenaed by the House Un-American Activities Committee. Among others, they rallied around Julius and Ethel Rosenberg, a pair of communist activists accused of spying on behalf of the Soviets by passing along secrets on the atomic bomb. They also defended the Hollywood Ten, a group of entertainment professionals who were incarcerated and blacklisted because they refused to answer questions regarding their communist affiliation. Labeled as the "legal bulwark of the Communist Party," the Guild itself was investigated and ostracized. Under President Eisenhower, Attorney General Herbert Brownell threatened to list the NLG as a subversive organization, and many affiliated attorneys left it in the course of the 1950s. As a result, the Guild almost collapsed, surviving on a shoestring for a decade.[19]

It was in the wake of the civil rights movement that the NLG came back to life and reconnected with the social movements. In the Guild's laboratory, the tradition of radical defense and legal mobilization was rediscovered and expanded, updated and recast. Indeed, most of the radical lawyers of the 1960s and 1970s were members of the NLG or had some ties with it. According to many testimonies, "radical lawyer" and "Guild lawyer" were practically synonyms at that time. More than any other organization, the Guild functioned as a magnet for those who wanted to foster systemic change and possessed legal skills, no matter what they intended to do with those skills. To be sure, some radical lawyers shared multiple affiliations and did not necessarily, or consistently, identify with the Guild in the first place. A few others found the NLG too overtly partisan, while others again refused to be part of any professional or political association. Notwithstanding, the Guild remained an unparalleled point of reference for both lawyers and activists who fiercely opposed the establishment.

For this reason, this book sharpens its focus on the NLG, unearths its main activities, and follows its trajectory from the early 1960s until the late 1970s, when a new political era opened up. But a caveat is in order: *Up Against the Law* is not conceived as an organizational history. Rather, it uses the NLG as both a thread and a frame for capturing a larger phenomenon. This research indeed builds from the assumption that the story of the attorneys, law students, legal workers, and organizers who were affiliated with the Guild or operated in its orbit provides a unique window into the collective engagement of radical lawyers in the social movements of the long sixties.

This story also offers a foray into bigger questions that illustrate the paradoxes inherent in radical activism pursued through law. First, each Guild member was forced to work through the intrinsic tension of being radical and being a lawyer at the same time and within the framework of a liberal democracy. In other words, this group of lawyers constantly strove to reconcile the norms and ethos of a profession conventionally linked to conservatism and law abidance with their own outright criticism of the legal foundations of the system. Could an officer of the court embrace such an oppositionist stance? Was there a place for lawyers in the revolutionary process?

Second, the practice of Guild attorneys showcases another related conundrum—that is, the use of legal resources and judicial procedures to uphold the rights and liberties of militants who advocated the overthrow of political institutions, rejected the legitimacy of courtrooms, and questioned the validity of the law. Was the law ultimately a guarantee for defiant subversives or a perennial threat? To what extent could a radical use the law? And, more generally, could the law serve liberation rather than domination?

The multilayered and elusive nature of lawyers' activism makes it intrinsically hard to trace and reconstruct. Extant literature is not of much help, as it mostly centers on the biographies or autobiographies of a few celebrated attorneys.[20] This scholarship delves into the life and achievements of these protagonists, offering some relevant details on radical lawyering but often missing the broader picture.[21] There is also a body of research surveying a few significant trials, such as the Chicago Eight, yet the experience of radical lawyers is never rendered in its collective dimension.[22] The literature on the antiwar movement, the underground revolutionary organizations, and the political repression of that period generally neglects the importance of lawyers; when it makes reference to their initiatives, it never examines their meaning and impact in depth.[23] The few historical studies that attempt to chart the organizational efforts of lawyers tend to focus on a few associations whose contributions were momentous, such as the American Civil Liberties Union (ACLU), but whose identity and scope were liberal and progressive, not radical.[24]

Therefore, we draw our basic knowledge about the Guild from a couple of publications edited by its own members and from a few coeval works written by movement sympathizers.[25] Albeit interesting and rich in details, these works deliver a self-portrait composed of collections of documents and autobiographical essays, lacking both historical contextualization and cross-checking of sources. Quite predictably, these reconstructions also betray a self-congratulatory perspective. For example, they tend to omit the ideological sectarianism of the organization or its indulgence toward confrontational forms of dissent, which jeopardized the Guild's cooperation with other groups and tarnished its reputation among the general public.

To produce a more detached and granular historical analysis, this book is based on extensive archival research on the records of the NLG and its sister organizations, and on the personal papers of a number of lawyers, all drawn from a number of different collections located across the country. A set of original interviews with members of the Guild who were active between the 1960s and the 1970s complement the documentary sources. Far from adding mere color to the chronicle, oral histories are key to understanding how protagonists revised their identity and constructed themselves as activists, with all the complexities that this process involved. They also provide a recorded account of individual trajectories, discourses, and everyday practices, of which no written traces remain.[26] To avoid a distorted, top-down perspective, testimonies include both prominent lawyers and unsung legal workers. All together, they convey the reality of an engagement that was truly collective.

The first chapter tells the story of a band of radical lawyers who traveled south to help the civil rights defendants and, in the process, cemented their relationship with the people they represented, questioned their faith in the justice system, thought anew about their professional duties, and brought back home an infectious enthusiasm about social change.[27] As soon as the new leftist activism erupted on campuses, spilled into the streets, and inevitably fell into the police's clutches, Guild lawyers were ready to shore it up. The second chapter examines how radical lawyers gradually structured mass defense strategies that not only enabled activists to exercise their rights in the face of mounting repression but also politicized justice and mobilized supporters. As the third chapter illustrates, the political and generational storm of the sixties did not spare the Guild and its milieu: youths' visionary fervor and palingenetic aspirations upset the organization and drew it closer to the most combative social actors. An utterly radical critique of law also gained currency and chimed with a new model of militant litigation—analyzed in chapter 4—that literally transferred contention into the courtrooms through a number of recurrent tactics.

In parallel, radical lawyers redefined their own identity, absorbing movements' values and practices. As chapter 5 makes clear, this attitude led to a creative revision of professional conventions and pioneering experimentation in legal education. Fatally, the antiwar zeitgeist called for engagement on the side of draft resisters, rebellious GIs, and domestic opponents of the conflict. Chapter 6 excavates the enormous outpouring of energies that radical lawyers offered to those who unashamedly fought against the war, either peacefully or violently, from East Asia to the United States. Chapters 7 and 8 shed light on the even more organic relationship between lawyers and prison movements, with particular attention to the lawyers' extralegal modes of engagement, including solidarity committees and unconventional forms of political and human support. As a matter of fact, lawyers' activism innervated the quasi totality of movements that shared a staunch opposition to the establishment and its values. Chapter 9 sets out to map some of the most crucial areas of intervention, such as rank-and-file unionism, Native American struggles, and women's and gay liberation battles. Finally, chapter 10 draws attention to a number of specific strategies that radical lawyers devised to deal with street-level policing, federal grand juries, electronic surveillance, and other tools of law enforcement and investigation that government agencies aggressively deployed against protesters—and against lawyers, too.

Overall, *Up Against the Law* engages the ongoing conversation about the social and political conflicts of the long 1960s. By integrating an overlooked category of actors into the historical account, this book seeks to provide the standard representation of that cycle of protest with a third dimension that often went unnoticed.[28] In other words, the following pages illustrate that the mobilization challenging the status quo was more profound and diffused than previously understood. As a fascinating sequence of projects, campaigns, experiments, conquests, victories, and tragedies testifies, an army of combative lawyers stood behind, alongside, and in connection with frontline militants. Far from being aloof technicians or protectors of uncontroversial rights, these practitioners of law bore unpopular messages, carried abrasive forms of contention, and deeply influenced other social actors.

1   With the New Abolitionists

The advent of massive resistance to desegregation in the South spurred national awareness that a legal emergency was underway. News of southern governors disobeying federal court orders, state legislators passing unconstitutional statutes, and white supremacists spreading fear and violence appalled many observers—and radical lawyers in particular. Countless Black and white civil rights activists were unjustly convicted of crimes and served time in jail without a lawyer to arrange bail or to appeal a verdict. Civil rights defendants also faced hostile judges and juries, who were hardly representative of the general population of the area: the deep-seated racism of many public officials favored all-white juries, and lawyers were reluctant to challenge the racial composition of jury panels. Moreover, it was difficult to find potential Black jurors, as in order to be eligible, they had to be registered to vote—and Black registered voters were traditionally scarce.[1] Not surprisingly, in numerous southern state courthouses, Black attorneys, defendants, and witnesses were treated with disrespect. Blacks were often segregated from whites in courtroom seating and rarely participated in the judicial apparatus.[2]

Against this background, defendants could rarely sustain the heavy financial burden of a competent legal defense and routinely struggled to find lawyers willing or able to handle civil rights cases. In fact, there were entire communities in the South without a single attorney providing representation in racially controversial lawsuits. And such cases were growing in number wherever southern Blacks tried to register to vote or attempted to desegregate public facilities. According to estimates, in the whole South, scarcely more than a hundred attorneys could be consulted for these matters. In Mississippi, the most troubled state, where Black Americans totaled nearly 1 million in a population of 2.1 million, there were twenty-one hundred white lawyers and four Black lawyers, of which only three—R. Jess Brown, Carsie Hall, and Jack Young—would handle civil rights cases. The landscape looked a little brighter in Virginia, where civil rights lawyers numbered approximately twenty, but in Louisiana, Georgia, South Carolina, and North Carolina, there were fewer than ten.

By all accounts, southern lawyers who undertook civil rights cases faced ostracism, financial losses, and threats of physical injury. They lamented being the target of attacks by state and judicial authorities, in particular through audits of tax returns and specious citations for contempt of court. Given the sheer volume of cases, lawyers were also forced to decline many cases. As a consequence, civil rights defendants, when they did not opt for self-defense or plead guilty, were commonly represented by court-appointed white attorneys, who were doing the absolute minimum just to preserve the formal right to counsel. These lawyers were hardly sympathetic with their clients and were generally reluctant to advocate constitutional rights in their defense. Unsurprisingly, lawsuits to compel integration and to restrain segregation also became problematic. When the 1964 Civil Rights Act passed, opening a number of new avenues for legal action, the demand for lawyers grew even more.[3]

While national and local bar associations did not substantially react to such a legal emergency, the federal government pronounced itself powerless. The president and the Department of Justice repeatedly stressed the limits of their mandate, as well as the lack of a national police force and other federal instruments to enforce the law.[4] As journalist Victor Navasky observed, until 1963 civil rights were "in the rear ranks" of the Kennedy administration's priorities. Despite sincere "emotional involvement" and "good intentions," the federal government preferred to encourage "the inevitable integration, but never at the cost of disturbing social equilibrium." Moreover, the tension between the Justice Department and the FBI, whose reluctance to intervene against white segregationists was notorious, severely limited the administration's commitment to civil rights. Although the administration eventually obtained more substantial bureau engagement in the South, its rule of thumb was "to avoid confrontation" with the FBI. As a matter of fact, the Kennedys were quite conservative in their judicial appointments. For example, they named at least five anti–civil rights judges to the U.S. Court of Appeals for the Fifth Circuit, thus solidifying resistance to desegregation where more vigorous action was needed—in the heart of the Deep South.[5]

As a partial remedy to this situation, civil rights organizations had turned to individual progressive lawyers in the North. For example, Ella Baker, executive director of the Southern Christian Leadership Conference (SCLC), had contacted Arthur Kinoy, a New York City attorney who had represented prominent left-wing clients such as the Rosenbergs and the United Electrical, Radio and Machine Workers of America. Baker had just returned from

Montgomery and wanted to talk with lawyers and other people in the North who could help in gathering support for a bus boycott campaign that Black activists were just starting. These young protesters needed funds and publicity as well as legal help. Therefore, Kinoy, with several organizers and lawyers who had worked together in the anti-McCarthy struggles, helped create the organization In Friendship.[6] This tiny group, however, ended up mainly assisting grassroots activists from New York, most frequently through donations.

Similarly, in June 1961, the American Civil Liberties Union asked William M. Kunstler, known as Bill, to fly to Jackson, Mississippi, to help civil rights lawyer Jack Young. Black activists—the so-called Freedom Riders, organized by the Congress of Racial Equality (CORE)—had just begun their interstate bus rides in May. At every place they stopped, they were harassed, arrested, and brutalized for their defiance of segregated seating, so they were in desperate need of legal aid. Kunstler, who at the time was a New York lawyer with a vague interest in liberal and progressive causes, agreed to help them and soon became one of Martin Luther King's trial advisers.[7] Yet these sporadic initiatives and individual interventions could hardly meet the legal needs of a growing and increasingly combative movement. Although they demonstrated a passionate sense of justice, they were mere drops in the ocean.

The Legal Defense Fund (LDF), the legal arm of the National Association for the Advancement of Colored People (NAACP), was the most organized and successful legal entity fighting against Jim Crow.[8] It functioned as a civil rights law firm, and the SCLC had traditionally relied on it. Legendary lawyer Thurgood Marshall, an early member of the Guild and the first Black American to become a U.S. Supreme Court justice, served as the LDF's first director-counsel. In 1961, Jack Greenberg, a white lawyer who had argued *Brown v. Board of Education* with Marshall, took over the reins of the organization.[9] However, in line with the NAACP's legalistic and moderate orientation, the LDF remained focused on test-case litigation and legislative lobbying to press for progressive laws and to resist the regressive ones.[10] Thematically, the LDF also concentrated on school segregation and, indeed, succeeded in winning some important cases it brought to the court. Its policy of representing people only if persecuted because of race, avoiding as much as possible controversial civil disobedience cases, coupled with its request to retain a large degree of control over litigation strategies, made the LDF's legal help quite selective. Activists thus sought out a different kind of support, and they eventually found it in the National Lawyers Guild.[11]

The Guild Goes South

The problem of legal representation in the South had never deeply troubled the NLG. Gravitating around New York and operating in line with the labor tradition, the Guild leadership treated the racial issue as one among many. In its view, the fight against segregation had to be considered within a broader transformative agenda that included, first and foremost, economic justice. It was also unclear how to provide substantive help in the South, as the Guild was a bar association and not a law firm. Before the early 1960s, only a few northern Guild lawyers had ever traveled to Mississippi or seen firsthand the iniquity of southern justice. Decimated after the intense repression of the 1950s, the Guild had embraced a minimalist agenda, simply aimed at surviving. It had limited its action to resolutions, amicus briefs, and cooperation with unions or progressive-liberal coalitions. Any broader engagement seemed out of scope and beyond reach.[12]

Things started changing after a few southern attorneys drew attention to their hardships at the Guild's national conventions and executive bureau meetings.[13] At the Guild's twenty-fifth national convention in Detroit in February 1962, six southern civil rights lawyers were honored for their fight to preserve and extend constitutional liberties. One of them, Leonard W. Holt (known as Len)—a Black attorney based in Norfolk, Virginia—took the floor and launched a heartfelt appeal: the South needed urgent legal help, and no delay was acceptable.[14] At the end of his talk, Holt asked everybody to stand up and join him in singing "We Shall Overcome." A full chorus followed.[15] It was a wake-up call that would significantly change the trajectory of the organization.

The 1962 convention—which elected twenty-one new young members to the executive bureau, including three female and eight Black attorneys— immediately passed a resolution to organize the Committee to Assist Southern Lawyers (CASL). As the Guild's narrative proudly emphasizes, CASL represented "the first organized attempt by American lawyers to provide large-scale legal aid to the southern civil rights movement."[16] The newly born committee was meant to compile a list of lawyers willing to contribute with their time, skills, or money to help their southern colleagues, to inform them of the availability of such assistance, and to undertake other activities, such as producing publications and attending conferences.[17] A Black attorney, George W. Crockett Jr., and a white colleague, Ernest Goodman, both of Detroit, were named co-chairs. Attorneys Len Holt and Benjamin W. Smith of New Orleans were appointed as southern coordinators.[18]

George Crockett, a founding member of the Guild, was a former U.S. Department of Labor lawyer and served as counsel for the United Auto Workers. A fierce critic of McCarthyism, he had been part of the legal team that represented the Communist Party leaders accused of advocating the overthrow of the federal government in the controversial Foley Square trial of 1949. This task had cost him his job and landed him in prison for four months for contempt.[19] Ernest Goodman was the driving force of the Guild during the early 1960s. A founding member of the NLG, in 1939 he had joined the legendary labor and civil rights law firm established by Maurice Sugar in Detroit and later became a nationally known labor lawyer.[20] In 1951, he created an integrated law firm with George Crockett—the first in Michigan and among the first in the whole country. As Goodman's biographers aptly wrote, two constants followed him through his professional life from the very beginning: "His clients were working class and poor, and more often than not they were African Americans." In other words, "he had crossed the color line early in his career" and then, in 1962, he saw an opportunity to keep on fighting his lifelong battle with a cohort of valiant colleagues.[21]

The Committee to Assist Southern Lawyers featured twenty-two members from ten states and boasted an interracial composition. In the beginning, CASL restricted itself to offering simple legal support to local lawyers, rather than representation to people or organizations.[22] The reaction on the field seemed nonetheless enthusiastic. In March 1962, Goodman spoke on behalf of the Guild at a large public meeting organized by the SCLC in Petersburg, Virginia, at the First Baptist Church. When he announced, in the presence of Martin Luther King, the creation of a Guild committee aimed at marshaling lawyers, the response from the audience was allegedly "tremendous."[23] "I can't sing at all," Goodman concluded, "but with all my heart, may I say, 'We shall help you overcome.'"[24] Within a couple of years, eighty-five lawyers agreed to devote their time, and fifty-nine of them provided assistance in the South with trial work, preparation of pleadings and briefs, consultation, and legal advice.[25] The CASL lawyers' docket was quite modest but showed the beginning of a convergence toward the movements. Cases ranged from omnibus desegregation suits to single issues involving Black defendants claiming jury discrimination, or cases opposing injunctions that prohibited public demonstrations.[26]

Given the unexpected interest shown by northern law students, CASL promptly set up a pilot project to send a few of them to clerk in the offices of southern civil rights lawyers during the summer. The program began in 1962, and until 1964 the participating students were no more than a handful, but the Guild welcomed the rapprochement of a younger generation.[27] CASL also organized one of the first interracial legal conferences on civil rights in the South, held in Atlanta in November–December 1962.[28] Meant to provide participants with a review of the latest developments in civil rights law, the conference had its highlight with the appearance of Martin Luther King. King acknowledged the "personal and economic sacrifice" of lawyers and praised their role in the South. He told the sixty-five attorneys in the audience that their efforts, combined with the mass movement for integration, were key to "making the American dream a reality."[29] His words were reportedly "more than inspiring," even "redemptive." His very presence validated that lawyers' engagement was just and valuable. It also ratified the union between "a new vanguard of lawyers" and the civil rights movement.[30]

Less than a year later, in October 1963, CASL co-sponsored a second conference in New Orleans. Its stated goal was, again, "to counteract the unwillingness or inability of all except a handful of southern attorneys to accept difficult and usually financially unrewarding cases arising from segregation." The conference also represented a chance for individual attorneys to share legal strategies and analyze the evolution of their functions and responsibilities.[31] The event, however, became a first crucial test for the Guild. In the afternoon of the opening day, Louisiana state troopers in uniform broke into the conference room and immediately arrested Benjamin Smith and Bruce Waltzer. A bit later, they arrested James Dombrowski. Meanwhile, troopers raided not only the law office of Smith and Waltzer and the headquarters of the Southern Conference Educational Fund (SCEF) but also the homes of the three, confiscating records and personal belongings.

Who were the three under arrest? A native of Arkansas, Benjamin Smith was a labor attorney in New Orleans. In 1959 he employed Bruce Waltzer, who was a Guild lawyer from Brooklyn, as his clerk, and the two partnered in a progressive law firm litigating civil rights cases. Neither a communist nor a liberal, Smith was mistakenly known within the FBI as a dangerous subversive.[32] Dombrowski was director of SCEF and Smith sat on its board. Established in the 1930s, SCEF was an interracial organization for civil rights that had provoked a great deal of controversy because of its communist supporters. The three men were charged with violating the state Subversive Activities and Communist Control Law and the Communist Propaganda Control Law. Dombrowski and Smith were accused of operating a subversive organization, the Southern Conference Educational Fund, while Waltzer was charged with belonging to a subversive organization, the National

Lawyers Guild. Later it emerged that both the raids and the arrests had been planned with the complicity of Senator James O. Eastland, a conservative Democrat and chair of the Internal Security Subcommittee of the Judiciary Committee of the Senate.[33]

The arrests came out of the blue and left everyone at the meeting outraged. It was an unsolicited flashback to the red scare and a bitter taste of southern justice.[34] Kinoy remembers having thought that if the "power structure" could illegalize SCEF and the Guild, it could use this technique against any radical organization in the South. If being a lawyer for the movement was a subversive crime, "no one who lifted a finger to help black people was safe."[35] Yet the arrest of three well-respected professionals attending a legal conference was also a powerful call to arms for the lawyers and a major publicity coup. The three were bailed out, and Smith was back at the conference the next day by noon, amid ovations. Our crime is "the act of desegregation," he said in a sharp accusation of prosecutors. The Guild was now united in a common purpose and was ready to counterattack.[36]

Led by Kinoy, the defense team sought to persuade a district court that the cases were in violation of the First Amendment, so that they could be promptly transferred to a higher court. Defense lawyers considered the justice system in Louisiana too dangerously rigged; therefore, filing a civil rights lawsuit in federal court seemed to be their only hope. The right to sue a federal court for protection of rights secured by the Constitution and to obtain injunctive relief against enforcement of state criminal statutes was spelled out in an almost forgotten statute of the Civil Rights Act of 1871. During Reconstruction, Congress wanted to protect the rights of the newly emancipated slaves dealing with former owners and vigilante violence; now, that logic could be replicated to shelter the new abolitionists from vindictive southern justice.[37]

The defendants initially lost in federal district court but persevered through appeal, and in 1965 they won the Supreme Court landmark decision *Dombrowski v. Pfister.* The Guild was intimately involved with this judicial turning point. The defense leading counsel and his team were part of the Guild's milieu, and the Guild itself filed an amicus brief arguing for the importance of the new approach brought by the defense. Eventually, the Supreme Court acknowledged that the mere existence of repressive legislation and repressive governmental activities created a "chilling effect" on the exercise of fundamental First Amendment rights. As a consequence, the court, in its opinion written by Justice William J. Brennan, ruled not only that Louisiana laws were unconstitutional and that the prosecution against Dombrowski, Smith, and Waltzer was unjust, but also—and most importantly—that it was incumbent on federal courts to exercise their judicial power to protect citizens from such a "chilling effect." As widely recognized, the so-called Dombrowski remedy opened up a new path in constitutional litigation. Citizens suffering under state procedures could cut through delays and get constitutional relief in federal courts.[38]

Guild lawyers meanwhile faced another test in Danville, Virginia, where the Black community, beginning in May 1963, had been organizing demonstrations to oppose segregation. SCLC and CORE representatives, including Martin Luther King, came into town to support the local movement, but the clash with law enforcement resulted in police violence, a large number of arrests, high bail, and injunctions limiting the right to protest. By August, more than three hundred people were awaiting trial.[39] In addition, attorney Len Holt was arrested for taking part in unauthorized demonstrations and indicted under the John Brown statute for inciting the Black population to acts of violence and war against the white population. The situation was desperate, and the Danville organizers, who had only Holt and a few other local lawyers to rely on, asked the Legal Defense Fund for help. Though open to covering legal fees, the LDF required that its resources be channeled exclusively to its trusted lawyers and that it supervise future demonstrations in order to avoid any unwise action. The organizers refused such a form of control, and a radical lawyers' team coalesced around Holt, with the help of Guild lawyers Dean Robb, Nathan Conyers, Kunstler, Kinoy, and a few local attorneys.[40]

Worn out by repression, the Danville movement was ultimately unsuccessful, but the legal crusade had interesting corollaries. To deal with such a great number of simultaneous arrests, Kunstler suggested employing the aforementioned statute of the Civil Rights Act. This mechanism forced federal judges to hold hearings on the validity of petitions for removal. Even though cases could still be sent back to state courts, the statute became a useful device to buy time and reverse many unjust indictments. All the Danville prosecutions were eventually stopped.[41] The Danville organizers had not won their battle, but Guild lawyers had opened up breathing room for them to fight another day.

Lawyers within the Movement

By 1964, it was clear that the Guild had entered the orbit of the most active and confrontational social movements in the country. In particular, the NLG developed an enduring relationship with the Student Nonviolent Coordinating Committee (SNCC), which would significantly alter radical lawyers' identity and practice. SNCC grew out of the sit-in movement, when a group of Black student leaders felt the need for a protest organization capable of broadening the focus of their militancy. Ella Baker sustained these efforts and signed, with Martin Luther King, the letter of convocation for the founding conference, held in Raleigh, North Carolina, in April 1960. At least in its first years of operation, the SNCC political platform merged Gandhian precepts, American pacifism, and Christian idealism. Together, these principles imposed a commitment to nonviolent direct action and special attention for disenfranchised people.

Described as "shock troops" of the civil rights movement, the young SNCC activists immediately stood out as they ventured into rural regions such as Southwest Mississippi, which was considered too dangerous by other groups, and sought to animate local community activists. Later, SNCC became a leading member of the Freedom Riders Coordinating Committee, together with CORE and the SCLC. Their "great discovery," as historian Wesley Hogan put it, was that "they themselves could dismantle the caste system," acting as if segregation did not exist when they entered restaurants, movie theaters, hotels, churches, courtrooms, and voting booths.[42] As a result of their engagement, SNCC militants experienced southern jails and retaliatory violence. Even so, their uncompromising militancy attracted plenty of white leftist students from the North, who were ready to abandon—at least for a while—their middle-class comfort and join a momentous struggle. In the name of an interracial pledge, SNCC welcomed them until the mid-1960s.

While arrests escalated and appeals for federal assistance seemed fruitless, the group radicalized. SNCC openly criticized the Kennedy administration, as well as the civil rights organizations, for accepting slow gradualism and for being complicit in racial oppression. At the same time, any residual anticommunist barrier evaporated in favor of a non-exclusion policy that would become controversial. The strict commitment to nonviolence also loosened. By 1963, SNCC endorsed protests even when they were likely to result in violence. Eventually, SNCC workers' "open defiance of segregationist authorities" and their "mixture of bravado and sincere moral courage" made them "the *enfants terribles* of the civil rights movement."[43]

Unsurprisingly, SNCC faced a formidable array of legal woes. In his opening press conference, Marion Barry—the first chair of the organization—exposed SNCC's principle of going to jail rather than accepting bail in order to heighten the iniquity of the system. Yet he immediately appealed to lawyers to help civil rights workers and to refrain from charging "exorbitant prices" in their cases.[44] SNCC was originally working with the Legal Defense Fund. However, the legal apparatus led by Jack Greenberg reportedly pushed SNCC for a slowdown. The arrests were growing excessively, whereas the legal resources were dwindling. As a result, SNCC explored the Guild's availability and asked Guild lawyers Irving Rosenfeld, Victor Rabinowitz, and Len Holt to address its staff at the third national conference in Atlanta, in April 1962.[45]

It was love at first sight.[46] There was indeed a special consonance between these "new abolitionists," as Howard Zinn defined them, and the most radical lawyers in the country. They shared a similar "disrespect for respectability" and a "tremendous respect for the potency of the demonstration," seen as the essence of democracy.[47] Guild lawyers admired SNCC's bravery to stay in the front line of the struggle and their commitment to empowering the people through activism.[48] SNCC militants, on their end, praised radical lawyers' "courage and willingness to openly fight the legal system of the United States" in a way that was "far ahead of the conservative legal profession."[49] Already warm to offensive action, the Guild rapidly made common cause with SNCC.

In 1963, the Mississippi Council of Federated Organizations (COFO)—an umbrella organization established by the NAACP, SNCC, CORE, the SCLC, and several voter and civil rights groups—sponsored a Freedom Vote Campaign to show that, given fair conditions, Black Mississippians would be willing to register and exercise their right to vote. Indeed, more than eighty thousand Black citizens cast their demonstrative ballots for a mock election for governor. Over one hundred white college students, mostly from Ivy League campuses, worked on the project, attracting attention from both the national press and the Department of Justice, especially when they were harassed by white reactionaries or arrested by Mississippi law enforcement.[50] Under these circumstances, civil rights organizers learned an important lesson: only the presence of a massive force of white civil rights workers could create media exposure, elicit a crisis, and force a confrontation between federal and state authorities.[51]

Consequently, in March 1964, COFO announced it would recruit one thousand students, teachers, technicians, nurses, artists, and legal advisers for a project called Freedom Summer. To challenge racial segregation in Mississippi, they would organize a voter registration campaign and set up Freedom Schools and community centers. Underlying the plan was a common understanding that Mississippi was "America written large, the ultimate end of racial policies practiced with lesser intensity in every American state."[52] Indeed, the media described the Magnolia state as "a besieged fortress," while anxiety that the summer-long drive might lead to "serious violence" was growing. Newspapers informed readers that "law enforcement agencies have joined in a program of paramilitary preparations," and Mississippi officials assured the public that they would deal firmly with any challenge to the state's racial codes and customs. Moreover, the state legislature passed a series of bills aimed at defeating "the coming invasion."[53]

Waiting for civil rights activists in Jackson was a riot-trained unit of 435 police officers, along with a specially armored battlewagon that could carry twelve people with shotguns, and three flatbed trucks enclosed with steel mesh—referred to by the police as "nigger wagons"—designed to transport demonstrators to newly enlarged stockades. Mississippi governor Paul B. Johnson had declared he would take whatever steps were necessary to avert violence and avoid federal intervention. His tactic would be sealing off civil rights workers from the white mobs who might attack them. However, the situation was hardly reassuring, especially because the Ku Klux Klan and other vigilante groups had perked up. Civil rights organizations denounced the fact that "a reign of terror" had been instituted in several counties, where intimidation and harassment were the order of the day. In the prior six months, five Blacks were reported killed in the area, and many others beaten. A number of buildings had been fired into or bombed, and wooden crosses were burning all over.[54]

The COFO staff were well aware of the judicial implications of their work and had put out a national call for lawyers to protect the workers.[55] For his part, COFO legal coordinator Hunter Morey addressed the Guild National Convention in Detroit in February 1964, drawing attention to the acts of intimidation and retaliation that the summer drive was likely to provoke. He voiced an "urgent need" for more attorneys, and the Guild rapidly drafted a plan to send at least sixty volunteer lawyers to represent civil rights defendants in Mississippi over the twelve-week summer period of COFO activities. Meanwhile, the Committee to Assist Southern Lawyers morphed into the Committee for Legal Assistance in the South (CLAS), while Crockett and Smith undertook the head of the organization as co-chairs. Goodman was elected president of the Guild, and the national office was moved from New York to Detroit, closer to Goodman's organizational machine. As the Guild's chronicles go, "When the convention chairman asked for a show of hands of those who might volunteer for Mississippi the response was electric. No one raised his hand; instead, scores of lawyers jumped to their feet."[56]

In April, the Guild issued its own call for lawyers to participate in a Peace Corps–type operation in Mississippi, defending, without fee, people who would otherwise be without defense.[57] The response was, as usual, passionate.[58] As a young attorney from Detroit put it, "It sounds so corny when you say these things. . . . But, fundamentally, you can't sit by."[59] The reaction of Jack Greenberg was quite a bit different. He had conceived the LDF as COFO's sole legal resource, and he worried that any connection to the Guild would serve to associate the LDF with the Communist Party.[60] As a result, Greenberg threatened to withdraw the plans for legal assistance during the summer if the Guild was involved in Mississippi. COFO, on the contrary, reaffirmed that any support was welcome. The volume of expected legal work compelled the council to seek and accept all possible legal help. Greenberg, as he had in the past, backed down.[61] Civil rights organizer and scholar Allard K. Lowenstein, then working to mobilize ivy leaguers to go South, similarly deployed strenuous efforts to dissuade COFO leaders from accepting the Guild's cooperation and urged students to withdraw if communist ties were not severed. He, too, was unsuccessful.[62]

As a matter of fact, the anticommunist debate seemed to interfere little with the Guild's operations. CLAS was organized around a field office with a full-time staff of two attorneys, two law students, and a secretary. The office was supposed to manage all requests for immediate assistance, until a Guild attorney could be assigned, and to back up lawyers on the scene. Defense would be accepted only upon request, and the Guild would not itself handle it, as the standard attorney-client relationship had to be respected.[63] However, the establishment of CLAS represented a great leap toward closer and more organic cooperation between lawyers and social movements.

Once in the field, CLAS lawyers operated primarily from three bases: Greenwood, Hattiesburg, and Meridian. A coordinating office was established in Jackson, on the same street where the first NAACP headquarters had been installed and where COFO had a legal office.[64] The week for volunteer lawyers generally began on Sunday, with the transition from the airport into Jackson. "Most of the trip was spent trying to quiet their fears without at the same time making them too complacent," confessed Crockett.[65] In Mississippi, Guild lawyers joined with the army of volunteers that COFO brought together, including attorneys and law students attached to other programs or to single firms, doctors and nurses, the cultural corps, the photographic staff, and clergy of the National Council of Churches.[66]

COFO workers eventually faced violence, acts of intimidation, and a large number of arrests. Data vary considerably, but many sources refer to approximately one thousand arrests during the summer, coupled with dozens of beatings and shootings, incidents of arson involving homes and churches, and six to fifteen murders. Concerning the arrests of civil rights workers, charges were usually misdemeanors, whereas felonies were extremely rare because the defendants were essentially nonviolent. Activists were accused of picketing without a permit, disorderly conduct, traffic violations, interfering with an officer in the performance of his duty, and other similar offenses.[67] The sheer number of arrests meant that many people were excluded from participating in the struggles, and a significant amount of money was required for bail, legal defense, and fines.

The Guild tried to limit this burden. Lawyers were constantly on hand to get people out of jail, arrange bail, or present papers before the appropriate judge in time to head off a trial. Drawing on the Danville experience, the Guild extended the practice of removal to the point that the majority of the thousand COFO arrests were transferred on the grounds that defendants could not get a fair trial in the state courts.[68] To be sure, tenacious guardians of the southern establishment like W. Harold Cox, chief judge of the U.S. District Court for the Southern District of Mississippi, made every effort to obstruct the removal process. In addition, the number of pending cases after the summer was still very high, whereas lawyers' engagement had decreased. Therefore, it remains difficult to quantify the extent to which the removal practice was successful.[69]

Even so, it is safe to conclude that Guild lawyers spared COFO activists countless days in jail as well as a large amount of money in fines. The Guild's presence in the streets, in the Freedom Houses, in the courtrooms, and in the jails helped affirm that legal rights could no longer be violated with impunity. Also, it arguably restrained police behavior. At the same time, Guild lawyers bolstered activists' confidence in the possibility of obtaining vindication of their rights and increased their morale.[70] Guild attorney Stanley Faulkner, who spent a week in Jackson and Hattiesburg to take depositions from civil rights demonstrators who were arrested, remembers that lawyers' presence had a twofold effect. On the one hand, it alerted white authorities, from judges to deputy sheriffs, that they were being watched by attorneys. On the other hand, it gave "strength to those struggling for their constitutional right to equality."[71]

Lawyers were also continually called on to give advice. For example, a Guild attorney who was placed in Hattiesburg recounted that some civil rights organizers contemplating a bus boycott asked her "to interpret the various Code sections involving boycotts." She did so and advised them about potential legal restrictions. COFO workers and local Black residents, she said, made Guild lawyers "keenly aware of the reassurance and security they felt" at their presence. The Guild also created the Mississippi Emergency Bail Fund when the "jail, no bail" policy was overwhelmed by massive arrests. COFO workers generally shared their cell with other white inmates who were likely to beat them, blaming them for being "white niggers" or "negro lovers." Usually, they were not even allowed to place a phone call from the jail, so even if their parents or "bail contacts" could afford the bail, they could not be freed. Thus, the fund was used to release them immediately.[72]

The Guild also played a key role in another SNCC campaign that emerged in parallel to Freedom Summer. Having grown disillusioned with Democratic party politics, particularly with the exclusionist Mississippi Democratic Party, SNCC founded the Mississippi Freedom Democratic Party (MFDP) in April 1964. The party, an integrated and progressive political force, soon began a separate registration process to allow voters to oppose the regular Democratic candidates for the national convention. This attempt however failed at the primaries. Then, the MFDP tried to unseat the regular Mississippi delegation at the national convention by sending sixty-eight alternative representatives. After a fierce battle, the convention voted a resolution that allowed only two MFDP representatives to sit. President Johnson's concern about preserving his white southern support prevailed, but the MFDP rejected the compromise.

In the course of such political maneuvers, the MFDP was assisted by Joseph L. Rauh Jr., a civil rights lawyer with strong connections to the liberal establishment. Cofounder of the Americans for Democratic Action and general counsel for the United Automobile Workers, Rauh pushed the MFDP to accept an agreement with the Democratic Party. He was also increasingly worried about the links between the MFDP and the Guild lawyers. In a few circumstances, he publicly suggested getting rid of the "Communist lawyers" and, in a COFO meeting, reportedly defined it as "immoral" to accept their help. Even in this circumstance, the MFDP, under the aegis of the SNCC leaders, opted for welcoming everybody's aid: it severed its relationship with Rauh and entrusted Kinoy, Kunstler, Smith, and their Guild partners.[73]

The MFDP thus planned a further challenge to the seating of the representatives from Mississippi to Congress, alleging that they had been elected at the exclusion of Black voters. Guild lawyers were called "to find a legiti-mate, realistic form for such a campaign" and, to the delight of the MFDP, they retrieved a forgotten federal statute that allowed the contestants to present evidence in support of their charges of illegality or impropriety in the elections. A campaign in favor of the challenge was then organized all over the country. Lawyers reached out to Democratic congressman William F. Ryan of New York and sixteen members of the House of Representatives, who agreed to challenge the right of the Mississippi regulars to be sworn in on the first day of the new Congress. Between January and February 1965, the Guild recruited about 150 volunteers to go to Mississippi and gather evidence on both the exclusion of Black people from the voting process and the climate of intimidation riveting the state. In the end, over fifty members of Congress objected to the swearing in of the Mississippi representatives, but the delegation was seated anyway.

Nevertheless, the challenge to the "illegal" election remained pending. More than four hundred people testified in Mississippi, including participants in Freedom Summer. In several cases, as Kinoy explained, lawyer-organizer teams used the federal subpoena power to bring representatives of the state institutions before community assemblies, where they were forced to testify on specific incidents of violence, intimidation, and exclusion of Blacks from the vote. The challenge was finally debated in the House of Representatives. Guild member John Conyers, a Black lawyer from De-troit who had just been elected to Congress, escorted MFDP delegates Fannie Lou Hamer, Victoria Gray, and Annie Devine onto the floor of the House and gave a rousing address. The challenge gained substantial backing, receiving 143 votes in favor, but it eventually lost, as another 228 representatives rejected it. The MFDP could be satisfied nonetheless, as the challenge set in motion a process for assembling radical social forces and showed that the proposition of an independent political party, free of the establishment's control and in sync with social movements, enjoyed ample support. In 1968, the Mississippi delegation of the Democratic Party was finally integrated. "No people's lawyer could ask for a greater fulfillment of role than to have taken part in this historic Challenge," wrote Arthur Kinoy years later.[74]

Red Baiting: Intended and Unintended Effects

The southern legal emergency pushed the NLG to seek the cooperation of the other national bar associations. The Guild constantly urged them to take more vigorous action to improve the administration of justice in the South and to join forces to sustain the movement in a collective endeavor. With this aim in mind, the NLG also tried to keep open a channel of communication with the federal government. Lobbying in Washington was still considered a crucial tactic, especially when more federal action was demanded. However, the pressure exerted at both levels did not immediately work. The call for cooperation remained largely unheard, the major obstacle being the deep-seated anticommunism that pervaded the mainstream lawyers' associations and the government. Still regarded as "the legal bulwark of the Communist Party," the Guild was ignored, ostracized, and occasionally opposed, as the arrests at the New Orleans conference confirmed.[75] Nonetheless, the Guild achieved its overall goals. The initiatives to supplant its presence in the South indirectly provided the civil rights movement with legal aid and drew plenty of other lawyers into action.

The Guild's initial concern was to "lead the [American Bar Association] unto the paths of righteousness," as Guild president Benjamin Dreyfus wrote in January 1962.[76] Being the largest national bar association, the American Bar Association (ABA) was considered a major source of potential help, together with the National Bar Association (NBA), the oldest national network of Black lawyers. At that point, nobody knew that only two years before, the former ABA president had met with FBI high officials, including director J. Edgar Hoover, to discuss how to hit the communist-inspired National Lawyers Guild.[77] So, in March 1962, Dreyfus asked the presidents of the two main bar associations to meet in order to join the Guild's effort and to draft a common program.[78] When the American Bar Association invited the NLG to present its plan, the reception was reportedly cordial. However, the ABA was persuaded that its own efforts were already adequate.[79] All the Guild could do was publicly criticize both the ABA and the Kennedy brothers for "standing idly" and "ducking their responsibilities on the Negro drive for equal rights."[80]

The Guild's attempt to establish a dialogue with the federal government on the legal emergency in the South was equally unsuccessful, and its offers of help and recommendations earned little attention.[81] Other external pressures—particularly the televised demonstrations in Birmingham, Alabama, where police clubbed people, employed fire hoses, and arrested thousands of people—were more effective in convincing the government to make a move and set up a first meeting with bar leaders.[82] On June 21, 1963, 244 prominent attorneys from across the country eventually convened at the White House to discuss the situation with President John F. Kennedy, Vice President Lyndon B. Johnson, and Attorney General Robert Kennedy.

Aimed at pushing the bar to become more vocal and more active in making legal aid available on a nondiscriminatory basis, the meeting testified to the persisting gap between the establishment and the Guild, which was not invited to the gathering.[83] On the one hand, both Lyndon Johnson and Robert Kennedy exposed their conception of what they defined as the "vital role" of lawyers in fighting racism. Instead of a combative function, it was the capacity of getting people around a table and keeping the problems off the street. "We must not let anyone believe they can only get justice by mobs and by going into the streets," summarized Johnson. On the other hand, the ABA, despite the proclamations of its president, confirmed its substantial disregard for the civil rights problem. As a matter of fact, it had waited until June 21, just a few hours before the White House conference, to launch a Special Committee on Civil Rights and Racial Unrest to work in the South during the following summer.[84]

The Guild's activism nonetheless exerted at least an indirect influence on both the Kennedy administration and the moderate sections of the bar, which feared a legal monopoly of communist-led Guild lawyers in the South. Between the summer of 1963 and the spring of 1964, two committees were created to draft lawyers for the civil rights struggles: the Lawyers' Committee for Civil Rights Under Law, also known as the President's Committee, and the Lawyers Constitutional Defense Committee (LCDC).[85]

The first committee was a direct by-product of the White House meeting of June 1963. More than one hundred lawyers volunteered for service, including officials of the NAACP, attorneys of the LDF, and the deans of twelve law schools. The committee's mission was to promote and coordinate activities to find legal solutions to the civil rights problem, including the enlisting of volunteers.[86] Interested in granting the formal right to counsel and, at the same time, taming the most belligerent civil rights organizations, the committee's attorneys eventually acted mostly for the sake of law and order. Berl I. Bernhard, the committee's executive director, explained it quite openly: "I am not a radical," he stated. "I just believe that lawyers and other responsible Americans must see that this racial thing comes out right. Otherwise, somebody else will, and their motives won't be as good."[87] Therefore, besides sending some northern lawyers, the President's Committee essentially negotiated with the southern bars to recruit lawyers who pledged to defend Blacks in their states.[88]

The fear of communist influence on the civil rights movement, together with a fair share of professional competition, was crucial in the establishment of the Lawyers Constitutional Defense Committee. When in 1963 the

Guild offered its legal assistance to CORE activists in the South, the leadership of the group declined the proposal, fearing that it would raise dangerous criticisms and political controversy. Instead, CORE legal director Carl Rachlin thought about creating a novel organization free of suspicion of red sympathies. He contacted his friend Melvin L. Wulf, the ACLU legal director. A democratic socialist, Wulf was not anticommunist but was admittedly worried about the Guild overtaking the ACLU. So CORE and the ACLU found themselves in agreement to build a network of lawyers willing to contribute to the movement under the guise of neutrality.[89]

On April 2, 1964, the new organization came to light, sponsored by the ACLU, CORE, the American Jewish Congress, the American Jewish Committee, the LDF, and the National Council of Churches. Henry Schwarzschild, a renowned civil rights activist, assumed the direction. The goal of the LCDC was to send a corps of volunteer lawyers to the South during the summer. Over 150 immediately responded to the call. The project mirrored the Guild's model of intervention. The main difference between the two initiatives lay both in the scale and in the designated recipients of the legal aid. The LCDC had a richer budget and a larger team of lawyers—approximately three hundred in 1964—that typically represented CORE workers. By contrast, the Guild tended to support SNCC workers, with a focus on the most controversial defendants. After a rewarding experience in 1964, many LCDC lawyers returned to the North and remained active in the fight against racism in their own cities, while others went back to the South.[90]

In the midst of such lawyers' activism, during the summer of 1963 a group of law students from Harvard, Yale, Columbia, and other prestigious universities volunteered for the civil rights movement in the South. Motivated by their experience, they founded the Law Students Civil Rights Research Council (LSCRRC), the first interracial organization of law students.[91] In 1964, the LSCRRC sent an increasing number of students throughout the South in support of the lawyers' organizations, particularly the Guild and the LCDC. According to estimates, sixty young law clerks were active during the summer of 1964, while about twenty-five law students served all or part of the summer of 1965 in Mississippi under the direction of COFO.[92] In addition to clerking, students prepared arrest data, collected affidavits, contacted the FBI, and gathered evidence of voting discrimination. Among these young volunteers were some of the lawyers who would enter the Guild in the upcoming years.[93]

In the meantime, during the summer of 1964, the Guild kept up its pressure on the White House, urging again that the federal government enforce the law in the South. With a letter addressed to President Johnson, the Guild sent a memorandum of law claiming that the federal government had "explicit and adequate powers" by which "it can protect the voting rights of the Negro citizens in Mississippi or any other state, through the use of whatever Federal agencies it deems necessary."[94] However, by that time—two years after its first initiatives—the Guild was hardly alone in its lobbying. At its annual convention in 1964, the NAACP had urged Johnson to take over the administration of the state of Mississippi and to employ the federal government's power to restore law and order.[95] Furthermore, twenty-nine renowned professors of law expressed public disagreement with Attorney General Kennedy's claim that the federal government lacked the power to take preventive police action in Mississippi. On the contrary, these jurists argued that the president was empowered to use the state militia and the armed forces of the nation to enforce the laws of the United States.[96]

The question of whether communists influenced the civil rights movement through lawyers continued to be, in the mid-1960s, extremely controversial. The specter of communist lawyers was noted and denounced by the red-baiting press, raising concerns among a large variety of observers, including the liberal supporters of civil rights, and prompted high-level pushback in Washington.[97] For instance, Washington Post columnists Rowland Evans and Robert Novak repeatedly accused SNCC of being infiltrated by left-wing revolutionaries and communists, making specific reference to the Guild.[98]

By the same token, in 1964 alone, the Congressional Record included at least two public denunciations of the Guild as a communist mastermind of the civil rights movement. The most structured attack came from the aforementioned Senator James Eastland of Mississippi, who marshaled what he considered faultless evidence of the "communist infiltration into the so-called civil rights movement." Eastland provided an intricate map of political links and family ties to prove that the Communist Party, in his words, "has continued to fish in the troubled waters of racial discontent." The NLG received the lion's share of attention. Guild lawyers—the senator charged—were sent "quite openly for the purpose of meddling into the problems of the State of Mississippi" and were "directing the agitators in the State." Many of the lawyers involved were "young people," Eastland conceded, but most of them were "old hands, with long Communist affiliations."[99] A few days later, Republican congressman James B. Utt of California, an outspoken opponent of civil rights, echoed Eastland's address, insisting that the "invasion of Mississippi, by expeditionary forces from other States, was carefully planned by the Communist conspiracy." "Working with the invaders" were pro-communist lawyers Crockett, Smith, and Martin Popper.[100]

Guild activism also raised liberal eyebrows, as exemplified in an episode revealed by SNCC leader James Forman. It all started the day Alfred M. Bingham—a progressive lawyer and author, descendant of a prominent family from Connecticut—came to Mississippi to visit his son Stephen, who was volunteering with the Summer Project and would later become a Guild lawyer. Alfred Bingham was reportedly disturbed after he saw the Guild operating in the field. Back home, he arranged a meeting at the Department of Justice to discuss the difficult situation in the Third Congressional District of Mississippi, where volunteers were working and much of the violence was happening.

The meeting—attended by Alfred and Stephen Bingham, Burke Marshall, John Doar, and Arthur Schlesinger Jr. for the administration, and Bob Moses, Lawrence Guyot, and James Forman for COFO—turned into a condemnation of the Guild. Schlesinger explained that many government officials had spent years fighting the communists and had worked hard during the 1930s and 1940s to defeat political forces such as the Guild. Therefore, they found it "unpardonable" that civil rights organizations were working with that organization. The old arguments against the Guild were given vent again. In response, COFO leaders reiterated their policy, stressing the circumstance that nobody at that point, with the exception of Guild lawyers, was willing "to take aggressive legal action in Mississippi."[101]

While the civil rights movement in the South gradually slowed down, red baiting persisted. As the FBI diligently reported, in early 1965 Goodman sent a letter to Martin Luther King expressing concern about the recent arrests in Selma, Alabama, where the reverend and the SCLC had just opened a voter registration campaign. By February 5, arrests had already reached three thousand. The civil rights activists had to deal with Governor George Wallace, a notorious opponent of integration; the local county sheriff, who was a rival of voter registration; and the white segregationists, who were capable of attacking peaceful demonstrators. Goodman offered King the assistance of Guild attorneys for the arrested. In a follow-up letter to King, Crockett added that the Guild was even prepared to open an office in Alabama for servicing volunteer lawyers.[102] King, however, under constant FBI surveillance and attack, gradually advocated the exclusion of communist lawyers.[103] Thus, while insisting that SNCC abjure any communist support and reject the aid of the Guild, King also gave up on Goodman and Crockett's offer of help.[104]

Lessons from the Civil Rights Movement

It goes without saying that the experience of the civil rights movement created a sea change in the South and in the whole nation at the cultural and political levels, while also altering the lives of its participants—both white and Black—their families, and their friends. It formed a generation of activists sharing similar aspirations, achievements, and traumas. It laid the groundwork for the passage of crucial legislation. It pioneered modes of political engagement, education, and lawyering. It set the stage for the ensuing social movements, such as the Free Speech Movement and the antiwar movement.

It was immediately clear that the microcosm of lawyers, and in particular the Guild lawyers, were deeply affected by this experience.[105] Those who worked in Mississippi, reads a booklet edited by the Guild in that period, almost invariably expressed profound changes in their attitudes. They had experienced "a new set of legal values, a different system of legal practice and a strange, uncomfortable set of human relations."[106] The transformation was inescapable and involved even those who joined the lawyers' crusade for personal reasons. A case in point is Kunstler, who admittedly started his civil rights work "as a selfish gesture" to find "a way out of the mundane and petty work of a regular law practice" and was nonetheless truly shaken.[107]

In general, lawyers first felt outraged and sometimes scared at the sight of racial segregation and intimidation by both private citizens and local officials; second, they were commonly radicalized and driven into action; third, they drew some lessons for their own practice, notably the unreliability of federal powers and the necessity of innovative legal strategies. This set of reactions explains to a great extent the shift in perspective of many Guild lawyers, the rise of a new generation of radical lawyers, and the sudden rejuvenation of the Guild during the second half of the 1960s. It is worthwhile to address these reactions in detail.

The enduring racism of a section of the white population and the hostility to civil rights workers came up again and again in lawyers' testimonies. One of the CLAS lawyers who ventured to Philadelphia, Mississippi, to investigate the disappearance of the three civil rights volunteers James Chaney, Michael Schwerner, and Andy Goodman recalled that before they could enter the county courthouse, a crowd of a hundred people closed in on them. He was blocked by an unknown person who demanded his identity, residence, and reason for being there. The sheriff's office was also filled with townspeople, giving the vivid impression that not even lawyers were safe. Anna K. Johnston Diggs, a Black lawyer who was part of the same Guild delegation, remembered that they were effectively "intimidated" by the number and threatening attitude of the locals. To go back to their car after meeting with police, the lawyers were forced to pass through a milling crowd screaming hate-filled epithets.[108] Claudia Shropshire, another Black lawyer who also participated in the search, similarly recounted, "There is no way to describe the complete breakdown of law and order in this state. . . . The conditions are terrible. . . . The resistance to integration is more massive than ever. . . . The fear of violence and death is all around us."[109]

The youngest civil rights volunteers were predictably the most frightened and still have crisp memories of those days. Future Guild lawyer Deborah Rand was only nineteen when she took part in the 1964 Summer Project with COFO. Born and raised in a left-wing Jewish family, she was a student at Carleton College in Minnesota. One day the Freedom Singers came on campus to recruit people to go to Mississippi, and she signed up without hesitation.[110] "We were just blown away," remembers Rand. Yet in the course of her training in Oxford, Ohio, fear gripped her. Lawyers and organizers came to talk to the new recruits. "The training was actually meant to protect ourselves and also to show us how scary it was, so that those of us who couldn't handle it could leave. A lot of us thought about leaving. I called my friends; I called my family. While we were there, Chaney, Goodman, and Schwerner disappeared. At that point, everyone suddenly freaked out."

She decided to continue anyway. "We went across the border, and the sign says 'Mississippi Law Stop.' . . . All of us still remember that sign. . . . Mississippi was terrifying. You knew it was the worst place in the country," she recalls. They finally reached Pascagoula in the Deep South, an area that was considered one of the safest in the state. However, when Rand arrived, several civil rights workers were already in jail, and the relationship with the white residents was hardly easy. When the volunteers walked in the streets, the locals sometimes veered their cars as if to hit them. "They didn't hit us," she explains, "but they wanted us to know how scary it was." For many students like Deborah Rand, their experience in the South was also their first encounter with firearms. Volunteers lived in the houses of the Black community, and the owners would sit out on the porch with their rifles at hand to protect their white guests. Nothing ever happened at the home she was staying in, but during one of the church meetings, the Klan came by and shot into the meeting, hitting one person: "Everybody was scared. I was never shot at before."[111]

Violence and intimidation, especially with regard to lawyers, often took other, more subtle forms. A volunteer with the Guild's 1964 Summer Project remembers that he never witnessed any open violence, but he knew it was there: "Cars of whites often waited in the darkness across the street from the Vicksburg project house." The house was indeed dynamited in September, right after he left.[112] A young law clerk for a Michigan Supreme Court justice took part in the same project and was assigned to Ackerman, Mississippi. Interviewed while he was there, he explained, "The strange thing is the people here are so pleasant. . . . They are pleasant until they find out why you're here. Then it changes. It becomes cold. . . . Walking out of the courthouses they yell at you. All the usual stuff. After a while you don't hear the words. You just see the lips moving."[113]

The most intense outrage probably resulted from the experience of racism and coercion against civil rights workers by local officials, including representatives of the justice system. Sanford Katz was asked by the Guild to go to Birmingham, Alabama, to try to assess what legal help was needed and to determine if the Guild's assistance would be welcome. At his arrival, he found the Black community "in a state of virtual occupation by the infamous Sheriff Bull Connor, his local police department and what seemed to be a battalion of German shepherds." Katz remembers staying at the Gaston Motel, the only structure in town that accommodated Black patrons, which served as the base for both local and out-of-town activists. Recently bombed, the motel "was entirely surrounded by members of every police agency in the State."[114]

Ralph Shapiro, a white lawyer dispatched to Columbus, Mississippi, recalls the little gestures of racism they faced. He was there with a Black attorney from Chicago to represent a few young Black activists. The two went to meet one of the city's prosecuting attorneys. Shapiro introduced himself. "He took my hand when I extended it," remembers Shapiro, but when his Black colleague extended his, the prosecutor "just refused to take it and turned his back on him." The intrepid Victor Rabinowitz, who had represented a large number of controversial clients during McCarthyism, also admitted his personal shock before that system of justice: "None of my extensive practice in the Federal Courts in New York, Washington, Boston and other so-called centers of civilization prepared me for the barbarism of the courts, court officials and police in Jackson (and indeed in Albany, Georgia, as well). We were all treated as alien invaders, as perhaps we were."[115]

As far as Guild lawyers were concerned, outrage and indignation usually stoked radicalization and a stronger commitment to act. Kunstler explained that after seeing Black people "beaten and bloodied," he felt "empty inside" and had to do whatever he could to stop their pain. As a result, he found himself "no longer satisfied practicing conventional law and talking liberal politics" and wanted to be "someone who had a real contribution to make" for his new constituency, namely "the poor, the uneducated, the powerless, the disfranchised."[116] "All too frequently," wrote Goodman, referring to Guild volunteers, "they went from one extreme to the other," and after a few days in the field, they wanted to be "just as militant as the COFO workers." "We constantly had to remind them that their job was to get people out of jail and not to land there themselves," glossed Goodman. Crockett also claimed that none of the lawyers actually wanted to leave after the week's tour of duty, and all tried to think of reasons to stay longer.[117] In sum, Guild volunteers "went, learned, experienced the terror that existed there, the difficulties of obtaining the most elementary justice, and came back as converts. They became fighters for the cause and wanted to do more."[118]

Looking back to the experience with the civil rights movement, Guild lawyers took away at least two main lessons from their practice. First, relying on federal powers to eradicate injustice and racism was not a safe plan. Second, legal strategies and the professional identity of movement lawyers had to be revamped to fit the shifting political context. Regarding the first point, Len Holt put it very straight: "The summer that wouldn't end—the Mississippi Freedom Summer of 1964—if it does nothing more, should teach some and remind others that with regard to ending the racism of America the Federal government is not so much helpless as it is unwilling."[119]

The belief that the evil substantially lay in the hearts of white Mississippians and Alabamans and that the federal government, somehow isolated and oblivious, just needed to be informed and properly activated was eventually regarded as pure "naiveté," wrote another Guild lawyer reflecting on his experience in the South.[120] To be sure, Guild attorneys did not abandon any hope in that respect. In fact, they experimented with and popularized the legal stratagem of removal, which was grounded on the confidence that federal courts, as opposed to state courts, could still guarantee a fair trial. Removal petitions had indeed profound effects upon the movement, slowing down the "power structure" in its attacks and boosting the morale of the movement.[121] Also, federal courts—the Supreme Court, the Fifth Circuit Court of Appeals, and some district courts—rendered many decisions favorable to the movement. For example, according to legal scholar Jonathan D. Casper, civil rights forces won fifty-seven out of sixty-one sit-in cases decided by the Supreme Court between 1957 and 1967. The Warren court, as many contend, was a powerful ally to the civil rights movement during that period.[122]

However, most of the court rulings were based on technical grounds and sidestepped both First and Fourteenth Amendment issues; thus, they did not frontally attack the system of segregation. Moreover, only a small portion of the civil rights convictions in the criminal courts ever reached the higher courts for appeal. When they did so, decisions took quite a long time to be delivered; meanwhile, people sat in jail.[123] As previously discussed, federal protection was also accused of being full of gaps. Enforcement of constitutional rights at the state level was lacking, beginning with the right to effective counsel. Finally, direct interaction between civil rights workers and the FBI was highly problematic, to say the least.

Karen Jo Koonan's experience provides a case in point. At the age of nineteen, Koonan traveled to Mississippi in the summer of 1964 to teach people how to pass literacy tests in order to be able to register to vote. Her encounter with the FBI was probably one of the key reasons she became a legal worker and a lifelong Guild activist. When someone set fire to the school where she was teaching, "two FBI agents, white Mississippians," approached her and asked if she had been threatened. "I said no," she remembers. But after a while, a car arrived carrying several people, including the deputy sheriff of the county. "They jumped down and started beating one of my co-workers— in front of the FBI. . . . I went hysterical. I said, 'Do something!' And they replied, 'It's not our jurisdiction.'" "That was the turning point for me," she confesses. "I realized that [the problem] was much bigger than some ignorant rednecks in some town of Mississippi. This was about a whole system designed to protect some people and not others. That changed my whole life."[124]

The need for a broad makeover in the legal practice was the second lesson that Guild lawyers typically learned. As a matter of fact, lawyers in the South had experienced a very unusual way of working. Performing nonlegal tasks for the sake of the movement had become a rather common habit.[125] As Kinoy wrote, "A merger of legal and political roles was inevitable." During the MFDP drive, Kinoy stood before organizers "primarily not as a lawyer but as a political person," being "on an equal level with the other movement people." He explained it in these terms: "Our ultimate function was not only to be skillful technicians creatively molding legal concepts to serve the needs of the people's movements, but also to be political beings in our own right, independent and equal members of the movement, participating in the formulation of policy and then aiding in its implementation."[126] Kunstler echoed this line of reasoning. Lawyers, his experience confirmed, could be an integral part of the movement: "I spent most of my time during the spring of 1963 marching in the streets of Birmingham. I realized that the paperwork and intellectual maneuvers in the courtroom were not the heart of the movement at all, but merely an appendage. Marching and protesting, being out on the streets—that was where the strength of the movement lay, and that would be how it would finally prevail."[127]

In spite of a rich dose of rhetoric, the testimonies of Guild lawyers frequently describe a fascination with the movement and a tight relationship with both civil rights workers and Black communities. The meetings in the churches, the prayers, "We Shall Overcome" intoned together, Martin Luther King's impassioned speeches, the nights of endless political discussion with others in the movement, and the warm personal reception are common themes among the personal memories.[128] Contrary to the majority of civil rights lawyers, who tended to avoid emotional involvement and remain dispassionate courtroom advocates, Guild lawyers did not make any effort to stay aloof; rather, they amalgamated with the communities. For example, they gave sermons in churches and participated in demonstrations.[129] In August 1963, the Guild president himself urged all members of the bar to support the March on Washington for Jobs and Freedom by actively taking part in the demonstration.[130] This was noteworthy, as it was the first time the Guild encouraged lawyers to literally take to the streets. Kunstler rushed there and listened to Martin Luther King's legendary speech: "It was the most profound speech I had ever heard and moved me as no speech had ever done—before or since."[131]

Lawyers' and law students' direct contact with the movement also brought together a deeper appreciation for the self-denial and courage of civil rights workers—a realization that would affect future choices. In a 1965 report about his experience in Mississippi during the previous summer, Stephen Bingham explained that among his civil rights companions, "no one was weighing risk against need in personal terms." Activists also knew that their death was a possibility and, to some extent, a necessity to wake up the nation. Yet, they did not withdraw.[132] The topic of courage also resonates in Deborah Rand's description of her encounter with SNCC field secretaries, whom she describes as "truly heroic people." Jimmie Travis, for example, who got a bullet in his neck while in Mississippi, "talked about being shot, beaten, and insulted. He scared us but also moved us and made us angry enough at what he suffered to want desperately to stop it." "Their courage and commitment," notes Rand, "demanded some act on my part to support the struggle for democracy and racial justice."[133]

This shift toward the movement also called into question the conventional trial strategies of civil rights lawyers. Hitherto, the nature of the southern legal system had affected defense strategies in criminal prosecutions essentially in one way, toward the depoliticization of proceedings. As sociologist Steven E. Barkan explains, the mere representation of civil rights clients was risky enough, and juries were generally hostile, so defense attorneys "could not afford the luxury of trying in court to talk at length about the larger issues or racism and segregation." As a result, technical questions largely prevailed over social issues, and political rhetoric was also avoided. Given that backdrop, many defendants did not feel it necessary to carry their radical protests into the courtroom. Racial issues were overlooked even in the well-publicized trials, such as those of Martin Luther King.[134] When not dealing with criminal trials, civil rights lawyers were mostly employed to set out test cases to dismantle the Jim Crow system.

The experience of Guild lawyers suggested a different reaction to the legal emergency in the South. Both social issues and defendants' political claims gradually came back to courtrooms. "I understood," wrote Kinoy, "that the more we tied the fate of the individual to the overall confrontation between the assertion of federal power and the effort to perpetuate the system of segregation, the more chance we had of touching a raw nerve." In so doing, Kinoy came to the realization that one of the crucial tasks of a radical lawyer was "to make this bridge between the individual defense and the strategic assault upon the entire repressive structure."[135] At the same time, by adopting a less litigation-centered approach, lawyers were not leading the movement but following behind as a way to protect direct action and the movement's initiatives. Their primary responsibility was no longer to fashion legal solutions to win freedom and equality through court proceedings—they had to shield and empower the movement.[136]

2 Mass Defense

· ·

There was a moment in the 1960s when writing down the phone number of the local NLG on an arm or wrist came to be a routine precaution before any demonstration, like wearing comfortable shoes or bringing a lemon to ward off the worst effects of tear gas. At a time when taking to the streets was becoming the new normal and encounters with law enforcement an increasingly common occurrence, any experienced protester knew that it was wise to have rapid access to legal first aid they could trust.[1] The NLG thus became a reference point among radicals by virtue of its mass defense work, namely a comprehensive strategy to deal with the legal troubles of activists arrested during demonstrations, especially if there were many who risked criminal charges. To be sure, the notion of mass defense already existed in the communist tradition and first emerged through the legal militancy of the International Labor Defense. In the first half of the twentieth century, however, the concept of mass defense generically implied the mobilization of the masses against bourgeois justice.[2] Responding to the evolving needs of 1960s movements and tackling an unprecedented wave of arrests, Guild lawyers developed a new set of practices.

Even before the civil rights movement shook the conscience of an entire generation, groups of white students across the country "felt there was a kind of nobility in being devoted to the public good," as Todd Gitlin wrote. These young idealists treasured morality, opposed a nation obsessed with the private pursuit of material wealth and expressed solidarity with the people who were excluded from rights and prosperity. They also believed in the value of direct action: putting their bodies on the line, they attempted to seize—not only advocate for—civil liberties, campus reform, and peace. Their imagination was clearly moved by the struggle in the South, but they also shared a distaste for corporate liberalism and affluent society.[3]

By 1960, this political attitude quickly coalesced into the New Left and shifted the campus mood across America, beginning in the Bay Area. Known for its open-minded culture and diverse community, this segment of California had been the favorite destination for scores of leftists, dropouts, and bohemians since the 1950s. A large and tolerant university such as UC Berkeley and a still vital Old Left community also contributed to making the area a radical hotbed.[4] It was precisely this well-known presence of leftists of various lineages that drew the attention of the House Un-American Activities Committee (HUAC). And when the committee opened its hearings at San Francisco city hall, in April 1960, for the first time a large contingent of students were there to oppose it. Indeed, anti-anticommunism had unified a nonpartisan front of young people. Some of them had formed the ad hoc committee Students for Civil Liberties, affiliated with the ACLU, which demanded that HUAC be abolished. Others were members of SLATE, a recently formed nonideological group that urged an end to compulsory participation in the Reserve Officers' Training Corps and challenged the restrictions on campus political activity at Berkeley.[5]

On May 12, a rally at city hall gathered up to a hundred protesters, who clamored for admittance to the hearings. Tickets had been assigned to sympathetic observers, and the few unruly spectators who managed to enter were dragged out by marshals. The day after, some five thousand demonstrators showed up outside the hall, chanting, "Witch hunters go home!" Suddenly the police opened fire hoses, and chaos erupted. Kicked and clubbed, students went limp in an act of passive resistance. A few of them, dragged down the marble steps by police officers, were left injured. In two days of protests, a total of sixty-eight people, mostly students, were arrested and charged with inciting a riot, disturbing the peace, and resisting arrest. Only one student, Robert Meisenbach, was singled out as a ringleader and charged with assault of a police officer with a deadly weapon.[6]

The HUAC protest was, all at once, a sign of the end of McCarthyism, a baptism by fire for a generation of student rebels, and the first direct experience of police violence for many. It is not surprising that the event also sent shockwaves through the law enforcement community and specifically the FBI. Wanting to demonstrate that communists were behind these protests—or better, all protests—Hoover commissioned *Operation Abolition*, a documentary based on sloppy and forged evidence. The film was so biased that it turned out to be one of the most powerful weapons against HUAC. It was even screened by radicals to show that the government would lie to its citizens about students who simply exercised their constitutional rights.[7]

The events of May 1960 also prompted new legal needs: there was a substantial number of protesters facing the same charges for political action, and no one was there to help. The director of the local ACLU made it clear that his organization could neither post nor guarantee bail. "It is not our function to defend breaches of the peace," he declared. If anything, the

ACLU could intervene on behalf of the spectators who were wrongly arrested as rioters.[8] Malcolm S. Burnstein—a recent graduate of UC Berkeley Law School, a clerk on the Supreme Court, and a member of the Guild—participated in the demonstration and was appalled by the sight of police violence on harmless students. He wanted to help a friend who had been arrested and, with no clue about what to do, called Charles R. Garry, whom he had met through the NLG. Garry, who had been a president of the San Francisco chapter of the Guild and was a renowned trial lawyer dedicated to unpopular clients, headed immediately to the jail. To the delight of the FBI, which was eager to prove a communist conspiracy, an avowed Marxist who in 1957 had refused to disclose his communist membership in front of HUAC bailed out all the demonstrators.

However, when the defendants came back to city hall to be sentenced, they waived their right to a jury trial and placed their fate in the hands of the judge. They also agreed not to sue the city for police brutality. They fought no battle but were lucky enough to find a liberal judge who dismissed all the charges. In 1961, Meisenbach faced a separate trial and opted for a defense team of two civil rights advocates. One of them was, once again, Garry. Meisenbach surprisingly refused to plea-bargain and consented to an aggressive defense strategy. The two attorneys attempted to politicize the trial and challenged eyewitnesses' and police reports. Yet they specified that Meisenbach was not a political activist and was unjustly singled out. The jury cleared Meisenbach of all charges.[9]

As a result of a wave of protests against job discrimination in San Francisco, masses of young activists were arrested again in 1964. Led by civil rights groups such as the Berkeley Congress of Racial Equality, demonstrators picketed and sat down to denounce ingrained discrimination against minorities in employment. They targeted Lucky's stores, the *Oakland Tribune*, auto row shops, and, most famously, the Sheraton Palace Hotel, where nearly three hundred people were arrested on March 6. The mass arrests, which generated a total of 474 defendants charged with disorderly conduct, disturbing the peace, and trespassing, brought back the need for lawyers who were both familiar with criminal law and able to establish a relationship with political clients.[10]

Many volunteer attorneys and law students participated in the defense efforts, and the Guild submitted a number of amicus briefs. Nonetheless, the briefs were disregarded, the coordination among counsels was scarce, and the organization was rudimentary. The prosecution also parceled defendants into thirty-seven group trials, enough to require a large number of lawyers and to dissipate defendants' energies but not enough to stall the local system of justice. While local government officials scourged civil rights activists in the media and "unusual tension" arose in the courtrooms, the quality of justice was unequal. More than a half of defendants were convicted, and sentences were generally harsh, similar to those given to the Freedom Riders in Mississippi.[11]

Guild lawyers were disappointed. Something had to be devised to protect the rights of protesters in the future. But what could they do?

A Tentative Defense in Berkeley

Without a break, another more daunting challenge barged in. A few miles away from the halls of justice, at the uproarious UC Berkeley, students came back to campus in the fall of 1964 with extraordinary intolerance for rules, hierarchies, and paternalism. Eager to put participatory democracy into practice, they demanded to be treated as citizens with a voice in the governance of the university. Incidentally, some of them had spent the summer in Mississippi and, after close encounters with the Ku Klux Klan, were hardly intimidated by academic authorities. Students were bold and knew the grammar of civil disobedience. Now they wanted to speak freely.[12]

Compared to other universities, UC Berkeley under the presidency of Clark Kerr was a reasonably accepting space for free speech, yet since that fall, school officials had enforced a rule banning the use of university grounds to promote off-campus political causes, such as civil rights. Hence, free speech, in a period of relentless politicization, did not mean free advocacy. What happened later—the first major campus revolt of the 1960s—has been widely recounted, and a few words suffice to bring it to mind. Everything started with petitions for free speech, a few pickets on the steps of Sproul Hall (the main administration building), and the ensuing suspension of students. Then, on October 1, Jack Weinberg—a former student and current civil rights worker—set up a table to distribute CORE materials, refused orders to leave, and was subsequently arrested. Loaded into a police car in Sproul Plaza, he received the solidarity of hundreds of students, who sat down around the vehicle and urged his release. For more than a day, students chanted civil rights songs and employed the roof of the car as a podium to address the crowd. They demanded to meet the chancellor and that no disciplinary actions be taken. A junior in philosophy, Mario Savio, enchanted the onlookers with his natural charisma.[13]

In the blink of an eye, the Free Speech Movement (FSM) was born and began holding rallies almost every day at noon on the steps of Sproul Hall. It was during these early days that the students who had obtained a committee to "negotiate" the exercise of political and civil rights on campus contacted sympathetic lawyers. Through Communist Party connections, Bettina Aptheker, an FSM leader and the daughter of renowned Marxist historian Herbert Aptheker, approached Guild attorney Robert E. Treuhaft to be advised on legal and constitutional issues. Treuhaft had been a member of the CPUSA in the 1950s, had represented HUAC witnesses, and had opened a small firm specializing in labor law in Oakland with another Guild attorney, Doris B. Walker—a former factory worker and a communist herself.[14] The aforementioned Burnstein had been hired by Treuhaft and Walker and, in that capacity, was designated to deal with the students. It is interesting to note that Burnstein knew that the students were absolutely right in their basic demands and could reject any compromise solutions on solid legal grounds. However, still imbued with a gradualist approach, he proposed to accept the university's middle-of-the-road offer. Students did not follow suit and, in retrospect, they were right.[15]

On December 2, 1964, a showdown could not be avoided any longer, as thousands of students amassed to protest the threatened suspension of Savio and other activists. After Savio gave a speech that would go down in the annals, and Joan Baez sang "We Shall Overcome," a mass of protesters took over Sproul Hall and occupied its four floors. The university requested police intervention. From the wee hours of the following morning, everyone inside the building was arrested and charged with trespassing, failure to disperse, and resisting arrest. Robert Treuhaft was the first to be taken into custody and brought to Santa Rita jail. At the end of the day, a total of 773 people were arrested, giving shape to the largest mass arrest in California since 1946. No legal organization was ready to help, though. While civil liberties lawyers phoned one another to gather volunteer counsel, a borrowed office on campus was designated as Legal Central. Since no bail money was available, faculty members who sided with students posted bail and released the arrested.[16]

Though fury over the mass arrest mounted, it was soon overcome by joy. After further negotiations, the university backed down and granted the right of political advocacy on campus. It was a great victory, proof that an uncompromising strategy paid off, and a source of inspiration for activists across the country. However, following this political success, the judicial battle proved dire. The criminal defense of those arrested during the sit-in resulted, as Burnstein wrote, in "an unvarnished legal defeat," namely the conviction of 99 percent of the arrested. How did it happen?

An emergency meeting right after the arrests gathered more than thirty-five lawyers who volunteered to help, but many more came on board later, nearly one hundred altogether. Some of them were radical lawyers, others were more neutral lawyers moved by the students' sacrifice, and still others were lawyers appointed by students' families. Burnstein, who was the best acquainted with the FSM, was chosen to coordinate the defense. He eventually teamed up with Richard Buxbaum, who was a left-leaning professor of law at Berkeley and a sympathizer of the movement; Henry Elson, who gravitated around both the ACLU and the NLG; Norman Leonard, who was a seasoned civil liberties lawyer and a longtime member of the NLG; and Stanley Golde, who was one of the leading criminal attorneys in the Bay Area. This lawyer lineup was meant to represent the various currents of the FSM.

Provided that all students pleaded guilty, the prosecution offered a very lenient sentence of probation for the majority and a more serious sentence for the few presumed leaders. But a large majority of the students refused. All of them were the same, they rebutted, and a "unified defense" seemed "the only way to honor the unified principles that had led to the sit-in." They also believed that they would win in the end, so they requested a "mass jury trial" of all the indicted students. However, the court denied the motion. At that point, both defendants and prosecutors risked having more than seventy separate trials, because in Alameda County it was customary to not try more than ten people together. This solution would have taken an extremely long time (up to five years, considering the regular schedule), would have led to unequal judicial outcomes for people charged with the same crimes, and would have required dozens of lawyers ready to commit. Even sympathetic lawyers were not available for such a lengthy crusade.[17]

After much debate, the majority of defendants agreed to accept a second deal offered by the prosecution, which was to waive a jury and proceed to a trial by judge of a representative number of defendants (155), whose ruling would apply to everybody. Defined as a "mass court trial," it was a sort of trial by proxy, which was irregular and unprecedented but seemed the lesser of two evils. Only one defendant got his case severed, and just a radical minority contested the decision. Pragmatism prevailed over politics. The judge was considered fair, and lawyers believed that the chances of obtaining a favorable verdict were good. At the same time, a trial of this kind was briefer than any other solution, and students didn't want to spend too much time and money trapped in the clutches of justice. Only a few of them thought about politicizing or exploiting the trial as a forum. The only overt political statement was the refusal to plead guilty, which implied the confidence of being on the right side.

In any event, the trial was quite ordinary and prompted scarce participation by the public or even the students themselves. Although the defense committee asked defendants and supporters to attend the proceedings whenever they could and to raise money to pay at least office costs, results were scanty. Rarely more than thirty defendants showed up during the trial.[18] In their correspondence, lawyers repeatedly lamented that they were in desperate need of funds and, most importantly, that many of their clients had shirked their responsibility of coming to court. Your absence, they wrote to the students, weakens your own defense. "If you feel no other obligations," they added, "you still have one to the lawyers—who are giving their days and nights in your behalf."[19] At the same time, lawyers did not envision a particular role for their clients and asked them to behave, to avoid talking with the press, and "to dress up and be neatly groomed" for all court appearances.[20] "None of the five of us ever got outraged," remembers Richard Buxbaum, one of the five defense lawyers. "No one shouted, screamed, played the game, and so on. . . . This was not a histrionic case." Buxbaum also confirms that the students "were not really interested in a provocative kind of confrontation." Mario Savio himself was apparently "very sincere in his belief in attempting to have a just result without having to screw up the court system."[21]

The verdict disappointed almost everyone. The judge acquitted all defendants of failing to disperse from an unlawful assembly but convicted them of trespass. Those who went limp were also convicted of resisting arrest. While the vast majority of students received only fines, ten of them were given harsher sentences (up to 120 days in jail, plus a fine and probation).

Upon reflection, the waiver of jury trials was singled out as the main reason for the legal defeat and taught a lesson to political defendants.[22] Since that verdict, radical activists of the 1960s and 1970s rarely relinquished their right to be tried by peers, hoping to find sympathetic jurors among common people. At the same time, it was clear that both FSM students and lawyers treated the trial as a conventional criminal proceeding and did not attempt to educate the public with political arguments. Around the defendants there was a frail committee, and the Guild failed to act. "We had been as cooperative as possible all the way through," lamented a student; hence, the government "has gotten its convictions with a minimum expense and embarrassment."[23]

Yet times were changing, and the defeat prompted reflection. Albeit in a contradictory way, students signaled their intolerance vis-à-vis a system of justice that had punished them for acting in the name of constitutional principles. Therefore, before sentencing, when the judge asked all defendants to write him a note explaining their position, they replied with more than six hundred letters in which they reiterated their faith in the freedom of speech. The letters were essentially ignored and ended up in the university archives, yet they represent the litmus test of a shift toward a more disenchanted view of justice. Instead of apologizing, demonstrators reaffirmed the lawfulness of their actions.[24] At the same time, in another minimal but contentious gesture, a number of students refused probation and accepted lengthened jail terms. A few of them also spoke out against the war in Vietnam in front of a dumbfounded judge.[25]

In the aftermath, Guild lawyers discussed the dangers and potentiality of mass defense, also inviting some FSM activists to speak at the Guild's 1965 national convention in San Francisco. But in August of the same year, during the Watts uprising, the Los Angeles chapter of the Guild found itself substantially powerless. For six days, ten thousand Black Americans protesting lack of jobs, inadequate schooling, and police brutality took to the streets, looted stores, set property ablaze, and exchanged fire with law enforcement. When the smoke cleared, 34 people were dead, including 3 police officers, and 1,032 were injured; 3,952 Black citizens (4,200 according to Guild records), including 500 juveniles, had been arrested. Eighty percent of those arrested were held in jail for more than two weeks, and bails were set on average $3,000 above normal. It was also impossible to obtain accurate information about the persons involved in the riot and detained. Confusion prevailed, and the Guild filed an amicus brief urging the release of those under arrest, either on their own recognizance or on low bail. Discussions and individual initiatives of volunteer lawyers were all that emerged from the Guild's participation—too little for a situation that was becoming explosive.[26]

When other so-called race riots broke out a couple of years later in Newark, Detroit, and plenty of other communities, radical lawyers felt a natural urge to help.[27] Once again, Black people rebelled to denounce enduring segregation, alienation, and poverty, and acted against symbols of white America. More than at any time before, as the Kerner Report denounced, it was clear that the civil rights movement remained unfinished, and the nation was still harboring "two societies, one Black, one white—separate and unequal."[28] Unsurprisingly, Guild lawyers rushed to create makeshift defense committees. One such lawyer was Dennis James, a graduate of the University of Michigan Law School who had just abandoned the Democratic Party to side with the New Left. Being in Detroit, he pooled with a group of lawyers he knew through the Guild and created the Metropolitan Defense Committee. This elementary organization offered pro bono representation to people arrested for alleged rioting or organizing riots.

Yet James felt that initiatives like this were not enough. A few months later, at an executive board meeting of the Guild, he sounded the alarm: demonstrations were growing exponentially, and activists were being busted every day. Radical lawyers had to act more consistently, open offices, and coordinate their work.[29]

Shaping Mass Defense

It was the Vietnam War that magnified the student movement, radicalized it, and dragged it off campus. As such, it stands to reason that the Vietnam War played a key role in electrifying Guild lawyers and prompting them into action.

Students for a Democratic Society (SDS)—the main student organization of the New Left, famously reborn in the early 1960s with the *Port Huron Statement*—had the intuition and the energy to stage the first national demonstration against the conflict. Up until those days, university-based teach-ins had been the most frequent form of antiwar protest. On April 17, 1965, between twenty thousand and twenty-five thousand people materialized at an SDS march in Washington, D.C., surprising everyone and giving life to the largest peace march in U.S. history up to that time. In a celebrated speech, SDS leader Paul Potter called for the creation of "a massive social movement" that would "understand Vietnam in all its horror as but a symptom of a deeper malaise."[30]

A few weeks later in Berkeley, Jerry Rubin, a still unknown working-class activist from Cincinnati, joined forces with a few antiwar organizers to create the Vietnam Day Committee (VDC) and sponsored a teach-in at the university. More than thirty thousand people flocked there. When the speeches were over, several hundred participants, led by members of the Young Socialist Alliance, departed campus and marched to the Berkeley draft board, where they hanged President Johnson's effigy and burned draft cards. In August 1965, when the army began to send troops to Vietnam, and military trains were running through Berkeley to the nearby Oakland Army Base, the VDC decided to picket the trains and disrupt their course, sitting on the tracks and jumping on wagons with leaflets.[31]

Direct actions increasingly implied breaches of the law, and people involved in the movement clearly needed a more structured, permanent, and specialized legal support system. Peter Franck, a Free Speech Movement activist and a young Guild lawyer in Berkeley, proposed creating an umbrella organization to coordinate the defense of antiwar demonstrators in the Bay Area. His friends Fay and Marvin Stender jumped in, and together they established the Council for Justice. Fay was a junior partner in the radical firm Garry, Dreyfus, and McTernan. With her husband Marvin, a committed radical lawyer, she had joined the San Francisco Guild in 1961. The two had taken part in the Guild's project in Mississippi and had already helped with campus sit-ins. Now they were ready to serve their first client, the Vietnam Day Committee. On behalf of that organization, they designed a system of intervention for direct action, with volunteer lawyers providing advice on the spot, dispatchers, and a bail center. They also secured permits for demonstrations and made themselves available almost anytime.[32]

And yet the efforts of the Council for Justice were drops in the ocean, as the antiwar movement kept growing. While Congress passed war appropriations by huge majorities, demonstrators resolved to break the myth that the war was backed by national consensus. It was time to raise the stakes and escalate contention from protest to resistance. In that context, groups of young antiwar activists based in Berkeley organized Stop the Draft Week, to be held on October 16–20, 1967. The goal of this concerted series of actions was "to promote mass civil disobedience against the war." Sit-ins, picket lines, rallies, and episodes of "active resistance" were geared toward the disruption of the Oakland induction center, where hundreds of young men entered the armed forces daily.[33] The planning of the weeklong action was meticulous, and the complex organizational chart that was drawn up placed the legal office in a central position, in direct contact with the headquarters. "No aggressive violence against the cops" was encouraged, but it was agreed that all demonstrators had "a right to defend themselves against attack." Peaceful moral witnessing was definitely over.[34]

Although dominated by a pacifist sit-in, the first day was already legally complex and ended with the arrest of 140 activists, including Joan Baez. The morning after, a few thousand demonstrators descended on the induction center and found five hundred police officers in riot gear, who welcomed them with mace and severe beatings. While protests during the following two days were more restrained, between six thousand and ten thousand people converged on Oakland on Friday with a spirit of anger and revenge. Wearing helmets and carrying homemade shields, many acted as mobile squads, erected barricades, overturned cars, threw bottles and rocks at police, and spray-painted buildings. When the police shielded the induction center, demonstrators went on a rampage through the business district of downtown Oakland. With unprecedented rage, protesters tried to paralyze police by slashing tires, blocking intersections, and derailing city buses. A few officers and demonstrators were injured, but only twenty-eight people were arrested. By the end of the week, arrests totaled 317.[35]

The legal safety net held, fending off potential disasters. In addition to the legal headquarters, the Guild's student chapter at Berkeley and the local lawyers managed an emergency phone line and sent observers to monitor arrests and police behavior in the field. Guild attorneys worked around the clock all week, interviewing activists in jail, helping to arrange for bail, and appearing in court to advise defendants on their rights. Other Guild attorneys remained on standby and counseled people who phoned their offices.[36] A system of mass defense for large arrest situations was finally born, and it was simultaneously employed in Washington, D.C.'s Stop the Draft Week. The NLG estimated that in the two cities, over two hundred law students worked with senior attorneys to assist with mass arrests, observe and prepare affidavits, and draft background memos for volunteer attorneys.[37]

Two months later, during another Stop the Draft Week in New York City, the scheme was replicated and, for the first time, the New York City Guild chapter set up an official Mass Defense Committee, chaired by Mary M. Kaufman. Described by the press as a "spirited red-headed" attorney, Kaufman was a courageous and talented woman.[38] She had been part of the Nuremberg trials U.S. prosecution team and later, during McCarthyism, had defended a number of activists against the Smith Act, including labor organizer and communist leader Elizabeth G. Flynn.[39] The New York demonstration began on December 5, 1967, when a coalition of antiwar groups led by progressive pediatrician Dr. Benjamin Spock took to the streets with the objective of closing down the induction center in lower Manhattan. To defuse possible tensions, the massive police contingent allowed Spock and a small crowd of protesters to penetrate the blockade and commit civil disobedience. Activists sat down for a few seconds in front of the building steps and were quickly ushered into paddy wagons, as expected. Although the entire process was arranged in cooperation with the police, the "almost liturgical protest" led to arrests and charges of disorderly conduct. By the end of the week, the police, especially its plainclothes officers, lost patience and enforced order with a vigorous intervention. All in all, more than five hundred demonstrators were arrested.[40] Since most of the demonstrators had avoided disruptive tactics, the ACLU lawyers handled many arraignments, but the NLG referral panel took care of approximately two hundred cases. For most of them, the Guild lawyers won dismissals.[41]

Columbia, 1968

New York's Columbia University was ripe for revolt, possessing all the ingredients for combustion. SDS had become a protagonist in campus politics and was increasingly dominated by a radical wing, the Action Faction, led by Mark Rudd—a firebrand with contagious energy and a talent for seizing the moment. As protests gained traction, in September 1967 the university ordered a ban on demonstrations on campus, which served only to radicalize the political climate, and put on probation a few student leaders who had simply marched to present a petition. In addition to white radicals, a number of Black students veered toward the Left and formed the Students' Afro-American Society, with roots in the Harlem community and an agenda that partially overlapped with SDS's program.

In the name of self-determination, radicals opposed a university administration that appeared remote from students and prone to the interests of corporate America, starting from the self-appointed board of trustees, which disposed of the power of last resort. More specifically, radicals denounced Columbia's affiliation with the Institute for Defense Analyses (IDA), an organization that conducted research for the Department of Defense. IDA was the smoking gun that exposed Columbia's involvement in the military-industrial complex and, simultaneously, proved Columbia's disregard of democracy. Without open consultation, the university had become affiliated with IDA, and both its president, Grayson L. Kirk, and a trustee joined the board of IDA. A further issue that fueled discontent was the planned construction of a gymnasium in Morningside Park, a narrow strip between Harlem and Morningside Heights. Being a green island for the local Black community, its partial occupation by Columbia came to symbolize the colonizing attitude of white institutions. Radicals contended that the "Gym Crow," as it was renamed, would have been an exclusive space for affluent students. Construction began on February 19, 1968; the next day, the first sit-in was held.[42]

Gradually, as Columbia was portrayed as the epitome of a corrupt system, the protest escalated into a revolt against American society as a whole—a society in which, on February 8, a group of unarmed Black demonstrators in Orangeburg, South Carolina, had been fired on by police, leaving three dead and thirty-three injured; a society in which, on April 4, Martin Luther King was fatally shot on the balcony of a motel by an unknown killer.[43] While contention at Columbia mounted, in more than one hundred cities across the United States people unleashed their rage over the death of King and were confronted by tanks and rounds of arrests: forty-six people lost their lives. The promise of liberation through nonviolence seemed to die with King, and scores of angry young people swelled the ranks of militant groups. As one student leader put it, "The force of logic having failed, the logic of force was fast becoming the only alternative."[44]

This is why, on April 23, when one thousand students and sympathetic faculty marched onto Columbia's campus, conflict proved hard to tame. While Black protesters barricaded themselves in Hamilton Hall, whites seized Low Library. Compromise solutions immediately clashed against a wall of mutual intransigence. Faculty repeatedly tried to work as peacemakers and organized meetings and committees, but all efforts became increasingly quixotic. The 750 striking students, who came to control five university buildings (coordinated by a Strike Central), were more interested in making a political point and in changing their lives than in winning over concessions. Against a society they saw as repressive and dehumanizing, they attempted to carve out liberated spaces and to reconstruct personal relationships. Only an amnesty in favor of the strikers—to avoid the much-feared expulsions—could have possibly shifted the balance.[45]

Such a scenario inevitably called for the presence of lawyers. And this time the Guild was ready to act. After the first occupations, New York City Guild members got in touch with the students, while the NLG student chapter at Columbia acted as a legal liaison to the various buildings. From inside the Black-led Hamilton Hall during the first night of the siege, the chapter gave its formal support to the occupation in a statement to the press. Over thirty law students picketed the law school, and a Guild student member served on the steering committee of the strike. To deal with the expected mass arrest, a legal defense apparatus was set up in advance. Preparations were made to obtain bail money and lawyers for the arraignments, while law students served as legal advisers for the various communes that were created in the liberated buildings. Despite their overconfident declarations, these young students on the barricades were often scared, so they constantly sought advice from lawyers about the consequences of their actions.[46]

In April 1968, Eleanor Stein, the daughter of Annie and Arthur Stein—communists, union organizers, and antiracist activists—was completing her first year at Columbia Law School. Absorbing her parents' ethos, she had been an organizer with CORE and with the National Committee for a Sane Nuclear Policy in New York City. Yet she was especially inspired by two family friends and Guild founding members David Rein and Joseph Forer, Washington lawyers who had done antidiscrimination litigation and represented a huge number of communists before HUAC. With a few friends, including Michael and Margaret Ratner and Gustin (Gus) Reichbach, Stein reopened the Guild student chapter at Columbia and, quite inevitably, found herself among the strikers.

"We were all working for the Guild office," she remembers today. "The protocol was that you were an observer so that you could not get arrested. Hopefully, your presence as a witness could prevent the worst police excesses from happening, and you could make sure that people didn't just disappear off the streets. So that distance was important. Functioning as a lawyer or law student, you created a cordon sanitaire between the police and the demonstrators. It was sort of a persona that law students used to have, also preserving a kind of psychological distance." Yet the attitude of Guild members was shifting. Stein, indeed, respected the protocol she described for one day only, before the distance disappeared and she definitively merged with the occupants.[47]

Even senior lawyers saw the involvement at Columbia in a different light. When the New York City Guild president wrote to his colleagues to urge them to join the new battlefield, he described the defense of Columbia students as "a unique opportunity of participating in a situation which is socially and politically very exciting and in which new legal concepts are being developed or initiated." Not only were "important legal issues" in constitutional and criminal law being raised, but radical lawyers were becoming "a significant factor in the social scene in the city and throughout the country," establishing the Guild "as a meaningful and effective organization."[48] The fact that picket lines and peaceful demonstrations were supplanted by an invasion of property, including vandalism in the president's office and even the hostage-taking of the acting dean, led to "an entirely different scene" that involved much more than civil liberties. "It was," read an internal memo, "a tug of war on Columbia's property between rebellious students and their supporters against an oppressive and irrelevant school administration, deaf and blind to the need for change. The issues involved racism, war and the alienation of the students." Contrary to the existing defense organizations, the Mass Defense Committee recognized that demonstrators had been forced to devise new contentious strategies.[49]

Six days after the first takeover, while the trustees undercut the last negotiating efforts, it seemed clear that strikers would prefer being arrested rather than giving in to the administration. Eventually, President Kirk authorized a police intervention to end the occupation. During the night of April 29, police began assembling on the periphery of the campus. Black strikers allowed themselves to be arrested peacefully and were reportedly treated with kid gloves, as everybody was concerned about the reaction of the Harlem community. By contrast, in the early morning of April 30, more than a thousand police officers forced their way into the other four buildings occupied by white radicals. Although the latter resisted arrest only by dragging their feet, they were brutally handled. Eleanor Stein was among them: grabbed by the hair, she was harassed and shoved into a police van. Uniformed and plainclothes officers also charged into the crowd of supporters that were gathered outside the buildings. In the end, 711 people were arrested, most of them charged with criminal trespass and resisting arrest.[50]

It was almost impossible for lawyers to restrain police on the spot. Some of them spent the night in jail to assist the young strikers and represented them at their arraignments, while other attorneys immediately drafted injunctive suits against the City of New York and the university to prevent further disciplinary proceedings.[51] In the meantime, Columbia closed for a week, and for the rest of the term, only some classes could resume their regular schedule. While pseudo-communes were created, the Strike Committee urged class boycotts and engaged students in counter-classes within a newly instituted free university, designed on the model of the Free University of Berkeley. Guild lawyers and law students also participated, by teaching courses on civil disobedience and how to deal with police.[52]

Before the summer, two other incidents around Columbia led to further arrests and additional legal needs. The first was the occupation of a Columbia housing building on 114th Street, where 117 people were arrested— including Rudd, who had escaped the previous mass arrest. The second incident arose from the disciplinary hearings of the six student demonstrators who had been singled out before the occupation. The students refused to appear in front of the dean on May 21, sending their parents and lawyers instead, and four of them were suspended. Supporters protested, barricades were erected on campus, and a building was seized. Clashes with police ensued and, by the morning after, another 174 people had been arrested.[53]

In this case, too, observers denounced police brutalities. According to a report by Columbia sociologists, in cooperation with ACLU and NLG lawyers, "The widespread abuses exhibited in the mass police actions at Columbia" were not simply the work of a few bad apples or the angry response of men under threat or provocation but forms of "violence undertaken coolly—usually—as a form of punishment."[54] Retrospectively, members of the Tactical Patrol Force—the elite group of one thousand police officers who were called to campus—denied any punitive intent against the "ungrateful" affluent kids but incidentally admitted an aggressive intervention, as for them it made no difference "dealing with middle class students or knife-wielding drug dealers on the Lower East Side."[55] In any event, Major John Lindsay also criticized police officers' excessive force, and student charges of brutality poured into Guild offices, together with requests for legal representation.[56]

Arguing that protest was an internal affair of Columbia, many asked the university to drop criminal charges. Columbia, however, maintained that the matter was out of its hands, as the trustees had already filed a complaint to the New York Police Department. Meanwhile, the district attorney's office discussed whether it made sense to prosecute these cases at all. Police had arrested people haphazardly, without much regard to reliable evidence or witnesses to document the events and prove that defendants had actually committed the crimes, especially trespassing.[57] Also, the large number of cases, approximately one thousand in all (later reduced), made it unlikely that the DA's office could try everybody if they all insisted on a trial. And this was precisely what strikers, backed by Guild lawyers, asked for. In a fundraising letter, student leaders threw down the gauntlet: "Although many of us have no confidence in our legal system we are demanding jury trials. Jury trials will enable us possibly to turn the court room into political public forums where the truth and nothing but the truth will be presented. The accused will become the accuser."[58]

In August 1968, after Columbia president Kirk announced his early retirement, the acting president, in a gesture of reconciliation, asked the DA to drop criminal trespass charges and requested that the courts apply maximum leniency in the pending cases. However, New York district attorney Frank Hogan—who also had a seat on the Board of Trustees of Columbia University—insisted on prosecuting the students. And the students were ready to fight the charges. By then, the Mass Defense Committee, coordinated by the tireless Mary Kaufman, had already recruited forty to fifty attorneys, who made themselves available to represent Columbia defendants pro bono. The Guild's call for volunteers brought a very quick and enthusiastic response, partly because of the shock of "the outrageous misconduct of the police" and partly because of the identification of the lawyers with the arrested.[59] Even senior lawyers felt an unparalleled empathy with these "urban, middle-class college kids, the kind of kids that attorneys have," a local reporter observed.[60] The response of the public was, in Kaufman's words, "heart-warming," and contrary to the past, thousands of dollars poured into the Guild's office to be used for bail.[61]

The committee worked as a referral center by connecting individual defendants with sympathetic lawyers.[62] Kaufman held countless meetings, sent updates, and discussed common strategies. She also took care of training many of the volunteers who lacked experience, as the committee sought to create a synergy among seasoned lawyers, young lawyers, law students, legal workers, movement groups, and students' parents.[63] Ultimately, the Guild provided lawyers for almost all Columbia cases, including those of the two leaders, Mark Rudd and Martin Kenner, who were facing serious charges such as conspiracy to murder.[64]

The Guild also commenced an action in U.S. district court to enjoin Columbia University from adopting disciplinary measures against the students on the grounds that the university was imbued with a public interest, and its denial of democratic participation violated basic constitutional standards. According to the lawsuit, the sit-in was peaceful, and students had been assaulted. Furthermore, Guild lawyers challenged the criminal prosecutions, arguing that DA Hogan, being a trustee of Columbia University, had a personal and biased interest, which deprived the defendants of due process. Finally, Guild attorneys demanded the right of jury trials in all cases where students required them "on the ground that these cases [were] in essence political trials[,] and under decisions of the U.S. Supreme Court they [had] constitutional right to such trials."[65] Some of these claims were founded while others were "purely political points," admits Michael Ratner, a student at Columbia Law School who joined the occupation and later found himself on the side of Guild lawyers. But one of the main goals of the suit was to publicize students' demands, "even if these arguments had little chance of legal success."[66]

When the criminal trespass cases went to trial, the prosecutor—according to one of his colleagues in the DA's office—made "a series of half-hearted arguments," "in contrast to the array of lawyers on the other side, all of whom made a series of convincing and impassioned statements." Eventually, the judge irrevocably dismissed every case.[67] The legal-political strategy of the Mass Defense Committee had delivered and was also successful in the other Columbia cases, ensuring an overwhelming number of dismissals.[68]

From Chicago to the Bay Area

The sense of urgency and the acceleration of time in those climactic months between 1968 and 1969 are particularly hard to imagine, decades later. To grasp them, it is crucial to remind ourselves that scores of activists had been marching against the war in Vietnam for over four years and against racism for more than a decade. From their perspective, these efforts—from orderly rallies to civil disobedience—were not leading to any tangible change. In fact, change was already in motion but was hardly visible from the vantage point of the present. Such a sense of impotence had already generated harsh confrontations, especially in Oakland. Now, the Democratic National Convention, which was to be held in Chicago in August 1968, provided an invaluable opportunity for a showdown.

While calls for a confrontation were on the rise, many in the movement came to believe that it was time to arouse the sleeping dogs on the right. "A movement cannot grow without repression. The Left needs an attack from the Right and the Center," wrote Jerry Rubin in January 1968, echoing an old revolutionary argument. And he pointedly added, "Life is theater, and we are the guerrillas attacking the shrines of authority, from the priests and the holy dollar to the two-party system." Polarization was extolled, and a clash between the New Left and the clerics of pro-war liberalism was fairly apt to enhance it.[69]

With spectacular synchronism, the rising star of the Black Panther Party (BPP) also captured the imagination of an increasing number of white leftists. Born in the fall of 1966 in Oakland, the BPP tapped into the lost promises of the civil rights movement and the deception behind the enduring economic and political marginalization of Black America. Its leaders Bobby Seale and Huey P. Newton portrayed the Black community as a colony, police as an occupying army, and the Panthers' struggle as an anti-imperialist war. Initially conceived as a self-defense organization, the party patrolled the police in Black neighborhoods to hold them accountable and to prevent harassment. Tellingly, the Panthers drove around the streets of Oakland with guns, tape recorders, and law books. As Bobby Seale explained, the Panthers sold copies of Mao's *Little Red Book* on the Berkeley campus and, with that income, bought their first stock of weapons. This way, the party increasingly presented itself as a disciplined armed force that could lead the Black liberation struggle.[70]

At the same time, the Panthers recognized that to win over hearts and minds they had to address other community needs, from education to housing and employment, so they started to collect donations and food from local merchants and offered hot meals to kids in a church—the famous and cherished Free Breakfast for Children Program. They also instituted, among other things, a Free Clothing Program and free health clinics. Always navigating "a narrow boundary between legal participation in U.S. politics and full-out war," as it has been perceptively written, until 1968 the only visible face of the Panthers was the contentious one. Under the glare of the media and chanting, "Revolution has come, time to pick up the gun," in May 1967 they marched on the California capitol to defend the right to bear loaded firearms in public (after a bill threatened to ban it). In a matter of six months, they reached international notoriety. Their boldness and idealism, coupled with their leather jackets, black berets, sunglasses, and afro hairstyles, mesmerized scores of young radicals. White activists were electrified too and were reassured by the Panthers' commitment to avoiding counter-racism.[71]

In the midst of such a hectic moment, the two main groups that organized the contestation to the 1968 Democratic National Convention—the National Mobilization Committee to End the War in Vietnam (the Mobe) and the Youth International Party (YIP)—had very different ideas on how to challenge the establishment in Chicago and accelerate the end of the Vietnam War. The first one, a multifaceted coalition led by activists as diverse as Rennie Davis, Tom Hayden, and David Dellinger, had already brought more than 100,000 peaceful protesters to Washington, D.C., in October 1967, and also marched on the Pentagon. The Mobe proposed a disciplined and nonviolent mass demonstration. By contrast, YIP, led by Jerry Rubin and Abbie Hoffman, hoped to funnel the irreverence of its members, known as Yippies, into a Festival of Life, which confusedly blended guerrilla theater, violent confrontation, and unpredictable provocations. Their invitation card announced that "Rock groups will be performing in the parks; newspapers will be printed in the streets; *provos* and police will play cops and robbers in the department stores; Democrats and dope fiends will chase each other through hotel corridors. Longboats filled with Vikings will land on the shores of Lake Michigan, and discover America!"[72] Guaranteed was only the fact that organizers expected a dangerous confrontation against a Democratic mayor and a police department that conflated all radical activists into the stereotyped image of un-American hippies.[73] As a matter of fact, city officials took at face value the Yippies' threats of burning the city down and dumping LSD in the water supply and responded by assembling a broad web of informers and infiltrators.[74]

An array of legal questions predictably emerged, including how to get permits and how to grapple with the expected mass arrest. As historian David Farber reveals, in late January 1968, Davis, Hayden, and Dellinger gathered in New York City to meet with a dozen members of the National Lawyers Guild. The connection and main organizer was Bernardine R. Dohrn, a spirited student at the University of Chicago Law School and a leader of SDS, who was also the national student organizer for the Guild. While Hayden recognized that tactics for the protest were not yet clear, he also thought that they "should have people organized who can fight the police, people who are willing to get arrested." There was no question that the police would attack demonstrators; thus, they needed people prepared to stop the police. Dohrn, on her part, showed pragmatism and suggested that they should establish a legal committee. Davis agreed for the group, announced that he would work on it, and later maintained contact with the NLG to set it up.[75]

Mass arrests in August were so predictable that even the Chicago Bar Association formed an organization of volunteer lawyers to arrange defense teams. However, when compared to radical lawyers, they seemed too close to judges and prosecutors and thus unreliable. In the wake of the Columbia crisis, Guild lawyers knew that a structured and sympathetic mass defense organization would be necessary. Therefore, the national office sent a student of the University of Pennsylvania Law School, Gene Cerruti, to Chicago, with the task of organizing a legal defense apparatus. Within a few weeks, the Chicago Legal Defense Committee had an office, a fundraising arm, and a core of lawyers and students committed to maintain ongoing vigilance.[76] Plans were made for having fifty committee-affiliated attorneys always available, assisted by about the same number of law students.[77] Immediately prior to convention week, the Guild also sponsored a workshop for lawyers and law students at the University of Chicago. Guild lawyers with experience in Detroit and New York trained their colleagues on methods and techniques to be used in defense of demonstrators.[78]

Permits for parades and the use of parks were requested in unorthodox ways—one application form was initially delivered rolled up in a *Playboy* poster, and later followed up with a last-minute federal suit—and all were repeatedly denied.[79] Demonstrations thus started without authorization to march. Hayden told a New York audience that people should come to Chicago prepared "to shed their blood," while Mayor Daley's statements overheated the already inflamed atmosphere. Police officers for their part felt preemptively justified in their hard-nosed response.[80] To be sure, there were a few hundred "movement toughs"—the so-called park people who refused to be intimidated, rebuffed militant discipline, welcomed street fighting, and spoke the language of Molotov cocktails and rocks.[81] But the approximately ten thousand citizens, most of them young, white, and middle class, were essentially nonviolent. And they were met by an extraordinarily large contingent of law enforcement agents.

On the night that pro-war candidate Hubert Humphrey was nominated for president, demonstrators approached the Hilton Hotel, where the delegates were staying, only to be met by police. Demonstrators, bystanders, and the press alike were beaten and gassed in the chaos that ensued. More than a thousand people were injured and 662 were arrested. TV news cameras, already on site, made "the whole world" watch police clubs swinging and blood flowing.[82] At the request of the president's Commission on the Causes and Prevention of Violence, a team led by Daniel Walker investigated the violent confrontation during that week, ultimately blaming law enforcement for initiating the unrest and defining it as a "police riot."[83] Guild lawyers kept the Chicago Legal Defense Committee open 24/7 during the week, but there was no contest before an overwhelming police power. Lawyers were reportedly "swamped, between bailing people out of jail all night and taking down endless affidavits against police brutality." All communication with city officials, police commanders, and the Justice Department was disconnected. The most meaningful assistance the committee could provide was legal advice and liaisons with trusted lawyers. As in the Columbia case, the committee challenged the technique of mass arrests through coordinated defense of each individual. Multiple trials—experience taught—weakened the prosecution.[84]

In the meantime, the Guild decided to further expand its efforts to assist the movement and opened a permanent regional office in California. It was essentially a legal headquarters, ready to intervene whenever a mass arrest occurred. Based in San Francisco, it was staffed with a young lawyer, Peter

Haberfeld, and a legal worker, the previously mentioned Karen Jo Koonan. After her experience in Mississippi, Koonan had become an organizer for Stop the Draft Week and joined the Guild. The office gave free legal counsel, worked closely with individual defense committees, was constantly on call to perform investigative functions, and contacted other lawyers to undertake cases, especially for people charged with felonies.[85]

"One of our main goals," remembers Koonan, was "to teach the people what was happening to them. We had these 'mass defense meetings' during which lawyers said: 'This is what an arraignment is. . . . The next step is a motion to dismiss the charges.' This gave useful information on what was coming ahead." Then, if the district attorney proposed a deal, "we set up meetings with the defendants where we said: 'This is what has been offered, and each person has to make his own decision about it.' So [the regional office] was a place and a method for conveying information to the collective."[86] Replicating what Kaufman had done in New York, the office also held training sessions, distributed informational materials, raised funds, and organized seminars.[87] By virtue of this buffer of protection, defendants were led to discover "that their fate [was] manageable," a 1969 Guild report explained. Defendants were "encouraged to convey their politics to the lawyer and to insist, if necessary, that their political content be injected and their political strategy implemented."[88]

The office was immediately called to support the mobilization at San Francisco State College (SFSC), later renamed San Francisco State University. Students were on a war footing to expose the Eurocentric curricula, persistent racism, and lack of diversity that—they argued—dominated in their school. Led by the Black Student Union, they formed a large minority coalition named the Third World Liberation Front (TWLF), which included Latin American and Asian students. Captivated by the Black Panthers' success and enthralled by the charisma of BPP minister of education George M. Murray, an instructor at SFSC who had been recently fired, the TWLF radicalized. From November 1968 to March 1969, it held an unprecedented five-month strike, which occasionally blocked all activities on campus, while demanding increased minority access and an ethnic studies school. Strikers turned to disruptive tactics and were repeatedly met with force by the police, who made hundreds of arrests. According to a government report, it was "one of the most distressing episodes in American higher education," but the strikers finally obtained a favorable agreement that also established a School of Ethnic Studies with a Department of Black Studies, a Department of Asian American Studies, and a Department of La Raza Studies.[89]

Guild members helped to create a Third World Liberation Front Defense Committee and coordinated the defense of almost seven hundred students who were arrested in the course of the strike.[90] The mission was taxing, especially because each student had to appear individually. In September 1969, four hundred individuals were still awaiting trial, and lawyers were constantly in need. Lawyers also lamented the inconsistent verdicts given for the same offenses, as well as the exorbitant appeal bonds. However, evidence shows that Guild lawyers obtained good results and were extremely gratified because mass defense could finally be extended to non-white students. Such interactions, they wrote, helped in "establishing the type of trust necessary for work with the characteristically suspicious student and racially-conscious organizations."[91]

Beginning in January 1969, a similar Third World Liberation Front materialized at UC Berkeley, where several minority associations joined forces to demand the establishment of a Third World College and an Ethnic Studies Department. The TWLF and white radicals declared a strike, and the conflict rapidly escalated. Governor Ronald Reagan and the Alameda County administration refused to open a dialogue, declared the state of emergency, and sent law enforcement, which started making arrests. Once again, a Legal Defense Committee and a bail fund were established, and the Guild was asked to recruit and coordinate attorneys to handle the cases.[92] Guild law students at Boalt Hall contributed by helping fellow students accused of violating campus rules deal with university disciplinary hearings. During the strike, they also defied the ban on campus demonstrations with a rally on the steps of Sproul Hall. "We thought that being white law students we would be better protected than students of color," remembers one of the young protagonists. "And we won! The university conceded and the rallies continued."[93]

Everything came to a close in February with a violent police takeover that led to brutalities and dozens of arrests. The prosecution overcharged the students with felonies instead of misdemeanors, thus imposing high bails that were unaffordable for the young people. The ill-concealed objective was to put the protesters on ice in order to deflate the tensions. Law professor and former FSM counsel Richard Buxbaum, who had made a plea to his colleagues at Berkeley for funding for the bail bonds, represented most of the defendants at arraignments. Choosing to go back to fight on campus, most of the students pleaded guilty and their cases evaporated, while only a handful of them were tried.[94] The strikers' efforts ultimately resulted in the creation of the first Ethnic Studies Department in the United States and the implementation of special admission standards.

A National Phenomenon

Mass defense required coordination, a measure of anticipation of events, human resources, and funds, but these were not always available at the same time. During the extraordinary outpouring of activism between the two decades, the Guild's safety net also faced setbacks. For example, in the Bay Area, within the space of a couple of weeks in January 1969, 286 students were arrested at San Fernando Valley College, 17 Black Student Union members were arrested at Southwestern Junior College, and 17 Black Panthers were arrested in various circumstances. The regional office was there to help. However, given the large number of open fronts, there were few lawyers available, and it was almost impossible to raise bail money for Black militants, who usually did not have families or bond agents prepared to provide succor. Thus, the Guild was forced to ask some people to stay in jail for the sake of "movement economy."[95]

Notwithstanding these and other issues that complicated the task, Guild mass defense initiatives took off across the country.[96] In Manhattan, Kaufman was able to institute a permanent Mass Defense Office (MDO) with a 24/7 answering service and a volunteer corps of over seventy-five lawyers. Between December 1967 and December 1969, the MDO represented over two thousand political activists arrested in demonstrations, from student strikers to the so-called welfare mothers. The MDO won more than 78 percent of the cases it handled: 108 acquittals and 843 dismissals (against 221 pleas of guilty, 42 convictions, and 900 cases still pending). It comes as no surprise that the young people felt "cherished" that a lawyer such as Kaufman could spend an entire week in court defending not a celebrity or a political leader but an unsung student in the movement.[97] As of November 1970, regional or defense offices were active in New York, San Francisco, Los Angeles, San Jose, Seattle, Detroit, Chicago, Boston, and Atlanta.[98]

To coordinate all local efforts, a National Defense Committee was created at the beginning of 1970, just in time to deal with the outbursts of activism—and repression—in the spring.[99] While students' criticism of the war rose sharply and students increasingly resorted to contentious actions, President Nixon unexpectedly announced on April 30 the extension of the war into Cambodia, with the goal of disrupting North Vietnamese supplies. Nixon had campaigned on the promise to end the war, so many citizens obviously felt betrayed. The day after the announcement, protests erupted on campuses and cities throughout the United States. The most significant was the May Day demonstration in New Haven, where the antiwar sentiment and the trial of the Black Panthers drew large crowds to the city's green. While Yale law students formed a committee (co-chaired by future first lady and U.S. secretary of state Hillary Rodham) to offer legal advice to demonstrators and prevent violence, the Guild's National Defense Committee coordinated the legal arrangements for the arrests. It is interesting to note that the night before the event, Yale's president invited Kunstler, together with a handful of leftist national leaders, to discuss how to avoid contentious episodes. Eventually, participants were less numerous than expected, the speakers counseled calm, and the police made only a few arrests.[100]

Anguished protests proliferated after National Guardsmen shot at peaceful protesters at Kent State University in Ohio on May 4, 1970, killing four and wounding nine. The event traumatized students, who had never before faced such blatant and lethal force, but also outraged and mobilized them. Within a few days, a national strike spontaneously materialized, asking for immediate withdrawal from Indochina, an end to political repression, and termination of university complicity in war-related activities. According to conservative estimates, strikes and walkouts spread across 883 campuses and involved over a million students. More than one hundred campuses were officially closed for at least one day, and twenty-one campuses remained shut down for the rest of the academic year. It has been defined as "one of the largest coordinated sequences of disruptive protests in American history."[101] Demonstrations were mostly pacific, but contentious minorities escalated at the encounter with law enforcement. Whereas Nixon insinuated that "when dissent turns to violence it invites tragedy," a presidential commission more wisely urged to "draw back from the brink" and "declare a national ceasefire."[102]

Guild chapters provided legal services for a large number of these strike actions. As soon as university and high school students marched, rallied, sat-in, taught-in, occupied, leafleted, picketed, shut down their schools, or tied up their cities, mass defense networks got activated. Legal observers attended demonstrations and went to precincts, while attorneys negotiated with school officials and provided counsel for injunction proceedings, arraignments, and hearings.[103] In New York, the MDO joined the ACLU and other groups in an affirmative suit attacking the police officers who had stood idly by when a group of construction workers had violently retaliated against young protesters in Lower Manhattan on May 8. Between March and May, the same office handled 397 new cases, and even law students at Columbia and New York University set up defense units that worked with the MDO to coordinate legal aid at the two institutions.[104]

This wave of campus unrest reached a symbolic truce in the early morning hours of May 15, when police officers fired more than four hundred rounds of ammunition in less than thirty seconds into a women's dormitory at Jackson State College, Mississippi, killing two men and wounding a dozen. A by-product of enduring racial tensions, the incident was unrelated to the antiwar movement, but it cast a chilling shadow on the nationwide strike. Indirectly, this tragedy, which went unpunished, signaled that social conflict stretched beyond the Vietnam War into broader and more troubled territory.

∙ ∙

When the first lawyers went South to offer help to the civil rights workers, the National Lawyers Guild was still a beaten-up and minuscule organization, decimated after the intense repression of the 1950s. Progressively deserted, its student chapters had closed. Belonging to a group that had been labeled "the legal bulwark of the Communist Party" was extremely problematic, especially for students and recent graduates who were about to enter the profession and were afraid of being tainted by simple association. Membership in the Guild was still considered the kiss of death for an attorney and could result in failure to be admitted to the bar or to find a job. Even law professors explicitly advised against it.[1]

Yet, since the mid-1960s, the number of Guild affiliates had skyrocketed. While in 1965 Guild members totaled only a few hundred, in 1971 they totaled more than 2,000, in 1975 over 4,800, and in 1977 nearly 6,000.[2] In 1966, the first student chapter was officially opened at the UC Berkeley School of Law; soon after, Hastings College of the Law at the University of California, San Francisco, followed suit.[3] In just a few years, then, the NLG had grown faster than it could effectively organize. As a 1971 internal staff report reads, the Guild was "literally besieged with requests for help in organizing additional Guild chapters." In a matter of eighteen months between 1970 and 1971, the organization expanded from seven to seventeen local chapters, about thirty new student chapters opened, and Guild regional chapters increased from three to eleven.[4] A young breed of radical legal people took over the NLG, invigorating the organization while imposing a more contentious style. What happened during this time, and what made the Guild such a powerful magnet?

As already mentioned, experience with the civil rights movement contributed chiefly to attracting law students and graduates. The struggle in the South had revealed both the relevance of lawyers in the fight for social change and the urgency to take action. Many young people who went South in various capacities came back feeling a moral duty to keep on fighting, possibly with legal instruments.[5] But they were hardly alone. Around them, rising numbers of recent graduates saw the law as a powerful tool to right wrongs and sought to work with the new social actors.[6] Inspired by their elders, plenty of students entered law school specifically to become more skilled and useful activists and to be able to make a change.[7] The choice to become a lawyer—in the words of a Guild attorney who enrolled in law school in 1964—gradually turned out to be "a political expression."[8]

Above all, it was the exceptional ideological climate that fostered lawyers' engagement. Leftist radicalization was contagious. This was the case, for example, for Barbara Handschu, who happened to be a student of law at the University of Michigan, Ann Arbor, where Students for a Democratic Society had held its initial meetings and Tom Hayden had organized the first teach-ins. The intense politicization of the university, as Handschu notes today, made her conversion natural, by osmosis. She graduated in 1968 and immediately joined the Guild.[9] Although leftist law students would eventually remain a minority in U.S. law schools, in the mid-1960s they represented a growing cohort and made their voices increasingly heard. Even if their demography varied considerably, they were predominantly red diaper babies (children of American communists) of Jewish origin with a middle-class upbringing. Similar to their peers, they felt a moral imperative not to be "good Germans," refusing silent compliance and complicity with unjust policies.[10]

As the practical need for a legal arm for the movement emerged, lawyers were catapulted into the midst of student struggles. Instead of waiting for clients and studying codes in their legal offices, they found themselves on the barricades—literally. For example, the aforementioned Peter Franck, a young Guild lawyer, took part in a sit-in at UC Berkeley in support of the FSM defendants. Mario Savio, who happened to be Franck's former roommate, asked him to get on top of a police car and instruct the protesters on their rights if the police came. "I didn't go with the intention of doing that," remembers Franck. "I just went there as a demonstrator, but then I found myself advising five thousand people on their rights."[11]

Dan Siegel, who went to Mississippi and North Carolina with COFO, wanted to be a newspaper reporter, but he grew weary of being a mere observer. Hoping to work for change in a more tangible way, he enrolled in law school at Berkeley. In 1967, during his first week of courses, he "jumped right into the NLG" and was dragged into the mass defense organization for Stop the Draft Week in Oakland.

> I went out there the first day of demonstrations, with my Brooks
> Brothers jacket that my mother bought me when I was in college,

and a tie, and a clipboard, and an armband, and promptly I got beaten on the head by an Oakland cop. Bleeding all over the place, I went back to law school, did not wash the blood off my head, went to my criminal law class, and demanded that the class be refocused on what the cops were doing in downtown Oakland. My professor very politely declined and went on speaking about the Latin roots of the standards for criminal law in the United States. That is how I got involved in the Lawyers Guild.[12]

As the legal profession played an increasingly visible role in supporting social movements, a new generation of young radical lawyers and law students yearned for ways to become even more active. Malcolm Burnstein later said that he and his friends "would have paid . . . for the chance to be involved."[13] In this context, the Guild represented a major rallying point for leftists. "If you saw yourself as an activist lawyer, that was the place to be," notes Emily J. Goodman, who graduated in 1968 and joined the Guild that same year.[14] As a matter of fact, Goodman's point of view was widely shared. The NLG was regarded, as the testimonies evince, as "a way to connect to the movement," a place "to find other like-minded people," and a resource "to develop some skills you got in law school in favor of the movement."[15] Carlin Meyer, who in 1971 was an antiwar activist who had just graduated from Harvard College and enrolled in law school, summarizes this feeling with an anecdote: "I was driving from Chicago to go to Rutgers. I pulled into a diner and sitting at the counter there were a bunch of long-hair guys. I hear them talking about things related to law. I walked over and I told them I was about to start law school. By the time I left the diner, I had joined the Lawyers Guild! It was very clear that these were the people who were doing what I wanted to do."[16]

To be sure, young lawyers willing to fight for those who were discriminated against could join other alternative or complementary organizations—for example, the Law Center for Constitutional Rights (LCCR), later renamed the Center for Constitutional Rights (CCR). Founded by William Kunstler, Arthur Kinoy, Benjamin Smith, and Morton Stavis in 1966 in Newark, New Jersey, the center was an outgrowth of the Guild's southern projects and retained the same movement-oriented perspective. However, it was not a membership organization but a small litigation center that was designed to supplement the individual efforts of the lawyers who created it.[17] The Law Students Civil Rights Research Council (LSCRRC) was another option. As previously mentioned, the LSCRRC offered a chance to volunteer in the South with a fellowship; however, as the civil rights movement drew to a close, it gradually dissolved its progressive function.

Established to offer legal services to the poor, legal aid societies also attracted many law school graduates. Indeed, legal aid had a radical tradition in the United States that harked back to nineteenth-century initiatives of combative women and lay lawyers.[18] Yet the most politicized within the new crop of lawyers found legal aid societies paternalistic and limited in scope—"good dude charity" in the words of Gerald B. Lefcourt, who entered the Legal Aid Society in New York with the explicit purpose of changing it and eventually got fired. Equal access to the law, radicals contended, was a negligible progress, while the law remained structurally prejudiced and social injustice endured.[19]

Lyndon Johnson's 1964 Economic Opportunity Act included a section on free legal services for the poor. For the first time, the U.S. government had taken a step toward a national aid program (the Office of Economic Opportunity's Legal Services Program), whose goal was to replace the privately funded system of traditional legal aid. By 1973, the program consisted of 250 agencies staffed by more than 2,600 full-time lawyers working out of 900 separate offices, and these lawyers were winning over 70 percent of their cases on behalf of millions of indigent citizens.[20] Within this framework, the government created the Volunteers in Service to America (VISTA), a domestic version of the Peace Corps through which citizens could serve in underprivileged communities. Putting stock in the president's War on Poverty, many young radical lawyers joined the program. Although VISTA represented an appealing way to practice poverty law and an excuse to defer draft calls, it fell short of expectations.[21] Another program offering training in poverty law for recent law school graduates was the Reginald Heber Smith Community Lawyer Fellowship. After 1967, several radicals became "Reggies," as the recipients of the fellowship were known, but they rapidly grew unsatisfied. What they termed "legal placebos" to poverty were increasingly less acceptable, and they reclaimed more transformative action to dismantle inequalities.[22]

An intrepid organization with more than eighty thousand members by the mid-1960s, the ACLU was another option for those who wanted to immerse themselves in legal-political cases.[23] As historian Laura Weinrib wrote, "No organization or individual was as instrumental in shaping contemporary understandings of civil liberties as the ACLU." Born in the aftermath of the First World War, it had been an important ally of the labor movement and took part in militant defense campaigns, like the one on behalf of Sacco and Vanzetti. However, the ACLU had gradually abandoned this early agenda, focusing instead on the preservation of the democratic debate.[24] According to radical lawyers, the ACLU had two structural flaws. On the one hand, its firm commitment to civil liberties, particularly to First Amendment rights, led its lawyers to represent everybody, including Klansmen, Nazis, and any other opponent of the Left whose rights of expressive freedom were in jeopardy. As a matter of fact, nonpartisan defense was the ACLU's hard-and-fast rule.[25] On the other hand, with the exception of its Bay Area chapter, the ACLU had barred communists from membership during the McCarthy period and refused to assist them.[26]

It is no coincidence that early in the 1950s, in response to the ACLU's anticommunism, a group of lawyers and intellectuals founded the National Emergency Civil Liberties Committee (NECLC), an organization that focused on helping suspected communists targeted by the McCarran Internal Security Act.[27] Moreover, the ACLU membership was predominantly white, and it was not openly engaged against the war in Vietnam, at least until 1968–70. To be sure, many ACLU lawyers were still regarded as heroic progressive fighters, and several radical lawyers participated in the ACLU's activities, even holding seats on the local boards of the organization. Yet, over the course of the 1960s, they became less active with the ACLU and more active with the Guild, whose primary goal was to protect the leftist movement, not necessarily the First Amendment.[28]

By contrast, the doggedness of the NLG played a crucial role in attracting young activists. Since its founding in 1937, the organization had defended tooth and nail all possible incarnations of the Left, with a partisan commitment that resonated well among the new radical youth. In other words, Guild lawyers had chosen their clients based on what they stood for, not on what rights were at issue. Thus, the NLG was the right place for those who staunchly refused to represent property interests and who sought to defend the advocates of fundamental social change.[29] The Guild also offered "a historically tested structure" around which students could organize "immediately."[30]

Of course, the new leftists, with their distrust of ideological dogmatism and Soviet-style communism, regarded such an Old Left organization with a measure of suspicion. The Guild's links to the unfashionable CPUSA were plain to all, and many of its founding members were colloquially known as "progressive friends of the Soviet Union."[31] Particularly in the New York City chapter, the party had been highly influential.[32] Still, anti-anticommunism was a strong sentiment within the New Left, and the combative attitude of

Guild lawyers, especially during the 1950s, was a source of immense respect and fascination. The young radical students were indeed forging their identity from the example of these founding fathers of the Guild, who had argued some of the most controversial political cases and refused to testify before the House Un-American Activities Committee. They had been excluded from law journals, disbarred for years, and even jailed for their political ideas. An aura of legend surrounded them.

For example, attorneys Leonard B. Boudin and Victor Rabinowitz were said to have won the revolutionary government of Cuba as a client over a poolside chess game with Ernesto Guevara at Havana's Hotel Riviera. Both lawyers had cut their political teeth in the labor law firm of Louis Boudin, Leonard's uncle and a famed Marxist jurist, and both were known as champions of civil liberties against the government's wrongdoings. Both of them had also represented alleged Soviet spies in cases that commanded nationwide attention: Boudin was able to exonerate on appeal Judith Coplon, charged with stealing U.S. government documents and passing them to a Soviet agent; Rabinowitz, who had joined the Communist Party in 1940, defended Alger Hiss, a government lawyer and State Department official who was accused of espionage on behalf of the USSR. It was difficult for a young leftist not to be thrilled at the prospect of joining these people.[33]

Though reluctantly, the Guild's leadership foresaw the potential of the younger radical generation and tried to channel it into its ranks. To foster the bond between the NLG and the movements, the organization resolved to recruit a few young coordinators. Kenneth Cloke, a sharp radical law student who had been president of SLATE at Berkeley, worked with Black attorney C. B. King in the South, and joined the Du Bois Clubs of America, was hired as the first student organizer. "I replicated what Marcello Mastroianni did in the movie *The Organizer*," remembers Cloke today. Like the fictional labor activist who lived on the run in Italy and helped workers escalate their struggles, Cloke helped lawyers foster their political consciousness. As a matter of fact, his first project was "the movement," and being a lawyer was "really secondary," especially because he hated law school.[34]

In 1967 he was named executive secretary, while Bernardine Dohrn, the flamboyant SDS leader, was appointed student organizer, namely the head of the Guild's newly created student division. Dohrn, who would later become a leader of the Weatherman (later Weather Underground), the radical group that broke away from SDS to pursue urban guerrilla warfare (see chapter 6), was kept on the NLG's payroll until February 1970.[35] Then she disappeared to go underground. Dohrn made a distinctive impression on everyone in the Guild, not only for her political commitment but also for her fearless and provocative stance.[36] Well embedded within the movement and extremely active, both Cloke and Dohrn showed inexhaustible energy. They generated hundreds of speaking engagements, set up countless meetings with dozens of groups on the Left, drafted a myriad of detailed reports, and opened a great number of new Guild chapters.[37]

In 1967, the Guild's national office was moved from Detroit back to New York, precisely to 5 Beekman Street, in a building that also hosted the headquarters of the National Mobilization Committee to End the War in Vietnam.[38] Victor Rabinowitz was elected president at the 1967 convention. An extremely respected founding member of the Guild, Rabinowitz was rightly considered the best candidate to keep the old and the new generation together. Yet his diplomatic skills would be needed soon, as hard times were on the way.[39]

1968

Within a few months, the task of bridging the New Left and the Old Left turned out to be arduous, to say the least. While some old-time members implored to let themselves retain their balance and provide "an association for liberal lawyers," the young generation revealed its truly revolutionary intentions and refused to bend.[40] The young leftists emphasized that the world had changed "qualitatively" in the course of the 1960s, together with the structural needs of the movements. What defined the New Left more than anything else, as Kenneth Cloke reported to the national executive bureau in 1968, was "the fact that existing forms of action and organization were no longer seen as appropriate merely because they had been useful before." If the Guild desired "to produce change" and wished to involve young people in that effort, it needed to recognize "the problem of generational difference" and allow "younger lawyers to organize on their own terms and around their own grievances." Otherwise, they would not participate.[41]

In particular, as Bernardine Dohrn echoed, first-year law students now represented a different and more radical generation compared to third-year or older students. As long as they had been in college, the United States had been at war. They had always witnessed opposition to the war, experienced the movement at a younger age, and felt the impact of older activists. As a result, they were more political, more vulnerable to the draft, and more skeptical of professionalism. A large portion of this "new generation of lawyers," wrote Cloke during this period, entered law school "because of the movement, either to help others whom they saw being oppressed, or out of some inchoate distaste for injustice."[42]

The students, indeed, burst onto the Guild's scene at the 1968 national convention in Santa Monica, California. While only about forty to fifty law students actually attended the conference, their unceremonious style, over-confident attitude, and radical statements stunned most of the audience. Cloke again intervened to reiterate that the transformation "had to be to-tal" and the organization "had to be rebuilt from bottom to top" in order to project "an image of the Guild that was young, activist, and which made younger lawyers and law students excited about what it was doing."[43] But he was hardly alone in his revolutionary fervor. The former president of SDS, Carl Oglesby, took the floor to urge "confrontation politics" and ended his speech by asking: "What is our job in this country? Perhaps it is to die a very violent death." Protected by his armed bodyguards, Reverend Milton Henry, vice president of the Republic of New Afrika, a newly founded Black nationalist organization, spoke of advocating Black separatism. An activist lawyer dedicated to the defense of Detroit's Black population, Henry had come to believe that Black people would never gain the power to change the United States according to their needs. So he called for the creation of an independent state between Louisiana and Virginia, by means of diplo-macy or militarily if needed. Surprising everybody, he was elected vice president of the Guild.[44]

Though eliciting a raucous debate and despite the opposition of moder-ate Black lawyers, a resolution that defined the right of a "separate black nation" as a "substantial and meritorious legal issue" was also approved. Meanwhile, on the initiative of a handful of young Black lawyers led by Len Holt, a Black caucus met independently. Eventually, the convention voted additional radical resolutions, such as one accepting the Guild's newly pro-claimed role as "the legal arm of the movement" and one advocating am-nesty for all those who resisted the efforts of the U.S. government to engage in wars reflecting imperialism and racism.[45] As a student organizer summed up, "Many older members felt like a tornado had hit."[46] Not only did the new-comers appear unconventional, but their attitudes were perceived as a com-bination of "personal arrogance and animosity."[47] Today, asked about what she recalls of the Santa Monica convention, Margaret Ratner Kunstler, who at the time was a young student in the Guild and later married William Kunstler, replies with a laugh, "I remember getting high!"[48]

To be sure, the dividing line was not merely generational. Several long-time members were also particularly receptive to the Young Turks' message and keenly welcomed it.[49] Yet the differences in age and political experience created the main gap. Rabinowitz himself admitted that the NLG was a rapidly aging organization: "We were radical in politics but were stuffy in our observance of organizational forms, and even more stuffy in our manner of speech and our attitude toward non-professionals. Although we despised the political views of the Establishment bar associations, we mimicked them in many ways—in the way we dressed, the way we behaved, the language we used."[50] And yet, he added, the young radicals "came on very hard. It was difficult to tell whether they were fighting fascism and reaction or they were fighting the older leaders in the Guild. They came on with equal fervor in both battles." An intermediate generation was not there to mediate, and the young refused to conform.[51]

The young radicals' attitudes were so provocative that some equally young leftist militants who had recently joined the Guild felt uneasy too. For example, Michael S. Smith—who had experience in the Young Socialist Alliance, a Trotskyist youth group of the Socialist Workers Party—remembers a sense of incongruity when he attended a caucus of the younger members of the Guild. Held on the beach, the meeting was "led by Dohrn who was wearing a bikini," with everybody sitting cross-legged on the sand around her. Similarly, Smith felt uncomfortable when, during an interview for the position of Guild student organizer, he saw on the coffee table a manual on how to make explosive triggers and was interrogated about his attitude toward leftist bombings.[52] Michael E. Tigar, who entered the Guild during that period and later became a famed radical lawyer as well as an eminent law professor, significantly remembers that "these folks . . . [had] plenty of activism, but many of them had this contempt for learning the craft of lawyering and studying deeply. . . . Everything was bourgeois bullshit. Of course it is, but it is the bourgeois bullshit that the lawyers have to speak."[53]

In any event, the turmoil within the Guild was considered better than the apathy of the 1950s. A general consensus was reached that the student members had to take a more active role in Guild activities, and in September 1968, fifteen students were elected to the national executive board.[54] In February 1970, after another quarrelsome convention in Washington, D.C., law students finally became full voting members. Yet proposals were already being made to open the membership to "everyone" who was committed to "the creation of a new system of political and economic relationships based on the dominance of human rights over property interests."[55] While some voices lambasted sexism in the law, the woman question also came home to the Guild, and a women's caucus for the first time met independently. As if that were not enough turmoil, some recent graduates and students claimed they could not afford the tickets for the traditional gala dinner. They remained outside and stole a platter of food. Kunstler joined them and, after making an incendiary speech and publicly burning his ticket, was carried into the dining hall on students' shoulders.[56]

Some older associates again cried foul. Doris B. Walker, who had just been elected as the first woman to lead the Guild, spoke against the admittance of students into the organization. As a matter of fact, she was a dedicated mentor who also ran a Marxist study group for Guild law students at her own place. Yet she was also an old leftist who paid respect to hierarchies and roles.[57] Abraham Unger, a founder of the NLG and a veteran radical lawyer with a communist past, after hearing Dohrn speak in a women's panel discussion, admitted that he waited for "someone in [a] white coat" to come in and take her back to a "mental institution."[58] Nonetheless, in the following years the turnover in membership continued at a blistering pace. At the 1971 national convention in Boulder, Colorado, it became clear that the old generation had dropped out while the younger had permanently moved in.[59] Catherine Roraback was elected president, and a young national executive board took office alongside her. Born in 1920, Roraback had been the only woman who graduated in her 1948 Yale Law School class. An activist in the Progressive Party, she was a trailblazing civil rights attorney known for her participation in the 1965 landmark case *Griswold v. Connecticut*, which legalized birth control in Connecticut, and, more recently, for representing the Black Panthers in New Haven.[60]

At the same time, the Guild took another important step. After a fierce debate, it was decided that legal workers—a category that included secretaries, stenographers, bookkeepers, typists, legal clerks, organizers, draft counselors, and jailhouse workers, none of whom had a bar card or were enrolled in law school—would be admitted as members.[61] Fears that a large number of legal workers would convert the bar association into "a trade union," whose effectiveness and prestige would be impaired, were overcome by the new radical majority. To acknowledge the critical mass of "nonlawyers," the Guild needed to water down its professionalism, insisted the youth. Echoing the political storm that was raging on the Left, the question of legal workers was also framed as a gender issue. The large majority of legal workers employed in law firms were indeed women; it would have been pure "male-chauvinism" to exclude them.[62] By the mid-1970s, nonlawyers surpassed 45 percent of total membership, while women constituted more than 30 percent of total membership and more than 45 percent of student membership.[63]

For a few years, the older members—especially the noncommunist lawyers—mostly disappeared, believing that the young iconoclasts had compromised their progressive bar association. In the fall of 1971, of the over 890 people who gathered for a Guild conference in Philadelphia, no more than six were longtime members.[64] However, after 1975, the generational divide gradually healed. Coping with the ebb of the ideological infatuation and missing a reliable political compass, the younger people asked lawyers with seasoned experience to come back and tutor them.[65]

Law Is "a Function of Power"

The renewal of the Guild's demography brought forth a critical attitude toward the system of justice that was defiant and profound enough to challenge the very notion of legality. To be sure, the NLG had always condemned all sorts of legal abuses. However, former Guild lawyers, including most of the hard-line communists, had never abandoned their confidence in the timeless principles of the Constitution. They had consistently retained a belief in the progressive use of legal resources. This attitude substantially changed around 1968, mirroring the growing distrust of political institutions. The cumulative impact of traumatic events, including the race riots, the political assassinations, the war in Vietnam, and the repression of domestic rebellion, suggested to many—as historian Jerold Auerbach duly noted—"the enormous disjunction between the beneficent promise of American life and its everyday performance." In this context, the young radical lawyers displayed shock and anger before "a legal system which reflected the values of a society that preached equality and practiced racism, that promised abundance and tolerated poverty, and that waged war in the name of peace."[66]

This climate of doubt about "the citizen's moral relation to a valid law" was also perceived by external observers. In the spring of 1970, for example, the Association of the Bar of the City of New York organized a conference to discuss the capacity of the American legal and political order to meet the needs of the people when "some deny the idea of law itself as the compass of our social system."[67] A few months later, renowned constitutional scholar Philip B. Kurland diagnosed "a crisis of confidence in American law and the American judiciary." In particular, according to Kurland, "the young and dissident" were right in charging the establishment with hypocrisy, for the system of justice did not even try to attain its highest ideals and remained at the mercy of political loyalties.[68] The legal profession itself was in the eye of the storm. The president of the American Bar Association, Leon Jaworski, conceded that the "surge of disrespect for law and law's enforcers" resulted in large part from lawyers' own abuses of the legal process, as well as from their failure to make adequate legal services available to those who could not afford them.[69]

Pushing such criticism to the extreme, the new radical lawyers went as far as describing the U.S. legal system as "an apparatus for the preservation of the status quo—a society based on race, sex, and class exploitation."[70] Law, as an old adage repeated, was unmistakably "class law." All legal relationships were "relationships of power, for the purpose of maintaining existing property relationships and increasing advantage to some by decreasing it for others." In other words, the law was just "one aspect of the control of social behavior by the ruling class." "Law," as the argument went, was "not justice, a norm, neutral principles, nor ideal social harmony. It [was] not truth, due process, fairness, or any other idealization." Law was "a function of power."[71]

Such a perspective was clearly grounded on the classic Marxist-Leninist legal theory and stood worlds apart from the American mainstream legal thought that cherished the rule of law and the consensual foundations of the Constitution. Marxist historical materialism taught not only that the law was inessential to live peacefully in society but also, and more immediately, that the law was determined by the relations of production and therefore reflected—and legitimized—economic interests, wealth distribution, and ultimately social injustice. Marx had first adumbrated this argument in his early writings on the "theft of wood," while Lenin had echoed the concept by emphasizing how the ruling class enforced the law to serve its own interest.[72] More recently, in his *Essay on Liberation*, Marcuse brushed up that perspective: "There is no (enforceable) law other than that which serves the status quo." Thus, "those who refuse such service are *eo ipso* outside the realm of law even before they come into actual conflict with the law."[73] So the message was as much clear as subversive: the law was intrinsically coercive, and the fetishism of the law—namely the adoration of the law, as if it were sacred and detached from human interests—had to be denounced and resisted.

Enthralled by such leftist predicaments, this new generation of radical lawyers regarded the judicial system as a mere "forum for the resolution of class disputes," where those with greater wealth stood the best chance of winning. The bail system indeed imprisoned the poor and let the rich go free, hence plea bargaining was the most common solution for the indigent.[74] Being "only another instrument of repression"—asserted Henry di Suvero, a young lawyer who graduated from Harvard Law School—"the courts must always be viewed by the movement as the territory of the enemy."[75] Following this logic, legal reforms were considered little more than palliatives. The law was "bankrupt," namely in a crisis that could not be cured by mere technical improvements. "This law," wrote Cloke with self-assuredness, "has been accomplice to the greatest criminals and should be sentenced to be hung by the neck until dead."[76]

According to the same line of reasoning, a legal system of the sort not only failed to offer protection to the radical, the poor, and the racially discriminated but also failed to offer a device to transform society. Michael J. Kennedy, who later became one of the most belligerent radical lawyers in the country, put it very directly in 1968: "There can be no social change through the law."[77] The same concept was echoed by Charles Garry: "The courts are the last place in the world to make social change. You've got to understand the role of the courts and who the courts represent. Our judicial system represents the status quo, to keep big business where it can continue its exploitation."[78] "I never believed that the law was a tool for social change," reflects Dan Siegel today, also adding, "Those of us who were Marxists knew that this government was run by capitalists and the legal system was at best like a pressure valve."[79]

The debate on this subject also led to a partial reconsideration of the experience of the civil rights movement. As Bernardine Dohrn explained in a 1967 memo, the civil rights movement and the peace movement had attempted to gain justice through legislation, the courts, and massive nonviolent demonstrations. However, more recently, activists realized that such tactics had brought "no more than token success." Lawyers who wanted to use their skills to assist these movements had to acknowledge the goals, methods, and philosophy of the new struggles.[80] Cloke added that the fact that the civil rights movement had begun with *Brown v. Board of Education* was a "myth" obscuring people's struggle. The rule of precedent, he explained, made legal decisions appear to be the dominant force in social history, with human, economic, and productive relations following. In reality, the opposite was true. Such a fiction squeezed reform inside the boundaries of law, where it could be more closely regulated.[81]

Similarly, some lawyers admitted that they had thought the best way to effect social change was to pick an important issue and bring a test case to appellate courts, whose decision would affect millions of people. However, they had learned very quickly that the test case approach was substantially "unproductive" and that major legal victories often did not affect the actual conditions of people's lives.[82] Others denounced the fact that constitutional rights had little meaning to "the cop on the beat" or to judges in the courts: "To rely on 'legal rights' [was] to ignore entirely the fundamental reality of a class society."[83] Still, others went so far as to attack civil liberties, which were "championed as the essence of the people's rights" but were "one of the darlings of the liberal rich." As Michael Kennedy clarified, freedom of speech was in fact "the freedom to say anything one wishes so long as it is sufficiently inane as to be inoffensive to the government."[84] According to this perspective, the ACLU lawyer and the public interest lawyer were considered complicit in a system they did not contest. To some extent, their work was also counterproductive, as it made the system appear slightly less oppressive and defused the efforts for more radical change.[85]

The logical consequence of this debate was an increasing distrust of the legal profession as such. Was it possible to be a political radical while being an attorney playing within the rules of the system in court? Was it possible to accept the role of interpreter of the law and, at the same time, to help people who were opposing the law? These questions had no straightforward or unanimous answers but echoed larger debates among the New Left, which challenged the monopoly of expertise and the class character of professions.[86] During the same period, for example, the Radical Education Project, an SDS offshoot, discussed how "radicals in the professions" could work without betraying their own political values. Young activists wanted to make a change through their working skills but were deeply dissatisfied with the conventions of professional practice.[87]

In the Guild's milieu, everybody recognized that the radical lawyer embodied the contradiction between the values of a conservative profession, wedded to the law, and the revolutionary politics of many practitioners who constantly challenged the law.[88] But opinions on how to solve the dilemma diverged quite a bit. A few members showed optimism and claimed that a lawyer could be a radical and still win important battles. Future NLG president Paul Harris wrote that as long as society maintained its capitalist-democratic approach, a lawyer had the power to free people and further the revolution. "You don't have to love the law to be a lawyer," he summarized.[89] While recognizing that "both the Russian and French revolutions abolished the legal profession" because of its inextricable association with oppression and privilege, Cloke himself accepted that one was not obliged to quit the practice to foster revolution. The solution to the dilemma was to stop being "attorneys for the partisan" and become "partisan attorneys."[90] Similarly, Kunstler recognized that the radical lawyer was in "an utterly impossible position," bound by the strictures of a system that the lawyer, along with the clients, may want to destroy. However, it was not coincidental that those who were most aware of the failure of social institutions and those who first articulated the need for fundamental change had always been lawyers. Lenin, Gandhi, and Castro served as illustrations. Lawyers only needed to shift from passive acceptance to "open resistance."[91]

Yet some other lawyers came to the more far-reaching conclusion that "there is no such thing as a radical lawyer." According to this view, lawyers could participate in radical actions only outside the legal system and only "as people and not in their role as lawyers."[92] The president of the New York City chapter of the Guild stressed that all lawyers should avoid the tendency to define their work as revolutionary, while the Guild should abandon its presumption to be a revolutionary organization. Similarly, a lawyer from Vermont asked the radical lawyers to abandon hypocrisy: "You, the lawyer, are a part of that system. And it doesn't matter what you wear, what you say or what you do. If you're there, you're a part of it." In fact, legal victories were not disruptive of American capitalism but more often "placebos."[93] All in all, this argument echoed Lenin's transparent skepticism toward lawyers. In an often-quoted letter to his comrades in prison, Lenin dubbed lawyers as "the most reactionary of people" and alerted communists to "be wary" of them, with only a few exceptions. While militants must rely on themselves for their political defense, lawyers—recommended the Bolshevik leader—should limit themselves to judicial matters, laying traps for witnesses and prosecution or nailing trumped-up charges.[94] It is significant, however, that such a standpoint was now expressed by radical lawyers, in the form of self-criticism.

From a different angle, female radical lawyers attacked the legal profession, dubbing it as a "bulwark of conservatism" and "a caricature of male society's attitudes toward women." Therefore, according to them, "change must come from outside the law."[95] Florynce "Flo" Kennedy, a fearless feminist activist and a lawyer for the downtrodden, jumped into the debate. With her usual abrasive language, she argued that in "a prostitute society," the lawyer was "analogous to a prostitute" and even less honest. Indeed, Kennedy typically refused to be identified as a civil rights lawyer. When people came to her with a legal case, she used to say, "This is not a case to go into courts, but I'll form a picket line with you for nothing."[96] Profoundly disillusioned with the transformative power of the judicial system, Kennedy always focused on organizing and garnering public support for the causes dear to her heart, such as Black power and women's rights.[97]

By contrast, other lawyers appeared way more cautious and suggested compromise solutions. They reaffirmed the transformative power of the legal profession and the need for competent lawyers for the movement.[98] Already in 1967, Doris B. Walker cautioned her colleagues that those who lambasted the legal system, dubbing the Constitution and the Bill of Rights as irrelevant, were also making the legal profession "incompetent and therefore irrelevant."[99] George Crockett, who meanwhile had become a judge on the Detroit Recorder's Court, believed that no one had a better opportunity than the lawyer to eliminate racial discrimination in American society. The Black judge, in particular, had to represent "a special guardian of the rights of minority groups" and "a symbol of hope."[100] Along the same lines, Arthur Kinoy repeatedly stressed that the delegitimization of the institutions of the law was "at once too narrow and too one-sided," as democratic liberties and judicial safeguards were the last ramparts against impending fascism.[101]

As the Guild's radicalization intensified, former presidents Ernest Goodman and Victor Rabinowitz—in a 1970 letter addressed to all Guild members—argued that "there is no reason, of course, why a lawyer cannot be a revolutionary." Nonetheless, lawyers who wanted to act as full-time revolutionaries were invited to carry out their activities "not as lawyers, but as political organizers," forming or joining revolutionary organizations beyond the Guild. The assumption that the NLG could be a center or even provide the leadership for the revolution was ultimately "a romantic and dangerous illusion." To the elders' relief, Goodman and Rabinowitz's wish eventually materialized.[102] A few revolutionary hard-liners stepped out, while the Guild continued to exist as an organization that recognized the elusiveness and the dangers of the law but kept on fighting in the legal arena. Ultimately, this reconfiguration of the Guild as a hybrid legal-political organization showcased both the effects of the youthquake of the sixties and the resilience of the old leftist generation that never disengaged completely. Together, these two forces gave life to an uncommon combination of radicalism and pragmatism.[103]

The New Radical Lawyer

In the wake of the leftist storm of the 1960s, two main functions emerged as the most appropriate for the radical lawyer. The first was keeping activists on the streets, namely out of jail, thus allowing them to devote their time and energy to organizing. As "the law was not a resource but a threat," radical lawyers had to find ways to limit its impact on the movement, protecting the latter from the courts and granting it "some breathing space." While test-case litigation was gradually moved to the background, radical attorneys increasingly focused on criminal defense and police control.[104]

The second function of the radical lawyer was to demystify the law and its discourse in order to expose the oppressive character, hypocrisy, limits, and contradictions lying within.[105] Codes and conventions of the legal profession, it went without saying, needed to be criticized and restyled. From the beginning, these two functions revealed an intrinsic tension, because an effective defense strategy was often incompatible with a full-fledged critique of the legal system or with a truly alternative law practice. Yet radical lawyers worked unabatedly to combine these two goals and—at least for a while—they seemed to succeed. This is what makes their experience especially unique.

By all accounts, the only way for lawyers to recast their role and fulfill their mission was to get closer to the movement and possibly merge with it.[106] The need to develop stronger ties with activists and militants was recognized as soon as the radical youth invaded the Guild. As a 1967 internal memo reads, the students were lamenting the lack of "flesh contact between many Guild members and movement people" and declared it was time "to participate more in direct action rather than in passing resolutions and defending demonstrators."[107] It was indeed urgent to establish mutual trust with the activists, who were increasingly being thrown into jail.[108] Some older lawyers, however, reacted with skepticism. During McCarthyism, they had been forced to defend not only their clients but also themselves. They remembered, and still believed, that it was wise to stay clear of the people they represented. As a matter of fact, the professional characterization of the Guild had been a safety net that allowed leftist lawyers to get through the red scare. However, according to the younger generation, the form of a bar association could well coexist with the status of a political association. In other words, it was time to reframe the Guild as "a political association of the bar," or a "movement bar."[109]

In particular, there was a growing consensus that the traditional role of servicing the movement with simple legal representation was out of date and too narrow. With their increasing identification with the people in need of legal aid, radical lawyers' task could not be limited to protecting "other people's rights." This became particularly clear after the arrests of white middle-class students, antiwar militants, and draft resisters reached unprecedented proportions.[110] As William Kunstler explained, the lawyers' perception of their role changed dramatically during this period. Describing his experience as a leading counsel for a group of Catholic antiwar dissenters known as the Catonsville Nine (see chapter 6), Kunstler conceded that for the first time in his career, he felt "as much a part of the judgment roll as the defendants." To represent "those who speak for truth and love and brotherhood," asserted Kunstler, "a lawyer cannot maintain the traditional aloofness and reserve that have characterized the profession from its earliest days." Kunstler, inspired by his Catholic clients, suggested that lawyers ought to emulate the concept of the French "worker-priests" who had become part and parcel of their communities and turned into "worker-lawyers," indistinguishable from ordinary activists.[111]

So radical lawyers were pushed to experiment with what they called "creative approaches" in order to stay connected with the movement. Grassroots organizing with minorities, students, military personnel, women, and prisoners became the new mantra. Indeed, the best defense seemed to lay in the strength of the movement.[112] In this regard, the following words of a young Guild lawyer from Boston, who admitted to spending most of his time organizing activists instead of trying cases, are hardly surprising: "I live with the people I represent. I represent very few people who are not friends, to a greater or lesser degree. I participate in their activities. My life style is different because I don't think of myself as a lawyer at all. I am a human being. . . . I have decided that I want to practice law less and less, and focus more and more on living the things that I believe."[113]

Identification also meant friendship, respect, admiration, and, in a few cases, even love between attorneys and clients. Examples are countless, but some of them are paradigmatic. Charles Garry, the son of poor Armenian immigrants who studied law by night while working as a dry cleaner during the day, was unquestionably one of the most beloved lawyers.[114] Thanks to his deep empathy with the Black liberation movement and his own familiarity with discrimination and indigence, he became the Black Panthers' most trusted counsel, winning over the objections of some Black militants who resented his "whiteness."[115] Huey Newton constantly reiterated his esteem for Garry and insisted that "he always empathized with his clients to the point that he would be on trial himself." As a reminder of such a political and human bond, Newton gave Garry a gold Panther ring.[116] It comes as no surprise that Bobby Seale, the other founder of the Black Panther Party and himself a client of Garry, defined his favorite attorney as "the Lenin of the courtroom."[117]

Beverly Axelrod—a San Francisco Guild attorney who went to Louisiana for CORE, coordinated the 1964 Sheraton Palace and Auto Row employment discrimination lawsuits, and represented Free Speech Movement activists in Berkeley—provides another example of this far-reaching integration between lawyers and activists. In 1965 she agreed to assist Eldridge Cleaver, who later became the Black Panthers minister of information and one of the most charismatic leaders of the party. Known as a petty criminal and a rapist of white women, Cleaver was serving his time across various California penitentiaries when he turned into a religious agitator of Black inmates. Stunned by his intelligence, Axelrod fell in love with him, and her sentiment was reciprocated, at least while Cleaver was in jail.[118] "I feel as though I'm on the edge of a new world," confessed Axelrod in a letter to her client, in which she also acknowledged that she was losing her "lawyerlike objectivity." "What I feel for you is profound," replied Cleaver five days later. "Beverly, there is something happening between us that is way out of the ordinary. Ours is one for the books, for the poets to draw new inspiration from, one to silence the cynics, and one to humble us by reminding us of how little we know about human beings, about ourselves."[119]

After the encounters of the couple moved from the lawyers' visiting room to the family visiting room of Folsom prison, the two even celebrated a mock wedding and promised each other a life together. Axelrod, who envisaged Cleaver as a new Malcom X and saw herself as his midwife, not only passed books and magazines across bars but also smuggled out Cleaver's writings within her legal papers, as prison authorities had forbidden their diffusion. She brought his manuscripts to the acclaimed novelist Norman Mailer and to the *Ramparts* office in San Francisco. Cleaver's sharp prose, "savage irony," and "sexual mysticism" impressed everybody, and while he was still in jail, his writings appeared on *Ramparts*' pages. Thanks to his newly acquired status of intellectual and the support of renowned public figures, Cleaver eventually obtained parole and was introduced into the radical milieu.[120] A collection of Cleaver's texts and letters was printed in 1968 under the title *Soul on Ice* and obtained extraordinary success. It was dedicated to his lawyer, "Beverly, with whom I share the ultimate of love."[121]

The whole romance ended in bitterness when Cleaver, finally out of jail, proved to be unfaithful and quickly abandoned Axelrod. He would marry a black woman, Kathleen, considered more suitable for a Black Power leader. In the meantime, Axelrod had built ties with Huey Newton. Interestingly, the iconic 1967 photo of Newton posing in a wicker chair handling a rifle and a tribal spear was taken in Axelrod's living room in San Francisco, in a house where the lawyer used to host Black Panther Party gatherings.[122] At her place, Axelrod also personally typed the first two issues of *Black Panther*, the official newspaper of the group.[123] In October 1967, Newton was charged with murdering white Oakland police officer John Frey, assaulting another officer, and kidnapping a man whose car he used for his dash to the hospital, where he was eventually apprehended, badly wounded. Right after the arrest, Axelrod reached out to his friend and mentor Charles Garry to rescue Newton. Garry and Fay Stender rushed to the hospital. Stender's life would be forever changed, as she ended up serving as counsel in the most notable case in terms of a lawyer's total identification with clients and, at the same time, the most tragic one.

The sight of Newton, lying half-naked as he recovered from surgery under the grim watch of police officers, left Stender deeply impressed. As her biographer, Lise Pearlman, explained, Stender instantaneously felt both a sense of indignation for Newton's powerless condition and a strong physical attraction. Therefore, she began making regular visits to the Alameda County Jail, where Newton had been transferred. During these interactions and through an impassioned correspondence, she also discovered Newton's charisma and intelligence and subsequently fell in love with him. To build trust, foster affection, and promote a shared political agenda, Stender disregarded any traditional code of conduct. She began treating Newton "as extended family," while prison guards witnessed sexual contact between her and Newton in a jail visiting room.[124]

Such profound empathy and physical desire drove her not only to work relentlessly for Newton's defense but also to renegotiate her own identity. In 1970, in the midst of a Guild seminar, she explained her personal evolution this way: "My identity is being almost antiprofessional and in some sort of way that of a political prisoner. In fact, I sometimes wonder whether my effectiveness will ultimately be enhanced or impaired. . . . I don't use the expression 'my clients' anymore. That expression is going out of my vocabulary and is certainly going out of my thinking. I feel that they are comrades."[125]

However, as had been the case between Axelrod and Cleaver, Stender felt increasingly humiliated by Newton's sexist attitude, and the relationship came to an end. Yet Stender's commitment to radical defendants was overwhelming. She formed an even tighter bond with another Black inmate, George L. Jackson, who was charged with killing a guard at Soledad State Prison with two other Black prisoners, Fleeta Drumgo and John W. Clutchette. Perpetrated in January 1970, the assassination appeared to be an act of revenge for the killing of three Black inmates by a white guard a few days before in the exercise yard of the same penitentiary. At the time of the murder, Jackson, twenty-eight years old, was serving an indeterminate sentence of one year to life for second-degree robbery charges. Since he was known as a troublemaker, he had never been paroled. Now Jackson was being charged not only with murder but also with assault, which meant that if convicted, the death penalty was mandatory.

Jackson became politicized in jail around 1968 through interactions with leftist prison gangs and revolutionary texts that were smuggled across bars. His popularity among inmates, who considered him a guide and a teacher, came to Newton's attention. Without meeting Jackson, the Black Panther leader did not hesitate to name him field marshal of the BPP at Soledad and entrusted him with recruitment. Fay Stender's first visit with Jackson in jail was indeed at the request of Newton, who wanted to provide the new Panther officer with legal help. After that, the young, sensitive radical lawyer took on Jackson's case with everything she had.[126]

Stender co-defended Jackson with John E. Thorne, a Guild attorney from San Jose, California. An experienced and belligerent criminal defense lawyer, Thorne had been a civil rights activist and a fierce opponent of the death penalty. Dazzled by Jackson's personal charm and revolutionary charisma, Thorne embraced the case with extreme devotion. Stender and Thorne built a defense committee for the three Soledad Brothers, orchestrated an international campaign asserting their innocence, and were crucial in forging the intellectual figure of Jackson, for whom they arranged the publication of his prison letters in a best-selling book (see chapter 7).

It is not surprising that in his correspondence, Jackson referred to Stender as "my small but mighty mouthpiece" and "my favorite person" and shared with her not only his political views but also his most intimate angst.[127] "I am really slow about taking humans into my heart, I have been too let down, but I need and enjoy your counsel, your friendship," explained Jackson in an unpublished letter to Thorne. "I loved that man," wrote Thorne in a laudatory review of Jackson's writings. "If anyone has ever deserved description as 'bigger than life' this is the person . . . one of the greatest [writers] of our time." As the lawyer revealed in awe, Jackson slept only two or three hours per night and worked into the early morning hours under a single lightbulb. Thorne was also mesmerized by Jackson's "magnificent and revealing smile" and by his uncommon "physical strength." "He told me," wrote Thorne, "that to repress the natural sexual drive he did a thousand fingertip push-ups a day."[128]

In all these cases, there is no doubt that such an extraordinary infatuation was grounded, at least to some extent, in convergent self-interests. On the one hand, there were the desperation and the isolation of Black political defendants serving jail time. Flattering and seducing sympathetic lawyers were obvious strategies to secure and exploit their legal skills. On the other hand, a white middle-class frustration, coupled with an unresolved quest for authenticity, existed among lawyers and legal workers. George Jackson's book editor, Gregory Armstrong, who was named a "legal investigator" by Thorne so he could meet with Jackson in prison, admitted it plainly. Overwhelmed by Jackson's mental and corporal vitality, he confessed that within the defense committee, they all felt they had "the right to live through him," as "identifying with George was like having a second self." This connection also allowed them to live politics, at least vicariously, as "a matter of survival" and not only as "a form of play."[129] Nonetheless, it is important to understand that such relationships were also the product of genuine admiration, real generosity, and intense political consciousness. Radical lawyers were eager to transcend professional barriers, challenge normativity, and join their clients' cause. In a context of intense politicization, they undeniably felt they were "on the edge of a new world," as Axelrod wrote in a letter to Cleaver.[130]

Yet this merger of forces entailed objective risks for lawyers. Exploiting the attorney-client privilege but also walking on a legal tightrope, Guild attorneys and legal workers aided fugitives.[131] Dean Robb revealed that he volunteered his farm in Metamora, Michigan—about one hour from the U.S.-Canada frontier—as a hiding place for leaders in the antiwar movement. Jane Fonda and Donald Sutherland used the farm as a retreat when they helped shuttle draft resisters across the border.[132] According to an FBI investigation, at least a dozen lawyers in the Guild's orbit actively helped the Weather Underground. Lawyers borrowed cars, hosted meetings, paid fines, offered mail drops, bought tickets, and raised money.[133] Significantly, the Weather Underground did not resort to robberies to sustain its subversive nuclei. According to journalist Bryan Burrough, Chicago attorney Dennis Cunningham, together with his wife Mona, "loaned" their children to "Weather couples" so that they could pretend to behave normally in their daily lives. Cunningham conceded: "Without the lawyers, I'm telling you, they couldn't have survived." "Money, strategy, passports, whatever it was we could do, you just did it," confessed Elizabeth M. Fink, a Guild lawyer from Brooklyn who later specialized in prison rights. Fink also added, "We didn't have the balls to go underground but those who did they were our heroes. You can't believe the excitement, the romance, the intrigue."[134]

Likewise, Kunstler, who occasionally went to see Weather Underground affiliates in their safe houses, confessed that he enjoyed "the cloak-and-dagger aspects of meeting clandestinely with people the government was eager to find and prosecute." The danger also appealed to him because he was always "a little uncomfortable with the fact that lawyers took no risks, while . . . clients took many." "Meeting with the Weather Underground," he candidly acknowledged, "gave me a chance to demonstrate that I was ready, willing, and able to take some chances; it increased the camaraderie we felt with each other."[135]

Being particularly close to Dohrn, Michael Kennedy was reportedly involved in the 1970 jailbreak of psychologist and psychedelic guru Timothy Leary. Serving a ten-year sentence at San Luis Obispo prison on charges of marijuana possession, Leary escaped with the support of the Weather Underground, who had been hired and paid (the large sum of $50,000) by the Brotherhood of Eternal Love, an organization of drug users.[136] For her part, Eleanor Stein experienced the state of being both a Guild student activist when she was attending Columbia and, later, a federal fugitive as a member of the Weather Underground. Although she prefers to avoid talking "about the people who helped us," she admits that "there were definitely some lawyers who played a very important role in protecting the organization and also in helping people who got arrested. Counseling, at the end of the organization, became also very important. At times, some lawyers were good intermediaries. They had a certain level of protection: I am their lawyer and I am supposed to meet with them. I have a lawyer-client privilege, so if the FBI asks me questions, I have the right not to answer."[137]

Against this backdrop, advising activists was considered an obvious task for lawyers, and activists were relying on lawyers more than ever. "The movement needed us so badly," remembers Paul Harris, who had been a civil rights organizer before practicing law. "Every progressive group needed us; everything like getting a press pass or avoiding suspension from high school, they didn't know how to do it, and they turned to us."[138] Even so, contrary to traditional practices, the lawyers were supposed to respect activists' inclinations and avoid legalizing or depoliticizing activists' agenda. In this regard, radical lawyers constantly reflected on ways to curtail their paternalistic and elitist influence on activists, while a challenge repeatedly came to the fore: how to make sure that people with privileged backgrounds and professional skills maintain humility.

The solution was to limit counseling to explaining the alternatives open to activists when planning their tactics, suggesting the most productive ways to challenge the law, and clarifying the legal consequences of their actions. In other words, counseling was meant to provide knowledge. Activists had to make informed choices without taking lawyers' advice as sacred, and lawyers had to learn how to take a back seat and make sure that their personality, skills, language, and confidence did not become overly imposing.[139]

The activity of Guild lawyers is documented in dense correspondence with movement organizers, who frequently asked for advice and received multiple yet never imposing suggestions. Typical requests for information regarded the violations implicit in civil disobedience, the risk of conducting sit-ins on federal property, and the recommended behavior when plainclothes police officers asked for identification or when narcotics were involved.[140] It is worth noting that Guild executive secretary Kenneth Cloke became an official legal adviser to the Students for a Democratic Society, sitting on the National Interim Committee, which was the executive branch of the SDS leadership. SDS itself passed a resolution calling on its members to refer to the Guild for all matters regarding repression and legal defense. "If I had been someone who came without a radical critique of the law," remembers Cloke, "they wouldn't have listened to me. . . . They appreciated that we did not impose our opinion."[141]

To foster the notion of attorneys and clients as "equal partners in struggle," radical lawyers revised their traditional style and methods of work. Even the most outspoken leftist lawyers of the former generation had maintained strict aplomb and respected most of the professional codes. Three-piece suits and ceremonial manners were the norm for attorneys who represented unpopular defendants and wanted to be flawless. By contrast, to show solidarity with their clients, radical lawyers—especially the young—began dressing casually, keeping their hair long, and growing beards. Thorne, for example, typically wore blue jeans, a Mao cap with a red star, and a denim jacket with propaganda buttons. His colleague Terence Hallinan regularly dressed in bellbottom jeans and a tie-dyed T-shirt. "His long hair comes down almost to his shoulders, and with his spectacles he looks more like a graduate student from Berkeley than a practicing lawyer," wrote a journalist. Fay Stender, likewise, hardly seemed a conventional lawyer. She usually wore a leather miniskirt and had her hair in a ponytail. Always pushing the boundaries, Florynce Kennedy exhibited cowboy attire even before judges, pairing it with conspicuous hats and false eyelashes.[142]

In courtrooms, formal ties and white shirts temporarily disappeared from men's costumes, and women often replaced skirts with pants, which were considered "radical fashion" because they crossed gender lines and made a statement of women's power.[143] Emily Goodman, who would later become a New York Supreme Court judge, was among the first female lawyers to wear pants during a trial in the United States. After being chastised by the presiding judge, at the following court appearance she received solidarity from a group of fellow Guild women who showed up in the gallery all wearing pants.[144]

Not to refer to a judge as "your honor" turned out to be a quirk, even "an article of faith," among young radical attorneys, who tried their hardest to avoid using that phrase in court, as Marvin Stender remembers.[145] Since the judge's "possession" of the room was perceived as abusive, standing up when a magistrate entered the room became annoying as well.[146] All rituals, languages, and codes that sanctified the law became increasingly unbearable. When they rarely ascended to judgeship, radical lawyers continued to defy law's majesty and mystique. Elected as a judge of the Detroit Recorder's Court (Detroit's criminal court) in November 1972, Justin Ravitz refused to stand for the Pledge of Allegiance at his swearing-in ceremony. His courtroom bailiffs would not say "all rise for the judge" but "all rise for the jury," paying respect to people's justice. Until compelled by the Michigan Supreme Court, Ravitz did not wear a judicial robe or display an American flag in the courtroom.[147]

In a tribute to the 1960s credo that "change is only in the streets," official Guild delegations began participating in sit-ins, demonstrations, and marches, often with their own banners. To be sure, individual lawyers had always taken part in public displays of protest, but now they did it more frequently and under the umbrella of an organized entity. With lawyers on their side—also physically—protesters could feel that they were not alone against an overwhelming state power, while the establishment was warned that social unrest had spread to difficult-to-marginalize categories.[148] On April 30, 1969, the day before Law Day—the anniversary dedicated to the reaffirmation of American justice—two hundred lawyers and law students picketed the federal courthouse in New York. Attorneys William Kunstler, Arthur Kinoy, and William Crain took the floor and demanded the end of preventive detention, the lowering of excessive bails, more representative juries, better detention centers, civilian control of police, and the abolition of certain crimes, such as abortion and homosexuality. The protest was probably the first lawyers' demonstration in the history of the United States.[149] A few months later, on October 15, 1969, the NLG convened at the Church Center for the United Nations in New York and urged its lawyers to observe the Vietnam moratorium in the streets or at least at their workplaces.[150] At the time of the 1971 May Day protests, the NLG encouraged its chapters again to plan antiwar activity, suggesting that demonstrations of any kind take place at federal installations such as courtrooms, draft boards, and military bases. That May Day rally, coinciding with Law Day, was particularly successful, as more than two thousand lawyers met in New York demanding an end to the war and drastic changes to the legal system.[151]

4 Revolution in the Courtroom

· ·

As radical lawyers and movements merged their trajectories, politics burst into courtrooms as never before in American history. What ensued was a new model of litigation—here defined as militant litigation and understood as a conscious and elaborate strategy deployed by defendants to manipulate and subvert legal proceedings to further a political agenda.[1]

It is important to remember that political trials were hardly new. In fact, trials can be defined as "political" whenever public authorities (and sometimes defendants) seek to affect the distribution of power by exploiting the courts. Classic examples are trials to curb dissidence. Through the modern era, as jurist Otto Kirchheimer warned, political trials have been recurrent, if not "inescapable," regardless of the dominant legal system.[2] However, since the 1920s, American citizens forced into the position of political defendants coped with their trials quite submissively. They typically expected their counsel to use their technical skills to exploit whatever could be gained from the ordinary functioning of the judicial system.[3] Even during the McCarthy period, conventional, by-the-book defense schemes were preferred. It was regarded as normal to "sanitize" trials, excising political elements in order to limit the burden of repression.

The only notable exception was the 1948–49 New York trial of twelve members of the National Board of the Communist Party, which gave rise to an extraordinary courtroom confrontation.[4] Held in the most hysterical phase of the Cold War, it was the first Smith Act trial of party leadership.[5] Defendants wanted to turn the proceedings into a vindication of Marxism and socialism and saw the trial as a setting in which they could emulate the performance of Georgi Dimitrov, the Bulgarian communist leader who had been accused of setting fire to the Reichstag in 1933. Refusing counsel, Dimitrov had turned the tables on his accusers and exploited the trial as a forum to challenge Nazism and advocate communism. "The hero of offensive defense," as he was cherished in the communist tradition, unexpectedly succeeded and transformed his trial into an archetype of political defense.[6]

Therefore, in the U.S. district courthouse in Foley Square, defendants and lawyers—almost all Guild members—frontally attacked prosecutors, jury selection, and the demeanor of judge Harold R. Medina, who was actually an abrasive and unfriendly figure. Elizabeth G. Flynn predicted, "Our comrades will make the trial court a mighty tribunal of the people so that the accused become the accusers and the enemies of the people find themselves on trial before the huge court of public opinion in America—and the world." Indeed, such a combative attitude gave rise to bitter engagements and polemic outbursts. Attorneys and clients were held in contempt and were punished with lengthy prison terms. The defense committee also rallied external supporters, who raucously picketed the courthouse, and tried to educate a general public largely hostile to communists. Eventually, the jury convicted all defendants, and the U.S. Supreme Court upheld the decision. In follow-up trials, lawyers and clients behaved more cautiously, focusing instead on technical issues.[7]

Political trials with oppositionist defendants—or "disorderly trials," as they were often defined by law-and-order advocates—largely disappeared from sight in the following two decades. In fact, a few trials that involved the Nation of Islam between the late 1950s and the early 1960s prefigured some future developments. With the help of NAACP attorneys, the Nation of Islam tentatively used the courtroom as a stage to articulate its political views and to denounce the police brutality that its members allegedly experienced on a daily basis. Malcolm X himself took the witness stand and catalyzed public attention with his eloquence. However, despite the intended politicization and mediatization of the proceedings, militant litigation was yet to come.[8]

As detailed in chapter 2, both the Free Speech Movement trial and the Columbia trial suggested that political and legal needs required a synthesis, but these trials were still rather conventional. When in May 1968 Benjamin Spock and four other defendants, known as the Boston Five, were brought into court and charged with conspiring to counsel young men to evade the draft, Spock hoped to use the trial to dramatize the immorality of the war and accelerate its end. His codefendant Michael Ferber, the only one of draft age, agreed with Spock and declared his willingness to go to prison to uphold the choice to return his draft card to the Selective Service. Activists also yearned to make the trial a showdown against the administration, while supporters lined up around the courthouse.[9]

However, the appointed lawyers—a mixed bag of personalities with divergent political views—opted for a civil libertarian strategy based on the First Amendment and ran separate defenses aimed at protecting their individual clients regardless of mutual solidarity. When Spock's attorney, Leonard Boudin, proposed a "cohesive cooperative defense," the other lawyers opposed it, fearing that it would be taken as evidence of a real conspiracy. Legalistic arguments and prudence prevailed, and collateral activities and publicity were banned.[10] And yet the intent of the prosecution was markedly political, for the government wanted to crack down on those who urged younger men to break the law. Political, too, was the attitude of the judge, who demonstrated his biases by ruling out all discussions on the legality of the war and the draft. A jury eventually found four defendants guilty of all charges (except counseling to turn in draft cards) and acquitted one.[11]

Only a few months later, however, the case of the Oakland Seven in California showed that a new approach had taken shape. It was the first known application of the new criminal conspiracy law to antiwar demonstrations, and activists were deeply concerned about the prospect of a wave of similar prosecutions.[12] The indictments also hit the first major act of resistance against the war—Stop the Draft Week. So stakes were high, and the trial of this group of UC Berkeley students, former students, and full-time activists immediately gained special significance. Charles Garry, Malcolm Burnstein, and Richard Hodge, a San Francisco lawyer focusing on criminal defense and entertainment law, undertook their representation and coupled a unitary defense strategy with an open and intentional politicization of the trial.

Since the Vietnam War had to take center stage, in his opening statement Garry linked the conflict in Southeast Asia to the Nuremberg judgments. He argued that the evidence showed that the war was illegal, immoral, and genocidal. Therefore, as the Nuremberg principles suggested, citizens had an obligation to do everything in their power to prevent the commission of inhumane acts by their government. As a consequence, those who opposed the war were simply upholding the law, not breaking it. Pioneering a tactic that would later be adopted extensively, the defense called in two expert witnesses on Vietnam who buttressed the argument against the conflict. Student demonstrators were also summoned to testify that the Seven had taken to the streets out of an irrepressible animosity against the war. It was a sparkling success for the defense. "For a few moments," noted Garry, "the stark reality of war came right into the courtroom."[13] And the trial turned into a teach-in.

From the beginning, the Oakland Seven discussed how to convert their legal defense into "a counterattack on the system." They were visibly satisfied as soon as they recognized that "the jurors [were] getting a political education" about the reasons behind the protest. "The defense," reads a propaganda leaflet from the time, "has turned the trial into an indictment of the system's repressive legal apparatus, and of its brutal and conspiratorial cops. . . . We tried to force the jury to vote not on our guilt or innocence, but rather for or against the war, for or against the police, and for or against the free speech."[14] The defendants, their followers exulted, "have not retreated in court, haven't shaved or dressed straight, or trimmed their politics, and made it plain that they are proud of what they did." Local activists also provided external support through gatherings and sit-ins "to indicate to the District Attorney and the Oakland power structure that the anti-war movement [was not] intimidated."[15]

If at the trial's opening the jury seemed to endorse the war, by the end of the proceedings it seemed to oppose it. Garry's empathy, together with his ability to "play the common person," was considered key in winning the jurors over. By all accounts, Judge George W. Phillips, a liberal, was also fair and sympathetic toward the defendants, allowing them "to educate the jury" and to explain "why they did what they did."[16] Most importantly, in his instructions to the jury, the judge consented to taking into account the defendants' beliefs about the legality and morality of the war.[17] Eventually, in his closing argument, Garry dared to assert that in the country there was "a conspiracy" that sought to impose U.S. military force on the rest of the world and create "a curtain of fear" over dissident voices. He ended by reading out the sonnet engraved on the pedestal of the Statue of Liberty. The defense received nearly 160 contempt citations, but the Oakland Seven were all acquitted.[18]

Along the same lines, Charles Garry provided another exemplary political defense in a coeval trial. This time, Garry represented Huey Newton, with the invaluable assistance of Fay Stender. The blueprint of militant litigation emerged sharper than ever. As previously mentioned, Newton was charged with murdering a police officer, assaulting another one, and kidnapping a man to get a car. To counterbalance the negative publicity and generate sympathy for the defendant, Garry immediately organized a series of press conferences through which Newton expressed his views on the Black liberation movement and stressed the necessity of self-defense in response to police persecution.

Garry also arranged a large number of interviews with Newton in the leftist press and included Edward Keating, a *Ramparts* reporter with a law degree, on the legal team so that he could have direct access to the proceedings and disseminate favorable coverage.[19] Keating ended up writing a successful propaganda instant book titled *Free Huey!*, and the whole strategy, according to Garry, obtained "tremendous public relations." The defense, indeed, managed to spread the notion that Newton "has been continually subjected to harassment, provocation and assault by the Oakland police and that in every case, including this latest incident, he has acted in self-defense." The "power structure" was explicitly targeting the political leaders of the Black liberation struggle and the antiwar movement: after H. Rap Brown, LeRoi Jones, and Bobby Seale, who had all been hit by the system of justice, it was Newton's turn.[20]

Since pretrial hearings, thousands of supporters gathered outside the Alameda County courthouse in Oakland, chanting, "Free Huey, jail the pigs." Prominent picketers such as Mario Savio and Jack Weinberg joined the crowd, while the Peace and Freedom Party, a newly born left-wing political party, officially named Newton as a candidate for Congress.[21] The Black Panther Party leaped at the chance to orchestrate a political campaign and disseminated stickers, signs, and buttons. The trial had to be a political contest—there was no other way to rescue Newton. In the Black community, declarations of support for Newton became a badge of honor. On February 17, 1968, fifty-five hundred people celebrated Newton's birthday at the Oakland Auditorium in the presence of Berkeley councilman Ronald V. Dellums and former SNCC leader Stokely Carmichael. Newton's African wicker chair was left empty.[22] As it was immediately clear, the sudden emergence of the BPP from a local group to a national organization was largely due to the catalyzing power of that trial.[23]

To reinforce their coalition with Black militants, white radicals also exploited the trial. A Berkeley activist organized the Honkies for Huey group, playing on the racial slur used against white people, and printed some famous buttons. Guild lawyer Alex Hoffman, a white man of Austrian origin who was part of the defense team, acted as a liaison between the Panthers and the imprisoned Newton, winning over the Panthers' total trust.[24] Since the out-of-court propaganda was considered crucial, the defense asked to postpone the trial as long as possible, so that the general public could be educated, and requested a larger venue to accommodate media operators and sympathetic spectators. The motion was denied, but on July 15, 1968, when the trial started, a mass of supporters, including antiwar leftists, militant Chicanos, and Panthers in uniform, besieged the courthouse. An American flag was lit on fire, and Seale famously warned, "If anything happens to Huey P. Newton, the sky's the limit."[25]

Garry consistently raised the fundamental question of whether a Black man, least of all a Black power militant, could receive a fair trial before a U.S. court given the entrenched racism that still characterized the U.S.

population. The National Advisory Commission on Civil Disorders had just published its appalling report, and the argument also resonated within liberal public opinion. Thus, Garry attacked the all-white composition of the grand jury that indicted Newton and staged what at the time appeared to be an extremely protracted jury questioning process, aimed at eliminating any potential juror with racist attitudes. One of the innovative aspects of the trial was indeed the introduction of "racial prejudice" as a legitimate area on which to test the jury panel.

The defense also marshaled six social scientists who were meant to demonstrate, on the basis of scholarly evidence, the need for an unbiased jury of peers representing a cross-section of the defendant's community. The guest star was Robert Blauner, a Berkeley sociologist and expert in race relations, who argued that racism was "a basic reality in America" and that the Black population had been "colonized within the borders of the U.S.," hence judicial authorities should select jurors not from a generic cross-section of society but from the "ghetto."[26] Asking more than 290 questions drafted by Stender, Garry examined almost 160 prospective jurors and eventually obtained a selection that included seven women and five minority people. However, as Garry admitted, he was not able to eliminate some individuals who arguably concealed preconceptions against Black people.

In any event, Garry continued educating the jury and, in the opening statement, declared that Newton was a militant who sincerely believed in the necessity of revolutionary change and stressed the systematic persecution of the Panthers. When Newton took the stand, Garry let him talk about his philosophy and explain the Black Panther Party's ten-point program with a lengthy pseudo-sociological disquisition. The kidnapping charge was subsequently dropped, as the alleged victim refused to testify in court for fear of self-incrimination. Interestingly, this person was represented by Doug Hill, a Berkeley-based radical lawyer and Peter Franck's partner. Concerning the murder charge, the defense argued that the backup officer who rushed in to rescue his colleague shot both the victim and Newton in chaotic circumstances. Finally, in a three-and-a-half-hour closing argument, Garry compared Newton to Jesus Christ, spoke of Frantz Fanon and W. E. B. Du Bois, and quoted *Alice in Wonderland*, leaving the courtroom reportedly "spellbound." The jury found Newton guilty of voluntary manslaughter but not of assault with a deadly weapon on the other police officer.[27]

Prodded by Stender, the Free Huey Committee collected twenty thousand signatures urging Newton's release, while the National Lawyers Guild supported Newton's federal bail petition with a brief arguing that white defendants, if sentenced for the same crime, would have been released pending appeal. In May 1970, the California Court of Appeals reversed Newton's conviction and ordered a new trial. In August, the Panther leader was released, to the delight of the ten thousand supporters who hailed their hero just outside the prison. The new trial ended in 1971 with the jury unable to reach a verdict. A later and final trial closed the case with another hung jury.[28]

Chicago: Dramatized Contempt

United States of America, Plaintiff, v. David T. Dellinger et al., Defendants, No. 69 Crim. 180, better known as the trial of the Chicago Eight (later Seven), began in the federal district courthouse of Chicago on September 26, 1969, and ended five months later, after some two hundred witnesses had been heard and twenty-two thousand pages of transcript had been accumulated.[29] Immediately, the trial became a national event and made its entrance into popular culture. Though it was not the first example of militant litigation, it came to stand as the most prominent and well known.

As writer Dwight Macdonald observed, the Chicago Eight exemplified "a *kulturkampf* between the extremes of American politics and lifestyle."[30] The major lines of division of society seemed to be "distilled and then acted out in the courtroom." On the one hand, the defendants embodied the various ramifications of the leftist movement, from the Black Panthers to religious pacifism, from the Yippies to SDS. And they all defied the court system in an unprecedented way, thrilling activists and sympathizers around the world. On the other hand, the elderly and conservative judge Julius J. Hoffman seemed to epitomize everything that was unfair, oppressive, and outdated in the establishment. Unable to suppress his contempt for the youngsters beyond the bench, he reacted with stiffness and stubbornness to their explicitly provocative and unruly attitudes. Circuit judges condemned his behavior and defined it "deprecatory and often antagonistic." The prosecutor, on his part, added fuel to the flames.[31]

As is widely known, in March 1969 Abbie Hoffman, Jerry Rubin, David Dellinger, Tom Hayden, Rennie Davis, John Froines, Lee Weiner, and Bobby Seale were charged with conspiring to incite a riot during the 1968 Democratic National Convention and performing acts to achieve that purpose. They risked a ten-year sentence.[32] Eventually, the government was not able to prove that they plotted to provoke a riot in Chicago. As was also true for the Oakland Seven, they had never met all together before the August demonstration. Seale, for example, had only made a couple of speeches in

Chicago and did not have any substantial contact with the organizers. Quite paradoxically, they had first met after the charges had been laid down, when they gathered in a Black Panthers' office to select their lead counsel.

While Seale's position was severed and a mistrial was declared in his case, the jury eventually acquitted the other seven defendants on the conspiracy count. Froines and Weiner, who were also charged with teaching and demonstrating the use, application, and construction of an incendiary device, were acquitted of this charge. The other five, who were individually charged with crossing state lines with the intent to incite a riot, were found guilty of this charge. In 1972, an appellate court reversed the rulings, and the government did not seek a new trial.[33]

From the very first day, the legal proceedings degenerated into what former U.S. Attorney General Ramsey Clark defined as a "legal atrocity," for everything appeared wrong and controversial, no matter the point of observation.[34] The fact that the Chicago trial represented one of the most extreme and barefaced challenges to the legal system by both radical lawyers and defendants remains indisputable. Indeed, what happened inside and outside that courtroom exerted considerable influence on at least two levels: the general confidence in the system of justice and the practice of radical lawyers. In other words, such a highly publicized trial contributed to desacralizing the courts of justice and to defining the key features of militant litigation.

The strategies and the attitudes of the defense echoed the debates of the NLG and leveraged the experience of Guild lawyers. Almost all lawyers who were involved in the case, including the two leading attorneys, William Kunstler and Leonard Weinglass, along with scores of legal volunteers, were indeed active members of the NLG. As a police intelligence report reveals, the legal team met in New York City in March 1969 already expressing the view that "demonstrators will be convicted"; hence, the lawyers should "work to force error on the part of the judge in order to get appeal." Weinglass reportedly planned "to discredit the judge sometime during the trial," while the defendants were meant "to turn the proceeding into a circus" and to "wear false faces during at least one day of the trial."[35]

Yet the belligerent defense tactics and the courtroom turmoil were not entirely concocted in advance. They gradually arose from negotiations between lawyers and clients and were influenced by the personality of the people involved on both sides of the bench. They were also distorted by the media exposure and reflected a great deal of improvisation.[36] In fact, Hayden and Froines wanted to win the case rapidly with a "rational defense" and get back to organizing, while Hoffman and Rubin sought to politicize the trial as much as possible by bringing the war into the courtroom and mocking the system of justice. They also pressed for taking the tactics of the Oakland Seven case even further. During that trial—they complained—Garry had insisted that defendants behave in the courtroom. Hoffman and Rubin did not want a tedious teach-in in which they would take back seats while lawyers called the shots.[37]

This latter and most radical strategy eventually prevailed. The two Yippies were media-savvy marketers who treated the courtroom as a theatrical space with a national audience. It is worth remembering that Hoffman had first acquired fame for burning dollar bills outside banks, while Rubin had come to the limelight by appearing before HUAC in 1966 in an American Revolution uniform. Disciples of Antonin Artaud, they were eager to repurpose language and to use the power of drama to unveil the most excruciating reality. Acting, for them, was a search for authenticity. But they were also disciples of Marshall McLuhan and realized that mass media, and notably television, had redefined political communication and could be weaponized for the revolution.[38]

Hungry for sensational news, the press seconded and amplified such a colorful approach.[39] Eager to follow their defendants' lead, counsel agreed to put the government on trial and to educate the jury and the people on the politics of the movement. As historian Marianne Debouzy put it, the courtroom turned into "a pedagogic place," where lawyers took charge of translating the language of rebellious youth for the general public.[40] Defending their clients on strictly legal grounds thus became a secondary goal—never abandoned but largely decentered—and Garry's "aggressive courtroom tactics" became the model to be developed.[41] Finally, the harsh reaction of the judge seemed to justify such a strategy, reinforcing its rationale and further radicalizing movement constituencies. Instinctively authoritarian and terrified by the chaos of those days, Hoffman systematically rejected defense motions and lost his temper. This was precisely what the Yippies expected, betting that authorities, "in their own self-protective hysteria," would raise the stakes.[42]

The list of antics, put-ons, and travesties that punctuated the trial is almost endless. Defendants refused to stand up when the judge entered and left the room, interrupted him, referred to him insolently, and laughed openly at his rulings. They screamed obscenities, made faces, spoke to the jury, and ridiculed the court—for example, by wearing judicial robes. Sometimes they blatantly disregarded the proceedings and read newspapers, mail, and books. More conspicuously, they brought a Vietcong flag into the courtroom during the October moratorium and placed Che Guevara's portrait on the defense table on the anniversary of his assassination. They tried to read the names of the war dead in the courtroom and arranged to bring in a cake to celebrate the birthday of codefendant Bobby Seale.[43]

Seale was under arrest for a separate murder charge, but his lawyer, Charles Garry, was temporarily hospitalized, recovering from surgery. Seale vehemently refused to be represented by any other lawyer and insisted on his right to self-defense. Urged by Garry to keep his protest up in court and to reject any appointed lawyer, he reacted with anger to the judge's choice to provide him with an attorney and was forcibly put into his chair by the marshals.[44] For two days he attended the proceedings bound and gagged. Eventually, he was tried separately, but Seale's treatment, reminiscent of slavery, gained immediate notoriety as a symbol of government racial oppression and contributed chiefly to delegitimizing the whole trial.[45] Also playing on the delegitimization of authorities, Abbie Hoffman, of Jewish origins, cast himself and his codefendants as "good Jews" in contrast to "bad Jews" Judge Hoffman and prosecutor Richard Schultz, of Jewish origins themselves, who were betraying their own people. Abbie Hoffman also verbally assaulted the judge in Yiddish, while Dellinger accused the judge of treating defendants like Jewish people on the way to concentration camps.[46]

In the meantime, on the very first day of the proceedings, the judge issued bench warrants for pretrial lawyers Michael Kennedy, Dennis Roberts, Michael Tigar, and Gerald Lefcourt, who did not show up in court.[47] Amid indignation, Tigar and Lefcourt were arrested and jailed, only to be promptly released. The defendants also packed the courtroom with a claque of supporters, who joined them in their parody and scoffing of the prosecutor and judge by yelling derisive comments, raising their voices, and laughing at crucial moments. Called to the witness stand, singers Arlo Guthrie, Judy Collins, Phil Ochs, Country Joe, and Pete Seeger attempted to sing for the jury but were rebuked. Allen Ginsberg, another witness for the defense, tried to perform the Hare Krishna mantra and later chanted the mantra Om. On redirect examination, he also recited his poem *Howl*, still outrageous at the time.[48]

The lawyers did nothing to quiet their clients; rather, they sustained and justified their outbursts. Kunstler, for example, requested a recess on October 15 to allow the defendants to participate in Vietnam moratorium activities and called for a moment of silence for Dr. King on January 15. Journalist Anthony J. Lukas, who covered the trial for the *New York Times*, noted that "after the two Hoffmans, William Kunstler was the most compelling figure in the courtroom."[49] With a fair share of narcissism, Kunstler gradually adopted many of the practices that would become his trademark, including attacking the presiding judge with gusto, endorsing the radical ideology of the defendants, engaging in theatrics, and employing humor to mock the government.

Photogenic and well spoken, Kunstler was conscious of his media appeal and eagerly played with it. He let his hair grow, wore casual shirts, and began living day and night with the defendants. Reporters spotted him eating, drinking, smoking, dancing, and demonstrating with them. The identification was absolute—literally, a conspiracy. When Judge Hoffman told Kunstler, "You get awfully chummy with your clients," he replied, "There is a certain intimacy that is bred in these cases." Quite paradoxically, at the end of the trial, the most punitive rulings hit the two lead defense lawyers, Kunstler and Weinglass, who were sentenced to jail terms for contempt: four years and thirteen days for Kunstler; one year, eight months, and five days for Weinglass.[50] Yet much to the scorn of the judge, the lawyers sported the contempt verdict as a badge of honor. "I am, in a way, proud to be convicted," declared Kunstler right outside the courthouse, "because I think too long lawyers have been immune, being a representative breed, immune from the slings and arrows that oppress their clients."[51]

Importantly, to sustain the defendants and publicize the trial, the Committee to Defend the Conspiracy (an organization raising funds for legal defense) and the Chicago Legal Defense Committee attracted a large number of young volunteers from all over the country, who saw in the trial a meaningful opportunity to fight the system.[52] "The defendants," wrote Lukas, "were the most glamorous, exciting leaders of the New Left, and their defense seemed to be where the action was in the Movement at that time."[53] The Legal Defense Committee operated out of a communal-style office near the courthouse, where volunteers performed a variety of tasks, from legal work to laundry, and prominent supporters such as Dustin Hoffman sometimes stopped by. Carlin Meyer was among the volunteers who joined the committee. During the trial, she sat in the courtroom watching the proceedings, while in the evenings and on weekends she worked in the office. Such experience, she admits today, changed her life forever, as she learned from Kunstler and Weinglass the importance of the law as "a focal point for organizing," the commitment to clients, and "the defiance of authority."[54]

Defendants, for their part, appeared in public almost nightly to give speeches, present books, raise money, and organize. The reception they encountered was passionate, and the Chicago Seven, together with their leading attorneys, became true celebrities.[55] They were often invited to demonstrations, parties, and university campuses, where they attracted thousands of listeners. "After I walked on the stage," recounted Kunstler, "the audience would stand up and cheer as if I were a superstar. We had an enormous and enthusiastic constituency of young people that kept increasing."[56] Tom Hayden maintained that they spoke in public perhaps five hundred times during the trial, including on the day of the Vietnam moratorium in front of a million citizens. He also remembered the genuine solidarity he felt many times when he saw, early in the morning, hundreds of people lining up outside the courtroom to get one of the fifty to sixty seats available to the audience.[57]

Public support endured even after the end of the trial. To protest a widely anticipated guilty verdict, dozens of Day After demonstrations, as they were called, were organized across the country, especially around courthouses. These often resulted in clashes with police and arrests. A National Conference on Political Justice, held at the University of Pennsylvania in March 1970, amassed between two thousand and three thousand students who cheered and hailed the panelists. Particularly applauded were Charles Garry, who emphatically kissed a Black Panther representative on the cheek and gave a stirring address, and William Kunstler—"the hero of Chicago"—who electrified the audience by thrashing the system of justice and urging young lawyers to join the movement.[58]

Solidarity with the conspiracy trial also came from lawyers' organizations. Right after the bench warrants hit the pretrial lawyers, the Guild, in cooperation with the NECLC, the ACLU, the LCCR, and the Chicago Legal Defense Committee, organized a lawyers' protest on September 29, 1969. Two hundred lawyers from all over the country demonstrated at the Chicago courthouse, attempted to file two amici briefs—calling the arrest of the lawyers "a travesty of justice [that] threatens to destroy the confidence of the American people in the entire judicial process"—and asked to sit in as observers during trial proceedings. After they were denied access, 150 of them continued picketing the courthouse. In the meantime, two hundred other members of the legal community, also mobilized by the Guild, took to the streets in San Francisco in solidarity with the Chicago lawyers. This wide-ranging contestation, which also involved thirteen Harvard Law School faculty members asking the Senate Judiciary Committee to investigate Hoffman's conduct, was arguably decisive in pressing the judge to drop all charges against the lawyers.[59]

In the wake of this victory, lawyers formed an ad hoc committee to stop the trial and rapidly organized a national demonstration of lawyers on October 17 in front of the Chicago courthouse, to focus attention on the legal-political repression and to denounce Judge Hoffmann's persistent bias in favor of the prosecution. Other minor but relevant expressions of dissent—such as the protest of thirty newly admitted members of the New Jersey bar, who wore black armbands at their swearing-in ceremony—followed through the end of the trial.[60] Meanwhile, the Guild drafted another amicus brief to denounce the inhuman and unprecedented treatment of Bobby Seale, which stamped "with a fresh badge of slavery" every Black person in America.[61]

Militant Litigation

Without a doubt, the Chicago trial and the first highly politicized cases emboldened those involved in the movement. Organizers explicitly pointed to political trials as invaluable opportunities to demonstrate how the ruling powers threatened civil liberties and instrumentalized justice to target ideas and stifle dissent.[62] On their part, radical lawyers began to reflect on the evolution of litigation at a time of social turmoil, when the realm of possibilities opened up, and they felt empowered. "We thought we could make a new world," recalls one of them.[63] Contrary to both the McCarthy era and the civil rights period, in 1969–70 the Left was neither intimidated nor isolated.[64] In such a context, lawyers could not "escape the need to transform themselves as political beings." They could cease to be skillful technicians who simply cut losses.[65] As Gerald Lefcourt vividly remembers, "Lawyers have never said 'we are in a conspiracy to change this country.' Lawyers used to say: 'My client was not involved in this. . . . I represent him. . . . He wasn't there. . . .' Baloney! We are part of the change, and you are trying to destroy us with funny baloney. So, this was a whole new approach to the legal system."[66]

With experienced Guild lawyers providing mentorship and guidance, the main features of this confrontational model of litigation were increasingly discussed and stood out with greater clarity. In fact, they were even systematized.[67] By 1975, the Department of Justice had recognized that new disruptive strategies were being employed in some "very visible" trials: "A recurring group of experienced personnel for trial work and research," mostly affiliated with the NLG and the CCR, employed the same techniques in the representation of "publicly controversial defendants," making the cases "untriable" and encouraging disrespect for the government.[68] Ironically, both the Department of Justice and the radical lawyers singled out the same techniques.

First, the defense had to uncover the political reasons that moved the trial and shed light on the real issues posed by the prosecution—for example, the fact that the case was engineered by an oppressive government to deprive dissenters of their constitutional rights. It was imperative to emphasize that "prosecution" actually meant "persecution." In Mary Kaufman's words, it was important "to strip the charges of their hypocrisy." From this perspective, a valuable strategy had to exploit the trial as a public stage in order to demonstrate that the defendants were being charged with political crimes and, at the same time, to discredit the establishment.[69] By turning the accused into the accuser, the trial could focus on the government's wrongdoings and exemplify how legality was a relative concept. Reversing the logic of old-time political trials, the trial could disseminate "political counterimages," in Kirchheimer's words. And defendants could take advantage of the intrinsic quality of trials to "re-create history" in front of a public.[70]

Second, the defense had to expose the economic, social, and cultural issues that propelled the crime under judgment. As Garry put it, it was essential to relocate the crime into a different context and to present the facts from that perspective.[71] The roots of the crime had to be tracked down to such factors as social inequality, racial discrimination, or labor exploitation, or to more specific acts of repression, such as police harassment. This reconfiguration of crime led, quite logically, to removing responsibility from the individual—an act that mirrored the intellectual developments of those years. Indeed, an increasing number of psychiatrists, psychologists, sociologists, and legal scholars suggested reframing the phenomenon of crime as "a process of social interaction in which the legal process itself plays a critical role, rather than seeing it as an objectively given form of individual conduct." Otherwise said, crime was not "the behavior of an individual offender" but the result of "a complex set of interactions and transactions."[72]

A practical application of these principles was what Guild lawyer Paul Harris defined as the "black rage defense," which was a strategy of exonerating defendants based on the racial oppression they experienced. "The black rage defense," wrote Harris, "raises fundamental issues regarding crime, race, and justice. It forces us to grapple with questions the criminal justice system does not want to hear. Why does a person commit a crime? What is society's responsibility for shaping the person who commits a crime?" To put it very simply, it was meant to show how "concrete instances of racial discrimination" impacted the mental state of the defendant, pointing to a direct causal relationship between racism and crime. Oppression led to rage, thus generating mental breakdown, hence the commission of the crime. This kind of political strategy was pioneered by attorneys such as Charles Garry and Terence Hallinan (see chapter 6) and gradually gained currency among radical lawyers in the early 1970s.[73]

Attorneys Kenneth Cockrel and Justin Ravitz—two Detroit courtroom wizards and renowned radical militants—adopted a similar strategy to defend James Johnson in a seminal case. Johnson was an indigent Black autoworker who, in July 1970, was charged with the murder of two foremen and a job setter at Chrysler's Eldon Avenue gear and axle plant, where he was employed. After being laid off for insubordination, Johnson grabbed a carbine and took justice into his own hands. On trial, Cockrel and Ravitz never disputed that he had killed the men but insisted that the whole social context that surrounded the defendant, from his upbringing in Mississippi to the miserable factory life and his harassment by union and company officials, could explain his "temporary insanity," hence the reckless gesture.

Black psychologist Clemens H. Fitzgerald determined that Johnson suffered mental troubles most of his life due to the stress of institutional racism, and Johnson's mother gave witness to the bleak and hopeless existence of a poor sharecropper family in the South. Other autoworkers testified about shop-floor violence, racial abuse, and unsafe conditions at the Eldon Avenue plant, which was known for the exploitation of its predominantly Black workforce. To further emphasize the influence of environmental conditions, the two lawyers took the exceptional step of bringing the judge, the twelve jurors, and the two alternates (nine out of fourteen were Black) to the scene of the murders, in the company of Johnson. Despite the prosecutor defining the murderer as "morally sick," the jury delivered a not-guilty verdict by reason of insanity.[74] It goes without saying that mental insanity as exculpatory evidence was hardly novel, but this emphasis on its economic and social roots was unprecedented and conceptually different. Mesmerized by such a victory, radical lawyers immediately sought to apply this line of defense to similar cases.[75]

Shepherding the jury, the judge, and the general public toward the comprehension and justification of the defendant's action thus became more crucial than ever in militant litigation. Radical lawyers were encouraged to study defendants' history and attitudes, and to translate into courtroom discussion their family background, ideological principles, claims, grievances, slogans, and language. Details on the events under judgment could wait. "Very frankly," wrote Charles Garry referencing the Newton case, "I didn't spend any time with Huey discussing the facts of the case. Until three or four days before he took the witness stand in July 1968, I did not even go into his story of the incident of October 1967."[76] Usually, the opening and closing statements were considered the most appropriate moments to bring into focus the defendants' beliefs, as they allowed lengthy sociological and political articulation without mentioning "mere" trial evidence.

During these phases of the proceedings, radical lawyers typically resorted to historical parallels to suggest that those who judged according to mainstream standards had often been shortsighted. In the course of the Chicago trial, for instance, Leonard Weinglass remembered the harsh criticism Abraham Lincoln was subjected to when, in 1848, he denounced the war in Mexico as immoral and illegal. At that time, people's judgment was so bitter that Lincoln was forced to forgo his political activity for a while. But standards were shifting and relative, and Lincoln would be elected president of the United States only fifteen years later. Likewise, the minority who dared to denounce the war in Vietnam and was severely reprimanded by conservative America would one day, in the near future, be blessed and cherished by the majority.[77] History was also helpful in suggesting comparisons between radical defendants and immaculate figures of the past, such as Socrates, Jesus, and Frederick Douglass, and pointing out that these admirable people had been wrongly condemned for putting morality above law.[78] At the same time, references to the past, and notably to the American Revolution, afforded persuasive arguments to claim that the "right to revolution" was an integral part of the national identity. Such a reasoning had been a trope of labor defense since the nineteenth century, but decades later it still appeared effective to counter the charges leveled against radicals of being "un-American."[79]

Even more important, however, was to ensure that defendants be judged by their own community standards and by a jury closest to their peer group, who could easily grasp the perspective of the people on trial. Unlike many European systems where professional judges administer justice, criminal cases in the United States were usually decided by juries of twelve laypeople who could be persuaded through moral and ideological arguments. Therefore, jurors had to be attentively selected. Militant litigation, in particular, suggested that the Sixth Amendment guarantee of a trial by an impartial jury be interpreted together with the Fourteenth Amendment's equal protection clause. As a result, a trial by "a jury of the defendant's peers"—and not only a trial by a generic cross-section of the community—became a standard request. Interestingly, a jury of peers was also one of the ten points of the Black Panther Party program.[80] In practical terms, if the defendant was a person coming from the "Black ghetto," lawyers requested that at least a majority of jurors had that same specific racial, demographic, and social profile. Thus, far from representing a technicality, jury selection—also known as voir dire—became a key militant device.[81]

During such questioning, radical lawyers were expected to energetically challenge any potentially prejudiced juror (for cause) and to make extensive use of all peremptory challenges (to excuse potentially hostile jurors without stating any reason).[82] Newton's trial represented a groundbreaking example of this procedure and was translated into a Guild handbook, titled *Minimizing Racism in Jury Trials*, which enjoyed large circulation even outside the radical lawyers' cohort. Defying the myth of a "colorblind" justice, the volume offered Garry's guidelines for selecting jurors and a long list of innovative voir dire questions to uncover "subjective" and "objective" racists. If, according to radical lawyers, it was almost unimaginable to get a jury free of any racial or political bias in the United States, it seemed nonetheless possible to single out a group of people with as little racism as possible.[83]

Following this blueprint, in preparation for the New Haven trial of Bobby Seale and Ericka Huggins, attorneys Garry and Roraback conducted what was at the time the longest and widest jury selection in the history of Connecticut courts. Seale and Huggins were charged with the torture and murder of Alex Rackley, a fellow Panther and a suspected police informer, and faced the electric chair.[84] As of March 11, 1971, when the twelfth and last juror was chosen, Garry and Roraback had interviewed more than a thousand prospective jurors over the course of seventeen weeks. Deviating from Garry's strategy, Roraback chose to emphasize "gender discrimination" in addition to racial bias in her defense of Huggins. An idealistic young woman, Huggins had endured discrimination within the male-chauvinist Black Panther Party, in which she lacked any substantial power. Since no one listened to her within the BPP—the reasoning went—she could not stop the torture of Rackley. Moreover, she was now subject to an all-male jury in a male-dominated courtroom. The argument ostensibly won many people over and would become a recurrent theme in women's rights cases.[85]

Famously, leftist supporters and Yale students raucously protested the incrimination of the Panthers. Yale president Kingman Brewster Jr. upheld the students' right to demonstrate against the trial and acknowledged that he was "skeptical of the ability of black revolutionaries to achieve a fair trial anywhere in the United States." The conservative judge presiding over the trial went a long way to prove that the opposite was true. Pressured by a vast mobilization in support of the defendants and perplexed by the flimsy evidence that linked Seale to the actual murder of Rackley, the jury was unable to reach a verdict. Eventually, the judge dismissed all charges against the two Black Panthers by recognizing that "without superhuman efforts," it was impossible to select "an unbiased jury."[86]

This attention to jurors exposed the constant and widespread discrimination in the drafting of jury pools—the body of prospective jurors summoned for jury duty—which resulted in the frequent exclusion of minorities, women, young, and indigent people. Methods of jury selection were more clearly discriminatory in the South than in the North or West, but radical lawyers identified similar biases everywhere. In the North and in the West, all-white middle-class jury pools often originated from voter lists, but it was common knowledge that only a few people of color and of limited means registered to vote. Prospective jurors were also drafted by means of literacy tests that presented similar biases. In the South, they were frequently selected from the county tax rolls, but everybody knew that racial minorities rarely owned property.[87]

While the government began to require federal courts to review their systems of jury selection, Guild lawyers worked on techniques to detect and fight racial, age, gender, and social bias both in the preparation and in the management of the pools. As a matter of fact, jurors' ideological and moral predilections could be even more decisive than evidence and legal arguments, especially in political cases. In addition to the aforementioned methods for the voir dire, militant litigation also incorporated findings of statistical analyses that social scientists like Jay Schulman were developing in the early 1970s and would become known as "scientific jury selection." The intention was to fully investigate the orientations of prospective jurors before voir dire. Drawing on large samples, statisticians, psychologists, and sociologists sought to identify fairly stable correlations between demographics, social background, and habits, on the one hand, and political preferences, on the other.

Working with the defense lawyers of the Harrisburg Seven (see chapter 6), Schulman and his team inaugurated this cooperation between social scientists and radical lawyers.[88] They first realized that the trial location did not look promising for a group of Catholic antiwar defendants, as the area had at least three Republicans for every two Democrats, an unusually low proportion of Catholics, and several military installations. The presumption of innocence, they believed, was seriously threatened. Therefore, they began with a phone survey of registered voters in the judicial district to compare the pool of prospective jurors with a random sample of registered voters. They discovered that the members of the available panel were older than the average, so they asked for and obtained a new panel. Next, they organized in-depth interviews with a number of people in the random sample, asking questions about their favorite newspapers, level of trust in the government, religious preferences, and attitudes toward protest activities. Among other things, they found that certain religious affiliations and contact with metropolitan news media were "negative" enough to warrant exclusion, while political party membership could be ignored for it was less predictive of specific standpoints.

Therefore, Schulman and his collaborators presented a memo for the defense suggesting a number of voir dire questions, which proved to be quite effective, and rated the remaining prospective jurors during the selection process. Through community contacts, they also developed "third party information" on the attitudes of the candidates. Predictions turned out to be quite correct, and the selected jury eventually voted ten to two for acquittal. Since then, Schulman cooperated extensively with radical lawyers.[89] Together with David Kairys, a successful public defender in Philadelphia, Schulman cofounded the National Jury Project of the NLG. While the National Jury Project toured the country to train lawyers, careful pretrial investigation, coupled with sophisticated techniques to include neglected categories in jury pools, became fixtures in militant litigation.[90]

As the Chicago Eight trial had made plain to all, militant litigation implied the courage and the resolution to directly confront the courts by denouncing the prejudicial views of the prosecution, the biases of judges, and the intrinsic limitations of the system of justice. Such an openly defiant stance was aimed at shifting the power relations and climate of the courtroom. It did not, however, exclude disorderly tactics by both counsel and defendants, which could be responses to specific unfairness in the handling of the trial but also provocative acts to draw the judge into overreaction. Indeed, many judges—as the Department of Justice was forced to admit—were not prepared to handle major disruptions and "exhausting ordeals"; thus, they made ingenuous mistakes and lost control. Yet from the perspective of militant litigation, the fact that a trial could go awry or lead to contempt charges was not problematic per se; on the contrary, it could show the bankruptcy of the system and the malignity of the prosecution.[91]

To make possible all the aforementioned tactics, militant litigation rested on a trusting relationship between counsel and defendants. Not only were lawyers expected to be sympathetic to their clients' views, avoid restraining them, and learn from them, but they also had to be open to being guided by their clients. As Kunstler used to say, defendants should handle their own cases in constant dialogue with their lawyers. Therefore, lawyers progressively accepted their clients as equal decision-makers or, if possible, co-counsels who participated in legal and political decisions of any sort.[92] Since defendants were given increasing responsibilities, it logically followed that self-defense was reevaluated and, in a few cases, perorated as an inalienable right. Lawyers' allegedly superior dialectical method and arcane knowledge had to be demystified; indeed, there was no reason why defendants should not be able to explain and justify their conduct in front of a jury. Also, to uphold the political character of the trial, no better strategy existed than self-defense, as it immediately revealed the attack on dissent, on class, and on minorities.[93]

Once the charismatic leading figures in trial proceedings, lawyers took a more collaborative role over the course of militant litigation. Their work necessarily hinged on a large and diversified legal team to back and extend courtroom work, including social scientists, expert witnesses of any kind, legal workers, and movement organizers. Militant litigation also implied the attraction of external support and a great deal of extra-judicial activism. The involvement of sympathetic audiences, whose physical presence in the courtroom was exploited to exert psychological pressure on judges and jurors, was deemed essential. Demonstrations, assemblies, and other propaganda actions were also considered key assets in winning media interest and informing the public. As the Chicago Eight confirmed, a well-advertised trial could galvanize a large spectrum of social movements and be perceived as a new front of struggle or a rallying point. Publicity also helped with developing financial resources and attracting legal talent.[94] This is why militant litigation often leaned on powerful and well-structured defense committees with multiple national and even international branches. The Soledad Brothers Defense Committee and the National United Committee to Free Angela Davis (see chapter 7) represented the most vocal organizations of this type, but virtually any political trial of those years prompted the creation of a defense committee.

To be sure, these principles had various degrees of acceptance and implementation among radical lawyers and militants. Eager to challenge the legal system to the fullest, some people wholly embraced them, ready to sacrifice personal freedom or professional reputation by making confrontational political statements and bringing their case to the public. Others, content with obtaining a lesser penalty or a convenient settlement, opted for a more neutral approach and paid greater respect to courtroom conventions. The nature of the crime, the notoriety of the defendant, the potential sentence, the economic resources at their disposal, and the political climate all influenced the extent to which lawyers and clients were willing to trade judicial risk for political coherence.

Success and Limits of Militant Litigation

Between the end of the 1960s and the beginning of the 1970s, the strengths and shortcomings of militant litigation were dramatically revealed. The so-called New Bethel trials, for example, confirmed that a challenge to jury pool selection could become a formidable tool in the hands of lawyers.

Everything began in March 1969, when the Republic of New Afrika rented the New Bethel Baptist Church in Detroit for a convention. Police raided the church, and in the ensuing shoot-out with members of the movement, one officer was killed and another was gravely wounded. In a massive roundup, police made 142 arrests, and prosecutors eventually charged four Black men for the murder. Being a reference point for controversial cases in the Motor City, the radical duo Cockrel and Ravitz undertook their representation. Defendants were judged in two separate trials. In the first one, Cockrel managed to sit a sympathetic jury by forcefully challenging prospective jurors on their racist attitudes and won a surprising acquittal.

In the second and more interesting trial, the defense team opted for an even more drastic challenge to the jury pool. Among a population that was almost half Black, why, asked the two radical lawyers, had only a few Black citizens ended up in the pool of prospective jurors? Cockrel and Ravitz argued that nonurban whites made it into jury pools way more often than did inner-city residents, and that recent migrants from the South, usually Black, were typically discharged from jury duty. Young people were also less likely to be included in the pools because voter registration lists, which represented the source of the pools, were not updated. The two attorneys also contended that jury pool questionnaires were used to profile candidates on the basis of their political preferences, manner of dress, physical appearance, and judicial records. The Wayne County Jury Commission, in other words, had worked to expunge minorities, the poor, and radicals. Therefore, the lawyers filed a motion to quash the entire jury panel.[95]

The judge suspended the trial and opened a full investigation into these unprecedented and potentially explosive allegations. A Wayne County circuit court judge condemned the jury commission and confirmed that it improperly excluded between two thousand and three thousand prospective jurors out of the seven thousand who were originally called for the pool. At that point, since jury selection for the trial had already begun and the defense did not seek a mistrial, some of the wrongly excused jurors were recalled. For the first time in Detroit's history, a predominantly Black jury—twelve out of fourteen jurors—was seated in the Recorder's Court. After deliberating for twenty-eight hours, the jury acquitted both defendants of all charges. In the meantime, new guidelines for screening prospective jurors were issued, while Black convicts, supported by Guild lawyers, began requesting jury commission records to determine if their past verdicts had been delivered by jurors selected in a racist manner.[96]

On April 2, 1969, a federal grand jury charged twenty-one New York Black Panthers with organizing coordinated dynamite attacks targeting police stations in Manhattan, a school building in the Queens, and the Bronx botanical gardens. Twelve of them were immediately arrested, two were already in jail on earlier charges, and seven were missing. Thirteen of them were tried in September 1970. Known as the Panther 21, this legal case—at the time the longest and costliest in New York State history—became a cause célèbre among the Left and showcased most of the ingredients of militant litigation.

The Panthers entrusted Kunstler as their leading counsel; hence, without much surprise, the atmosphere in the courtroom quickly heated up. While the prosecutor presented the defendants as "terrorists," Kunstler, who reportedly moved into the room as "an entertainer," depicted the Black militants as activists interested in their communities and families, who were victims of society's injustice—a society that included, as he made explicit, the judge and the prosecutor. Immediately, it was clear to observers that lawyers and clients were behaving as equal partners in the struggle. Presiding over the trial was judge John M. Murtagh, a former assistant attorney general, who was described as "solemn, severe, unbending, and without humor or humility."[97] As soon as he heard Kunstler's first attacks, he rebuked him: "As a lawyer, I suggest that you have every obligation to defend the rights of the accused, but you have an equal obligation not to insult the court or to insult society."[98]

However, Kunstler was forced to leave the stage very soon. The parallel Chicago trial required his constant presence; therefore, a young radical lawyers' team replaced him. All of these lawyers operated in the orbit of the Guild. Leading counsel was Gerald Lefcourt, who had just left the Legal Aid Society to found the New York Law Commune (see chapter 5). At the time he was only twenty-eight years old, but he had already represented a few Panthers in New York and personally knew some of them. Two other members of the commune—twenty-six-year-old Carol Lefcourt, Gerald's sister-in-law, and twenty-seven-year-old William Crain, neither of whom had ever tried a jury case before—jumped on board. The three worked pro bono, receiving only a small contribution for office costs and retaining part of the royalties on *Look for Me in the Whirlwind*, a collective autobiography written by some of the defendants.[99]

Other leftist lawyers who were not connected with the commune also joined the defense team, including Sanford Katz, who belonged to the famed law firm Rabinowitz, Boudin, and Standard. Charles T. McKinney, one of the most talented Black lawyers of the moment, was recruited to add experience and diversity to the team. Yet paradoxically, the defendants were quite skeptical about him, as they saw him as a successful attorney, too integrated into the system. The law commune people, on the contrary, exuded spontaneous interest in their clients' condition and even a "white envy of the black style," as journalist Murray Kempton remarked. Lefcourt's "identification with the defendants," Kempton added, "violate[d] every tradition."[100]

With such a legal team on their side, the defendants were determined to carry their political message into the courtroom, one way or the other. The Panthers fiercely contested the legal proceedings and argued that the trial was rigged from the beginning, being "a political trial" rather than a criminal trial. They defined the American system of justice as "a hideous sham and a revolting farce" that enforced a law that had been imposed on Black people without their consent.[101] Insults and threats directed at both the judge and the prosecutor, along with interruptions, cheers, jokes, and protests from the boisterous audience, were the order of the day. In a couple of instances, fights between defendants and court attendants broke out, as well as melees during which tables and chairs were thrown around. Judge Murtagh charged two people in the audience with summary contempt and ordered others to be removed from the room. The judge also suspended the pretrial hearings and sent the defendants back to jail until they promised to behave.[102] As often happened with these trials, it was hard to tell exactly who was provoking whom and who was reacting. Legal scholar Peter L. Zimroth, who attended the proceedings as a neutral observer, concluded that although the defendants were explicitly disruptive, the prosecutor and judge misused their powers and transformed the whole trial into "a holy war against dissent."[103]

Counsel openly endorsed the conduct of their clients and persistently rebutted the court's criticism of not being "lawyer-like." Lefcourt and his team also requested the judge to withdraw from the case for lack of fairness and mutual respect. The motion was denied, but the message seeped through. Putting into practice a key lesson of militant litigation, defense attorneys staged a particularly aggressive and lengthy questioning of prospective jurors. Evidence of guilt seemed overwhelming; thus, a compassionate jury appeared indispensable. More than two hundred New York voters were attentively screened, until six white, five Black, and one Latino juror were chosen to decide the destiny of the New York Panthers. Even a journalist who was admittedly sympathetic with the defense was shocked at the lack of mercy and the personal attacks against prospective jurors. He commented, "We were being treated to that rarest of spectacles in a courtroom, the exercise of the despotism of the oppressed."[104]

In the meantime, demonstrations, also in the presence of the legal team, grew in force. They arose not only around the courthouse but also in other cities, rallying extraordinary support and media attention. "In New York you couldn't walk two blocks without seeing a sign that said 'Free the Panther 21!,'" remembers Lefcourt today.[105] Lefcourt also asked activist Martin Kenner, whom he had defended after the Columbia occupation, to help coordinate propaganda activities around the Panther 21. Kenner accepted and attracted a group of people that included renowned journalists Gail Lumet Buckley and Hannah Weinstein, who organized fundraising gatherings and social events. It was a huge success, and "unbelievable amounts" of money—at least $100,000 according to Kenner—were collected.[106]

To the delight of Tom Wolfe, who chronicled the happenings in his caustic account titled *Radical Chic*, a party was organized at Leonard Bernstein's Upper East Side apartment. While some Guild people collected donations, Lefcourt took the floor and compared the persecution of the Panthers to the Nazi repression after the Reichstag fire.[107] Thanks to generous contributions, two defendants among those who had been jailed—Michael Tabor and Richard Moore—were bailed out. Tabor and Moore were selected because they were considered the most skilled agitators and promoters. According to this logic, they would be able to raise additional money to free their comrades from prison. However, they both disappeared, losing $150,000 in bail money. Tabor resurfaced in Algeria alongside Eldridge Cleaver, who had fled to Algiers and obtained accreditation as ambassador of a national liberation movement. Moore was found hiding in the Bronx.

The trial was troubled, and even more politicized, by the explosion of a bomb at the judge's home in upper Manhattan. A gesture of solidarity with the Panthers devised by the Weather Underground, the potentially murderous attack was bloodless and caused only material damages. Yet it was interpreted as a proxy of the legal battle against American justice. Although defendants and lawyers expressed solidarity with the judge, a group of New York Panthers, including some of the defendants, wrote an open letter praising the Weather Underground for the violent act.[108]

Tensions were high but never exploded, as the case unexpectedly turned in favor of the defendants. As a matter of fact—and without going into the intricacies of the case—the New York Panthers had been infiltrated by the police, and most of the evidence against them proved to be poisoned. The undercover agents who served as witnesses for the prosecution became the ace in the hole for the defendants, as they testified about teaching the Panthers how to shoot and assemble explosive devices. In a quintessential radical style, Lefcourt used his closing argument to trace a daring historical parallel and assert that the revolutionaries of the past, after being persecuted, turned out to be on the right side of history. In 1670, William Penn, "the Panther of that time," was charged with conspiracy. However, he was found not guilty and was later celebrated. Penn, insisted Lefcourt, was the one who started the process of Black emancipation.[109]

Though probably guilty of several counts out of the 156 contested, all defendants were acquitted after only ninety minutes of jury deliberations. The jurors, who grew fond of the indicted, unanimously decided that evidence was missing and thus, there was no case. The radical front scored a legendary victory and framed the verdict as a political statement: the American people recognized that society, in many instances, forced people into crime.[110] However, the prosecution succeeded in one major goal. If the point of the trial was to wear the Black Panther Party down, the legal battle certainly contributed to this outcome. Almost all the economic resources and activist energies of the New York Panthers had been channeled into this single trial for almost a year. While internal rifts in the BPP had increasingly widened, most notably on the subject of revolutionary violence, expulsions and scissions followed. Paranoia and fear of infiltration, as Lefcourt recalls, grew exponentially; as a consequence, the more moderate activists left the BPP, while the most radicalized became "soldiers" and went underground.[111]

A similar twofold outcome emerged from the coeval trial of the Seattle Seven. The sequence of events began with the foundation, in January 1970, of the Seattle Liberation Front (SLF), a leftist antiwar group. The SLF was the creature of Michael Lerner, a young assistant professor of philosophy at Washington University in Seattle. Lerner sought to reunite local collectives with the remaining activists of Students for a Democratic Society, which had recently crumbled at the peak of its success. In February 1970, the SLF sponsored a rally to protest the anticipated guilty verdict of the Chicago Seven trial—one of the many Day After demonstrations that were held across the country. For the majority of demonstrators, this was meant to be a teach-in. Instead, it turned into a riot around Seattle's federal courthouse that spread downtown, generating disorder, damages, clashes with police, injuries, and eighty-nine arrests.

Local authorities considered the SLF a branch of the Weather Underground and suspected that the group was behind all instances of disorder that were troubling Seattle, including some bombings whose responsibility was unclear. In fact, the two political entities marginally overlapped but were separate. Nonetheless, in April a federal grand jury indicted eight members of the SLF on charges of conspiracy to incite a riot and damage government property. As in Chicago, the eight defendants had never met all together before the February demonstration. One of them immediately disappeared. Lerner and another militant opted for self-defense, while the other five were represented by a team that included at least two radical attorneys. Since lawyers were afraid of replicating the Chicago Eight "circus," the politicization of the trial was not fully agreed upon and emerged in a spontaneous and improvised way.[112]

As in other political cases, however, the role of the defense committee was crucial in mobilizing an external audience and affected the course of the trial. A member of the SLF was also a legal worker in the People's Law Office in Chicago, a radical law firm very close to the NLG (see chapter 5). She took the lead on creating a defense committee, which was named Conspirare and attracted personalities such as Howard Zinn, Noam Chomsky, I. F. Stone, and Jane Spock. As Kit Bakke explained in her book on the case, the defense committee gathered scores of raucous supporters who raised their clenched fists, chanted antiwar songs, marched, and cheered the defendants—both inside and outside the courtroom. As usual, they mocked the judge and were expelled from the courtroom because of their disrespectful conduct. Chicago Eight defendants, together with Kunstler, also came to Seattle to give speeches and help raise money. This strategy backed and reinforced the Seven, who repeatedly accused the judge of unfairness, voiced their opposition to the war in Vietnam, and contested the proceedings, eventually refusing to be present in the courtroom.[113]

However, according to the judge, the disorder was so unbearable and the jury so prejudiced that a mistrial was the only possible outcome. Because of their misconduct, six of the seven defendants were cited for contempt of court. This sensational outcome sparked further protests and led to the arrest, without bail, of ten spectators in addition to the defendants. In 1972, the Seven pleaded nolo contendere to the contempt charges (they did not take or deny responsibility for the charges but agreed to accept punishment), while the original charges of conspiracy were dropped after the discovery of an FBI infiltration into the group. All but one of the Seattle Seven were sentenced to light prison terms for minor charges. Ultimately, the aggressive posture during the trial and the collective defense efforts paid off, but only partially. The defendants spent some time in jail essentially because of the courtroom disorder, and most importantly, the Seattle Liberation Front collapsed in 1971 as a result of the dire judicial battle and internal divisions. Entrapped in the halls of justice, the leftist organization lost momentum, energy, and money.[114]

As a consequence of these and other mixed results, intentional disruption of proceedings remained episodic and mostly related to a handful of trials. When in 1970 the Association of the Bar of the City of New York began fearing the spread of contentious courtroom tactics and appointed a special committee to report on the incidents of courtroom disorder, the rarity of this behavior was confirmed. The committee sent a questionnaire to every trial court judge of general jurisdiction in the country and to lower criminal court judges in New York City and California, obtaining 1,602 responses. The survey showed that by 1972, there was "no serious quantitative problem of disruption in American courts." For the most part, disruption did not occur in politically oriented cases but rather in ordinary felony cases. The Chicago, New York, and Seattle trials were not the tip of an iceberg, as many had feared.[115]

The testimonies of many radical lawyers seem to corroborate these findings. While they brought politics, pugnacious defenses, and new techniques into courtrooms, they remained pragmatic, avoiding excesses and mostly accepting the need to play by the rules. They demonstrated awareness that acting on a principle was a double-edged sword. "I was never held in contempt," remembers Paul Harris, who also adds, "I defended Huey Newton and I juggled before the court: one ball was the prosecutor's case, one ball was my case, one ball was justice. The judge said, 'What are you doing, Mr. Harris?' I said: 'At Law School they told us to use visual aids!' He loved it. . . . If you acted as a lawyer, you were not disrespectful; that's where the adversary system is so powerful. You can push, and push, and push, as long as you are not disrespectful. And, personally, I was known as someone who pushed the rules quite a lot."[116]

Michael Tigar, who participated in the legal teams of both the Chicago Eight and the Seattle Seven, agrees with Harris. "I thought it was possible to connect with the judges and jurors rather than getting in their face."[117] Similarly, Emily Goodman confirms that Guild lawyers "would know how far they could go." They had long hair and radical ideas, but their attitudes proved to be highly flexible: "They could change their demeanor according to the jury. A lawyer like Michael Kennedy could be the most elegant and respectable person and then he could become a street fighter. You are always playing in court!" In line with the principles of militant litigation, strategies and tactics were also dictated by defendants' preferences. Sometimes, as Goodman recalls, radical clients were not interested in making any political point and just wanted to be released from jail. They simply asked lawyers to be "as much professional as possible," avoiding any behavior that could jeopardize their acquittal.[118]

And yet, militant litigation sent shockwaves into the legal community and appalled both conservative and moderate members of the bar. U.S. Supreme Court justice Warren E. Burger repeatedly implored greater decorum in the halls of justice and called on the legal profession to develop stronger disciplinary procedures to deal with disruptive and insulting trial lawyers—practitioners of the "new litigation."[119] At its 1971 annual meeting, the ABA passed a major resolution demanding that lawyers and judges conduct themselves with more dignity.[120] Along the same lines, Stanley H. Fuld, chief judge of the New York State Court of Appeals, publicly alerted that no grievance, however meritorious, could possibly justify the degeneration of courtroom proceedings "into a chaos of deliberate insults and purposeful disruption."[121] Even more excoriating was the Board of Governors of the Tennessee Bar Association, which voted through a resolution blaming "the consistent patterns of unlawyer-like conduct on the part of William Kunstler" and urged all Tennessee trial judges to deny him the privilege of practicing law.[122]

The American College of Trial Lawyers, an organization of about two thousand of the country's leading trial lawyers, also denounced "the tactics of trial disruption which on occasion had converted trials in spectacles of disorder," warning that they run the risk of "becom[ing] systematized and popularized among small but militant segments of the profession and the general public." Lawyers responsible for courtroom disruption, it was noted with apprehension, "have been warmly welcomed by university students—even law students—as if, somehow, their conduct was responsible and heroic."[123] Bruce Littlejohn, an associate justice of the Supreme

Court of South Carolina, defined those who upset courtroom proceedings as "legal vandals," while Hal H. Rowland, a veteran trial lawyer, referred to those who hampered the orderly process of government as "vicious elements more dangerous than any disease" and stated that the courtroom must be respected as "a hallowed temple," for "justice, per se, approaches the divine."[124]

In the same period, several state legislatures passed new norms dealing with different aspects of militant litigation and disruptive behavior during trials. California, for instance, approved a law in 1970 making it a crime to picket or parade in or near a building housing a court with the intent to interfere with, obstruct, or impede the administration of justice. Massachusetts voted through a similar act, making it a criminal offense to disrupt court proceedings.[125] Fearing courtroom theatrics and disorders, some judges, such as the one who presided over the New Haven trial of Seale and Huggins, requested small rooms with limited capacity.[126] Most importantly, with its decision in *Illinois v. Allen* (1970), the U.S. Supreme Court ruled that defendants could lose the right to be present at trial if, after being warned by the judge, they nevertheless insisted on conducting themselves in a manner so disorderly, disruptive, and disrespectful of the court that the proceedings could not be carried on.[127]

Such a barrage of reprimands and norms ultimately confirmed that militant litigation could not hinge on a defiant and oppositional stance in the courtroom. Rather, it had to lean on more sophisticated—and often invisible—strategies, which contextualized crimes, garnered sympathetic juries, and educated the public. When lawyers focused on those aspects, trial victories were frequent and resounding.

5 Alternative Law

. . . .

Working on his acclaimed photographic portrayal of the sixties, Richard Avedon could not resist the temptation to take a group picture: they looked like a large, awkward family with all the requisite characters, including the baby, the nerdy schoolgirl, the bushy-haired guy, and the rebel wearing striped pants and a black leather vest.[1] Yet they were a Manhattan law firm. It was 1969 and they represented the New York Law Commune, one of the first legal offices that challenged the conventions of ordinary law firms, sought to transpose leftist ideals into professional practice, and tried to identify with clients' political positions.

Tensions between the assertion of revolutionary principles and the values of the legal profession were inescapable and the subject of constant debate among radical lawyers and students. The competitive and hierarchical relationships of the majority of law firms were seen as dehumanizing; the impersonality and neutrality of most practitioners were perceived as intolerable. The use of technical competence, when divorced from personal responsibility, was considered unethical.[2] Therefore, since the mid-1960s, young radical lawyers increasingly felt the urge to renounce potentially lucrative careers and experiment with governmental poverty offices or public interest law firms. However, a deeper cultural conflict persisted: the transformation of legal practice could not be limited to the objects of cases; it had to affect attorney-client relationships, lawyers' moral standards, firms' internal hierarchies, gender dynamics, and lifestyles.

The idea of a New York Law Commune first emerged in the wake of the arrests at Columbia University. Lawyers and law students immediately identified with the people in trouble and understood that, if they wanted to fully cooperate with them, they could not work in the same way their predecessors used to. A few months later, in March 1969, four organizers and four young attorneys, including Gerald Lefcourt and his sister-in-law, Carol, opened an office space in Manhattan, in Union Square West. The label "commune" was more an homage to the sixties than a faithful description, as the people involved continued to live on their own, and the law firm was officially named Lefcourt, Garfinkle, Crain, Cohn, Sandler, Lefcourt, Kraft, and Stolar.

However, in many respects, the commune's novelty was substantial. Its members asserted their loyalty primarily to the movement and only subordinately to their profession. They sought to offer effective counsel but also to advance the goals of the defendants. They also operated on the assumption that "legal service should be free for everyone," while most of the profession followed market rules. Only those clients whose cases did not challenge social, economic, and political relationships were invited to pay. Typical sources of revenue were non-political draft cases, middle-class drug arrests, personal injury cases, and divorces. Commune participants handled finances together, and each member received "a survival salary," being remunerated according to needs. Gerald Lefcourt, for example, was paid less than the secretaries because he came from a wealthier background. Lawyers and legal workers had an equal voice in meetings, and in order to defeat lawyers' "elitism," the commune housed not only attorneys and clerks but also law students, artists, writers, organizers, and volunteers. "Panther posters and radical slogans are on the walls instead of diplomas," noted the *New York Times* with a measure of sarcasm.[3]

Gerald Lefcourt dreamed of recruiting graduates at law schools and creating a "national commune," with offices in several cities and dozens of attorneys who would be ready to embrace the new "alternative life-style" and confront the "mounting repression."[4] Yet, in rapid succession, tensions erupted not only between lawyers and nonlawyers but also between men and women who demanded to handle relevant cases and felt discriminated against. There were also frictions over the legitimacy of political violence and, specifically, on the opportunity to employ resources in assisting people who were accused of murdering police officers or claimed to be a revolutionary vanguard but lacked any consistent following. As a result, the commune dissolved in July 1971. However, in its short life, it was able to defend the Panther 21, Abbie Hoffman, Jerry Rubin, and many other leftist dissenters. It also served as an example of alternative law practice, inspiring multiple similar initiatives across the country, and laid the groundwork for one of the first feminist and women-only law offices, Lefcourt, Kraft, and Libow (later Arber).[5] Drawing on this experience, Carol Lefcourt ended up teaching one of the first law school courses on women and the law and wrote a pioneering book on the same subject.[6]

The Lafferty, Reosti, Jabara, Papakhian, James, Stickgold, Smith, and Soble law firm was established in 1968 in Detroit and gradually became a law commune.[7] The founding partners were all Guild supporters and political activists; hence, the Guild used to refer cases to them, notably draft cases, which increased in number and became their specialty. Their rule of thumb was to charge only rich people or activists whose parents were wealthy and give free representation to the indigent. The lawyers organized themselves on the basis of full equality, received the same salary, and gave a portion of their income to the movement. As one of them explained, the partners had decided that they were willing "to live on a fairly modest scale and to structure the economics so that the overhead [would] be low." They rented an old house near Wayne State University, cutting expenses by building and painting the walls themselves. Given the sheer number of political cases of the period, they were extremely busy, and in addition to draft resisters, they represented local welfare mothers, the Dodge Revolutionary Union Movement, and several tenants' unions.[8]

Excitement for these alternative forms of legal practice was contagious. A lengthy news story published in *Fortune* in 1971 described with curiosity how young law graduates increasingly wanted to quit what they considered "straight" jobs to experiment with an alternative law practice in "sometimes bizarre" organizations. Even graduates of Harvard Law School, it seemed, were ready to give up a lucrative and conformist future. Jerry Billow, one of the founders of the Cambridge Law Commune, explained it this way: "Mostly, lawyers out of Harvard, where I went, go to work in big corporate-practice firms. But I have no intention of increasing corporate profits. And once you decide you don't want to do that, the alternatives are limited. I don't think I could consume $50,000 a year anyway." So Billow, along with two other young lawyers in the area, two nonlawyers, and a student, began operating as a law commune in the fall of 1970, sharing quarters with a karate school a few blocks away from Harvard Square. The usual egalitarian rules applied, and participants devoted their time to defending Boston-area youths charged with marijuana possession, suing the Boston police for using illegal tactics, and attacking landlords for violations of rent-control laws.[9]

As documents show, the finances of many law communes and similar legal experiments were often in trouble and represented a recurring concern.[10] To face this problem, it was necessary to deploy some creativity. The Bar Sinister Collective, which emerged in 1970 in Los Angeles with twelve young leftist lawyers and legal workers, found a solution to sustain its free-of-charge practice for the movement with money earned from other socially meaningful cases. The collective observed that after the Civil Rights Act of 1964 became effective and Title VII allowed workers to file complaints about employment discrimination, a lot of cases were ready to go to trial, but knowledgeable lawyers were still few.[11] Such a groundbreaking law was not self-enforcing and risked remaining a dead letter. The Equal Employment Opportunity Commission (EEOC)—the government agency that aided workers in applying the law—was indeed overwhelmed by the unexpected number of cases. So the collective contacted the EEOC, received training on handling these complaints, and began doing some of the early employment discrimination cases.[12] "This was the main way we supported our demonstration work," remembers Koonan, who was a legal worker for the collective.

Having some financial security, these young lawyers who described themselves as "political people who happened to be lawyers" could start defending the Black Panthers in murder cases or channel their energies into other contentious cases. Like in similar experiments of alternative law, "everybody had a vote and it was not the lawyers making the decision and the staff having no power." This is because the principle of equality also extended to the division of labor. "I could not speak in court," specifies Koonan, who never became an attorney, "but I went to the training and I learned the legal framework, how to do legal research, prepare people for depositions. I went to court with lawyers . . . and the lawyers had to do their 'phone duty' and their own typing. It was really revolutionary."[13]

In the meantime, on Berkeley's uproarious Telegraph Avenue, the law office of Peter Franck and Doug Hill, which had already been focusing on free speech and movement cases, morphed into a law collective. When Fay Stender felt suffocated by Charles Garry's personality, she joined the collective too. In the Bay Area, young lawyers also tended to live together communally. When Stephen Bingham bought a house in Oakland with two friends, plenty of local people in the Guild's orbit joined that radical cluster, including Patricia (Patti) Roberts, a law clerk who cooperated with Stender on the Soledad case and later became a pioneering LGBT legal activist, and Doron Weinberg, a young law professor at Stanford University who worked as a regional organizer for the Guild. A few blocks away, on Berkeley's Regent Street, Dan Siegel shared another communal arrangement with a few Guild lawyers, including Jennie Rhine, a graduate of UC Hastings College of the Law and a future Alameda County Superior Court judge. The neighborhood, Siegel remembers, was dotted with communes—most notably the Red Family, led by his friend Tom Hayden—and militant energies were contagious.[14]

The Bay Area was definitely in ferment, and in San Francisco, Paul Harris and a few other young Guild lawyers theorized the notion of "community law firm," with the aim of "working both legally and extra-legally with organizations of people." The group soon established the San Francisco Community Law Collective. At a conceptual level, their project replicated many of the features of the New York Law Commune. For example, inclusive decision-making, voluntary limitation of income, and egalitarian organization according to which chores—such as cleaning the office or answering the phone—must be done by everyone. But more emphasis was placed on the embeddedness of the law firm in the community. Boasting its multiracial composition, the collective operated from a storefront office in the Mission District, decorated with Ho Chi Minh's quotations and furnished with items donated by supporters.[15]

The challenge to the corporate downtown offices was explicit. Even so, the underlying logic was to reproduce the function of the in-house lawyers of big corporations, acting as internal advisers and counsel. "We went to community groups and radical groups, saying, 'We will be your lawyers and will do political work for free. You just have to bring us your paying cases.' It was a big success," recalls Harris.[16] The members of the collective believed that the "community lawyer" had to dissipate the hostility and suspicion that generally surrounded lawyers, living and operating in the neighborhood and behaving like "an equal human being who happens to have special technical skills." According to this reasoning, the lawyer was supposed to debunk and explain the law, as well as involve political clients in the decisions affecting their cases. It was also important to avoid the high fees of "downtown lawyers" who denied legal services to the poor. To some extent, reflects Harris in hindsight, "what today is a regular client-centered practice, at the time was revolutionary."[17]

The collective, for example, gave in-house counsel to seven young Marxist-Leninist Latinos prosecuted for killing a police officer after an altercation in San Francisco in 1969. Known as Los Siete de la Raza, six of them went to trial, while one hijacked a plane to Cuba. A whole organization was built around them in the Mission District, stressing their innocence, denouncing the oppression suffered by Latinos, and advocating radical social change. A labor caucus, a newspaper titled ¡Basta Ya!, a children's breakfast program, and a free clinic were also created. The collective provided pro bono legal representation but also helped Los Siete in multiple situations, from finding locations to sell their newspaper to forcing their landlord to negotiate their rent. "It gave them extra power," remembers Harris, "but also informed their tactics." The Los Siete organization became a model of successful grassroots mobilization, and the murder trial ended with the acquittal of all defendants in November 1970. Led by Garry, the team of radical lawyers that undertook the case successfully persuaded the jury that the defendants suffered constant racial prejudice and daily police harassment; hence, the murder represented a sort of collateral damage.[18]

But it was in Chicago that the largest, longest-lived, and arguably most radical of these legal experiments emerged. The original idea of "an office that would be part of the movement in some real way, with a workload determined by political events and involvements, and thus free of the normal constraints of a law firm," surfaced in 1968, following the mass arrests at the Democratic National Convention. It took almost a year, but in August 1969, Ted Stein, Dennis Cunningham, Skip Andrew, Donald Stang, and Jeffrey Haas were ready to open the People's Law Office (PLO). The *New York Times* described its premises as follows: "The client is greeted by no secretaries and is not ushered into an air-conditioned office in which a natty lawyer sits beneath shelves of imperious looking lawbooks. Rather he parks on the front lawn, strolls past the cluttered fly-ridden porch and enters the house, where he might find his lawyer cooking dinner, washing the dishes or lounging in his underwear."[19] The collective soon attracted other radical lawyers and volunteers, including Marc Kadish, who moved to Chicago to organize the local Guild chapter and established its headquarters in the PLO building.

December 4, 1969, represented a watershed not only for the PLO but also for the entire radical movement. At 4:30 a.m., a rainfall of police gunfire left Fred Hampton, chairman of the Illinois chapter of the Black Panther Party, and his comrade Mark Clark dead and four others wounded. Immediately, the PLO and other observers documented the facts with pictures and videos, while collecting and removing pieces of evidence to a secret location.[20] The young lawyers realized from the beginning that contrary to official statements, police forces raided the apartment by shooting first, whereas the victims did not have a chance to fight fire with fire, with the exception of a single shot. For years, the PLO's lawyers engaged in a legal crusade demonstrating the police cover-up and fought to assist both the Hampton family and the survivors. In particular, Flint Taylor and Jeffrey Haas worked full-time on the case, in cooperation with the Rutgers Law School Constitutional Law Clinic.[21]

The identification of the PLO with the Panthers was so indisputable that the lawyers feared of being exposed to their clients' same risks, including direct violence. So a six-inch-thick concrete wall and a steel gate were placed to protect the storefront office in case of an armed incursion. Eventually, in 1979, a landmark decision on the Panther case acknowledged the existence of a conspiracy between the FBI, Cook County state's attorney Edward Hanrahan, and the police to murder Hampton and to crush the local chapter of the BPP. The court also recognized that the FBI had obstructed justice by suppressing two hundred volumes of documents that would have exposed that the raid was part of the FBI's Counterintelligence Program and involved an agent provocateur. But the efforts of the collective were not limited to this mammoth case. The People's Law Office was strong enough to open a branch in Carbondale, Illinois, to help local Black defendants such as the Panther Six. In those years, the PLO did trailblazing work in prisons and defended a wide array of activists, including members of the Weather Underground and Puerto Rican nationalists. The collective was also constantly engaged in Guild initiatives and, more than fifty years after its foundation, still operates, affirming that "the purpose and philosophies of the NLG and PLO are virtually inseparable."[22]

The synergy between most of these law collectives and the Guild contributed to circulating this model of "non-hierarchical and non-capitalist" legal practice and sustained these often-inexperienced lawyers by referring cases to them and by providing knowledge and mentorship.[23] "When we were in our collective," explains Carlin Meyer, who was part of the Brooklyn Community Law Office, "there were Guild lawyers who offered themselves to train us in different areas of practice we didn't know. So, for example, there was a judge in the NLG who trained us in how to get an eviction petition knocked out. He went over every word so that we could become landlord-tenant lawyers. . . . People in the Guild's network would spend endless hours training us."[24]

The Brooklyn Community Law Office was yet another example of this kind of alternative organizations. It started at the very end of 1975, when six radical lawyers sublet a space "in a grungy part of Brooklyn," repainted it, and refused to hire a staff, doing their own typing and answering the phones. Clearly, the period of ebbing mass mobilization had an impact on the type of cases that the collective undertook and on its radical ambitions. The law office gradually converted into a community- and labor-oriented entity, working, for example, to stop the closing of a Manhattan public hospital or to challenge racial discrimination at school. It did not try to pay each lawyer according to needs, but it did agree to pay its members' loans. It did not work pro bono but was committed not to overcharge, and typically its lawyers were more involved in their cases than ordinary lawyers would be. "We would be going the extra mile," remembers Meyer. "We did hours and hours of research. We worked on weekends if we had to.

We also closed the office every Friday afternoon at 2 or 3 p.m. to study labor history together. An ordinary lawyer obviously wouldn't do it."[25]

Eventually, the external political climate and its contradictions proved fatal for the Brooklyn office's project. The ephemeral Maoist craze that swept across the U.S. Left pushed three of its lawyers to join the October League, a pro-Chinese organization. According to the October League's political line, any sexual orientation that was not straight denoted bourgeois decadence. But one of the other lawyers in the office was gay, and another was bisexual. The "non-straight" lawyers felt discriminated against and abandoned the group. Then other problems came to the fore. The workers who were assisted by the collective increasingly criticized the egalitarian organization: "What the f*** are you doing? You have legal skills, you should use your skills, somebody else should type and answer the phone." A lawyer of the group, Amy Gladstein, recalls that these people thought "the organization was sort of silly, a waste after three years of law school."[26] The collective, in fact, did not dissolve but became a labor law firm that still exists today.

Legal Education under Fire

"Law school was pretty awful. Students were privileged . . . read the *Wall Street Journal*, and got their shoes shined at the corner. Professors were smug, some were abusive, there were no Blacks, and there were no radicals in the freshmen class." This is how Michael S. Smith recalls his experience at New York University, beginning in 1964. "When I took property law, from a reactionary southern professor, of course I got a D," he remembers jokingly.[27]

Almost unanimously, radical law students who were educated in the 1960s have unenthusiastic, if not nightmarish, memories of their years in law school. Surely, as historian Laura Kalman perceptively noted, law school capitalized on the rising myth of the Warren court, attracting scores of liberal students for whom "the law seemed like a romance" and the prospect of becoming social reformers was thrilling.[28] Yet those who had a progressive or radical mindset and were about to join the civil rights movement or the New Left regarded the study of law as "demoralizing and conservative," even though some of them enrolled in open-minded institutions such as UC Berkeley.[29]

Criticisms were consistent with both the demystification of the legal system and the leftist discourse on capitalist pedagogy. Echoes of Paulo Freire, who famously attacked the system of education for serving the interests of the oppressors inculcating passivity and a body of knowledge disconnected from experience, are easy to discern.[30] Indeed, all radicals' objections pointed in the same direction. Law schools were seen as one of the primary institutions for the defense and preservation of those economic and political interests that dominated American society. According to this view, specially trained and selected law professors were teaching, with authoritarian methods, a restricted pool of students that excluded women and minorities. Courses reflected the status quo of capitalism and rarely questioned existing legal institutions, while they trained business-oriented specialists.

Almost every facet of this "so-called education"—explained a Guild graduate of Harvard—revealed itself "to be concerned more with the protection of property and wealth than with the protection of human lives and the satisfaction of human needs." The courses, the system of prerequisites, and the typology of teachers all testified to this bias.[31] The absence of clinical programs to experiment with the practice of law before graduation also made the experience of law school "limiting" and "narrow."[32] Some Guild lawyers went as far as contending that the education they had received in law school was "irrelevant"; the real training started later, on the streets and defending their comrades in courtrooms.[33] Experience, the leftist canon went, outstripped expertise.

Standard legal education, as the critics argued, also denied students adequate tools for the recognition of urgent social problems. During the three years of law school, according to many voices, students literally undertook "a metamorphosis." "Their ideological indoctrination and limited training" destroyed the development of social consciousness.[34] We are constantly taught that we should operate "as hired gun for whoever can pay us," lamented a young Guild member who had recently graduated from the University of Washington, Seattle.[35] Many other radical students echoed this reasoning, which undermined one of the foundations of the legal profession: "We are told that a good lawyer should be able to argue any side, take on any client, defend or prosecute any claim. We are told that it is irrelevant whether we believe in our clients or their causes, or whether we share their values." However, they maintained, it would be impossible to put aside personal convictions and argue on behalf of the state prosecuting a dissident.[36]

According to a group of Los Angeles students, law schools programmed people into "aggressive and competent apologists for the status quo," destroying "humanism, idealism, and rebelliousness." By choosing this course of study, youths actually did capitalist society "an enormous favor," they insisted, as students accepted being subdued and standardized by professors, entering a sort of slave-master relationship. Unsurprisingly, "left-leaning students" and those who advocated social change were treated "like freaks" in law school and soon became "alienated." "Law School is lonely and deadening," echoed another young radical graduate. "It took me all my first semester to find a few people I could be with and talk to, who could help me regenerate some humanity and sense of perspective."[37]

This sentiment was also reinforced by the fact that women and minorities were still largely excluded from law schools, at least until the late 1960s.[38] "I believe there was just one Black student, perhaps James Meredith, and there were no people of color in the faculty," remembers Eleanor Stein, who studied at Columbia Law School in the mid-1960s.[39] This gross underrepresentation was a reality, not only a radical's interpretation. According to estimates, in 1969 there were less than two hundred Black students graduating from American law schools, compared to ten thousand white students. While in the entire nation there were approximately 300,000 lawyers, no more than 3,000 of them were Black. As a result, if there was 1 lawyer for 640 people in the United States, the ratio of Black lawyers to Black citizens was 1 to 8,000—a proportion that dropped to 1 to 28,500 in the South.[40]

Racial discrimination was not alone, for it was coupled with persistent gender biases that operated in a twofold manner. On the one hand, social conventions discouraged women from undertaking a legal career. As feminist lawyer Carol Arber put it, law school "just wasn't an acceptable thing for a woman to do." When she decided to go to law school in 1965, everybody discouraged her because there was still "a kind of stigma attached to being a career woman." Neither law firms nor most government institutions hired female attorneys. If employed, women were meant to be secretaries.[41] Indeed, until the academic year 1969–70, only 6.3 percent of law degree candidates were women.[42] Even in a liberal institution such as the University of Michigan Law School, in the late 1960s "it was still difficult to be a woman," remembers Barbara Handschu. "It was six of us, out of 350 people. We couldn't live in the law triangle where all students lived. They separated the six women into a different section. It was horrible."[43] On the other hand, male chauvinism was perceived as overwhelming in law schools, perhaps more than in any other segment of education.[44] Ann Fagan Ginger, a pillar of the NLG and the founder of the Meiklejohn Civil Liberties Institute, said it without equivocation: "Law school was my real first encounter with professors and students who openly accepted and acted on the theory that women are inferior to men."[45] Lectures, critics lamented, were filled with anti-feminist remarks, sexist innuendo, and bad jokes.[46] Vocabulary itself, beginning with the expression "reasonable man standard," proved that law schools crystallized "the oppressiveness of the English language towards women."[47]

Yet, insofar as radical students perceived law school as a deceiving and even damaging experience, law school enrollments doubled in the course of the 1960s and were still on the rise in the early 1970s. Between 1968 and 1971, for example, the number of candidates taking law school application tests doubled.[48] It goes without saying that the majority of them were still craving conventional careers, corporate practice, and financial success, but as mentioned before, law schools increasingly attracted college graduates who saw the law as the best available means to effect social change. Among these future lawyers, there were many radical-minded students who contested the system of education. And educators themselves recognized that discontented students were raising both a direct challenge to the viability of law schools and "a frontal assault upon certain venerable legal doctrines nourished by middle-class liberal values."[49]

It was time for a radical reassessment of the process of learning that would break down the rigidly controlled atmosphere of the classroom, encourage risk-taking, disregard formalism, reject pure abstraction, and integrate the findings of social and behavioral sciences. As Lawrence Friedman wrote in his *History of American Law*, in the 1960s "volcanic rumblings began disturbing the peace of law schools," and in those "unusual times," it was not easy to say where the profession was going.[50] Many of the Guild-sponsored initiatives were indeed part of this tumultuous trend and contributed to the shake-up, and ultimate reform, of legal education in the United States.

Law for the People

As soon as the Guild's demography rejuvenated and began absorbing student radicalism, the leadership of the group started discussing the hypothesis of organizing some "free law schools," in order "to prepare students for certain aspects of law which they do not get in Law School."[51] The idea remained on paper until 1968, when the Columbia University occupation once again worked as a catalytic moment. The law students involved in the protest reportedly "felt that the law school, and everything they were studying, was irrelevant to serious social problems." The result was the creation of a Liberation School, and the NLG was asked to prepare courses for it.[52] In the meantime, as internal reports confirm, the Guild increasingly targeted law schools as strategic bases for its expansion. The organization had no choice but to build a student membership and be a protagonist.[53]

As mentioned before, Guild activism in law schools between the late 1960s and the early 1970s was hectic. Students and organizers were restless and built an incredibly strong network, while radical lawyers carried out countless speaking engagements on campuses. Archives are full of leaflets and invitations that attest to the profusion of forces committed to disseminating a different take on the law and the legal system. Practicing attorneys volunteered their time to share their experiences and ideas with students, who were reportedly very receptive.[54]

But the Guild's activism at the educational level extended beyond the traditional boundaries of education. In a number of law schools, Guild students organized "free law schools" or "people's law schools" to provide free legal education to the community. These schools typically had no cost, no grades, and no degrees. The purpose was to spread legal knowledge to nonlawyers or young students and "to demystify the law in order to break down the unequal relationship between the professional lawyer and the layperson."[55] Topics varied widely, but they usually included tenants' rights, military law, women and the law (treating issues such as divorce, child custody, abortion, and employment discrimination), workers' rights, alternative legal systems (e.g., China, Soviet Union, and Cuba), health and the law, welfare law, immigration law, prison law, and gay rights.[56] Students planned courses, recruited teachers (other students or sympathetic professors), arranged meeting spaces, promoted classes, and worked closely with community groups. In 1971, for example, the Wisconsin Guild chapter was able to reach out to 150 people with its free law school.[57] In 1972, the New York City chapter provided teachers for four people's law schools throughout the city, and even high school students were a recipient of targeted programs.[58] In 1973, there were eleven people's law schools in the United States, ranging from Seattle to Minneapolis.[59]

Guild-affiliated students also set up "law student matchup programs" to link interested law students with seasoned NLG lawyers, so that the students could "learn what it really means to be a people's lawyer" and to get the chance to work on politically interesting cases. Finally, to strengthen the expertise of younger Guild attorneys, some local chapters provided lawyers law schools, namely seminar classes in which experienced trial lawyers taught newly graduated radical students.[60]

Shortly after, in the fall of 1974, the dream to create a Guild law school materialized in Los Angeles. The idea was to provide a true alternative to official legal education. Stated goals were essentially two: first, to offer a solid legal instruction, which allowed students to pass the bar examination yet retained "a special emphasis on the use of the law as an instrument for social change and as a means of protecting the constitutional rights of those seeking social change"; and second, to develop a curriculum that would "bridge the gap between legal education and the practice of law."[61] In order to reduce discrimination and set an example, the school geared its admission policies to have approximately two-thirds of its student body representing minority groups and one-half of it female, with pioneering attention to the gay population. As a matter of fact, admission criteria affirmatively took into consideration economic and educational deprivation, as well as political engagement. In practical terms, excellent academic achievement, as measured by the applicant's grade point average or high score on the "culturally biased" Law School Admission Test, were not prerequisites for admission. Moreover, applicants were interviewed on their interracial attitudes and their stance toward the radical left. The school, which was run collectively and without "bosses"—that is, deans—also offered second-year legal clinics, whose cases ranged from immigration to police brutality, and evening session courses to help working students.

The Peoples College of Law, as it came to be known, made every effort to eliminate "traditional law school elitism and competition" and fostered discussions on political aspects of the law in each class. It was a law school that, instead of celebrating the law, had to bring into light "the limits of the law" by integrating legal expertise and a consciousness of social injustice.[62] To keep contacts with outside political and community groups and to increase minority enrollment, the Guild joined forces with the Asian Law Collective, La Raza National Law Students Association, and the National Conference of Black Lawyers.[63]

The students' immediate reaction was good and met the Guild's expectations, yet the relatively small numbers suggest that it was still a niche phenomenon. In 1975–76 there were twenty-five second-year students and ninety-six first-year students. The new class was 56 percent white and 44 percent nonwhite (16 percent Chicano, 28 percent Black); 42 percent of students were women, and 19 percent were openly gay. Marshaled by Guild attorney Henry di Suvero, who represented the driving force behind the school, the faculty listed twenty-five attorneys who were active in social and political causes, including Leonard Weinglass, one of the attorneys for the Chicago Eight; Antonia Hernández, a young attorney with the Los Angeles Center for Law and Justice; and Terry L. Smerling, a staff attorney with the Greater Watts Justice Center who worked on prisoners' rights.[64]

Despite its innovative offerings, the Peoples College underwent periods of deep crisis. With just 369 students in five years, the financial burden was overwhelming, especially for an organization devoted to providing legal education to those who had neither social nor economic capital. Remaining an unaccredited institution, the Peoples College also required an additional test for its student to be admitted to the bar examination.[65] However, the college has managed to survive, and its radical perspective has found other incarnations, such as the New College in San Francisco, "a public interest law school" that operated until the early 2000s, enrolling a few dozen students every year.[66]

Radical lawyers' influence in the realm of education also extended to established law schools in many different ways. The most visible one was the presence of Guild-affiliated professors who disseminated unconventional ideas and inspired scores of students. A case in point is Arthur Kinoy, who began teaching at Rutgers Law School in 1964. "He was an incredible person," remembers Jim Reif, who enrolled in the New Jersey institution in 1966 and later became a Guild attorney working at the Center for Constitutional Rights and in the Brooklyn Community Law Office.[67] Kinoy was singlehandedly responsible for attracting to the school a large number of law students who later became progressive or radical attorneys. Carlin Meyer, who entered law school in 1971, has no doubt: "I applied to Rutgers because Arthur Kinoy was there. I also went to hear him arguing the case *U.S. v. U.S. District Court* about domestic wiretapping at the Supreme Court. . . . We were all mesmerized. He was an extraordinary lawyer and the most imitated person in the Guild."[68]

Under the pressure of mounting social convulsions and by virtue of an increasingly radical student population, Rutgers University itself began to change in the second half of the 1960s. The 1967 Newark riots and their aftermath left a particularly deep mark: not only did they shock the local citizenship, but they stirred Black students' protests on campus and led to occupations. The law school intercepted the quest for drastic transformation and, within a year, expanded its curriculum, incorporating courses and seminars such as Legal Representation of the Poor, Social Legislation, and Urban Poverty. The school also started a clinical program, which dealt with urgent issues like the relationship between Black citizens and local police, and began to engage students in public interest advocacy.

Between 1960 and 1967, only twelve nonwhite students had graduated from Rutgers. Since 1968, however, a groundbreaking Minority Student

Program diversified admission standards and, in 1971, 110 Black students—almost 20 percent of the student body—enrolled in the law school. An increasingly larger number of women, both students and professors, joined Rutgers, which became known as "the People's Electric Law School" for its vivacity. Ruth Bader Ginsburg was famously among them and, along with a few other colleagues, established the *Women's Rights Law Reporter*, a legal periodical focusing on women's rights. Significantly, the journal's board included only one man: Arthur Kinoy. Nadine Taub, a Guild member and a professor of law, founded the Women's Rights Litigation Clinic, and by 1977, Rutgers was the first law school in the United States to have a majority of women students.[69]

It comes as no surprise that Rutgers turned out to be a radical lawyers' hotbed. "It was incredibly active. I loved that school," confirms Deborah Rand. "When I arrived, it was almost half women, which at the time was remarkable, and there was a large number of minority people, which mattered a lot to me." Rutgers was a magnet for radicals also because the NLG had established a large and active chapter there. "We all worked in the Guild office. I joined the Guild in 1971, as soon as I arrived," remembers Rand. Meyer, who renounced Harvard to study at Rutgers, has similar memories: "Rutgers was a continuation of the anti-war movement in a lot of ways." She joined the local Guild chapter and hung out with a law collective that was based just a block away from the school and operated under the aegis of Morton Stavis, one of the founders of the Center for Constitutional Rights. Clinics at Rutgers, according to Meyer, were enthralling for radical people, because teachers were often "movement lawyers" and because students could start practicing "socially meaningful law" while they were still at school. "The students pressed for it," she recalls, and Rutgers was among the first schools to allow this opportunity. "We also did wild things," she confesses. "We invited this group to come and teach vaginal self-examination in the lounge of the law school. There were these glass doors, and we had to hang blankets over there to cover all these women spreading [their] legs and taking [the] speculum."[70]

A similar evolution also occurred at Boalt Law School at UC Berkeley, where students' activism was arguably more heated and impassioned than at any other university in the country. As research shows, the excitement for the Free Speech Movement and the following waves of protest stimulated the interest in law careers; thus, the applications "grew dramatically" between 1964 and 1972: from 1,490 to 4,958. However, the incoming students altered the patterns of legal education permanently, bringing hostility toward conventional subjects and teaching methods. Legal scholar

Sanford Kadish, who at the time taught criminal law at Berkeley, observed that students had traditionally come to law school because of their interest in becoming lawyers, whereas "in the sixties many students were more interested in becoming 'antilawyers,' or learning how to beat the system." While the classroom atmosphere drastically changed, becoming more contentious and distrustful, the school had to adapt to the new trend. It renovated its programs and challenged its white middle-class male composition with a special admissions program.[71] The Guild, quite naturally, recruited with both hands in this radical hotbed, and its student chapter ballooned.

Over the next few years, other schools also diversified their student bodies, implemented scholarships, established clinical programs, hired more progressive and diverse faculty, oriented their attention to the underrepresented, and started giving back to their communities.[72] This implied the dissemination of advanced—if not radical—legal ideas, the spread of interracial law firms, and the entrance of minorities into the profession. If until the late 1960s law school had been a frustrating experience for most radical students, in the course of the 1970s it became an inspiring moment of growth. Gladstein remembers that even an elite institution like the NYU School of Law, which she entered in the fall of 1971, had become somehow progressive. "I would say that there were many people, including myself, who went to law school to be lawyers for the movement. There was also a really big Guild chapter of about 100 or 150 people." "It was pure accident that the day my class started," recalls Gladstein, "was the day of the Attica rebellion, and a lot of people in my class volunteered to work there."[73] Only five years before, this would have been inconceivable.

These conquests in education, especially those related to diversity, were deemed too precious to be left unprotected. Therefore, in the years to come, the Guild guarded them zealously. Quite predictably, charges of reverse discrimination of white people were soon made against affirmative action programs. While the economic recession of the early seventies tapered the job market and increased competition, segments of the population felt more insecure and reacted to the expansion of civil rights by denouncing compensatory treatment for minorities and invoking a "colorblind constitution."[74] In 1973, for example, a white engineer, Allan P. Bakke, filed a suit against the Board of Regents of the University of California, arguing that he had been unfairly rejected from UC Davis School of Medicine due to a special admissions program. The program reserved sixteen first-year seats out of a hundred for disadvantaged applicants of any race, yet no white applicant had ever been accepted through it.

Trial judges ruled that the program violated the equal protection clause of the Constitution, as well as Title VI of the 1964 Civil Rights Act. The university appealed, and the NLG collaborated with the National Conference of Black Lawyers on two amicus curiae briefs in support of the university, but the California Supreme Court ruled that special admissions programs were unconstitutional and ordered Bakke admitted to the school. While the university petitioned the U.S. Supreme Court, the Guild joined other civil rights organizations in a vociferous campaign to create a climate of opinion that would pressure the justices to overturn the decision.[75] The NLG insisted that only quotas, to be implemented through special programs for minorities, would be effective in fighting institutional racism and giving these communities "what they have been robbed [of] for years." In other words, only reparations would end oppression.[76] However, in 1978, the Supreme Court, in a much-contested plurality opinion (none of the six opinions reached a majority), decided that affirmative action was permissible only under certain conditions, and racial quotas were unconstitutional. Since then, the battle has continued, with the aim of retaining and expanding affirmative action programs in higher education—especially in law schools.[77]

Lawyers without Borders

Fully embracing leftist internationalism, Guild lawyers always conceived their endeavor as part of a global struggle against various incarnations of fascism and imperialism. Early in the 1930s, several members of the organization had enlisted in the Abraham Lincoln Brigade and joined the transnational coalition supporting the republican forces in the Spanish Civil War; a handful of them also died in combat. When the volunteers of the brigade came back to the United States and, in view of their links with the Communist Party, were identified as a security problem and charged with espionage and sabotage, Guild attorneys rushed to defend them.[78] At the same time, the NLG was involved in the founding of the United Nations as one of the forty-two official consultant organizations of the U.S. delegation, and Guild lawyers Mary Kaufman and Abraham L. Pomerantz were part of the U.S. prosecution team in the Nuremberg military tribunals, notably for the cases against German industrialists. Two Guild members were also sent to the Nuremberg trials as observers on behalf of the U.S. government.[79]

In 1946, with a group of French lawyers who participated in the antifascist resistance, the Guild cofounded the International Association of Democratic Lawyers (IADL). The scope of the association was to continue the struggle against violations of human rights and threats to international security after the war. The first secretaries of the IADL were NLG executive secretary Martin Popper and Joë Nordmann, a renowned French communist lawyer. René Cassin, who would become a major contributor to the Universal Declaration of Human Rights and a Nobel Peace Prize laureate, served as the first president, while NLG president Robert W. Kenny was named vice president. The IADL's transnational campaigns and investigating commissions soon attracted lawyers and lawyers' organizations from about one hundred countries. It was a great achievement, but the Stalinist orthodoxy of the association jeopardized the participation of the NLG. As a matter of fact, the IADL suffered from the incongruence of defending communists from repression while upholding the extremely problematic record of repression under communist rule. Following the IADL's exclusion of the delegates from Yugoslavia, who had been expelled from the Cominform, in 1951 the Guild disaffiliated from the IADL, concentrating for a while on domestic issues.[80]

It was the Cuban Revolution that brought back a consistent engagement of Guild lawyers across borders. While Castro's government turned to the firm of Rabinowitz and Boudin for representation in the United States against the blockade, transnational campaigns and cooperation with radical lawyers in foreign countries intensified. In tune with the global revolutionary tempo, the realm of the possible extended geographically. In 1967, the Guild started discussing its reaffiliation with the IADL and formally obtained it a couple of years later.[81] Meanwhile, Mary Kaufman took part as an observer in the opening session of the Bertrand Russell War Crimes Tribunal in Paris, and a few months later, Guild lawyers were present at the World Conference of Lawyers for Vietnam in Grenoble, France.[82] When in 1969 SDS arranged the first Venceremos Brigade, namely a group of U.S. leftists who traveled to Cuba to work in sugarcane fields in solidarity with the Castroist revolution, young Guild affiliates jumped in with both feet. Circumventing the U.S. travel ban, the brigades that followed one another in those years were invaluable opportunities to see the reality of "Third World socialism" firsthand, to build anti-imperialist consciousness, and to weave transnational ties. Since then, Guild delegations visited the Caribbean island frequently, at the invitation of official organizations or for individual projects.[83] Meanwhile, the NLG reconstituted its International Law Committee, and at the end of the decade, the Los Angeles chapter of the Guild hosted the first official delegation from the government of Cuba.[84]

Without a doubt, Cuba struck a chord with the Guild. In the extensive and glamorized reports of their trips, lawyers not only felt they were "part of a global revolution" but also seemed particularly captivated by popular tribunals.[85] Karen Jo Koonan still remembers her excitement when she bumped into one of these community courts in Havana, just a few hours after she underwent an abortion.[86] Indeed, a number of aspects of these popular tribunals captured Guild lawyers' attention. First, these experimental institutions—created in 1966 to deal with misdemeanors and civil cases—were predicated on the concept of community self-control. Judges were not professionals but citizens elected by the community, who worked during the day and offered judicial service in the evening, without pay. Second, these community courts were geared toward problem-solving, education, and rehabilitation—a far cry from the U.S. courts, which were dominated by strict procedure, arcane language, and the logic of punishment. Popular tribunal judges, observed Guild lawyers in awe, were guided by their own experiences as workers and revolutionaries and by their contact with the community. Hence, they took into consideration not only the narrow details of cases but also "the entire range of circumstances concerning the defendant." As militant litigation suggested, "Crime [was] viewed as a product of historical and existing social and economic conditions." Finally, the prosecutors themselves seemed to work in the interest of the entire society, including the defendant, as there was no contradiction between the interests of the state and the interests of the individual.[87]

It must be noted that a few Guild lawyers objected that women were persistently marginalized from the Cuban judiciary system, and a few others reproved the existence of military courts with exclusive jurisdiction over counterrevolutionary offenses. However, all interactions with the Cuban legal structure—including meetings with the minister of justice, the Supreme Court justices, the director of the Havana Law School, and the director of the correctional system—suggested that "socialist legality . . . function[ed] not to keep people in their place and protect the privileges of the wealthy, but to serve and protect the interests of all the people." As a matter of fact, citizens fully participated in the legal system: laws were promulgated in response to needs expressed by the people and were enacted after criticism and discussion. In such a system, noted Guild lawyers with delight, the role of lawyers was "de-emphasized," private practice had been virtually eliminated, and law collectives mushroomed across the community.[88] "In every facet of Cuban life," concluded the enthralled report following a 1975 visit, "people are the axis around which things revolve. The society exists, after all, to meet human needs."[89]

Later, China also became a sought-after destination for lawyers' trips. In 1977, after twenty Guild members spent eighteen days in the People's Republic of China, their reaction was positive, at times even "starry-eyed." But they were not completely taken in, as testimonies evince.[90] Guild lawyers also visited North Vietnam during the war and, in May 1975, celebrated the Vietnamese victory with over two hundred representatives of progressive organizations in Vancouver, Canada. After the conflict, the Guild supported the Vietnamese struggle for the implementation of the Paris Peace Agreement with "fact-finding" trips and public statements.[91]

In the mid-1970s, international relationships and missions increased at a hectic pace: some Guild attorneys cooperated with Chilean lawyers to defend antifascist prisoners indicted after Pinochet's coup; others monitored the military trials of prominent writers, film directors, and journalists in Iran; and others attended the trial of the Carabanchel Ten, a group of Spanish labor organizers charged by the Francoist regime of being communist driven and ultimately convicted despite a far-reaching mobilization.[92] Along with their presence abroad and their resolutions, Guild lawyers also supported the attorneys who were under attack by the authorities of the Federal Republic of Germany and faced conspiracy charges because of their controversial participation in the defense of the Red Army Faction, a leftist guerrilla group.[93]

Amid such a proliferation of international contacts, the resurging national liberation struggle of Puerto Ricans emerged as another beacon in the global movement against imperialism. While in New York a robust relationship between the Guild and the Young Lords solidified (see chapter 10), new overseas links were created with the Puerto Rican Socialist Party (PRSP), which also operated in the United States and was recognized by Non-Aligned Movement countries as the rightful representative of the Puerto Rican people. The colonial relationship between the island and the United States appeared utterly anachronistic, and the repression that proindependence groups suffered, especially by means of the English-speaking federal court system, seemed equally intolerable.

The secretary general of the PRSP was invited to be the keynote speaker at the Guild's national convention in the Twin Cities in August 1974, where it was resolved that the Guild would commit itself to actively work with groups struggling for the independence of Puerto Rico. Only a few months later, Kinoy took the floor at a massive rally at Madison Square Garden in solidarity with Puerto Rico. In the following years, Guild initiatives multiplied and included political support for demonstrations, legal representation of militants and union workers, and assistance to indigenous attorneys, all through the establishment of a Puerto Rico Legal Project operating from Hato Rey, a barrio of San Juan.[94]

If internationalism became a tenet of Guild lawyers' engagement—and most of the people in the organization were involved in international projects at one time or another—political disagreements on world politics provoked constant and passionate debate.[95] The question of the Israeli-Palestinian conflict proved to be the most divisive issue during that period. After a long phase of study, a lawyers' delegation went to the Middle East in 1977 and met with both the Palestine Liberation Organization and progressive Israelis, concluding that the Israeli government was an occupying power oppressing Palestinians in the West Bank and the Gaza Strip.[96] The condemnation of Israeli human rights violations and the support to the right of nationhood for the Palestinian people was nonetheless hard to digest for many Guild members. A debate erupted, also spilling into the national press. Famed lawyer Alan M. Dershowitz, known as "America's most public Jewish defender," publicly denounced the Guild's position as being one-sided, for it overlooked Palestinian terrorism.[97] The NLG ended up drafting a compromise statement in favor of the establishment of an independent Palestinian state but requesting protection for the security of Israel.[98]

To be sure, such a declaration, as well as many others that inflamed Guild lawyers' discussions, had very little if any practical consequences. However, it demonstrated the extent to which the global dimension of militancy was taken seriously—in line with the tradition of International Red Aid—and gave political lifeblood to the legal profession. Ultimately, internationalism represented for lawyers yet another way to immerse themselves in the waters of radical politics, even if only to debate, study, travel, forge connections, and take a stand. Although this may sound like a vicarious or virtual engagement, it was fully attuned to the "spirit of '68" and served the needs of a group of professionals whose intellectual abilities far exceeded their guerrilla skills.

6 Opposing the War Machine

· ·

"Dear Mr. President, the purpose of this letter is to let you know what one citizen thinks of the Viet Nam problem. Ever since Election Day, I have had the uneasy feeling that a concerted move is afoot to embroil our country fatally in that part of the world." So began a letter to the White House written by Guild founder Abraham Unger in November 1964, the first of a series, expressing his distress for President Johnson's "startling change." After campaigning for peace following the incident in the Gulf of Tonkin, in August 1964 Johnson asked and obtained authority to take all necessary steps to protect U.S. armed forces in Vietnam, initiating a military campaign without formally declaring war. Soon he began sending troops and ordering aerial bombings.[1]

Radical lawyers' reaction to the escalation of the conflict rapidly shifted from bewilderment to indignation and rage, as Unger's later letters to Johnson testify. Whereas in February 1965 the revered New York lawyer wrote that the United States was "itself the aggressor," by April he was lambasting the president, saying that his "floundering excuses merely generate[d] disgust and cynicism." "Your statements," Unger hammered, "are mystifyingly inconsistent with your actions; your words are words of peace, your deeds are acts of war." "Then," he rhetorically asked, "what is it you want?"[2] Other lawyers during the same months penned scorching letters to the president, and the message was univocal: the "horror in Vietnam is beyond relief." The war must end immediately.[3]

As soon as the Guild membership met for its national convention in November 1965, the organization adopted a definitive position against the war and in support of the UN Charter, guaranteeing that the people of every land have the right to establish whatever form of government they desire.[4] Through conferences and participation in cases, the Guild pioneered efforts to revitalize the Nuremberg principles and apply them to the Vietnam War, under the assumption that international law had the power to declare a war crime and to deal with those who aided and abetted their states in its commission. According to this logic, citizens had both individual rights to refuse criminal orders and international duties that transcended the obedience imposed by their states.[5]

The NLG and its larger community fought tirelessly against the U.S. intervention in Vietnam and Southeast Asia, and they did so while politicizing as much as possible the contestation of the draft, supporting the rebellion of enlisted GIs, and representing defendants who had openly breached the law to denounce the war. As always, Guild lawyers weaved relationships with the antiwar movement at all levels and directed their resources toward those who seemed most unprotected. While participating in lobbying efforts promoted by other sections of the bar to influence the government's foreign policy, Guild lawyers predominantly opted for a direct-action approach.[6] By contrast, the American Civil Liberties Union resolved that the conflict in Vietnam was not a civil liberties question and decided it would not defend those who violated a valid law to protest the war.[7]

Guild lawyers plunged into this work as early as 1966. Dennis James, who would become executive secretary of the Guild, recalls that during those months he had a job at the legal service in Detroit but started doing draft counseling at night. Then, with a group of friends, he set up the Detroit Draft Counseling Center, which operated until 1973. With Jim Lafferty, another executive secretary of the NLG, they also trained numerous young draft counselors, including some of the first Black draft counselors.[8] Michael Smith, who went to law school to avoid the draft, also joined the group. Spurred by his socialist faith, Smith got expelled from ROTC and was "proudly" court-martialed. Smith remembers that the center was moving so aggressively against the draft that it received a complaint from the fitness committee of the Michigan Bar Association.[9]

Meanwhile, between 1965 and 1967, teach-ins on the war had spread across campuses, and the first antiwar demonstrations had amassed thousands of students in the streets. It was "an electric time for peace activists."[10] Most importantly, young people resisted the draft with unprecedented force, giving rise to what has been defined as "the largest eruption of public outrage since the Civil War."[11] Increasing numbers of registrants claimed to be exempt from service or deferred it through school, draft classification appeals to review boards boomed, and conscientious objector registrations steadily grew to a total of more than sixty-one thousand in 1971. Despite byzantine procedures and complex requirements, in 1972 there were more conscientious objectors than draftees. Thousands obtained "phantom disabilities" or dodged the draft by escaping abroad. To be discharged, many others just drew an unsightly tattoo on their body, like "fuck the Army" on their saluting hand or a portrait of Chairman Mao on their chest, as Mark Rudd defiantly did. Moreover, the draft system became the target of a growing number of attacks, ranging from the burning of draft cards to the sabotaging or destruction of draft records. ROTC enrollment fell from 218,000 in the 1968 academic year to 72,500 in 1972, and ROTC installations were routinely disrupted.[12] During the fiscal year ending June 30, 1967, 1,424 cases were filed with the Department of Justice for violation of the Selective Service law.[13]

The year 1967 marked a turning point for the Guild. Demands of legal advice on all aspects of Selective Service were rising, and the NLG had recently adopted an internal resolution opposing the draft, calling on its members to assist people who needed counsel "whether they [were] C.O.s or going to Canada or passing out leaflets to inductees." However, while the number of people who were challenging the draft ballooned, the number of lawyers and counselors who were knowledgeable was still limited. So, once again, the Guild mustered its troops. The war imposed a "moral responsibility," and the organization had to fall in line behind a specific program.[14]

In New York, a meeting of lawyers was held in April 1967, just a few days before the spring mobilization against the war showed the massive strength of the movement. By September, a draft committee was set up, and workshops on draft litigation and counseling for lawyers, law students, and laypeople immediately began. The close relationships that already existed with movement groups helped strengthen the connection with a vast array of local initiatives that were flourishing in the city, including the Lower East Side Anti-Draft Front, the Vietnam Summer West Side Project (run by the Columbia SDS), and the Brooklyn Draft Resistance Union. Soon the Guild was receiving referrals and requests for assistance from a vast spectrum of national organizations, such as the Committee for Nonviolent Action, The Resistance, and the War Resisters League.[15]

The choice of concentrating on the draft was also strategic in a moment of expansion for the Guild. Achieving expertise and organization in that area was a way to attract young lawyers and law students who were themselves personally concerned with the draft. "The Guild with Bernardine [Dohrn] and Ken [Cloke]," remembers Eleanor Stein, "wanted to focus on the Vietnam War and, in particular, to become the central force for counseling people about resisting the draft. . . . The draft counseling project became a mass organizing project and provided real material support for the anti-war movement in a way that I don't think any other organization of lawyers was doing. It was a really courageous and brilliant thing to do. That's the way they became so popular among young people and, at the same time, so unpopular with the government."[16]

As a matter of fact, within a couple of years the national office staff planned and sponsored about a dozen conferences on draft and military law, taught classes in law schools, trained approximately 450 draft counselors, advised 2,500 registrants, spoke at over 400 meetings, and distributed more than 20,000 copies of Guild pamphlets on the topic, including 9,000 copies of *The New Draft Law: A Manual for Lawyers and Counselors*.[17] Lawyers also began to intervene publicly against the war, so the organization sent speakers outlines to guide them through the basic issues and legal points to be raised in a speech about Vietnam.[18]

Soon, every active chapter had developed a corps of lawyers prepared to defend draft resisters and antiwar activists, while law students circulated "We Won't Go" petitions and assisted antiwar organizations in mass demonstrations against the conflict. In 1967, the New York City office received an average of fifty to seventy-five calls or visits per week; in 1968, it received almost a hundred. Frequently, as many as twenty to twenty-five young volunteers worked in the office, while senior lawyers began asking for assistance and guidance.[19] Given the sheer number of requests, however, attorneys capable of handling Selective Service and draft resistance cases were constantly in short supply.[20] "Never in the history of the Guild had we, as an organization, been so busy and so successful," conceded the president.[21]

Thanks to connections with lawyers in Canada and Europe, the Guild also provided special help for those who chose to flee beyond borders. The organization offered suggestions, such as entering as a visitor into Canada by car or appearing "clean-cut and well dressed," and provided contact information for complicit lawyers with whom dodgers could connect once they crossed the border. If Canada was indicated as the most recommended solution, European countries were considered valuable options, too. None of them, explained a Guild memorandum, would have repatriated an American who had broken the draft law. In particular, deserters seemed most secure in Sweden, France, and Switzerland, where a network of complicit civilians was active. The safest way to reach these countries, advised the same document, was through Canada, of course without declaring the real intention at the border.[22]

Lawyers' initiatives against the draft also proliferated spontaneously without the Guild's input. Michael Tigar, for instance, began editing a publication titled *Selective Service Law Reporter*, a loose-leaf service to inform lawyers, draft counselors, and registrants about the evolution and technicalities of the draft law.[23] At Berkeley, a Campus Antidraft Network emerged and was animated by radical law students such as Dan Siegel, who refused to be drafted in Oakland by declaring he belonged to subversive organizations.[24] A Lawyers Selective Service Panel coalesced in San Francisco and provided free services to people who opposed the war and refused induction. By 1968, it announced the availability of more than 120 lawyers.[25] The earlier-mentioned National Emergency Civil Liberties Committee (NECLC), a lawyers' group set up in 1951 for the preservation of the Bill of Rights, also took an open position against the war and the Selective Service law, vowing to help those who opposed the draft.[26]

Since the NECLC was not specifically connected with the movements, it joined forces with the Guild, and in 1968, the two organizations established the New York Draft and Military Law Panel (NYDMLP). The goal was to create a brain trust on these matters and develop specialized counsels committed to helping draft-eligible men who were "politically and morally opposed to the war." With a virtual membership of over 100 lawyers in New York and more than 250 cooperating attorneys throughout the country, by the end of 1968 the NYDMLP had a docket of fifty-two Selective Service suits and twenty military cases. The panel coordinator managed phone referrals, made emergency calls to attorneys, assigned resisters to panel members, planned monthly seminars, and organized an extensive training program. Typically, the resister who was picked up by the FBI on a sworn complaint that he had violated the Selective Service Act could have the immediate assistance of an NYDMLP lawyer to handle the preliminary appearance. The resister was made aware of his rights and given access to competent and sympathetic counsel.[27]

While the Guild constantly hardened its stance against the war and passed resolutions that unabashedly condemned the government's conduct, its language also escalated as the unfolding conflict disclosed incredible atrocities and giant losses.[28] The Guild mirrored the semantic shift that characterized the discourse of the student movement, whose contempt for the war was growing swiftly. At its uproarious 1968 national convention, the NLG not only defined the war as "illegal" and "in violation of the United States Constitution, traditional International Law, the United Nations Charter and the Geneva Accords of 1954," but also described it as "remarkably similar to the campaign waged by the Japanese military forces in World War II." "We are being viewed," lamented the Guild resolution on Vietnam, "as successors to Hitler Germany in our efforts to impose our will on peoples striving to achieve national independence."[29]

At that point, radical lawyers began questioning the political meaning of their efforts, which had been hitherto focused on the draft. "The individual solution to the problem of being drafted," pointed out Cloke, "although an important and necessary facet of organizing opposition to compulsory military service or to the war in Vietnam, is hardly resistance; it is draft dodging." Only a few people, indeed, sought counseling to stay out of the armed forces for political reasons. Even among radical lawyers, it had become common to make money out of draft counsel and sustain pro bono radical practice by representing white upper-middle-class youths whose parents were willing to pay substantial fees to keep their sons at home. As a result, lawyers risked merely "helping one person evade the draft at the expense of another," especially because the Selective Service proved able to enlist as many people as it needed. Also, the burden of military service tended to fall more heavily on minorities and the poor, namely those who were not enrolled in universities, did not have access to counsel, or did not fulfill the Selective Service requirements for deferment because they were deemed "essential."

Given these premises, counseling had to be seen as an organizing tool and not an end in itself. A wider attack "on the entire oppressive political structure," of which Selective Service was only a part, was necessary. Lawyers were called on to "turn people to resistance" and to help active-duty GIs who had been jailed and harassed because of their political stance.[30] After President Nixon announced the first withdrawal of troops in 1969 and the upcoming end of the draft, the conviction rate in draft cases gradually plummeted.[31] Reflecting public distaste for the war, judges and juries proved to be less and less hostile, while lawyers developed more sophisticated tactics. The U.S. Supreme Court also ruled in favor of draft resisters—for example, banning punitive reclassification without due process. Between 1967 and 1975, the share of defendants convicted of Selective Service Act violations dropped every year, and by 1975, less than 17 percent of draft law defendants were being found guilty. The emergency was over. At that point, the attention of radical lawyers could turn toward those who seemed politically more committed and legally more vulnerable: the GIs rebelling against the war.[32]

Against the Military, with the GIs

Though military dissent was not new in the nation's history, it reached unprecedented diffusion and magnitude during the most unpopular war ever fought by the U.S. armed forces. According to estimates, around 1970–71, one out of four enlisted persons engaged in dissident activities, and an equal proportion participated in acts of disobedience. By 1972, as scholar and activist David Cortright contends, rebellion within the ranks and the ensuing breakdown of morale and discipline became major obstacles to carrying on the war and were key reasons behind Nixon's choice to gradually withdraw troops and shift the burden of combat to the South Vietnamese Army.[33] "By every conceivable indicator, our army that now remains in Vietnam is in a state approaching collapse, with individual units avoiding or having refused combat, murdering their officers, drug ridden, and dispirited where not near-mutinous," wrote Robert D. Heinl, a retired colonel in the Marine Corps and a military analyst.[34]

Symptoms of disaffection and protest abounded. Active-duty soldiers, and to a lesser extent sailors and airmen, went increasingly AWOL (absent without official leave) or deserted (absent without authorization for over thirty days) at record levels. AWOL rates grew from 4.3 percent in 1967 to 7.7 percent in 1973, while desertion rates rose from 1.2 percent to 2.4 percent during the same time frame. Toward the end of the conflict, in 1971, the desertion rate in the army was three times higher than the highest Korean War rate.[35] Minor acts of sabotage and obstruction were countless. So too were discharges for misconduct, unfitness, and unsuitability. Tacit avoidance of combat was coupled with open mutiny, blatant insubordination, stockade revolts, and acts of violence against commanders, especially in the form of assaults with explosive devices. By July 1972, when the last troops were leaving Vietnam, 86 people had died and over 700 had been injured as a result of 551 incidents of this kind, known as fragging.[36] Commanders minimized the extent of such dramatic acts of resistance, but the press and the antiwar movement granted them wide resonance.[37]

In addition to individual gestures of contention, a more structured movement of resistance was growing. To be sure, political activity in uniform was prohibited, and organizing was extremely difficult and risky, as GIs were the object of psychological conditioning and were under constant surveillance. Their constitutional rights were also severely limited. If the participants in a sit-down of the civil rights movement of the 1960s were charged with trespassing, those who performed analogous actions in the military were tried for mutiny, a crime punishable by death. Yet GI resistance seemed contagious. New tactics were adopted and new dissent organizations were created, including the American Servicemen's Union (ASU), which advocated the right to refuse illegal orders, and the Movement for a Democratic

Military (MDM), which was an openly revolutionary organization.[38] Rebellious soldiers agitated, met in assemblies, organized fasts, led demonstrations, published up to 250 underground newspapers, distributed dissident literature, and wore partisan symbols, both off and on post.[39]

At the same time, radical counterculture was seeping into the armed forces, bringing not only peace signs and rock music but also extensive drug use, which was considered another symptom of frustration and disaffection. According to official sources, in 1971 almost 14 percent of army soldiers in Vietnam smoked marijuana, and 9.2 percent used heroin or opium every day. Indifference to or plain rejection of authority, martial discipline, and patriotic duty multiplied, but coffeehouses near military bases came to represent the hotbed of this antimilitary counterculture. With the generous support of the U.S. Servicemen's Fund and under the leadership of Fred Garner, a San Francisco–based activist and journalist, coffeehouses became resource centers and strategic bases for active-duty soldiers organizing against the war. Located both across the country and abroad, they provided a space to gather, discuss, share publications, and relax with music and food, but they also offered contacts with civilian antiwar entities and radical lawyers.[40] Last but not least, racial tensions deeply permeated American ground troops in Vietnam. Black soldiers and other minorities refused to accept the paradox—famously denounced by Martin Luther King—of being sent thousands of miles away to drop bombs on people of color, supposedly to protect liberties they did not enjoy at home. So they voiced their resentment with the language of revolutionary groups.[41]

The opening of a third front against the war within the military, in addition to the Vietnamese front and the antiwar front at home, galvanized radical lawyers' enthusiasm. Like many others, Michael Smith immediately thought about Trotsky and the history of the Russian Revolution: it had been "the greatest antiwar movement in history," as soldiers rebelled and ended Russian participation in World War I.[42] Cloke echoed this reasoning and, in his widely reprinted manual on draft resistance, noted that one of the slogans of the Bolsheviks just prior to the seizure of state power was "Turn the imperialist war into a civil war." Moreover, he reminded readers that "contradictions and antagonisms which exist[ed] in society as a whole [were] intensified, polarized and sharpened by the army in its ordinary actions and particularly in its attempts to suppress them." From this perspective, the army was undeniably a hotspot of class struggle.[43]

As a consequence, military justice appeared to be a more corrupted version of civilian justice: its purpose was "not even remotely related to protecting the innocent" but rather to "conditioning a man into docility." More concretely, radical criticism of military justice pointed to the fact that juries consisted of military people for whom obedience was paramount. Theoretically, the military defendant could be represented by an attorney (civilian or military) at any level of court-martial (summary, special, and general), but soldiers only rarely obtained counsel for a summary court-martial, which judged minor offenses. Until 1969, only about 5 percent of defendants in special courts-martial were represented by an attorney. In the general courts-martial, where soldiers could be sentenced to death, all defendants were guaranteed trained legal counsel. However, military lawyers had no power to call military witnesses and enjoyed little freedom of cross-examination. Most importantly for political cases, an appointed lawyer, being answerable to military authority, only rarely embraced the defendant's point of view or dared to question the system.[44]

While rebellious GIs seeking counsel started flocking to Guild offices or were referred to Guild lawyers, the organization began discussing ways to provide effective support.[45] The number of qualified attorneys across the country was still limited, and the movement in the military seemed to call for the kind of assistance that the Guild had been developing since the late 1960s. Named coordinator of the NLG Military Law Project (MLP), attorney Tim Coulter observed that "a consciously higher level of struggle [was] underway," leading to outright rebellion and physical resistance, far from the spirit of civil disobedience. As a matter of fact, the military movement was rarely directed toward securing legal or constitutional rights as such. "GIs are the first to recognize that rights per se often have little relevance to their fight, that the real problems are inherent in the nature of a draftee Army and the nature of war itself," wrote Coulter. Since the military literally controlled every aspect of soldiers' lives, winning limited legal rights, focusing on test-case litigation, and working on reform projects offered only small protection and little change.

On the contrary, the core of lawyers' involvement had to be political. The Guild ought to be "an integral part of the GI movement," making every effort to engage lawyers more directly. Efforts to avoid a conviction or to minimize a sentence should not be entirely abandoned, but legal counselors ought to make GIs aware of the political context of their acts, raise their consciousness, convince them of their strength, attract them to the movement, and help them with planning and carrying out political actions. "A lawyer can do a tremendous amount to clarify or remove legal impediments and to combat fear and doubt about legal consequences," insisted

Coulter, who also encouraged his peers "to take the initiative in suggesting and organizing" in order to influence the development of the GI movement. Of course, this role had to be performed "from a responsible position within the movement" and not from an "arrogant" superior position.[46]

New York and the Bay Area became the two major poles of the Military Law Project, which had a few staff lawyers who directly handled cases and a referral service that directed GIs to project attorneys. In the summer of 1970, the New York office alone gathered a panel of over one hundred lawyers and took on cases at Fort Dix, Fort Hamilton, Fort Monmouth, and other bases, handling thirty to fifty referrals per month. To ensure "absolute ties to the GI movement," representatives of the ASU, the Coffeehouse Collective, and the Soldiers Liberation Front sat on the steering committee that managed the project, while Guild lawyers became official counsels for GI organizations and coffeehouses.[47] In 1971, the MLP opened an office in Wrightstown, New Jersey, a few hundred yards from the entrance of both the McGuire Air Force Base and the U.S. Army's Fort Dix, with the aim of creating a movement foothold—a place for GIs to get legal assistance and organize.[48] A Bay Area Military Law Panel, with an office on San Francisco's Mission Street, also operated at least until 1976, offering low-cost or free legal advice and representation to antiwar GIs, reservists, and veterans. With its referral system of twenty to thirty attorneys, it handled five hundred to six hundred cases per year and also published a very influential manual of military law titled *Turning the Regs Around*.[49]

The case of Kenneth Cloke is, once again, paradigmatic of radical lawyers' engagement. While serving as executive secretary of the Guild, he became one of the lawyers for the coffeehouse movement and helped them get in touch with other friendly attorneys. Coffeehouses were indeed under attack by law enforcement and entangled in complex legal battles. They fell under surveillance, were frequently infiltrated, and were charged with distributing dissent literature, giving "dissident counsel," and maintaining a public nuisance.[50] Drawn to the GI movement, Cloke left the Guild in 1969–70 to work full-time with antiwar soldiers and, in particular, with the Movement for a Democratic Military. "Every time I went to the military base of Camp Pendleton [where the MDM operated]," remembers Cloke, "I would be greeted by a sea of clenched fists; it was just exploding, it was unbelievable." GIs wanted to do "something dramatic and profound, and I helped them to frame that," he recalls. Specifically, he made sure that the act of protest was not causing GIs to be arrested but was "completely outside the realm of the law and challenged the fundamental nature of the system." Eventually, it was decided that GIs would refuse saluting or "sir-ing" their officers. The effect, assures Cloke, was "stunning."[51]

Bay Area lawyer Terence Hallinan did not miss the chance to participate in the GI movement either. The opportunity arose in October 1968, when twenty-seven prisoners in the Presidio stockade, a military jail in San Francisco, staged a peaceful sit-in. They read their list of demands against the harsh conditions in the jail and protested the murder of an imprisoned GI who had been shot by a guard as he jogged away from a work detail. They were charged with mutiny, one of the most serious military offenses. With a few exceptions, they were not particularly militant: they were very young, poor, and white (except one). Yet they were united by their aversion to military conscription and their urge to get out from a facility that was known for its overcrowded cells and its high suicide rate.

Even before this episode, Hallinan had represented a military inmate and had become quite a legendary figure at the Presidio. Many prisoners had put their trust in this eccentric attorney, who himself was standing trial on charges of assaulting a police officer at San Francisco State College. According to testimonies, in one of his visits to the stockade, Hallinan had encouraged prisoners to stage a nonviolent protest, downplayed the chances of mutiny charges, and confirmed radical lawyers' readiness to help. A couple of days before the protest, he came once again to the jail gate with about one hundred demonstrators to show solidarity. As if that were not enough, the day of the sit-in, when the twenty-seven inmates were forced to go back to their cells, they chanted, "We want Hallinan." Finally, right after the demonstration, Hallinan drove to the stockade to see if any of the prisoners needed counsel. While the guards shoved him out of the gate, he gave prisoners his address. Although he always denied any active role in the alleged mutiny, it is understandable why military authorities saw him as an external agitator.

Hallinan received nineteen letters, and seventeen prisoners eventually became his clients, while the remaining defendants opted for ACLU lawyers or military lawyers. Hallinan based his line of defense on the assertion that conditions at the stockade constituted cruel and unusual punishment, which meant that the GI's protest was truly legitimate and had no intention of overriding authority. Applying a classic technique of militant litigation, he hoped to spur outside pressure from an irate public and mounted a political campaign around the case. He made himself available to every interviewer, spoke at rallies to laud such a "heroic act" of disobedience, and filled the courtroom with sympathizers. The fanfare about the case reached politicians, who began visiting the Presidio stockade to ascertain its deplorable conditions.

A Special Civilian Committee for the Study of the U.S. Army Confinement System was also established, while the army, increasingly embarrassed, ceased to support the prosecution.

Recognizing that a defense based on free speech was perhaps too fragile to win, Hallinan also argued that defendants were in a state of "temporary insanity" due to the recent cold-blooded killing of a prisoner.[52] Pioneering the "black rage defense," Hallinan called to the witness stand Price Cobbs, a professor at the University of California and coauthor of *Black Rage*, a best seller at the time.[53] Developing a convoluted reasoning, which nonetheless received the plaudits of the public, Cobbs maintained that the defendants, who all shared low self-esteem and a sense of oppression, had become "niggerized." Finding themselves in a "transient situational reaction psychosis," they were convinced that what they were doing was right. In the end, all but two GIs were found guilty of mutiny. However, sentences were relatively light, for a maximum of fifteen months, and a military court of review later threw out the mutiny charges for insufficient evidence. In the meantime, however, the case undeniably shed light on the flaws of military justice and fanned the flames of an escalating GI rebellion.[54]

To be sure, radical lawyers operated along more conventional lines, too. Moved by a concern for the protection of the constitutional rights of all citizens, in the fall of 1968 Lord Bertrand Russell and Dr. Benjamin Spock created the GI Civil Liberties Defense Committee (GICLDC). Defending the principle that those who were forced to fight in a war must be allowed to express their opinion about the war, the committee attracted numerous lawyers, including a few Guild attorneys such as Leonard Boudin and Michael Smith, and was backed by a list of illustrious supporters.[55] The GI-CLDC scored impressive victories, among them the famous case of the Fort Jackson Eight.

In 1969, a group of enlisted men at Fort Jackson (in South Carolina) formed a cross-racial organization named GIs United Against the War in Vietnam and circulated a petition to their general requesting permission to hold a meeting on base to discuss the war. Thrilled by Malcolm X's speeches, the group was backed by the Socialist Workers Party leadership and advised by Leonard Boudin, who suggested forcing the army to comply with First Amendment rights and treat GIs as equal citizens. After the general rebuked the petition, the GICLDC provided a team of attorneys to file a suit on behalf of the GIs.

When a large and peaceful meeting on the barracks' lawn was held, nine of the petitioners faced charges, including breach of the peace and disobeying an order, and suffered retaliatory and punitive treatment. Interestingly, because one of the nine turned out to be an informer, the Fort Jackson defendants became eight. In the spirit of militant litigation, the GICLDC not only mobilized legal counsel but also developed a persuasive campaign that succeeded in creating a cause célèbre on a national scale. Michael Smith, who was part of the defense team, assisted the GIs while they were awaiting trial in the stockade, bringing them radical literature and information. Facing adverse publicity, the army retreated, and all charges were dropped. Following the dismissal of the Eight, the Pentagon issued a memorandum cautioning military commanders against overreacting to soldiers' manifestations of dissent.[56]

By virtue of these and other judicial victories, the use of trials as political forums as well as radical lawyers' support of antiwar efforts within the military came out into the open.[57] Increasingly aware of the "deterioration of morale among members of the Armed Forces" and worried about the "attempts of militant revolutionaries to subvert the military," the House Internal Security Committee ordered an investigation and held hearings in April 1971. Unsurprisingly, the inquiry denounced a communist infiltration in the armed forces with the scope of spreading a defeatist spirit and eventually taking control of soldiers. It was, the report goes, the "same old line with different trappings"—a strategy already tested during World War I in Russia and during the 1920s and 1930s in the United States. The Guild, "a long-time legal bulwark of the Communist Party," was one of the organizations at the center of this dangerous web, sustaining both the fight against the draft and the most threatening GI organizations. As Colonel Heinl put it, the army was the victim of "legal harassment." While "well-established lawyer groups" such as the NLG and the GICLDC were given free rein, the First Amendment shelter was extended to "any form of utterance."[58]

On the Battlefront: East and Southeast Asia

Despite the significant rebellion raging at home, the real epicenter of GI resistance was not on U.S. soil but in East and Southeast Asia. At the same time, given that the military was reluctant to send rebellious GIs back to the States for judgment, most of the trials of dissenters were conducted on overseas bases.

Since 1968, Guild lawyers had advanced proposals to open legal offices on the war front, and the organization had passed a resolution to implement this idea.[59] Cloke also traveled to Japan to meet with a group of local radical lawyers and members of Beheiren, a Japanese peace coalition working with American deserters. The Japanese were excited, offered help, and suggested setting up an office in Tokyo, where a large number of U.S. soldiers used to go while on leave.[60] Time passed, however, and the plan remained unrealized. The Lawyers Military Defense Committee, a project sponsored by the ACLU, proved to be more effective and opened an office in Saigon at the end of 1970. The committee received nearly one thousand requests for legal counsel during its first year, yet it resolved to end its operations quite soon.[61] But rebellious GIs reportedly "begged" radical lawyers to come to Asia. They lamented the shortcomings of military justice, which included racial biases and lack of effective representation, and pointed to the absence of civilian defense counsel and sympathetic observers as a blatant violation of their rights.[62]

Eric Seitz, a young Guild lawyer, explored the option of setting up an office in Vietnam and, after spending five weeks in Asia, was ecstatic at what he had witnessed. The movement in the military, he wrote to Charles Garry, "simply blew my mind. . . . Not only have the GIs essentially stopped the ground war in Vietnam, they are literally destroying the U.S. military throughout Asia." Much of the impetus, explained Seitz, came from Black GIs, who tended to identify very strongly with the Panthers at home and, indeed, craved news about Angela Davis and Bobby Seale.[63] But Seitz soon discovered that he could not get a visa to travel there because his name, along with the names of many other Guild lawyers, was included on a list of potential agitators. Moreover, troops were already being removed from that theater of war, as the conflict was morphing into an air war. It seemed more useful to be closer to the bases outside Vietnam and be able to travel to the neighboring countries where U.S. troops were stationed.[64]

Eventually, the NLG resolved to set foot in the Philippines, where Seitz landed in September 1971, followed by four others from the Guild (three lawyers and a legal worker). Two months later, the NLG opened a GI center near Clark Air Force Base, about forty miles northwest of Manila. In the following months and years, the so-called Southeast Asia project spread to various locations, setting up offices or simply sending lawyers for a few weeks near U.S. bases in Olongapo (Philippines), Yokosuka (Japan), Okinawa (Japan), Iwakuni (Japan), and Nam Phong (Thailand). A few lawyers were also dispatched to South Korea and Vietnam. For a while, the Guild house in Olongapo City represented the project's main office, also serving as a GI coffeehouse and organizing hotspot. It was adjacent to Subic Bay Naval Base, where the Pacific Fleet was headquartered, in a town where thousands of GIs spent their rest and recuperation time after their missions in Vietnam. In Guild lawyers' memories, Olongapo was a surreal place, "full of drugs, prostitutes, and rock and roll," where GIs on short leave let loose. Even so, at the local Guild house, lawyers managed to gather GIs together every night. They had torrential discussions, played a lot of chess, and drank gallons of beer. Politics went with the flow.[65]

The official purpose of the mission was to provide free legal advice and representation to American servicemen and women stationed in Asia. Yet Guild lawyers immediately refocused their effort on more complex political activities. As Seitz remembers, those who spoke up against the war and the Nixon administration could be confined to their bases on the other end of the world, without any external contact except their own lawyers. Therefore, it was crucial for Guild lawyers to "educate them about their role," "link them up," "forge connections," "get information back and forth," and "provide support for them in the larger communities." When not engaged in courts-martial, Guild lawyers provided counseling for nonjudicial cases, developed literature on legal self-defense, distributed radical publications, animated political education sessions, and provided concerts and movie screenings for GIs. They also built bridges with local anti-imperialist groups and U.S. organizers both in the Philippines and in Japan.[66]

The project also leveraged its partnership with the Pacific Counseling Service (PCS), an organization established in 1969 by Unitarian minister Sidney Peterman to help GIs with legal and political counseling. Based in Monterey, California, the PCS had grown into an international structure, with a dozen offices employing recently discharged GIs, clergy, draft resisters, and leftist activists. Now it was in need of lawyers who could effectively handle its growing caseload; thus, the NLG and the PCS joined forces.[67] Immediately, GIs looking for legal aid began to seek them out, especially if they were working class and Black.[68] Cases ranged from simple conscientious objector discharges and illicit distribution of political newspapers to refusals of orders for combat and episodes of fragging. A large number of legal issues were drug related. Some appeared to be politically motivated, others seemed racially tinged (as the large majority of officers were white and tended to adopt biased policies), and still others were by-products of severe military discipline. All of them were fought resolutely by Guild lawyers who dared to use social and political arguments in courts-martial.

In September 1971, at the age of twenty-five, Barbara Dudley was not yet a member of the bar, but she traveled to the Philippines to join the Guild office and obtain her first legal job ever. Robert Brake, a young Black man who served in the marines, was one of her first clients. "He was the sweetest guy in the world," she recalls, "but he had just killed six fellow GIs. So he was being charged with murder." After being in Vietnam, Brake had gone to Subic Bay Naval Base for some rest and recuperation. He had recurring nightmares about the old Vietnamese women he had blown up and was allegedly tortured by these visions. One night he woke up screaming, put the gun under his pillow, and started firing. The six GIs he murdered were sleeping in the same barrack. Dudley managed to mount a case. By calling on two classmates of hers, one working at the *New York Times* and the other at CBS, she was able to arouse the interest of the U.S. public. She based her defense strategy on the assumption that the young marine was a victim of shocking combat experiences. Although post-traumatic stress disorder was not yet a formal diagnosis, Dudley succeeded in demonstrating that a battlefield trauma led to a physical reaction. Eventually, Brake was sent to a psychiatric hospital and never went to prison.[69]

Around the same time, another Black GI, Lee King, was charged in Okinawa with the murder of his twenty-month-old son. Guild lawyers, however, succeeded in presenting the accusation as a form of "military racism"—an act of revenge against a politically active GI who, in the past, had brought charges against two officers and obtained their removal from command. By demonstrating that King's baby had died falling from a crib onto a concrete floor, they won an astounding acquittal and denounced the fact that Black GIs were subject to "extraordinary punishment" for minor or fabricated crimes.[70]

In an even more controversial case, Guild lawyers were able to dismantle murder charges against another Black GI, Billy Dean Smith, accused of killing two officers and wounding a third with a fragmentation grenade in Bien Hoa, Vietnam. In what appeared to be a by-the-book case of fragging, and indeed contributed to raising awareness of such a practice, Smith was arrested and held in solitary confinement at the Fort Ord stockade in California for over fifteen months. Once again, Guild lawyers insisted that the defendant was framed due to racism and his open opposition to war. Despite the lack of evidence against him (only a grenade pin was found in his pocket), he was subjected to exemplary punishment. The Guild and other GI organizations advertised the case and held demonstrations across Fort Ord, also at the start of the proceedings. The courtroom, purposely built for Smith's trial, was mysteriously firebombed twice, and various military facilities were destroyed. Even Angela Davis, who traveled to Havana after her acquittal and spoke in front of hundreds of thousands of people, mentioned the case of Smith. Fidel Castro, in response, vowed that Cubans would raise their voices to demand the freedom of this Black GI, while posters demanding the liberation of Smith covered the walls of Havana.

Not only was Smith eventually acquitted of all charges in the Court of Military Appeals, but his case prompted the escalation of antiwar political rhetoric to the point of justifying the practice of fragging. As a Guild bulletin read, the murder of officers was one manifestation of the "consciousness" that was emerging among GIs who rightly refused combat and rejected authority. "Fraggings," the article went on, "occur when GIs are pushed up against the wall. Most GIs who kill their officers are acting in self-defense, avoiding combat by any means necessary. Fragging is an act of class warfare and a concrete aid to the Indo-Chinese liberation forces who teach GIs what the real enemy is and how to fight against it."[71]

On a similar note, the case of the aircraft carrier USS *Midway* illuminates the extent to which Guild intervention was able to set off an effective out-of-court mobilization, leveraging local and transnational networks. The case arose when a group of navy personnel refused to go on board and sail with the *Midway*, which was stationed in Yokosuka, a major U.S.-controlled harbor in Japan. Most of these rebellious sailors were nonwhite and expressed their outrage at the racism of the command structure, but they also refused to be on a ship that transported nuclear weapons in violation of agreements with Japan. The NLG immediately offered its help. The case made a sensation in Japan, as the *Midway*'s protest resonated with the massive discontent of the Japanese who demonstrated against the presence of U.S. nuclear weapons in their country. During the trial, all major Japanese newspapers rushed to send their journalists to cover the proceedings, and attention was so impassioned that the judge ordered the courtroom closed for the sentencing. Defendants pleaded guilty and were convicted, but they eventually appealed and were released on the grounds that a public trial had been denied.[72]

As in all these cases, courts-martial were not necessarily an antagonistic environment for radical lawyers and their clients. Dan Siegel, who spent eleven months with the project in the Philippines and in Japan, remembers that he discovered to his surprise that military lawyers were often "nonpartisan" and quite "open-minded." Since they were typically rotating, they acted as defense lawyers for a few months, prosecutors for another few months, and judges for a few months again. "Most of them were draft dodgers," explains Siegel. "They had joined the JAG [Judge Advocate General's Corps] to avoid being drafted. They often were our age; they were not hostile." Sometimes they even offered their cooperation and resources at the bases. By virtue of this atmosphere, it was possible to win cases that under civil jurisdiction would have been testing or even impossible. The whole military establishment, concludes Siegel, was "very mixed" in the treatment of Guild lawyers. Whereas some officers, especially high-ranking ones, attempted to ban them from bases, others invited them to share lunch at their clubs and treated them amicably.[73]

Serious troubles arose only once, in October 1972, when Guild attorney Douglas Sorenson and two organizers representing the PCS were arrested by the military authorities of the Marcos regime (in cooperation with U.S. Naval Intelligence) following a raid on the project office in Olongapo City. In the beginning, the charges were unclear, and possession of subversive literature looked like the only apparent crime. But the martial law that had been proclaimed in the country allowed expedite arrests. As a matter of fact, U.S. authorities had been investigating the NLG engagement in Asia for months. The pro-American Philippine government itself had previously raided the Guild's office, claiming that lawyers were violating the local jurisdiction by practicing law without being admitted to the bar. According to Philippine authorities, the office also represented a dangerous center of political activity, and indeed, "Communist literature and illicit drugs" had been found during the bust. Alleged links between the NLG and a communist front organization in the Philippines also emerged. Now, it was easy to blame them.[74]

The NLG rapidly assembled a rescue team to be sent to the Philippines, which included, among others, Charles Garry, former U.S. Attorney General Ramsey Clark, and *New York Times* reporter Tom Wicker. Congressman Ronald Dellums and other politicians were also ready to join in order to exert further pressure. Due to the great extent of publicity and scandal, the Philippine authorities released Sorenson and the organizers ten days later and eventually deported them. Such a repressive measure ended the Guild's presence in the country but did not stop its activism in the region, as it redirected its legal energies to other bases in Japan.[75]

The War at Home

Quite inevitably, radical lawyers' engagement extended to the representation and advocacy of those who sought to bring the war home. As previously mentioned, Guild attorneys were protagonists in some of the first and most controversial cases involving antiwar militants, from the Vietnam Day Committee to the Oakland Seven. As the sixties wore on, they stood as legal ramparts for those civilians who resolved to adopt disruptive means to end the war. To begin with, some lawyers belonging to the Guild assisted the radical Catholics who voluntarily breached the law to uphold their rights of conscience. Inspired by the burgeoning liberation theology, these activists spearheaded some of the most evocative antiwar acts.[76]

In May 1968, for example, Jesuit priests Daniel and Philip Berrigan, with seven other Catholic militants, removed 378 draft files from a Selective Service office in Catonsville, Maryland, and set them on fire with homemade napalm. After performing this symbolic gesture denouncing the U.S. involvement in Vietnam and the corruption of American politics, they prayed and waited to be arrested. As a matter of fact, the so-called Catonsville Nine were proud of their action, expected to face charges, and yearned for a public trial during which they could condemn the war and the bankruptcy of the legal system. The trial, in their words, had to be "a morality play, a celebration, [and] a massive teach-in."[77] This is why, declining the aid of a trusted lawyer who envisioned representing them in a conventional manner, the Nine turned to Kunstler to form a defense team.[78] Unwilling to cooperate with the Baltimore court, which they considered part of the "war machine," the Nine found a compromise solution with their counsel: they followed Kunstler's advice to request a jury trial but refused to take part in the process of jury selection.

In the meantime, a local defense committee organized vociferous demonstrations, raised funds, and attracted considerable media attention. Interestingly, neither the committee nor the attorneys ever disputed the facts or argued for the defendants' innocence. Instead, Kunstler asked jurors to exert their power of "nullification," namely to acquit on the basis of the morality of the defendants' acts. But the judge and the prosecutor constantly reminded the jurors that neither the reasons behind civil disobedience nor the legitimacy of the Vietnam War were at stake. Kunstler also brought up the trials of Socrates and Jesus to recall how revered figures had been tragically condemned for putting morality above the letter of the law. The Nine testified extensively about their intent, stressing that they had obeyed a higher law and committed a minor crime to avert the perpetration of worse crimes. After the jury left, the defendants led everyone in a Catholic prayer, which was exceptionally authorized by the judge. Nonetheless, in November 1968 the Nine were convicted on charges of destroying government property and were sentenced to prison terms ranging from two to three and a half years. When the U.S. Supreme Court rejected the appeal, the two Berrigans, George Mische and Mary Moylan, respectively a peace movement organizer and a nurse who had taken part in the raid, evaded capture and went into hiding.[79]

And yet the trial hardly represented a setback for the antiwar movement. Despite the hardship of prison or underground life, which were truly expected, the trial touched a chord among the public by showing a group of people who put their freedom on the line in the name of peace. The trial also gave a boost to the antiwar movement in the United States, creating opportunities to organize and protest, and won a transnational audience. Daniel Berrigan's book, titled *The Trial of the Catonsville Nine* and based on the transcript of the trial, was turned into a play that was staged across the world and also inspired Gregory Peck to produce a movie that premiered at the Cannes Festival in 1972.[80]

The case also had a sequel. In the first months of 1971, seven other antiwar Catholics, mostly nuns and priests led by Philip Berrigan, were arrested in Harrisburg, Pennsylvania. They were charged with conspiring to kidnap Henry A. Kissinger, assistant to President Nixon for national and security affairs; blow up heating tunnels in Washington, D.C.; and vandalize draft boards in several areas. The accusations were based on prison correspondence between Berrigan, who had been apprehended and was by then behind bars, and his wife, Sister Elizabeth McAlister. The letters had been smuggled by a police informer who had earned the trust of Berrigan. Ramsey Clark—who in the meantime had crossed the barricades and joined the antiwar front—led a radical attorneys' team that included Leonard Boudin. In this case, defendants and lawyers maintained innocence, arguing that the letters were authentic, but the contents were amorphous and hyperbolic. While a defense committee loudly denounced the frame-up of innocuous activists, a team of social scientists helped select a sympathetic jury based on probabilistic calculation. Sure enough, the case ended in a hung jury.[81]

Meanwhile, in August 1971, twenty-eight antiwar Catholic militants were arrested in Camden, New Jersey, halted just minutes before raiding the local draft board and destroying its files. Based in Pennsylvania, these pacifists had been under strict surveillance, because a few months earlier, in Media, Pennsylvania, a mysterious group of activists (the Citizens' Commission to Investigate the FBI) had broken into an FBI office and stolen thousands of classified files. Secretly advised by Boudin, they had famously revealed the existence of the COINTELPRO operation and the Security Index, namely the two main instruments of the FBI war on dissent.[82] Since investigators believed that a single conspiracy was underway in the state, the Camden activists had been infiltrated too. In fact, their plan to burglarize the draft board had been outlined back in April, but it stalled. The arrival of an undercover FBI agent made it possible for the group to find the necessary money, know-how, tools, and other recruits. Thus, the plan was soon executed under the eye of the Internal Security Division of the Department of Justice, whose agents were ready to handcuff the burglars as soon as they approached the draft board.

The aforementioned expert in jury selection, David Kairys, led a radical defense team that included two other Guild lawyers, Carl Broege and Martin Stolar, and was supported by a group of Georgetown Law School volunteers. A common strategy was nonetheless hard to reach. As a matter of fact, all seventeen defendants who eventually went on trial acted as co-counsel or opted for pro se representation, having very different plans for their defense. Some of them expected to be acquitted based on their motivations— namely the moral rightfulness of their act of disobedience—and so they insisted on making the proceeding an indictment of the war and claimed responsibility for the raid. Others wanted to emphasize the disruptive role of the FBI in order to minimize their sentence as much as possible, for they risked up to forty-seven years in prison. Eventually, both strategies were cleverly combined.

When the trial began in February 1973, the war was leaning toward its end, and both the media revelations and the Watergate scandal had shifted attention to the government's misdeeds, implicitly justifying the raiders' action. In addition, the undercover FBI agent refused to back up the prosecution, agreed to sign an affidavit in which he confessed he had become the leader of the group and acted as a provocateur, and also testified for the defense. All of this was simply unprecedented. Known as a pro-government hard-liner, the judge told the jury that the defendants' motivations were not an admissible defense or justification. Yet he allowed the defendants to educate the jury on their opinion on the war and on the reasons why they chose to willingly violate the law. He also let the defendants participate in the trial, including cross-examination.

Following the militant script, a plethora of expert witnesses illustrated the defendants' backgrounds and beliefs. Under the glare of the national media, Boston University professor Howard Zinn surveyed the history of U.S. involvement in Vietnam and stigmatized its economic interests. He also reiterated the fact that civil disobedience was at the heart of the American democratic ethos. Two Vietnamese women recounted the effects of the war on their people, while Yale psychiatrist Robert J. Lifton exposed how the war traumatized veterans. Then Frank Donner, a renowned civil liberties lawyer and director of the ACLU's Project on Political Surveillance, explained the implications of the FBI's use of provocateurs.

"It was quite a show," remembers Kairys, who, in his summation, stressed both the overreaching participation of government agents in the plot and the advisability of jury nullification, arguing that the Camden defendants destroyed property to preserve life and liberty. Such an act of civil disobedience descended from the Boston Tea Party and had been constantly replicated throughout U.S. history by heroes such as Rosa Parks. When the jury released its verdict of not guilty, the courtroom exploded with joy, and spectators intoned "Amazing Grace." It was a masterpiece of militant litigation: defendants had been acquitted on the assumption that their crime was justified.[83]

Compared to the antiwar Catholics, the Weatherman (later Weather Underground) would prove much harder to defend, yet radical lawyers never abandoned it. The intensity of these militants' hatred of the war in Vietnam—and of capitalism, imperialism, "white skin privilege," and "male chauvinism"—was only paralleled by the radicalism of their tactics, which ranged from street fighting to violence against property. Under the leadership of former Guild officer Bernardine Dohrn, the Weatherman stood out as the most radical expression of SDS and the only one attuned to the "oppressed people of the world."[84] These "mother country radicals," as they self-identified, felt compelled to bear witness against injustice and to share the sacrifice of the "Third World revolutionaries."[85] Their allure of transgression and barbarism, their call for "seizing the time" and bringing "armed chaos," and their push for liberated sexuality and drugs seduced many white leftists eager to defy bourgeois morality.[86]

In October 1969, the trajectory of the Weatherman's escalation reached a turning point with the so-called Days of Rage, an explicitly violent demonstration held in Chicago. Wearing helmets and heavy jackets, the most boisterous leftist militants in the country carried Molotov cocktails, metal bars, and Vietnamese flags. They did everything they could to "bring the war home," as their rallying cry promised.[87] Contrary to expectations, only a few hundred participants showed up, but they blew up a police statue in Haymarket Square—the site of the 1886 massacre—and went on a rampage through the city's business district. They ravaged shops, broke bank windows, and engaged in full-contact fights with police officers. Dozens were hospitalized on both sides, and up to 287 people were arrested.[88]

It was in that circumstance that the Weatherman first requested Marc Kadish—the reference person of the Guild in Chicago and a member of the People's Law Office—to advise them on the legal implication of their upcoming actions and to help them establish a legal defense office.[89] Immediately, a problem of political compatibility arose and was taken up by the executive board of the NLG. The Guild had a policy of "assisting all groups who [were] part of the movement for social change," but the Weatherman's rhetoric and tactics were controversial and divisive. Even the Chicago Panthers voiced their criticism for the Days of Rage, and Fred Hampton defined them as "anarchistic, opportunistic, adventuristic, and Custeristic." Kadish himself was torn. But after much debate, the NLG reaffirmed "its continued commitment to provide[,] to the extent possible, legal support and assistance to all groups and individuals who [were] under attack as a result of repression of the ruling powers."[90]

Therefore, Guild representatives met with Weatherman leaders and agreed on specific forms of legal aid. A person was also sent to Chicago to prepare the first major case regarding the group. Dozens of militants lay in jail, waiting to be bailed out, and sixty-four of them soon faced a grand jury indictment.[91] A few months later, the attorney general leveled federal conspiracy charges against twelve leaders of the Weatherman for the events in Chicago (twenty-eight co-conspirators were also cited). Building on prior movement acquaintances and lawyers' hospitality, a legal collective gathering Weatherman militants and PLO lawyers readily emerged.[92] The PLO also represented Brian Flanagan, a member of the Weatherman charged with the attempted murder of a Chicago Corporation attorney, who remained paralyzed during the street battles of the Days of Rage. Flanagan was acquitted, as the defense was able to demonstrate his noninvolvement.[93]

During the early months of 1970, however, the Weatherman broke away from SDS. Feeling powerless before the horrors of war, the group had resolved that only violence would meet violence. In a tragic nemesis, however, three members of the organization perished in the explosion of the Manhattan townhouse they were using as a bomb factory. Kathy Boudin, Leonard's daughter and a militant of the group, was one of the two survivors of the incident. Together with Cathy Wilkerson, another Weatherman affiliate and the daughter of the building owner, Kathy Boudin was able to flee from the scene of the massacre and take refuge at her parents' house a few blocks away. In spite of her father's requests to turn herself in, she disappeared, remaining on the run until 1981.[94] The core of the organization, indeed, went underground. Structured as an urban guerrilla group and yearning to set an example, the Weather Underground made itself heard through bombings against targets related to war and capitalism, including the Capitol, the Pentagon, and the California attorney general's office. The organization also hit symbols of law enforcement, such as police facilities, departments of correction, and halls of justice. The Weather Underground claimed a total of twenty-seven attacks in about seven years, which they always made sure to contrast with the two thousand victims per day of the Vietnam War.[95]

As mentioned in chapter 3, contacts between lawyers and clandestine militants remained open so that the latter could receive information and gestures of solidarity. As soon as some members of the group resurfaced or were arrested, they always found radical lawyers ready to assist. To be sure, Guild lawyers were not immune to the widespread skepticism, even contempt, that was growing among U.S. leftists vis-à-vis the strategy of the Weather Underground.[96] Yet they consistently resolved to help this group and most of the other leftist guerrilla organizations.

Guild affiliate Lewis Steel, for example, admitted that there was "an ocean" separating himself from the radicalism of the Weather Underground. He was an heir to the Warner Bros. fortune, had a house in the Hamptons, and liked to go to the opera. Nonetheless, he was committed to serving the movement and agreed to represent Dionne Donghi, a member of the Weather Underground Cincinnati collective who was arrested for forging checks. An undercover FBI agent had infiltrated the group and driven Donghi, along with another member of the collective, straight into the arms of the police. The agent had also made her pregnant. Among other things, Steel managed to get her out of jail in time to have an abortion, despite the federal judge having denied bail. Distance between the affluent lawyer and the young zealots, full of anger and guilt, never healed. Nonetheless, solidarity was imperative. "I wasn't on their side," explained Steel, "but I wasn't on whatever was the other side either."[97]

Quite predictably, William Kunstler was more approving of the Weather Underground. He admired their dedication to a world without racism and oppression, as well as their willingness to risk their lives to attain it.[98] In a 1971 interview, he condensed radical lawyers' most shared sentiment, suspended between criticism of violence at a tactical level and the need to close ranks against a common enemy:

> I feel now that it is a bad tactic to employ violence. I understand the reasons why the Weathermen resort to a philosophy of terrorism. I am not one who says that terrorism is not a part of a revolution. Terrorism was used in the American Revolution, in the Russian Revolution, certainly in the Algerian Revolution and in the struggle to free Palestine from the British mandate and control. But it

normally occurs at a time of the transfer of power, not at a time when that transfer appears to be distant. Because the result of isolated acts of terrorism is to disunite the movement and to bring on a whirlwind of repression at a time when we're not prepared for it. It only alienates our friends and unites our enemies and may well bring on a second Reichstag Fire. So my feeling is that as a tactic—and I talk only in tactical terms—I don't have more scruples against violence—violence at the moment is bad for the movement. On the other hand, this view should not lead us to abandon the Weathermen and other practitioners of violence. We should debate this question of violence, and not turn on the Weathermen, just as the Weathermen should not turn on the liberals because they engage in electoral politics. If there was ever time for absolute unity it is now, or the only unity we will find will be in a common grave with the help of a bulldozer.[99]

To some extent, such an enduring solidarity was facilitated by the Weather Underground's resolution to avoid violence against human beings and to target property. "I have never countenanced killing people," explains Ratner today, but "I had no problem with symbolic bombings in which no one was injured."[100] Indeed, after some initial missteps and internal tribulations, the group made warning calls ahead of its attacks to police and the media in order to clear the buildings. It also set explosive charges to blow up in the wee hours and, in general, avoided political assassinations and other acts endangering civilians.[101] The Weather Underground gradually understood violence as a propaganda tool: bounded, symbolic, and comprehensible to the people. Most of the sympathizers still held human life as sacred and rejected bloody rhetoric, and it would have been suicidal for the organization to lose them entirely. Therefore, the Weather Underground's concern with avoiding total isolation, retaining mass support, and securing private aid encouraged a policy of relative restraint.[102] In 1975, toward the end of the group's trajectory, Leonard Boudin could write without much scandal that the conduct of the Weather Underground was "a highly moral, even idealistic reaction to governmental behavior," as its actions "for the most part were directed at property rather than people."[103]

But someone like Kunstler, and a handful of others like him, were willing to go even further in the public backing of antiwar militants, justifying them even when violent acts led to fatalities. That was the case of Karleton (Karl) Armstrong, one of the four young leftists, known as the New Year's

Gang, who bombed the Army Math Research Center, a military-funded think tank at the University of Wisconsin, Madison. In August 1970, Armstrong drove onto campus a stolen van filled with a ton of explosives, which detonated early in the morning, devastating the building that hosted the center. Despite a last-minute warning call, a researcher who was still working in the basement was killed, and five other people were injured. The radical community went into shock and mostly criticized the incautious attack. The bombers fled to Canada and disappeared. Armstrong was the first to be arrested in Toronto, in 1972, and later extradited.[104]

Given the overwhelming volume of evidence, Armstrong was compelled to plead guilty to second-degree murder and other related crimes. And yet Kunstler and his team opted for a defense based on the Nuremberg principles, hoping to lessen the sentence in the mitigation hearings of 1973. They managed to bring to the witness stand the usual lineup of testimonies and experts, including thirty-eight Vietnam veterans; Lifton and Zinn; Senator Ernest H. Gruening, who had voted against the Gulf of Tonkin Resolution; Pentagon Papers defendant Anthony Russo; and Harvey Goldberg, a famed History professor. They all insisted on the magnitude of war atrocities and on the rightfulness of resistance. Kunstler also participated in community events that were held in Madison for Armstrong's release. In what has been described as "one of the most impassioned summations of his career," the New York lawyer lauded the "children" who, alone, were opposing the conflict. While Armstrong himself hesitated to justify his reckless gesture, Kunstler emphatically declared he did not want to be "a good American anymore," mentioning the "good Germans" who stood idle before Dachau. In spite of Kunstler's efforts, Armstrong got the maximum sentence, and the case, which never occupied the Guild directly, remained a source of embarrassment within the Left.[105]

In the meantime, the specter of domestic terrorism haunted the government. According to official estimates, bombings between January 1969 and April 1970 tallied 4,330 (excluding threats and attempts). More than twelve hundred of them were attributable to campus disturbances and extremists, whereas half of them remained unattributed. The phenomenon appeared as a "grave danger," "unparalleled" in U.S. history.[106] The Weather Underground thus became the catch-all name for a plethora of groups that independently resorted to attacks against political targets, both before and after the period of the Weather Underground's activity.[107] In July 1970, a federal grand jury in Detroit leveled charges of conspiracy to commit bombings and murders and illegally carrying weapons against thirteen Weather Underground members. Their response came in a communiqué, addressed to Attorney General John Mitchell: "Don't look for us, Dog; we'll find you first."[108]

It goes without saying that the FBI boosted its investigation of the Weather Underground. Mitchell regarded the group as "the most severe internal security threat this country has seen since the Depression," and President Nixon pushed for lifting all restrictions on inquiries. Between 1970 and 1974, eight of the twenty-four new entries on the FBI's Most Wanted list of fugitives were white radical leftists. The squads assigned to follow the Weather Underground multiplied, increased their size, and were equipped with the most advanced technologies. At least informally, warrantless break-ins, mail opening, and wiretapping were authorized. But despite invasive surveillance and harassment, which also targeted the People's Law Office in Chicago as well as scores of Weather Underground's sympathizers, results were modest. This tiny organization remained almost impermeable to infiltration and continued operating unperturbed.[109]

Due to the massive volume of surveillance obtained without search warrants, by January 1974 the government had dropped all federal charges against the Weather Underground in both Chicago and Detroit. Rather than revealing the extent of such illegal and publicly embarrassing conduct, the government turned a blind eye on its former number one enemy. As a matter of fact, in June 1972 the Supreme Court had unanimously rejected the government's claim that it could conduct electronic surveillance of domestic groups or individuals without prior approval or probable cause, even when national security was involved. The Fourth Amendment's barrier could not be breached. For once, the much-deprecated legal system had curbed the government's surveillance (see chapter 10).[110]

Later on, the Weather Underground tried to reconnect with those above ground and envisioned a long-term strategy. A widely circulated pamphlet titled *Prairie Fire* encapsulated the principles of the new course, while the Prairie Fire Distribution Committee, which also co-opted radical lawyers, was entrusted with promoting the debate with social movements and recruiting followers.[111] And yet sectarianism and paranoia bent the organization.[112] As the 1970s drew to a close and the political context appeared more favorable, the Weather Underground militants voluntarily resurfaced. With the help of radical lawyers, they negotiated for charges to be dropped, short sentences, or fines and probation.[113] As historian Arthur M. Eckstein rightly observed, "The defendants in the only federal trial ever held involving Weatherman were not radicals but top FBI officials." Associate director Mark Felt and assistant director Edward Miller, together with a number of other FBI agents, were eventually convicted, in November 1980, for twelve warrantless burglaries of Weather Underground supporters and relatives. President Reagan, quite predictably, rushed to pardon them in April 1981.[114]

Meanwhile, a handful of former Weather Underground affiliates, including Kathy Boudin, had pursued their militancy under the banner of the May 19 Communist Organization (M19CO). This group saw itself as a cohort of white people supporting the armed struggle of revolutionary people of color in the name of anti-imperialism. May 19 was indeed the birthday of both Malcom X and Ho Chi Minh. Faithful to their solidarity pledge, attorney Susan Tipograph, a future president of the New York City chapter of the NLG, and Dana Biberman, a Guild legal worker who often assisted the Black Panthers and Puerto Rican radicals, were in the orbit of the M19CO.

In particular, the M19CO was ancillary to the Black Liberation Army (BLA), a loosely connected network of underground units that embraced outright violence against the U.S. government. Gaining traction after the BPP lost strength, the BLA assembled former Black Panthers and Republic of New Afrika militants, among others. The number of the BLA's actions is disputed, because of uncertain attribution and because the group was a primary target of the COINTELPRO, which may have provoked or faked some attacks. It remains the fact that BLA affiliates were responsible of several police shootings and bank robberies from as early as 1971. Among the presumed leaders of the BLA, JoAnne Chesimard, aka Assata Shakur, featured prominently. Branded as a cop killer, she collected an outstanding number of indictments and was defended by an assortment of Black lawyers, including Evelyn Williams (her aunt) and Florynce Kennedy. Kunstler also jumped on board, but white radical lawyers were not particularly vocal in Shakur's defense. Sentenced to life imprisonment (pending appeal) for the murder of a state trooper in May 1973, Shakur escaped from prison in 1979 with the help of the M19CO.[115]

On October 20, 1981, on a day that it is remembered as a fateful confrontation between the government and the leftist insurgents, a group of white and Black militants belonging to the M19CO and the BLA were arrested. They had orchestrated and executed the robbery of a Brink's armored truck in New Jersey, which went awry and claimed the lives of a guard and two police officers. Even in that thorny case, radical lawyers did not fail to provide assistance, while members of the M19CO and the Republic of New Afrika mobilized to reframe the crime in political terms. A Coalition to Defend the October 20th Freedom Fighters was also created. Even so, it was difficult to justify a murderous robbery as a revolutionary act. The leftist community of the 1960s had largely disintegrated, along with the support of white antiwar sympathizers. Many observers saw the incident as the disastrous epilogue of an entire season of activism that was falling apart.[116]

A few militants—those who were more directly involved with the robbery—opted for a principled defense, refused to recognize the legitimacy of the courts, and reaffirmed their wholehearted commitment to the oppressed.[117] Not only were they consistently prevented from discussing political issues, but they also obtained severe prison sentences.[118] Conversely, Kathy Boudin, whose role in the robbery was more indirect, adopted a more pragmatic approach. She acted under the expert guidance of her father and a pool of Guild lawyers. While her defense team sought to distance her from the rest of the group, arguing that she was a last-minute recruit, she pleaded guilty to one count of felony murder and robbery. After spending more than twenty years at the Women's Correctional Facility in Bedford Hills, New York, Boudin was paroled in 2003.[119]

Until the early 1960s, the inner workings of U.S. prisons received relatively little scrutiny from activists and the press. Authorities projected a sense of confidence in the rehabilitative mission of penitentiaries and emphasized their pledge to treat and reform inmates instead of simply punishing them. Many states also introduced indeterminate sentence laws that redefined, at least in theory, the logic of incarceration. Instead of sentencing the offender to a specific period of time, judges gave prison authorities—the parole boards—the power to tailor the length of incarceration according to the time needed to rehabilitate the subject. To stress its commitment to thera-peutic treatment, the American Prison Association rebranded itself in 1954 as the American Correctional Association, encouraging its members to re-place "prison" with "correctional institution" and to refer to their "punish-ment blocks" as "adjustment centers," alluding to their curative function.[1]

As soon as civil rights activists were forced into jail, many of whom re-fused to be bailed out in order to dramatize their condition, confidence in the carceral system was deeply shaken. On the one hand, activists denounced racial violence behind bars and portrayed prison life as a mirror of segregated life, especially in the South. On the other hand, activists made use of jail and repurposed it. As historian Dan Berger pointed out, jail be-came at once "a rite of passage, a form of community, and a tool of political mobilization." It turned into "an extension of the mass meeting" and, quite paradoxically, was seen as "a place of freedom."[2] In jail, activists could gather forces, organize, and dream of a brighter future.

For those who remained in prison, however, racial prejudice, unequal sentencing, denial of rights, cruel punishments, and inadequate facilities made life hell. If a more acute concern for individual rights helped them single out their grievances, religion provided a moral compass and a badge of identity. A large number of Black inmates, indeed, embraced the Muslim faith and became the "in-prison political arm" of the civil rights movement.[3] Many of them joined the Nation of Islam, a radical organization that preached total separation along racial and religious lines to restore Black dignity. Since the late 1950s, Black Muslims initiated direct-action protests and filed a number of successful lawsuits to challenge prison authorities' attempts to prevent them from meeting together, proselytizing, and praying. These prisoners envisioned the courts as "a breach in the walls," which allowed them to state their political claims before the world and bring their struggles to national attention.[4] Therefore, they flooded the courts with writs. On their part, judges intervened quite substantially on behalf of inmates and established—at least on paper—rights to adequate medical care, to communicate with lawyers, to be free from arbitrary censorship, to express political opinions, and to enjoy recreation and visitation. Petitioned by a Muslim inmate, the Supreme Court in 1964 explicitly determined that prisoners retained their constitutional rights, ending the "hands-off" doctrine that since the nineteenth century had made captives legally powerless.[5]

Fanning the flames of inmates' radicalism, a few Black prisoners with unquestionable charisma and writing skills emerged as political leaders and ideologues. Eldridge Cleaver was arguably the forefather and one of the most admired figures of this kind. Through his writing, Cleaver helped popularize the idea that the inmate represented the most authentic outcast, who would ignite the revolution in the United States. While prisons became "universities for political education," as the *New York Times* reported, a tremendous process of teaching and indoctrination spread oppositional messages among inmates.[6] The increasing presence of Black Panther Party militants in prisons just added fuel to the fire. The BPP lionized its own "political prisoners," recruited easily among inmates, established prisons as a critical battleground, and worked from the outside on behalf of Black inmates. As a matter of fact, the Panthers' most prominent leaders, including Seale, Newton, and Cleaver, spent many years behind bars and, from that specific condition, managed power and exerted influence.

At the same time, a large number of white draft resisters, antiwar activists, radical militants, and drug users experienced the trauma of incarceration for the first time. These people elicited the interest of the Left in the struggles for prison rights and were functional in breaking down the racial antagonism that still pervaded prison life. A new militancy gradually took shape, and prison activists became less and less preoccupied with improvements in the conditions of incarceration and increasingly questioned the legitimacy of their incarceration. If the whole system of justice was an instrument of class and race oppression, as the leftist canon went, it logically followed that the detention of both Black and white radicals was truly abusive. They were "political prisoners" whose alleged crimes had to be understood and justified.[7]

Quite predictably, the radicals grew infatuated with these "wretched of the earth" who were literally in shackles. At the end of the 1960s, a large section of the anti-capitalist and antiracist front shared a positive attitude toward lawbreaking that sometimes resulted in a "romantic fetishization of crime." As Marx had argued, indeed, criminals, thieves, and vagrants were able to perform "the most heroic deeds and the most exalted sacrifices, as of the basest banditry and the dirtiest corruption."[8] Thus, prisoners—as Berger neatly summarizes—became "symbols of political possibility," while prisons were taken as the truest revelation of the state's naked power.[9] Such a sentiment was reinforced by the impressive growth in prison incidents, disorders, and insurrections that occurred between the late 1960s and the early 1970s. Whereas only five prison riots troubled the peace of U.S. correctional facilities in 1967, there were already fifteen in 1968, twenty-seven in 1970, and forty-eight in 1972—marking the highest point in American history.[10]

Steered by Black nationalists and other radical inmates, these upheavals were racially mixed and highly contentious. In August 1970 at the Manhattan House of Detention for Men, known as the Tombs, a group of roughly eight hundred inmates took a few guards hostage and occupied several floors to make their grievances heard. It was one of the first major prisoner blowups in New York City. Inmates protested poor food, overcrowded conditions, lack of medical care, racial violence, and exceedingly long trials. After eight hours of negotiations, the hostages were released unharmed. Mayor Lindsay, the commissioner, the warden, and the district attorney acknowledged that the grievances were meritorious. However, nothing changed in the aftermath of the riot, and inmates allegedly suffered reprisals.

Prisoners' self-awareness nonetheless developed, coupled with a public recognition that most of the inmates who inhabited U.S. jails were "Third World," poor, and awaiting trial under harsh conditions, without the possibility to meet bail. In October 1970, just a few months after the protest at the Tombs, the whole New York correctional system was shaken by insurrections in five of its major facilities in Manhattan, Queens, Brooklyn, and the Bronx. An estimated four thousand inmates revolted, demonstrating an increasingly radical spirit and, in some cases, operating like an organized guerrilla movement. They set up barricades, secured hostages, set fires, and mustered outside supporters. They were eventually forced to surrender, but they succeeded in elevating the prison as a space of warfare.[11]

The following November the contagion spread to Auburn, New York, the state's oldest prison and the site of the first execution by electric chair in the United States. Inmates seized control of the overcrowded facility for eight hours, holding nearly fifty hostages. After negotiations, they released the hostages unharmed, returned to their cells, and agreed to discuss their grievances with the authorities, who vowed to implement reform and avoid ex post retaliation. Yet pledges were broken, reforms stalled, and six leaders of the revolt—the so-called Auburn Six—were singled out and charged with a long list of felonies. Awaiting trial, they were sent to Attica prison in upstate New York.

The rebellion at Folsom, the oldest and largest prison in California, was arguably the most resonant of that already turbulent period. In November 1970, almost the entire population of the facility refused to leave their cells to go to work for nineteen days—an unprecedented length of time in U.S. history. Showing both class consciousness and racial unity, prisoners advanced a number of demands that were spelled out into a manifesto. They dubbed correctional institutions as "fascist concentration camps of modern America" and put forth requests ranging from better medical facilities and adequate visiting conditions to political asylum in foreign countries for "political prisoners." None of the demands were met, but external support for the insurgents was surprisingly large, and a group of former convicts and lawyers established the United Prisoners Union.[12]

As a matter of fact, inmates' militancy could hardly be dismissed. More work stoppages, hunger strikes, riots, and other moderate efforts of unionization followed, shedding further light on the degrading conditions to which captives were often subjected. Teach-ins, student demonstrations, and leftist publications also began addressing prison issues, while advocacy groups for prisoners took action across the country. Former inmates were brought to campuses to discuss their personal experiences behind bars, while conferences criticized prison as a mode of treating social ills.[13] In solidarity with the prisoners who, through their struggles, showed the vulnerability of the U.S. empire, the Weather Underground bombed several buildings belonging to the justice and penal systems, creating further havoc.[14]

Even beyond the radical milieu, a large spectrum of observers, including journalists, politicians, lawyers, judges, and members of the administration, began discussing the future of incarceration and urged reforms.[15] The earlier blind confidence in rehabilitation also ebbed, opening the door to qualms about a system that seemed to punish and manipulate inmates instead of redeeming them. The indeterminate sentence also came under attack. According to critics, it increased the average terms, proved substantially ineffective, and was used to quell internal resistance targeting political troublemakers. Adjustment centers in medium- and maximum-security complexes—employed to punish unruly inmates and known as "the holes" in prison jargon—were described as "prisons within prisons" that coupled total isolation with sensorial deprivation. Since many prisoners began asserting that they did not need any "correction," as they were innocent victims of a sick society forcing them into crime, the notion of rehabilitation appeared increasingly difficult to defend.[16]

All Inmates Are "Political Prisoners"

The traditional seclusion of U.S. penitentiaries had been breached by prison authorities themselves in the early 1960s. With the best of intentions and hoping to strengthen the correctional system, they had invited outside experts to participate in convict reform programs. At San Quentin, for example, these external specialists proved to be particularly sympathetic to the rebellious inmates and began smuggling a few seditious readings into the once insulated cells. The Bay Area radical winds thus blew across the bars for the first time. Thanks to an initial lack of control of the prisoners' reading diet, a number of detainees voraciously read the "outside" literature, which helped them to elaborate a firmer critique of the prison institution and to redefine their own identity. Something like a "prisoner intelligentsia" coalesced and assumed the role of a revolutionary vanguard, turning previous defeatism into an aggressive stance.[17]

Together with the external experts, an ever-growing number of lawyers and legal workers took up the habit of passing through prison gates to visit inmates and to hear their complaints. Lawyers were indeed crucial to making the walls of penitentiaries more porous. The majority of them belonged to the new breed of young radicals that gravitated around the Guild. Increasingly deluged with letters from prisoners who required their help, they resolved to intervene in a space they perceived as both outside judicial control and strategic for political engagement. A classic example of the *extra legem* procedures of correctional facilities was the system of disciplinary hearings in which the prisoner, without the presence of counsel, was not permitted to confront or cross-examine the accuser or to call witnesses in defense. Therefore, all infractions of internal rules, which were increasingly violated for political motives, were enforced under a regime of unfettered discretion.

Of course, radical lawyers could not stand idly by. According to Fay Stender, in the mid-1960s only half a dozen lawyers sporadically represented convicts, whereas in the early 1970s there were between three hundred and five hundred, and fifty of them did only prison work.[18] The Guild was at the forefront of this mobilization, but the NAACP Legal Defense Fund and the ACLU had been focusing on inmates' issues since the end of the 1960s. In 1970, for example, the ACLU national office created a National Committee on Prisoners' Rights (later National Prison Project). In addition to lawyers, scores of legal workers, investigators, fundraisers, former inmates, and political agitators made their energies available and, in some instances, colluded with inmates in crippling the normal operations of penitentiaries.

Given their degree of familiarity with prisoners, lawyers became the most trusted—and sometimes the only authorized—intermediaries between captives and the outside world, carrying secret verbal messages, confidential letters, political documents, and other items across jail bars. As officers of the court, attorneys were indeed accorded attorney-client privilege and special legal protections. In addition, Section 2600 of the California Penal Code had recently granted inmates the right to correspond confidentially with any member of the state bar or holder of public office, together with the right to purchase, receive, and read all newspapers, periodicals, and books accepted for distribution by the U.S. Postal Service, with only a few exceptions. So correspondence with lawyers and the exchange of reading materials were legally safeguarded, at least in California.[19]

Since the Folsom riot in 1970, the NLG explicitly asked its lawyers to back up the strike and protect the demonstrators, while the rebellious inmates entrusted attorney Charles Garry as one of their negotiators.[20] As mentioned earlier, the riot did not achieve the expected results, yet organizers were satisfied with the fact that "contact with the outside, mostly through lawyers, had been good, and at the same time a crowd of supporters with picket signs were gathered beyond the gates. The men inside knew they were there, and that counted."[21] As the California Board of Corrections noted, the San Francisco chapter of the NLG played a substantial role, as its lawyers held press conferences, contacted news media in support of the strike, and were present during demonstrations, including a rally at the West Capitol Steps featuring Fay Stender and Tom Hayden.[22]

When protests erupted in New York, Guild lawyers were there, too. In October 1970, Gerald Lefcourt acted as legal counsel to the insurgent prisoners of the Branch Queens House of Detention who forced three state Supreme Court justices, under threat of lethal violence, to hold a bail review hearing of forty-seven detainees in a makeshift court arranged within the prison. The forced hearing unexpectedly obtained the immediate release of twelve prisoners, thanks to drastic bail reductions and the impromptu fundraising by supporters who had gathered outside the jail. Lefcourt defined it as a "legal jailbreak."[23] The so-called Tombs Brothers, namely the seven men who were indicted on charges ranging from kidnapping to obstruction, were also represented by Guild lawyers, who volunteered to help them.[24]

Later on, when thirty-four inmates were indicted for the Brooklyn and Queens rebellions on charges that included kidnapping, NLG lawyers undertook the representation of all but two of them. The Guild also denounced the "outrageous deterioration" of both penal institutions and argued that prisoners had no alternative but to seek more aggressive means of publicizing their plight.[25] A legal team that included Guild vice president Lewis Steel and Herman Schwartz, a law professor at the State University of Buffalo and a founder of the ACLU's National Prison Project, represented the Auburn Six. Brought into court in shackles, the six inmates appalled the audience by talking about the "near-starvation rations that were offered under the glare of lights that were never turned off," the "guards banging their sticks on the bars to wake them at all hours," the unnecessary "cavity searches," and other acts of gratuitous barbarity.[26]

A few months later, a Brooklyn Law School Prisoners' Rights Committee was established in New York and focused on the Catskill Reformatory, a state prison for men in Napanoch, New York, currently named the Eastern Correctional Facility. The committee's goal was to help prisoners with research and preparation of their legal papers, while mobilizing and "politicizing" law students and other interested people. From the very outset of their involvement in prison work, however, radical lawyers and legal students began to question the meaning of their own efforts. Prisons represented "the pinnacle of an oppressive system," and lawyers, by helping inmates to ease their conditions, ran the risk of "disguis[ing]" such a form of extreme coercion.[27]

As a matter of fact, since 1970 a critical discourse on prisons was developing within the Guild milieu and revolved around four main notions. First of all, the "system of injustice," which oppressed its citizens by denying bail and discriminating racially and sexually, made all inmates "political prisoners, regardless of the offenses with which they [were] charged."[28] Put another way, the judiciary was so rigged that all alleged criminals could consider themselves victims. Such a statement was reinforced by a second notion, namely the idea that prison could be considered "a place of banishment" for those who did not accept the status quo.[29] Nonconformists, rebels, and "Third World people" were systematically thrown into jail, for prisons were "the ultimate weapon of domestic social control."[30] A third related principle equated the nation with its prisons, which could be viewed as "a reflection" of the values and goals of American society. Prison, indeed, replicated and intensified the political, economic, racial, gender, and cultural conflicts that permeated the United States.[31] Fourth, and finally, the prison system symbolized the institution where the government was most unreservedly allowed free rein, even more than the military. It was pure, unrestrained oppression. It was the epitome of "lawlessness."[32] "Working with the prisoners as I do is like being present at Dachau," maintained Stender, who added that "convicts [were] literally at the mercy of an arbitrary system which [was] almost completely above and beyond the law."[33] Interestingly, on the other side of the Atlantic, Michel Foucault, who had just plunged himself into prison militancy, adopted very similar images to describe how "justice puts the prisoner outside the law" through incarceration.[34]

However, since prisons represented such a dangerous "experiment in dehumanization and victimization," those who were able to resist them developed unique qualities. They were "a new breed of humanists, victors over oppression, men and women who have dared to win their freedom, their rights, their humanity."[35] Ultimately, prisons were at once "concentration camps" and microcosms of revolution.[36] Rebellious inmates had learned capitalist exploitation the hard way and were ready to show the path to liberation.

Confronted with a movement replete with promise and danger, the NLG pondered on whether there were more effective ways to connect with it. While a few doctrinaire Marxists still argued that prisoners could not be considered a revolutionary class, most Guild lawyers hailed the exceptional development of the prison movement with enthusiasm and rushed to help the new rebels behind bars.[37] Consistent with its general approach, the Guild agreed that the work in the prisons must be oriented "to increasing prisoners' powers" and provide "a vital link between the world within the walls and the world outside."[38]

With the "Brothers"

Defense committees for political prisoners were not only key components of militant litigation but also important bridges between lawyers and radicalized inmates. Indeed, they were hardly new, and since the nineteenth century they had contributed to shaping the modern notion of legal militancy. As previously noted, the anarchists, the Wobblies, the Communist

Party, the NAACP, the ACLU, and the NLG itself had sometimes resorted to defense committees to advocate the innocence of people awaiting trial in jail and to demand clemency for those who were sentenced to death or long prison terms. Depending on the context and the nature of the crimes under judgment, these committees were either broad based—in the form of "popular fronts"—or very divisive and sectarian.[39] This tradition had somehow faded by the sixties, but the memory of some of these mobilizations, notably those on behalf of the Scottsboro Boys and the Rosenbergs, remained alive.[40] A common thread reemerged, and interestingly, the thundering campaign that developed on behalf of Huey Newton was masterminded not only by his attorney, Charles Garry, but also by William L. Patterson, a legendary communist lawyer and former head of the International Labor Defense. Patterson himself had spent inexhaustible energy in both the Rosenberg and the Scottsboro cases.[41]

During the 1960s and 1970s, defense committees resurrected and played an even more significant role than in the past, leveraging the state of agitation of entire sectors of society and taking advantage of the diffusion of mass media. Committees turned into formidable tools to bring people into the streets, contributed decisively to building and celebrating the heroism (or martyrdom) of militants, and worked as platforms for a radical analysis of American society. While providing legal talent, money, and moral support, and putting pressure on juries and judges, they also challenged dominant values and educated large audiences, way beyond the usual constituency. With an unprecedented alliance of legal and extralegal energies, the Soledad Brothers Defense Committee (SBDC) set the standard for most of the ensuing political cases.

As previously mentioned, in January 1970 a racially mixed group of inmates was taken to a recreational area of Soledad, a high-security prison located in Salinas, California. The penitentiary was known for its violent outbursts, including rapes and murders. By all accounts, a scuffle broke out in the exercise yard. A white guard fired four shots with his rifle, killing three Black prisoners and wounding one white prisoner. One of the victims was W. L. Nolen, arguably the most respected Black inmate at Soledad, a New Afrikan, and a mentor to many. Soledad inmates instantly protested the murderous repression, and many of them went on a hunger strike. Minutes after a grand jury found the homicide "justifiable" and the verdict was broadcast on television, a white guard at Soledad was found dead.

Black inmates George Jackson, Fleeta Drumgo, and John W. Clutchette were interrogated, held in solitary confinement for almost a month, and charged with assault and murder. Black prisoners throughout California exploded in rage, and so the leftist movement did. Attorneys Fay Stender and John Thorne represented Jackson, while Floyd Silliman, a Salinas liberal lawyer, and Richard Silver, a young partner in a Carmel law firm, defended Drumgo and Clutchette, respectively. In the Bay Area, a Soledad Brigade was organized to ensure that every inmate who testified on behalf of the Soledad Brothers had a lawyer who could protect him from reprisals. According to the defense, many prisoners had already been threatened and intimidated by guards and officials. Immediately, between fifty and sixty lawyers stepped up to the plate.[42]

Having spent a few years at the side of Garry, Stender knew very well that public relations, press coverage, public participation, influential endorsers, and generous donations were essential to politicize a trial. And the Jackson case offered the ideal conditions for a structured organization that could weave together a legal defense on a specific case, a general critique of imprisonment, Black power claims, and the solidarity spirit of white radicals. The NLG participated in this endeavor only marginally, but local Guild lawyers and legal workers were fully involved. While Stender began corresponding with Jackson and visiting him in the spring of 1970, she also started recruiting volunteer law students, paralegals, and activists to help with the pretrial work and the campaign. The Soledad Brothers Defense Committee was set up in Berkeley, and by the following summer it had expanded into an organization with seven subcommittees. Secondary branches soon opened in San Jose, Santa Cruz, Los Angeles, and Marin County.

Lawyers contributed their services, but funds were necessary for travels to interview witnesses, transcripts of court hearings, research, and experts' reports. Thus, the committee urged everyone to raise money through parties, dinners, flea markets, concerts, and art auctions. It also arranged for supporters to speak on campuses and in churches, booked rock groups, issued press releases, sent letters to politicians, and secured media coverage.[43] The organization was so meticulous that the committee even suggested the content of speeches and the best arguments for winning over hearts and minds.[44] Not only did committee members ask activists from Berkeley and Oakland to go to Salinas to observe the trial proceedings— wearing pins, carrying signs, and distributing propaganda materials—but they also drove them to the courtroom. As a result, a large number of supporters generally showed up at the courthouse, including hippies who changed their haircuts and outfits to look like random locals. Stender herself was reportedly impressed by the turnout.[45]

Public demonstrations, like a rally at the San Francisco Civic Center in August 1970, were organized to increase awareness of the case, lessen the impact of adverse publicity, and "create an atmosphere of acquittal," which was the committee's constant concern.[46] Propaganda was hardly limited to California and even expanded abroad through a network of European contacts, especially in France and Britain, where both Stender and Thorne traveled. An official SBDC chapter was opened in London, and in April 1971, three thousand people convened at the Central Hall Westminster (a historic place that hosted the first UN General Assembly meeting) to hear Thorne, Jackson's mother, and other speakers purporting the innocence of the Soledad Brothers.[47] As historian Rebecca Hill underscored, the SBDC sought to exploit the desperate pleas of the defendants' mothers and sisters, thus replicating a strategy employed in the past by the ILD, for example in the Scottsboro case.[48] Somehow echoing the ancient Greek tragedies, the supplication of mothers and sisters deprived of their children or brothers prompted spectators' compassion and solidarity.

And yet publicity, attraction of press coverage, and fundraising were contingent on the support of big names. Therefore, the committee soon gathered prominent endorsers, including democratic representatives such as Julian Bond, Ronald Dellums, and Mervyn M. Dymally; intellectuals such as Lawrence Ferlinghetti, Jean Genet, and Allen Ginsberg; and public figures such as Jane Fonda, Benjamin Spock, and Pete Seeger. Other Guild lawyers enthusiastically joined the fight, including C. B. King, Arthur Kinoy, William Kunstler, Leonard Weinglass, and Morton Stavis. Meanwhile, defense lawyers endlessly activated their contacts to expand this network. Albeit unsuccessfully, Thorne also tried to get Pablo Picasso on board.[49]

From the beginning, the committee argued that the three Black inmates were innocent. To buttress its argument, the committee whitewashed Jackson's criminal record and reduced it to a $70 gas station robbery that allegedly locked him behind bars (due to the indeterminate sentence). Jackson, in fact, had a more troubled criminal record, constantly refused to comply with prison rules, and likely killed the prison guard. The committee also contended that the Soledad Brothers' right to a fair trial was "systematically and intentionally destroyed" by prison administrators, who held them in solitary confinement for almost a month, negated immediate counsel, censored their communication, barred them from appearing at their codefendants' proceedings, and denied them fundamental legal information. Furthermore, according to the committee, prosecutors had psychologically coerced other prisoners in order to avoid unfavorable witnesses, prohibited the defense from releasing media statements about the case, placed the scene of the crime off-limits until it was remodeled, and chained the three defendants during pretrial motions thus presuming their guilt. In sum, defendants' rights to a fair trial had been blatantly violated, owing mainly to their Blackness and poverty.[50]

The political scope of the SBDC was indeed broader than simple legal defense. As the propaganda materials made clear, the case of the three Black inmates "[did] not merely involve the guilt or innocence of specific individuals. An entire legal system [was] called upon to defend its validity."[51] The committee sought to uncover "the link between the selective repression of political prisoners and the general repression of the people at large." Public opinion, in other words, had to come to terms with "the depth of State Repression which manifests itself in the many attempts at legal lynchings" and, ultimately, with "the total bankruptcy of American democracy and jurisprudence." Supporting the Soledad Brothers meant defending not only Jackson, Drumgo, and Clutchette or "all political prisoners" but "all people who have been victimized by the society and the judicial system." "People"—warned the Soledad Brothers Newsletter—"[could] no longer afford to ignore the rise towards fascism in this country."[52]

To succeed in its resolve, the committee also required as much time as possible and needed a favorable environment offering both a supportive public and a sympathetic jury pool. For this reason, the defense team filed a motion to move the trial to San Francisco—a location with a more progressive population than the small provincial town of Salinas and that was easier to reach by loyal audiences. Granted by the judge, the change of venue also helped buy some time, which was crucial for building a counternarrative of the events at Soledad, for raising awareness of the conditions of imprisonment, and, even more importantly, for shaping the heroic figure of Jackson.

Assisted by a number of law students and legal workers who were part of the committee, the legal team spent months interviewing more than one hundred Soledad inmates in order to offer an alternative, albeit fragile, version of the killing of the prison guard. Then the defense strove for bringing to public view "the barbaric conditions" at Soledad. The committee called on the California Legislative Black Caucus and requested an official investigation of the treatment of prisoners. In June 1970, a delegation led by Senator Mervyn Dymally, assemblyman John J. Miller, the director of the California Department of Corrections, and Stender visited the prison, including the infamous O Wing—the maximum-security section. They met with the warden and collected the grievances of several prisoners, who denounced the contaminated food, inadequate medical attention, and harassment. They also interviewed inmates' families and collected their letters.[53]

A disturbing report was eventually published. The document concluded that "inmates' charges amount[ed] to a strong indictment of the prison's employees (on all levels) as cruel, vindictive, dangerous men who should not be permitted to control the lives of the 2,800 men in Soledad." Inmates, the report stressed, were also unanimously "convinced that racist attitudes and practices on the part of correctional officers were common." Prison officials admitted that inmates were often punished by assignment to isolation and maximum-security cells before any hearing on the charges against them—a practice that was "honored only in the most totalitarian societies," according to the report. Worse still, prisoners had "no real avenue to seek redress for violation of law or breaches of morality by employees," as civilian control over prison employees was absent. As a result, the legislators urged further investigation, together with the cessation of intimidation and discrimination behind bars. To be free from guards' reprisals, Jackson applied for transfer to San Quentin, while a federal action filed by Stender and Thorne, known as *Clutchette v. Procunier*, successfully challenged the constitutionality of disciplinary hearings in prison.[54]

Flooded by a stream of prison letters, Stender immediately recognized the literary genius of Jackson. A few years before, her colleague Beverly Axelrod had succeeded in rehabilitating her controversial client and lover, Eldridge Cleaver. Despite Cleaver's highly debatable statements and hot-blooded language, Axelrod had collected his writings in a popular book and made him a literary star. Now Stender could do something similar with Jackson, who was far from being a confessed rapist (like Cleaver) and could be presented as an innocent victim of the system. Jackson's letters powerfully blended the longing for a leftist revolution with the hardship of growing up in a poor Black community, the racist discrimination of the justice system, the rage of Black inmates, and the horror of prison life. Stender foresaw great potential and contacted an editor at Bantam Books, Gregory Armstrong, who became enamored of the project and joined the SBDC. After "extensive editing" that removed Jackson's most abrasive calls for retaliatory violence and frequent invocations of armed revolt, his correspondence was published under the title *Soledad Brother*.[55]

The book was an instant success. It was enthusiastically reviewed, widely translated abroad, and awarded a number of prestigious literary prizes. It also generated a large amount of royalties, which were channeled to an overseas corporation, specifically designed by Guild lawyer Harry Margolis.[56] Jackson attracted a great deal of curiosity, becoming a much-sought-after interview subject. Stender was also able to garner an introduction to the book from Jean Genet, which further elevated Jackson's intellectual and political standing. A playwright of global fame and a former convict himself, Genet was a tireless supporter of the Black Panthers, for whom he had fervently campaigned and raised funds. In addition to offering his writing, Genet arranged for a French edition with his publisher Gallimard and mobilized intellectuals of the caliber of Jean-Paul Sartre, Michel Foucault, and Jacques Derrida.[57] Contacted by Thorne in Paris, acclaimed novelist James Baldwin also joined the legal crusade and took the first steps toward creating a movie on the Soledad case.[58]

Ultimately, Stender's intuition proved to be right. The book became one of the most influential examples of prison literature worldwide, Jackson stirred the revolutionary imagination across the globe, and the Soledad Brothers were worshipped as heroes by both the Black liberation movement and the radical Left.[59] Even liberals with no previous contact with the prison resistance finally had a glimpse of that incredibly problematic universe. However, the experience of the SBDC was not entirely a bed of roses. First of all, Jackson himself was scarcely convinced that his legal team could persuade a jury of his innocence. To be sure, he enjoyed being supported, sought after, and protected by a wide array of people, including militants, journalists, lawyers, and women in love. Yet he never abandoned his belief that only a prison escape would save him from the gas chamber. He talked about breaking out with lawyers and other visitors who came to the prison, repeatedly asking for material help.[60]

As is well known, George Jackson's younger brother Jonathan made an ill-fated attempt to rescue the Soledad Brothers on August 7, 1970. He stormed the Marin County courthouse and took Superior Court judge Harold Haley, prosecutor Gary Thomas, and three jurors hostage. Black radical inmates James McClain, Ruchell "Cinque" Magee, and William A. Christmas, who were in the courtroom for a trial, cooperated in the assault. The assailants reportedly demanded the release of George Jackson and his co-defendants. The ensuing shoot-out with police left Jonathan Jackson, the judge, and two inmates dead, while Thomas and Magee remained wounded.[61] On the one hand, the failed plot shed more light on the Soledad case and made Jonathan a new martyr of the Black liberation. On the other hand, it opened the doors to a new judiciary attack on the prison movement, further radicalized George Jackson, and deeply troubled the SBDC. In memory of Jonathan's gesture, a number of Black radical inmates in California's maximum-security institutions created the August 7th Movement, which advocated armed rebellion and was headed by James Carr, a member of George Jackson's prison gang.[62]

While increasingly boasting his commitment to revolutionary violence, Jackson sharply reduced his cooperation with both the defense team and the SBDC. After a series of harsh disagreements concerning legal strategies and use of funds—he wanted to channel his royalties and donations to the Panthers' guerrilla training—Stender left the defense team in February 1971.[63] Thorne alone took the lead of the defense apparatus, but the effort appeared increasingly futile. Stephen Bingham did not think so and joined the team, filling Stender's vacancy on the visiting list at San Quentin, where Jackson awaited trial in solitary confinement. Bingham also helped Thorne in drafting a civil suit, made in cooperation with the Guild, that challenged the conditions of maximum-security detention. He was often in and out of the prison and, according to reports, had been mesmerized by Jackson. Like almost everyone in the SBDC, Bingham glamorized and revered him.[64]

In the meantime, however, Jackson was putting increasing pressure on all his supporters to get behind his plan of smuggling in arms for a prison insurrection and privately admitted that he had killed the prison guard as an act of revenge.[65] Writing to his book editor, he affirmed that "the fight to live like Che prescribes living isn't too very important anymore" and declared, "it's become very important to me to put up a total resistance, it's been too long. . . . We all hold this power, to give life and take it away."[66] Jackson was equally transparent with Thorne, to whom he wrote in July 1971: "Things have not gone the way I would have had them go. . . . This is coming. The dragon is coming."[67] His confidence in the efforts to demonstrate his innocence had permanently vanished. Jackson's letters of this period were collected in a book, *Blood in My Eye*, which went to press posthumously, with limited editing. Unsurprisingly, it turned out to be a brazen celebration of revolutionary violence, penned by a convict who had nothing to lose.[68]

Bingham was the last outsider to meet with Jackson before his death, on August 21, 1971. At the urging of the Black Panthers, he agreed to bring to San Quentin a legal investigator and Panthers' aide, Vanita Anderson (née Witherspoon), who was the daughter of a communist lawyer. She wanted to meet Jackson, was denied access, and perhaps handed a tape recorder to

Bingham. What happened next has been the object of conflicting narratives and endless speculations. Anderson subsequently disappeared from the Bay Area and was never fully questioned, giving vent to conjectures about her possible role as an agent provocateur. A private firm conducted its own inquiry on behalf of Bingham's family but was not able to shed further light.[69] What is indisputable, nonetheless, is that Jackson came into possession of a gun and, with a group of inmates, took control of the adjustment center. Later, three white guards and two white inmates were murdered as a result of what prison authorities described as a failed jailbreak. Shot by a tower guard, Jackson lost his life in the prison yard.[70]

Jackson's death was ruled "justifiable homicide" by the grand jury investigating the case, while Bingham was charged with smuggling a gun, concealed in a tape recorder, into the hands of Jackson, who was reportedly able to hide it under an Afro wig, together with two clips of bullets.[71] According to the government's case, Jackson managed to carry the weapon inside the adjustment center even though he had been skin-searched. Sympathizers and other observers suspected that prison officials conspired to make the weapon available to Jackson as a pretext for killing him.[72] The SBDC, indeed, denounced what they considered a blatant execution—the culmination of years of cynical attempts to "get rid of George Jackson," a dangerous political leader.[73]

Interestingly, a few months after the massacre, the committee conceded that nobody knew in detail what had happened on August 21, not even whether Bingham had smuggled the gun. They just knew that Jackson had been murdered by the system he denounced.[74] In the beginning, the NLG itself was publicly silent and avoided taking up its cudgels for its young affiliate Bingham. Given the full-fledged radicalism of many lawyers and legal investigators, their complicity in such a plan could not be entirely ruled out. Bingham's closest comrades were also quite careful: they wanted to protect him but also avoid getting in trouble themselves. They repeated that he was innocent and a "scapegoat" but acknowledged that they did not know what happened.[75] For all parties, it was unclear how best to manage the situation.

Dan Siegel to this day believes that Bingham was "framed" and that the police version was "impossible," given the evidence that emerged during trial. However, he admits that "it was not inconceivable that any one of a number of us would have tried to be helpful to these Panthers who were in prison, including Steve, who was extremely committed." Around the same time, Siegel himself was asked by someone if he could smuggle a weapon into jail to the benefit of James Carr, the leader of the August 7th Movement.

"I said: 'No thank you!'" he recalls. "It was probably one of the few sensible things I have ever done in that period of time! But it's not that I was completely against the idea that Jimmy Carr should have a gun; I just thought it was a crazy thing to ask me to do it and I didn't quite trust the person who asked me."[76] In any event, Bingham contributed to the controversy by disappearing within hours of the bloodshed and staying underground for thirteen years, mainly in France.

The Guild milieu nevertheless remained secretly supportive while Bingham lived in hiding. Radical lawyers also helped him when, in July 1984, he decided to turn himself in. The backing of NLG attorneys, "who knew how to develop a political trial and how to mobilize a community," admittedly influenced his decision to come back to the United States and surrender.[77] Once he resurfaced, the Friends of Stephen Bingham Defense Committee was created, rallying some of the old sponsors, from Haywood Burns to Noam Chomsky. Assisted by Guild attorneys Paul Harris and Leonard Weinglass, Bingham claimed that he "might be a victim of a careful cover-up," that authorities obstructed a thorough investigation, and that he went underground only because he knew that prison officials were anxious to discredit radical lawyers, since their work "highlighted the unbearable harshness of the prison system."[78] Always maintaining his innocence, Bingham was cleared of all charges after his trial.[79] No one, however, ever proved how a gun ended up in Jackson's hands.

Opening Prison Doors

All in all, the story of the Soledad Brothers defense and its tragic epilogue illuminates the multifaceted engagement of lawyers on behalf of the prison movement, their sincere empathy with politicized inmates, and their willingness to take extraordinary risks by acting on a legal tightrope. If the SBDC's judicial results came up short, at least in the beginning, the case nonetheless awakened public opinion and shed light on a secluded dimension of social life. The mobilization in support of these three Black inmates provided a template of organization that was adopted simultaneously and afterward, for example in the campaign on behalf of Angela Y. Davis.

A native of Birmingham, Alabama, Davis had been a graduate student of Herbert Marcuse and a philosophy instructor at the University of California, Los Angeles, where she had been fired by the regents because of her communist militancy. With her lawyer John McTernan, a founding member of the Guild, she had decided to "assume the offensive" and openly acknowledged her political affiliation before the academic administration.[80] Davis, indeed, was a Black radical and a member of the Los Angeles Che-Lumumba Club, an all-Black section of the Communist Party USA that had raised its voice against the "legal lynching" of the Soledad Brothers. After attending a court hearing of the case, she began corresponding with Jackson, became one of the most outspoken supporters of the three defendants, and eventually co-chaired the SBDC in Southern California. For Davis, the Soledad Brothers were "descendants of a long line of black heroes" who "refused to pattern their lives after the authoritarian behavior of the apologetic victim." "No wonder they have resolved to kill this man," she wrote, alluding to the prison guard; they were fighting "unwaveringly in the most dangerous arena of struggle in America."[81]

To Fay Stender's dismay, Davis and Jackson also fell in love with each other. The letters of these two charming revolutionaries blended passion and subversive proclaims in such an intriguing way that they became the object of obsessive interest, especially by judicial authorities.[82] Thorne, who described Davis as "one of the warmest, kindest, most brilliant people I have ever met in my life," agreed to name her as a legal investigator so that she would be authorized to enter the penitentiary and meet George Jackson.[83] In the meantime, Jackson arranged for his brother Jonathan to become a sort of disciple of Davis and to serve as her bodyguard against possible attacks by racists and reactionaries. This implied that Jonathan had access to a stock of firearms that Davis had reportedly bought for self-defense and registered under her name. Embracing some of these weapons, Jonathan took over the Marin County courthouse in August 1970.[84]

A week after the incident, Davis was charged with aggravated kidnapping, first-degree murder, and conspiracy in the attempted liberation of the Soledad Brothers. The death penalty was likely, but she was already on the run. Within days her name appeared on the FBI's Ten Most Wanted list. She remained underground for a couple of months and was eventually arrested and jailed in Manhattan. Her case is well known, but what is worth noting here is the way her defense substantially built on previously tried and analyzed experiences: a defense committee was organized on her behalf, and militant strategies of litigation were adopted to discharge her. The tension between legal and political defense proved to be so fruitful that Guild lawyers came to see Davis's case as "the prototype of government prosecution[s] and people's fightback."[85]

Franklin Alexander, chair of the Che-Lumumba Club of Southern California, and Fania Davis Jordan, Angela's sister, co-coordinated the National

United Committee to Free Angela Davis (NUCFAD), which was established in November 1970 at a mass meeting in Los Angeles. The underlying assumption was that Davis's freedom could not be won by "legal maneuvering" but by "massive pressure, exerted by millions of Americans on state and local authorities."[86] As in the Soledad case, the committee's energies were geared toward publicity, propaganda, and fundraising. Under the rallying cry "Free Angela, Free All Political Prisoners," the committee distributed posters, buttons, bumper stickers, leaflets, trial bulletins, local and national newsletters, press releases, and pamphlets. It organized conferences, rallies, and concerts. The NUCFAD also managed the publication of Davis's incendiary writings and interviews, which justified crime in unequal societies, denounced impending fascism, chastised a racially biased justice system, and urged the liberation of political prisoners.[87]

Once again, a wide array of celebrities joined the campaign, including Aretha Franklin, who pledged to post Davis's bail; Ossie Davis, who helped with fundraising and became the chair of the Angela Davis Legal Defense Fund; and James Baldwin, who wrote an impassioned "Open Letter to My Sister, Miss Angela Davis," which appeared in the *New York Review of Books*.[88] Five months after her arrest, local branches of the committee numbered two hundred, and additional spontaneous groups were also bringing their support, from the Black People in Defense of Angela Davis, founded by Black writers, to the Committee of Black Women for the Freedom of Angela Davis, established in Harlem. Hundreds had gathered in the streets of New York City around the Women's House of Detention since the morning of her arraignment, asking for her release. People who wanted to visit her in jail were so numerous that the NUCFAD had to parcel them into a rigid schedule. The NUCFAD also held "mail parties" to sort the huge flow of letters that were sent to Davis—an estimated 500,000 during the first six months of 1971. Davis, on her part, was obviously delighted by such an outpouring of solidarity.[89]

The level of support Davis enjoyed clearly exceeded any previous experiences. Four main factors help explain it. First of all, the case for Davis's innocence was more plausible, at least for the general public, when compared with the Soledad case. The young, good-looking, middle-class, and cultured professor could easily have been completely oblivious to the plot to free George Jackson. Mainstream media sensationalized her arrest and trial, and this amplification eventually played into the defense's hands. Given the fractious political climate, even those people who were not persuaded of her innocence were nonetheless concerned about her right to a fair trial, so they vowed to help her.

Second, the communist parties across the globe, from France to the German Democratic Republic, mobilized their followers and acted as sounding boards for the campaign. Their organizing skills and structures were formidable. When a lawyer on her defense team toured Hungary and Bulgaria in the fall of 1971, he remained shocked by the extent of the solidarity toward Davis. "It is literally true," he wrote to a colleague, "that there is not a man, woman or child in either country who doesn't know about and feel the closest kinship to her." "People everywhere," he added, "not only identify with her but see her freedom struggle as indissolubly linked with their own aspirations."[90] Davis's intellectual connections across borders, built through the CPUSA and during the years she had spent abroad, were also unparalleled. Hungarian communist philosopher Georg Lukács, for example, circulated a petition demanding freedom for "an innocent human being," victim of a "judicial murder," and secured the signatures of a long list of European intellectuals, including philosophers Ernst Bloch and Jürgen Habermas, and writers Heinrich Böll and Günter Grass. A similar letter, sent to California governor Ronald Reagan asking to set Davis free on bail, was signed by icons of the cultural and artistic scene, such as Michel Foucault, Louis Aragon, and even Pablo Picasso, who had not endorsed a similar plea for the Soledad Brothers.[91] Greek-French film director Costa-Gavras and the cast of his Oscar-winning movie *Z* also penned a letter to New York governor Nelson Rockefeller asking to avert David's extradition to California.[92]

Third, Davis was a woman and a feminist whose charges were largely based on the gendered assumption that her "boundless and all-consuming passion" had driven her to conspire to free her lover by any means. The prosecutor, indeed, had tried to depoliticize the trial while stressing the motive of womanly desire. Therefore, Davis could lean on the support of the burgeoning feminist movement and, in particular, the Women's International Democratic Federation, which played a crucial role and circulated another petition calling for Davis's freedom that was signed by 600,000 supporters.

Fourth, the fact that Davis was a Black woman, who militated in the Black liberation movement and denounced racial discrimination as well as the values of affluent white America, turned out to be another key strength. While she emphasized her Blackness in a moment when Blackness epitomized the ideal of resistance—her silhouette with Afro haircut and her colorful outfits became transnational icons—mobilizations and petitions surfaced all across the world, from Africa to India.[93] Thus, Davis rose as a global symbol of an intersectional struggle against capitalism, imperialism, prisoners' repression, male chauvinism, and racism all together.

The National Lawyers Guild participated strongly in the mass defense effort, although the solidarity lineup was quite overcrowded and, paradoxically, Davis was seen as less an underdog than other unknown political prisoners.[94] Guild lawyers took part in the legal team who represented Davis, including John Abt, general counsel for the CPUSA and a longtime member of the NLG; Howard Moore Jr., who was involved with the NAACP Legal Defense Fund and had tried many civil rights cases; and former Guild president Doris B. Walker. They co-counseled Davis with Leo Branton, a lawyer for the Communist Party and the Black Panthers, and one of the first Black attorneys to own a law firm in California; and Margaret Burnham, a young staff attorney for the NAACP Legal Defense Fund and Davis's friend since childhood.

To demonstrate that Black lawyers were "every bit the equal" of their white colleagues, Davis had requested to be defended by a Black lawyer, so Branton acted as lead counsel.[95] But she had also asked Walker, an avowed Marxist-Leninist, to enter the case. Davis insisted on having "at least one member of the legal team who substantially shared her politics, and who could help her translate her politics into a form which would be useful, educational, and effective in the courtroom."[96] Davis also welcomed Walker's participation because she felt it was "politically important" for women to assume visible roles on defense teams.[97] Guild lawyers Sheldon Otis, Michael Tigar, Dennis Roberts, and Allan Brotsky, together with members of the National Conference of Black Lawyers and the ACLU, assisted in the preparation of pretrial motions, while the NLG, the California Federation of Teachers, and the ACLU joined as friends of the court in a writ of habeas corpus to release her on bail (denied until February 1972).[98]

Following the blueprint of militant litigation, Burnham masterminded an in-depth jury selection that lasted thirteen court days, as the specter of racial and political prejudice loomed large.[99] Branton, on his part, asked the judge to have the entire trial televised for the sake of publicity and transparency. Denied this motion, he demanded a larger courtroom to accommodate as many spectators as possible, once again to make the trial a political forum and to pressure the jury for an acquittal. The judge opposed this request, too. Having verified the extensive public sympathy and Davis's intentions, the defense team also opted for an aggressive strategy that put racism on trial. In Davis's words, since one could not expect justice from an inherently racist, repressive, and class-biased judicial system, "an exclusively legalistic approach . . . would be fatal."[100]

Such a strategy implied not only a classic politicization of the trial but also the role of Davis as co-counsel. More specifically, Davis tried to combine legal arguments elaborated by her attorneys with political issues delineated by herself. Fearing a disrespectful and outspoken defendant, the California Supreme Court denied her right to self-defense, but Davis nonetheless remained very active in the planning of legal moves.[101] She also spoke powerfully in court, notably at her arraignment when she defined herself as the target of "a political frame-up."[102] Finally, Branton played on a consummate tactic. In his closing argument, he framed Davis's behavior in the context of centuries of racism and abuse against Black people, and traced a historical parallel between Davis and the heroic Frederick Douglass, who had run away from justice after being charged with conspiracy in the antislavery raid on Harpers Ferry. According to the defense's argument, Douglass had been prosecuted "for having spoken so eloquently on the right of all men to be free." Precisely like Davis.[103]

In June 1972, after California abolished the death penalty and the two surviving Soledad Brothers were discharged, an all-white jury acquitted Davis of all charges. Even radical critics admitted that the trial had been relatively free from racial prejudice and political bias.[104] The tremendous agitation of millions of people had clearly set a favorable political climate that boded well for the defendant and likely influenced the jury. Interestingly, months before the verdict, when the judge granted bail, he had acknowledged the reception of an incredible number of letters, phone calls, and telegrams from foreign countries, all asking to free Davis. The judge did not admit he had yielded to public pressure, but recognized the impact of the unprecedented mobilization.[105] The legal-political campaign to free Angela Davis was so successful that the NUCFAD was not dissolved after the trial victory but renamed the Campaign to Free All Political Prisoners (later the National Alliance against Racist and Political Repression). Such organizations directed existing funds and resources to help other political prisoners, starting with Davis's co-defendant, Ruchell Magee.[106]

Magee's case was less fortunate, though. He was the only surviving participant of the August 7 raid and was now facing charges of kidnapping and murder in a separate trial.[107] In and out of jail since he was thirteen, and most recently convicted of kidnapping in 1963, Magee had taught himself to read using a legal dictionary and the Constitution. While developing quite advanced legal skills, he had become a "jailhouse lawyer," widely known across California penitentiaries. He had helped many fellow inmates in their cases and filed numerous suits exposing brutalities in prison. Given his knowledge, he opted for self-defense. However, since he had scored a low IQ on the tests, he was denied this right. A small defense committee formed in San Francisco but was backed only by Guild lawyers and lacked a broad and vociferous constituency.[108]

The stark contrast between Magee and Davis did not go unnoticed and was emphasized by the media. Davis stunned everyone with her intelligence and "imperious beauty," while enjoying "the best-organized, most broad-based defense effort in the recent history of radical political trials." Magee, "dressed in a formless gray prison jacket" and entering the courtroom shackled, looked "sullen" and desperately alone.[109] Eventually, Ramsey Clark agreed to represent him. After a hung jury, a retrial, and a guilty plea of kidnap, in 1975 Magee was finally given a sentence of seven years to life. Although the case was itself problematic and many factors contributed to the final outcome, the absence of a wide-ranging involvement of lawyers and outside supporters arguably exerted a considerable impact.

In the meantime, the experience of the Soledad case had generated further legal mobilization, once again animated by Fay Stender. Although she had left Jackson's defense team in early 1971, Stender had not given up her commitment to prisoners. "I certainly feel that, person per person, prisoners are better human beings than you would find in any random group of people. They are more loving. They have more concern for each other. They have more creative human potential," she wrote in 1972, leaving no doubt about her intentions.[110] Stender thus retained a nucleus of lawyers, legal workers, and activists who had cooperated with her in the previous months. While interviewing prisoners for the Soledad case and receiving an increasing number of letters from prisoners who requested assistance, this group of radicals had grown convinced that a task force was needed to operate across the California prison system. A dozen of them created the Prison Law Project.

Together, they investigated allegations of arbitrary behaviors on the part of prison guards and administrators, filed suits challenging illegal practices, recruited lawyers or volunteered to undertake indigent prisoners' cases themselves, assisted inmates who represented themselves, negotiated with correctional authorities to obtain better medical care or to increase visiting rights, and made sure to inform the public, particularly law students. Their "uninhibited manner to reach out to inmates," as Pearlman wrote, "was deemed as therapeutic for both lawyers and inmates" and reportedly included sexual acts between female legal assistants and male inmates.[111]

While funds were running dry and forced the Prison Law Project to halt its activities in 1973, a faction of the group, led by Patricia Roberts, formed an even more radical Prison Law Collective, which was housed in the San Francisco NLG office. The split between the two groups was tumultuous and bitter, anticipating the more traumatic divisions to come in the following years.[112]

The endless California prison turmoil and the Soledad Brothers case left yet another legacy, namely the legal struggle of the San Quentin Six—the Black and Latino prisoners who were charged with murder, assault, and conspiracy (also with Bingham) to help George Jackson escape. The case involved Guild lawyers, an aggressive trial strategy, and a defense committee. However, it already reflected a shift in the political mood. The extent of the public mobilization was not comparable with that of the cases of the early 1970s. Although the defense obtained the endorsement of a wide range of personalities, including Father Daniel Berrigan and Congressman Ronald Dellums, and attracted a few hundred demonstrators at initial support rallies, media coverage and fundraising were both scarce. Defense committee lawyers also seemed mostly concerned about keeping unity and solidarity among the six defendants in order to protect Bingham from possible betrayal. They feared that some of them would accept a deal and become prosecution witnesses.[113]

The case took nearly four years of legal maneuvering before coming to trial, losing its appeal among the public and wearing down prisoners' constituencies. Only the Guild resisted, working behind the scenes to challenge the grand jury indictments.[114] Charles Garry entered the case on behalf of Jonny L. Spain, a Black Panther and the youngest defendant. Thus the trial, which began in March 1975, was managed according to the customary principles of militant litigation. The defendants agreed to fight the case collectively and to challenge the indictments, arguing that the grand jury represented neither a jury of peers nor a cross-section of the community. Later on, the defense contended that a conspiracy to escape from San Quentin had never existed. Instead, law enforcement agencies had conspired to kill Jackson, while the six inmates had been brutally sacrificed for the sake of the plot.

To reinforce its offensive stance, the defense also filed a lawsuit challenging the brutal conditions of the adjustment center where the defendants were detained. Replicating the usual scheme, experts were invited to testify and explain the effects of solitary confinement, racial segregation, and power dynamics within prisons. Among them, Philip G. Zimbardo, the social psychologist at Stanford University who had just become famous for his controversial jail experiment, was called to the witness stand. Zimbardo argued that authoritarian and sadistic attitudes naturally emerge among guards within any prison environment, to the detriment of all inmates. Building on Zimbardo's findings, lawyers maintained that the dehumanizing conditions of maximum security had generated the spontaneous outburst of violence on August 21, 1971, regardless of individual acts. In other words, any prisoner could have killed those guards.

In August 1976, the jury delivered a mixed verdict by exonerating three defendants and convicting three others of various charges. An inmate conspiracy had occurred, and a gun had been smuggled in, but crucial responsibilities remained undetermined. As the whole case suggested, the prison movement had already ceased to exist as a mass phenomenon, making principled defense and public engagement for acquittal less effective.[115] In the meantime, however, the politics of prison rebellion had grown more important, and the case of Attica had shaken a generation.

· ·

"I have never quite recovered from Attica," admitted William Kunstler, remembering his involvement in the most violent prison rebellion in U.S. modern history. Kunstler's feeling was widely shared among Guild lawyers, who offered their characteristic legal, political, and emotional support in this momentous case. By all accounts, the engagement at Attica was at once seen as dreadful, because of the bloodshed; instructive, for the revelation of the darkest side of American law enforcement; and emboldening, thanks to the inspiration provided by the prisoners' courage. It was indeed a life-changing event for many radical lawyers, for the army of legal activists and law students who volunteered, and for the NLG itself, which promptly rallied around the rebellious inmates.[1]

Such a complex series of events has received a great deal of attention. Most recently, Heather A. Thompson has provided a fine-grained historical reconstruction that sheds light on even the most obscure and disputed details of this story. However, the meaning and the implications of the presence of radical lawyers and legal activists both during and after the Attica revolt continue to warrant a closer look. How, and to what extent, did they change the course of the events?

First of all, it is worth emphasizing that inmates' life inside Attica Correctional Facility had long been abysmal, in terms of food quality, medical care, working conditions, and internal discipline. Built in the 1930s to deal with prisoners' revolts, the fifty-acre penal complex was an archaic, overcrowded facility that housed more than twenty-two hundred inmates—54.2 percent Black, 8.7 percent Puerto Rican, and only 36.6 percent white—under the supervision of an almost all-white and poorly trained corps of correctional officers.[2] As political consciousness developed among the inmates, protests bubbled to the surface. The formation of groups who were affiliated with the Nation of Islam, the Black Panthers, and the Young Lords served to further catalyze and amplify existing discontent, as did the transfer from Auburn of a few dozen radicalized inmates. Samuel Melville, known as the Mad Bomber, had recently relocated to Attica and helped ignite these spirits. Highly regarded among inmates, Melville promoted cross-racial solidarity against the system and cofounded the Attica Liberation Faction, an informal group that came into being in May 1971 and submitted a manifesto with a list of demands soon after. In July, Melville also started writing and distributing an underground newsletter significantly titled the *Iced Pig*.[3]

Being a reformer who sincerely believed in the possibility of humanizing prisons, the recently appointed New York commissioner of corrections, Russell G. Oswald, had tried to address inmates' grievances. However, the long-awaited changes in prison conditions were hard to obtain, and inmates were impatient. Above all, inmates were distrustful of any government promise, especially after they heard rumors of the broken pledges at the Tombs and Auburn.[4] Reacting to the news that Jackson had been killed on August 21 at San Quentin, seven hundred prisoners participated in a day of mourning on August 22 by wearing armbands, sitting down in silence, and refusing meals. A stream of incidents and scuffles between inmates and guards took place in the following days, touching off the explosion of September 9, when a group of prisoners attacked a group of guards and unexpectedly succeeded in gaining control of D Yard—one of the central lawns of the facility. In the process, they injured some correctional officers and left one of them, William E. Quinn, mortally wounded.

By the afternoon of the same day, 1,281 prisoners—two-thirds of them Black—secured control of a large section of the prison. Wearing baseball helmets and brandishing bats, pipes, shovels, and other improvised weapons, they held fifty hostages, both correctional officers and civilian employees. Some of them would later be released due to injuries. The prisoners' first hours of freedom were predictably anarchic and violent, giving rise to abuses, rapes, and vandalism. Yet under the leadership of Black Muslims and thanks to a few respected inmates, such as Richard X. Clark and Elliot James "L. D." Barkley, order was partially restored. A committee was formed, food distribution was organized, a security force was established, hostages were given protection, and a pseudo-democratic system of deliberation was implemented. For four days, rebellious inmates assembled in D Yard, sleeping under the stars in a makeshift camp.[5]

In a rousing address, the bespectacled Barkley, now the informal spokesperson of the prisoners, shouted, "We are men! We are not beasts and do not intend to be beaten or driven." He warned that what happened at Attica was but "the sound before the fury" of the oppressed, who had just begun to cast light on the "ruthless brutalization and disregard for the lives of the prisoners." After making clear that they would "not compromise on any terms except those that [were] agreeable to [them]," Barkley called on "the conscientious citizens of America" to assist them and set forth a few urgent demands. These included "complete amnesty, meaning freedom from any physical, mental and legal reprisals"; "speedy and safe transportation . . . to a non-imperialist country"; and intervention by the federal government to place them under its jurisdiction. Finally, the prisoners requested the intervention of a group of sympathetic observers who were meant to witness the negotiation with the state for the release of the hostages in exchange for concessions—a negotiation they wanted to conduct under the eyes of the press.[6]

More than thirty people gathered at the prison's gate by the end of the second day (September 10), including most of the observers called on by the inmates, individuals recruited by the government, and those who spontaneously offered their services. The heterogeneous team consisted of, among others, New York State Democratic assemblymen Arthur O. Eve and Herman Badillo, Democratic senator Robert Garcia, Republican senator John R. Dunne, Rockefeller's urban affairs adviser Reverend Wyatt Tee Walker, publisher of the Harlem daily *Amsterdam News* Clarence B. Jones, former prisoner and Muslim leader Jaybarr Kenyatta, professor and civil rights lawyer Herman Schwartz, and *New York Times* political columnist Tom Wicker. Guild lawyers William Kunstler and Lewis Steel were also part of the group: Kunstler had been explicitly requested by the prisoners, while Steel joined the very first day of the revolt at the urge of the NLG, who believed it was key to have at least a Guild official on the scene.[7]

Commissioner Oswald bore responsibility for leading the negotiations, but he appeared constrained and rigid, despite his initial openness. Superior and inferior chains of command in the administration, not to speak of law enforcement, were eager to avoid concessions and retake the prison as soon as possible. The inmates drafted fifteen proposals, which Oswald could not entirely satisfy, hence tensions immediately grew. While the two radical lawyers pushed for a full (or at least partial) amnesty, Schwartz tried to play the card of legal appeasement and obtained a federal injunction, signed by a judge, against reprisals. The rebellious crowd rejected it and literally tore it up, on the (mistaken) grounds that it had no seal and could be appealed. In the following hours, Oswald decided to avoid further direct interactions with the rioters, and the ball passed to the observers, who entered the yard—for the first time all together—on the night of September 10. For thirty hours, they worked to achieve a settlement. Without a clear mandate—neither simple witnesses nor full negotiators—they found themselves in an ambiguous position.[8]

Kunstler, on the other hand, had a crystal-clear idea of his role. He militated on one side and was there to advocate that side's position. He later explained, "I felt that these men, society's outcasts, were my people, my constituents. . . . I wanted to demonstrate that I was with them completely and that I recognized the significance of this moment. I wanted them to know I was not just another lawyer with a briefcase saying, 'I'll do the best I can.' I wanted them to know that I was willing to go to the wire for them."[9] As he stood up in the yard, he shouted into the microphone, "*Palante*! All power to the people!" and inmates applauded and cheered. The disheveled lawyer reassured the insurgents, confirming that they had bargaining power and they could "reach ears." Prisoners, he said, had to lay down what they wanted, not what outsiders wanted. Casting a spell on the audience, he also stated that many of the observers loved inmates and despised the "shitty decrepit system." And specified: "We are your brothers . . . we hope." At that point, one of the prisoners took the microphone and asked him, "Brother Bill, will you be our lawyer? Will you represent the brothers as only you can?" After a theatrical pause, Kunstler returned to the microphone and accepted. Enthusiasm hit the roof.[10]

Later, another inmate moved forward and, making implicit reference to the battle in the Chicago courtroom and the contempt charges, demanded, "Brother Kunstler! What did they do with you in court?" Kunstler, as observer Tom Wicker recalled, rose like someone surrendering to a lover and threw his arms around the inmate. "There was pain and rapture in Kunstler's face, in his voice, as he cried out, 'The same thing they did with you, Brother!' The two men embraced, and once again there were cheers." When asked what he thought about the injunction that his colleague Schwartz had obtained, Kunstler replied that it was "not worth the paper it's written on." Amnesty still looked like a negotiable issue, and Kunstler, together with Steel, immediately recognized that judicial pardon was becoming the sine qua non for the resolution of the crisis.[11]

As one of the leaders of the revolt later revealed, inmates "wanted Kunstler for his legal mind. [They] felt that an involved lawyer like him would be the last person to allow a whitewash." They believed that "if he saw the conditions himself, he would definitely commit himself."[12] On his part, Kunstler was admittedly impatient to take part in a high-profile case that was both politically decisive and under the spotlight.[13] As a matter of fact, while accepting to serve as "inmates' attorney," Kunstler also took charge of collecting grievances; managed to let into the yard Thomas Soto, a Puerto Rican militant who had been denied entrance because he was considered a dangerous firebrand; and urged Bobby Seale to come to the prison, as re-quested by the inmates. As Thompson rightly put it, "Every observer could see that Kunstler was going to be an entirely new force with whom the state would have to reckon. He was assertive, unapologetic, and damned certain of himself."[14] Contrary to some of the other observers, such as the divisive Kenyatta, Kunstler was widely respected across racial lines and possessed much needed legal experience.

At that point, Kunstler suggested that inmates submit a second draft of demands to the government. Therefore, an executive committee of six, which also included Kunstler, took care of preparing the document. Com-missioner Oswald surveyed the thirty-three demands included in the draft and accepted twenty-eight of them. Although some of these points were de-liberately vague or contingent on legislative actions, most of them portended major advances in prison reform. No authority, however, was open to the hy-pothesis of an amnesty for penal crimes involving physical injury; the only acceptable concession was amnesty for civil charges. Fearing a violent fi-nale, the observers almost unanimously urged the inmates to approve the settlement. Kunstler himself insisted that they give full consideration to the twenty-eight points, though inmates alone had to make their own deci-sion. "I'm speaking to you now as a lawyer," he reportedly said, "and that may destroy my credibility with you, but as a lawyer I can tell you this is the best we can do for you at this time." And he added, "We don't want people to die. You can turn it down, though. You have an absolute right to do that, but I wouldn't be fair to you if I didn't tell you what the consequences might be. . . . I recommend that you accept it."[15]

With a heavy heart, Kunstler also confirmed that the injured officer Quinn had died and murder prosecutions were possible, potentially hitting any participant in the insurrection. Implicitly, the amnesty became even more vital. Seale's appearance in the yard hardly helped to reach a settle-ment. The Black Panther leader delivered a brief speech refusing to endorse the twenty-eight-point compromise and asking for more time to discuss the matter with the Panthers' leadership. He came back to Attica the day after, was denied entry into the prison, and eventually read a communiqué that rejected any compromise solution.[16] In the meantime, however, the barri-caded inmates had already concluded that the proposal was unacceptable and refused to properly discuss it. The leadership had ripped the document up, amid roars of approval.

While a brutal retaking of the prison was already in the air, Kunstler ex-plored at least two options that might hold off the worst. First, with other observers, he called on Governor Rockefeller to come to Attica to meet with the inmates and assure them he would not seek judicial revenge. Rockefeller, who was firm in his intransigence and also nurtured presidential ambitions as a law-and-order candidate, staunchly refused to open a dialogue with violent captives.[17] Second, Kunstler made some moves to allow prisoners to be rescued by a "non-imperialist country," such as Algeria or North Vietnam, as they had initially requested. Forlorn as it was, this hypothesis was still mentioned in Kunstler's last speech on September 12, when observers entered the yard for the last time. In a highly nervous and gloomy atmosphere, Kunstler said that there were "four third-world and African country people across the street from [the] prison prepared to provide asylum for everyone that want[ed] to leave this country." He later testified that he had spoken with members of the BPP who claimed they carried offers of asylums, but he admitted that "there was no one waiting across the street and the Panthers' proposals were limited to providing asylum only after inmates had completed their sentences."[18]

The observers' mediation ended bitterly. Some have accused Kunstler of raising false hopes among prisoners and encouraging their intransigence— for example, by maintaining that amnesty was negotiable or that transfer abroad was a viable option. Kunstler has also been charged with jeopardizing the unity of the observers' team with his unbending defense of the inmates' will and of generating a conflict of interest by assuming the task of inmates' attorney instead of remaining a neutral witness. According to critics, he also mistakenly gave confidence to the "democracy" of prisoners in the yard, who were, on the contrary, prey to radical leaders and hardly unanimous. Kunstler's "ego trip" and unconcealed desire to please rebellious inmates, the reasoning goes, did nothing but complicate the task.[19]

All these criticisms contain a grain of truth. Kunstler undeniably raised expectations and helped to prolong a deadlocked negotiation. However, other factors were decisive in leading toward the tragic end. Authorities' and inmates' uncompromising stances and reciprocal distrust contributed more than anything else to the failure of a settlement. Suffice it to read the memories of Richard X. Clark, a Black Muslim minister and a leader of the revolt, to realize how radical inmates distrusted white men's promises, doubted the negotiating power of the observers, and felt that they had nothing to lose if they went on a rampage.[20] The death of officer Quinn also hardened mutual incomprehension and pushed the two parties to a dead end.

Kunstler, on his part, given his revolutionary credentials and the confidence he inspired among inmates, was not necessarily an obstacle on the way to a settlement. By contrast, a truly competent yet politically moderate lawyer such as Schwartz was jeered when he told prisoners that their demand to be flown out of the country was unrealistic. Schwartz himself admitted that inmates were in no mood to hear him saying that their requests were impractical, so he left the yard on the second day.[21] Moreover, Kunstler insisted that the twenty-eight points were, at that stage, the best possible outcome and sincerely hoped that Bobby Seale could endorse them. As it has been recognized by fellow observers, he put "all his prestige on the line at the one moment when it really mattered."[22] Kunstler also believed, as many others did, that Rockefeller was interested in reaching an agreement. Ultimately, Kunstler's somehow groundless and daring statements have to be seen not so much as forms of narcissism or unethical behavior but as quintessential expressions of militant lawyering. Contrary to other observers in the yard, he totally refused to impose a legal strategy, strove to support militants even at the psychological level, and identified with the inmates' struggle. Of course, such an attitude entailed high risks and was politically debatable, but it would be inaccurate to blame it for the failure of negotiations.[23]

By the evening of September 12, Oswald decided that the dialogue had to end, and access to D Yard would need to be barred. He felt that he had given everything but received nothing, so the revolt had to be quelled. Rockefeller authorized the New York State Police to lead an armed assault on the prison, backed by the National Guard and correctional officers. Persuaded that the takeover was planned for the day after, eight observers decided to stay overnight in the administrative building of the prison, hoping to exert a moderating influence on the law enforcers and to be ready to assist. Oswald sent another ultimatum the morning after, September 13, but the inmates rejected it. They began arming themselves and moved eight of the hostages to a visible catwalk, surrounding them with men handling rudimentary knives. Although the majority of prisoners did not expect an attack with firearms, they were now ready, as they pledged, "to die like men."[24]

As the official report of the New York State Special Commission on Attica made clear, the assault "was not carefully planned to minimize the loss of life"; "no safeguards were established to protect against excessive use of force by those who were authorized to fire"; "no adequate arrangements were made for medical care" of the casualties, which should have been anticipated; and "no responsible system was established to prevent vengeful reprisals against inmates after the retaking." At 9:46 a.m., an orange helicopter dropped a cloud of tear gas on the yard. A few seconds later, troopers opened fire on the inmates, killing twenty-nine prisoners and ten hostages, and wounding approximately eighty people in less than fifteen minutes.[25] "With the exception of Indian massacres in the late 19th century," asserted the report, "the State Police assault which ended the four-day prison uprising was the bloodiest one-day encounter between Americans since the Civil War."[26]

Predictably, troopers and correctional officers unloaded their rage and let off their frustration about the long breakdown of order. Racial and political hatred did the rest. With no clear strategy for rescuing the hostages, no signs of identification, and no ammunition accountability, police forces killed in cold blood and exerted hideous abuses and tortures on prisoners—even on those who surrendered, and particularly on the leaders of the insurrection. Medical neglect—to some extent intentional—worsened the already dramatic situation. The official spokesperson for the Correctional Services Department immediately stated that prisoners had murdered all hostages and that several of them had been found with their throats slashed. This was a blatant lie to cover a disastrous law enforcement operation. In fact, all victims died from bullet or buckshot wounds, as autopsies soon revealed. Moreover, many of them were shot in the back, suggesting that they were running away without posing any imminent danger. Prisoners, it must be recalled, did not possess any firearms.[27]

Attica: After the Fury

"The very day of the Attica takeover," remembers Emily Goodman, "I happened to be at the Guild office when Kunstler's call came, saying that the place was going to blow up and that lawyers, and probably doctors, were needed. I was one of the lawyers who went there immediately." A group of lawyers thus drove to the airport, flew to Buffalo in the afternoon of September 13, prepared the papers to obtain access to the prison through a federal order, and got a judge to sign it. On the spot there was already a small contingent of attorneys and legal workers from Chicago, Boston, Philadelphia, and New York, who had rushed to Attica's gates on September 11. Now there were about fifteen of them, accompanied by medical personnel.

"But, when we got there by car," explains Goodman, "we realized that our court order was not worth anything. We found armed police and military. A person checked our papers. I said: 'I have a court order.' He said: 'I got a bayonet.' That was a startling moment, not only for me but also for other people. We went to law school, we believed in lawyers, court orders, judges: that gave us some power. But that was one quick lesson about how little all that meant. . . . Justice was very elusive, and it didn't matter that we were lawyers."[28]

Denied access to the prison by the warden, the lawyers spent the night outside the gate, as they wanted to get into the penitentiary as soon as possible. They were still there the morning after, when medical analysts said that all the prisoners had been shot by government agents and not by inmates. Rage escalated, but the Correctional Services Department still denied access, allegedly for security reasons. On September 17, only lawyers, without medical personnel, were allowed to step into the prison. The Guild immediately sent five persons to interview inmates and preserve evidence, which ran the risk of being contaminated.[29] In the meantime, the Guild sponsored the first class action on behalf of the Attica prisoners to compel the State of New York to institute criminal prosecutions against Rockefeller, Oswald, Attica warden Vincent R. Mancusi, and other state police and correction officers for committing, conspiring to commit, or aiding and abetting in the commission of crimes against inmates and guards at Attica, including murder, manslaughter, and assault.[30]

To be sure, Guild lawyers were not alone at the prison. The Legal Aid Society, the ACLU, and the Council of New York Law Associates were also present, feeling the urge to provide their support.[31] A hundred alleged prison leaders had been placed in solitary confinement and denounced it as a violation of their civil rights, while other prisoners wanted to sue the state for damages. Since the very beginning, however, Guild lawyers differentiated themselves by regarding inmates as "political prisoners" and sought to capture their political claims and channel them into a common strategy—something that other, more neutral legal organizations disregarded.[32] Guild lawyers also promised absolute identification with defendants' plight. As a dense correspondence confirms, many of the inmates, who lamented persisting intimidation, dehumanization, and victimization, specifically requested the exclusive "commitment" of Guild lawyers for "a total defense."[33]

Despite divergent approaches, a loose coalition of these legal groups, plus the NAACP Legal Defense Fund, the Harlem Lawyers Association, the National Conference of Black Lawyers (NCBL), and the Center for Constitutional Rights, was rapidly set up under the name Attica Defense Committee (ADC). In January 1972, the ADC was formalized with the institution of a "non-profit charitable trust," whose scope was raising funds and providing legal talents for the defense of inmates in cases arising out of incidents related to prison conditions. The ADC also committed to work on affirmative legal actions for the rights of detainees and to disseminate information on prisons. "To forestall feelings of isolation and hopelessness," the ADC pledged to foster links between the movements inside and outside prisons, thus creating a broader base of support for inmates. Legal workers, ex-prisoners, concerned citizens, and students joined the group in addition to lawyers. Haywood Burns, a former counsel to Martin Luther King and a co-founder of the NCBL, was named president, while Guild lawyers David Scribner and Barbara Handschu served as vice presidents. Three young Guild lawyers began staffing an office in Buffalo, initially funded by the Legal Aid Society and the ACLU.[34]

As mentioned, surviving prisoners were the objects of brutality and hu-miliating retaliation in the days after the takeover. They were stripped na-ked, beaten with clubs, threatened, kept in solitary lockup, and denied elementary rights. Guards also confiscated or destroyed most of their per-sonal property. In response, Guild lawyers filed several suits to denounce these punitive treatments. In conjunction with other groups, the Guild also filed motions challenging the special Attica grand jury, which was seated in Warsaw, New York, to investigate the events. They unsuccessfully con-tested both its venue—Wyoming County, a predominantly white and con-servative area where the prison was a major employer—and its composition, which was unsurprisingly all white. A speakers bureau was also created to inform the public about the development of the case, its main goal being to present the inmates' view of the rebellion and counteract the false re-ports that abounded from both official sources and the press. It is worth noting that radical lawyers were among the very few who denounced the campaign of systematic disinformation that, years later, would emerge. As a matter of fact, in the immediate aftermath of the takeover, the governor's office, prison administrators, and police authorities tried to remove or con-taminate evidence; spread false rumors, such as the unfounded claim that inmates had castrated an observer; and cultivated a common version of the events to cover up their misconduct.[35]

Guild lawyers were particularly active in this campaign to shape a coun-ternarrative, and Kunstler figured prominently among them.[36] Speaking at the State University of New York at Buffalo the day after the takeover, the "inmates' lawyer" defined Rockefeller as a "murderer" and called for his resignation. The "real murderers," he accused, "wore uniforms" and "had state-issued weapons and ammunition." Hosted by the *David Frost Show* that same night, Lewis Steel also railed against Rockefeller, whose "class pre-rogatives," according to the lawyer, were so entrenched that he had been ready to sacrifice white guards for the sake of order.[37] A few days later, invited to participate in a "counterdedication" for a new law school building at Georgetown University, Kunstler spoke from a truck and eulogized the rebellious prisoners of Attica: "the heroes who died there," "the finest men I have ever known." Echoing a standard argument of those years, Kunstler admitted that in the course of the negotiations in the yard he realized that "there are many more decent persons in prison than on the outside."[38]

Such a celebration of the revolt and its protagonists was indeed very common within the Guild milieu. Some Chicago lawyers, for example, acknowledged that the insurrection had shown both "the heights that a revolutionary society can reach," given the inmates' heroism and spirit of loyalty, and "the darkest side of Amerikan [sic] fascism and genocide," as "thousands of rampaging state troopers" attempted to destroy "the most noble of all struggles against Amerika."[39] Similarly, Guild lawyer Dan Pochoda, who had been at Attica since September 13, reported how he was inspired by inmates' courage, perception, political understanding, solidarity, and will to resist. He was taught "that a person must resist the forces of oppression, of racism and exploitation in every context, that a person must constantly fight the humiliations and indignities or die." An act of resistance at the highest level, Attica had shown that "an effective, multi-racial organization under third-world leadership" was able to take control "in the most controlled of institutions" and to expose worldwide that "Amerika's rulers" were liars and murderers.[40]

Since many inmates indicated that they wished to communicate only with Guild attorneys, with whom they could "exchange views and speak freely," the NLG strove to maintain a daily presence around the prison for several months. However, in May 1972, fifty-five leaders of the rebellion, who had worked together on their defense with the help of the Guild, were transferred to six different prisons. This was hardly surprising, as correctional authorities were afraid of their collective power and wanted to break their link with alleged outsider agitators. The Guild tried to stay the transfers, but it proved to be impossible.[41]

Reportedly "swamped with hundreds of inmate letters containing a myriad of requests," from complex legal issues to demands for books, the Guild increasingly realized that one of the main prisoner concerns—at Attica but also elsewhere—was the need to share problems and to correspond with someone who was possibly sympathetic. Hence, not only did the NLG constantly look for volunteers who could answer this torrent of mail, but it also began publishing a monthly newsletter called *Midnight Special*, whose first issue was printed in November 1971. Through this paper, inmates could communicate with one another, express their grievances, cut their sense of isolation, get basic legal and medical information, and develop their politics.[42]

Russell T. Neufeld, a young Guild lawyer who had been close to the Weatherman and had jail experience of his own, served as first managing editor, giving the paper a radical edge. A collective of eight people—a mix of leftist activists, legal workers, and former convicts—compiled the newsletter from the basement of the New York City Guild office. Published under the Guild logo so that it could be accepted as "legal mail" inside penitentiaries, the paper was sent to prisoners throughout the state of New York. Although many deliveries were confiscated, *Midnight Special* gradually acquired a total circulation of forty-five hundred, without considering hand-to-hand dissemination. Given the scarcity of inmate publications allowed within correctional facilities, its impact was significant, and the number of prisoner contributions constantly increased. The pages of the newsletter were filled with inmate letters, poems, and artworks that related to concomitant struggles, expressed similar complaints, and adopted strikingly homogeneous rhetoric. Interestingly, in order to respect prisoners' voices, the editors refrained from proofreading and polishing the texts, which were indeed printed in their original form.[43]

In the meantime, in December 1972, after thirteen months of hearings, the special Attica grand jury handed down its initial thirty-seven indictments—it was just a first batch, and the jury remained in session. Sixty Attica Brothers were charged with crimes ranging from murder to possession of a prison key. Only prisoners were indicted. The ADC immediately accelerated the recruitment of lawyers, so that any defendant could have a trusted attorney instead of a court-appointed counsel, and demanded that the state officials responsible for the conditions that led to the revolt and for the "mass murder" be brought to justice. The committee also urged sympathizers to "pack the courthouse" in order to demonstrate their solidarity with the Attica Brothers and to show the authorities they were being watched.[44]

A few days later, when the arraignments took place in Warsaw, inmates declined to enter pleas and, to dramatize repression, refused to walk into the courtroom, often forcing prison guards to drag them. The defendants turned to their supporters in the audience and rhetorically asked them if they—the people—indicted them. The answer was a loud no.[45] Richard Bilello, a white jailhouse lawyer and a member of the NLG, protested that he had been kept in chains for the previous eight hours, was not permitted to shave or shower, was not allowed to use the restroom, and could not call his lawyer. Theatrically, he opened his shirt to show five scars on his abdomen that he got when prison guards put cigars on him after Attica was retaken. While the sympathetic audience cheered, the judge removed him from the courtroom. Right after, Franck Smith, aka Big Black, called the indictment "toilet paper" and sent "greetings of love and power" to the spectators.[46]

Serious problems, however, soon surfaced. Defendants were numerous, and the ambitious pledge to "get every brother a lawyer" had to be honored, together with the commitment to preserve "a unified resistance against the prosecution." A large number of experienced attorneys were promptly needed—not just the activists and legal workers who represented the majority of the volunteers. And yet, despite their generic proclamations of solidarity, many lawyers had no intention of getting embroiled in complicated cases that were to be tried in a remote place over a period of up to eight months. The ADC could make no commitments about covering expenses, let alone fees.[47]

A legal coordinator was needed, and Donald A. Jelinek was recruited. A prison attorney who lived in a Berkeley commune, Jelinek had given up a Wall Street job to work with the civil rights movement in the South. He had later assisted the Native Americans who had seized Alcatraz prison and worked alongside Fay Stender. In March 1973, he agreed to fly to upstate New York "to mold a disparate defense effort into one well-oiled legal and political machine."[48] Meanwhile, the legal defense of the Attica Brothers became a Guild national project and a summer project for 1973. Beginning in mid-June, lawyers, legal workers, and law students gathered in a two-hundred-year-old farmhouse in Victory, New York, to work together on the defense effort. Victory was near Auburn prison, where most of the Attica defendants had been sent. The group was aware of facing "one of the most massive political prosecutions in [the] country's history." However, disorganization, divergent political outlooks, lack of resources, sexism, and elitism seemed to put a spoke in the Guild's wheel. Indeed, Jelinek had a hard time dealing with the younger volunteers, which he portrayed as "callow sloganeering young crusaders." According to him, they had alienated community organizers, refused to be directed by seasoned lawyers, and advocated a "suicidal" politicization of trials.[49]

The old-time contrast between radicals and moderate leftists risked compromising everything. But that strange communal house did not collapse, and by the fall, attorneys from all over the country were rushing to the Brothers' aid, ready to file pretrial motions and to investigate state claims. On September 7, 1973, the second batch of forty-two felony indictments, totaling 1,289 counts, was handed down against sixty-three prisoners. The key indictments regarded the killing of officer Quinn and implicated two Native Americans who were represented by William Kunstler and Ramsey Clark.[50] On September 21, the ADC morphed into the Attica Brothers Legal Defense (ABLD), which explicitly combined legal and political goals. Based in New York City, the ABLD built branches in Victory, Buffalo, Syracuse, and Rochester, New York, as well as in Detroit, Chicago, and Berkeley. Its fifty-to sixty-person staff included eighteen defense attorneys and at least twenty-eight investigators. Funds finally began pouring in, mostly through community groups such as FIGHT (Freedom, Integration, God, Honor, Today) and BUILD, and through lawyers' networks, such as the Association of the Bar of the City of New York.[51]

Since the task seemed colossal—the legal defense planned to contact over four thousand witnesses, volumes of physical evidence had to be sorted and filed, and a massive jury selection needed to be prepared—during the summer of 1974 the Guild sent another twenty law students to New York and Buffalo to assist the ABLD, and also to contribute in the community network and fundraising.[52] The legal-organizational machine was now working well, particularly because the ABLD was able to recruit Haywood Burns to go to Buffalo and coordinate the team when Jelinek stepped down. Young leftist lawyer Elizabeth Fink and Big Black were sent along to back him up. "The three were a successful triangle," remembers Martin Stolar, who managed the New York office.[53] Fresh out of law school, Fink was deeply outraged after watching the revolt and the takeover on television. Later, when the indictments were handed down, she felt the urge to do something: "I decided that I needed to find out what it was like to be a lawyer," she recalled. In July 1974, she entered the ABLD and, for twenty-six years, she represented one of the pillars of the legal mobilization.[54]

The ABLD succeeded both in forcing the state to disclose any evidence it planned to use and in moving the trial venue from the secrecy of the Attica prison to Buffalo. Following the radical lawyers' playbook, the ABLD organized the Fair Jury Project, which worked earnestly to gather data on the jury pools and their probable opinions. Beth Bonora, a young Guild lawyer, was in charge of this mission, welcoming on board statisticians, social scientists, and a team of investigators that included Jay Schulman and David Kairys. The Fair Jury Project successfully contested the Buffalo jury pool, which was known to be overwhelmingly composed of aged white men. Through a survey of random people in the area, the project documented racial disparity and underrepresentation of women, which was due to the fact that women typically asked for exemption or excuse, so their husbands were selected ex ante.[55]

After a $4 million state investigation that involved twenty specially appointed attorneys general and required three years of work, the trials began in September 1974. The hardest challenge for the ABLD was to fashion and keep together a common political strategy for the Brothers—a strategy that combined militant goals and effective judicial outcomes without loosening the solidarity pact among defendants. However, two dominant legal philosophies emerged within the ABLD. Moderates intended to discharge inmates by demonstrating their innocence on legalistic grounds, whereas radicals were eager to mount an aggressive political campaign to put the state on trial and justify inmates' violation of the law as a response to the barbarous conditions of imprisonment. Radicals were also identifying with the defendants, building strong human bonds and even romantic liaisons.[56]

But the Attica Brothers' attitudes were not monolithic either. Some of them preferred to be simply discharged, postponing or avoiding political contention, while others were ready to risk their judicial position to denounce state brutality. The same held true with respect to the agency in the defense: some prisoners opted for entrusting their lawyers with all responsibilities, while others, usually the most politicized, claimed a more active role and typically demanded to act as co-counsel. Others again directly contested the "white leadership" in the legal field and invoked self-defense.[57]

As always, the enhanced commitment of lawyers brought together discussions and divisions. Therefore, trial strategies varied quite a bit, and so did their outcomes. The aforementioned Richard Bilello surprisingly refused radical lawyers' help and pleaded guilty in the very first Attica case that went to court. On the contrary, in the prosecution for the death of officer Quinn, for which Native American prisoners John Hill and Charles Joe Pernasalice were indicted, two lines of defense emerged. William Kunstler and his girlfriend Margaret Ratner defended Hill with an openly militant strategy, while Ramsey Clark, Herman Schwartz, and others represented Pernasalice with a more traditional and by-the-book approach.

Kunstler sought to politicize the case as much as possible, so he participated in street demonstrations, insisted on denouncing state violence, decried the neglect of prisoners, and vehemently challenged the jury selection on the basis of the data collected by the ABLD. He also attempted to expose the racial prejudices that allegedly motivated the prosecution. Therefore, he referred to Hill by his Indian name, Dacajeweih; wore Indian ornaments in the courtroom; and beat an Indian drum outside the courtroom for the press. At the same time, Hill showed up with a ribbon in his long hair and was escorted by a claque of tribesmen, including Mad Bear, a spiritual leader who sported conspicuous traditional garments. Kunstler concluded with a poignant seven-hour summation that needed an additional day to be completed.

However, the judge systematically denied defense motions and barred any evidence that was not strictly related to the murder. Although only faltering evidence linked the two inmates to the actual beating that left Quinn dead, the jury found Hill guilty of murder. He was sentenced to twenty years to life. By contrast, Pernasalice was sentenced to second-degree attempted assault and received an indeterminate sentence of up to three years. As Kunstler's biographer, David Langum, noticed, the temper of America in 1975 was far more conservative than it had been during the Chicago Eight trial, and the case of Attica failed to catalyze the same level of sympathy and mobilization, even on the Left. Once again, militant litigation was contingent on environmental conditions. The judge and the jury, who were visibly unreceptive to Kunstler's showy style, were indeed more sensitive to what public opinion demanded—namely, someone to blame for the officer's death.[58]

Clearly different was the following trial for the murder of inmate Barry Schwartz, whose dead body was found in a deserted area of the prison along with the remains of two other prisoners. Bernard Stroble, aka Shango—a Black inmate with a turbulent and violent past—was charged with first-degree murder and kidnapping of his fellow inmates during the insurrection. Shango, who always denied all charges, had the chance of being represented by Ernest Goodman and Haywood Burns, who not only volunteered to defend him but also accepted him as a co-counsel. In Goodman's words, "a process of mutual education" developed, and Shango, who proved to be articulate and profound, earned "enormous respect."

As Goodman explained, the defense team resolved to strike a balance between legal and political goals. They sought "to develop a strong, forward-looking, consistent logical attack," making every effort "to show the jurors they were 'humane and concerned'" and to demonstrate they were "personally, intimately, and fully committed" to the vindication of both a person and a cause they believed in. The defense purposely avoided picket lines outside the courtroom and other overtly contentious tactics. Unexpectedly, the judge granted a motion that challenged the entire jury pool, for it was white, male, and middle class, and had close relationships with law enforcement. The Fair Jury Project once again scored a crucial point. The defense also succeeded in discrediting the prosecution's witnesses, revealing that they had been coached and manipulated. In his closing remarks, Burns deplored the treatment of Shango and defined it as "part and parcel of the 400-year victimization of Black people after being kidnapped from Africa." While the kidnapping charges were reduced to unlawful imprisonment, the jury acquitted the defendant of the murder charge. Pandemonium broke out in the courtroom. It was a victory of "moderate" radicalism and a success for the whole ABLD. Goodman wept.[59]

In fact, the wind had already shifted a few months before, when one of the special prosecutors of the case decided to blow the whistle. It was April 8, 1975, when Malcolm N. Bell, a chief assistant prosecutor in the Attica case, spoke to the *New York Times* to tell the world that the prosecutors who investigated the revolt had systematically prevented any legal action against the law enforcement officers who ended the siege, despite a large volume of evidence against them. "I couldn't call witnesses, I couldn't ask questions, I couldn't pursue leads," he protested, suggesting that authorities had pushed for a cover-up. As a matter of fact, Bell had resigned from the team, written a letter to the state attorney general outlining his complaints, and sent a report to the newly elected New York Governor, Hugh L. Carey, alleging that he had been thwarted from the top.[60]

Similar complaints of "fabrication and selective prosecution" were neither unrealistic nor isolated. Before anyone else, the ADC had denounced them, then lawyers had spelled them out in court, and later two state commissions—in particular the one headed by the dean of the NYU School of Law, Robert B. McKay—had reiterated them. Even state legislators had questioned why only inmates had been indicted, whereas state troopers and guards had been left out of any prosecution. And yet no legal action had been taken, and the fact that in August 1974 President Gerald Ford had nominated Rockefeller vice president hardly helped. Now, however, it was no longer possible to overlook the facts. By December 1976, Governor Carey halted all prosecutions, issued a pardon for some Attica inmates, and commuted the sentence for John Hill, who would be eligible for parole shortly after.

A bittersweet feeling pervaded Guild lawyers and activists. It was a victory, if only an elusive, deferred, and painful one. Former prisoners and their families, as well as hostages' families, had been denied justice for years and still lamented that authorities had forgotten them. Then, in the early 1990s, ex-prisoner Big Black brought attention to the fact that a class action, filed in 1974, which sued the governor and other state officials for damages, was still alive albeit dormant. Twenty years after the revolt and with little hope of winning anything, Elizabeth Fink decided to reopen the case. So Big Black and Fink set up the Attica Justice Committee. With the help of other radical attorneys and volunteers, they won a historic decision establishing that the civil rights of Attica inmates had been violated—also with "cruel and unusual punishment"—and that the state had to refund them. A settlement was reached only in January 2000, when the state finally agreed to pay $12 million, to be apportioned between prisoners and attorneys. Since some prisoners were not being adequately compensated, lawyers gave up a portion of their share. Although the state never admitted wrongdoing nor issued official apologies, defense lawyers and militants could stand tall. They had not fought in vain.[61]

From Total Engagement to Disillusion

In the wake of San Quentin, Soledad, and Attica, Guild attorneys and activists channeled unprecedented attention and energies toward prisons. A myriad of small, or simply lesser-known, battles on behalf of rebellious inmates were initiated across the country: prison task forces, committees to analyze inmates' and ex-inmates' needs, groups to provide post-conviction legal services, constituencies to advocate the release of prisoners, conferences on prison legal-political work, and suits to lessen the consequences of political actions and to keep prison administrators under watch.[62]

Considering that coercion and isolation were the traditional strategies for dealing with unruly prisoners, the fight against "punitive segregation" was a constant of Guild lawyers' engagement during that period. The case of Martin Sostre, a Black Puerto Rican, raised particular attention. Sostre was first incarcerated on drug charges in 1953 and remained in prison until 1964, spending four years in solitary confinement due to his Muslim activism. Only three years later, he was once again incarcerated, after the police found several heroin doses in the bookstore he had opened in Buffalo. Sostre's detention conditions, his repeated seclusion in punitive segregation, and his stubborn opposition to prison discipline troubled many. A lawsuit filed on his behalf began a series of inquiries into the issues of due process and prison punishment. Eventually, a judge awarded him compensatory damages and forbade prison officials to isolate him without a hearing. Sostre remained incarcerated until 1975, when his sentence was commuted by Governor Carey in response to pressures from Amnesty International and the Martin Sostre Defense Committee.[63]

Remarkable success also came in August 1973, when the Court of Appeals for the Seventh Circuit rendered its decision on a class-action lawsuit—filed by Taylor and Deutsch of the People's Law Office—challenging the unconstitutional incarceration of 103 inmates of the Marion Federal Penitentiary. A maximum-security prison built in 1963 to manage difficult male felons in rural Illinois, Marion ended up secluding some of the most rebellious prisoners in the federal system. As a matter of fact, during the spring of 1972, federal authorities had transferred there approximately one hundred inmates who had taken part in political disturbances across the country's penitentiaries, with the aim of insulating them and making them undergo behavior modification programs. And yet by that summer, a multiracial group of prisoners was organizing coordinated protests and strikes against the harshness of the disciplinary methods. As a result, the prisoners suffered brutalities, harassment, and indefinite segregation in special units where isolation was coupled with sensory deprivation.

As always, Guild lawyers, together with ACLU and NAACP lawyers and Congressman Dellums, came to their aid. The aforementioned lawsuit charged prison officials with cruel and unusual punishment and the denial of access to courts, of procedural standards for prisoners placed in solitary confinement, and of rights to freedom of religion and freedom of speech in the mail. After a long battle and a series of setbacks, the lawyers succeeded in convincing the judge that indefinite confinement in the special units could be disproportionate punishment—therefore cruel and unusual—and it was always so if it was retaliation for a strike. The convicts held in isolation at Marion for eighteen months were promptly released.[64]

A couple of years later, Guild lawyers intervened again on the same terrain, this time at Bedford Hills, a New York State correctional facility that housed about 380 female prisoners serving sentences above one year, mostly Black and poor. After episodes of beatings and revolts, twenty-eight women were singled out as ringleaders of the rebellion and placed in segregation, while another fifty were put in twenty-four-hour lockup in their cells. Those "in seg," as they used to say, were permitted neither showers nor recreation for the first week. As this and other cases made clear, incarcerated women suffered the mutually reinforcing discrimination of being both female and prisoners. A Guild attorney filed a class action on behalf of the twenty-eight segregated women against the Bedford administration to declare the punishments unconstitutional. Prisoners were eventually granted due process rights before any confinement in punitive segregation.[65]

The attempts to establish some limited rule of law inside penitentiaries, the increasing external attention on prison conditions, and the inmates' enduring agitation forced prison officials to develop programs that could enforce order while avoiding open physical violence and adverse publicity. These techniques could be presented as nonpunitive but rather based on treatment and rehabilitation. It was a throwback to the early sixties. Ten years later, however, these special programs increasingly targeted rebellious prisoners. Radical lawyers immediately cried them down: in their view, these were pernicious forms of control and behavior modification that continued to segregate prisoners while denying them due process. Treatment and rehabilitation, denounced the lawyers, simply transferred authority to professionals who arbitrarily assessed the state of inmates' minds.[66]

At a time when the subject was still taboo, Guild lawyers revealed that behavior modification techniques included severe sensory deprivation, electroshock, and drug conditioning. They also exposed that the practice of psychiatry guided and legitimized these methods. Echoing the leftist criticism of "total institutions" and the anti-psychiatric zeitgeist, Guild lawyers dubbed prisoners' behavior modification as a form of "psycho-fascism" and condemned its experimentation.[67] According to a Guild report based on clients' information, prisoners denounced electroshock on the penis to cure homosexuality, lobotomy to leave individuals in a totally passive state, and "psychosurgery" to stimulate specific areas of the brain. The newly created National Behavioral Research Center in Butner, North Carolina; the Illinois State Penitentiary in Joliet; and the Federal Medical Facility in Springfield, Missouri, were the main institutions where these treatments allegedly occurred. Obviously, lawyers pledged to halt them.[68]

Yet the prison engagement of radical lawyers rapidly faded around the mid-1970s. Although a broad movement had shed light on the dark side of penitentiaries, gained undeniable victories, and obtained the implementation of a set of protections for prisoners, disillusion loomed large.[69] After titanic efforts, many radical lawyers viewed prison work as increasingly fruitless and even dangerous. Two main circumstances played a role in shifting perception. First, success in federal and state actions appeared to some "negligible." A comprehensive "prison reform" or a change of paradigm with respect to prison conditions did not materialize.[70] Meaningful relief was perceived as "uncertain at best," even when inmates had won formal protection of constitutional rights. If anything, suits helped to catalyze public attention on the "cruel mockery" of a system that promised equal justice under the law and denied it.[71] Scarred by cover-ups and human tragedies, the outcomes of the Soledad and the Attica cases obviously contributed to raising skepticism.

Second, the confidence that the whole leftist movement, including radical lawyers, had placed in prisons, elevating them as the most advanced battle-front in the new American revolution, had often proved exaggerated if not misplaced. As the Attica massacre confirmed, "revolution from within," in the absence of an external political force, appeared "futile" and "a sorry waste of human life." Without a leading movement in civil society, radical prisoners felt abandoned when they discovered that free citizens were not necessarily on the barricades.[72] Interviewed by Guild lawyers, Huey Newton reiterated this concept: "A revolution in the prison will not take place without revolution in the outside society." Hence, in the early 1970s, those who called for a revolution in the United States were "infantile leftists."[73]

Even Guild members doing prison work in California—the epicenter of prison radicalism—began questioning both the revolutionary potential of in-mates and the meaning of their efforts. In a position paper, for example, they admitted that their idealization of prisoners and the "incredible amounts of romanticism" they injected into the struggle had been "very petty bourgeois" and stemmed from their own "self-hate." The great majority of prisoners were not, "in the strict sense," "political prisoners" and, because of their per-sonal vicissitudes, were often individualist and without discipline. This led them to impatience, militarism, or despair.[74] As a journalist put it, lawyers realized they had been "purblinded" by their own rhetoric.[75]

Far from being an exemplary and reliable vanguard, radical inmates had sometimes behaved disastrously. Indeed, taking inspiration from George Jackson, Donald D. DeFreeze, a Black inmate serving a sentence for armed robbery at Vacaville Prison, California, had created a prison self-improvement group, the Black Cultural Association. DeFreeze, who would take the battle name of Cinque from the leader of a slave ship rebellion, turned the prison group into a Black nationalist organization. He also wove relationships with white middle-class radicals from the Bay Area who vis-ited Vacaville to support revolutionary inmates. Having escaped from Va-caville in March 1973, Cinque joined his allies in Berkeley, notably some prison activists belonging to the Maoist group Venceremos. Together, they created the Symbionese Liberation Army (SLA), a self-styled revolutionary organization.

As obscure and nonsensical as its name, the SLA pledged to destruct the prison system, quash racism, defeat fascism, and liberate monogamous mar-riage. In fact, it stepped onto the public stage in November 1973 with the absurd assassination of Marcus Foster, a Black superintendent of education in Oakland, who was beloved in his community. Foster was shot nine times in the back with cyanide bullets, which were designed to kill. According to the SLA, he deserved such retribution for his plans to introduce ID cards and guards into the school district.[76] The small organization swiftly began losing appeal in the radical community.

This isolation temporarily cleared when the group was able to kidnap rich heiress Patricia C. Hearst, the nineteen-year-old granddaughter of media tycoon William Randolph Hearst. The SLA eventually recruited her under the nom de guerre Tania (inspired by Tamara Bunke, the guerrilla fighter who battled alongside Che Guevara), converted her into a revolutionary and a bank robber, and forced her father to organize a grand food distribution for the poor.[77] It was one of the most sensational acts of political theater of the period. For a while, the SLA hit the headlines and seemed to fight with a purpose. Yet this was just another illusion. Decimated by arrests and devastated by a gun battle with the LAPD that left six militants dead, the SLA managed to commit another, albeit unintentional, murder during a bank robbery in April 1975. Now firmly isolated from the prison movement, the SLA gradually disappeared. It secretly merged with the New World Liberation Front, an underground network of guerrilla units that claimed responsibility for a long stream of bombings during the mid- to late 1970s.[78]

Times were also changing within the Guild, which found itself divided regarding the wisdom of assisting the SLA. An internal debate opened, but lawyers failed to rally around these controversial leftists. For the first time, unpopular defendants on the Left did not receive enthusiastic and unanimous support from radical attorneys. Some lawyers were outraged by the defendants' actions, while others were even fearful that defendants would go after them if convicted. Marvin Stender was adamant on the subject and spoke for the majority of Guild attorneys, stressing that such prisoners did not deserve militant litigation, with its manifold and compassionate engagement: "The SLA should be denied a special defense . . . by us! . . . I feel the strongest priority to speak out against the SLA . . . this small group with nothing to do with anyone, no roots in the community, killing innocents, shooting bystanders in banks. . . . They must be accountable for what they have done and a movement holds them accountable by holding back skills." Garry echoed this reasoning, even recalling how he had represented many on the Left whose ideas he disagreed with. "But the SLA are not even on the left. Read Lenin, *What's to Be Done?* Terrorists are enemies of the masses and retard the revolutionary movement. The SLA are enemies of the left."

Kunstler, however, dissented and declared that he would take the case of the SLA—"the kind of case which tests the radical lawyer." "Even if I thoroughly despised their acts," he explained, "I would not criticize them, or anyone in the Movement, to the general public."[79] Likewise, the Prison Task Force of the San Francisco chapter admitted having problems with the politics and tactics of the SLA, but reminded the others that the state made no fine distinctions between brands of revolutionaries. Unity among those dedicated to radical change was "absolutely necessary." Hence, it offered its "political and legal support" to the SLA's fight for freedom.[80] The Prison Task Force also endorsed and took part in a scarcely attended rally in solidarity with the SLA, held in Berkeley in September 1975.[81]

Although refusing to take an official position, the San Francisco chapter of the Guild censored the Prison Task Force and distanced itself from its impromptu show of solidarity.[82] Jennie Rhine, president of the chapter, acknowledged that she was "not sure" about what to do. The general guideline, she said, was "I don't have to agree, but I must not strongly disagree." And the SLA case was indeed testing that limit. What would finally settle things once and for all would be the appearance of a statement by two SLA defendants who went for the jugular of radical lawyers. In a letter to the Guild, they wrote that they did not expect "anything more than egotistical lies and excuses" from an "elite gang" who gave credibility to a judicial system that relied on them "as intellectual interpreters of legalized fascism." The two insisted that they did not trust Guild lawyers because they were "reformists at heart, bourgeois democrats who pose[d] as revolutionaries but stifle[d] real revolutionary action." Being "superstar lawyers for the superstars," they were just interested in seeing their pictures in the papers.[83]

The SLA defendants eventually retained court-appointed lawyers who were far from being radical. Only later, a few Guild lawyers—such as Susan B. Jordan and other maverick attorneys like J. Tony Serra—accepted to represent them.[84] Regardless, the most important outcome of this case was that it confirmed that mutual trust and empathy between lawyers and political inmates were rapidly vanishing. Indeed, in the same period, a strong internal current pushed the Guild to cut off its ties with the prison newsletter *Midnight Special*, whose contributors were increasingly advocating armed struggle. In fact, the New York Prison Task Force, which had marshaled the project, almost unanimously sustained the paper, scorning "legalistic approaches" and justifying the call for a violent insurrection as "a direct response to the material conditions of prisoners' lives." The New York City chapter, however, dissociated itself from the newsletter, arguing that the line of the armed struggle had no place within a broad-based legal organization like the Guild.[85]

Eventually, the symbolic endpoint of the romance between radical lawyers and inmates arrived in 1979. Once again, the protagonist was Fay Stender, who was this time the victim of an appalling act of retribution. By the mid-1970s, when the prisoners she had released started going back to jail, Stender had stopped representing inmates and begun focusing on feminist and gay issues. This new path also reflected a desire to take up a new life. Yet, within the prison movement, rumors circulated that she was a sellout who had abandoned the brothers behind bars, notably George Jackson, and taken advantage of the money that had poured into the accounts of the defense committees. Of course, these were unfounded allegations. But the Black Guerrilla Family (BGF), the prison gang that Jackson had originally created in 1966 at San Quentin, had put a death warrant on the heads of a number of people, including Fay Stender.[86] In 1979, Edward G. Brooks, a recently paroled BGF member, entered Stender's house at night. At gunpoint, he forced her to write and sign a confession of betrayal of Jackson. Then he shot her six times. Stender survived but remained paralyzed below the waist and racked by chronic pain. She left the hospital under an assumed name and began to live in hiding, always carrying a gun.[87]

Stender's tragedy extended to the whole prison movement and its lawyers. Marvin Stender, who at that point had divorced Fay but remained in the Guild, remembers how the failure of the alliance between lawyers and inmates was agonizing and hard to accept for many, even within the NLG. Shortly after Fay was shot, he joined the annual meeting of the San Francisco chapter: "This was before anybody had been charged with the shooting. I went there and I heard this undercurrent . . . 'It must have been the cops or the Department of Corrections or the Attorney General of California who had Fay shot as retaliation for the work she was doing on behalf of inmates' . . . and that was just stupid, ugly, and literally being captive of your own propaganda machine. There was a lot of that going on." Hopefully, he adds, many other lawyers realized that it was not only dangerous to keep on doing this kind of work, "because you couldn't really count on your own comrades," but also politically improper to put the blame on the establishment.[88] Marvin then announced a reward for any information about the crime. A few days later, the NLG condemned the attempted assassination, and friends and colleagues established a Fay Stender Trust Fund to raise money on the victim's behalf.

Yet contradictions were surfacing all around as the web of lawyer-client solidarity, so patiently knitted, was unraveling. A week after the attempted assassination of Stender, Fleeta Drumgo—one of the Soledad Brothers and a member of the BGF—went to Charles Garry's office and admitted he was aware of plans to shoot Fay two weeks before the fact. Willing to sell information, Drumgo confided that Hugo Pinell—one of the San Quentin Six and a leader of the BGF—was the person who ordered the attack on Stender. While Pinell denied accusations, Garry was placed under police protection, and Drumgo was shot dead in Oakland. At that point, radical lawyers unanimously declined to help the alleged shooter of Fay Stender and his accomplices, no matter the color of their skin and their political affiliation. Only a former employee of Stender and a member of the Prison Law Collective took part in the defense team of the BGF, arguing for coherence.

After testifying against her killer, Fay Stender left for Hong Kong, where she committed suicide in May 1980. In 1981, one of her former colleagues in the Prison Law Project stated, "Her funeral marked the end of an era in my life, and I think the end of an era, period." He further specified, "I still represent clients who have varying levels of criminality. . . . My attitude toward them is strictly professional: I am their lawyer, and I don't make the mistake of thinking I'm anything more than that."[89]

9 With Militant Labor and Minorities

Alongside their work with students, soldiers, and prisoners, Guild lawyers threw themselves wholeheartedly into the struggles of rank-and-file labor organizations and rebellious minorities throughout the 1970s. Militant workers opposing bureaucratized unions, Mexican American farmers struggling against authoritarian growers, Native American activists challenging the government's disrespect of treaties, feminists battling against sexism and patriarchy, and gay people mobilizing against discrimination and for child custody were all "wretched of the law," so to speak. All deserved radical lawyers' engagement and promptly obtained it.

According to historian Jefferson Cowie, in the 1970s "workers were back, but in ways that were simultaneously profound and strange, militant and absurd, traditional and new, insurgent and reactionary." While many white- and blue-collar workers declared their allegiance to segregationist presidential candidate George Wallace, radical workplace militancy reached the pinnacle of the postwar years, at levels not seen since the 1930s.[1] A new generation of workers, which included people of color and women, especially the young and unskilled, entered the workforce with a relentless attitude, pushing to unionize, contesting authority, and demanding economic power. To a large extent, these workers had won access through the 1964 Civil Rights Act and "reformulated" the identity of the working class. But now they faced a rapid and dangerous increase in employer resistance to union organizing. As companies grappled with global competition and falling rates of profit, a classic scheme of capitalist restructuring unfolded. While inflation was on the rise, workers' real wages were declining, and unemployment was growing. In many circumstances, employers went all out on evading social welfare obligations, with the help, among others, of "antiunion" management consultants and lawyers.[2]

Inspired by international labor insurgency and domestic social movements, workers' rage simmered. And yet unions appeared to adopt a submissive posture. This is why these radicalized workers challenged not only their employers but also—and sometimes most aggressively—union leaders and bureaucrats. In their view, mainstream unions were unwilling to defy companies, engaged in centralized "concessionary bargaining," stole elections, and disciplined troublemakers. Thus, rank-and-file labor not only raised issues of wages and working conditions but also advocated "a more aggressive, inclusive, democratic, and politicized union movement." Slowdowns, sabotages, stoppages, and collective insubordination grew together with rejection of contracts, lawsuits against union leadership, and workplace self-organization in the form of caucuses and alternative unions.[3]

While strikes spread exponentially and crested in 1970, when sixty-six million workdays were lost and one union member in six stopped working, unofficial wildcat strikes also boomed. According to estimates, they more than doubled between the early 1960s and the mid-1970s, accounting for more than a third of all strikes in the country. As one labor organizer pointed out, wildcat strikes were the most dramatic and authentic expression of this movement, for they bypassed altogether grievance processes, formal union procedures, labor contracts, employer regulations, and union officials.[4] Far from being neutralized, class struggle was alive and well, underscored a Guild report. After few decades of relative quiescence, labor was back at the forefront of social change. It was time for lawyers to help the more vulnerable, those who were written off by industrial unions and were effectively unorganized.[5]

Since its onset, the Guild had gathered many of the most skilled labor lawyers in the country, and a National Labor Committee united them within the organization. Without a doubt, labor had been in the DNA of the Guild and represented a privileged area of intervention, at least until the social movements of the sixties temporarily moved workplace militancy and class struggle to the background. In the mutated context of the 1970s, however, it was necessary to rethink the role of labor lawyers. A debate opened up within the NLG, with the bottom line being that the legal arena, once again, could not be trusted. The law had been used to shift workers' struggles from the shop floor, the picket line, and the streets, to the labor board, the arbitration room, and the courts, where disputes were resolved without disrupting production. Such mechanisms had fatally stripped workers of their power and transferred it to professional experts. Workers' feeling that "all they need to do is get a lawyer" to match the power of the employer was a dangerous misperception. It was necessary, argued Guild lawyers, to show that legal channels could be totally "useless." In this domain, too, the force of rights was directly correlated to the strength of activism.[6]

Given that U.S. unions were not revolutionary organizations but often functioned as counterrevolutionary organizations, radical lawyers had to decide whether to assist them or not. The answer was generally (albeit not unanimously) positive, because workers instinctively related to unions and those workers could not be abandoned. But a series of conditions would apply. First of all, the lawyers would contribute to efforts to make unions more democratic and progressive, instead of accepting the status quo. Second, lawyers would not operate as mere technicians but would participate in political and organizational decision-making with workers. In practical terms, radical lawyers had to join in contentious worker actions like wildcat strikes, not only by fighting injunctions against the strikes or defending those who were arrested but also by debating goals and tactics and helping to organize beforehand.[7] Working full-time as union employees seemed possible too, provided that lawyers engaged with progressive unions and did not remain in their legal offices or cloistered inside the headquarters. Sure, this task was not "free of contradictions," but there were countless services that a legally trained person could provide from within unions.[8]

Accordingly, in the summer of 1972 the Guild revitalized its National Labor Committee, organized a labor law conference to mark its comeback to the field, and began publishing a newsletter. While resuming roadshows and seminars to train attorneys in labor law, the NLG also printed a referral directory of resource people and established a Brief Bank where lawyers could obtain legal forms and pleadings. Numbers of lawyers instinctively joined the bourgeoning militant labor movement across the country, helping workers of any kind to fight their battles.[9]

In particular, Guild lawyers engaged with the most contentious unions, such as the Teamsters for a Democratic Union (TDU), a grassroots organization that was born within the International Brotherhood of Teamsters, known as the Teamsters. The Teamsters was the largest union in the country by the late 1960s, but it had grown authoritarian and undemocratic, with open ties to organized crime. Therefore, in 1975–76, rank-and-file internal dissension had developed into a movement of thousands. The International Socialist activists, who had been sent into the union with the aim of organizing class struggle, played a significant role in these activities and gave them a political imprint that many in the Guild appreciated.[10] The Fruitvale Law Collective, created in 1973 in Oakland by Dan Siegel and other Guild lawyers to represent activists victimized by employers and unions, was among those who cooperated with the TDU for many years.[11]

Other lawyers worked with dissidents within the United Steelworkers of America (USWA). While the steel sector was losing jobs and plants were closing, in 1973 the union leadership signed an Experimental Negotiation

Agreement—that is, a national no-strike pledge that exchanged the right to strike in return for cash bonuses, cost-of-living adjustments, and other small benefits (steelworkers retained the right to strike only on a few local issues). Protest erupted within the union, as the rank and file asked to end the agreement, retain their right to ratify contracts, and elect a new leadership. Guild lawyers found such a "co-operative venture" between labor and management unbearable and brought a legal suit on behalf of the Right to Strike Committee. The suit maintained that by negotiating a no-strike agreement without consulting workers through a vote, USWA officials had breached their fiduciary obligation and their duty of fair representation toward their membership. The legal maneuver was politically ambitious, attempting to demonstrate a direct relationship between the right to strike and rises in wages. The court, however, dismissed the suit, and the opposition candidate was defeated too.[12]

More fortunate was the Rank and File Coalition of the New York City Taxi Drivers Union, Local 3036 of the AFL-CIO (American Federation of Labor and Congress of Industrial Organizations), which represented approximately thirty thousand taxi drivers. With the help of Guild lawyers Richard Levy and Michael Ratner, this rebellious group of drivers filed suit against the union leadership, charging it with violation of members' rights and, specifically, the right to vote on the contract negotiated on their behalf. They won in court, and the Taxi Drivers Union was restrained from entering into contracts without membership approval. The NLG rejoiced, as it was a victory against both employers and union leadership.[13]

Another positive experience emerged out of the cooperation between the Newark Law Collective and the caucus ACTION, created in 1970 by members of the United Auto Workers (UAW) at the New Departure–Hyatt Bearings, the world's largest bearing manufacturer. ACTION wanted to take over the local union, hence it was under attack by both union officials and management. Supported by radical lawyers, these rank-and-file workers filed state and federal complaints challenging the union's undemocratic practices. The suits led nowhere and the UAW disregarded them, but the failed legal strategy encouraged other workers to join the group and organize. The more the union fought back, the more its militancy escalated and drew consensus. Eventually, ACTION won the local elections.[14]

As radical lawyers never ceased to repeat, legal resources could be used to the benefit of worker organizing even in the absence of unions, as was the case for the Gulf Coast Pulpwood Association (GPA). In the early 1970s, this multiracial organization of about twenty-five hundred pulpwood cutters and haulers from Mississippi, Alabama, and Florida battled for recognition as a bargaining agent with the international pulp and paper trusts, primarily International Paper and Scott Paper. The GPA denounced exploitative and dangerous work conditions—woodcutters were among the least paid in the nation and were victims of frequent incidents—in the peculiar situation of the absence of unions. Indeed, these workers were not considered employees but independent contractors.

While the GPA called strikes, radical lawyers from across the country pledged to help, including veteran labor attorney David Scribner, as well as groups of young law students and legal workers sent through the Guild's summer projects. On the one hand, they contributed with defense against the injunctions to restrict picketing and the suits brought by the companies charging restraint of trade and interference with business. On the other hand, they devised creative solutions to cope with the lack of unionization and took part in the organizational activities of the GPA as rank and file themselves. Within a few years, the GPA succeeded in shedding light on the "violence and bruising labor" of this sector, as the *New York Times* characterized it, and obtained a substantial pay raise.[15]

Despite such an unprecedented mobilization of labor across different fields, lasting results were marginal or barely visible. By the end of the 1970s, all unions except one—the United Mine Workers—succeeded in crushing internal rank-and-file opposition. Employers regained the upper hand, too. Changes in the economic context, political wind shifts toward the Right, resilient unions' cultures, and divisiveness of the militant front all contributed to normalizing workplace relationships. Nonetheless, before the decline of labor during the 1980s, workers scored an extraordinary victory, once again with the participation of radical lawyers.

Huelga!

When, in the mid-1960s, he accepted an invitation to fly from San Francisco to Delano to meet with a group of Mexican farmworkers, Marvin Stender could hardly imagine the destiny of such a seemingly unassuming labor organization that operated in the center of California grape production. Indeed, Stender was mostly concerned about the pilot skills of his colleague Peter Franck, who flew him there in a small plane. Once the two lawyers managed to touch down on "a landing strip, not even a real airport," they met a still relatively unknown labor leader and community organizer named Cesar Chavez.

Chavez reached out to the Council for Justice (see chapter 2) because the organization he had been building since 1961 was evolving from a community benefit association to an aggressive labor union capable of calling strikes against growers. Quite predictably, local law enforcement and growers had begun fighting back. Stender and Franck offered their legal assistance and persuaded Chavez to adopt them, and the Council for Justice, as farmworkers' legal representatives. The two lawyers had to roll up their sleeves immediately, as Chavez was arrested and convicted for using a loudspeaker without a permit. In fact, he had applied for a permit, the sheriff had denied it, and he had nonetheless flown over the fields with a plane to call a strike, shouting the unmistakable rallying cry *"Huelga!"* Stender appealed this conviction and, much to his surprise, got a technical reversal. Starting with this first victory, Chavez came to recognize that lawyers would be vital.[16]

According to sociologist J. Craig Jenkins, it was a combination of perseverance, shrewd organizing, and external sponsorship that helped the National Farm Workers Association (later the United Farm Workers [UFW]) become the first successful farmworkers' union in U.S. history and a model for organizing the powerless. In its first years, solidarity and loyalty were crucial, so Chavez and his staff held house meetings to discuss local problems, organized festivals and parades, made sapient use of Mexican and Catholic symbols, instilled a morale of sacrifice, and inspired new recruits with a frugal lifestyle. Chavez was also aware of the importance of weaving political ties and soliciting external support, thus he rallied important allies and donors within the Democratic Party, the United Auto Workers, and the AFL-CIO, showing that the farmworkers did not shun moderate means and monies to pursue radical goals.[17]

The Delano grape strike inaugurated this organizing strategy. First called by Filipino grape pickers in the Coachella Valley, the strike gained traction when Chavez's farmworkers decided to join it and transfer it to Delano in September 1965. Playwright Luis M. Valdez, who was among the first to conceptualize the Chicano identity, wrote up his influential "Plan de Delano," which announced the dawn of a new social movement—a nonviolent revolution of all poor farmworkers demanding social justice. Valdez advocated for those with a nonwhite Indigenous past and a working-class history, but Chavez pressed for a broader multiracial constituency.[18] Chavez's line prevailed, and students from Berkeley and other California campuses flocked to Delano, where they were recruited to serve as volunteer union staff and organizers. Called derisively *gabachos*, meaning North Americans, they came to represent both a key asset and a source of controversy because of their supposed tendency to patronize farmworkers. In any event, these volunteers kept contentious actions alive in a problematic context in which farmers' families desperately needed income and the labor season was short.

In particular, when the 1965 grape strike was about to fail, the commitment of thousands of students and civil rights activists made possible its conversion into a long-term boycott of wines, liquors, and table grapes produced by hostile growers. After a march from Delano to Sacramento, where farmworkers attended hearings for labor legislation and met Senator Robert Kennedy, who endorsed their goals, the boycott gained national momentum. Five years after its inception, it would lead to a historic victory. In 1970, dozens of growers finally recognized the union, asked for negotiations, sat at the bargaining table, and signed approximately 150 grape contracts.[19] In the meantime, radical lawyers of the Council for Justice represented grape boycotters arrested for leafleting or picketing grocery stores. However, the legal needs of a movement that now comprised up to ten thousand workers had grown exponentially. Thus, the UFW began to hire its own legal staff and named attorney Jerry Cohen, a civil rights organizer who did not identify with the Left, chief legal counsel.[20]

At that point, some radical lawyers who were mesmerized by the farmworkers' movement insisted on participating, whereas others grew very critical and reluctant to work with a union that was not radical enough for them. As usual, an internal debate opened up within the NLG. "The ultra-left thought that we, as lawyers, working with the farmworkers were misleading them to believe that there were legal solutions," remembers Peter Haberfeld, who remained with the UFW for years. Animated discussions divided Guild lawyers, but eventually Chavez himself settled things once and for all. The farmworkers' leader encouraged the lawyers who were willing to join forces to forget about leftist criticisms. He reportedly said, "With all due respect, we are much more radical than the people on the Left. . . . People on the Left were trying to organize farm workers for at least fifty years. On the contrary, we have managed, by a coalition of liberals, church people, and students, to put together a force capable to organize a nation-wide grape boycott and we have changed the power relationships in the valley."[21]

As a matter of fact, a flow of Guild volunteers continued to offer their help, especially when the UFW turned its attention to the lettuce growers in Salinas and Santa Maria valleys. Growers had signed "sweetheart contracts" with the aforementioned Teamsters, a moderate union that appealed to many seasonal workers. The UFW called strikes, and the Teamsters' guards broke them with severity.[22] Encouraged by the Teamsters, in 1973 some grape growers refused to re-sign the contracts that had been forced by the 1970 boycott. Strikes to challenge "illegal contracts" followed, and hundreds of workers were arrested for breaking court orders that limited striking and picketing. According to Guild sources, over four thousand strikers and supporters were arrested over the summer of 1973 for violating injunctions. A UFW striker was also shot dead.[23]

In June, the Guild sent eight students and two attorneys to scattered locations from Coachella to Salinas. Coordinated by Haberfeld, they went to picket lines from 4:30 a.m. until noon, six days a week, trying to prevent harassment of protesters by police and private security. They took statements about incidents from workers and also attempted to force the police to collect reports—for example, on the growers' use of firearms to tame disturbances in the fields. In the afternoons, volunteers typically did legal research for the hundreds of lawsuits that were being filed for deprivation of civil rights. While assisting in mass defenses and visiting jails to help the arrested, a few lawyers also savored repression and ended up behind bars.[24] During trials, Haberfeld recalls, volunteers filled the courtroom with farmworkers, bringing in front of the judge "the sea of faces of the people who picked the crops that his family ate at the table." Courtroom power relations had obviously shifted.[25] A year later, in 1974, the Guild replicated the project and sent additional lawyers and legal students to participate in criminal defense and boycott activities.[26]

As had happened a decade earlier with the civil rights movement, Guild students and lawyers found themselves enchanted by farmworkers. One of the participant attorneys, for instance, noted that they were all struck by "the spirit and total commitment of the farmworkers." While organized labor staff was made of "well-paid bureaucrats with half-hearted concern for the interests of workers," the UFW was "a militant union of third world people who have been fighting for survival and the interest of working people." For lawyers, even jail time seemed to be a formative experience, "because the spirit of the strikers was incredible." It was somehow thrilling, recounted a young Guild participant, to be in a cell "with a sixty-year-old woman with a heart condition and 7 children at home who tells you that she doesn't care how long she stays in jail so long as her children do not have to live most of their lives as she did."[27]

In a coeval report, another young volunteer explained that the "uniqueness" of such legal work stemmed primarily from lawyers' "total involvement with a strong movement that is dedicated to bettering the lives of all farmworkers." Much as had been the case for their predecessors in the South, legal workers got the feeling that they had more to learn from activists than vice versa. Farmworkers, wrote the same volunteer, "have taught us about the need for more than legal skills detached from a political environment." Finally, he confessed, "Working within such a strong movement gives us much encouragement, energy and stimulus. . . . We often wonder how other law students survive in the dry, remote environment of corporate law which is attached to no movement at all."[28]

Meanwhile, Jerry Brown, a Democrat who had marched with the UFW, became governor of California, succeeding Reagan. After much discussion, in 1975 the state legislature passed the California Agricultural Labor Relations Act, the first farm labor certification statute in U.S. history, which guaranteed basic rights to organize and select union representatives.[29] Although it was a compromise solution between growers and farmers, it represented a historic breakthrough and was considered "the most union-friendly legislation in the United States."[30]

However enthusiastic about the victory, Guild lawyers found themselves once again divided on the question of working with the UFW. This time, the vexing issue was the presence of undocumented Mexican immigrants who entered the United States or were smuggled in by growers, sometimes with the alleged complicity of the Immigration and Naturalization Service (INS). Not only were these workers exploited at slave wages and intimidated by the constant threat of deportation, but they were also used to damage striking farmworkers and to weaken their bargaining power.[31] To address this issue, Chavez and UFW officials had started filing complaints with the INS and petitioning Congress, asking them to deport undocumented individuals. Union interests were weighed against workers' solidarity, a delicate balancing act that put radical lawyers' political and moral rigor to the test.

Hard-core Marxists within the Guild, including many who had worked with the UFW, had no doubt: the NLG supported "the just struggles of all working people" in the country, no matter if the U.S. government deemed they were legal or not. The four million to ten million "illegal people" on national soil constituted "the most super-exploited section of the working class" and a potentially powerful political force. The presence of "a reserve labor supply of third world and women workers," they explained, had historically been used as a threat to the economic position of white male workers. Now, the undocumented were being pitted against the native-born national minorities, and the UFW was guilty of splitting the Latino movement. Guild members had to abandon the farmworkers' projects unless volunteers were exempted from doing any "anti-working-class action" in support of these policies.[32]

On the contrary, a pragmatist front within the Guild argued that the UFW was "too progressive and too threatened to permit a withdrawal of support." The UFW stood as a rampart against capitalist exploitation and was under major threat by agribusiness. Its position on undocumented workers, some lawyers maintained, had to be seen as a defensive strategy. These workers were being imported by growers with the explicit intent to break strikes. The Guild should not abandon the UFW at this critical juncture.[33] Other lawyers proposed to support farmworkers on both sides of the border "in their efforts to survive, to eat, to organize, to liberate themselves and to achieve class consciousness and class solidarity." After all, these people were all indigent and sought employment.[34]

Eventually, the Guild expressed an official position that echoed the first stance. Lawyers and students would keep supporting the UFW on the condition that the farmworkers did not engage in efforts to deport undocumented people, even when they were "acting as scabs." Indeed, the Guild fully supported illegal workers' rights. The UFW replied that it could not accept such terms and formally severed its relationship with the Guild. UFW cofounder and civil rights icon Dolores Huerta labeled the Guild's resolution as a "very vicious attack," comparable to the actions of the Teamsters and the growers. Chavez himself branded the Guild as "a chicken-shit outfit." The few Guild members who were part of the UFW's legal staff, including Haberfeld, were delivered an ultimatum. Forced to choose between the NLG and the UFW, they resigned from the Guild, as their primary loyalty lay with the workers' movement.[35]

Only a few months later, the UFW convention passed a resolution calling for amnesty for all illegal aliens, softening its position on immigrants and advocating a broad coalition across minorities. The union ended up attacking Border Patrols and even organizing "*sindocumentos*."[36] Yet its cooperation with the Guild had been largely compromised and, in the meantime, the background had significantly evolved. While the passage of the Agricultural Labor Relations Act had convinced many that support for farmworkers was no longer a matter of life and death, the UFW had revised its strategy by moving its officers to the city of La Paz, purging most of the white leftists from its ranks, and strengthening its centralization.[37] It was a transition to the mainstream and, as experience showed, something that fatally alienated radical lawyers.

At Wounded Knee, against "Domestic Imperialism"

Persistently, unmistakably, and irremediably a minority, Native Americans were the darlings of radical lawyers. Their legal issues invariably turned into political disputes; their entrenched segregation demanded fierce courtroom battles.[38] Therefore, the NLG provided them with scores of volunteer combatants as their long confrontation with the U.S. government escalated on numerous fronts.

The Native Americans' conflict with the political authorities of the United States and the ensuing chain of hardship and anguish are sadly well-known. Suffice it to remember that the controversial Treaty of Fort Laramie (1868), negotiated between the federal government and the Sioux, guaranteed Native Americans a territory and the right to independent nationhood. However, white settlers and fortune hunters blatantly disregarded it from the beginning. The subsequent discovery of gold in the Black Hills—Native lands in western South Dakota—did nothing but further erode Native Americans' land rights. Genocidal wars, spoliation of territories, and erosion of Native jurisdiction followed, together with the progressive restriction of the reservations where Native Americans had been confined. Policies of forced assimilation into the American way of life progressively wore down the fabric of Native society and culture.[39]

Only President Roosevelt attempted to reinstate Native American self-government, but in 1934, under his own tenure, the Bureau of Indian Affairs (BIA) was created. A federal agency entrusted with supervising tribal councils and running social programs for Native Americans, the BIA communicated the idea that Native Americans could not manage their own affairs without the help of white federal bureaucrats. Indeed, during the 1950s, the government was already back on the track of assimilation. In addition, it pursued a road map for the "termination" of reservations and the relocation of their inhabitants to urban areas. The eventual displacement of Native Americans to cities fostered racial discrimination, unemployment, poverty, and social plagues such as alcoholism.[40]

The 1960s saw growing demands for Native self-determination. Inspired by the bourgeoning radicalism and identity politics, Native Americans shared a sense of continuous betrayal and victimization. They increasingly asserted treaty rights, which was a different way to claim their civil rights, seeking their place not within but outside the system.[41] Even Democratic administrations, they contended, made conciliatory announcements but paid only lip service to their rights.[42] Electorally and economically voiceless, Native Americans were realizing the singularity of their grievances and felt compelled "to play the political game outside the designated conventional arena of institutional politics."[43]

Inaugurating a new era, the National Indian Youth Council held its first annual meeting in 1963. More radical than previous organizations, it decried Native Americans' loss of control over their own destiny. In July 1968, the American Indian Movement (AIM), the first major radical organization advocating "Red Power," saw the light in Minneapolis. Its leaders, Clyde H. Bellecourt, Dennis Banks, and Russell C. Means, who all had prison records, were charismatic agitators and persuasive speakers. They shrewdly mastered both their relationship with traditional tribesmen and their connection with the younger generations. Wearing long hair and ceremonial garments but also blue jeans and sunglasses, they played the role of selfless warriors and unrepentant outlaws, forging a political language and a seductive aesthetic that captivated plenty of activists. Clearly inspired by the Panthers, they became famous for patrolling police and going to the scenes of arrests with cameras, recorders, attorneys, and bondsmen.

Native American activism soon hit the news with a few resounding actions, such as the seizure of the abandoned prison of Alcatraz on November 29, 1969, by a group of militants who wanted to dramatize their condition and asked for Native American study programs. It was in that circumstance that radical lawyers first engaged with the escalating Red Power movement. During the action planning, which was mostly held at San Francisco State College and UC Berkeley, Guild lawyer Aubrey Grossman was called on to untangle legal questions, such as the validity of Native people's rights to abandoned federal property or the consequence of an act of appropriation of federal land. Already familiar with Native American issues, Grossman encouraged the young militants to stage the occupation and reassured them that there were attorneys like him who were ready to help in the aftermath. Initially sustained by a wide front, the occupation turned out to be long and wearing, without accomplishing much. After nineteen months of self-restraint, the federal government sent law enforcement and arrested the occupiers.[44]

Always to protest the government's failure to abide by its treaties, Native American activists also staged fish-ins, attempted to occupy Ellis Island and Mount Rushmore, and seized a replica of the seventeenth-century ship *Mayflower*. While urban communities of Native Americans, from Minneapolis to Denver to Los Angeles, increasingly discovered radical politics, AIM chapters also mushroomed on reservations, where they opposed tribal governments and BIA rule. In November 1972, six hundred Native American caravanners headed to Washington, D.C., to present to the White House a twenty-point program asking for renewal of treaty rights, reconstruction of communities, and tribal sovereignty. They hoped to find an ally in President Nixon's administration, which had recognized the century-old discrimination of Native Americans and favored self-determination. Yet things went immediately awry, and activists took over BIA headquarters. Negotiations (with promises) ended the standoff, but once the activists headed back home, treaties were never rediscussed. In January 1973, the White House rejected the twenty points, arguing that Native Americans were not foreign nations but ordinary citizens. The Trail of Broken Treaties, as organizers named it, had totally flopped.[45]

Frustration inevitably grew, and one reservation more than any others—Pine Ridge, in South Dakota—became a key flashpoint as these issues magnified and converged. First of all, the reservation comprised Wounded Knee, the site of the infamous 1890 massacre of up to three hundred Lakota—the Sioux tribe of Sitting Bull and Crazy Horse—by the U.S. Seventh Cavalry. It consisted of a tiny hamlet with a church, a trading post, and a handful of houses, but it remained a powerful symbol of white America's violence. With the 1970 publication of Dee Brown's bestseller *Bury My Heart at Wounded Knee*, the place regained notoriety, especially among leftist youth.[46] Second, living conditions at Pine Ridge, as on all reservations, were dire: 56 percent of the people did not have electricity, and 78 percent did not have running water. Infant mortality and suicide rates were the highest in the United States, not to speak of unemployment and alcoholism.[47] Finally, the BIA's tribal council on the reservation was headed by a contested chair, Richard Wilson, whose tenure was unanimously described as corrupt, nepotistic, and authoritarian. Wilson had also built an unofficial security force, whose agents were commonly known as "goons," to enforce his orders and overstep the BIA police that legally operated on-site.[48]

To fight back against these conditions, the Oglala Sioux Civil Rights Organization was established, and the tribal council considered impeaching Wilson. AIM militants also began speaking against the mismanagement of tribal government. However, AIM was banned from the reservation, and both the FBI and the BIA increased their presence to monitor any suspect subversive activity. Tension further mounted after the death of an Oglala Lakota man, who was harassed and beaten by four whites in a small Nebraska town close to Pine Ridge. A tragic event that in the past would have barely raised eyebrows, this time it generated vocal demands for justice and spurred the intervention of AIM, which played the role of the avenger.

Against this background, the Oglala Sioux Civil Rights Organization and tribal chiefs at Pine Ridge agreed to call AIM onto the reservation to publicize their plight and defend their people. On February 27, 1973, eighty-three years after the last massacre on that land, three hundred Native American militants occupied Wounded Knee. Claiming to act under the provisions of the 1868 treaty, they addressed a list of demands that included the removal of the tribal chairman, free elections for the tribal council, and Senate investigations into the government's failure to honor its agreements and the handling of reservations by the BIA and the Department of Interior.[49] Eleven hostages were taken, but they clearly sided with the Native Americans. Once they were released, ten of them decided to stay at Wounded Knee. Trenches and bunkers were built by the militants, who were otherwise poorly armed and faced a large contingent of heavily equipped FBI agents, BIA police, U.S. marshals, and military personnel, who encircled and blockaded the area.[50]

Both sides negotiated and even smoked the pipe together under the tepee, but exchanges of gunfire, arrests, and indictments continued nonetheless. From the very beginning, it was clear that legal support was essential. Guild attorney Kenneth E. Tilsen, known in the region for representing antiwar activists, was immediately contacted to assist fifty Native Americans who had been arrested in the course of the takeover and lay in jail in Rapid City, South Dakota. Ramon A. Roubideaux, a Rosebud Sioux who had also served as an attorney general in the state, was named chief negotiator. In the meantime, more lawyers headed there to help with arraignments and bond hearings and to assist in discussions with the government.[51]

Undeniably, the Native American cause inflamed radical lawyers. Within the Guild, the subjugation of this population was seen as "the first manifestation of class exploitation in North America," and Native Americans' resistance to "domestic imperialism" was linked to the liberation struggle waged by Black and Chicano communities.[52] Employing an overstated analogy, the siege of Wounded Knee was also compared to the war in Southeast Asia: "Here, too, the government was held at bay by a force who, though few in number and lacking in arms and supplies, resisted with the strength and perseverance that only a struggle for survival can produce," read a Guild report.[53] "Wounded Knee is precisely the type of situation to which the Guild has always responded," declared an article in the NLG official magazine, and indeed, the organization immediately fulfilled AIM's request for legal aid.[54]

On March 22, the Wounded Knee Legal Defense/Offense Committee (WKLDOC, pronounced "Wickledoc") opened in Rapid City. In addition to processing cases and acting as advisers for negotiations, committee members also functioned as couriers of food and medical supplies, as they claimed access to Wounded Knee by virtue of their attorney-client privilege. Being an "offense" committee too, WKLDOC initiated a series of civil lawsuits against the tribal council and the federal government—for example, to secure access for lawyers into the village (as they were often stopped at roadblocks), to halt Wilson's abuses on the reservation, and to challenge the deployment of the military against U.S. civilians in the absence of congressional action or executive order.[55]

WKLDOC had approximately thirty full-time members, working alongside a larger number of part-time volunteers. They all operated without salaries, relying on small contributions. Later, at its national convention in June 1973, the Guild made an official pledge to provide legal help for Wounded Knee. While lawyers who operated primarily east of the Mississippi River would supply the recruitment base for the concomitant Attica cases, those who operated on the west side would focus on Native American struggles. In addition to attorneys, students and legal workers would be sent through the Guild's summer projects. Some of them would end up serving as an investigative team and live and work on the Pine Ridge reservation; others would remain in the WKLDOC office, which was located in Sioux Falls, South Dakota.[56]

The Guild was hardly alone in its support of AIM's venture, as lawyers of different affiliations joined the fray. For example, the National Association of Criminal Defense Lawyers sent a delegation to South Dakota and pledged to help. Provisions of food, medicine, and ammunition also came from other tribes and from a miscellaneous coalition of white college students, leftist organizations, Vietnam veterans, progressive churches, and Chicano, Asian, and Black militants. They all flocked to the tiny hamlet under siege. In some cases, these supporters flew with planes over the village and dropped supplies; in other cases, they drove from across the country and traveled by foot during the night with their backpacks in the hope of reaching Wounded Knee without being arrested. "When the red man will begin to unite, all other races will join with him," advised an old Native American prophecy, and reality seemed to fulfill it.[57] Enthusiasm ran high, especially because support extended to the larger public. Marlon Brando created havoc by declining the Academy Award for Best Actor in *The Godfather* in solidarity with the protest, and a Harris Poll of April 1973 revealed that 93 percent of U.S. citizens were following the siege, and 51 percent of them sided with the occupiers.[58] According to Guild lawyers, this was already "a clear-cut victory." For the first time in U.S. history, a public opinion survey attested that the majority of U.S. citizens supported "an armed uprising against the U.S. government."[59]

The occupation lasted seventy-one days. In the course of that time (in March and April), tentative agreements had been reached, but clashes followed right after. Kunstler himself advised the occupiers not to "give in so easily." "In the long run, the danger had to be secondary to the political protest," he stated.[60] The Native Americans established an Independent Oglala Nation, which was enthusiastically greeted by radicals as the first territory ever liberated from U.S. government control.[61] Eventually, after two occupants were killed during exchanges of fire and a marshal was left paralyzed, a final agreement led to the deposition of weapons, with the promise of a discussion of the 1868 treaty with White House officials. On May 8, the siege was over.[62]

All in all, the secessionist action led to just one formal meeting with government emissaries, during which the Native Americans reiterated their demand to enforce the treaty and to obtain an amnesty for the charges arising from the occupation. Later on, government attorneys raced to argue that treaty making with Native American tribes had been abolished in 1871 and only Congress could modify the status quo, definitively burying AIM's ambitions. The Watergate scandal had already flared up, and the administration had a tougher nut to crack. In addition to massive publicity, the most tangible effect of the takeover at Wounded Knee seemed to be the 562 arrests and 185 federal indictments, mainly for crossing state lines to incite a riot, interfering with federal officers, and illegal possession of firearms. Other charges, such as larceny and unlawful assembly, were brought at state and tribal levels.[63]

Native Americans on Trial

In light of the mass arrests and indictments, the defense work suddenly appeared overwhelming, and a meeting was convened to plan a strategy. On May 31, 1973, in Rapid City, more than fifty people attended, including AIM militants, WKLDOC volunteers, various supporters, and a number of lawyers, such as William Kunstler, who were contacted through defendants. Consistent with the mass defense standards, Guild workers pushed for coordination of all cases under the political direction of defendants. They also expressed a wish to be educated by Native Americans on culture and life on the reservation. A few nonradical lawyers predictably withdrew, and a number of young and idealistic legal workers, law students, and investigators were thrown into the breach without much experience. Above them, however, were a handful of seasoned attorneys. Roubideaux headed WKLDOC, while Tilsen acted as day-to-day coordinator and Leonard L. Cavise—a Washington, D.C., attorney—operated as a local reference for the Guild. Bronx lawyer and civil rights activist Mark Lane directed investigations from a house on the reservation.[64] Lane, who was himself a Guild affiliate, was a colorful and controversial figure who had campaigned against the Vietnam War and published a best-selling book that trashed the Warren Commission, arguing for Lee Harvey Oswald's innocence in the murder of John F. Kennedy.[65]

Organized in a number of subcommittees, WKLDOC members gathered evidence, recruited lawyers, managed witnesses, administered subpoenas, and indexed materials. While mounting a massive defense campaign that flooded the media with a constant stream of statements, WKLDOC also generated community awareness through initiatives in schools and churches, raised funds, arranged appearances of supporters such as Dick Gregory and Angela Davis, and secured speaking engagements for "celebrity lawyers." WKLDOC also shepherded hundreds of Native Americans from across the country to lend their support.[66]

Even so, defending this population was not a bed of roses. The lack of previous substantial contacts between white lawyers and Native Americans represented a major obstacle. Guild lawyers reiterated their willingness "to learn" from Native Americans, but AIM's leadership was inconsistent, and cultural differences proved to be deep—for instance, at the level of respect for women.[67] Moreover, AIM's self-aggrandizing rhetoric and flamboyant style increasingly appeared phony to many outside observers. Banks, Means, and other leaders were accused of seeking friendly publicity with "a game of charades played by an Indian Nation that had lost its soul and all hope of resurrection."[68]

Finally, Guild lawyers were red-baited. Prominent Sioux chief and civil rights activist Robert Burnette remembers that the arrival of New Left activists and radical lawyers "who [had] hurried west to jump on the Wounded Knee bandwagon . . . was resented by many of the more conservative Indians and even by some sincere white liberals with long records of support for Indians." Leftists' presence cemented the conviction that AIM activists had communist ties, as the tribal council repeated. "You didn't have to be a master psychologist," Burnette significantly added, "to realize the effect on a South Dakota jury of having William Kunstler or Mark Lane as an attorney. Some members of AIM's legal advisory staff, who had worked with the activists since before the Trail of Broken Treaties, tried to warn the head-strong militants that association with people like Kunstler and Lane would ultimately do more harm than good. But the short view—that big-name attorneys would bring in more publicity and money—won out, at least initially."[69]

That said, defense efforts did not substantially suffer from these criticisms, and a mix of full-fledged dedication, legal talents, and government missteps ensured unexpected victories in the majority of trials that arose from the occupation. In particular, the so-called leadership trial, involving Dennis Banks and Russell Means, polarized much attention. Means was represented by Lane and Kunstler, while Banks retained Larry Leventhal, Douglas Hall, and the aforementioned Tilsen. Leventhal, who had been among the first lawyers to gather at the village during the siege, was an expert on Indian treaty rights and an enthusiast advocate of AIM. Hall was a civil rights attorney and the cofounder of the Legal Rights Center, a non-profit law firm created in 1970 to fight against racial biases in the judiciary system.

The leadership trial closely followed the blueprint of radical litigation, from pretrial motions to closing statements. First of all, lawyers filed a change of venue motion. Since South Dakota was deemed "the most racist and repressive court system in America, vis-a-vis the Indian people" and, in Tilsen's words, comparable to Mississippi or Alabama in the 1930s, "when lynching in and out of the courtroom was the order of the day," the defense team tried to demonstrate with a survey that Native Americans could not receive a fair trial anywhere in that state.[70] The motion was approved and the Banks-Means' trial was relocated to St. Paul, Minnesota, before Fred J. Nichol, a liberal judge. Eventually, only a few trials remained in South Dakota, whereas the others were all moved to neighboring states. Second, jury selection was attentively prepared, with a team of volunteers who conducted an opinion survey and collected data on registered voters' demography, once again under the direction of Jay Schulman. After a voir dire of three weeks, the twelve jurors who were seated had an average age of thirty-two and seemed sufficiently unbiased.

Quite obviously, politics and law were intentionally enmeshed. While Kunstler declared that he wished the case would be tried "through the media and the people" and lambasted the system of justice, Means repeated, with a standard rhetorical artifice, that the United States was on trial for violating treaties, not himself. Indeed, the trial was devised as a forum to educate the public on the broken treaties, on the discrimination of Native Americans, and on the corruption of the BIA, shifting legal arguments to the background.[71] The defense insisted on "bad faith prosecution," namely the fact that the government harnessed expensive trials and potential massive sentences to silence AIM leadership and tie it up in never-ending court battles. The defense also contended that the government enforced the law selectively, by employing criminal statutes against Native American militants but not against tribal chair Wilson and his goons.[72]

Opening statements were also played by the book. As Banks recalled, his and Means' appearance was utterly theatrical: "We wore our hair neatly braided and wrapped in strips of red cloth, each of us with an eagle feather dangling from one braid to give us strength."[73] Banks spoke about treaties and racism, accused the government, and concluded by pleading guilty of participating in the siege. Means was even more bombastic and talked profusely on topics ranging from "Indianness" to religion. Lawyers seconded their clients, embraced them and, at some point, were expelled from the courtroom because of their unrelenting objections. Due to their "courtroom theatrics talking," Kunstler and Lane spent a Friday night in jail for contempt. Strategically, the defendants announced they wanted to fire their attorneys and were granted co-counsel status with the right to conduct cross-examination, which was their objective. Expert witnesses, including best-selling authors Dee Brown and Vine Deloria Jr., and dozens of reservation residents followed one another to the stand. They all insisted on the U.S. record of unfulfilled promises vis-à-vis Native Americans. Summoned by Kunstler, Harry Belafonte and Marlon Brando appeared in the audience, sitting right behind their beloved defendants.[74]

And yet the actual game changer was the monthlong hearing into the FBI wiretaps. The defense produced witnesses who alleged that the government had used illegal electronic surveillance, wiretapping activists' phones during and after the takeover. On the contrary, the FBI had assured the court that electronic surveillance was absent and also denied that informants were present at any defense meeting. Even Mark Felt, the FBI associate director who had secretly leaked information about the Watergate scandal to the press, initially confirmed it. To unravel the knot, the judge interrupted the prosecution's case and ordered that the government's entire Wounded Knee file be available to the defense. The existence of a number of informants, the manipulation of a witness (who blatantly lied under oath), and the adoption of a party line to keep phones under surveillance were disclosed. Although no breach of the attorney-client privilege was proven and the court refused to dismiss the charges, the fact that the FBI had extensively interfered and clumsily covered its operations was plainly revealed. Eventually, wiretap evidence was suppressed, and over five hundred previously undisclosed documents were made public. The judge was left visibly upset, irremediably shifting the mood in the courtroom.[75]

After the close of the proceedings, Tilsen obtained from another trial record an FBI report on AIM that had been drafted by an undercover agent by the name of Douglas Durham (see chapter 10). It just so happened that Durham had been Dennis Banks's right-hand man, who had also been present when defense strategies were discussed. The shocking revelation confirmed that the FBI had deeply infiltrated AIM and also, according to Banks, tried to disrupt it. Durham allegedly sought to bring in "heavy weapons" for the militants and suggested that they "kidnap the governor." When publicly confronted, Durham admitted his role.[76] Suddenly, the assault and harassment charges that WKLDOC had repeatedly leveled against the FBI looked realistic. The FBI was active in a complex series of actions against AIM, which followed the blueprint of COINTELPRO, even after its official demise.[77]

Going back to the trial, the proceedings closed with the usual emotional climax while demonstrators marched outside the courtroom asking to free Banks and Means. Attorney Leventhal argued that this was "not a criminal conspiracy, but a joint action to honor the 1868 treaty—to enforce the law, not to break it." Kunstler compared the occupation of Wounded Knee to the American Revolution and solemnly stated, "Those who never speak never bring about change." To conclude, he read the last verses of *American Names*, a poem by Stephen V. Benét.[78] After eight months of trial proceedings, deliberations began. However, since a juror had suffered a stroke and his alternate was probably pro-acquittal, the government asked for a mistrial. The judge, who had already acquitted both defendants on several counts, dismissed all pending felony charges and attacked both the prosecution and the FBI "in a way rarely seen in an American courtroom," noted Guild observers with satisfaction. In his final summation, he admitted that "the waters of justice have been polluted."[79]

The other Wounded Knee trials attracted much less attention, less community support, and less prominent lawyers, sometimes resulting in hasty proceedings and convictions. Attorneys Thorne and Leventhal filed a motion (and a massive brief) to dismiss all remaining cases for lack of jurisdiction. Between December 1974 and January 1975, they conducted a special hearing to support this motion, marshaling historians, anthropologists, and tribal chiefs in front of the judge to testify that the U.S. government did not have authority to try "an Indian" for alleged crimes committed in the territory of the "Indian nation." Since Native Americans had no written language and transferred history from generation to generation verbally, the hearing turned into an extraordinary exercise in oral history to ascertain how the Sioux who had signed the 1868 treaty had understood its terms. Witnesses established that the signers of the treaty believed the Sioux retained the right to self-government over the lands they had designated as their permanent home, including criminal jurisdiction. The judge congratulated them on the reconstruction but denied the motion.[80]

In any event, when the whole legal battle ended, out of the forty cases that had been brought to trial for the occupation, only five resulted in guilty sentences.[81] According to Tilsen, WKLDOC did an excellent job, ensuring a 7.7 percent conviction rate, whereas the average in the circuit was 78.2 percent.[82] While some scholars agree that the legal victory was substantial, resulting in positive outcomes for Native Americans, including monetary compensation, greater control over the BIA, and favorable legislation, others argue that the government emerged as "the real victor," as it succeeded in avoiding charges against law enforcement and wearing out AIM, which lost its momentum. A "low-level civil war," indeed, continued after the occupation both within and outside Pine Ridge, where Wilson once again won a contested tribal chair election against Means.[83]

Yet legal-political success depends on perspective. By zooming out, it is possible to see—after the siege of Wounded Knee and the whole cycle of mobilization—an unprecedented recognition of Native American grievances, which also translated into favorable norms. While the Indian Self-Determination and Education Assistance Act of 1975 guaranteed Native Americans more power and federal funds to govern their own reservations, the Supreme Court ruled in 1980 that the United States had effectively breached the 1868 treaty and must pay compensation for the stolen land.[84] By zooming in on Native American radicalism, however, it is clear the AIM did not capitalize on the legal victory and imploded in the ensuing years, disintegrating under the weight of internal divisions, endemic violence, and enduring repression. The majority of Native Americans, indeed, turned back to mainstream strategies.[85]

After the occupation, federal marshals and FBI agents remained within the reservation for months, and a "reign of terror," according to Native sources, began. In October 1973, Pedro Bissonette, the adopted son of an Oglala elder, was mysteriously assassinated before testifying in court, and BIA police were fingered for the murder. The atmosphere was so tense that a Guild delegation was sent to the funerals to grant some protection.[86] In February 1975, a repressive action hit the remaining forces of AIM and WKLDOC. Two Guild attorneys and other committee members were set upon and beaten by BIA police and the goons at the Pine Ridge airport. The day after, Russell Means was arrested on an unrelated charge of attempted murder. On his way to jail, Means attempted to flee and was eventually apprehended after a shoot-out that resulted in one person being killed. At that point, Means found himself under judgment in fourteen separate trials.[87] In June, in the course of another shoot-out, two FBI agents and a Native American were murdered. Four AIM militants were charged: one was acquitted, two were successfully defended by Kunstler—who persuaded the jury that the FBI had caused the death of its own agents with its reckless conduct—and one, Leonard Peltier, fled to Canada. He was later convicted, paying the price for everybody.[88]

While WKLDOC gradually demobilized and the struggle in the region morphed into a gun battle, the NLG shifted its attention toward more constructive political projects. At its 1976 national convention, a group of lawyers adopted a formal national committee structure and named themselves the Committee on Native American Struggles. Based in the Twin Cities, the committee gathered between fifty and one hundred Guild members who pledged to work on behalf of Native American rights of sovereignty and self-determination. In addition to representing individual people or tribes in political cases, it offered its resources to grassroots initiatives such as the Native American Solidarity Committee, whose mission was to build support for Native Americans through public education and organizing in non-Indian communities.[89]

Confronting Sexism

Guild lawyers' fight against sexism dates back to the early days of the NLG, when many of the few women lawyers in the country joined the organization. Carol Weiss King, for example, had been active since the very first meeting of the Guild. A pioneer of militant defense, King devoted her entire life to representing aliens accused of political crimes and became an undisputed authority in immigration law. Although she was a young widow and a mother, she worked unabatedly and often pro bono. She also founded the U.S. section of the International Juridical Association, a communist-oriented organization that focused on civil liberties and labor rights, and later established one of the earliest female law firms in 1948. Yet like most of her female colleagues of that period, she never fought openly for the rights of women; rather, she assumed and exercised them. Being an example was, for King, the strongest feminist statement. Indeed, until the 1960s, women's issues were rarely spelled out and remained marginal, even within the NLG.[90]

This picture dramatically changed with the increase in the Guild's female membership, especially via students and legal workers. Such a critical mass was impossible to ignore and carried the message of second-wave feminism, usually in its more radical version. Well aware of the class nature of society, feminist lawyers wanted to fight sexism and racism first, deferring or recasting class struggle.[91] Without much surprise, 1970 proved a pivotal moment for the women in the Guild. In the year of the publication of Firestone's *Dialectic of Sex* and Millet's *Sexual Politics*, the questions of sexual discrimination and patriarchy barged into the radical lawyers' debate.[92] Since that time, Guild lawyers began to address these issues in three different yet overlapping domains: the NLG, legal education and the profession, and American society at large.

Starting from the organizational sphere, Guild women expressed their determination to reconcile legal-political work with their commitment to the women's movement. To discuss their own issues and establish programs to overcome them, they not only organized conferences and workshops but also began creating "small groups," potluck gatherings, and caucuses of "Guild sisters" that mirrored the separatist stance of radical feminist groups.[93] In 1974, the Massachusetts chapter decided to host its first meetings to debate how sexism polluted the NLG. Since the problem was still pervasive, the "awakening" was reportedly "rude." The Guild, some women complained, had focused too exclusively on representing male political defendants and those engaged in male-dominated struggles. The organization also wrongly assumed that the vanguard of the movement was "closely identifiable with the more para-military struggles of men," primarily in prison and within Black communities. As if that were not enough, the "stars" of the Guild's legal work were male lawyers—aggressive, competitive, and impatient—while those who frequently bore the cost of day-to-day organization were female workers.[94]

Other voices raised questions about leftist lawyers' persistent ostracism of women issues. If a woman lawyer delved into "her own oppression," overlooking for a while "the panoramic oppression of the legal system," severe criticisms from male colleagues were still common. For many male attorneys, especially old-style Marxists, such a perspective was "petty and self-indulgent." "I have been repeatedly told I'm thinking like a woman and not like a lawyer," admonished a young female lawyer.[95] Women legal workers were particularly sharp in their criticisms. One of them, for example, after stating that law was "a macho profession" and "a fascist tool to rape, murder and rob," stressed the idea that gender discrimination crystallized into the relationship between lawyers and legal workers, even in movement circles.[96] Indeed, legal secretaries at the radical law firm Rabinowitz, Boudin, and Standard in New York City came up with the proposal for a Women Office Workers Conference, to be organized in cooperation with the National Organization for Women, the Radical Feminists, and the Lesbian Feminist Liberation. Held in October 1973 in Manhattan, the meeting assembled four hundred legal workers to discuss common grievances, including lack of job security, low pay, limited mobility, inadequate fringe benefits, and unpleasant working conditions due to sexism and ageism.[97]

As previously mentioned, criticism of sexism in legal education and in the legal profession, as well as in the judiciary system, was ubiquitous within the Guild. Law was frequently depicted as an instrument that enshrined "woman's secondary role in society," since women had been unfairly excluded from participation in the legal apparatus as lawmakers, judges, jurors, and litigants. The definition of crimes also bore witness to that prejudice. Low acceptance rates of women in law schools, lack of hiring in law firms, and a gender pay gap were as much normal as painful.[98] If admitted into court, women were rarely treated fairly and equally, being either overlooked as non-important people or objectified in terms of their bodies.[99]

In addition to raising awareness about these cultural and social biases, Guild lawyers also discussed how anti-sexism could translate into trial practice. For instance, the defense of rapists became a hot topic, and after much discussion and an influential workshop held in Boston in April 1973, consensus emerged that representing rapists would mean subscribing to the idea that women ultimately cause rape. Thus, Guild lawyers resolved not to engage in the standard defense at rape trials, with the only exception being political frame-ups. To be sure, the NLG could not "politically support" any prosecution "in The Man's courts," but in the case of rape, it committed to stand by women.[100] Consistently, the Guild also sustained the case of Joan Little, a young Black woman who admittedly killed, in self-defense against sexual assault, a white guard at Beaufort County Jail in Washington, North Carolina, where she was incarcerated. A victim of racism and sexism, Little was eventually acquitted, establishing an important, albeit controversial, precedent.[101]

Guild women also experimented with feminist defense methods that supplemented militant litigation. San Francisco lawyer Mary C. Morgan recounted that she, along with two other female lawyers, had represented six women who went on trial in Berkeley on charges growing out of feminist demonstrations. They were accused of a variety of misdemeanors, such as disrupting a public meeting, resisting arrest, and trespass. Feminist commitment cemented these very different women, who together created a defense team that took care of preventing legal, political, and, most importantly, emotional isolation. As Morgan admitted, "lawyerism" was hard to elude, but they managed to work together, and three of the defendants also acted as co-counsel, revealing themselves as "both eloquent and outrageous." The absence of men made the difference and opened up "a wonderful new dimension." "We must have created a unique scene in the courtroom, a traditional bastion of male supremacy," explained Morgan, elated. While the judge, prosecutor, and bailiffs were men, all the other protagonists were women, including spectators and jurors, thus molding a supportive atmosphere. The defense relied heavily on showing the jury that the six women were being tried for "unlady-like" acts, not for real crimes. The jury eventually acquitted them on five counts and convicted them on two. "We were part of them. I had the feeling that we were defending ourselves, as well as them," explained Morgan, who would become the first openly lesbian judge appointed in the United States.[102]

The Guild's National Commission on Women's Oppression emerged in 1975 to promote the study of women's issues, develop a national program, organize local projects such as "anti-sexism committees," and foster a connection with the burgeoning women's movement.[103] The same year, the struggle against sexism was the main topic of the NLG's national convention in Columbus, further acknowledging the relevance of this area of engagement. By then, Guild lawyers had indeed offered their contribution to countless cases centered on women's issues, beginning with some of the early abortion cases.

Estimates of the number of illegal abortions in the United States at the end of the 1960s ranged from 200,000 to 1.5 million. Reliable statistics were impossible to gather, but the picture looked grim and terribly problematic. Many women found the situation unbearable. In that context, women's rights groups begun discussing the idea of launching an affirmative attack in federal court against New York State abortion laws, to declare them unconstitutional. Importantly, at stake was the right of women to terminate a pregnancy and not, as it had been in the past, the right of doctors to practice medicine. While a list of plaintiffs rapidly built up, a coalition named Women's Abortion Project coordinated the "women's law suit."

Radical women lawyers Nancy Stearns (lead counsel and staff attorney at the Center for Constitutional Rights), Ann Garfinkle, Emily Goodman, Florynce Kennedy, Carol Lefcourt, and Diane Schulder took the lead on the main case, known as *Abramowicz v. Lefkowitz*, whose plaintiffs were 314 people, mostly women. Three other companion lawsuits—brought by medical doctors, community activists, and a reverend—also joined the legal battle. Defendants in all cases were New York attorney general Louis J. Lefkowitz, New York district attorney Frank Hogan, and Bronx district attorney Burton Roberts.

Nancy Stearns and her colleagues relied on a twofold strategy: first, women's direct testimonies on the physical and psychological damages of illegal abortions or unwanted pregnancies, and second, public demonstrations by women's liberation groups. In January 1970, dozens of women flocked to the Foley Square courthouse to give their depositions in front of lawyers and reporters. They carried either babies or coat hangers, the symbol of illegal abortion.[104] Under oath, a select number of plaintiffs described the ordeals of finding complicit abortionists, explained the do-it-yourself unsafe methods for abortion, and disclosed the functioning of the homes for unwed mothers and the cruel system of forced adoptions. They also confessed their "shotgun weddings" and revealed the isolation they suffered when they got pregnant before marriage. Meanwhile, various public events drew attention to the case and, at the end of March, a large march of women under the banner of the Women's National Abortion Action Coalition invaded Manhattan. Just a few days later, and before the trial opened, the New York State legislature voted to amend the abortion laws. As of July 1970, abortion prior to the twenty-fourth week of pregnancy became legal.[105]

The women's victory was indisputable and confirmed that aggressive legal-political strategies bore fruit even outside the judicial system. Yet women's rights activists were far from being fully satisfied, as their stated goal was to raise the issue of the constitutionality of abortion laws at the national level. Soon, indeed, similar initiatives blossomed in other states. In the spring of 1971, Guild president Catherine Roraback, who had already been a protagonist in the legal fight for the legalization of the purchase and use of contraceptives (*Griswold v. Connecticut*), led a team of women lawyers representing a dozen feminists who filed a class action challenging the constitutionality of Connecticut's abortion law of 1860. In this case, too, the activists chose the judicial avenue as a mere first step in a larger mobilization, mistrusting the transformative power of the law. A federal court ruled in favor of the women plaintiffs, but the governor called a special session of the state legislature to write a new statute to protect the sanctity of life. The bill passed and further restricted the abortion law. In the meantime, the plaintiffs reached out to their peers, became nearly two thousand strong, and went back to the halls of justice, bringing with them two pregnant women in need of an abortion. In 1972, a federal court overturned the state's anti-abortion law.[106]

In accordance with the Guild's approach, once a right was gained, it was equally important for lawyers to preserve it and extend it across society. And so it was with the right to abortion. In deciding *Roe v. Wade* (1973), the U.S. Supreme Court recognized a woman's right to terminate unwanted pregnancy in the first trimester as absolute. Early-term abortions thus passed from the realm of prosecutorial scrutiny into that of a woman's right to privacy. During the second trimester, however, the state interest in promoting the health of the mother and prenatal life competed with a woman's freedom of choice.[107] According to Guild lawyers, far from being a momentous victory, the ruling was "an O.K. decision," coupled with a "loosely-knit standard." Sure, two justices had supported it on libertarian bases, but it was still unclear what would happen in the future, especially for women on welfare and "Third-World women."[108]

Abortion had to be fully available to every woman, as sterilization, self-induced or illegal abortions, and unwanted pregnancies were now, more than ever, unacceptable. With this aim in mind, radical women lawyers worked unabatedly in the following years.[109] For example, in 1973, Roraback successfully argued another case in which a federal judge ruled that the State of Connecticut had to pay for a welfare recipient's abortion if a doctor certified that it was necessary. In 1976, after the Hyde Amendment (and its following reformulations) barred the use of federal funds to reimburse the cost of abortions under Medicaid, Guild lawyers went back to the game. With the ACLU and Planned Parenthood attorneys, they filed a lawsuit to defend the rights of an indigent woman. The case initially brought a favorable ruling in the district court (*McRae v. Califano*), holding that the recent restrictions violated the First Amendment and the establishment clause of the Fifth Amendment. A June 1980 Supreme Court decision (*Harris v. McRae*), however, upheld the constitutionality of the original Hyde Amendment, whose exceptions remained for a long time only cases in which the woman's life was endangered.[110]

Central as it was, abortion was far from the only issue of interest during that period. Male-inflicted domestic violence, for instance, was increasingly being reported but remained largely ignored by police and the judiciary. One of the few means of protection were shelters for battered women, first ideated by feminists. So, in the second half of the 1970s, Guild lawyers worked to help create these "refuges," which not only subtracted women from home violence but also undermined the "patriarchal" institution of the family.[111] For example, Peggy Wiesenberg, a young attorney who worked for Minneapolis Legal Aid, was among the founders of the Harriet Tubman Women's Shelter, one of the first structures of this kind in the country, which hosted both mothers and kids. Led by the Battered Women's Movement, the shelter was created in 1977 and, thanks to Wiesenberg's legal knowledge and connections, was framed within the Minneapolis Housing and Redevelopment Authority, from which it acquired a building for $1 and garnered state welfare funds.[112]

While the feminist movement found larger audiences, the defense of gay rights also attracted increasing attention, as it rapidly grew from an invisible phenomenon to a significant factor of social concern. By 1973, four years after the groundbreaking Stonewall riots in New York, gay organizations already numbered eight hundred in the country and were voicing their discontent. And yet they still faced both legal and social discrimination. The majority of American states enforced sodomy laws that prohibited sexual acts between persons of the same sex, and gay people could not serve in the armed forces, could not be hired in many government offices, and were commonly excluded from many jobs.[113]

As had happened in the case of women, radical lawyers' struggle for gay rights first developed within their own milieu. At the Guild's 1971 national convention in Boulder, Colorado, a few gay lawyers began discussing the formation of a gay caucus. Yet, even within such a young and progressive environment, homosexuality was still a peripheral concern. Criticism, indifference, and even disdain were common; on the one hand, radical lawyers replicated the very conservative habits of the legal profession, where gay discrimination was widespread; on the other hand, they resented the ideological climate of the Left. The Revolutionary Union and the October League, two Maoist organizations that attracted many radical lawyers, defined homosexuals as "unnatural and perverts," while gay people dubbed the former "doctrinaire heterosexists."[114]

"In all but a few states it is illegal for lesbians and homosexual men to express their love openly. This is compounded by anti-gay attitudes either clearly stated or merely left understood in state bar associations," reads a 1972 letter by a group of gay lawyers to a Guild local chapter. According to them, not only did gay lawyers hide their sexual preferences, but they were also "unable to be open, let alone publicly fight for their gay sisters and brothers." The enemy front included all "oppressive institutions," from the nuclear family to the church, but also the leftist groups that maintained "the same sexist racist attitudes of America." Tired of adducing justifications, gay lawyers asked for comprehension, guidance, and support.[115]

Times were changing, however. A gay caucus was officially formed at the 1974 national convention of the NLG, when the organization officially recognized that gay people were part of the revolutionary movement. In 1975, the first Gay Rights Summer Project was held in Los Angeles. Law students began working together with older local lawyers to address discrimination, and local gay caucuses were built in different cities. That same year, a Gay Rights Task Force was established to serve as a clearinghouse for legal work on gay rights, in areas such as child custody, police harassment, and employment discrimination. The chair of the task force was Thomas Steel, a gay lawyer in San Francisco who undertook prominent cases involving free speech, freedom of religion, and rights of minorities. Projects focusing on anti-discrimination laws thrived for a few years, operating closely with community groups.[116]

Lesbian custody, in particular, attracted much attention within the Guild, for it was an intrinsically controversial topic and a largely unmapped legal territory. Until the late 1960s, same-sex sexuality was still understood as antithetical to parenting and, at the judicial level, "the best interest of the child" persistently lay in the heterosexual household. Yet things began to change rapidly, also by virtue of radical lawyers.[117] In 1972, Madeleine Isaacson and Sandy Schuster—two mothers who openly identified as lesbians and had committed to each other—were granted custody of their minor children, who were born out of their previous relationships. However, custody was contingent on the women's promise not to live together. In April 1974, the fathers petitioned for a modification of the custody order, arguing that the children and their mothers lived together as a family. Furthermore, the two mothers had become prominent advocates of lesbianism: they had indeed made a documentary, written a book, appeared on TV shows, and given various media interviews. The children, the fathers argued, were being led to approve homosexuality and would likely become juvenile delinquents.[118]

It was a dream case for radical lawyers. Four Guild attorneys, in cooperation with the ACLU, represented the two women, who were also included in the defense team. To discuss strategy and strengthen their union, they met weekly for several months. Previous lesbian-mother cases had typically led to adverse rulings and revealed, according to Guild lawyers, the "homophobic nature of the judicial system." Moreover, in this case a prominent conservative lawyer, who consistently analogized lesbianism to epilepsy and leprosy, represented the fathers and called experts who testified that lesbianism was incompatible with the role of parent. Yet the fact that the American Psychiatric Association had recently (1973) removed "homosexuality" from the psychiatric nomenclature as a "mental disorder" boded well for the mothers. So the defense presented a vast array of expert testimonies on contemporary sexual mores, emotional development of children, sociological theories on homosexuality, and gender. The defense also consistently argued that children should have the freedom to choose their sexual identity. After a six-day trial during which the courtroom was constantly packed with women supporters, the court ordered that the two mothers retain custody of the children, refused to limit their right to publicly speak about their sexuality and lifestyle, and determined that they could live together as a single household. The tribunal also ruled that homosexuality per se was not a proper basis for denying custody to a parent.[119]

The victory was resounding and contributed making the Guild a point of reference for gay custody rights. During the summer of 1977, for instance, the New York Guild's Anti-Sexism Committee hosted a Lesbian Custody/Gay Rights Summer Project to help women learn how to run a custody counseling clinic for lesbian mothers. For six weeks, radical lawyers held workshops to train twenty women from Dykes and Tykes—a community organization of lesbian mothers—in paralegal and peer counseling. The Dykes and Tykes Legal Custody Center eventually opened in December 1978.[120] The Guild also wrote and published a pioneering manual on lesbian mother custody rights and offered seminars on gay rights, protracting its solitary engagement until the end of the decade, when this area of law ceased to be a niche for open-minded, progressive attorneys.[121]

10 Against Political Repression

Richard Nixon put it plainly in his 1968 presidential campaign and reiterated it countless times thereafter: "In a system that provides for peaceful change, there is no cause that justifies resort to violence. Let us recognize that the first civil right of every American is to be free from domestic violence." Those who were wreaking havoc in the United States, insisted the President, were "not romantic revolutionaries" but "the same thugs and hoodlums that have always plagued the good people."[1]

Between the late 1960s and early 1970s—and more resolutely under Nixon—law enforcement responded to the growth of radicalism and the breakdown of social order with a new approach. As historian Elizabeth Hinton carefully documented, this transformation of policing had already emerged from the ashes of the 1964–65 urban rebellions, when policy makers resolved that only intensified enforcement of the law in Black neighborhoods would tame anarchy and avoid chaos. Indeed, President Johnson's war on crime officially began with the September 1965 passage of the Law Enforcement Assistance Act, which secured for urban police departments federal funds to increase recruits, professionalize them, and arm them with military-grade weapons. Johnson's legislation also instituted the Office of Law Enforcement Assistance (OLEA), initially headed by Ramsey Clark, to fund public and private programs to modernize law enforcement technologies and strategies. While Johnson insisted that law and order should not be separated from a robust intervention on poverty and education, police officers increasingly assumed a role in the administration of urban social programs.

When Nixon took office, he disregarded Johnson's social agenda and incentivized the expansion of policing that his liberal predecessor had initiated. The Law Enforcement Assistance Administration (LEAA), formerly OLEA, became the key agency to design and implement the "punitive intervention" against crime in American cities, and its budget swelled from $63 million in 1969 to $871 million in 1974.[2] Inevitably, the policing of protest expanded too, especially because the Nixon administration tended to subsume political contention under crime. Police forces shifted from passive monitoring, crowd control, and peacekeeping to active suppression of dissent, often assuming an adversarial role. What materialized was, in Frank Donner's words, "a pattern of hostility and harassment, usually haphazard and unplanned," which included indiscriminate targeting of a wide range of peaceful groups and individuals; stop-and-frisk policies; racial profiling; intrusive, extensive, and frequently illegal surveillance; and aggressive measures, such as incitement to violence, provocation, and disruption. Police countersubversive units—commonly known as red squads—expanded greatly in all major cities, employing an increasing number of agents. They adopted new technologies, amassed an unprecedented volume of information, and cooperated with federal agencies such as the FBI and the CIA.[3]

At the urging of Nixon, who wanted to defeat "revolutionary terrorism" at any price, the FBI was indeed building the nation's first institutions dedicated to preventing and opposing terrorism. Some of the projects devised during that period never took shape, and results were mixed. But in the short term, between July 1969 and July 1972, the bureau increased new domestic surveillance investigations by over 50 percent and expanded covert operations.[4] According to historian Robert J. Goldstein, around 1971 the FBI had at its disposal approximately 2,000 intelligence agents, 7,000 so-called ghetto informants, and 1,700 regular domestic intelligence informants who could rely on another 1,400 confidential sources.[5]

Those who first and foremost suffered from this wave of heightened policing were, predictably, Black Power militants—most notably, the Black Panther Party. As a matter of fact, the group's size had skyrocketed in a matter of a few years, upgrading a local organization into a national movement. By 1969, it comprised approximately five thousand members across forty local chapters. While denouncing police harassment, the Panthers themselves were violent and fear-inducing. Their "police patrolling" was actually aggressive and intimidating, at least in the eyes of many observers. The "distinction between using firearms to repel aggression and employing them as existential symbols of self-assertion sometimes became blurred," historian and former activist Mark D. Naison noted.[6] Indeed, the rhetorical appeal to "pick up the gun" and "kill the pigs" remained hardly abstract, as the Panthers often refused to submit to police control and confronted police with firearms. They killed and were killed.

In January 1968, Huey Newton had also ordered all Panthers to keep weapons in their homes so they could react to warrantless police searches, further increasing the likelihood of armed clashes. As if this were not enough, internal discipline in the BPP was hard to maintain, especially because national leaders spent considerable time in jail. Strategic divisions, purges, and personal disputes propagated; thus, endogenous violence, including beatings and murders, also grew. While the leadership continued to emphasize community service, a faction led by Eldridge Cleaver (who would later be expelled from the party) openly advocated military escalation and prepared to wage urban guerrilla warfare. A parallel underground organization also took shape.[7]

And yet the evolution of Panthers' violent conduct was deeply intertwined with policing. To some extent, it was a by-product of both the aforementioned wave of police repression and the unleashing of a specific branch of the FBI's COINTELPRO, initiated in November 1968 and intended to disrupt or otherwise neutralize the BPP. The array of counterintelligence activities targeting the Panthers was larger than ever, including disinformation, fostering antagonism with parent groups, harassment of supporters, infiltration of informants and provocateurs, instigation of internal feuds, raids at local offices, and even assassinations. In the two-year span between 1968 and 1970, at least 233 FBI counterintelligence operations targeted the Panthers.[8] Commenting on the growing number of arrests that hit the BPP, Charles Garry reported that during the spring of 1969 alone, he had received two hundred separate requests for legal representation from members of the group who had been victims of the unprecedented police and intelligence crackdown.[9] According to other estimates, by the end of 1969, at least thirty Panthers were facing the death penalty, forty were facing life imprisonment, and fifty-five were facing sentences of up to thirty years. About 155 Panthers were in jail or underground.[10]

To save the situation, in September 1968 a group of Guild attorneys filed a suit on behalf of the BPP in New York, charging the New York Police Department with systematic "violence, intimidation and humiliation," asking for community control of the police, and seeking injunctions forbidding the police from harassing the Black Panthers. Answering the Panthers' call for a Conference for a United Front against Fascism, a few radical lawyers, including Kunstler and Garry, took part in a massive gathering that was held in Oakland in July 1969. The two lawyers solemnly promised to develop a plan to provide an ongoing legal defense for Black militants and pledged to enlist a thousand colleagues.[11] Yet these and other legal maneuvers, albeit well-intentioned, looked increasingly futile.

In such an overheated context—and specifically after the raid in Chicago, which had left Fred Hampton and Mark Clark dead, and after the five-hour gun battle between a SWAT team and the Panthers at the BPP headquarters in Los Angeles[12]—white supporters, including lawyers, decided to offer their presence at Panthers' premises.[13] Conceived to de-escalate police intervention, this form of assistance seemed more urgent than legal representation; in fact, it was a survival strategy. As Dan Siegel recounted, external supporters like him created the Committee to Defend the Black Panther Party, which organized all-night vigils at the BPP headquarters. They also exerted pressure on the city governments of Berkeley and Oakland to avoid hazardous attacks.[14] Tony Serra, an eccentric radical attorney and a quintessential hippie, slept at Panthers' quarters many nights in the company of other lawyers. He vividly recalls a state of war, with the buildings sandbagged, the Panthers armed with guns, and everybody ready for a shoot-out. Since lawyers risked being bugged with electronic devices, they had to sleep naked. They stayed in sleeping bags in front of the door, explains Serra, "so in case the police came you would go out to mediate, or you would be a witness, or . . . you would be shot!" The police, thankfully, never showed up in their presence.[15]

Far from being chastised like the Panthers, the white New Left was nonetheless a victim of this recrudescence of police repression, especially through mass arrests and unbridled interventions during demonstrations. Moreover, in May 1968, the FBI started a branch of COINTELPRO specifically designed to hit the New Left, which put into effect more than 450 documented covert actions in three years. Tactics included disinformation, instigation of internal conflicts, infiltration, and provocation.[16] In this case, too, Guild lawyers wanted to do more than providing mere representation. They recast Panthers' idea of "policing the police" by sending "legal observers" to demonstrations and offering on-call systems with constant availability of lawyers (see also chapter 2).[17]

This system reportedly prevented and halted countless "interrogation-cell beatings," deprived police of opportunities for harassment or retaliation, and gave people who were abused by police a chance to file civil damages claims.[18] As a Chicago activist who was arrested during a raid explained, as soon as NLG lawyers arrived at the police station where he and his comrades were being detained, the police officers changed their attitude. The people under custody were not interrogated or intimidated: "It was as if someone higher up was very up-tight about the publicity that might arise from the attack. We were charged with the lightest charges that could have been trumped up. . . . We were given relatively low bonds the next morning."[19]

Legal observers were duly trained in workshops, while the Guild offices produced a large number of materials to inform activists of their rights vis-à-vis police controls, arrests, or harassment in various circumstances, like in their cars, in their houses, and on the street. Tips included how to hide dope, where to buy a gun, where to store weapons, when to consent to a search, and when to confess or sign anything (never). "There is no such thing as security paranoia. Things are getting heavier," warned one of these "legal street sheets."[20] A *Bust Book* was also assembled by a few Guild lawyers and Columbia University law students in 1969. It described, in practical terms, the encounter with the police in the street and the usual process of arrest and detention, making them less obscure and intimidating. It also offered a myriad of suggestions, from what to wear at a demonstration to how to call an attorney from a police station. Initially printed under the name of a phantasmal organization, an extended version of the *Bust Book* was later published by Grove Press and sold fifty thousand copies, becoming a must-have in the movement.[21]

A remarkable case of Guild legal observers' intervention occurred in support of the New York chapter of the Young Lords (YL), a group of Puerto Rican revolutionary nationalists. Born as a Chicago street gang during the 1950s, the YL had grown following the Black Panthers' lead. In a thirteen-point document, the Lords pledged to fight for the dignity of the racially oppressed and to advance basic human needs in the barrio, including food, housing, and health. Wearing their signature purple berets and speaking their unmistakable "Spanglish," these young militants also advocated armed self-defense and socialism. In the fall of 1968 they opened a chapter in East Harlem, where locals regarded them with sympathy and supported their community service programs, but the media often depicted them as thugs and lawbreakers.[22]

Looking for a place to host their breakfast for children program and to run their health clinic, the Lords hoped to employ East Harlem's First Spanish United Methodist Church and negotiated for weeks with the local minister. However, the priest denied the use of the building. On December 28, 1969, arguing that the church had ignored people's suffering, the Lords barricaded inside the church for ten days. As historian Johanna Fernández has documented, the occupied building was renamed the People's Church and transformed into a staging ground for the Lords vision of society: "a liberated space offered as a sanctuary for East Harlem poor." The YL enjoyed strong support among both the New Left and the BPP, and approximately 150 activists permanently rotated in and out of the church. Even BPP leader Kathleen Cleaver and former SNCC chair H. Rap Brown visited the building. Charles Garry went there too, to read Huey Newton's solidarity greeting, which reportedly "thrilled the packed chapel with clenched fists raised in spread-armed salute."[23]

Among these enthusiastic devotees were also a number of NLG lawyers who were already in contact with the group. As soon as the occupation was proclaimed, they immediately filed court injunctions to uphold the Young Lords' right to protest and acted as legal observers at the church. "With the knowledge of recent Black Panther shootings hanging heavily over the Lords," read a Guild report, "it was decided that extraordinary legal services were essential to prevent a repetition of the Panther incidents." Therefore, teams of lawyers accompanied the Lords to the church each Sunday, sat in their office every night, and provided around-the-clock "legal coverage." Several of them also set up a legal clinic within the church to interview community members and give legal advice. According to various sources, on more than one occasion the presence of legal observers did in fact help to de-escalate police and avoid incidents. In all, sixty lawyers and law students, coordinated by attorney Carol Goodman, participated in the six-hour shifts at the church for ten days. Police finally came in on January 7, 1970, to enforce the injunction originally filed by the priest requiring the Lords to vacate the church.[24]

Yet the presence of twenty-four lawyers and law students inside and outside the church avoided what could have been a bloody confrontation. Those outside moved quickly to cool the three hundred riot police who were ready for action, while those inside assisted in arranging the exit of supporters who wanted to leave peacefully. Observers kept a channel of communication with the police open and searched the church thoroughly to certify that—contrary to rumors—there were no weapons inside the building. They also reassured the authorities, explaining that the Lords did not intend to resist arrest. Because of the police's good faith in counsel, only eight unarmed sheriff's deputies eventually entered the church. Escorted by lawyers, police managed to walk out the 105 occupiers who still remained inside the premises.[25] Not only were the arrests performed in a peaceful way, but the subsequent phases of the case were handled coolly, to the point that the judge released all 105 defendants on their own recognizance. Guild attorneys took care of them and created a Young Lords Committee, while Puerto Rican congressman Herman Badillo acted as a mediator. As a result, charges were dropped, and the church agreed to initiate a day-care center and a clinic for a drug rehabilitation program. Lawyers from the Guild's Mass Defense Office also successfully represented thirteen Young Lords who were charged with crimes such as riot, trespass, and unlawful assembly for a previous bust at the church.[26]

The success of the action did nothing but enhance the Lords' visibility and popularity, followed by a quick and stellar growth of its ranks. One incident, however, seemed to interrupt the ascent. In October 1970, two YL militants were arrested by undercover narcotics officers for attempted arson. Two Guild lawyers were ready to help, but they had limited access to their clients, who were jailed at the Tombs. Right after, one of them, Julio Roldan, was found hanging in his cell, without a clear motive. Crying scandal and denouncing a murder, the YL carried Roldan's body to the First Spanish United Methodist Church with a funeral procession. They forced their way into the church and proclaimed their intention to remain indefinitely in the building from which they had been evicted ten months earlier. This time, however, they carried weapons and threatened an insurrection by the East Harlem community to protect them.

Occurring in the wake of the New York prison rebellions, this second occupation drew enormous attention. The Lords' demand to investigate both the death of their comrade and the whole city's penitentiary system resonated among progressive and liberal public opinion. Fearing the subversive contagion of the Lords, Mayor John Lindsay stated that no violation of the law was occurring within the church and assured that he would take no legal action to oust them. While an independent investigative commission—led by Puerto Rican attorney Geraldo Rivera—scrutinized the events at the Tombs, the Young Lords animated political and social activities in the church. Ordered to leave the premises six weeks after the takeover, the Lords walked out without police intervention.[27]

Since the early seventies, as mass rallies and contentious actions ebbed, red squad activities began retreating too. A larger public acknowledged that police behavior had been frequently unbridled, and red-hunting units had sometimes exaggerated or fabricated the subversive threat.[28] Even so, the Guild kept mobilizing its ranks to monitor less visible police abuses. In 1975, for example, the NLG created a National Task Force on Police Crimes, which undertook the task of exposing the work of the LEAA. Ahead of the times, the Guild pointed to the manifold risks of a "corporate managerial model" applied to police and fiercely denounced it. As would become clear in the following years, the LEAA had turned into a system of corruption and patronage.[29]

The Specter of Federal Grand Juries

Grand juries are bodies of citizens convened to decide whether there is sufficient evidence to hold another citizen for trial. Historically, grand juries were people's panels that protected suspects against unjust prosecutions. They acted as independent checks on prosecutors' discretion, upholding a right guaranteed by the Fifth Amendment.

By many accounts, these functions and prerogatives were valid up until 1969–70. At that point, the Justice Department of the Nixon administration turned the power of these "people's tribunals" into a weapon against political dissent, using them as a kind of intelligence agency. Since the HUAC congressional investigations were no longer acceptable instruments to quell subversion, the government established a political grand jury network, which was managed by a revitalized Internal Security Division (ISD) of the Justice Department and led by Republican Party official Robert C. Mardian. Mardian, by the way, would later be involved in the Watergate scandal and indicted by a grand jury himself. U.S. attorney Guy L. Goodwin became the head of the Special Litigation Section of the ISD and served as a sort of field marshal, organizing federal grand juries across the nation to locate enemies of the state and gather evidence against them. At the same time, ISD staff increased from seven to sixty lawyers.

Being entrusted with the sensitive job of weighing prosecutors' evidence, grand juries were given ample investigatory powers and protected secrecy, as well as extraordinary authority to compel testimony and punish recalcitrant witnesses. In particular, a federal prosecutor could subpoena anyone to appear before a grand jury without explaining the purposes of the investigation—not even whether the person was being questioned as a potential defendant or mere witness. Also, there was no limit to the number of witnesses who could be called, to the number of questions that could be addressed, and to the number of subpoenas. The witness entered the chamber alone, had no right to retain a lawyer, and had no right to a transcript of the testimony. Most importantly, after the Organized Crime Control Act of 1970, which expanded the power of federal grand juries, the witness also lost the right to remain silent. Through the institute of the "use immunity," also known as "forced immunity," if a witness did not agree to testify, claiming Fifth Amendment rights (privilege against self-incrimination), a prosecutor could force immunity upon the witness. Accordingly, the witness could not be prosecuted for any offense coming out of the investigation but could not assert the right to remain silent. In the case of a persisting refusal to testify, the witness could be jailed for contempt (refusal to obey an order of the court) until the grand jury was active. The same 1970 act also empowered the Justice Department to convene special investigative grand juries for up to eighteen months, renewable.

It goes without saying that this configuration of federal grand juries made them one of the most formidable devices for intelligence gathering and political disruption, especially in the hands of an administration that felt under the assault of subversive forces. According to estimates, between 1970 and 1973, the ISD conducted over one hundred grand juries in eighty-four cities, called between one thousand and two thousand witnesses by subpoena, and returned some four hundred indictments, often pro forma. Up to fifty of these grand juries were openly political, with their targets including the Black Panthers, the Catholic left, and the American Indian Movement. Essentially no one on the radical front was exempt. Blaming grand juries' proliferation and their unfettered discretion, even Senator Ted Kennedy went as far as saying that "the abuses of power of the Department's overzealous prosecutors do not even know the bounds of a Joe McCarthy." After an interruption caused by the Watergate scandal, a second wave of grand jury investigations took off in 1975, hitting a number of radical groups, including the Symbionese Liberation Army and the Weather Underground, but also subpoenaing an increasing number of radical lawyers.[30]

Since the very beginning of this redefinition of grand juries, Guild lawyers cast a wary eye on them. In a cruel twist of history, this citizens' counterforce—also designed to protect political dissent—was transformed into a weapon in the hands of the Justice Department and a tool to intimidate advocates of disfavored ideas. As Guild attorney Jim Reif recalls, grand juries "could force people into essentially a secret proceeding on very short notice without having lawyers sitting next to them. They committed people to travel thousands of miles in a few days and asked them far-reaching, invasive questions on political activities that really did not have anything to do with genuine criminal investigation."[31] While no one could be directly compelled to answer questions posed by FBI agents or produce other evidence for them, as the FBI did not retain subpoena power, these new grand juries were used to circumvent this limitation and discover evidence that would have otherwise remained out of reach.[32]

It naturally followed that counseling witnesses subpoenaed before political grand juries became a priority for the NLG and looked like a throwback to past efforts to protect witnesses before HUAC. In a sense, being at the forefront of such a legal fight seemed the best way to close ranks against what radical lawyers labelled the "Gestapo tactics" of Nixon.[33] In 1971, attorneys began sharing information and acquiring expertise on this area of law, which lacked a significant caseload but was developing rapidly. A year later, the Grand Jury Defense Office opened in San Francisco. The office worked as a center of national coordination, a clearinghouse, and a training hub. Since lawyers had no prior exposure to this matter, workshops to instruct counsel representing witnesses were held across the country. Jim Reif, who worked with the Center for Constitutional Rights and focused on grand juries, toured the United States with a core group of a dozen lawyers to support other colleagues and witnesses, somehow tailing the trajectory of Guy Goodwin. The Grand Jury Defense Office also published a booklet for prospective grand jury witnesses and, in 1974, authored *Representation of Witnesses before Federal Grand Juries*, at the time the only legal manual on grand jury law. In the meantime, the Guild proposed the formation of a national Coalition to End Grand Jury Abuse, to initiate an educational and legislative campaign calling for the reform of this misused judicial tool. The ACLU, the NECLC, the NCBL, and the Women's Strike for Peace joined the initiative, which also led to the drafting of a bill.[34]

The opportunity of testifying or not, even in cases of forced immunity when witnesses faced the risk of prison, was widely discussed. Should we ever talk with the enemy? Is it more convenient for the movement the jailing of a militant who remains silent or the freedom of a militant who accepts to testify and potentially endangers others? These and other questions haunted Guild lawyers and, once again, inner divisions formed. For some, mostly hard-core radicals, non-collaboration was imperative, and the NLG, they argued, should be entitled to protect it. The movement could not afford to be further divided and weakened by tipping off the authorities. For others, immunity was a trap against the movement, and it was essential to defuse it by testifying. Eventually, a middle-of-the-road and flexible approach prevailed: it seemed wise to take into consideration a range of factors, from the kind of information the witness knew to the effective risk of perjury, and let the activists decide, case by case.[35]

In practical terms, the whole effort succeeded in both publicizing to the legal community the repressive use of grand juries and providing substantial know-how to lawyers and militants. According to rough estimates, 75 percent of the lawyers working on political grand juries were Guild lawyers, and 90 percent of them were trained by the Guild. Coordination among cases and exchange of opinions and briefs through the Guild were also crucial. And victories in court came frequently. A team of radical lawyers, for instance, successfully represented Joanne Kinoy, Arthur's daughter and a leftist activist, who was involved in one of the first grand jury cases in which the government tried to leverage the immunity mechanism. She refused to testify on the whereabouts of two Weather Underground militants, but the government's application for immunity was rejected.[36] In a number of other cases, radical lawyers either impaired the grant of immunity or were able to delay the contempt hearings until the end of the relative grand jury session, so witnesses avoided talking and were not jailed.[37]

The radical community that gravitated around the Weather Underground seemed quite impenetrable and essentially complied with the instructions that the group itself sent to its sympathizers. "Grand juries," read the document, "are a way of getting information that the pigs couldn't get in any other way." Hence, it was necessary to refrain from talking or, in the worst case, it was advisable to answer without providing any reliable evidence.[38] As a matter of fact, the Weather Underground resisted the assault of federal grand juries, also with the help of radical lawyers. The 1972 grand jury that was impaneled in San Francisco and subpoenaed seventeen leftists from the area is a case in point. By virtue of a legal and extralegal battle led by a Guild team—to get subpoenas quashed and to denounce in the media a preposterous investigation—only a couple of activists, allegedly devoid of any relevant information, testified, while the others avoided cooperation. Only one of them was charged with contempt and spent a month in jail, but indictments were never issued.[39]

Despite lawyers' unrelenting efforts, however, it was hard to cope with this pernicious mechanism of intelligence gathering and its chilling effects. Supportive communities sometimes broke down under the attack of grand juries. For example, a number of radical lesbians and feminists in Massachusetts were approached in an attempt to seek information on two women, Susan Saxe and Katherine Power, who were on the FBI's Most Wanted list for their participation in a radical group that committed robberies and murdered a police officer. Between forty and fifty of them were subpoenaed and eventually only six among them decided not to talk. They were granted use immunity and, after a second refusal to testify, were held in contempt and jailed. However, five of them decided to free themselves by going back to the grand jury for a third time and finally cooperate. Only one remained in jail. Although the defense claimed that these five witnesses did not disclose any sensitive information, Saxe was arrested, and the unity of the radical front was clearly damaged.[40]

All in all, it is hard to assess the extent to which lawyers and militants were able to substantially impair the work of political grand juries, although they certainly slowed it down and forestalled it several times. One aspect, however, emerges quite distinctly from such mixed evidence. Many federal grand jury investigations failed to achieve their goals because the government refused to disclose whether "illegal electronic surveillance"—essentially, wiretapping conducted in the absence of a properly issued warrant—formed the basis for the questions that were addressed to witnesses. The repressive apparatus stumbled upon that major obstacle, and radical lawyers were ready to take advantage of it.

Turning Surveillance against Itself

Since the beginning of the 1970s, the menace of all-pervasive monitoring of human activities loomed large in American society. More than at any time before, multiple voices raised awareness of such a threat and leveled charges against the government. "The exponential growth of privacy-invading technology"—wrote, prophetically, Senator Charles E. Goodell, a moderate Republican of New York—"is whittling away our privacy so rapidly that soon we may not be able to prevent our government, employers, and others who pass judgment upon us from knowing virtually everything about us from the moment of birth to the date, amount, purpose, and recipient of our last check. In this computer age, virtually everywhere we go we leave electronic tracks on somebody's computer."[41]

The escalation and increasing sophistication of surveillance protocols mirrored broader social trends but were also correlated with the approval of the Omnibus Crime Act in 1968 and the subsequent expansion of policing under Nixon. Red squads and the FBI routinely collected and exchanged an extraordinary volume of data concerning any kind of dissident activity, including peaceful and lawful organizations whose menace to national security was at best unrealistic. In fact, the network of political surveillance was more intricate than that, involving both the CIA and the army. In principle designated to intercept and counter foreign threats, the CIA and the army had extended their mission in order to monitor domestic dissent through a variety of projects and operations. For example, they scrutinized phone calls and correspondence, generated tens of thousands of dossiers on presumed radicals, and tracked down alleged foreign influences on alleged extremists.[42]

While Senator Samuel J. Ervin's Subcommittee on Constitutional Rights tried to uncover the extent of military spying, conservative voices took up the cudgels for the government and its right to surveil citizens. William H. Rehnquist, who at the time was an assistant attorney general in the Office of General Counsel at the Department of Justice, insisted that the Constitution empowered the president to prevent violation of the law through extensive, warrantless surveillance if necessary. It was an "inherent power" of the executive branch, mandated by the need to protect the "national interest."[43] Before taking his seat on the U.S. Supreme Court and changing his mind, Lewis F. Powell, former president of the American Bar Association, wrote a widely read essay arguing that the charges of repression leveled against law enforcement were "false" or, otherwise said, "standard leftist propaganda." In particular, the impression of massive eavesdropping was almost "a conspiracy to confuse the public," as wiretaps numbered only a few hundred annually. Law-abiding citizens, indeed, had "nothing to fear."[44]

Radical lawyers could not help but engage in this arena of political and legal confrontation. One of the first steps was taken in 1971, when a group of Guild lawyers filed a class action against the City of New York, its police commissioner, and the Intelligence Division of the New York City Police Department. Drafted by Martin Stolar, Jethro M. Eisenstein, and Paul G. Chevigny, the class action charged the NYC red squad with a wide array of abuses that revolved around illegal surveillance, infiltration, and provocation, all to the detriment of First Amendment rights. Plaintiffs of *Handschu v. Special Services Division*, as the case is known, were a group of individuals that Guild lawyers drew from the movement milieu, including Abbie Hoffman and Jerry Rubin, who gave sworn statements about being surveilled and provoked. For a laugh, the name of Barbara Handschu, who helped to organize the class action, appeared first on a list of plaintiffs that increasingly grew bigger. In 1985, a settlement was finally reached. Although the Guild harshly criticized the settlement for being a meager compromise, the class action, which is still open, led to the creation of evolving guidelines that police should follow and citizens can invoke.[45]

At the same time, radical lawyers began to delve into electronic surveillance to unhinge the grand juries' mechanism. In this regard, it is worth remembering that since the 1930s, the government's policy had been to use electronic surveillance only against suspected spies working on behalf of foreign countries. Then the controversial Omnibus Crime Act of 1968 had authorized police wiretapping and eavesdropping in investigations of many crimes, going largely beyond national security cases. A warrant based on "probable cause" was always needed; however, in case of "emergency," warrantless surveillance was allowed for up to forty-eight hours. For the first time, the law also permitted the admission of the results of such surveillance in federal court.

While the number of authorized wiretaps ballooned, it was common knowledge that government agencies were operating in the absence of judicial authorization in countless circumstances.[46] For example, under the pressure of Guild attorneys, the Justice Department admitted that it had conducted electronic surveillance without a warrant on at least some of the lawyers in the Chicago Eight case. The government argued that the taps were valid due to their internal security relevance.[47] In March 1969, however, the Supreme Court not only confirmed that defendants were entitled to the suppression of evidence violative of the Fourth Amendment but also held that a court hearing was always required to show whether evidence was "the fruit of the poisonous tree"—namely, tainted.[48] Such a favorable legal backing was immediately exploited.

The first major victory came from the grand jury subpoena of Sister Jogues Egan, in connection with the investigation of the Harrisburg Seven in 1971 (see chapter 6). Following her refusal to testify on Fifth Amendment grounds, she was granted immunity. Her lawyer, Jack Levine, an associate of the NLG, contacted his Guild fellows for consultation. Together they raised the possibility that illegal electronic surveillance could be at the core of the investigation, and this liability could be used to avoid interrogation. When Egan declined to testify a second time, she contended that the information that had caused the government to subpoena her flowed from illegal electronic surveillance. The district court judge refused to consider that argument; thus, she was held in contempt and jailed. The case was appealed to the third circuit judges, who in May 1971 recognized that the government failed to reveal whether Egan was a victim of illegal surveillance and granted her the right to remain silent. "The Government," reads the majority opinion, "now seeks to profit from its unconstitutional conduct by propounding questions based on the improperly seized information. To deprive Sister Egan of a shield to ward off such activity would seriously rend the armor of the Fourth Amendment." As Reif remembers, it was a tremendous victory for the radical front and provided a solid ground to avoid testimonies before grand juries.[49]

Other similar cases followed in the ensuing months, bringing about further victories.[50] Altogether, such legal developments led to a wholesale repudiation of the government's policy of unrestricted surveillance with *U.S. v. U.S. Dist. Ct.*, a landmark Supreme Court decision. The case arose from charges brought against John Sinclair, Lawrence "Pun" Plamondon, and John Forrest, accused of conspiracy to destroy government property, notably a CIA office in Ann Arbor, Michigan. The three defendants were leaders of the White Panthers, a radical collective operating between Detroit and Ann Arbor, and were represented by Kunstler, Weinglass, and Hugh M.

Davis, another Guild lawyer. Sinclair, by the way, was a national figure who had been sentenced to prison (up to ten years) for possession of marijuana. Represented by Guild lawyer Ravitz and supported by a parade of celebrities that included John Lennon and Yoko Ono, he had been released in December 1971.[51]

Evidence against these three militants was contained in tape recordings of conversations they allegedly had with employees of the Cuban embassy. The prosecution acknowledged warrantless wiretapping, claiming that national security was at risk, and the Department of Justice confirmed it. As these admissions transpired, Guild lawyers were puzzled. Why didn't the government just deny it? Soon they discovered that the administration was explicitly seeking a stamp of legitimacy from the Supreme Court on the notion that the president could easily overlook the Constitution in the name of national interest. Radical attorneys viewed this attack to the limitations of power as "unprecedented" and seriously thought that a "transition to fascism" was underway.[52]

In any event, the judge did not accept the government's argument, and when the case was finally taken to the U.S. Supreme Court, things went awry for the administration. Robert Mardian himself—the head of the ISD—argued for the government, while Kinoy argued for the defendants. "I was facing head on an ominous bid for unlimited power by the top forces in the ruling establishment, and it was overwhelming," remembered Kinoy, who opted for avoiding legal technicalities and emphasized the suspension of constitutional guarantees. The court unanimously rejected Nixon's claim of unlimited power. In a shocking reversal, Nixon's appointee Lewis Powell, by then a justice, wrote the decision establishing that warrantless electronic surveillance could not be sustained by claiming national security exemption.[53]

U.S. v. U.S. Dist. Ct. led the government to drop its charges in numerous prosecutions, instead of releasing the illegally obtained logs. Conversely, it opened the door to surveillance claims in political cases and provided grounds for civil suits for damages by all persons victimized by "domestic security" wiretapping. By 1973, the Guild recognized that electronic surveillance was a primary area of struggle and turned the Grand Jury Defense Office into the Electronic Surveillance Project, also based in San Francisco. The new project publicized this avenue of litigation, served as a clearinghouse of legal materials, established a network of contacts, and organized training sessions across the country to teach lawyers and defendants how a victim could prove its status through discovery motions and disclosure demands.[54]

Meanwhile, illegal surveillance emerged as a favorite method through which the White House dealt with political opponents in the corridors of power. Therefore, in April 1973, the Guild embarked on a lawsuit to set aside the 1972 election, which had confirmed Nixon in a landslide. Retrospectively overambitious and quixotic yet characteristic of the combative spirit of the Guild, the idea of a legal action to declare null and void the election was based on the assumption that "the American people had been deprived of their right to choose their highest elected officials by a widespread conspiracy that operated through a series of illegal acts." They included unlawful surveillance, misuse of government agencies, campaign fraud, intimidation, extortion, and perjury. The goal was to prove this whole range of crimes in court and mobilize the public. Eventually, on May 21, 1974, the NLG filed its class action. The complaint contained 171 pages of factual allegations detailing how Nixon conducted a fraudulent campaign, and it was signed by eight thousand people. But history ran faster: formal hearings in the impeachment inquiry of Nixon had already begun, and the president's destiny was doomed.[55]

Over the following years, further revelations of broad intelligence targeting and questionable tactics surfaced in numerous political cases. Public pressure, indeed, led to the disclosure of police intelligence documents at various levels. In 1976, the Seattle chapters of the NLG, the ACLU, and the American Friends Service Committee formed the Coalition on Government Spying (COGS), which launched a successful campaign to ban indiscriminate police surveillance. In June 1977, a number of local organizations under the banner of COGS filed a complaint for the release of their intelligence files. Police reluctantly disclosed these records: they showed not only a wide range of surveillance tactics against political activists and community leaders but also "misinformation, irrelevance, inaccuracies, and trivia" about the people under scrutiny, including Guild lawyers. While the chief of the intelligence unit, who had attempted to remove some embarrassing files, was held in contempt and fired, the COGS published a list of recommendations for legislating on the matter. These guidelines were embraced by the mayor of Seattle and, in 1979, the city council passed a landmark ordinance banning political surveillance without criminal investigation. The ordinance also requested rigorous authorizations for investigations that could interfere with the rights to free expression or association and for the deployment of infiltrators and informers. It was the nation's first local ordinance limiting police intelligence gathering.[56]

Lawyers under Attack

As soon as the Roosevelt era came to an end and the Guild ceased to be an ally to the government, repression became a daily companion of radical lawyers. As a matter of fact, prosecutors, police, and FBI agents lucidly recognized the influence of lawyers and feared it. While inflating the threat that radical attorneys posed to democracy, they sought to discredit or neutralize them. To appreciate the extent and the impact of the repressive measures that hit the Guild and those in its orbit, it is useful to unpack them on the basis of the main deployed strategies—namely, public condemnation and blacklisting, attempts to impair professional activity, direct policing, grand jury investigation, and surveillance and infiltration.

As previously mentioned, efforts to tarnish the reputation of radical attorneys and marginalize them had a long history. The first major blow against the NLG was delivered in August 1953, when the attorney general announced in a speech to the American Bar Association that he wanted to include the Guild on his list of subversive organizations. The attorney general stated that evidence showed that the NLG was "a Communist-dominated and controlled organization." The blacklisting was supposed to assist the government in determining the loyalty of its employees, but the attorney general specified that it should also help citizens disassociate themselves from such groups. To begin with, NLG members ought to be excluded from the ABA. Guild president Earl B. Dickerson replied that the government's charges were unfounded and the Guild was "an independent, liberal bar association" that always acted "in the best traditions of American democracy." Without disowning the defense of the constitutional rights of communists, Dickerson recapped the Guild's credentials, such as support for the UN, and sought the help of the bar to challenge this procedure.[57]

The blacklisting was never implemented, but the shadow of McCarthyism loomed over the Guild. Not only did many lawyers leave the organization out of fear of losing respectability and business, but a number of the Guild's associates ran the gauntlet of HUAC hearings.[58] When lawyers typically refused to tell the committee whether they were communist or not—many were indeed staunch communists—they were charged with contempt of Congress.[59] Attorney Maurice L. Braverman, on his part, served more than two years in federal prison for acknowledging his membership in the CPUSA.[60] In a 1959 report, the House Un-American Activities Committee claimed that Communist Party lawyers were practically required to become members of the Guild, making the NLG "a focal point" of "legal subversion."[61] Essentially, until the early 1960s, all publications and reports issued by HUAC cited the Guild as a "Communist front" or "the foremost legal bulwark of the Communist Party."[62]

Judicial activism was variously denounced, especially when it involved illustrious figures such as Arthur Kinoy, who was convicted for his energetic defense of witnesses before HUAC, citing "loud and boisterous talking." Only a long legal battle supported by the NLG was able to clear him of these charges.[63] George Crockett was another victim of public condemnation. During his tenure as a judge in Detroit, he made a big name for himself reducing sentences in all cases in which he suspected that police had committed brutality. Crockett also pressed for the release of the quasi-totality of the 142 Black nationalists rounded up at the New Bethel Baptist Church in 1969, affirming that they were illegally deprived of their liberty. As a result, the Detroit Police Department and the local press began a campaign of defamation against him and circulated a petition of impeachment and removal. A support committee for the judge, also endorsed by Democratic national politicians, successfully neutralized the attack.[64]

Given the lawyers' full-fledged commitment to prisoners, law enforcement and government officials came to perceive the engagement across bars as a major threat to public order. As already mentioned in chapter 7, the crisis of the California prison system was regarded as the outcome of a concerted attack unleashed by a front of subversive forces, among which radical lawyers featured prominently. San Quentin director Raymond K. Procunier openly attacked "a small group of lawyers who are feverishly involved with left-wing activist activities throughout the state." When a prison guard was killed in July 1971, San Quentin associate warden James W. Park also reprimanded the lawyers: "You can lay some of the blame for this at the door step of some of these radical attorneys who come in here and encourage the men to do this sort of thing." Right after the murder of George Jackson, Park once again blamed lawyers: "I think that a lot of this bullshit talk by dilettante revolutionaries—and they aren't here getting killed—contributed to this kind of thing." And he added, "We are not going to have a goddam parade of lawyers coming in here anymore."[65] The FBI, indeed, nurtured this interpretation: "Most of the influence" in connection with Black prisoners and extremist activities "comes from outsiders, mainly attorneys and other pseudo groups," asserted a memo released in 1971.[66]

Prison authorities alleged that Fay Stender and John Thorne and other associate attorneys encouraged inmates to provide testimony on behalf of the Soledad Brothers. According to an FBI report, prisoners testified that

NLG lawyers made promises to help inmates in exchange for false testimony.[67] In the wake of the bloody events at San Quentin, Governor Reagan commissioned the California Board of Corrections to conduct a study to address the problem of violence and revolutionary activities behind and across prison walls. The report specifically charged the Soledad Brothers Defense Committee, Stender, and the San Francisco chapter of the NLG of circulating "false reports" about correctional facilities; fomenting disturbances, such as hunger strikes and riots, at Folsom and San Luis Obispo; introducing subversive publications; and acting as message carriers between prisons. Among its recommendations, the board of corrections emphasized the need to exclude from penitentiaries "outside groups or persons advocating violence or revolutionary activities."[68]

It goes without saying that concrete actions to impair the professional activity of radical lawyers quite naturally followed. For example, more stringent rules for lawyers and clients were introduced across California. While under a prior rule any member of the state bar could visit an inmate, only one attorney of record was now entitled to visits. Only officially licensed legal investigators—and not any person as before—were allowed to work with prisoners, and the infamous tape recorders were banned from prisons. Time for interviews with external visitors was reduced, and the presence of guards during all visits was mandated. By consenting to mail inspections against contraband and other possible crimes, the secrecy of attorney-client correspondence was breached. Justified as sensible and rational measures after a wave of bloody incidents, these and other restrictive measures were perceived by radical lawyers as explicit attempts to curb their activities and neutralize their engagement.[69]

Punitive reviews by character committees hampering or retarding admission to the bar were also quite frequent. As is known, the bar investigates the character and fitness of its applicants and enforces professional discipline. Radical lawyers' allegations of political discrimination through this review process were countless. For instance, the previously mentioned Terence Hallinan—who was the son of Progressive Party presidential candidate Vincent Hallinan, had been a member of the W. E. B. Du Bois Clubs of America, had a juvenile criminal record, and had been arrested during civil rights demonstrations—passed the bar examination in California, but the Committee of Bar Examiners delayed his admission to practice. He was not a person of moral character, argued the committee. Represented by Benjamin Dreyfus—a doyen of radical lawyers—and supported by a Guild amicus curiae, he was forced to appeal to the California Supreme Court in order to be admitted to the bar. Ironically, he would later be elected as a district attorney in San Francisco.[70]

Similarly, Dan Siegel was admitted to the bar, but having received criminal charges for inciting a riot during the People's Park crisis at Berkeley, he was suspended for being morally unfit. To be reinstated, he had to undergo a three-year legal fight, obviously with the help of Guild lawyers.[71] When a character committee asked Martin Stolar if he had ever been a member of any organization that advocated the overthrow of the government, he refused to answer, pleading the Fifth Amendment. His admission stalled, but his lawyer, Leonard Boudin, took the case up to the Supreme Court and obtained a resounding victory.[72]

As mentioned earlier, contempt citations and threats of disbarment dotted radical lawyers' history. Famously, Harry Sacher and Abraham J. Isserman, two legendary Guild lawyers, were punished for their defiant courtroom manners during the Foley Square trial. In 1952, the Supreme Court confirmed their conviction: Sacher was disbarred and had to spend six months in prison; Isserman was suspended for two years and sent to jail for four months.[73] In the context of the 1960s and 1970s, disciplinary measures of this kind increased in number, giving the impression of a concerted attack against the leftist legal community.[74] However, these attacks also boomeranged, laying bare their specious motivation or simply offering the lawyers a badge of honor for being persecuted.

The case of Kenneth Cockrel is worth remembering because it turned a contempt proceeding against a single lawyer into an offensive against racism in the courtroom. As described in chapter 4, Cockrel was a young Black lawyer from Detroit, but he was also a notorious leftist. In April 1969, while representing one of the defendants in the New Bethel trial, Cockrel reacted with rage to the judge's refusal to allow the defense to present witnesses and to the judge's order to double the bond without a hearing. Outside the courtroom, he gave an interview and referred to the judge as a "racist honkey," "racial bandit," and "fool."[75] Contempt charges closely followed, but tremendous legal and political support was mobilized for him. The prosecutor was confronted by eleven defense attorneys and a jammed courtroom, with hundreds of spectators in the corridor and outside the building. Six amicus briefs were submitted by representatives of the Guild and by liberal organizations such as the ACLU. Instead of focusing on free speech, the Guild insisted on bashing judicial racism and contextualized Cockrel's intemperance within "the necessity of a Black attorney defending a Black client." Every day during the four-day hearing, scores of people gathered at

5 p.m. to attend the "People's Court" where Cockrel, his attorneys, and movement spokespeople explained the trial proceedings and commented on race and class biases in the legal system. Cockrel did not retract his statements and maintained that his comments were "a correct characterization." To prove that the judge was indeed a "racist" and a "criminal," Cockrel and his team amassed an enormous volume of evidence. Facing such a legal barrage, the prosecutor voluntarily dismissed the case, making Cockrel a celebrity.[76] A few months later, a bar disciplinary proceeding was nonetheless instituted against Cockrel, but a petition to support him immediately circulated among radical lawyers, suggesting that "the Bar should investigate the people who are seeking to punish him rather than the other way around." Over three hundred lawyers from all over the country signed it. The bar had no choice but to pull back.[77]

Albeit less thundering, a similar victory ensued in Louisville, Kentucky, where Daniel T. Taylor was under attack by both the judiciary system and the bar. Undeniably a firebrand, Taylor had for a long time been the only lawyer in Louisville who would take unpopular and indigent clients. He fully embraced militant litigation and was described as someone who "collected contempt citations from judges the way some people run up parking tickets." Representing a Black man accused of killing a police officer in 1971, Taylor was so theatrical in his defense and so enraged against the presiding judge that he was sentenced to four and a half years for contempt (surpassing Kunstler's contempt sentence in Chicago). Taylor served only six days before being released from jail, but his case went up to the U.S. Supreme Court. Justices held that the judge had violated Taylor's right to a hearing, providing new protections for lawyers. At the same time, after a long investigation the Kentucky State Bar Association brought various charges against Taylor, including contempt and assault and battery on a fellow attorney, and recommended a five-year suspension. While a solidarity committee publicized the case, Kunstler agreed to represent him, bringing to court a parade of witnesses, including radicals and sex workers, who testified on Taylor's generosity toward the outcasts. His suspension was eventually limited to six months.[78]

In other circumstances, however, repression of lawyers took more immediate and material substance by means of arrests and criminal charges. As previously explained, lawyers were brought into custody and tried during both the civil rights movement and the Free Speech Movement. The case of Robert Treuhaft, arrested on December 3, 1964, during the occupation of Sproul Hall at UC Berkeley, made a sensation, for he was a veteran lawyer and a communist whose influence on young people was deemed as dangerous.[79] While the prosecutor maintained that Treuhaft had advised Berkeley students to "go limp" so that police would have difficulty handling them, Treuhaft argued that he was simply extending his services to demonstrators. The case was dismissed in April 1968, thanks to the untiring work of a team of Guild lawyers.[80] Jim Donnelly, another Guild eminence and founder of the organization, was arrested a few years later. In his case, charges stemmed from a courtroom confrontation in Cambridge, Massachusetts, for which he was accused of assault and battery on a police officer and disorderly conduct inside a courthouse. Donnelly represented himself and, with the constant presence during the trial of about two hundred supporters from the leftist community, won an acquittal.[81]

Arrests also occurred overseas, in Olongapo (see chapter 6), leading to the deportation of the Guild delegation back to the United States. After the military law office in the Philippines closed, other forms of harassment followed in the remaining East Asian offices, always to discredit and undercut the engagement of lawyers. Not only were they spied on, but they were also searched, held in custody, and restrained of their professional rights in multiple circumstances.[82] As part of Operation CHAOS—an espionage project to unmask foreign influences on the radical movements—the CIA monitored and occasionally disrupted the Guild's activities abroad. One lawyers' delegation to Cuba, for example, was arrested during its transit in Mexico. The lawyers were held for four days, questioned about their political beliefs, subjected to searches, and eventually expelled from the country.[83]

In a handful of documented cases, radical attorneys also served time in prison for criminal charges. They argued that they were victims of repression, while judicial authorities maintained it was a plain application of the law. Arthur Turco was one of the targets. A junior partner in the Kunstler firm and a dedicated lawyer for the Black Panthers, Turco was charged with participating, together with twelve BPP militants, in the torture and murder of another Black Panther, under the impression that he was either a law enforcement officer or a police informer. Specifically, Turco was charged with conspiracy to murder, assault with intent to murder, solicitation to murder, solicitation to kidnap, and accessory to murder. Turco left the country and, six months after a warrant for his arrest had been issued, was caught in Montreal, Canada. He agreed to be deported from Canada and returned to Baltimore, where he served eleven months before receiving a hung jury and being freed on bond.

Radical lawyers saw the indictment and imprisonment of Turco as a threat to their entire community. In August 1971, a pool of first-class Guild lawyers, which included Garry, Kunstler, Weinglass, and Lefcourt, filed a class action on behalf of Turco, "all other attorneys similarly situated," the Black Panther Party, and "all other organizations similarly situated" against the state's attorney for Baltimore City, his assistant, the police commissioner of Baltimore City, and the chief of criminal investigation of the Baltimore City Police Department. The plaintiffs alleged that the criminal proceeding against Turco was brought "in bad faith and without reasonable expectation of eventual success in order to have a chilling effect on the exercise by him and his clients . . . of their fundamental rights of expression." The complaint also argued that police officials conspired to fabricate the criminal charges in order to "harass, intimidate, deter and destroy" the Baltimore chapter of the BPP. According to the plaintiffs, the police secured "by terrorization, intimidation, coercion, grants of immunity and payments of money" the agreement of three former members of the BPP to serve as false witnesses. While asking to drop the charges against Turco and the Panthers, the suit also demanded that the police and judiciary avoid infiltrating, surveilling, or otherwise interfering with the activities of the BPP. Coming ahead of the torrent of revelations about police and FBI abuses, the suit fell on deaf ears and was rejected for lack of factual evidence. At retrial, however, Turco was given the offer to plead guilty to assault charges; he accepted the deal and was immediately freed.[84]

Quite predictably, radical lawyers did not escape the tentacles of grand juries either. It was the demonstration against the Democratic National Convention in Chicago that first put investigators on the Guild's trail. In February 1969, a federal grand jury sitting in Chicago subpoenaed the administrative assistant of the NLG, essentially because most of the meetings for planning the legal defense of the Chicago protesters took place in the New York Guild office where she worked. "This is a clear infringement of the right of people involved in political and social movement to confer with their attorneys in advance of mass action," rebutted the Guild.[85] But it was a shock. "This was the beginning of the turn against the lawyers," remembers Cloke. "Within the NLG you could feel it. The movement was starting to collapse."[86] Other lawyers were later subpoenaed by grand juries who were investigating, among other things, the Weather Underground, the radical bomber Sam Melville, and deserters who were going to Canada.[87]

During the course of the 1970s, the use of subpoenas against lawyers increased, essentially to force them to disclose information and whereabouts obtained in the course of their representation of political defendants. Within the Guild, this was seen as "a concerted strategy to harass . . . the political defense bar," which "flied [*sic*] in the face of the canons of ethics, the code of professional responsibility, and the Sixth Amendment." It was arguably so. However, the hybrid role of Guild lawyers, forever suspended between political and legal action, inevitably exposed them to attacks of this kind.[88]

The Bureau and the Guild

The Guild and the FBI shared a long history of monitoring each other's activities. Documents prove that the NLG was under the FBI's radar at least since 1941, when the bureau started investigating it as a "Communist front organization."[89] The Guild's bold criticism of FBI surveillance practices in the 1940s could not help but stir Hoover's attention. And FBI documents evince the use of break-ins and eavesdropping to investigate the Guild during the entirety of the 1950s, coupled with attempts to impair its activities.[90]

As soon as lawyers set foot in the South in the early sixties, the alarm regarding Guild activism sounded again. The main concern was that radical lawyers would have instilled into the movement what the FBI considered a pernicious communist influence. A 1965 letter from Ernest Goodman to Martin Luther King offering the assistance of radical lawyers circulated within the bureau as proof of this danger. The NLG drive for the desegregation of southern public facilities was a source of apprehension, too, and a Guild memorandum on the topic was disseminated through the Department of Justice and other agencies.[91] As mentioned, lawyers frequently perceived the FBI surveillance in the South; however, they primarily criticized the bureau's inaction vis-à-vis racial discrimination.

The feeling of being in the grip of the FBI and the red squads grew exponentially between the late 1960s and the early 1970s. And it was not simply an illusion. In those months, individual lawyers, law collectives, and defense committees were monitored and harassed on multiple occasions. People's Law Office attorneys and clients, for instance, discovered that they were under constant surveillance, their mail was controlled, and their phones were tapped. Unmarked vehicles with plainclothes officers inside began parking near the office, and the cars of some of their clients were stopped and searched.[92] As a matter of fact, the NLG was the object of an ongoing investigation regarding its connections with the Communist Party, simultaneously appeared in several FBI investigations on radical organizations, and was an official target of COINTELPRO, at least since March 1969.[93]

Defying Hoover's staunch obsession with communism, however, the FBI was forced to attest to the emancipation of the Guild from the CPUSA. In

1969, a source belatedly advised that the NLG had developed from a "complacent old left type organization" into a strong, active supporter of the "new left," whose purpose seemed to be the advancement of "social revolution."[94] Two years later, the FBI finally acknowledged that there was "little or no Communist Party influence on current Guild activity" and that the organization came to represent "the activist arm of the radical movement."[95] Such a conclusion was reiterated in a 1973 report: a special agent confirmed that the NLG "has broken ties with the CP as an organization" and recommended that the case "be placed in a pending-inactive status." "It should be noted," glossed the report, "that the NLG although the champion of many liberal causes is not itself considered a subversive organization and does not espouse the use of force, violence, or assassination."[96] In 1974, the investigation into the Guild's communist ties was officially closed.

Even so, the scrutiny of radical lawyers was far from over, as their "liberal causes" were still being regarded with a measure of suspicion, to say the least. A paper drafted in February 1975 at the request of the number two person in the FBI, James B. Adams, underscored the threat the Guild still posed, which revolved around two main poles: prisons and subversive groups. On the one hand, the lawyers' celebration of prisoners as a "revolutionary vanguard" and the promotion of disruption within correctional facilities were intolerable. On the other hand, the ties between the NLG and the Weather Underground appeared particularly close, way beyond the professional level.[97]

Therefore, the bureau duly investigated both sources of danger, but conclusions were negative. It was impossible to detect any illegal organized activity of the Guild with inmates, and no evidence was found with respect to its promotion of discontent and disorder inside penitentiaries, with the exception of the introduction of literature into prisons.[98] Similarly, reports on the alleged relationship between the NLG and the Weather Underground failed to reveal any justification for researching and monitoring the activities of the NLG. The line between what constituted a lawyer-client relationship and what constituted an illegal act was admittedly "thin," and the Guild "could foment much adverse publicity claiming violation of its client's constitutional rights, should information of [an] active FBI investigation . . . become public knowledge." Therefore, even the collection of evidence was problematic.[99] As of March 1976, any further investigation of the Guild was not warranted. Future indications of illegal activities on the part of individuals associated with the organization, the Department of Justice recommended, should be handled through individual cases in accordance with established procedures.[100]

And yet to reach these unsatisfying conclusions, the FBI subjected the Guild, its affiliates, and its allies to extensive surveillance, infiltration, and disruption. First of all, dozens of Guild lawyers were included in the Security Index, a list started by FBI director Hoover in 1939 comprising citizens whom the FBI believed would be dangerous to national security during a war or other major emergencies and thus could be arrested and held indefinitely without a warrant.[101] In addition, most of them were constantly surveilled, both collectively and individually. Eight special agents, for example, were assigned to cover the People's Law Office and its attorneys in Chicago, while nine others secretly monitored the Guild's national convention in Boulder in July–August 1971.[102]

Some prominent figures were also the object of singular attention, Charles Garry being a case in point. Since 1947, Garry had been under the FBI's radar for his alleged membership in the Communist Party, his representation of radicals, and his official roles in the San Francisco chapter of the Guild.[103] Garry's FOIA files are as much revealing as they are monotonous. For years, the FBI kept track of his residence and his employment, with little or no indication of any illegal activity, while reiterating his ominous affiliation with the communist-led NLG.[104] Clearly worn out by the investigation, in March 1968 a San Francisco special agent in charge (SAC) asked the FBI director to remove Garry from the Security Index. However, the request was denied. Although Garry had last been reported as a member of the Communist Party in 1950, there was "no indication that he has changed his sympathies." Moreover, he had been very active in the NLG, had frequently represented communists in their legal actions, and was counsel for the minister of defense of the BPP.[105] Following a common pattern, surveillance escalated in the late 1960s, when the Black Panthers replaced communism as a major threat. Garry was also listed in the Key Agitator Index, which was a new FBI list of dangerous antiwar militants.[106] Predictably, Garry's ebullient out-of-court advocacy of the Panthers was rummaged, including his speeches and interviews, which were invariably antiracist and harshly critical with the system of justice.[107]

The FBI director further intensified surveillance in January 1970, explicitly requesting "sources close to Garry who [could] identify his contacts and keep [the] office apprised of his activities on a daily basis." It was "essential that a determination be made as to whether he [was] maintaining contact with the CP and whether the CP [was] exerting influence over the BPP through Garry." The bureau, in other words, feared that Garry could be "the link between the CP and the black extremist movement in this country."[108] The lawyer was indeed wiretapped at his residence, at his law office, and through the phone of the BPP headquarters. Actually, according to the logs, many people called the Black Panthers to speak to Garry. Additional sources followed him at Guild conferences and during various BPP events, such as fundraisers and rallies. A source also checked on him from inside the prison of San Luis Obispo to monitor his visits to Newton, while another source advised the bureau from within the BPP milieu, where "he feels and acts like a 'little God.'" Garry's private encounters in various cities were all duly recorded. Yet no trace of any contact with the CP was ever found.[109]

In a major escalation, in February 1970 the FBI director informed the San Francisco SAC that "available information indicates Garry is in reality the leader of the Black Panther Party (BPP) although he does not identify himself as such. The influence which he exerts over the BPP programs and activities and his propagandizing in behalf of that revolutionary group clearly shows [sic] that he is at least as much of a threat to this nation's security as the top leadership of the BPP." Accordingly, Garry was elevated to Priority I in the Priority Apprehension Program.[110] Somehow reinforcing this interpretation, the director stressed that considerable information indicated that Garry also coordinated BPP finances, because money poured into his office and was redistributed for bail and other activities.[111] As time wore on, the director increasingly stressed the fanaticism of Garry, who "would not pass up any opportunity to criticize or embarrass the Bureau," and repeated his request of "daily" surveillance.[112] Although local SACs complied with the directives, they could not help but repeat that it was difficult to single out criminal conduct by Garry. His activities, in legal terms, did not go "beyond the scope of his capacity as a BPP attorney."[113] At the same time, the FBI obsessively pursued connections between Garry, the CPUSA, and the BPP that could not be substantiated.[114]

Although Garry's relationship with the Black Panthers had no parallel, the San Francisco lawyer was hardly alone in the FBI's agenda. A still undisclosed number of Guild lawyers were regularly followed, and for most of them the real or alleged affiliation with the Communist Party weighed heavy. The case of Mary Kaufman, under surveillance since 1941, is paradigmatic. Her intelligence records show that the FBI constantly monitored her meetings at CP headquarters, her attendance at communist leaders' gatherings, and her political travels abroad. Her earnings were also checked, as well as her academic record, but in 1978 the investigation was called off, having accomplished little.[115] For other Guild lawyers, it was their direct engagement in the leftist movement that attracted FBI attention. John

Thorne, for instance, was constantly tracked at picket lines, during campus demonstrations, at events on behalf of the Soledad Brothers in the United States and Europe, and in the course of activities with the group Vencere-mos. In his case, too, the investigation was fine-grained but led nowhere by the late 1970s.[116]

The bureau gathered much of its intelligence on radical lawyers through electronic surveillance, bogus calls, mail opening, continuous physical ob-servation, surreptitious entries into premises, and informers disseminated across the movement.[117] In addition, infiltration into the NLG and its sister organizations was also employed, and three major cases stand out. The first one stars John H. Rees and his wife, Sheila O'Connor (aka Louise Rees), as protagonists. An alleged conman and impersonator, Rees worked under-cover for HUAC during the August 1968 protests in Chicago and published a newsletter, *Information Digest*, which provided information on movement activities to government agencies and conservative politicians. According to a Guild investigation, Rees and O'Connor were also on the payroll of Con-gressman Larry McDonald, a right-wing Democrat and a member of the national council of the John Birch Society.[118]

Playing the part of an Anglican priest, in 1970 John Rees moved to Wash-ington, D.C., with his wife. The two infiltrated the radical milieu by living in a commune, participating in demonstrations, joining various progressive groups, and opening a leftist bookstore named Red House. While John worked with the Institute for Policy Studies (a progressive think tank) and developed into a police informer, Sheila became an office manager for the local chapter of the Guild. Gaining access to privileged information and hosting parties and political meetings at their house, the Rees sent reports on both organizations and copies of internal records to government agen-cies. Sheila also caused dissension among Guild members, sabotaged a legal conference, and interfered with the press. Looking like an enthusiastic and overzealous activist, she was ultimately elected to the Guild's national executive board, but in 1976 she suddenly disappeared.[119]

Twenty-six-year-old Mary Jo Cook was a leftist activist and a legal vol-unteer both in the Attica Brothers Legal Defense and in the Fair Jury Proj-ect. Yet, between 1973 and 1974, she was also an FBI informant.[120] After much soul-searching, she decided to unveil her role. Guild members were mostly worried because she could have meddled with statistical studies for the jury selection, compromising the precious work, but evidence of sub-stantial disruption was never found. It only emerged that one of the legal volunteers knew about Cook well before her confession but kept the secret, thus engendering a deep sense of distrust within the group. Informed about the breach, the judge in the Attica trial ruled that the information provided by Cook, which had been shared with prosecutors, had not been employed in the investigation, so everything went on like nothing had happened.[121]

The third informer who indirectly spied on Guild lawyers was the previously mentioned Douglas Durham. A former police officer in Des Moines, he was a pilot, a photographer, a locksmith, and a scuba diver. He also had contacts in the underground press and, most importantly, had the complexion of a Native American. Contacted by the FBI, in March 1972 he traveled to the encampment at Wounded Knee, where he smoothly settled in. A year later, he was already chief of security for the Wounded Knee Legal Defense/Offense Committee, administrator of the AIM national office in St. Paul, and Dennis Banks's closest confidant and adviser. In 1975 he confessed his story. He had access to relevant information and passed it to the FBI. Despite the fact that the government swore it did not make use of informants, Durham's intelligence also ended up in the hands of the prosecutors in the Wounded Knee trials. As is known, the revelation about the infiltration and illegal surveillance on the Native American defendants contributed to the dismissal of charges in the Banks and Means' proceeding.[122]

All in all, disruption through infiltrators was discomforting, but its effects were quite negligible. Yet it was coupled with other irritating forms of harassment, such as frequent and "unnecessary" tax investigations of the NLG, its officers, and its members.[123] Break-ins into lawyers' premises were also particularly disturbing. For example, the offices of the Soledad Brothers Defense Committee and those of Fay Stender were raided.[124] Cloke believes that FBI agents broke into his office in Venice, Los Angeles, and stole some files related to the Guild.[125] In 1975, the Guild national office was mysteriously burglarized, documents went missing, and information that had been locked up in the office was subsequently published in a right-wing publication that attacked the Guild.[126] There were also cases of anonymous mailings designed to promote internal factionalism or to tarnish external reputation.[127] Finally, according to various testimonies, the presence of agents fraudulently posing as clients was another frequent act that demanded constant vigilance. Bogus clients, for instance, sought to induce lawyers to counsel blatant violations of the law or offered payments in drugs instead of money, with the obvious intent of exposing lawyers' misbehaviors.[128]

The impact of this array of repressive actions was hard to pin down and demonstrate. Nevertheless, in 1977 the Guild filed a massive complaint against the FBI, the CIA, and a number of government agencies. The suit argued that the government had engaged in a "conspiracy" to deter persons from joining the Guild, to interfere with and disrupt the Guild's activities, and to prevent the Guild from expressing its views. The government, in other words, systematically spied on the organization and adopted a whole range of illegal or preposterous tactics, thus depriving the Guild and its members of rights, privileges, and immunities secured by the Constitution. As compensation for the damages, the Guild requested $10 million. Despite the massive volume of evidence that was mobilized in support of such claims, in 1983 the assistant attorney general dismissed the case in its entirety. Even if the Guild were right on the facts and all government actions were unconstitutional—the judicial authority observed—this type of case should not be entertained by the federal courts. And in any event, the government was immune from any suit for conduct taken in the course of a national security investigation, since high-level officials had taken measures to protect the security of the United States against threats of subversion, terrorism, and unrest.[129]

Seen from the Guild's perspective, this legal outcome added insult to injury. A partial consolation was that the FBI turned over copies of roughly 400,000 pages of its files on the Guild, which essentially corroborated the charges. However, it also remained the fact that the public shaming, red-baiting, disciplinary actions, policing, invasive surveillance, infiltration, and disruption left radical lawyers mostly unperturbed. Clearly, they knew they were the target of repressive actions, some of their projects were unsettled, and a number of them had to fight in court to see their rights restored. Without a doubt, loss of clients and income, violations of privacy, and disaffection weighed heavy. Their First and Fourth Amendment rights were often violated. A number of lawyers arguably never joined the Guild out of fear. Yet retrospective testimonies are almost unanimous in stressing that lawyers felt they were "under surveillance, but not under threat." "Everybody assumed or knew that the FBI was tracking us," confirms a lawyer. "But nobody was restrained or intimidated because of it."[130]

For someone like Margaret Ratner Kunstler, for example, the main concern was just to prevent the FBI, which was ostensibly tailing her, from learning the whereabouts of the fugitives she was meeting. "I was lucky," she admits. "People who had normal jobs could have lost them. I had a safer job. Even seeing a fugitive was not a crime for a lawyer."[131] "I remember being in the federal court in San Francisco," recalls Peter Franck, "and I was getting an injunction for an antiwar march in Oakland. I used a pay phone in the hall of the courthouse. I asked to call my office, and someone answered from the office of the Oakland Army base! I thought that someone in my office was kidding, but it was the Oakland Army base, which proved that my phone was being tapped by the army." "I was aware of it," he concedes, "but it didn't bother me. You know, I come from a Jewish family who suffered Hitler's repression."[132]

Scaling down and contextualizing repression are indeed common tropes in lawyers' memories and confirm at least two dynamics. First, government agencies were partly unable and partly unwilling to crack down on white middle-class professionals. In other words, there was an invisible line that could not be crossed, and lawyers were aware of it and took advantage of it. Second, lawyers were always prepared to face a certain degree of disruption, as they knew that repression was inescapable if they ventured onto slippery ground.[133] "Our attitude was not to be afraid," clarifies Siegel, who also adds: "On one hand, I felt privileged, being white and a law school graduate. . . . Our comrades in the Panthers and other African Americans were just killed. On the other hand, I felt that I would always face charges, that it would have been a constant factor in my life, whether through civil cases, the bar, or criminal cases. . . . It was just the price of doing this."[134]

Conclusion

Since the end of the 1970s, radical attorneys have scored countless crucial victories. More than eighty years after its founding, the National Lawyers Guild is alive and well and steps up to the plate whenever a contentious front opens up. Nowadays, the Guild supports the victims of law enforcement misconduct, assists immigrant groups, participates in the resistance to oil and gas pipelines, defends the rights of protesters through its signature mass defense and legal observer programs, and promotes initiatives to end mass incarceration. Even some of the people interviewed for this research are still involved in a broad range of projects and operate in continuity with their commitment of decades ago. As a matter of fact, the form of legal-political activism described in this book cannot be considered a onetime, idiosyncratic experience. Lawyers' political engagement endures—often underneath—and cyclically resurfaces. It is an undercurrent of social movement life, mirroring the ebbs and flows of contentious politics.

However, more often than not, during the last forty years radical lawyers' political ambitions had to be downsized and circumscribed. Radical lawyers were forced to reassess their areas of intervention and to adjust their strategies in a way that was hardly expansive. Sometimes they had to surrender to the fact that their law practice could not be "offensive" any longer.[1] This dynamic confirms that the growth of a wholesale legal-political intervention, its creative development, its uncompromising criticism of institutions, its chances of success in court, and its ability to resonate in broad sectors of society were, and still are, contingent on specific conditions. As this book illustrates, the multifaceted engagement of lawyers during the 1960s and 1970s grew out of a context that combined worldwide revolutionary hopes, integration of disenfranchised segments of the population, mass mobilization across different domains, an unpopular war abroad, and a crisis of political legitimation in the country. If forms of radical lawyering existed in the nineteenth century, resurfaced in the interwar period, and survived after the 1970s, the long sixties represented the golden age of this phenomenon.

More specifically, the diffusion of radical lawyers' engagement cannot be explained without considering the civil rights movement, which offered a laboratory in which a new relationship between lawyers and activists could be forged. The legal emergency in the South also afforded a glimpse of the limits of the conventional avenues for redressing legal problems. Joining the civil rights struggle proved transformative at the emotional level, too, as anger and enthusiasm were contagious among lawyers. The apprenticeship of a new crop of radical lawyers began there, between Mississippi and Georgia, but blossomed on liberal campuses from Berkeley to Columbia, which were swept by the winds of the New Left. Without the rising tide of the student rebellion and the antiwar movement, a novel generation of combative lawyers would never have materialized. Spaces of contention, such as the military and prisons, also offered unprecedented calls to action and a panoply of new allies. The burgeoning Black Power movement, the political awakening of other minorities, and the resurgence of militant labor further emboldened lawyers' commitment, projecting a political mission into a solidarity struggle. By jeopardizing the fundamental rights to dissent, freely speak, and associate, the government's unbending response against social protest commanded immediate and resolute involvement.

The encounter of a new cohort of "radical legal people" with the NLG was as much spontaneous as explosive. The existence of an alternative bar association with leftist credentials was arguably another sine qua non for the expansion of the radical lawyers' phenomenon. In a rare instance, New Left and Old Left managed to find a constructive synergy. The NLG provided attorneys and law students with a recognized forum for getting in touch with political organizers and for meeting other like-minded people. The presence of a nationwide structured network defeated the sense of isolation among many radical lawyers and reinforced their pledge to fight collectively. In particular, shared experiences—such as gathering at conventions, meeting at local chapters, demonstrating, taking part in solidarity committees, or traveling abroad—radicalized many lawyers and enhanced their feeling that a segment of the legal profession was marching together. While connecting young and seasoned lawyers, the Guild offered role models, alternative education, specialized training, coordination, and a cordon sanitaire to protect its members. Not least, the organization featured a space of political and professional discussion that constantly reassessed the role of radical lawyers against an evolving context. Ultimately, this group of lawyers found a way to reconcile, at least tentatively, the impulses of radicalism with the constraints of the legal practice.

On the outside, the NLG also exerted a "leftward pressure" on mainstream lawyers and their associations, who were sometimes timid or reluctant to rally around some causes.[2] Although its influence was clearly diminished by its haunting association with communism, the Guild gave the established bar "a sense of its obligation to represent groups that haven't had representation, a real commitment to serve society as opposed to performing merely a mouthpiece function," as Philip Kurland put it.[3] The Guild milieu also showcased that a democratization of the legal profession was possible and urgently needed. Ahead of its times, the NLG lifted the curtain on the lingering sexism, racism, elitism, and political discrimination that still characterized both law firms and law schools. If it is true that the Guild could not entirely remove its own biases, as it remained—much to its concern[4]—a largely white, middle-class association, its efforts to transform the professional practice were nonetheless significant and bore fruit in the following decades.

Importantly, radical lawyers' critique of the law reminded those who embraced legalism, both conservatives and liberals, that an alternative view of the legal system existed and was also innervated by a robust logic. Being a major instrument for shaping and maintaining social, economic, racial, and gender relations, the law, they argued, was far from being neutral and objective; it was politics by other means. Hence, every trial was, to some extent, a political trial. Indeed, the very concept of criminal behavior could be dismantled, relativized, and correlated to the illness of society, while the idea of justice through the courts could be demystified and reassessed. Judges, lawyers, scholars, and even sympathetic observers have later criticized some of these assumptions on the basis that they were ideological or simplistic, if not dangerously romantic when they justified ordinary crime with revolutionary arguments. And yet, regardless political and moral evaluations, this radical approach contributed to shifting paradigms and redefining interpretative canons. Part of its legacy is still visible to this day in the scholarly domains of critical legal studies and critical race theory.[5]

On a different level, the Guild offered leftist militants a legal network animated by sympathetic, expert, and mostly pro bono attorneys—attorneys who would go the extra mile to advocate defendants' cause, attorneys who would consider themselves "co-conspirators." Tracing the contours of militant litigation, these lawyers ensured that defendants' politics were injected and translated into courtroom discourse, unveiled the social roots of the alleged crimes, fought to obtain a jury of defendants' peers, dared to assume a defiant stance during proceedings, justified defendants' disorderly behavior, employed a wide array of experts, drew sympathetic audiences to exert psychological pressure, and orchestrated out-of-court propaganda.

In so doing, lawyers and defendants could reverse the logic of political prosecutions against itself. Instead of enduring the politicization of justice, as regularly happened during McCarthyism, they could lay it bare, enhance it, and take advantage of it. The accused could turn into the accuser. Trials thus became public forums to raise thorny questions about imperialism, racism, the right to resistance, and so on. Justice figuratively exited the tribunals to return to the people, often with the help of the mass media. Ultimately, at least three goals could be achieved: first, discredit the establishment; second, educate and convert the jury; and third, radicalize larger constituencies. This is why, under certain conditions, trials of militants ceased to be a mere impediment and could be understood as a continuation of protest or disobedience by other means.

Buttressing the radical upsurge of the 1960s, the Guild provided opportunities for self-help legal knowledge and made available legal observers capable of restraining law enforcement (also with their bodily presence), skilled fundraisers, compassionate advisers, and complicit mediators. It also delivered fearless public statements, for example on the Vietnam War, and pugnacious amicus curiae briefs. Lawyers in the Guild pioneered a discourse on racism in trials, proposed a trailblazing critique of the government's surveillance of citizens, and staunchly condemned the very logic of incarceration. In those decades, no other lawyers' network or organization at the national level was so unashamedly partisan and so unreservedly available to radicals. This does not detract from the historic contributions of legal organizations such as the NAACP and the ACLU. The NLG, however, operated on a different terrain and responded to other necessities, remaining unique in that respect.

Unforgiving critics of legal liberalism, radical lawyers in and around the NLG mostly avoided test-case litigation and constantly explored unconventional patterns of action. Their skepticism for everything that could be accepted and incorporated by the establishment led them to advocate the most controversial defendants and the most divisive causes. Paradoxically, as soon as an issue that radical lawyers had enthusiastically embraced shifted from the margins to the mainstream, that issue ceased to be worthy of their commitment, as if institutionalization would fatally compromise even the most meritorious claim.[6] And yet this crop of radical lawyers, with all their limits and biases, complemented the work that other, more moderate professionals were undertaking. They persistently strove to expand both the contents and the boundaries of legal rights. In hindsight, they should be credited as legitimate and sometimes key actors of "the rights revolution of the 1960s," namely that process that transformed the notion of American freedom "from a finite body of entitlements enjoyed mainly by white men into an open-ended claim to equality, recognition, and self-determination."[7]

Additional research would be necessary to assess in more detail the impact of radical lawyers on social movements' internal dynamics and strategies. It would be interesting to fathom how the presence of complicit lawyers affected the patterns of radicalization, escalation, and de-escalation of individuals and groups. But this would require interrogating an extraordinarily large set of sources, which falls outside the scope and the limits of this book. For now, it is safe to conclude that lawyers' material, political, and moral support did not necessarily make militants more reckless or more restrained in their conduct. Rather, it empowered them. It made them more confident in challenging the law, whether they breached, ignored, contested, ridiculed, or creatively abided by it. This multilayered protection and cooperation became especially vital when state repression hardened and many activists, in the absence of a "legal arm of the movement," would have been paralyzed and neutralized even more rapidly than actually happened.[8]

The same radical lawyers who recognized that the legal order mirrored the structure of power and legitimized it also came to terms with the fact that the legal order expressed limits on government power and protected the rights of underdogs. They acknowledged, in Stephen Bingham's words, that the tribunal, on occasion, was "the only place where David could beat Goliath."[9] Otherwise said, radical lawyers conceded that the law may not redistribute power, eliminate inequality, or erase exploitation, but it could safeguard any category of citizens, even those who resolutely fought against the establishment. Therefore, they made a "defensive" and "temporary" use of the legal order on behalf of the people who were most seriously victimized.[10] Thanks to their engagement, protesters who deliberately violated the law for political motives were acquitted, agents of repression were restrained, due process of law seeped through prison walls, and the Bill of Rights was enforced to the advantage of unpopular defendants.

This is why radical lawyers' posture vis-à-vis the legal system cannot be dismissed as a contradictory or provocative stance. On the contrary, it was the logical outcome of their notion of justice, which was quintessentially progressive. As this book reveals, radical lawyers held firm an ontological distinction between law and justice, whereby the law is the ratification of unfair economic and social relations, and justice is an ideal of equity. While they went up against the law, radical lawyers saw justice as a horizon to aim for—a tension that could never be fully resolved, an approximation that always deserved criticism. This is why, for these lawyers, fighting for justice was more significant than attaining the formal sanction of justice in the courtrooms.

In 2000, after obtaining a $12 million settlement for the victims of the carnage of Attica, Guild lawyer Elizabeth Fink commented, "What we got might have been a victory, but it was not justice. . . . So, you ask, well, why do we do this? And the answer to that is: because this is struggle for justice, and the struggle for justice is what makes this meaningful and what makes life meaningful."[11]

Acknowledgments

Many people listened to my arguments, read my work, and offered precious comments; I owe many thanks to all of them. Special gratitude goes to Ellen Schrecker, who first discussed this project with me, helped me to frame it, and encouraged me to pursue it. I am also extremely grateful to Giuliano Bellezza, James Fontanella-Khan, Carlo Invernizzi Accetti, and Clara E. Mattei for their insightful reviews, which came with sharp suggestions and affectionate endorsement.

This project started at New York University's Tamiment Library, where I found not only an archival treasure trove but also superb research assistance. In particular, I cannot thank enough Michael Koncewicz for his expert advice and constant readiness. The European Institute at Columbia University provided an outstanding intellectual and professional environment where I could develop and complete this book. I am grateful to Victoria de Grazia and Adam Tooze for their invaluable support, and I thank François Carrel-Billiard and Sharon Kim for their always generous assistance.

I am also indebted to Traci Yoder, who welcomed me when I first set foot in the NLG offices in New York and kindly helped me start this research. I deeply appreciate all the people who agreed to be interviewed: they spoke about their lives with passion and honesty, while sharing emotionally complex recollections. I hope this book provides at least a glimpse of their incredibly rich experiences. Ken Cloke, a protagonist of the events narrated in these pages, deserves a special mention for his illuminating and thought-provoking comments.

I wish to extend my sincere appreciation to the Justice, Power, and Politics series' editors, Heather Ann Thompson and Rhonda Y. Williams, for the confidence they placed in this project. While preparing this manuscript for publication, I was very fortunate to work with a talented editor at UNC Press, Brandon Proia. I thank him very much for his perceptive and enthusiastic guidance. In New York, Tony Lenti and Johann Marcotullio also made available their help; I am very grateful.

I also want to express special appreciation to Paolo Colombo, Marc Lazar, Elizabeth Leake, Daniela Saresella, and Lisa Tiersten for their steadfast encouragement and inspiration over the years—it has meant a lot to me. A number of colleagues from various disciplines, who are first of all friends, gifted me with engaging conversations and warm conviviality, which were key to achieving this book. Among them, I am very pleased to thank Matteo Albanese, Franco Baldasso, Naor Ben-Yehoyada, Alessandro Citanna, Roberto Colozza, Stefano Costalli, Beatrice Mazzi, Javier Osorio, Luca Peretti, Guido Vestuti, Lorenzo Vigotti, Julien Zanetta, and Paolo Zanini. Family and friends, from Milan to Brussels, have been an unremitting source of joy and peace: I need not say more, for they already know.

Notes

Abbreviations

Armstrong Papers: Gregory Armstrong Papers Relating to the Publication of *Soledad Brother: The Prison Letters of George Jackson*: ca. 1970–1971, BANC MSS 84/27c, Bancroft Library, University of California, Berkeley

Beinecke Library: Beinecke Rare Book & Manuscript Library, Yale University

Brown Special Collections: Brown University Library Special Collections, John Hay Library, Brown University

Burnstein Papers: Malcolm Burnstein Papers, 1963–1994, BANC MSS99/294c, Bancroft Library, University of California, Berkeley

CCR Records: Center for Constitutional Rights Records, TAM 589, Tamiment Library—Robert F. Wagner Labor Archives, New York University

Cleaver Papers: Eldridge Cleaver Papers, 1963–1988, BANC MSS 91/213c, Bancroft Library, University of California, Berkeley

Cleaver Photograph Collection: Eldridge Cleaver Photograph Collection, 1966–circa 1982, BANC PIC 1991.078, Bancroft Library, University of California, Berkeley

Cockrel Collection: Kenneth V. and Sheila M. Cockrel Collection, UP001379, Walter P. Reuther Library, Wayne State University, Detroit

Davis Papers: Papers of Angela Y. Davis, 1937–2017, MC 940, Schlesinger Library, Harvard University

Goldring Papers: Benjamin and Muriel Goldring Papers and Photographs, TAM 347, Tamiment Library—Robert F. Wagner Labor Archives, New York University

Hall and Hoag Collection: Gordon Hall and Grace Hoag Collection of Dissenting and Extremist Printed Propaganda, John Hay Library, Brown University

Hayden Papers: Tom Hayden Papers, Special Collections Research Center, University of Michigan Library, University of Michigan, Ann Arbor

Kaufman Papers: Mary Metlay Kaufman Papers, SSC-MS-00300, Sophia Smith Collection of Women's History, Smith College, Northampton, Mass.

Kennedy Papers: Papers of Florynce Kennedy, 1915–2004, MC555, Schlesinger Library, Harvard University

Meiklejohn Collections: Meiklejohn Civil Liberties Institute Collections, BANC MSS99/281c, Bancroft Library, University of California, Berkeley

New Left Collection: New Left Collection, 69001, Hoover Institution Library & Archives, Stanford University

Newton Collection: Dr. Huey P. Newton Foundation Inc. Collection, M0864, Special Collections, Stanford University

NLG Records, Bancroft: National Lawyers Guild Records, BANC MSS99/280cz, Bancroft Library, University of California, Berkeley

NLG Records, Tamiment: National Lawyers Guild Records, TAM 191, Tamiment Library—Robert F. Wagner Labor Archives, New York University

Oral Histories, Bancroft: Regional Oral History Office, Bancroft Library, University of California, Berkeley

Oral Histories, Columbia: Individual Interviews Oral History Collection, Rare Books & Manuscript Library, Columbia University

PCS and MLO Records: Pacific Counseling Service and Military Law Office Records, 1969–1977, BANC MSS86/89c, Bancroft Library, University of California, Berkeley

Popper Papers: Martin Popper Papers, TAM 680, Tamiment Library—Robert F. Wagner Labor Archives, New York University

Rabinowitz Papers: Victor Rabinowitz Papers, TAM 123, Tamiment Library—Robert F. Wagner Labor Archives, New York University

Roberts Papers: Patti Roberts Papers, 1968–2009, GLC 111, James C. Hormel LGBTQIA+ Center, San Francisco Public Library

Thorne Papers: John E. Thorne Papers, MS.423, Special Collections and Archives, University Library, University of California, Santa Cruz

Treuhaft Papers: Robert E. Treuhaft Papers, TAM 664, Tamiment Library—Robert F. Wagner Labor Archives, New York University

Unger Papers: Abraham Unger Papers, TAM 157, Tamiment Library—Robert F. Wagner Labor Archives, New York University

Introduction

1. See, most notably, Tocqueville, *Democracy in America*, 247–48.

2. Barkan, *Protesters on Trial*, 1.

3. Friedman, *Law in America*, 13.

4. Handler, *Social Movements and the Legal System*, 1.

5. Kalman, *Strange Career of Legal Liberalism*, 2–4.

6. Scheingold, *Politics of Rights*, 7, 49. For a discussion on legalism as a political ideology, see Shklar, *Legalism*, particularly 1–24. In his seminal research on the outcomes of the Supreme Court, Gerald N. Rosenberg also concluded that Americans credit courts and judicial decisions with a power of producing "significant social reform" that they simply do not have. See Rosenberg, *Hollow Hope*, 338.

7. For a theoretical assessment, see McCann, "Law and Social Movements."

8. Tocqueville, *Democracy in America*, 276–79.

9. See Sarat and Scheingold, "What Cause Lawyers Do *for*, and *to*, Social Movements"; Hilbink, "Profession, the Grassroots and the Elite."

10. In addition to the expression "radical lawyers," previous literature has adopted the expressions "movement lawyers," "people's lawyers," and "activist bar" to denote the most contentious segment of the profession. For a theoretical discussion, see Scheingold, *Politics of Rights*, particularly 170–71, 181. See also Black, *Radical*

Lawyers; James, *People's Lawyers*. For a more recent review of the debate, see Hilbink, "Constructing Cause Lawyering." In the present book the term "radicalism" describes the belief in a need for fundamental political, social, and economic change. Radicalism is theoretically distinct from the use of extremist tactics, although sometimes radicals adopt unconventional or illegal means. Radicalism is not employed as a synonym of courage, as many lawyers proved to be extremely brave without being radical. In the U.S. context, radicalism was common to several political families, including the Communist Party, the Socialist Party and the anti-Stalinist Left, the civil rights movement, religious-based pacifism, and the New Left. See Sánchez-Cuenca, *Historical Roots of Political Violence*, 20–21; Brick and Phelps, *Radicals in America*, 5–7; Gosse, *Rethinking the New Left*, 20.

11. The notion of "long sixties," embracing the period 1959–74, is credited to Marwick, *Sixties*. Regarding the projection of the movements of the 1960s into the 1970s, see S. Hall, "Protest Movements in the 1970s."

12. On the watershed of the 1960s at the level of legal mobilization, see Kraft, "Contention in the Courtroom." See also McCann and Dudas, "Retrenchment . . . and Resurgence?"

13. The communists would later establish the Civil Rights Congress to assist both the victims of racism and political defendants, with a radical approach that openly defied the more liberal organizations. See Avrich, *Haymarket Tragedy*, particularly 260–333.

14. Such a long and complex evolution of legal defense organizations is thoroughly examined in Hill, *Men, Mobs, and Law*, 72–238. With regard to the ILD, see Ginger, *Carol Weiss King*, 82–141.

15. Established in 1922 by the Comintern, the International Red Aid (IRA) was also known by its Russian initials MOPR. The first IRA conference was convened in Moscow in 1924. For an overview of the Red Aid's first campaigns, see IRA Executive Committee, *Ten Years of International Red Aid*, 97–128. For a historical assessment, see Finkel, "'Political Red Cross' and the Genealogy of Rights Discourse in Revolutionary Russia."

16. The 1937 founding convention was held in Washington, D.C., and gathered together approximately six hundred lawyers. One of the first motions approved was the plan to pack the Supreme Court in order to protect Roosevelt's social legislation. See Ginger and Tobin, *National Lawyers Guild*, 7–11. See also *Constitution of the National Lawyers Guild*, folder NLG-NEB 1971, carton 57, NLG Records, Bancroft.

17. The first executive committee included, among others, Wisconsin governor Philip F. La Follette; Washington senator Homer T. Bone; retiring chief justice of the Minnesota Supreme Court John P. Devaney; Illinois federal district court judge William H. Holly; and state court judges from Missouri, California, and New York. However, internal rifts soon developed on the issue of anticommunism. Since the anticommunists were defeated, people such as Judge Ferdinand Pecora, who had been a national president of the NLG, and Adolf A. Berle, a Columbia University professor, resigned. See Ginger, *Carol Weiss King*, 219–37; "From the New Deal to the

'Crisis of Confidence,'" in *Law for the People*, ed. NLG (New York: NLG, 1979), 30–42, folder 348B:27, box N-35, pt. 2, Hall and Hoag Collection.

18. John Corwin, "The Guild Then and Now," *Blind Justice* 3, no. 2 (December 1973): 12–13, folder "Blind Justice" 1970s, carton 57, NLG Records, Bancroft.

19. Doron Weinberg and Marty Fassler, *A Historical Sketch of the National Lawyers Guild in American Politics, 1936–1968* (New York: NLG, n.d.), 9–11, folder 25, box 6, Goldring Papers.

20. See, for instance, Kunstler, *My Life*; Garry and Goldberg, *Streetfighter in the Courtroom*; Kinoy, *Rights on Trial*; Klebanow and Jonas, *People's Lawyers*.

21. A notable exception is the compelling research by Auerbach, *Unequal Justice*, which is a social history of the legal profession.

22. See, among others, Schultz, *Chicago Conspiracy Trial*; Ely, "Chicago Conspiracy Case"; Wiener, *Conspiracy in the Streets*.

23. See, for instance, the otherwise insightful Gitlin, *Sixties*; Goldstein, *Political Repression*; Varon, *Bringing the War Home*.

24. See, for example, S. Walker, *In Defense of American Liberties*.

25. See, above all, Ginger and Tobin, *National Lawyers Guild*.

26. On the use of 1960s activists' oral testimonies, see Gildea and Mark, introduction to *Europe's 1968*.

27. Zinn, *SNCC*.

28. The recent and growing European literature on the subject makes a partial exception. See, for instance, de Graaf and Schmid, *Terrorists on Trial*; Israël, *À la gauche du droit*; Malatesta, "Défenses militantes."

Chapter 1

1. See, among others, Kinoy, *Rights on Trial*, 166; Holt, *Summer That Didn't End*, 64; "Lawyers Guild Eyes Dixie Aid," *Michigan Chronicle*, August 16, 1962, folder 22, box 15, NLG Records, Tamiment.

2. Ann F. Ginger, "The National Lawyers Guild and the Civil Rights Movement," NLG, Chicago National Convention, Commemorative Dinner, August 20, 1983, 5–58, folder 2, box 1, Popper Papers. See also C. B. King's testimony in James, *People's Lawyers*, 294–96; Wulf, interview.

3. "Len Holt Depicts Struggle of Civil Rights Lawyers in South to N.Y. Guild Meeting," *New York Guild Lawyer* 20, no. 3 (March–April 1962): 4, folder 2, box 68, Kaufman Papers; "Summer Project: Mississippi, 1964."

4. Burns, "Federal Government and Civil Rights."

5. Navasky, *Kennedy Justice*, 97–101, 243–45.

6. Kinoy, *Rights on Trial*, 152–53.

7. Kunstler, *My Life*, 103–11. On the towering figure of Kunstler, see also Langum, *William M. Kunstler*; Kunstler and Kunstler, *William Kunstler*. For a critical perspective, see "Lawyer for Hire."

8. NAACP lawyers had been fighting against disenfranchisement and racial segregation since the 1910s. For an examination of their action before *Brown v. Board of Education*, see Goluboff, *Lost Promise of Civil Rights*.

9. An early member of the NLG's national executive board, Marshall left the organization at the onset of the Cold War. See Babson, Riddle, and Elsila, *Color of Law*, 274. On *Brown v. Board of Education*, see Kluger, *Simple Justice*.

10. Minow, "Political Lawyering."

11. Barkan, *Protesters on Trial*, 41–42; Greenberg, *Crusaders in the Courts*, 346.

12. Ginger and Tobin, *National Lawyers Guild*, xviii.

13. See, for example, Joseph Jordan, Edward Dawley, and Leonard W. Holt, "An Urgent Plea from America—South," memo, n.d. [1962?], folder 7, box 67, Kaufman Papers.

14. "Guild Honors Six Leading Southern Civil Rights Lawyers," *New York Guild Lawyer* 20, no. 3 (March–April 1962): 1–16, folder 2, box 68, Kaufman Papers.

15. Ginger and Tobin, *National Lawyers Guild*, 188.

16. Doron Weinberg and Marty Fassler, *A Historical Sketch of the National Lawyers Guild in American Politics, 1936–1968* (New York: NLG, n.d.), 17, folder 25, box 6, Goldring Papers.

17. See the resolution adopted at the 1962 convention in Detroit, "Assistance to Southern Lawyers," folder 43, box 45, NLG Records, Tamiment.

18. Chester Bulgier, "2 Detroiters Lead Attorneys Aiding South's Integrationists," *Detroit News*, October 7, 1962.

19. "George Crockett to Speak," *Conspiracy* 3, no. 1 (September 1972): 6, folder 267B:25, box N-35, pt. 2, Hall and Hoag Collection.

20. An early member of the NLG, Maurice Sugar had been general counsel of the United Auto Workers until 1946.

21. Babson, Riddle, and Elsila, *Color of Law*, 3.

22. George Crockett et al., "Interim Report of the Committee to Assist Southern Lawyers," June 9, 1962, folder 14, box 15, NLG Records, Tamiment.

23. Ernest Goodman, "Report on Assistance in Contempt Case at Hopewell, Virginia," March 1962, folder 14, box 15, NLG Records, Tamiment.

24. "Address by Ernest Goodman at the First Baptist Church, Petersburg, Virginia," March 28, 1962, folder 14, box 15, NLG Records, Tamiment.

25. Ernest Goodman and George Crockett, "Convention Report on the National Lawyers Guild's Committee to Assist Southern Lawyers (CASL)," n.d. [1964?], folder 14, box 15, NLG Records, Tamiment.

26. "Outline of Cases in Which National Lawyers Guild Committee to Aid Southern Lawyers Has Participated," n.d. [1963?], folder 17, box 15, NLG Records, Tamiment.

27. Aryay Lenske, "Guild Program Directed toward Law Students," June 1962, folder 6, box 67, Kaufman Papers.

28. CASL co-sponsored the Workshop Seminar for Lawyers on Civil Rights and Negligence Law with the National Bar Association's Civil Rights Committee and the Southern Christian Leadership Conference. See *Workshop Seminar for Lawyers on Civil Rights and Negligence Law*, flyer, n.d. [1962?], folder 14, box 15, NLG Records, Tamiment.

29. See the NLG press release "King Lauds Civil Rights Lawyers at National Meeting in Atlanta," December 2, 1962, folder 22, box 30, NLG Records, Tamiment. See

also "Over 60 Lawyers Attend Two-Day Atlanta Meeting," *Guild Lawyer* 20, no. 9 (December 1962): 1–2, folder 14, box 15, NLG Records, Tamiment.

30. Robb, *Dean Robb*, 229–30.

31. Kinoy, *Rights on Trial*, 213–14.

32. S. H. Brown, *Standing against Dragons*, 47–48, 155–61.

33. Rogers, *Righteous Lives*, 101–2. See also Kinoy, *Rights on Trial*, 220–27.

34. Benjamin Dreyfus to Robert Kennedy et al., wire, October 5, 1963, folder B. Dreyfus Papers, NLG-Independence of the Bar, carton 10, NLG Records, Bancroft.

35. Kinoy, *Rights on Trial*, 217.

36. See Benjamin Smith's speech at the conference, New Orleans, October 5, 1963, Folder B. Dreyfus Papers, NLG-Independence of the Bar, carton 10, NLG Records, Bancroft.

37. In 1871, the U.S. Congress approved "An Act to enforce the Provisions of the Fourteenth Amendment to the Constitution of the United States, and for other Purposes," which came to be known as the Third Enforcement Act or the Ku Klux Klan Act. Signed by President Ulysses S. Grant, the act authorized the president to intervene in the former rebel states by deploying the U.S. military or other means and to suspend habeas corpus. Moreover, section 1 of the act gave those deprived of a constitutional right by someone acting under color of law the opportunity to seek relief in a federal district or circuit court. This section was later amended and codified at 42 U.S.C. § 1983, allowing federal court lawsuits against state and local officials. In 1958, the act was first rediscovered and applied in the case of a victim of a warrantless raid by Chicago police. Filed by the ACLU, the suit led to a 1961 Supreme Court decision, *Monroe v. Pape*, 365 U.S. 167 (1961), that authorized federal remedy to parties deprived of constitutional rights by state officials. See Sobieski, "Civil Rights Act of 1871"; Foner, *Reconstruction*, 454–59; Berger and Losier, *Rethinking the American Prison Movement*, 62–63.

38. Dombrowski v. Pfister, 380 U.S. 479 (1965). In the following years, the "Dombrowski remedy" was adopted in some civil rights cases, but since the early 1970s, the Supreme Court tended to protect state criminal proceedings from federal interference. See Kinoy, "Brief Remarks on *Dombrowski v. Pfister*"; Ginger, *Law, the Supreme Court, and the People's Rights*, 175–82. See also K. L. Hall, *Nation of States*, 262–63.

39. Emma C. Edmunds, "Danville Civil Rights Demonstrations of 1963," Encyclopedia Virginia, https://encyclopediavirginia.org/entries/danville-civil-rights -demonstrations-of-1963/.

40. Holt, *Act of Conscience*, 109–17, 192.

41. Kinoy, *Rights on Trial*, 187–207.

42. Hogan, *Many Minds, One Heart*, 235.

43. Carson, *In Struggle*, 92. See also SNCC, *Story of SNCC*.

44. Carson, *In Struggle*, 25.

45. Holt, *Summer That Didn't End*, 89–90. By contrast, Greenberg denied any pressure on SNCC leaders. See Greenberg, *Crusaders in the Courts*, 353.

46. SNCC Executive Secretary James Forman to Aryay Lenske, May 2, 1962, folder 30, box 30, NLG Records, Tamiment.

47. Zinn, *SNCC*, 7–13. See also Abraham Unger to SNCC, June 12, 1964, folder 10, box 1, Unger Papers.

48. Irving Rosenfeld, "Report on Guild Committee Participation at Two Conferences in the South," n.d., folder 14, box 15, NLG Records, Tamiment.

49. Forman, *Making of Black Revolutionaries*, 380–81.

50. Holt, *Summer That Didn't End*, 6.

51. Carson, *In Struggle*, 114.

52. Bond, preface, 4.

53. Claude Sitton, "Mississippi Is Gripped by Fear of Violence in Civil Rights Drive," *New York Times*, May 30, 1964.

54. See Ivi and "Allen's Army," *Newsweek*, February 24, 1964.

55. Forman, *Making of Black Revolutionaries*, 380–81.

56. Goodman and Crockett, "Convention Report on the National Lawyers Guild's Committee to Assist Southern Lawyers (CASL)."

57. See the NLG press release "A 'Lawyers' Peace Corps' Moves into Mississippi," April 23, 1964, folder 22, box 15, NLG Records, Tamiment. See also "'Lawyer Peace Corps' Officially Launched," *Jackson Daily News*, April 24, 1964, folder 52, box 46, NLG Records, Tamiment.

58. See the correspondence in folder 24, box 44, NLG Records, Tamiment.

59. Don Hoenshell, "'Can't Sit By,' Lawyer Says; Going to Mississippi," *Detroit News*, July 12, 1964.

60. Greenberg, *Crusaders in the Courts*, 351.

61. Carson, *In Struggle*, 105–7, 320. See also Lewis, *Walking with the Wind*, 271.

62. Dittmer, *Local People*, 230–34.

63. Ernest Goodman to Guild members, April 15, 1964, folder 18, box 56a, NLG Records, Tamiment.

64. See Babson, Riddle, and Elsila, *Color of Law*, 338.

65. "Summer Project: Mississippi, 1964."

66. Holt, *Summer That Didn't End*, 77–78.

67. See the data in Carson, *In Struggle*, 122; Holt, *Summer That Didn't End*, 93.

68. Barkan, *Protesters on Trial*, 84–85; Holt, *Summer That Didn't End*, 60.

69. On the effectiveness and limits of the removal jurisdiction, see Spriggs, "'Summer Vacation' in Mississippi," 141–46.

70. See David P. Welsh and CLAS, *Project Mississippi: An Account of the National Lawyers Guild Program of Legal Assistance to Civil Rights Workers in Mississippi: Summer 1964*, folder 43, box 45, NLG Records, Tamiment; Ginger, *Civil Rights & Liberties Handbook*, 72a; Hilbink, "Profession, the Grassroots and the Elite."

71. Miriam Clark and Sofia Sequenzia, "Remembering Freedom Summer 25 Years Later," NLG, NYC Chapter, 52nd Anniversary Dinner, March 3, 1989, 14–23, folder 2, box 1, Popper Papers.

72. "Summer Project: Mississippi, 1964."

73. Carson, *In Struggle*, 137; S. Walker, *In Defense of American Liberties*, 265; Wulf, interview.

74. Kinoy, *Rights on Trial*, 267–95. See also Ginger, "National Lawyers Guild and the Civil Rights Movement," NLG, Chicago National Convention, Commemorative Dinner, August 20, 1983, 5–58, folder 2, box 1, Popper Papers.

75. The definition was first employed in U.S. House of Representatives, *Report on the National Lawyers Guild*.

76. Benjamin Dreyfus to Aryay Lenske, January 18, 1962, folder 18, box 56a, NLG Records, Tamiment.

77. Emerson, Krinsky, Moore, and Buitrago, "National Lawyers Guild v. Attorney General."

78. See Benjamin Dreyfus to Robert E. Lillard (NBA), Alfred J. Schweppe (ABA), Eugene W. Rostow, and Ernest Angell, March 9, 1962, folder 14, box 56a, NLG Records, Tamiment.

79. George Crockett and Benjamin Smith, "Report on the Conference with the American Bar Association, Committee on Civil Rights," May 26, 1962, folder 14, box 15, NLG Records, Tamiment.

80. "Kennedy, Bar Association Denounced by Law Group for Stand on Rights," *Washington Post*, June 10, 1963.

81. See, for example, "Lawyers Guild Vows Support," *San Francisco Chronicle*, October 1, 1962.

82. Barkan, *Protesters on Trial*, 71–73.

83. See, respectively, Benjamin Dreyfus to John F. Kennedy, telegram, June 20, 1963; "Lawyers Who Attended President's Meeting," memo, June 21, 1963; Robert Kennedy to Benjamin Dreyfus, July 9, 1963, folder 16, box 15, NLG Records, Tamiment.

84. See "American Bar Association Response to President's Plea in Civil Rights Crisis," *New York Law Journal*, July 2, 1963; Attorney General to all participants to the June 21 conference, June 28, 1963; George Crockett to Benjamin Dreyfus, June 26, 1963, folder 16, box 15, NLG Records, Tamiment.

85. See John Herbers, "Mississippi Drive Is Being Widened," *New York Times*, July 1, 1964.

86. William G. Weart, "100 Lawyers Join New Rights Group," *New York Times*, July 11, 1963.

87. "Civil Rights Lawyer Berl I. Bernhard," *New York Times*, February 8, 1965.

88. Hilbink, *Filling the Void*, 14–16.

89. Wulf, interview. See also Hilbink, *Filling the Void*, 8–10.

90. In the meantime, the ACLU established a Southern Regional Office in Atlanta with a few staffed lawyers. In April 1965, the ACLU incorporated the LCDC. On the LCDC, see S. Walker, *In Defense of American Liberties*, 266; Hilbink, *Filling the Void*, 36–39; Aronson, "Politics of Civil Rights Lawyering."

91. See the flyer *Know Your Rights*, Law Day Seminar, Detroit, May 1, 1965, folder 26, box 5, NLG Records, Tamiment.

92. "Summer Project: Mississippi, 1964." See also "Minutes of the National Executive Board Meeting," October 18, 1964, folder 26, box 5, NLG Records, Tamiment.

93. Cloke, interview; Haberfeld, interview.

94. See the NLG press release, July 14, 1964, and attached Ernest Goodman and Herman B. Gerringer to Lyndon B. Johnson, July 14, 1964, folder 18, box 51, NLG Records, Tamiment.

95. M. S. Handler, "F.B.I. Augments Mississippi Forces," *New York Times*, June 25, 1964; M. S. Handler, "N.A.A.C.P. Bids U.S. Rule Mississippi," *New York Times*, June 27, 1964.

96. John H. Fenton, "29 Jurists, Disputing Kennedy, Say U.S. Can Act in Mississippi," *New York Times*, July 1, 1964.

97. For an overview of the impact of Cold War anticommunism on the civil rights movement, see Lieberman and Lang, *Anticommunism and the African American Freedom Movement*.

98. See, for instance, Rowland Evans and Robert Novak, "Freedom Party Postscript," *Washington Post*, September 3, 1964; Rowland Evans and Robert Novak, "Danger from the Left," *Washington Post*, March 18, 1965.

99. James Eastland, "Communist Infiltration in the So-Called Civil Rights Movement," 110 Cong. Rec. 16593–7 (1964).

100. James B. Utt, "Communists Promote Mob Violence," 110 Cong. Rec. 17241–2 (1964). See also, in the same vein, "National Lawyers Guild," 110 Cong. Rec. 24041 (1964).

101. Forman, *Making of Black Revolutionaries*, 381–82.

102. FBI SAC, Detroit, to Director, memo, April 22, 1965, folder 1, box 293, NLG Records, Tamiment.

103. This was at a time when King's close association with Stanley Levison, a New York lawyer and champion of left-wing causes, was under scrutiny and nurtured the FBI's allegations of a communist influence over the reverend. See "Levison, Stanley David," King Encyclopedia, https://kinginstitute.stanford.edu/encyclopedia /levison-stanley-david.

104. Fairclough, *To Redeem the Soul of America*, 263. To the contrary, Kunstler insisted that King sidestepped rivalries and made use of all lawyers without distinction. See Kunstler, *My Life*, 118–19.

105. The involvement in the civil rights movement was a "life-changing experience" also for lawyers who belonged to other organizations. See Aronson, "Getting Punched by Sheriff Clark and Other Misadventures," 196–99.

106. Welsh and CLAS, *Project Mississippi*.

107. Kunstler, *My Life*, 112.

108. "Summer Project: Mississippi, 1964." On the Guild's involvement in the case, see McCray, *Mississippi, America*. See also Popper, "Goodmans and Schwerners," which explains how Popper, a friend of the Goodman family, went to the White House several times, met with President Johnson, and urged him to help in the search for the three volunteers.

109. Both Anna K. Johnston Diggs (aka Anna Diggs Taylor) and Claudia Shropshire (aka Claudia C. House Shropshire Morcom) became prominent judges in Michigan. See "3 Lawyers in Search for Missing Rights Workers," *Worker*, July 5, 1964, folder 34, box 52, Popper Papers.

110. Founded in 1962, the Freedom Singers was a music band that toured the country singing church and movement songs in order to educate people about the civil rights movement, raise funds, and recruit activists for SNCC. See R. M. Harris, "I Love to Sing."

111. Rand, interview.

112. Clark and Sequenzia, "Remembering Freedom Summer 25 Years Later," 17–20.

113. Van G. Sauter, "Young Detroit Attorney Joins 'Freedom' Fight," *Detroit Free Press*, June 23, 1964.

114. Clark and Sequenzia, "Remembering Freedom Summer 25 Years Later," 20–23.

115. Clark and Sequenzia, "Remembering Freedom Summer 25 Years Later," 14.

116. Kunstler, *My Life*, xiii–xiv.

117. "Summer Project: Mississippi, 1964."

118. Babson, Riddle, and Elsila, *Color of Law*, 340.

119. Holt, *Summer That Didn't End*, 72.

120. Jelinek, "Evolution of a Radical Lawyer."

121. Ginger, *Civil Rights & Liberties Handbook*, 44d–44f.

122. Casper, *Lawyers before the Warren Court*, 145.

123. Barkan, *Protesters on Trial*, 28–31.

124. Koonan, interview.

125. Stavis, "Mississippi Freedom Democratic Party Challenge."

126. Kinoy, *Rights on Trial*, 262–70.

127. Kunstler, *My Life*, 126.

128. See, for instance, Rosenfeld, *Report on Guild Committee Participation at Two Conferences in the South*, n.d., folder 14, box 15, NLG Records, Tamiment.

129. Kunstler, *Deep in My Heart*, 359–60; M. S. Smith, *Lawyers You'll Like*, 67; Holt, *Act of Conscience*, 155–59.

130. Benjamin Dreyfus, "National Lawyers Guild Urges All Members of the Bar to Support the March on Washington," press release, August 16, 1963, folder 3, box 52, NLG Records, Tamiment.

131. Kunstler, *My Life*, 135.

132. See Stephen Bingham's open letter, February 15, 1965, folder Bingham Stephen—"Mississippi Letter," carton 51, NLG Records, Bancroft.

133. Clark and Sequenzia, "Remembering Freedom Summer 25 Years Later," 14–16.

134. Barkan, *Protesters on Trial*, 38, 49–53.

135. Kinoy, *Rights on Trial*, 167–68, 193.

136. See, for example, John Lewis and Lawrence Guyot in McCray, *Mississippi, America*.

Chapter 2

1. Katrina Leefmans, "Lawyers against the System," *Juris Doctor* 1, no. 4 (April 1971): 17–18, folder NLG Convention 1971, carton 57, NLG Records, Bancroft.

See also the leaflet Massachusetts Lawyers Guild, *In a Demonstration*, n.d., folder 555, pt. 2, box M-21, Hall and Hoag Collection.

2. Hill, *Men, Mobs, and Law*, 209–63.

3. Gitlin, *Sixties*, 26–27, 84–132.

4. Rorabaugh, *Berkeley at War*, 89–90.

5. Though styled as an acronym, SLATE did not stand for anything. See Rosenfeld, *Subversives*, 77–78.

6. Malcolm S. Burnstein, "The Un-American Committee in San Francisco," *New University Thought* 1, no. 2 (Autumn 1960): 9–15, folder ILWU–HUAC San Francisco Hearings, May 1960, carton 76, Meiklejohn Collections.

7. Rosenfeld, *Subversives*, 94–96.

8. "63 Rioters Face Court Today," *SF Examiner*, May 16, 1960.

9. Malcolm Burnstein, interview by Lisa Rubens, 2000, transcript, Free Speech Movement Oral History Project, Oral Histories, Bancroft.

10. Rorabaugh, *Berkeley at War*, 18.

11. Frederick D. Smith to Colleagues, August 14, 1964; *Petition for Writ of Habeas Corpus*, August 11, 1966, folder Miscellaneous, carton 64, NLG Records, Bancroft. See also Malcolm Burnstein, interview by Lisa Rubens, Oral Histories, Bancroft.

12. Gitlin, *Sixties*, 163–64.

13. Rosenfeld, *Subversives*, 153–207.

14. Walker was employed in a pharmaceutical company where she also ran a union. After being fired because of her communist affiliation, her union unsuccessfully appealed to the Supreme Court to demand her reinstatement. In a well-known decision, the Supreme Court refused to rule on the substance of the case—that is, whether a communist had the right to a job in the United States. See Black v. Cutter Laboratories, 315 U.S. 292 (1956). See also Schrecker, *Many Are the Crimes*, 299–300.

15. Burnstein, "FSM"; Burnstein, interview with the author.

16. Pearlman, *Call Me Phaedra*, 99–100; Rosenfeld, *Subversives*, 221–22.

17. Siegfried Hesse, interview by Lisa Rubens, 1999, transcript, Free Speech Movement Oral History Project, Oral Histories, Bancroft; Buxbaum, interview with the author; Burnstein, "FSM," 438.

18. *The Defender: Free Speech Trial Newsletter*, April 18, 1965, folder 7, box 4, Robert E. Treuhaft Papers; Malcolm Burnstein to appellants in the FSM case, October 24, 1967, folder Lawyer's Committee, carton 33, Meiklejohn Collections.

19. See the letter addressed to all defendants, n.d., folder Lawyer's Committee, carton 33, Meiklejohn Collections.

20. FSM Legal Central, *Defendants: Read This Carefully*, instruction sheet, n.d., folder Lawyer's Committee, carton 33, Meiklejohn Collections.

21. Richard Buxbaum, interview by Lisa Rubens, 2000, transcript, Free Speech Movement Oral History Project, Oral Histories, Bancroft.

22. Burnstein, "FSM." Peter Franck, who was among the youngest lawyers helping the defendants, thought it was a mistake to waive the jury. See Franck, interview. Other protagonists argue that the choice of a bench trial was not necessarily the main reason for the legal defeat. See Buxbaum, interview with the author.

23. Marvin Garson, "The Politics of Justice," *The Trial*, July 19, 1965, 2–4, folder 7, box 4, Treuhaft Papers.

24. The letters are in folders 3–14 and 1–17 of, respectively, box 3 and 4, Burnstein Papers.

25. Richard Buxbaum, interview by Lisa Rubens, Oral Histories, Bancroft.

26. For an overview of the facts, see Platt, *Politics of Riot Commissions*, 263–306. On the Guild's initiatives, see Civil Liberties Docket et al., "Watts Revolt and the Los Angeles Chapter Response"; Doron Weinberg and Marty Fassler, *A Historical Sketch of the National Lawyers Guild in American Politics, 1936–1968* (New York: NLG, n.d.), 22, folder 25, box 6, Goldring Papers.

27. On the extended geography and temporality of race revolts, see Levy, *Great Uprising*, 9.

28. U.S. National Advisory Commission on Civil Disorders, *Report*, 1.

29. James, interview.

30. Anderson, *Movement and the Sixties*, 61–66. Potter's quote is in Sale, *SDS*, 115–27.

31. Rorabaugh, *Berkeley at War*, 92–93.

32. Franck, interview. See also Pearlman, *Call Me Phaedra*, 101–3.

33. *Stop the Draft*, leaflet, n.d. [1967?], and *A Time to Groove and a Time to Disobey*, leaflet, n.d. [1967?], folder 10, box 12, New Left Collection.

34. See the document "What Stop the Draft Week Is All About," n.d. [1967?], folder 10, box 12, New Left Collection.

35. Rosenfeld, *Subversives*, 384–85.

36. "Anti-Draft Activities Involve Many Local Guild Lawyers," *News, Notes and Activities* 1, no. 1 (October 1967): 1–2, folder NLG–1968 Convention, carton 31, NLG Records, Bancroft.

37. Bernardine Dohrn, "Report from the Student Division," November 1967, folder NLG Students, carton 58, NLG Records, Bancroft.

38. David Lubell to NLG members, December 16, 1968, folder 37, box 7, Unger Papers.

39. On Kaufman's previous activity, see M. M. Kaufman, "War Crimes and Cold-War 'Conspiracies.'"

40. Mary Kaufman to NLG members, January 9, 1968, and Mary Kaufman to NLG members, January 16, 1968, folder 58, box 3, Unger Papers; "The Battle of Whitehall Street," *Civil Liberties in New York (NYCLU)* 16, no. 1 (January 1968): 1, 7, folder 36, box 8, Unger Papers. See also Homer Bigart, "246 Seized Here in Draft Protest," *New York Times*, December 6, 1967.

41. Data are in the paper by Mary Kaufman, "The Mass Defense Office—A Lawyer's Weapon Against Repression," July 9, 1970, folder 3, box 71, Kaufman Papers.

42. See the Columbia Strike Committee's booklet *Why We Strike*, n.d. [1968?], folder 18, box 11, New Left Collection.

43. See Mark Rudd's comment in Avorn, *Up against the Ivy Wall*, 291–97.

44. Gitlin, *Sixties*, 305–13. The quote is in Hayden, *Reunion*, 255.

45. Avorn, *Up against the Ivy Wall*, 117–52.

46. See the convention package, June 28, 1968, folder McTernan—1968 NLG Convention, carton 31, NLG Records, Bancroft. See also *Student Guild Newsletter*, no. 1 (May 1968), folder NLG Students, carton 58, NLG Records, Bancroft.

47. Stein, interview.

48. Jonathan Lubell to NLG members, August 2, 1968, folder 36, box 8, Unger Papers.

49. Kaufman, "Mass Defense Office."

50. Avorn, *Up against the Ivy Wall*, 195–203. On Stein's arrest, see Jones, *Radical Line*, 167–68.

51. *Student Guild Newsletter*, no. 1 (May 1968).

52. See, for instance, Columbia Liberation School, *The Courts and Legal Repression*, August 8, 1968, folder 6, box 28, Kennedy Papers. See also Ratner Kunstler, interview. On the phenomenon of free universities, see Horn, *Spirit of '68*, 198–205.

53. Avorn, *Up against the Ivy Wall*, 242–76.

54. Baker et al., *Police on Campus*, 7, 117–18.

55. Poka, "Impressions of a Rookie Cop"; Reynolds, "Hats and Bats."

56. See the correspondence in folder 40, box 45, NLG Records, Tamiment. The Civilian Complaint Review Board (CCRB), an oversight agency of the New York City Police Department, received 162 complaints, but only three officers were the object of disciplinary charges. The CCRB spread the blame on both the police and students. M. Johnson, *Street Justice*, 261–65.

57. Gershman, "In the Spirit of Reconciliation."

58. George H. Hickerson and Mark Rudd to friends, August 21, 1968, folder 6, box 28, Kennedy Papers.

59. Kaufman, "Mass Defense Office."

60. Jonathan Black, "Lawyers of the Left: A Crisis of Identity," *Village Voice*, May 1, 1969, 12, 54.

61. Mary Kaufman to NLG members, May 14, 1968, and "Minutes of Board Meeting," June 5, 1968, folder 24, box 20, NLG Records, Tamiment.

62. See, for example, Katherine Ellis to Abraham Unger, August 22, 1968, and Roberta Manning to Unger, August 26, 1968, folder 16, box 1, Unger Papers.

63. See, for instance, Mary Kaufman to NLG members, August 29, 1968; Kaufman to NLG members, November 26, 1968; and Kaufman to NLG members, December 20, 1968, folder 16, box 1, Unger Papers. See also James, *People's Lawyers*, 94–96.

64. See the section "Marty Kenner" in Payne, *What We Want, What We Believe*.

65. *News Letter*, September 1968, folder 24, box 20, NLG Records, Tamiment.

66. The lawsuit eventually failed. See Ratner, *Moving the Bar*, 98.

67. Gershman, "In the Spirit of Reconciliation."

68. With the help of Gerald Lefcourt, Guild students also disrupted the internal disciplinary trial of Gus Reichbach. Reichbach risked being suspended or expelled from Columbia Law School because he had led an "illegal" demonstration at the University Hall in September 1968. After a contested hearing before academic authorities, he was eventually placed on disciplinary probation. See Columbia University School of Law, *Opinion of the Disciplinary Tribunal*; Ratner, *Moving the Bar*, 101–104.

69. Rubin's quote is in Gitlin, *Sixties*, 289.

70. Seale, *Lonely Rage*, 153–58.

71. Hilliard and Cole, *This Side of Glory*, 116–22, 163. See also the testimonies in Kitchell, *Berkeley in the Sixties*. The quote and further information are in Bloom and Martin, *Black against Empire*, particularly 386, 57–59. See also Shames and Seale, *Power to the People*.

72. Youth International Party, *People Get Ready*, n.d. [1968?], folder Chicago Yippies, box 32, CCR Records.

73. D. Farber, *Chicago '68*, xiv–xvi.

74. Donner, *Protectors of Privilege*, 116–17.

75. D. Farber, *Chicago '68*, 80, 99. See also Hayden, *Reunion*, 258–62.

76. See "Documentation of National Mobilization Committee, December 27, 1967, to August 30, 1968," and "Projected Legal Defense Budget," April 8, 1969, unnamed folder, box 32, CCR Records.

77. "Minutes of August 18th Noble Street Administrative Meeting in Chicago," n.d. [1968?], folder Overt Act 6, box 32, CCR Records.

78. "Chicago Mass Arrests and the Guild," *National Lawyers Guild Newsletter* 14, no. 1 (May–June 1968): 1, 3, folder 23, box 83, NLG Records, Tamiment.

79. Raskin, *For the Hell of It*, 136–54.

80. Hayden, *Reunion*, 297.

81. Gitlin, *Sixties*, 327–29.

82. DeBenedetti, *American Ordeal*, 228. On the effects of this coverage, which unintentionally contributed to the polarization of society, see Gitlin, *Whole World Is Watching*, 186–96.

83. D. Walker, *Rights in Conflict*, vii.

84. "Chicago Mass Arrests and the Guild," *National Lawyers Guild Newsletter*. See also Hayden, *Reunion*, 303–4.

85. Rabinowitz and Ledwith, *History of the National Lawyers Guild*, 46.

86. Koonan, interview.

87. See NLG, SF Bay Area chapter to colleagues, June 6, 1969, folder San Francisco Chapter 1969, carton 58, NLG Records, Bancroft.

88. "San Francisco Regional Office," *NLG Newsletter* 15, no. 1 (May–June 1969): 1–2, folder 25, box 6, Goldring Papers.

89. Orrick, *Shut It Down!*, particularly ix, 92–96.

90. NLG, "SF Bay Area chapter executive board meeting," February 12, 1969, folder San Francisco Chapter 1969, carton 58, NLG Records, Bancroft.

91. "Current projects of the S.F. Bay Area Regional Office of the National Lawyers Guild," memo, September 8, 1969, folder San Francisco Chapter 1969, carton 58, NLG Records, Bancroft. See also Bloom and Martin, *Black against Empire*, 282–83.

92. See Stender, interview; Peter Franck and Marvin Stender to friends, February 8, 1969, folder San Francisco Chapter 1969, carton 58, NLG Records, Bancroft.

93. Siegel, interview.

94. Buxbaum, interview with the author.

95. Joan Anderson, "Report on Activities," January 25, 1969, folder 36, box 5, NLG Records, Tamiment.

96. "NLG: The Legal Arm of the Movement for Social Change," memo, n.d. [1969?], folder 25, box 6, Goldring Papers.

97. "The Mass Defense Office of the National Lawyers Guild," memo, n.d. [1970?], folder 1970 NLG Convention Reports, carton 57, NLG Records, Bancroft. See also Stuart Schwartz, "Guild Speaker Urges: Become Radical Lawyers," *Justinian* 31, no. 1 (October 30, 1970): 1, 4, folder 2, box 1, Kaufman Papers. On the welfare mothers, see Nadasen, *Welfare Warriors*.

98. "NLG Regional and Defense Offices," memo, n.d., folder 3, box 61, Thorne Papers.

99. "Co-ordination of Movement Legal Defense," memo, n.d., folder 10, box 71, Kaufman Papers.

100. "National Office Projects and Activities, March 1970 – July 1971," memo, folder 6, box 67, Kaufman Papers. See also Bass and Rae, *Murder in the Model City*, 133, 150–59.

101. Amanda Miller, "The May 1970 Student Strikes," Mapping American Social Movements Project, University of Washington, https://depts.washington.edu/moves/antiwar_may1970.shtml. For a coeval survey of campus reactions, see Peterson and Bilorusky, *May 1970*, 1–27.

102. Platt, *Politics of Riot Commissions*, 522; President's Commission on Campus Unrest, *Report*, 2.

103. The Detroit chapter, for example, was particularly active. See NLG, Detroit Chapter, "1970 Annual Report," folder 21, box 18, Cockrel Collection.

104. See "May Belonged to the People," *Defense Notes*, May 1970, 1, folder 3, box 16, Thorne Papers.

Chapter 3

1. See, among others, Michael Steven Smith, "1965: How I First Found the Guild," Michael Steven Smith's Notebook, May 29, 2007, http://michaelstevensmith.com/2007/05/how-i-first-found-the-national-lawyers-guild; Stender, interview; Doron Weinberg and Marty Fassler, *A Historical Sketch of the National Lawyers Guild in American Politics, 1936–1968* (New York: NLG, n.d.), 22, folder 25, box 6, Goldring Papers.

2. Data are in the document "NEB Delegates for August, 1975," folder NEB Ohio 1975, carton 57, NLG Records, Bancroft; Donald J. Stang to Friends of the Guild, August 8, 1977, folder NLG–SF Chapter 1972–3, carton 58, NLG Records, Bancroft.

3. The Boalt Hall Student Chapter of the NLG, "Preamble," n.d., folder NLG Students, carton 58, NLG Records, Bancroft.

4. Eric Seitz and Alicia Kaplow, "Staff Report," n.d. [1971?], folder NLG-NEB 1971, carton 57, NLG Records, Bancroft.

5. For example, Fassler, interview; Bingham, interview.

6. Bernardine Dohrn, "Report from the Student Division," November 1967, folder NLG Students, carton 58, NLG Records, Bancroft.

7. Among others, Gladstein, interview; Rand, interview; Meyer, interview.

8. Haberfeld, interview.

9. Handschu, interview.

10. For a reflection on how the burden of the Holocaust and the hurdles of assimilation affected Jewish leftists in the United States, see Grossmann, "Shadows of War and Holocaust."

11. Franck had graduated in 1962 from Columbia Law School and started practicing in 1963 in Berkeley. Franck, interview.

12. Siegel, interview.

13. Burnstein, "FSM."

14. E. Goodman, interview.

15. Fassler, interview; Bingham, interview; Stolar, interview.

16. Meyer, interview.

17. For an overview of the history of the Center for Constitutional Rights, see Ruben, *People's Lawyer*; Ratner, *Moving the Bar*, 128–33.

18. On the genealogy, evolution, and shortcomings of legal aid, see Batlan, *Women and Justice for the Poor*, particularly 4–13.

19. Concerning the leftist skepticism about legal aid, see Jonathan Black, "Lawyers of the Left II: New Channels of Sacrifice," *Village Voice*, May 15, 1969, 11–12, 29; SDS, *Legal Aid Society—Up against the Wall*, leaflet, n.d. [1970?], folder 48, box 9, Unger Papers. Also Lefcourt, interview.

20. E. Johnson, *Justice and Reform*, xxix–xxx, 40, 71.

21. Testimonies are consistent in that respect. See Stolar, interview; Smith, interview; Reif, interview. On the shortcomings of the EOA and community action, see Matusow, *Unraveling of America*, 243–70.

22. The fellowship was named after the author of the groundbreaking essay *Justice and the Poor* (1919), who first challenged the bar to provide free legal assistance for low-income Americans. See Seitz, interview; Stolar interview.

23. S. Walker, *In Defense of American Liberties*, 217.

24. Weinrib, *Taming of Free Speech*, 9; see also 1–13.

25. For instance, Gladstein, interview; E. Goodman, interview.

26. Reif, interview. See also Margaret Burnham, foreword, ix.

27. The Internal Security Act of 1950 required communist organizations to register with the federal government and established the Subversive Activities Control Board to investigate persons suspected of engaging in subversive activities. The NECLC was born to deal with the legal cases arising from this statute that many considered an infringement of political liberty. Progressive journalist I. F. Stone and philosopher Corliss Lamont were among the founders. Leonard Boudin served as chief counsel. See NECLC, *Questions and Answers about the National Emergency Civil Liberties Committee*, leaflet, 1968, folder 8, NLG Records, Tamiment.

28. This opinion was widely shared, as expressed in interviews with Stein, Koonan, Franck, and Meyer.

29. Gespass, interview.

30. *Law Students and the National Lawyers Guild*, flyer, n.d., folder NLG Bd. Meeting Jan. 25, 1969, carton 58, NLG Records, Bancroft.

31. Smith, interview; Dudley, interview.

32. Ken Cloke, interview by Lisa Rubens, 2004, transcript, Free Speech Movement Oral History Project, Oral Histories, Bancroft.

33. On the life and legal cases of Boudin and Rabinowitz, who had worked together since the 1930s, see "Reminiscences of Victor Rabinowitz, 1990" and "Oral History Interview with Leonard Boudin, 1983," transcript, Oral Histories, Columbia. The "real" and more prosaic story of how Cuba became their client in 1960 is fully chronicled in Rabinowitz's interview. Michael Tigar emphasizes the young lawyers' fascination vis-à-vis these figures in his interview with the author.

34. As a student at UC Berkeley's Boalt Law School, Cloke had met a number of NLG members who provided legal support for local demonstrations. He had also worked with Guild lawyer Ann F. Ginger at the Meiklejohn Civil Liberties Institute. See Cloke, interview.

35. Born as Weatherman, the group was subsequently renamed Weather Underground. The media and law enforcement agencies used to refer to the group as Weather Underground Organization, and its affiliates were typically called Weathermen. Later, the group also introduced gender-neutral variations, such as Weatherpeople, and began using the term Weatherwomen when indicating female members. For the sake of simplicity and conforming with the group's self-description, this book employs the terms Weatherman to indicate the aboveground organization and Weather Underground to indicate its clandestine form.

36. See Bernardine Dohrn to Victor Rabinowitz and Kenneth Cloke, February 22, 1967, folder 9, box 7, NLG Records, Tamiment. See also Rabinowitz, *Unrepentant Leftist*, 185; James, interview.

37. Kenneth Cloke, "Report of the Executive Secretary to the 1968 Convention," n.d. [1968?], folder 4, box 8, Rabinowitz Papers.

38. Cloke, interview.

39. See Samuel Rosenwein to Victor Rabinowitz, February 16, 1967, folder 9, box 7, NLG Records, Tamiment; Victor Rabinowitz to George Crockett, August 22, 1968, folder 15, box 8, Rabinowitz Papers.

40. Stanley Mayer to Guild members, January 5, 1968, folder 37, box 7, Unger Papers.

41. Kenneth Cloke, "Executive Secretary Reports to N.E.B.," *NLG Newsletter* 13, no. 5 (January–February 1968): 1–4, folder 16, box 8, Rabinowitz Papers.

42. See, respectively, Bernardine Dohrn, "Report from the Student Division II, February 1968," folder NLG Students, carton 58, NLG Records, Bancroft; Cloke, "The National Lawyers Guild," *Radicals in the Professions* 1, no. 4 (February 1968): 1, 19–22, folder 16, box 8, Rabinowitz Papers.

43. Cloke, "Report of the Executive Secretary to the 1968 Convention."

44. Milton Henry, "Black Separation: New Africa," *Guild Practitioner* 27, no. 4 (Fall 1968): 169–75. On the Republic of New Afrika and the figure of Henry, see Onaci, *Free the Land*, particularly 16–24.

45. See the convention resolutions in folder 5, box 8, Rabinowitz Papers. For an interesting rebuttal of the Black separatist resolution, see George Crockett to Victor Rabinowitz, July 29, 1968, folder 15, box 8, Rabinowitz Papers.

46. For a chronicle of the 1968 national convention, see Joan Andersson, "1968: The Way We Were," *Guild Notes* 9, no. 1 (January 1980): 16, folder NLG Anth., box 84, NLG Records, Bancroft; Rabinowitz and Ledwith, *History of the National Lawyers Guild*, 46.

47. Ben Margolis to Doris B. Walker et al., August 26, 1968, folder 15, box 8, Rabinowitz Papers.

48. Ratner Kunstler, interview.

49. Don Newton, "Guild Goes Activist," *Guardian*, July 20, 1968.

50. Rabinowitz, *Unrepentant Leftist*, 168.

51. "Reminiscences of Victor Rabinowitz, 1990," transcript, Oral Histories, Columbia. See also Dan Lund, "NLG: The Way We Were 1968," *Conspiracy*, Spring 1986, 5–8, folder 17, box 9, Rabinowitz Papers.

52. M. S. Smith, *Notebook of a Sixties Lawyer*, 29–30.

53. Tigar, interview. Tigar also wrote a history book on the role of law in the capitalist rise to power in Europe. See Tigar, *Law and the Rise of Capitalism*.

54. Jonathan Lubell to NLG Board Members, September 30, 1968, folder 24, box 20, NLG Records, Tamiment.

55. See Massachusetts Lawyers Guild's proposals for changes in the NLG constitution (February 1970), folder 1970 NLG Convention Reports, carton 57, NLG Records, Bancroft.

56. Langum, *William M. Kunstler*, 235.

57. Siegel, interview.

58. Abraham Unger to Samuel Rosenwein, February 12, 1967, but 1970, folder 27, box 1, Unger Papers.

59. "Reminiscences of Victor Rabinowitz, 1990," transcript, Oral Histories, Columbia.

60. See Rabinowitz and Ledwith, *History of the National Lawyers Guild*, 43; Norgren, *Stories from Trailblazing Women Lawyers*, 83–86. See also Griswold v. Connecticut, 381 U.S. 479 (1965).

61. See the document "Definition of a Legal Worker," n.d., folder 1, box 72, Kaufman Papers.

62. Doris B. Walker, "Report of the President to the National Executive Board on the State of the Guild: A Personal Evaluation," February 1, 1971, folder 6, box 67, Kaufman Papers. See also Mary Kaufman, "Draft on Legal Worker Point," n.d., and "Statement of Detroit Chapter of National Lawyers Guild on Admission of Law Workers," n.d., folder 1, box 72, Kaufman Papers. Other professional organizations were grappling with the same issues at the same time. See Schmalzer, Chard, and Botelhox, *Science for the People*, 3.

63. Data are in "NLG Demographic Breakdown (1974–1975)," folder 5, box 67, Kaufman Papers.

64. Dan Lund, "Guild Survives in Changing Times," *Conspiracy*, Fall 1986, 12–13, folder 17, box 9, Rabinowitz Papers.

65. See, for example, Ann F. Ginger to "Practiced Practitioners," December 10, 1975, folder NLG Survival Conference Dec. 1975, carton 57, NLG Records, Bancroft; Seitz, interview.

66. Auerbach, *Unequal Justice*, 284, 300. It must be noted that a few of these young lawyers always retained their confidence in the legal institutions and, notably, in the federal courts. In particular, they regarded the U.S. Supreme Court of the sixties as a positive and effective agent of change. See Silver, interview; W. Goodman, interview; Rand, interview.

67. Rostow, *Is Law Dead*, 13.

68. Philip B. Kurland, "The Judicial Process," *New York Times*, December 12, 1970.

69. Vanderwicken, "Angry Young Lawyers."

70. Boudin et al., *Bust Book*, 14.

71. See Cloke, "Economic Basis of Law and State"; Kenneth Cloke, "Law and the Radical Lawyer," unpublished paper for the Conference on Radicals in the Professions, Ann Arbor, Michigan, July 14–16, 1967, folder 3, box 67, Kaufman Papers.

72. Marx, "Debates on the Law on Thefts of Wood." On the Marxist legal theory, see Collins, *Marxism and Law*, 1–34; Pashukanis, *General Theory of Law and Marxism*.

73. Marcuse, *Essay on Liberation*, 67.

74. Columbia Liberation School, "The Courts and Legal Repression," report, August 8, 1968, folder 6, box 28, Kennedy Papers.

75. di Suvero, "Movement and the Legal System," 52.

76. See, respectively, R. Lefcourt, "Law against the People," 21; Cloke, "Law Is Illegal," 43.

77. See Michael J. Kennedy's testimony in Jonathan Black, "Lawyers of the Left: A Crisis of Identity," *Village Voice*, May 1, 1969, 12, 54.

78. Garry, "Political Lawyers and Their Clients," 90–91.

79. Siegel, interview.

80. Bernardine Dohrn et al., "Working Draft Program National Lawyers Guild," 1967, folder 41, box 11, NLG Records, Tamiment.

81. Cloke, "Economic Basis of Law and State," 76. For a scholarly appraisal of the role of the Supreme Court in the civil rights movement, see Rosenberg, *Hollow Hope*, particularly 39–169.

82. "Counter Culture Law," *Up against the Bench* 1, no. 2 (April 1972): 2, folder Chapter Newsletters Chicago, carton 57, NLG Records, Bancroft. See also Paul Harris, "The Community Law Firm—San Francisco," memo, n.d., folder 1970 NLG Convention Reports, carton 57, NLG Records, Bancroft.

83. Boudin et al., *Bust Book*, 14.

84. Both quotes are in M. J. Kennedy, "Civil Liberties Lie," 143.

85. See Black, *Radical Lawyers*, 12. See also "New Public Interest Lawyers."

86. For a taste of the debate, see Gorz, "On the Class Character of Science and Scientists."

87. See the presentation by Dick Magidoff, Conference on Radicals in the Professions, May 16, 1967, and the document "The Radical Education Project: An Introduction and an Invitation," n.d. [1967?], folder 39, box 30, NLG Records, Tamiment. For a broader discussion, see Champy and Israël, "Professions et engagement public."

88. See, for example, Kinoy, "Role of the Radical Lawyer and Teacher of Law."

89. P. Harris, "You Don't Have to Love the Law to Be a Lawyer."

90. Cloke, *Law and the Radical Lawyer.*

91. Kunstler, "Open Resistance," 269–73.

92. di Suvero, "Movement and the Legal System," 57. In the same vein, see "The Movement and the Lawyer," pt. I.

93. See, respectively, Jonathan Lubell, "Revolutionary Analysis and Lawyers Work: A Reply to Arthur Kinoy," memo, n.d. [1970?], folder 3, box 67, Kaufman Papers; Condon, "Comments on You Don't Have to Love the Law to Be a Lawyer."

94. *A Letter to Y. D. Stasova and to the Other Comrades in Prison in Moscow* was written in 1904 but first published in 1924. See Lenin, *Collected Works*, vol. 8, 66–70.

95. Garfinkle, Lefcourt, and Schulder, "Women's Servitude under Law."

96. See F. Kennedy, "Whorehouse Theory of Law," and Kennedy's testimony in Avedon and Arbus, *Sixties*, 66.

97. On Kennedy's life and militancy, see Randolph, *Florynce "Flo" Kennedy*, particularly 7–9. See also F. Kennedy, *Color Me Flo*, for the autobiographical account.

98. Leonard, "Movement Lawyer as Seen by One over Fifty."

99. Doris B. Walker to Rabinowitz and Cloke, letter with proposed statement, October 13, 1967, folder 8, box 7, NLG Records, Tamiment. See also D. B. Walker, "Class Role of US Courts."

100. Crockett, "Racism in American Law."

101. Kinoy, "Role of the Radical Lawyer and Teacher of Law."

102. Ernst Goldman and Victor Rabinowitz to NLG members, December 3, 1970, folder 11, box 5, Unger Papers. Regarding the positive reception of the letter, see Martin Popper to Victor Rabinowitz and Ernest Goodman, December 17, 1970, folder 5, box 3, Popper Papers.

103. Ann F. Ginger to Arthur Kinoy and Morton Stavis, January 8, 1968, folder 3, box 67, Kaufman Papers; Harris, interview.

104. Among others, see Tigar, "Lawyer's Role in Resistance"; Axelrod, "Radical Lawyer."

105. See, for instance, "Counter Culture Law," *Up Against the Bench.*

106. See the notes drafted by the National Office Collective, April 7, 1975, folder 6, box 67, Kaufman Papers.

107. Gene Cerruti, "Initial Perspective on Guild Organizing," n.d., memo, folder 24, box 20, NLG Records, Tamiment.

108. Southern California Regional Guild Office, memo to Arthur Kinoy et al., n.d. [Summer 1969?], folder 24, box 20, NLG Records, Tamiment.

109. For the two positions, compare Andersson, "1968: The Way We Were," 16, folder NLG Anth., box 84, NLG Records, Bancroft; Cloke, "Executive Secretary Reports to N.E.B.," 1–4, folder 16, box 8, Rabinowitz Papers.

110. See Gus Reichbach's testimony in Black, "Lawyers of the Left," 2, 54.

111. Kunstler made reference to the initiative of a group of French Roman Catholic priests who, since the 1940s, shared the experience of factory workers while attempting to reconcile them with the official church. See Kunstler, "Some Thoughts

about the Berrigans et al." On Kunstler's total identification with his clients, see Black, "Interview with William Kunstler," 301–2.

112. "1967 Statement of Policy and Program," *NLG Newsletter* 13, no. 1 (May 1967): 1–3, folder 16, box 8, Rabinowitz Papers. See also Seitz and Kaplow, "Staff Report."

113. "New Public Interest Lawyers," 1144.

114. Outraged by the execution of Sacco and Vanzetti, Garry felt compelled to study law. After working as a volunteer in Upton Sinclair's campaign for governor of California in 1934, Garry began attending San Francisco Law School. He passed the bar examination in 1938, immediately joined the NLG, and became a labor law expert. See Garry and Goldberg, *Streetfighter in the Courtroom*, 11–24.

115. For instance, Seale admitted that before meeting Garry, he wished to retain a Black lawyer. See Seale, *Lonely Rage*, 174–75. See also Jeffries, *Huey P. Newton*, 68–69.

116. See Garry's introduction in Keating, *Free Huey!*, xviii. See also Forbes, *Will You Die with Me?*, 214–15. Newton's quote is in the documentary Bezjian, *Charles Garry*.

117. Freed, *Agony in New Haven*, 43.

118. For further details on Cleaver, see Bloom and Martin, *Black against Empire*, 74–80.

119. Cleaver, *Soul on Ice*, 146–49. The dense correspondence between the lawyer and her beloved client is almost entirely collected in box 2, Cleaver Papers.

120. Cummins, *Rise and the Fall*, 96–99; Kask, "Soul Mates," 3–9, 37–72. See also Cleaver, introduction, 10–11.

121. The book was named as one of the ten best books of 1968 by the *New York Times*. See Cleaver, *Soul on Ice*; John Berriman, "Ten of Particular Significance and Excellence in 1968," *New York Times Book Review*, December 1, 1968.

122. Kask, "Soul Mates," 118–19. See also the pictures of Axelrod, folder BPP Album: Beverly Axelrod (1967), box 1, Cleaver Photograph Collection.

123. For this information and other details, see Axelrod's video interview, in the section "Movement Lawyers," in Payne, *What We Want, What We Believe*.

124. Pearlman, *Call Me Phaedra*, 18–22, 141–45.

125. Stender, "Prisoners' Rights and Community Concern," 284–85.

126. For an overview of the case, see Liberatore, *Road to Hell*, 47.

127. See Jackson, *Soledad Brother*, particularly 17, 212, 228, 232.

128. Thorne's review of *Blood in My Eye*, n.d., folder 5, box 11, MS 423, Thorne Papers.

129. Armstrong, *"The Dragon Has Come,"* ix–x, 42.

130. Cleaver, *Soul on Ice*, 150.

131. Guild lawyers insisted that such a privilege be extended to legal workers. See Marty Fassler, "Lawyer, Secretary . . . Client Privilege," *Conspiracy* 3, no. 3 (November 1972): 3, folder 5, box 25, New Left Collection.

132. Robb, *Dean Robb*, 296.

133. At least to some extent, the FBI investigation overstated these connections, including in the ranks of the Weather Underground militants who were close to the

group but never joined the underground. Furthermore, many of the lawyers who were mentioned in the report (twenty-two in total) did not build any stable bond with the Weather Underground. Nonetheless, the FBI gathered evidence of multiple links and "borderline areas." See SAC Chicago to FBI Director, airtel with enclosed document titled "The Relationship between the Weather Underground Organization (WUO) and the National Lawyers Guild (NLG), Internal Security," September 16, 1975, folder 4, box 235, NLG Records, Tamiment. See also SA William F. Dyson to SAC Chicago, memo, "Weatherman—Legal Support," February 28, 1975, folder 3, box 235, NLG Records, Tamiment.

134. Burrough, *Days of Rage*, 142–43; FBI, "Weatherman Underground, Summary," August 20, 1976, 2:268, FBI Records: The Vault, https://vault.fbi.gov/Weather%20Underground%20%28Weathermen%29/Weather%20Underground%20%28Weathermen%29%20Part%205%20of%206/view.

135. Kunstler, *My Life*, 200.

136. See FBI, "Weatherman Underground," 2:311; Jones, *Radical Line*, 221–24; Cloke, interview.

137. Stein, interview.

138. Harris, interview.

139. Stein, interview; Koonan, interview; Haberfeld, interview.

140. See, for example, Eric Frumin to Victor Rabinowitz, April 23, 1967; Rabinowitz to Frumin, April 27, 1967; Frumin to Rabinowitz, November 1, 1967, folder 9, box 1, Rabinowitz Papers. See also, in a similar vein, Richard Fried to Bernardine Dohrn, October 2, 1967; Vernon W. Urban to Dohrn, December 7, 1967, folder 28, box 56a, NLG Records, Tamiment.

141. "Executive Secretary's Report (as adopted at the National Executive Board meeting, Feb. 10–12, 1968)," folder 34, box 5, NLG Records, Tamiment; Cloke, interview.

142. See the pictures in folder 1, box 298, NLG Records, Tamiment. For a description of Hallinan, see Kenneth Lamott, "In Search of the Essential Angela," *Los Angeles Times*, May 30, 1971. Kennedy's eclectic outfits are well documented in F. Kennedy, *Color Me Flo*. Further details appear in Harris, interview; E. Goodman, interview.

143. Norgren, *Stories from Trailblazing Women Lawyers*, 103.

144. Handschu, interview. On the women's condition in the legal profession, see, among others, Hesse, "On Women Lawyers and Legal Secretaries."

145. Stender, interview.

146. See John Thorne et al., "Speeches from the Soledad Brothers Rally," Central Hall, Westminster (UK), April 20, 1971, folder 6, box 11, Thorne Papers.

147. Georgakas and Surkin, *Detroit*, 181. See also Jerry M. Flint, "Detroit Lawyer Becomes First Radical Judge in U.S.," *New York Times*, November 12, 1972.

148. Some pictures document the earliest marches in 1963; see folder 1, box 298, NLG Records, Tamiment. For examples of later demonstrations, see *Call to Participation*, October 3, 1969, folder San Francisco Chapter 1969, carton 58, NLG Records, Bancroft; "Guild Marches for ERA," *Women's Newsletter*, Summer 1978, 11, folder NLG Women & NCWO, carton 23, NLG Records, Bancroft.

149. *Lawyers Picket Line*, flyer, n.d. [1969?], folder 24, box 20, NLG Records, Tamiment. See also G. B. Lefcourt, "Radical Lawyer under Attack," 254.

150. Jonathan Lubell and Gene Cerruti to Guild members, n.d. [1969?], folder 37, box 7, Unger Papers.

151. "National Lawyers Guild Plans: May 1 Anti-War Activity," memo, n.d. [1971?], folder NLG-NEB 1971, carton 57, NLG Records, Bancroft.

Chapter 4

1. Earlier attempts to conceptualize these courtroom strategies made reference to "ideological litigation" or "revolutionary litigation." See Hakman, "Old and New Left Activity in the Legal Order."

2. For a theoretical discussion, see Kirchheimer, *Political Justice*, 4–18, 47. See also Belknap, introduction.

3. The trial of Sacco and Vanzetti made a partial exception, but lawyers and conflicting groups of supporters quarreled over defense strategies, which ended up being volatile and hardly effective. See Hill, *Men, Mobs, and Law*, 162–99.

4. The case of William Z. Foster was severed from the trial because he was seriously ill. The trial of the remaining eleven defendants began in January 1949 and ended ten months later. See Burnstein, "From Arrest to Verdict," 42.

5. The Smith Act was a 1940 statute prohibiting the teaching and advocacy of the violent overthrow of the government.

6. Dimitrov's strategy is described and celebrated in a book written by Marcel Willard, who was one the most popular communist lawyers in France during the 1930s and 1940s. Willard volunteered to represent Dimitrov, but German judicial authorities barred him. He nonetheless counseled Dimitrov and was incarcerated in Germany. See Willard, *La défense accuse*, 105–205.

7. Ten defendants were sentenced to five years in prison, while one was sentenced to three years. With the help of the ACLU and the NLG, the defendants appealed to the Supreme Court, challenging the constitutionality of the Smith Act. However, the Supreme Court upheld the trial court's decision. See Dennis v. United States, 341 U.S. 494 (1951); Belknap, "Cold War in the Courtroom." See also Redish, *Logic of Persecution*, 82.

8. Felber maintains that these trials were already "public spectacles" and forms of "political theater," yet most of the defining features of militant litigation seem to be unexpressed. See Felber, *Those Who Know Don't Say*, 77–103; 123–44. In France, however, since the early 1960s radical lawyer Jacques Vergès and the attorneys who represented the Algerian Front of National Liberation experimented with their version of militant litigation, known as "defense of rupture." See Vergès, *De la stratégie judiciaire*; Israël, *L'arme du droit*.

9. The more accurate historical reconstruction of the trial is in Foley, *Confronting the War Machine*, 226–94.

10. Boudin himself did not intend to use the courtroom as a forum and was focused on winning the case. See "Oral History Interview with Leonard Boudin, 1983," transcript, Oral Histories, Columbia.

11. A year later, a court of appeals overturned the convictions. For a critical perspective on the trial, see Mitford, *Trial of Dr. Spock*.

12. As civil disorders spread in 1967, some commentators blamed Black militants such as H. Rap Brown, who allegedly toured the country inciting riots. In April 1967, Congressman William Cramer (R-FL) proposed an anti-riot bill outlawing travel across state lines with the intent to incite, organize, or participate in a riot. After the events of Newark, the House passed the bill, and in April 1968, the president signed a civil rights statute that included the anti-riot amendment. See Ely, "Chicago Conspiracy Case," 237. On the activists' concerns, see the booklet of the Stop the Draft Week Defense Fund, *The Oakland Seven*, n.d., folder "The Oakland Seven" (draft resisters) pamphlet, c. 1969, carton 180, Meiklejohn Collections.

13. Garry and Goldberg, *Streetfighter in the Courtroom*, 176.

14. Frank Bardacke, "The Oakland 7," *Realist*, no. 86 (November–December 1969): 1–8, The Realist Archive Project, www.ep.tc/realist/86.

15. *With a Little Help from Our Friends*, leaflet, March 1968, and *Support the Oakland Seven*, leaflet, May 1968, folder 10, box 12, New Left Collection.

16. Malcolm Burnstein, interview by Lisa Rubens, 2000, transcript, Free Speech Movement Oral History Project, Oral Histories, Bancroft. See also Bardacke, "Oakland 7."

17. Bannan and Bannan, *Law, Morality and Vietnam*, 117–23.

18. Garry and Goldberg, *Streetfighter in the Courtroom*, 153–80.

19. As an example of these interviews, see Mark Lane, "Exclusive: Mark Lane Interviews Huey Newton in Jail," *Los Angeles Free Press*, July 24, 1970, Harold Weisberg Archive, http://jfk.hood.edu.

20. Independent Socialist Club, *Defend Huey Newton*, leaflet, n.d., and Direct Action Committee, Peace & Freedom Party, Stop-the-Draft-Week, *Free Huey—Support the Leaders of Stop the Draft Week*, leaflet, n.d. [1968?], folder 10, box 1, New Left Collection.

21. The party also nominated Eldridge Cleaver for president, Mario Savio for the California State Senate, and Cleaver's wife, Kathleen, for the California State Assembly.

22. Anthony, *Picking Up the Gun*, 83.

23. Coeval sources confirm it. See Keating, *Free Huey!*, xix.

24. Rorabaugh, *Berkeley at War*, 81–82; Hilliard and Cole, *This Side of Glory*, 145, 261.

25. Bloom and Martin, *Black against Empire*, 136.

26. Blauner, "Sociology in the Courtroom."

27. Garry and Goldberg, *Streetfighter in the Courtroom*, 97–151. For a more detached and fine-grained analysis, see Pearlman, *Sky's the Limit*, 334–473.

28. Pearlman, *Call Me Phaedra*, 134–35.

29. The fifty-two volumes of the transcript have been digitized and are available in the World Trials Library, https://heinonline.org.

30. Macdonald, introduction, xxiii.

31. Wiener, *Conspiracy in the Streets*, 1–41, particularly 1–2. See also Paul Schachter, "Chicago Conviction Reversed," *Guild Notes* 1, no. 4 (December 1972): 1, 4, 14, folder 1, box 73, Kaufman Papers.

32. More specifically, the eight were charged with conspiring to use interstate commerce with intent to incite a riot. Six of the defendants—David Dellinger, Rennie Davis, Tom Hayden, Abbie Hoffman, Jerry Rubin, and Bobby Seale—were also charged with crossing state lines with the intent to incite a riot. The other two defendants, John Froines and Lee Weiner, were charged with teaching demonstrators how to construct incendiary devices that would be used in civil disturbances.

33. At the end of the trial, the seven defendants went to jail; ten days later, they were granted bail.

34. Klebanow and Jonas, *People's Lawyers*, 320. It is worth remembering that attorney general Clark objected to the anti-riot provisions of the Civil Rights Act of 1968 and did not agree with the idea of a conspiracy trial for the Chicago demonstrations. He also opposed sending federal troops to Chicago, refused to authorize wiretaps of radicals, and did not endorse a grand jury investigation. As soon as Richard Nixon won the election and John Mitchell replaced Clark, the prosecution was activated. See Raskin, *For the Hell of It*, 182.

35. Chicago Police Department, Intelligence Division, "Interview Report on the subject of Democratic NC, March 27, 1969," folder: United States v. David T. Dellinger, et al., 1969–1987, box 33, Hayden Papers.

36. Evidence of these negotiations is in Leonard Weinglass to Jerry Rubin, September 15, 1969, folder Jerry Rubin, box 32, CCR Records. For a reflection on the legal strategies, see Lukas, *Barnyard Epithet and Other Obscenities*, 32–33.

37. Hayden, *Reunion*, 382; Hoffman, *Autobiography of Abbie Hoffman*, 192.

38. Foner, foreword, xiv. Hoffman himself conceded that TV coverage worked perfectly for rendering Yippies' politics. See Hoffman, *Autobiography of Abbie Hoffman*, 188.

39. Protagonists were well aware of it. See Hayden, *Trial*, 69.

40. Debouzy, "Le procès des Huit de Chicago (1969–1970)," particularly 42.

41. Langum, *William M. Kunstler*, 19–22, 14.

42. Gitlin, *Sixties*, 234. On the judge's conduct, see Lahav, "Chicago Conspiracy Trial."

43. For some examples of these behaviors, see Dellinger, *Contempt*.

44. Kunstler confirmed it in Roxanne Bezjian's documentary *Charles Garry: Streetfighter in the Courtroom*. For Seale's version, see Seale, *Lonely Rage*, 179–97.

45. As an example of the influence of this event, see the powerful artwork *Injustice Case* (1970) by David Hammons in Godfrey and Whitley, *Soul of a Nation*, 104.

46. Raskin, *For the Hell of It*, 200–201, 212–13.

47. These lawyers had been retained only for pretrial motions and had already withdrawn by telegram. Tigar, interview.

48. These and other episodes are recounted in Louis Nizer, "What to Do When the Judge Is Put Up against the Wall," *New York Times Magazine*, April 5, 1970; Hayden, *Trial*, 33–39; Lukas, *Barnyard Epithet and Other Obscenities*, 27–28.

49. Lukas, *Barnyard Epithet and Other Obscenities*, 88.

50. See Macdonald, introduction, xiv–xv; Lukas, *Barnyard Epithet and Other Obscenities*, 88–91.

51. See Kunstler and Kunstler, *William Kunstler*.

52. The Committee was launched with a letter signed by a number of intellectuals, including Noam Chomsky and Susan Sontag, and published in the *New York Review of Books*. See Peter Babcox et al., "The Committee to Defend the Conspiracy," *New York Review of Books* 12, no. 12 (June 19, 1969): 37–38.

53. Lukas, *Barnyard Epithet and Other Obscenities*, 67.

54. Meyer, interview. See also Hayden, *Reunion*, 377–78.

55. See, for instance, *Stop the Trial*, leaflet, November 1, 1969, in Brown Special Collections. See also Hoffman et al., *Conspiracy*.

56. Lukas, *Barnyard Epithet and Other Obscenities*, 64–65; Kunstler, *My Life*, 15, 34.

57. Hayden, *Trial*, 91.

58. Kalba and Beste, "Lawyers and Revolutionaries."

59. "Fact Sheet on Events Surrounding the Chicago 8 Conspiracy Trial," n.d. [1969?], folder 23, box 7, Unger Papers; NLG, San Francisco-Bay Area Chapter to Fellow members of the legal community, October 3, 1969, folder San Francisco Chapter 1969, carton 58, NLG Records, Bancroft; Stolar, interview.

60. "Conspiracy Protest," *SLAM* 1, no. 1 (October 1969): 4–6, and "Lawyers Rally to Stop Trial," *Rights*, November 1969, 2–6, folder 10, box 48, Kaufman Papers. See also *NLG Newsletter* 15, no. 4 (November–December 1969), folder 25, box 6, Goldring Papers.

61. Alicia Kaplow to NLG colleagues, letter with enclosed amicus curiae brief, November 6, 1969, folder 5, box 3, Popper Papers.

62. See, for instance, Organizer's Manual Collective, *Organizer's Manual*, 143–44.

63. Handschu, interview.

64. Rod Such, "Radical Lawyers: 'Turn the Accused into the Accuser,'" *Guardian*, May 26, 1971.

65. Gene Cerruti, "San Francisco: Report and Criticism," July 16, 1970, folder 25, box 6, Goldring Papers.

66. Lefcourt, interview.

67. Southern California Regional Guild Office, "Proposed Lawyers Guild Seminars on Criminal/Political Trials," memo, n.d. [summer 1969?], folder 24, box 20, NLG Records, Tamiment.

68. U.S. Department of Justice, *Disruption in the Courtroom*, 1–10.

69. This concept was frequently reiterated. See, for example, Such, "Radical Lawyers"; Hayden, *Trial*, 98.

70. Kirchheimer, *Political Trials*, 256, 423.

71. Garry, "Attacking Racism in Court before Trial."

72. Savoy, "Toward a New Politics of Legal Education."

73. P. Harris, *Black Rage Confronts the Law*, 31–58.

74. For a step-by-step chronicle, see John Griffith and Louis Heldman, "Ousted Worker Kills Three in Chrysler Plant Shooting, *Detroit Free Press*, July 16, 1970; Tom Ricke, "Murder Trial Jury," *Detroit Free Press*, April 29, 1971; Tom Ricke, "Murder Trial Witnesses Tell of Violence at Auto Plant," *Detroit Free Press*, May 6, 1971; Tom Ricke, "Old Mental Scars Blamed in Killing of 3 at Factory," *Detroit Free Press*, May 19, 1971; Bill Black, "Mom Describes a Squalid Life in 'Other America,'" *Chron-*

icle, May 22, 1971; Tom Ricke, "Jurors, Slayer Visit Factory Where 3 Died," *Detroit Free Press*, May 14, 1971. See also Thompson, *Whose Detroit?*, 136–43; Georgakas and Surkin, *Detroit*, 85–86.

75. See, for instance, George Colbert to Kenneth Cockrel, July 21, 1971; Colbert to Cockrel, July 21, 1971, folder 16, box 16, Cockrel Collection. Harris employed a "Black rage defense" for the first time in the case of Steven Robinson, a twenty-nine-year-old Black man who robbed a bank in the Fillmore district of San Francisco in January 1971. The case went to trial in the summer. See P. Harris, *Black Rage Confronts the Law*, particularly chap. 2.

76. Garry, "Attacking Racism in Court before Trial," xv.

77. Clavir and Spitzer, *Conspiracy Trial*, 561.

78. It is interesting to note that during the 1912 murder trial of labor organizers Joseph Ettor and Arturo Giovannitti, which became legendary in the radical tradition, Giovannitti compared himself and his co-defendant to Socrates and Jesus Christ. See Giovannitti's address to the jury in Ebert, *The Trial of a New Society*, 144.

79. On the previous use of this historical parallel, see Hill, *Men, Mobs, and Law*, 6, 135.

80. "What We Want Now!," *Black Panther*, May 15, 1967.

81. According to some observers, the focus on jury selection was the key factor explaining the numerous acquittals in the so-called political trials of the early 1970s. See Ginger, *Law, the Supreme Court, and the People's Rights*, 319–27.

82. Since 1931, lawyers could ask jurors questions about racial prejudice. However, very few lawyers would pose such questions because they were afraid of triggering further racial hostility. See P. Harris, *Black Rage Confronts the Law*, 74.

83. Ginger, "Part of the Answer." See also Community Assistance and Education Fund, *La Raza Defendants and Voir Dire: A Manual to Help Combat Racist Juries*, 1972, folder 11, box 204F, Davis Papers.

84. All in all, fourteen Panthers were arrested and nine of them were tried. Seale faced murder, kidnapping, and conspiracy charges for ordering to "off" the suspected spy. Huggins was charged with assisting in the (taped) interrogation and torture of Rackley. Both of them denied charges. By contrast, the two actual murderers, George Sams and Warren Kimbro, confessed. Sams also claimed that Seale had personally requested the execution. See Bass and Rae, *Murder in the Model City*.

85. The whole jury selection process is chronicled in the sympathetic account by playwright and Yale University teacher Donald Freed, *Agony in New Haven*, 15–174.

86. Neil MacFarquhar, "Harold M. Mulvey, 86, Judge at Tense Black Panther Trials," *New York Times*, March 1, 2000; Bloom and Martin, *Black against Empire*, 253–62.

87. Ginger, *Law, the Supreme Court, and the People's Rights*, 501–2.

88. It must be remembered that a form of collaboration had already existed in the Angela Davis trial, with sociologist Jeffrey M. Paige and psychologists Harold Dent, Thomas Hilliard, William Pierce, and William Hayes.

89. Schulman et al. "Recipe for a Jury."

90. Kairys, *Philadelphia Freedom*, 294–97. See also Kairys, Schulman and Harring, *Jury System*. As an example of the project's activities, see the leaflet of the workshop at the NYU School of Law, *Jury Selection: Strategies for Success*, May 10, 1975, folder 25, box 6, Goldring Papers.

91. U.S. Department of Justice, *Disruption in the Courtroom*, 7.

92. See, for instance, Paul Harris, "Stephanie Kline and Her Lawyer's Ego," *Conspiracy* 3, no. 1 (September 1972): 1, 10–11, folder 267B:25, box N-35, Hall and Hoag Collection.

93. Willard, *La défense accuse*, 321–22.

94. Kalba and Beste, "Lawyers and Revolutionaries," 49–54.

95. John Oppedahl, "Commissioner Accused of Bias in Juror Screening," *Detroit Free Press*, March 27, 1970. See also People of the State of Michigan v. Rafael Viera and Clarence Fuller, "Joint Motion to Quash Jury Panel and for Other Relief," March 26, 1970, folder 18, box 17, Cockrel Collection.

96. John Oppedahl, "Jury Commission Blasted by Judge," *Detroit Free Press*, April 14, 1970; John Oppedahl, "Bethel Case Jury Finally Selected," *Detroit Free Press*, May 1, 1970. See also the order establishing the new guidelines, signed by Robert. E. De Mascio (Recorder's Court of Detroit), March 31, 1970, folder 18, box 17, Cockrel Collection. More generally on the case, see Thompson, *Whose Detroit?*, 134–35.

97. Zimroth, *Perversions of Justice*, 15–17.

98. Kempton, *Briar Patch*, 26.

99. Balagoon et al., *Look for Me in the Whirlwind*.

100. Kempton, *Briar Patch*, 32–35, 141.

101. Committee to Defend the Panther 21, *What Do the Panthers Stand For*, booklet, n.d. [April 1970?], folder 14, box 26, New Left Collection.

102. Nizer, "What to Do When the Judge Is Put Up against the Wall"; Rod Such, "Panther 21 Trial Opens," *Guardian*, February 19, 1971.

103. Zimroth, *Perversions of Justice*, 282–86, 399.

104. Kempton, *Briar Patch*, 152.

105. Lefcourt, interview.

106. Hilliard and Cole, *This Side of Glory*, 280–81.

107. Tom Wolfe, "Radical Chic: That Party at Lenny's," *New York Magazine* 3, no. 24 (June 8, 1970): 26–56.

108. The letter appeared in various radical and underground publications. See "Open Letter: Panther 21 to Weatherman," *Berkeley Tribe* 3, no. 4 (February 12–19, 1971): 8–9.

109. Kempton, *Briar Patch*, 186, 267.

110. Edith Evans Asbury, "Black Panther Party Members Freed after Being Cleared of Charges," *New York Times*, May 14, 1971; Catherine Breslin, "One Year Later: The Radicalization of the Panther 13 Jury," *New York Magazine* 5, no. 22 (May 29, 1972): 53–63.

111. Lefcourt, interview.

112. Crowley, *Rites of Passage*, 163–75. See also the testimony of one of the defendants in Stern, *With the Weathermen*, 261–93.

113. Bakke, *Protest on Trial*, 67–152.

114. David Aikman, "In Seattle: Up from Revolution," *Time* 115, no. 15 (April 14, 1980): 14–16.

115. Dorsen and Friedman, *Disorder in the Court*, 5–9.

116. Harris, interview.

117. Tigar, interview.

118. E. Goodman, interview.

119. Fred P. Graham, "Burger Assails Unruly Lawyers," *New York Times*, May 19, 1971. See also, in the same vein, "Order in Court," *New York Times*, December 8, 1973.

120. Vanderwicken, "Angry Young Lawyers."

121. Fuld, "Right to Dissent: Protest in the Courtroom," 594.

122. Karlen, "Disorder in the Courtroom," 998–1000.

123. "American College of Trial Lawyers."

124. See, respectively, Littlejohn, "Legal Vandalism"; Rowland, "Crucial Code."

125. Dorsen and Friedman, *Disorder in the Court*, 3–5.

126. In that case, only twenty-nine spectators could be seated in the room, and as many as fifty people a day were turned away. Eventually, 850 people who were denied seats signed a petition requesting to be admitted. See Bass and Rae, *Murder in the Model City*, 175–76.

127. Illinois v. Allen, 397 U.S. 337 (1970).

Chapter 5

1. The picture did not ultimately appear in the final publication—Avedon and Arbus, *The Sixties*—but a copy of it is in Lefcourt's possession.

2. See, for instance, "New Public Interest Lawyers."

3. "Activist Lawyer with a Cause: Gerald Bernard Lefcourt," *New York Times*, February 17, 1970.

4. Rod Such, "Law Commune: Alternative Institution," *Liberation News Service*, no. 187 (August 21, 1969): 4, GI Press Collection, 1964–1977, Wisconsin Historical Society Online Collections.

5. See, among others, Biderman, "Birth of Communal Law Firms"; Black, "Interview with Gerald Lefcourt"; R. Lefcourt, "First Law Commune"; Stolar, interview; Lefcourt, interview. On the first feminist law firms, see Fuchs Epstein, *Women in Law*, 141–44.

6. C. H. Lefcourt, *Women and the Law*. At the same time, Diane Schulder, who had worked with Leonard Boudin on the Spock case and later became a Legal Aid attorney and a feminist activist, taught courses on women and the law at the University of Pennsylvania Law School and NYU School of Law.

7. James, interview.

8. "Movement and the Lawyer," pt. II. On the Dodge Revolutionary Union Movement (DRUM), a radical organization of Black workers born at Chrysler's Dodge Main assembly plant in Detroit, see Pizzolato, "Transnational Radicals."

9. Vanderwicken, "Angry Young Lawyers."

10. See, for instance, Paul Boas to Civil Liberties Legal Defense Funds, letter with enclosed document, September 11, 1970, folder Correspondence, box 34, CCR Records.

11. Title VII prohibited employment discrimination based on race, creed, national origin, or sex.

12. NAACP lawyers were the most active in that field. See McLean, *Freedom Is Not Enough*, 76–113.

13. Koonan, interview. See also Gibbs, "Alternative Forms of Practice," *Guild Notes* 3, no. 4 (May 1974): 14–15, folder 2, box 73, Kaufman Papers.

14. Siegel, interview; Liberatore, *Road to Hell*, 66.

15. Paul Harris, "Community Law or Second Base!," in *Law for the People: An Alternative for Law Students*, ed. NLG (New York: NLG, n.d. [1975?]), 11–14, folder 2, box 67, Kaufman Papers.

16. Harris, interview. See also Paul Harris, "The Community Law Firm—San Francisco," memo, n.d. [1970?], folder 1970 NLG Convention Reports, carton 57, NLG Records, Bancroft.

17. Harris, interview. See also Douglas, "Organization, Ego, and the Practice of Alternative Law."

18. The defense team included R. Jay Engel, Michael Kennedy, Charles Garry, and Richard Hodge. See Diane Middleton, "Los Siete de La Raza: Strictly Ghetto Property," *Conspiracy* 2, no. 10 (June 1972): 13, folder 6, box 68, Kaufman Papers. For an overview of the case, see (the overtly sympathetic) Heins, *Strictly Ghetto Property*.

19. Robert Reinhold, "'Law Communes' Seeking Social Change," *New York Times*, September 5, 1971.

20. Some of the footage documenting the shooting is in Alk and Gray, *The Murder of Fred Hampton* that also features Skip Andrew of the PLO.

21. It must be recalled that given the outrage for the raid, the outpouring of solidarity for the Panthers was remarkable, also involving the ACLU, the NAACP, and national Black politicians who offered help and called for an independent investigation. See Bloom and Martin, *Black against Empire*, 239–44.

22. On both the history of the PLO and Hampton's murder, see Haas, *Assassination of Fred Hampton*. See also "History," People's Law Office, https://peopleslawoffice .com/about-civil-rights-lawyers/history.

23. See, for instance, "Alternative Practices," *Up Against the Bench* 3, no. 2 (April–May 1974): 20–21, folder 7, box 68, Kaufman Papers; "Students Explore Alternative Practice," *Guild Notes* 4, no. 3 (May 1975): 5, folder 3, box 73, Kaufman Papers.

24. Meyer, interview.

25. Meyer, interview.

26. Gladstein, interview.

27. Smith, interview.

28. Kalman, *Strange Career of Legal Liberalism*, 52.

29. Bingham, interview.

30. Freire, *Pedagogy of the Oppressed*, particularly 57–74.

31. David Rockwell, "Taking on the Law School," *Crossing the Bar* 1, no. 1 (March 1972): 2, 6–7, folder 208B:80, box M-21, pt. 2, Hall and Hoag Collection.

32. "Classroom Lawyers?," *Up Against the Bench* 1, no. 5 (September 1972): 1, folder Chapter Newsletters Chicago, carton 57, NLG Records, Bancroft.

33. Steve Dobkin, "The Court Street School of Law," *Blind Justice* 5, no. 2 (April 1975): 19, folder 2, box 68, Kaufman Papers.

34. Rockwell, "Education of the Capitalist Lawyer."

35. Bob Gibbs, "Peoples Law . . . in Practice," in *Law for the People: An Alternative for Law Students*, ed. NLG (New York: NLG, n.d. [1975?]), 10–11, folder 2, box 67, Kaufman Papers.

36. Lynda Mills-Erickson and Wayne Saitta, "Open Your Eyes Alice, You Are in Wonderland," in *Law for the People: An Alternative for Law Students*, ed. NLG (New York: NLG, 1978), 4–6, folder Law Student, carton 23, NLG Records, Bancroft.

37. See Los Angeles Guild Law Students, "Make the Best of a Bad Situation," and "A Different Kind of School: The People's College of Law," in *Law for the People*, ed. NLG (New York: NLG, n.d. [1975?]), respectively 6–9 and 1–3, folder 2, box 67, Kaufman Papers. As for the comparison between the student-professor relationship and the white master–Black slave relationship, see J. Farber, *Student as Nigger*.

38. With respect to Columbia University Law School, see Jim Mauro, "Law Student Organizing," memo, n.d. [August 1969?], folder 24, box 20, NLG Records, Tamiment.

39. Stein, interview.

40. Crockett, "Racism in American Law." Crockett's data are consistent with those in Stevens, *Law School*, 234.

41. "Woman Lawyering—Two Perspectives," in *Law for the People*, ed. NLG (New York: NLG, n.d. [1975?]), 15–20, folder 2, box 67, Kaufman Papers.

42. Stevens, *Law School*, 234.

43. Handschu, interview.

44. Handschu, interview; Goldstein, interview.

45. Ginger, *Relevant Lawyers*, 14.

46. "This Is a Divided Courtroom . . . ," *Blind Justice* 1, no. 2 (December 1971): 9, folder 2, box 68, Kaufman Papers.

47. "The Reasonable Man Is a Woman!!," *Up Against the Bench* 1, no. 6 (October 1972): 8, folder Chapter Newsletters Chicago, carton 57, NLG Records, Bancroft.

48. Stevens, *Law School*, 235.

49. Savoy, "Toward a New Politics of Legal Education."

50. Friedman, *History of American Law*, 595.

51. "Minutes of Meeting of Board of Directors," June 7, 1967, folder 24, box 20, NLG Records, Tamiment.

52. *Student Guild Newsletter*, no. 1 (May 1968): 1, folder NLG Students, Carton 58, NLG Records, Bancroft.

53. Gene Cerruti, "Initial Perspective on Guild Organizing," memo, n.d., folder 24, box 20, NLG Records, Tamiment.

54. See, among others, Stephen A. Sandler to NLG members, January 27, 1969, and the enclosed tentative program, NLG Law Student Division, "Second Radical Law Student Conference at Columbia Law School on Radical Uses of Legal Skills," folder 24, box 20, NLG Records, Tamiment. See also the leaflet of the conference, *Political Repression in the United States*, with lawyers Weinglass and Lefcourt, Harvard University, n.d. [October 1970?], folder 82A:128, box M-21, pt. 2, ms. 76, Hall and Hoag Collection.

55. "Peoples Law School," *Up Against the Bench* 1, no. 5 (September 1972): 3, folder Chapter Newsletters Chicago, Carton 57, NLG Records, Bancroft. As an example of free law school, see *Rocky Mountain Law School,* flyer, n.d., folder NLG, Southwest, carton 24, NLG Records, Bancroft.

56. See, for instance, "People's Law School," *Conspiracy* 2, no. 10 (June 1972): 7, and "Peoples Law School Winter Session," *Conspiracy* 3, no. 5 (January 1973): 9, folder 6, box 68, Kaufman Papers.

57. "National Executive Board Meeting, Atlanta, February 13–14, 1971," minutes, folder NLG-NEB 1971, carton 57, NLG Records, Bancroft.

58. "Summary of N.Y. City Chapter Projects and Board Contact People—Summer, 1973," folder 38, box 7, Unger Papers. See also Robert Lefcourt, "On Being a Legal Organizer," *Blind Justice* 1, no. 3 (February 1972): 13–15, folder 2, box 68, Kaufman Papers.

59. Lynn Siiter, "Peoples Law Schools National Clearing House," *Guild Notes* 2, no. 5 (October 1973): 24, folder 1, box 73, Kaufman Papers.

60. Los Angeles Guild Law Students, "Make the Best of a Bad Situation," in *Law for the People,* ed. NLG (New York: NLG, n.d. [1975?]), 6–9, folder 2, box 67, Kaufman Papers; "Lawyers Law School," *Conspiracy* 2, no. 10 (June 1972): 7, folder 6, box 68, Kaufman Papers.

61. Henry di Suvero to Victor Rabinowitz, January 21, 1974, and enclosed prospectus "A Different Kind of School: The People's College of Law," folder 16, box 1, Rabinowitz Papers.

62. See the admission package, "Peoples Law School of the National Lawyers Guild," n.d.; Peoples Law School of the National Lawyers Guild, "Interviewing Guidelines—Admissions Committee," August 1975; "Peoples Law School of the National Lawyers Guild," information sheet, n.d., folder 47, Carton 2, PCS and MLO Records.

63. Operating since 1971, the Asian Law Collective was a group of progressive law students and community workers based in Los Angeles. La Raza National Law Students Association was founded in 1969 to federate Spanish-speaking law students across the country. The National Conference of Black Lawyers was established in 1968 by Black attorneys who saw the need for a racially-defined organization to defend the Black power movement.

64. Peoples College of Law of the National Lawyers Guild, "Report on Operations #2," March 1, 1975, folder 8, box 3, Popper Papers; Peoples College of Law of the National Lawyers Guild, "Report of Operations #4," March 1, 1976, folder 2, box 3, Popper Papers. See also "A Radical Law School Enters Its 2nd Year," *New York Times,* October 16, 1975.

65. Ted Winchester, "People's College of Law—the First Five Years," in *Law for the People,* ed. NLG (New York: NLG, 1979), 23, folder 348B:27, box N-35, pt. 2, Hall and Hoag Collection.

66. Harris, interview. Less directly, the People's College of Law also inspired the creation of the CUNY School of Law in 1983.

67. Reif, interview.

68. Meyer, interview.

69. Tractenberg, *Centennial History of Rutgers Law School in Newark*, 53–61.

70. Meyer, interview. The fact that women created havoc at Rutgers is confirmed in "Woman Lawyering—Two Perspectives," folder 2, box 67, Kaufman Papers.

71. Epstein, *Law at Berkeley*, 271–76.

72. Between 1969 and 1976, minority law students' enrollment increased by 211 percent, while female law students' enrollment increased by 535 percent. However, this data must be placed against the rapid expansion of the total number of law students. Thus, in relative terms, gains were respectively 3.9 percent and 18.2 percent. See the ABA data quoted in NLG, National Conference of Black Lawyers, Minority Admission Summer Project, *Affirmative Action in Crisis*, 11–12.

73. Gladstein, interview.

74. NLG, National Conference of Black Lawyers, *Affirmative Action in Crisis*, i–iii, 133–34.

75. June Moroney, "Minorities Need Not Apply," *Guild Notes* 4, no. 3 (May 1975): 5, folder 3, box 73, Kaufman Papers. For a review of the Bakke case, see Ball, *The Bakke Case*, 46–144.

76. Frank Del Olmo, "Lawyers, Ethnic Groups Opposed in Bakke Case," *Los Angeles Times*, September 16, 1977; NLG Southern California Chapter, "The Guild Position on Bakke," press release, n.d. [1977?], folder NLG—Minority Legal Task Force, carton 23, NLG Records, Bancroft.

77. See, among others, *National Committee to Overturn the Bakke Decision*, leaflet, June 28, 1978; "A Call for Unity in Defense of Affirmative Action," *AACC News* 1, no. 1 (November 1978): 8–9; "Rutgers University Law School–Newark," *AACC News* 1, no. 1 (November 1978): 3, folder NLG—Minority Legal Task Force, carton 23, NLG Records, Bancroft. See also Jack Hartog, "The Wake of Bakke," in *Law for the People: An Alternative for Law Students*, ed. NLG (New York: NLG, 1978), 14–15, folder Law Student, carton 23, NLG Records, Bancroft.

78. FBI, "Summary Memorandum on the Veterans of the Abraham Lincoln Brigade, 1937–1948," n.d. [1948?], www.governmentattic.org; Ginger and Tobin, *National Lawyers Guild*, 30.

79. Ellen Chapnick, "NLG Slide-Show Script," n.d. [1987?], folder 8, box 67, Kaufman Papers; Ginger and Tobin, *National Lawyers Guild*, 75–76.

80. Doris B. Walker, *International Association of Democratic Lawyers: An Extremely Brief and Incomplete History*, n.d. [1975?], folder NLG International Committee, carton 26, NLG Records, Bancroft; Popper's testimony in Ginger and Tobin, *National Lawyers Guild*, 79–80. On the foundation of the IADL and its Stalinist dogmatism (until 1968), see Nordmann and Brunel, *Aux vents de l'histoire*, 225–35. For a critique of the IADL, see Kirchheimer, *Political Justice*, 257.

81. On the Guild's reaffiliation with the IADL, see Joë Nordmann to Victor Rabinowitz, 20 December 1967, folder 8, box 7, NLG Records, Tamiment; William L. Standard to Ben Margolis, September 26, 1968, folder 15, box 8, Rabinowitz Papers; "Minutes—N.E.B. Meeting," October 18, 19, 1969, folder 37, box 5, NLG Records, Tamiment.

82. See Mary Kaufman to Ken Cloke, April 9, 1967, folder 31, box 5, NLG Records, Tamiment; the flyer of the World Conference of Lawyers for Vietnam, Grenoble, France, July 6–10, 1968, folder 60, box 10, Unger Papers.

83. Hal Mayerson to friends, January 11, 1979, folder Cuba NLG, carton 24, NLG Records, Bancroft. On the Venceremos Brigades and the influence of the Cuban Revolution on U.S. radicals, see Latner, *Cuban Revolution in America*, 28–74.

84. See, respectively, "Memorandum on Proposed Activities of the International Law Committee," n.d., folder NLG International Law Committee, carton 26, NLG Records, Bancroft; "First Official Cuban Delegation to Visit Los Angeles," press release, 1979, folder Cuba NLG, carton 24, NLG Records, Bancroft.

85. Ratner, *Moving the Bar*, 157–61.

86. Koonan, interview; E. Goodman, interview.

87. "Popular Tribunals . . . Justice by the People," *Up Against the Bench* 1, no. 3 (May 1972): 6–7, folder Chapter Newsletters Chicago, carton 57, NLG Records, Bancroft; "Cuba," *Guild Notes* 1, no. 3 (September–October 1972): 1, 12–14, folder 1, box 73, Kaufman Papers. Enthusiasm for popular tribunals was not isolated; see Berman, "Cuban Popular Tribunals."

88. NLG Delegation to Cuba, "Guild Delegation Travels to Cuba," *Guild Notes* 3, no. 6 (October 1974): 3, 16–18, folder 2, box 73, Kaufman Papers.

89. Pam Britton, "Cubans Send Greetings!" *Guild Notes* 4, no. 5 (July 1975): 4, folder 3, box 73, Kaufman Papers.

90. Meyer, interview. See also Vernell Pratt, "China Trip," *NLG Gay Task Force Newsletter*, February 1978, 5, folder NLG–Gay Task Force, carton 24, NLG Records, Bancroft.

91. See International Committee to all NLG Chapters and NEC, 29 November 1974, folder NLG International Committee, NLG Records, Bancroft; Bruce Bentley, "Vietnam Is Free!," *Guild Notes* 4, no. 4 (June 1975): 6, folder 3, box 73, Kaufman Papers.

92. See *International Committee Newsletter* (February 1974), folder NLG International Committee, carton 26, NLG Records, Bancroft. Details on these missions are also in Chapnick, "NLG Slide-Show Script." Specific information on the Carabanchel Ten are in Eric Schmidt, "Carabanchel Ten Convicted in Spain," NLG, NYC Chapter, Annual Membership Dinner, February 4, 1974, 11–16, folder NLG 1975, carton 26, NLG Records, Bancroft.

93. William Schaap and Ellen Ray were particularly involved in the German cases and traveled to Hamburg. See "Groenwald Disbarment Stopped," *Guild Notes*, pre-convention issue (August 1977): 11, GI Press Collection, 1964–1977, Wisconsin Historical Society Online Collections; Larry McDonald, "The National Lawyers Guild Reaffirms Support for Revolutionary Terrorism," 125 Cong. Rec. 10518–25 (1979).

94. See Hal Mayerson to Joan Anderson, Jeff Segal, and Emily De Falla, July 30, 1975, with enclosed proposal for a Puerto Rico Project of the NLG, folder 1, box 68, Kaufman Papers; Franklin Siegel and Joan Lobis, "Fighting Imperialism on Its Home Court," in *Law for the People*, ed. NLG (New York: NLG, 1979), 26–29, folder 348B:27, box N-35, pt. 2, Hall and Hoag Collection; Lipofsky, interview. On the Puerto Rican independence movement in New York City, see Starr, "'Hit Them Harder': Leadership, Solidarity, and the Puerto Rican Independence Movement."

95. Joan Andersson, "Report on the Guild International Committee," May 1976, folder NLG International Committee, carton 26, NLG Records, Bancroft.

96. NLG, Middle East Delegation 1977, *Treatment of Palestinians*, particularly 119–21.

97. Alan M. Dershowitz, "Can the Guild Survive Its Hypocrisy?," *American Lawyer* 1, no. 1 (August 1978): 30–31. See also Dershowitz, *Taking the Stand*, 455–57.

98. Jabara, interview; "Reminiscences of Victor Rabinowitz, 1990," transcript, Oral Histories, Columbia.

Chapter 6

1. Abraham Unger to President Johnson, November 30, 1964; James L. Greenfield (assistant secretary of state) to Unger, n.d. [December 1964?], folder 10, box 1, Unger Papers. Greenfield, who later became a *New York Times* editor and was directly involved in the publication of the Pentagon Papers, replied that Vietnam was under the siege of "Communist terrorists," and the risk of a domino effect from Asia to Africa was high. On the early path toward the war, see Gardner and Gittinger, *Vietnam*.

2. See, respectively, Abraham Unger to President Johnson, February 16, 1965; Unger to Johnson, April 2, 1965; Unger to Johnson, November 26, 1965, folder 10, box 1, Unger Papers.

3. See John E. Thorne to President Johnson, November 17, 1965. See also Thorne to Johnson, April 22, 1965; Thorne to Johnson, September 29, 1965, folder 3, box 48, Thorne Papers.

4. NLG, "Convention Resolutions."

5. Douglass Archer, "Vietnam War Crimes and Nurnberg Trial," *Worker*, December 11, 1966. On the importance of the Nuremberg precedent, see Victor Rabinowitz to William Fullbright (Chairman, United States Senate Committee on Foreign Relations), letter with enclosed NLG statement on Songmy, December 11, 1969, folder 5, box 3, Popper Papers.

6. On the "Lawyers' convocation on Vietnam," on the occasion of the October 15, 1969, moratorium, see Jonathan Lubell and Gene Cerruti to NY NLG members, n.d. [1969?], folder 37, box 7, Unger Papers. As proof of the lobbying efforts, see Lubell to NY NLG members, May 15, 1970, folder 38, box 7, Unger Papers; Lawyers Committee for Effective Action to End the War, "Political Briefing Paper," n.d. [1970?]; "An Action Program to End the War in Indochina," *New York Law Journal*, May 14, 1970; Lawyers Committee to End the War, "The War," press release, March 31, 1971, folder 44, box 9, Unger Papers.

7. After a raucous internal debate, in 1968 the ACLU revised its earlier approach, let its lawyers represent antiwar activists and, in 1970, denounced the war as a presidential usurpation of power. See S. Walker, *In Defense of American Liberties*, 282–87.

8. James, interview.

9. Smith, interview.

10. Wells, *War Within*, 35.

11. Cortright, *Soldiers in Revolt*, 4.

12. Cortright, *Soldiers in Revolt*, 5–6. See also Cloke, interview.

13. "Justice Department Files 1,424 Cases . . . ," *Selective Service* 28, no. 4 (April 1968): 2, folder Selective Service Prosecutions & Results Statistics 1968–1969, carton 64, NLG Records, Bancroft.

14. Ken Cloke to all groups concerned with the draft, 29 March 1967, folder Draft Law—Attorneys 1967, box 48, NLG Records, Tamiment. See also Samuel A. Neuburger, "The Role of the National Lawyers Guild in the Coming Period," memo, n.d. [1967?], folder 33, box 5, NLG Records, Tamiment.

15. See the convocation letter by the chair of the Draft Committee of the New York chapter, William Crain, to colleagues, September 14, 1967, folder 8, box 7, NLG Records, Tamiment. See also "National Draft Program Report," n.d. [1967?], folder 12, box 70, Kaufman Papers.

16. Stein, interview.

17. Doron Weinberg and Marty Fassler, *A Historical Sketch of the National Lawyers Guild in American Politics, 1936–1968* (New York: NLG, n.d.), 22, folder 25, box 6, Goldring Papers. As examples of workshops and conferences, see the leaflets NLG, CCCO (Central Committee for Conscientious Objectors), *Lawyers' Conference on the Draft*, New York, February 9, 1967, folder Draft Law—Attorneys 1967, box 48, NLG Records, Tamiment; NLG, *Lawyers' Workshop "Draft Law: Selective Service Litigation,"* University of Chicago, April 28, 1967, folder 30, box 5, NLG Records, Tamiment. As examples of materials edited by the Guild, see Draft Law Group, Yale Law School, *The Draft and Antiwar Protests—an Introduction for Laymen*, November 1967, folder 1, box 52, NLG Records, Tamiment; Ginger, *New Draft Law.*

18. Terry Shtob to NLG members, November 30, 1967, with enclosed "Speaker's Outline on the War in Vietnam," folder 8, box 7, NLG Records, Tamiment.

19. Bernardine Dohrn, "Report from the Student Division," November 1967, folder NLG Students, carton 58, NLG Records, Bancroft. Data are in "Brief Summary of New York City Chapter Activities," n.d. [1967?], folder 33, box 5, NLG Records, Tamiment; "Minutes of the Board of Directors Meeting," March 27, 1968, folder 24, box 20, NLG Records, Tamiment; Ken Cloke, "Report of the Executive Secretary to the 1968 Convention," n.d. [1968?], folder 4, box 8, Rabinowitz Papers.

20. Requests to provide help were numerous. See, for example, Kenneth Cloke to NLG members, n.d. [December 1967?], NLG Records, Tamiment; Ralph Shapiro to NLG members, December 1, 1967, folder 37, box 7, Unger Papers.

21. Rabinowitz, *Unrepentant Leftist*, 184.

22. NLG, "Emigration to Canada and Europe," memo, n.d., folder 16, box 8, Rabinowitz Papers. See also Franklin, *Vietnam and Other American Fantasies*, 60.

23. Tigar, *Fighting Injustice*, 117–18.

24. Siegel, interview.

25. Lawyers Selective Service Panel to friends, n.d. [1968?], folder Selective Service Prosecutions & Results Statistics 1968–1969, carton 64, NLG Records, Bancroft.

26. Statement of Dr. Corliss Lamont (chair of the NECLC), February 2, 1968, folder NLG—1968 Convention, carton 31, NLG Records, Bancroft.

27. On the functioning of the NYDMLP, see "The New York Draft and Military Law Panel," *Anti-Draft Notes* 1, no. 1 (November–December 1968): 1, folder 21, box 10, Unger Papers; NECLC, "Minutes of 4th Seminar," n.d. [1968?], folder 8, box 10, Un-

ger Papers. On the training programs, see Loni Levy (panel coordinator) to draft counselors and panel attorneys, n.d. but 1968; Levy to panel members, n.d. [1968?], folder 24, box 20, NLG Records, Tamiment.

28. "Convention Passes a Wide Variety of Resolutions on Pressing Issues of Day," *NLG Newsletter* 13, no. 1 (May 1967): 4–5, folder 16, box 8, Rabinowitz Papers.

29. Jonathan Lubell to NLG board members, September 25, 1968, and enclosed "Resolution on the Illegality of Our Involvement in Viet Nam," July 1968, folder 24, box 20, NLG Records, Tamiment.

30. Ken Cloke, *A Pocket Manual on Draft Resistance* (New York: Weekly Guardian Associates, 1968), folder 10, box 16, New Left Collection. Cloke's manual was also printed by the San Diego Committee to Defend the Bill of Rights, the People's Commune, and the Industrial Workers of the World. References to the use of draft counsel money are in the author's interviews with Koonan, Stolar, and Lefcourt.

31. The draft system was first converted into a lottery and eventually ended in December 1972. President Nixon, on his part, admitted that draft resisters influenced the way he approached the war. See Nixon, *No More Vietnams*, 102, 125. On the draft, see Flynn, *Draft, 1940–1973*, 181, 236.

32. Data are in Kohn, *Jailed for Peace*, 89. See also Foley, *Confronting the War Machine*, 327–28.

33. Cortright, *Soldiers in Revolt*, vii, 207; Stanton, *Rise and Fall of an American Army*, 293–94.

34. Robert D. Heinl, "The Collapse of the Armed Forces," *Armed Forces Journal*, June 1971, in U.S. House of Representatives, *Investigation of Attempts to Subvert the United States Armed Services*, Pt. 2, 92nd Cong. 2nd Sess. (1971–72), 7132–40.

35. Data are in Cortright, *Soldiers in Revolt*, 10–13. Larger figures are reported in "Latest Pentagon Figures on AWOL's and Deserters," *Tricky Dix*, May 1971, 3, folder 2, box 72, Kaufman Papers.

36. Cortright, *Soldiers in Revolt*, vii–xiii, 43–45.

37. U.S. House of Representatives, *Investigation of Attempts to Subvert the United States Armed Services*, Pt. 1, 92nd Cong. 1st Sess. (1971), 6690–93.

38. See "Thoughts on the G.I. Movement" and "Desertions on the Rise," *Tricky Dix*, n.d. [January 1970?], respectively 3–4 and 2, folder 2, box 72, Kaufman Papers.

39. Gitlin, *Sixties*, 417–19.

40. Cortright, *Soldiers in Revolt*, 19–25, 53.

41. See the speech by Martin L. King Jr., "A Time to Break Silence," New York City, April 4, 1967, in King, *Testament of Hope*, 231–44.

42. Smith, interview.

43. Cloke, *Pocket Manual*, 21.

44. Sherrill, *Military Justice*, 65–69, 83–92.

45. See "Report of the Summer Military Law Project," July 4, 1969, folder 46, carton 2, PCS and MLO Records.

46. See the convention report by Tim Coulter, "Military Law: The Lawyers Participation in the GI Movement," n.d. [1970?], folder 1970 Convention Reports, carton 57, NLG Records, Bancroft. These observations are echoed in Kenneth Cloke, *Military Counseling Manual: A Guide to Military Law and Procedures for GIs, Counselors*

and Lawyers (Los Angeles: National Lawyers Guild, n.d. [1970?]), folder 21, box 83, NLG Records, Tamiment.

47. See Linda Borus to Luke Hiken, June 16, 1970, folder 1, carton 2, PCS and MLO Records. See also "Organized Professionals and Professional Organizers," *Tricky Dix*, n.d. [January 1970?] 4, folder 2, box 72, Kaufman Papers.

48. Tim Coulter was staffed there. The office was partially funded by a grant from the Civil Liberties Legal Defense Fund. See "Military Law Project," *Guild News* 1, no. 1 (January 1971): 2, folder 2, box 68, Kaufman Papers; "Law and Orders," *Tricky Dix*, n.d. [January 1970?], 1–2, folder 2, box 72, Kaufman Papers.

49. See Paul Albert, "Report on the Military Law Panel to the Executive Board," June 3, 1975, folder 13, carton 2, PCS and MLO Records; "Report of the MLO and the Bay Area Military Law Panel–1976," folder 3, carton 2, PCS and MLO Records. See also *Turning the Regs Around: A Handbook on Military Law and Counseling: An Aid to Organizing for GIs and Civilians* (San Francisco: Bay Area Turning the Regs Around Committee, 1973), folder 26, carton 2, PCS and MLO Records. On the success of the manual, see Stewart Purkey to Herb Allen, May 22, 1973, folder 23, carton 2, PCS and MLO Records.

50. "Lawyers for G.I. Coffee Houses," memo, n.d., folder 5, box 25, New Left Collection. On the coffeehouse movement, see Parsons, *Dangerous Grounds*, 73–86.

51. Cloke, interview.

52. Gardner, *Unlawful Concert*, 177.

53. Sherrill, *Military Justice*, 21.

54. Gardner, *Unlawful Concert*, 196.

55. Among others, James Baldwin, Noam Chomksy, Alan M. Dershowitz, Conrad J. Lynn, Susan Sontag, Paul M. Sweezy, and Kurt Vonnegut endorsed the GICLDC.

56. On the GICLDC, see GI Civil Liberties Defense Committee, *Are Soldiers Citizens?*, leaflet, n.d., folder 5, box 25, New Left Collection. On the Fort Jackson Eight, see M. S. Smith, *Notebook of a Sixties Lawyer*, 34–35; Halstead, *GIs Speak Out against the War*, particularly 44–47, appendix F; Smith, interview.

57. Bannan, *Law, Morality and Vietnam*, 212.

58. U.S. House of Representatives, *Investigation of Attempts to Subvert the United States Armed Services*, Pt. 1, 92nd Cong. 1st Sess. (1971), specifically 6381–84, 6545, 6627–28.

59. Ernest Goodman, "The Guild and the Civil Rights Movement, Part II," *Guild Notes* (May–June 1981): 3–9, folder 16, box 9, Rabinowitz Papers; Eric Seitz, "Report on Establishment of Guild Asian Office," *Tricky Dix*, May 1971, 9, folder 2, box 72, Kaufman Papers.

60. Kenneth Cloke, "Proposal for NLG Office in Saigon," August 20, 1968, folder Draft Resistance 1968, box 48, NLG Records, Tamiment.

61. David F. Addlestone to MLO, September 22, 1972, folder 1, carton 2, PCS and MLO Records.

62. For an example of the requests of assistance, see Sgt. Bob Salard to MLO, January 24, 1973, folder 1, carton 2, PCS and MLO Records.

63. Eric Seitz to Charles Garry, June 2, 1971, folder 28, box 2, PCS and MLO Records.

64. Seitz, interview. See also the copious fundraising correspondence that documents a vast network of supporters. For instance, Eric Seitz to Howard Zinn, March 24, 1971; Zinn to Seitz, April 5, 1971; Seitz to Joë Nordmann, April 6, 1971; Seitz to Nguyen Thi Binh (Vietnamese Communist leader who negotiated at the Paris Peace Conference on behalf of the Viet Cong), June 9, 1971; Kenneth Cloke to Seitz, June 7, 1971, folders 28 and 30, carton 2, PCS and MLO Records.

65. Siegel, interview. See also Barbara Dudley, *Defending GI's in Vietnam*, January 8, 2015, http://vietnamfulldisclosure.org. For a different perspective, see U.S. House of Representatives, *Investigation of Attempts to Subvert the United States Armed Services*, Pt. 3, 92nd Cong. 2nd Sess. (1972), 7532–37.

66. Seitz, interview.

67. See "Fact Sheet on Pacific Counseling Service" in U.S. House of Representatives, *Investigation of Attempts to Subvert the United States Armed Services*, Pt. 1, 92nd Cong. 1st Sess. (1971), 6660–61.

68. In the meantime, the ACLU transferred its Asian docket to the NLG.

69. Dudley had worked on the War on Poverty in 1968 and had just graduated from UC Berkeley's Boalt Law School. See Dudley, interview. On the notion of post-traumatic stress disorder, see Horowitz, *PTSD*.

70. MLO, "Annual Report, 1972–3," October 10, 1973, folder 3, carton 2, PCS and MLO Records.

71. Details about the case are in "Billy Dean Smith," *Up Against the Bench* 1, no. 5 (September 1972): 12, 19, folder Chapter Newsletters Chicago, carton 57, NLG Records, Bancroft; "Trying Times," *Guild Notes* 4, no. 1 (January 1975): 20–21, folder 3, box 73, Kaufman Papers. On Davis's and Castro's support, see Davis, *Angela Davis*, 398. The quote about fragging is in "Free Billy Smith," *Conspiracy* 3, no. 1 (September 1972): 8–9, folder 267B:25, box N-35, pt. 2, Hall and Hoag Collection.

72. Gespass, interview. See also Aaron Zaretzsky to Doris B. Walker, letter with enclosed proposal, October 25, 1974, folder NLG Military Law Office, carton 26, NLG Records, Bancroft.

73. Siegel, interview.

74. For the army's version, see U.S. House of Representatives, *Investigation of Attempts to Subvert the United States Armed Services*, Pt. 3, 92nd Cong. 2nd Sess. (1972), 7532–37. See also FBI San Francisco to FBI Acting Director, 19 October 1972, folder 2, box 293, NLG Records, Tamiment.

75. Art Simon, "Military Law Office Staff Arrested/Deported," *Conspiracy* 3, no. 3 (November 1972): 1, 13, folder 5, box 25, New Left Collection; Seitz, interview. As an example of the activities in the following years, see Bart Lubow, "S. E. Asia Project," *Up Against the Bench* 2, no. 8 (November–December 1973): 11–12; Bart Lubow, "The Fight against U.S. Entanglement in Okinawa," *Guild Notes* 3, no. 2 (February 1974): 3, 28, folder 2, box 73, Kaufman Papers.

76. On the Catholic Left in the 1960s, see Meconis, *With Clumsy Grace*.

77. Peters, *Catonsville Nine*, 161.

78. The ubiquitous New York lawyer assembled a team that included Harrop A. Freeman, an expert in civil disobedience and a professor at Cornell University;

Harold Buchman, a communist attorney; and Rev. William C. Cunningham, a Jesuit attorney and a professor at Loyola University.

79. The Berrigans and Mische were apprehended rather soon. Moylan managed to stay underground until 1979, when she voluntarily surrendered. She later spent one year in prison. See Kunstler, *My Life*, 188–92; Peters, *Catonsville Nine*. Other details on the case are in the overtly sympathetic Berrigan, *Trial of the Catonsville Nine*, 102–207. See also Catonsville Nine Defense Committee, *The Catonsville Nine: An Act of Conscience*, leaflet, 1968, Dean Pappas Papers, Enoch Pratt Free Library, http://c9.digitalmaryland.org/artifact.php?ID=DPCN003&PT=2; Sachs, *Investigation of a Flame*.

80. Robert Berkvist, "Gregory Peck Goes to Catonsville," *New York Times*, May 21, 1972.

81. "The Case of the Harrisburg 7," *Rights*, March 1972, 12, folder 1, box 28, Kennedy Papers. See also Homer Bigart, "Berrigan Case a Mistrial on Main Plotting Charges," *New York Times*, April 6, 1972.

82. Boudin advised the Citizens' Commission on how to securely release the files to the press. On Boudin's role, see Braudy, *Family Circle*, 226–28.

83. For a participant observation, see Martin Stolar, "Camden 28: 'A Fine Group of Christians,'" *Guild Notes* 2, no. 3 (May 1973): 24, 22, folder 1, box 73, Kaufman Papers; Kairys, *Philadelphia Freedom*, 183–223. See also Medsger, *Burglary*, 5–8, 285–324.

84. "You Don't Need a Weatherman to Know Which Way the Wind Blows," *SDS New Left Notes*, June 18, 1969, 3–8; Bill Ayers, "A Strategy to Win," *SDS New Left Notes*, September 12, 1969, 3.

85. See Naison, *White Boy*, 115.

86. For an in-depth analysis of the mindset and behavior of the group, see Varon, *Bringing the War Home*, particularly chaps. 2 and 4.

87. "Chicago 69," *Fire!—SDS New Left Notes*, October 21, 1969, centre-page poster.

88. FBI, "Weatherman Underground, Summary," August 20, 1976, pt. 1, 109–17, in FBI FOIA Library, https://vault.fbi.gov. For a journalistic chronicle, see John Kifner, "Vandals in the Mother Country," *New York Times Magazine*, January 4, 1970.

89. The testimony of an FBI infiltrator confirms it. See Grathwohl, *Bringing Down America*, 33–36.

90. "Minutes—N.E.B. Meeting, October 18–19, 1969," folder 37, box 5, NLG Records, Tamiment. Hampton is quoted in Thomas, "Second Battle of Chicago," 207–8.

91. See the "Executive Secretary's Report," n.d. [1970?], folder 1970 NLG Convention Reports, carton 57, NLG Records, Bancroft.

92. Wilkerson, *Flying Close to the Sun*, 308–12.

93. See "History," People's Law Office, https://peopleslawoffice.com/about-civil-rights-lawyers/history.

94. Kathy Boudin had been a brilliant student at Bryn Mawr College, traveled with her father to Cuba, and studied in Leningrad. After being rejected from Yale Law School, she joined an SDS project. She was first arrested in Chicago during the protests against the Democratic National Convention. On the townhouse episode and the (troubled) relationship between Kathy and Leonard Boudin, see Braudy, *Family Circle*,

particularly 119, 180, 205–12. It must be noted that Braudy's portrayal of the Boudins' saga, albeit replete with interesting information, is at times too focused on titillating details and tends to excessively psychoanalyze the father-daughter relationship.

95. Dohrn, "When Hope and History Rhyme." FBI sources list thirty-four attacks. See FBI, "Weatherman Underground, Summary," 176–85.

96. Meyer, interview; M. S. Smith, *Notebook of a Sixties Lawyer*, 31.

97. Steel, *Butler's Child*, 21, 189–90.

98. Kunstler, *My Life*, 199.

99. Black, "Interview with William Kunstler," 306.

100. Ratner, *Moving the Bar*, 107.

101. According to some sources, the Weather Underground was responsible for at least one attack that killed one police officer and wounded another. See Burrough, *Days of Rage*, 94–97. On the risks of hurting people, see Wilkerson, *Flying Close to the Sun*, 339–43. For a different and more self-absolving perspective, see Ayers, *Fugitive Days*, 207, 263.

102. The new strategy was announced on December 6, 1970, with a communiqué titled "New Morning—Changing Weather" and signed by Dohrn. See *Outlaws of America: Communiques from the Weather Underground* (New York: Liberated Guardian, 1971), 31–38, folder 6, box 67, New Left Collection. On the constant presence of aboveground supporters, see Gilbert, *Love and Struggle*, 158–59. For an analysis of the Weather Underground's policy of restraint, see Falciola, "Bloodless Guerrilla Warfare."

103. Boudin, "Reflections on Violence in the United States," 106. It must be noted that only a few years later and after many family tribulations, Leonard Boudin's opinions would change. Interviewed in 1982, he declared, "I happen to dislike the Weathermen very much. I mean, personally. And I didn't approve of a number of things that Kathy was doing, but she was and is my daughter." Boudin also defined the Weatherman's choice to go underground as "a terrible mistake." See "Oral History Interview with Leonard Boudin, 1983," transcript, Oral Histories, Columbia.

104. David Fine, the youngest in the group, was apprehended in California in 1976, while Dwight Armstrong, who was Karl's brother and another member of the Gang, was arrested in Toronto in 1977. The fourth member of the Gang, Leo Burt, vanished without a trace.

105. Bates, *Rads*, particularly 376–427.

106. U.S. Senate, *Riots, Civil and Criminal Disorders*, pt. 24, 5313–15, 5342. It must be noted that more recent estimates are lower, suggesting, for example, that between 1969 and 1974, U.S. radicals detonated approximately six hundred bombs. See Chard, *Nixon's War at Home*, 3.

107. National Advisory Committee on Criminal Justice Standards and Goals, *Disorders and Terrorism*, 507–95.

108. U.S. House of Representatives, *Terrorism*, 112–14.

109. Chard, *Nixon's War at Home*, 100–106, 136–61; Eckstein, *Bad Moon Rising*, 124–26, 165–87. For the historical record of the Ten Most Wanted list, see FBI, "Ten Most Wanted Fugitives 60th Anniversary, 1950–2010," https://www.fbi.gov/file -repository/ten_most_wanted_60th_anniversary.pdf/view.

110. "Weather Case Dropped," *Up Against the Bench* 3, no. 1 (February 1974): 15, folder Chapter Newsletters Chicago, carton 57, NLG Records, Bancroft.

111. Weather Underground, *Prairie Fire*. On the lawyers' involvement, see James B. Adams to [Richard L. Thornburgh] Assistant Attorney General, Criminal Division, and [Clarence M. Kelley] Director, FBI, March 13, 1975, folder 2, box 293, NLG Records, Tamiment.

112. Berger, *Outlaws of America*, 204–42.

113. Mark Rudd, for example, easily settled his two criminal cases. He was released on his own recognizance, receiving two years' probation and a $2,000 fine for charges stemming from the Days of Rage. Gerald Lefcourt assisted him and negotiated the deal. See Rudd, *Underground*, 285–99. Morton Stavis was able to have all charges against Eleanor Stein dropped and to reduce the sentence of Stein's partner, Jeff Jones, to a year and a half of probation and six months of community service. See Jones, *Radical Line*, 279. Margaret Ratner and Elizabeth Fink represented Cathy Wilkerson, who pleaded guilty to the charge of possession of illegal explosives. In 1980, she was sentenced to zero to three years in prison. After serving her prison time, she joined her friend Fink as an office assistant. See Wilkerson, *Flying Close to the Sun*, 386.

114. Eckstein, *Bad Moon Rising*, 238–39.

115. See Williams, *Inadmissible Evidence*.

116. See Ronald Smothers, "Brink's Robbery Casts Shadows From the Past," *New York Times*, October 31, 1981. For a first-person account of the legal case, see Gilbert, *Love and Struggle*, 278–325. For a journalistic but in-depth chronicle, see Castellucci, *Big Dance*, particularly 212–54. For a more recent and documented appraisal with information on both the BLA and the M19CO, see Reverby, *Co-conspirator for Justice*, 85–116.

117. In particular, former Weather Underground member (and Kathy Boudin's partner) David Gilbert, former Weather Underground member Judith A. Clark, and former BPP members Sekou Ondiga and Kuwasi Balagoon refused to cooperate and opted for self-defense.

118. Subpoenaed by the grand jury investigating the case, Bernardine Dohrn refused to testify and to disclose information about her brothers and sisters in arms. She was jailed for contempt for seven months.

119. Kathy Boudin's legal team included her father, Leonard; Victor Rabinowitz; Martin Garbus; and Leonard Weinglass. On Boudin's defense, see Braudy, *Family Circle*, 320–37.

Chapter 7

1. Useem and Kimball, *States of Siege*, 9–10.

2. Dan Berger, *Captive Nation*, 38.

3. Cummins, *Rise and Fall*, 65.

4. The Nation of Islam (NOI) was founded in 1930 in Detroit. Among the earliest prisoners' rights movements, the organization refused to take part in racial desegregation campaigns, focusing instead on seeking religious freedoms. The NOI mem-

bership swelled during the 1950s and early 1960s, also by virtue of the popularity of Malcolm X, who became the second in command of the organization. Quite predictably, the government profiled the NOI as a racial hate group and targeted it with repressive measures in and out of prisons. See Felber, *Those Who Know Don't Say*, particularly 9–12, 66, 73.

5. With the decision in *Cooper v. Pate*, 378 U.S. 546 (1964), the Supreme Court also maintained that prisoners were entitled to file actions under Section 1983 of the 1871 Civil Rights Act (allowing citizens to appeal to federal courts in order to avoid unsympathetic state courts). By the end of the 1960s, federal courts had decided more than two thousand cases citing Section 1983. See Felber, *Those Who Know Don't Say*, 82. See also Useem and Kimball, *States of Siege*, 12, 17.

6. Steven V. Roberts, "Prisons Feel a Mood of Protest," *New York Times*, September 19, 1971.

7. Atkins and Glick, *Prisons, Protest, and Politics*, 2.

8. Cummins, *Rise and Fall*, 108–9. Marx's quote is in Davis, "Political Prisoners, Prisons and Black Liberation," 27. The original source is Marx, *Class Struggles in France*, 50.

9. Berger, *Captive Nation*, 3–6; quote on p. 4.

10. Useem and Kimball, *States of Siege*, 17.

11. For a more detailed examination, see Losier, "Against 'Law and Order' Lockup."

12. Berkman, *Opening the Gates*, 62–66.

13. See, for instance, the leaflet for the conference organized by the Soledad Defense Committee and the Santa Cruz Radical Action Project at UC Santa Cruz, *The Prison Empire*, n.d., folder 1, box 15, Thorne Papers.

14. *Outlaws of America: Communiques from the Weather Underground* (New York: Liberated Guardian, 1971), 10–13, 19–21, folder 6, box 67, New Left Collection.

15. See, for example, Clark, *Crime in America*.

16. Mitford, *Kind and Usual Punishment*, 80–121.

17. Cummins, *Rise and Fall*, viii, 74.

18. Mitford, *Kind and Usual Punishment*, 252–57.

19. As soon as penitentiaries were in turmoil, prison authorities attempted to toughen up censorship and fought in court to restrict inmates' rights. They also targeted the principle of confidentiality with lawyers. See Cummins, *Rise and Fall*, particularly 124, 134, 195.

20. See the four-page insert "Prisoners Union on Strike," along with the Folsom manifesto and a call to picket at the Folsom gates on November 3, 1970, in *Conspiracy* 1, no. 3 (November 1970), folder NLG Internal Struggles and Speeches, carton 26, NLG Records, Bancroft.

21. Frank Browning, "Organizing Behind Bars," *Ramparts* 10, no. 8 (February 1972): 40–45, 132–39.

22. State of California, Board of Corrections, *Report to Governor Ronald Reagan*, 8.

23. Burton, "Organized Disorder."

24. One of the seven opted for self-defense. Five defendants were eventually acquitted; the two remaining pleaded guilty to felonies but were not sentenced to

additional jail time. See "Corrections," *Blind Justice* 1, no. 3 (February 1972): 7, 9–10, folder 2, box 68, Kaufman Papers; The Tombs Seven Defense Committee, "Fact Sheet," May 1972, folder 9, box 28, Kennedy Papers.

25. "Mass Defense Office," *Guild News* 1, no. 1 (January 1971): 1, folder 2, box 68, Kaufman Papers.

26. Steel, *Butler's Child*, 183.

27. Joani Temko, "Brooklyn Law School," *Guild News* 1, no. 1 (January 1971): 2, folder 2, box 68, Kaufman Papers.

28. "N.E.B. Minutes," October 3, 1970, folder NLG-NEB 1971, carton 57, NLG Records, Bancroft.

29. NLG, *San Quentin to Attica: The Sound before the Fury* (New York: NLG, n.d. [1971–72?]), 17, folder 4, box 10, Thorne Papers.

30. Bay Area Prison Task Force, "On the Midnight Special," *Guild Notes* 4, no. 5 (July 1975): 25, folder 3, box 73, Kaufman Papers.

31. Temko, "Brooklyn Law School," 2.

32. Greenberg and Stender, "Prison as a Lawless Agency."

33. Stender, introduction, 9–10.

34. Bourg, *From Revolution to Ethics*, particularly 92.

35. NLG, *San Quentin to Attica*, 17.

36. MS [Midnight Special] Collective, "Prison Movement: Are the Guild and the Special on the Right Track?," *Blind Justice* 5, no. 1 (January 1975): 1, 6, 16, folder "Blind Justice" 1970s, carton 57, NLG Records, Bancroft.

37. Stender, interview.

38. NLG, *San Quentin to Attica*, 17–18.

39. Hill, *Men, Mobs, and Law.*

40. Stender, interview.

41. Hilliard and Cole, *This Side of Glory*, 145.

42. "Guild Protects Prisoners," *Conspiracy* 1, no. 2 (October 1970): 4–5; Regional Office Committee, "Minutes for 22 September 1970," folder NLG Internal Struggles and Speeches, carton 26, NLG Records, Bancroft.

43. "What You Can Do to Help Defend the Soledad Brothers," n.d. [1970?], folder 1, box 14, Thorne Papers. As an example of the many initiatives, see the leaflet NLG, Peninsula Chapter, *A Symposium on Prisons and Prison Law*, University of Santa Clara, September 30, 1971, folder 6, box 11, Thorne Papers.

44. Soledad Brothers Defense Committee, "Guide to Education and Fundraising in Churches," n.d., folder 1, box 14, Thorne Papers.

45. See Pearlman, *Call Me Phaedra*, 189, 196, 508–10.

46. See the leaflet *National Rally*, San Francisco Civic Center, August 19, 1970, folder 7, box 13, Thorne Papers. See also Soledad Brothers Defense Committee, "For Immediate Release," September 10, 1970, folder 1, box 15, Thorne Papers.

47. With respect to Britain, see Friends of Soledad (London), *Marin: August 7th*, leaflet, n.d., folder 4, box 10, Thorne Papers; Friends of Soledad (London), *George Jackson Has Been Killed*, leaflet, August 30, 1971, folder 6, box 11, Thorne Papers; and the booklet John Thorne et al., *Speeches from the Soledad Brothers Rally*, Central Hall, Westminster, April 20, 1971, folder 6, box 11, Thorne Papers. With respect

to France, see Thorne to Angela Davis Defense Fund and Soledad Brothers Defense Committee, December 30, 1970, folder 8, box 5, Thorne Papers.

48. Hill, *Men, Mobs, and Law*, 293–94.

49. Thorne, for example, secured the endorsement of Jane Fonda. See John Thorne to Franklin Alexander, January 20, 1971, folder 8, box 5, Thorne Papers. As for Picasso, see Cathy [Catherine Roux] to Thorne, August 18, 1971, folder 4, box 10, Thorne Papers.

50. Soledad Brothers Defense Committee, *Soledad Brothers*, leaflet, n.d., folder 1, box 14, Thorne Papers.

51. See the document Soledad Brothers Support Committee (Santa Cruz), *Soledad Brothers: To Save Three Lives*, n.d. [1970?], folder 1, box 14, Thorne Papers.

52. See, respectively, *Soledad Brothers Newsletter* 1, no. 1 (March 1971), and *Soledad Brothers Newsletter* 1, no. 2 (May 1971), folder 6, box 15, Thorne Papers.

53. *Soledad Brothers Newsletter*, n.d. [June 1970?], folder 1, box 14, Thorne Papers. See also "Attorney Fay Stender: 'We Are Fighting to Change the Conditions That Destroy Life,'" *Berkeley Barb* 10, no. 24 (June 19–25, 1970): 5, 12.

54. Mervyn M. Dymally and John J. Miller, *Treatment of Prisoners at California Training Facility at Soledad Central* (Sacramento: California State Legislature, 1970), folder 5, box 14, Thorne Papers. By virtue of Stender and Thorne's legal action, the court of appeals held that, in a disciplinary proceeding, an inmate was entitled to counsel, prison authorities should provide reasons in writing to inmates who were denied the privilege of cross-examination or confrontation of witnesses against them, and minimum due process was necessary where inmates were deprived of privileges. See Clutchette v. Procunier, 497 F.2d 809 (9th Cir. 1974).

55. The genealogy of the publication is summarized in Mary Clemmey to Gregory Armstrong, May 22, 1970, folder Personal Correspondence Jackson, George, 1970–71, carton 1, Armstrong Papers. See also Pearlman, *Call Me Phaedra*, 186–222. Still advocating her son's innocence, Jackson's mother disliked the fact that the book depicted George as an "outlaw." See Armstrong, *"The Dragon Has Come,"* 166–68.

56. The book received the Black Academy of the Arts' nonfiction award and was named one of the American Library Association's Notable Books of 1970. See "Selected Books of the Year in Nonfiction," *New York Times*, December 6, 1970.

57. Genet's original preface to the book is in folder 6, box 11, Thorne Papers. On Genet and the BPP, see Sandarg, "Jean Genet and the Black Panther Party." See also the classic biography by Sartre, *Saint Genet*.

58. John Thorne to James Baldwin, December 1, 1970, folder 4, box 11, Thorne Papers.

59. Stender, interview.

60. Pearlman, *Call Me Phaedra*, 179–80.

61. According to a self-proclaimed informant for the FBI and the Los Angeles Police Department, Louis Tackwood, the attack had been masterminded, or at least facilitated, by the police in order to divide and disrupt the BPP. Tackwood made his revelations through a radical research group whose lawyers were Guild attorneys Joan Andersson and Dan Lund. See Citizens Research and Investigation Committee and Tackwood, *Glass House Tapes*, 107–29.

62. Berger and Losier, *Rethinking the American Prison Movement*, 85–86.

63. The shifting relationship between Jackson and Stender is reflected in the extent of the powers he granted her, which evolved from the initial appointment of attorney-in-fact to the separation of the last months. After Jackson's death, there were also disagreements between Stender and Thorne on the sale of the letters that would be included in Jackson's second book. See the correspondence in folder 16, box 9, Series 2, Newton Collection.

64. Liberatore, *Road to Hell*, 114, 128.

65. Armstrong, *"The Dragon Has Come,"* 97–99.

66. George Jackson to Gregory Armstrong, August 11, 1971, folder Personal Correspondence Jackson, George, 1970–71, carton 1, Armstrong Papers.

67. George Jackson to John Thorne, July 8, 1971, folder 6, box 11, Thorne Papers.

68. See Jackson, *Blood in My Eye*.

69. According to available sources, the parallel investigation only confirmed that Anderson's fingerprints were never collected, that a note in Bingham's files suggests she had confessed to Charles Garry that she had taken the gun into prison, and that Anderson's handwriting did not match with the handwriting on the prison's register of August 21, 1971. See Josiah Thompson to Dennis Riordan, January 19, 1983, and Thompson to Riordan, March 23, 1983, with enclosed memoranda. See also Jo Durden-Smith, "Jackson's Smoking Gun," *California*, January 1985, 92–93. All are in folder Prison Reform, box 1, Roberts Papers.

70. "Coroner's Report in the Matter of the Death of George Jackson," folder Prison [Bingham Case] 1971, box 1, Roberts Papers.

71. From the beginning, it seemed quite implausible that a gun, and notably a 9 mm Astra, could fit under a wig.

72. Corroborating this hypothesis, an inmate testified that the commander of the San Quentin guards asked him to participate in a plot to kill Jackson. See "Quentin 'Plot' Report," *San Francisco Chronicle*, September 17, 1971.

73. *Soledad Brothers Newsletter*, n.d. [October 1971?], folder 7, box 15, Thorne Papers.

74. Ivi.

75. Betsy Callaway et al., "Back Steve Bingham," *Berkeley Gazette*, September 6, 1971, folder Prison Reform, box 1, Roberts Papers. See also John Thorne to Friends engaged in social struggles, 9 September 1971, folder 3, box 14, Thorne Papers.

76. Siegel, interview.

77. Bingham, interview. On the lawyers' support, see also Bingham to Barbara [Dudley], December 17, 1984; Bingham to Atlanta NLG, April 9, 1985; Nancy Stearns and Barbara Dudley to Fellow Guild members, November 5, 1985; *Friends of Stephen Bingham Defense Committee*, flyer, November 1985, folder 11, box 72, NLG Records, Tamiment.

78. See Durden-Smith, *Who Killed George Jackson?*, 74–83; "This Is Bingham's Version," *California*, January 1985, 94–95, folder Prison Reform, box 1, Roberts Papers.

79. After the preliminary hearings, M. Gerald Schwartzbach took over as lead counsel. Susan Rutberg and Bruce E. Cohen acted as co-counsels. See *The Friends*

of Stephen Bingham Defense Committee Newsletter, October 1985, box 72, folder 11, NLG Records, Tamiment; Bingham, interview.

80. Davis, *Angela Davis,* 220.

81. Angela Y. Davis, "Call for Unity to Free the Soledad Brothers," *Soledad Brothers Newsletter* 1, no. 2 (May 1, 1971): 3–4, folder 6, box 15, Thorne Papers. On Davis's resolve to help the Soledad Brothers, see Davis, *Angela Davis,* 256–57.

82. Later on, at Davis's trial, the prosecution read in the courtroom an edited version of a private letter written by Davis while she was in jail. The document, which included references to her infatuation, had been allegedly found in Jackson's cell. See Aptheker, *Morning Breaks,* 11, 237–40. See also Earl Caldwell, "Love Letter Read at the Davis Trial," *New York Times,* April 20, 1972. Regarding Jackson's feelings, see his published letters to Davis dated May 29 and June 2, 1970, in Jackson, *Soledad Brother,* 300–303, 304–5.

83. Jane Hoyt, "John Thorne Talks About Soledad Brothers," n.d. [1971?], folder 6, box 11, Thorne Papers.

84. Liberatore, *Road to Hell,* 81–92.

85. Ginger, *Angela Davis Case Collection,* v.

86. *Free Angela and All Political Prisoners: Newsletter of the UCFAD,* December 8, 1970, folder 8, box 5, Thorne Papers.

87. See, for instance, Davis, "Political Prisoners, Prisons and Black Liberation."

88. Ralph Abernathy et al., *On Trial: Angela Davis or America?* (New York: Angela Davis Legal Defense Fund, 1971), and James Baldwin to John Thorne, November 30, 1970, with enclosed original manuscript by James Baldwin, "Open Letter to My Sister," folder 3, box 16, Thorne Papers. Baldwin's famous letter would be finally published as James Baldwin, "An Open Letter to My Sister, Miss Angela Davis," *New York Review of Books* 15, no. 12 (January 7, 1971): 15–16.

89. On the mobilization and the torrent of solidarity, see Aptheker, *Morning Breaks,* 27–29, 75; Davis Jordan, Alexander, and Alexander, "Political Campaign"; Aptheker, "Statements and Appeals." Some envelopes of the letters to Davis are in folder 12, box 204F, Davis Papers. On the positive effects of solidarity on Davis's morale, see Davis, *Angela Davis,* 31.

90. "Document 40A: John J. Abt to Margaret Burnham, 1 October 1971," in Aptheker and Gore, *Free Angela Davis.*

91. See "Document 13B: George Lukács's Statement and lists of signers, [January 1971]" and "Document 46: [French] National Committee for the Defense and Liberation of Angela Davis to Governor Ronald Reagan, 27 October 1971," in Aptheker and Gore, *Free Angela Davis.*

92. For a review of the international endorsements, see *Free Angela and All Political Prisoners: Newsletter of the UCFAD,* December 8, 1970, folder 8, box 5, Thorne Papers.

93. See, for instance, "Document 39: Teachers' Forum and Delhi Students' Joint Letter and Resolution sent to Prime Minister of India, 24 September 1971," in Aptheker and Gore, *Free Angela Davis.* For an example of the aesthetic power of Davis's image, see the 1971 poster by Cuban artist Félix Beltrán in the online collection

of the Oakland Museum of California, http://collections.museumca.org/?q=collection -item/2010547402.

94. Interestingly, Eldridge Cleaver also criticized the excessive attention on the Davis case. According to him, the trial was exploited by both reactionaries and communists, in order to cast a shadow over the issue of revolutionary violence and to overlook the most pressing case of Bobby Seale. See Eldridge Cleaver, "On the Case of Angela Davis," *Black Panther*, January 23, 1971, 5.

95. Abt and Myerson, *Advocate and Activist*, 274.

96. Ann F. Ginger, "Interview with Doris B. Walker," *Conspiracy* 2, no. 12 (August 1972): 2–21, folder NLG Internal Struggles and Speeches, Carton 26, NLG Records, Bancroft.

97. See Davis, *Angela Davis*, 328.

98. Some Detroit Guild attorneys also provided assistance in jury selection. See Ginger, *Angela Davis Case Collection*, xxii–xxiii.

99. Davis confirmed they were directly inspired by Garry's voir dire in the Newton case. See Davis, *Angela Davis*, 312.

100. See NUCFAD, *San Rafael, March 16: Your Day in Court*, flyer, n.d. [1971?], and *Newsletter of the National United Committee to Free Angela Davis*, no. 6, n.d. [March 1971?], folder 8, box 15, Thorne Papers. See also Davis, "Prison Interviews," 177.

101. On the right to self-representation, see Burnham, "Ruchell and Angela Want to Represent Themselves"; Davis, "Angela Davis."

102. *Newsletter of the National United Committee to Free Angela Davis*, January 15, 1971, folder 8, box 15, Thorne Papers.

103. Berger, *Captive Nation*, 204–10.

104. Ginger, "Interview with Doris B. Walker."

105. Davis, *Angela Davis*, 335.

106. See "Document 67: Angela Davis, Statement upon Release, 20 August 1972," in Aptheker and Gore, *Free Angela Davis*. See also "National Defense Organizing: Getting Down to Business," in *National Defense Bulletin* 1, no. 1 (August 21, 1972): 1–6, folder 8, box 5, Thorne Papers.

107. Initially tried with Davis, Magee gradually devised a different strategy and asked for a severance of his case.

108. See "Free Ruchell," *Soledad Brothers Newsletter* 1, no. 2 (May 1, 1971): 5, folder 6, box 15, Thorne Papers; "People's Lawyer," *Soledad Brothers Newsletter*, n.d. [October 1971?], 8–9; *Ruchell Magee: $10 = Life Sentence*, booklet, n.d., folder 8, box 5, Thorne Papers; R. Kaufman, "Ruchell Magee."

109. Sol Stern, "The Campaign to Free Angela . . . and Ruchell Magee," *New York Times Magazine*, June 27, 1971.

110. Stender, introduction, 13.

111. See the section "The Prison Law Project" in Pell and Prison Law Project, *Maximum Security*, 249–50. See also Pearlman, *Call Me Phaedra*, 141, 240–74.

112. For an example of the PLC's activities and philosophy, see Prison Law Collective, *The Jailhouse Lawyer's Manual: How to Bring a Federal Suit against Abuses in Prison* (San Francisco: Prison Law Collective, 1973), folder 11, carton 2, PCS and MLO Records.

113. Patti Roberts to Steve Bingham Defense Team, October 18, 1971, and enclosed memo, "Difficulty in Interviewing AC Prisoners," folder Prison Reform, box 1, Roberts Papers.

114. Joel Kirschenbaum and Jae Scharlin, "Indictment Quashed!," *Conspiracy* 4, no. 6 (February 1974): 5, folder 555, box N-35, pt. 2, Hall and Hoag Collection.

115. See Garry and Goldberg, *Streetfighter in the Courtroom*, 257–59; Wald, "San Quentin Six Case."

Chapter 8

1. Kunstler, *My Life*, 231, 217. See also E. Goodman, interview; "Attika," *Up Against the Bench* 1, no. 1 (Têt Issue, n.d. [January 1972?]): 1, 6, folder Chapter Newsletters Chicago, carton 57, NLG Records, Bancroft.

2. New York Special Commission, *Attica*, xiv, 490.

3. See the bulletin of the Buffalo chapter of the NLG: "Statement of September 23," *Attica . . . Did Not Start Here nor Will End Here!* 1, no. 1 (November 1971): 2, folder Materials on the BPP and Surveillance, box 83, CCR Records. See also Melville, *Letters from Attica*, 65–68, 175–81.

4. At Auburn, inmates wrongly accused commissioner Oswald of breaking the pledge. See Wicker, *Time to Die*, 22.

5. The events are thoroughly surveyed in Thompson, *Blood in the Water*, 64–69; Useem and Kimball, *States of Siege*, 22–37; Lichtenstein, *Ghosts of Attica*.

6. NLG, *San Quentin to Attica: The Sound before the Fury* (New York: NLG, n.d. [1971–72?]), 1, folder 4, box 10, Thorne Papers.

7. New York Special Commission, *Attica*, 229.

8. New York Special Commission, *Attica*, 237–42.

9. Kunstler, *My Life*, 218.

10. Wicker, *Time to Die*, 76–80.

11. Wicker, *Time to Die*, 97. See also New York Special Commission, *Attica*, 243–47.

12. Clark, *Brothers of Attica*, 65.

13. Kunstler, *My Life*, 216.

14. Thompson, *Blood in the Water*, 110.

15. "I'm Speaking to You," *Newsweek*, September 27, 1971, cited in Langum, *William M. Kunstler*, 187.

16. New York Special Commission, *Attica*, 257–64. Seale's version was slightly different, but the BPP leader conceded that he was not "an astute negotiator" and felt like "some of the death and brutality at Attica happened because [he] failed." See Seale, *Lonely Rage*, 221.

17. Wicker, *Time to Die*, 200–22. See also New York Special Commission, *Attica*, 271–75.

18. New York Special Commission, *Attica*, 290–91. Kunstler had reportedly spoken with Afeni Shakur, one of the Panther 21 defendants. See Wicker, *Time to Die*, 185.

19. New York Special Commission, *Attica*, 247, 264, 291. See also observer Alfredo Mathew's criticism of Kunstler "playing with the other people's lives" and Wicker's

reservations about Kunstler's radicalism. See Wicker, *Time to Die*, respectively 118 and 76–77. While recognizing that Kunstler acted "nobly," a few legal scholars also expressed reservations about his conduct. See Schornhorst, "Lawyer and the Terrorist."

20. Clark, *Brothers of Attica*, 75, 109, 114.

21. See Schwartz's memoir, unpublished, quoted in Jelinek, *Attica Justice*, 51.

22. Wicker, *Time to Die*, 174.

23. On the failed negotiation, see the chapter "William Moses Kunstler Oral Histories" in M. S. Smith, *Lawyers You'll Like*, 63–77. Albeit critical with Kunstler's tendency to please and radicalize inmates, Wicker confirmed this hypothesis and praised Kunstler for his passion and the force of his personality. See Wicker, *Time to Die*, 67, 241, 336.

24. Wicker, *Time to Die*, 241–45.

25. The final death toll was forty-three. In addition to the thirty-nine who were killed during the attack and the correctional officer killed during the insurrection, three prisoners were found dead after the takeover. Their murderers remain unknown.

26. New York Special Commission, *Attica*, xi.

27. Thompson, *Blood in the Water*, 183–88, 209–16.

28. E. Goodman, interview.

29. See the testimony of Elizabeth Fink in NLG, Speaking Freely Video History Series (2015), https://vimeo.com/channels/996070; E. Goodman, interview.

30. The district court eventually denied the inmates' application for preliminary injunctive relief and dismissed the complaint. See Inmates of Attica Correctional Facility v. Rockefeller, 453 F.2d 12 (2d Cir. 1971). See also "Wanted for Murder," *Blind Justice* 1, no. 3 (February 1972): 2–6, folder 2, box 68, Kaufman Papers.

31. The Council of New York Law Associates (today Lawyers Alliance for New York) was founded in 1969 by a group of young lawyers working in Wall Street and Midtown firms who were driven by a spirit of political activism and the desire to offer pro bono legal services.

32. "A Lawyer at Attica," *Blind Justice* 1, no. 1 (October 1971): 1–3, 8, folder 2, box 68, Kaufman Papers.

33. See, for instance, Bernard Shipman to William Kunstler, January 25, 1973, folder unnamed, box 84, CCR Records; Richard X. Clark to Kunstler, November 13, 1971, folder Attica Correspondence, box 84, CCR Records. On the harassment of prisoners, see Brothers in Attica, "From Attica," *Blind Justice* 1, no. 2 (December 1971): 12 folder 2, box 68, Kaufman Papers.

34. The three lawyers were Kenneth Kimerling, Dennis Cunningham, and Michael Deutsch. On the ADC, see the act that established it on January 24, 1972, folder Attica Defense Committee, box 84, CCR Records. For a chronicle of the Guild's engagement, see Dan Pochoda, "Attica and the Guild," *Guild Notes* 1, no. 1 (April–May 1972): 2–3, folder 1, box 73, Kaufman Papers; Handschu, interview.

35. Joshua Roth, "The Brothers behind Bars," *Blind Justice* 1, no. 2 (December 1971): 1–2, folder 2, box 68, Kaufman Papers; "Attica," *Guild Notes* 1, no. 3 (September–October 1972): 8, folder 1, box 73, Kaufman Papers. On the contamination of evidence and disinformation, see Thompson, *Blood in the Water*, 233–34, 266–74.

36. As an example of counterinformation, see Attica Defense Committee, *We Are Attica*.

37. Steel, *Butler's Child*, 18.

38. Langum, *William M. Kunstler*, 207–208.

39. "Attika," *Up Against the Bench*.

40. Pochoda, "Attica and the Guild," *Guild Notes*.

41. Mike Deutsch, "Attica!," *Conspiracy* 2, no. 10 (June 1972): 15, folder 6, box 68, Kaufman Papers.

42. Roth, "Brothers Behind Bars," *Blind Justice*.

43. Bay Area Prison Task Force, "On the Midnight Special," *Guild Notes* 4, no. 5 (July 1975): 25, folder 3, box 73, Kaufman Papers.

44. *Attica News*, January 1973.

45. "Brothers in Court," *Attica News*, March 1973.

46. "Attica Brothers Demand: Indict Real Criminals," *Guild Notes* 2, no. 3 (May 1973): 6–7, folder 1, box 73, Kaufman Papers.

47. W. Goodman, interview; Stolar, interview; Dennis Riordan, "Attica Battle Enters Courtroom," *Guild Notes* 2, no. 4 (August 1973): 5, 25, box 42-14, pt. 1, Hall and Hoag Collection.

48. Jelinek, *Attica Justice*, 170–71.

49. "Attica Summer," *Guild Notes* 2, no. 5 (September 1973): 7–8, folder 1, box 73, Kaufman Papers. On the divisions between New York and Buffalo, see Jelinek, *Attica Justice*, 188, 210–26; "Minutes of the ADC Meeting," November 19, 1972, folder Attica Defense Committee, CCR Records.

50. Only a single state trooper was charged with brutality, but he was soon discharged. See Kunstler, *My Life*, 228–29.

51. Thompson, *Blood in the Water*, 313–18. FIGHT had been created by community organizer Saul Alinsky in the wake of the Rochester riots of 1964. In 1967, after similar riots erupted in Buffalo, Black leaders and clergymen, always in cooperation with Alinksy, created BUILD. See Jelinek, *Attica Justice*, 191–92.

52. NLG, *Summer Projects*, booklet, 1974, 11, folder 718, box N-34, pt. 2, Hall and Hoag Collection; "Attica," *Guild Notes* 3, special issue (September 1974): 4–5, folder 1, box 73, Kaufman Papers.

53. Stolar, interview.

54. Lichtenstein, *Ghosts of Attica*.

55. Kairys, *Philadelphia Freedom*, 287–88, 293.

56. Among others, Guild legal investigator Linda Borus fell in love with Bernard Stroble, aka Shango, while Barbara Handschu wove a relationship with Mariano "Dalou" Gonzalez.

57. Jomoe Joko Omowale [born as Cleveland McKinley Davis, aka Eric Thompson, aka Jomo Joka Omowale], "A Dragon Today," *Midnight Special* 5, no. 2 (March 1975): 15–16, folder NLG 1975, carton 26, NLG Records, Bancroft.

58. Langum, *William M. Kunstler*, 211–12. See also Thompson, *Blood in the Water*, 346–61. On the lack of broad support, see Ed Mead, "Remembering Attica: Twenty Years Later," *Prison Legal News* 2, no. 9 (September 1991): 1–2, www.prisonlegalnews .org/news/1991/sep/15/remembering-attica-twenty-years-later.

59. Information on the Shango trial are in E. Goodman, "The Shango Trial," and Ernest Goodman, *The Shango Trial*, unpublished manuscript, tentatively titled *Carrying the Struggle into the Courtroom*, folder 67, Microfilm, NLG Records, Bancroft. See also "Shango Acquitted," *Guild Notes* 4, no. 5 (July 1975): 9, folder 3, box 73, Kaufman Papers.

60. Lee Dembart, "Outspoken Lawyer," *New York Times*, April 10, 1975; Michael T. Kaufman, "Cover-Up at Attica: Often Charged but Never Investigated," *New York Times*, April 16, 1975.

61. In January 2005, the state of New York consented to pay a $12 million settlement with the hostages and their families. See Thompson, *Blood in the Water*, 460–557.

62. See, among others, the initiatives listed in *Prison Law Project* 1, no. 1 (January 1972), folder 654, box M-21, pt. 2, Hall and Hoag Collection; "The Struggle Continues at Walpole," *Mass Dissent* 2, no. 11 (September 1972): 3, 10, folder 164A:12G, box M-21, pt. 2, Hall and Hoag Collection; Jeanne Mirer and Alex Palamarchuk, "Prison Conference," *Guild Notes* 2, no. 4 (August 1973): 7, 16, box 42-14, pt. 1, Hall and Hoag Collection.

63. During his detention, Sostre became a jailhouse lawyer and was known for helping other prisoners with their suits. Attorneys Victor Rabinowitz and Kristin B. Glen appeared on Sostre's behalf but always credited him for his legal work. In 1972, however, Sostre rejected the assistance of Rabinowitz, calling him "a sellout lawyer." See William Worthy, *The Anguish of Martin Sostre* (Buffalo, NY: Martin Sostre Defense Committee, October 1970), folder 9, box 28, Kennedy Papers; "Sostre Convicted . . . the Struggle Most Definitely Continues," *Up Against the Bench* 4, no. 1 (March–April 1975): 6, folder Chapter Newsletters Chicago, carton 57, NLG Records, Bancroft; Martin Sostre, "Letter to a Sellout Lawyer," *Right On!* 2, no. 1, (February 1972): 14, 18, 21, GI Press Collection, 1964–1977, Wisconsin Historical Society Online Collections.

64. On the Marion case, also known as *Adams v. Carlson*, see "Looking to the South," *Up Against the Bench* 1, no. 7 (November 1972): 8–9, folder Chapter Newsletters Chicago, carton 57, NLG Records, Bancroft; "Marion Inmates Win Appeal," *Up Against the Bench* 2, no. 6 (September 1973): 9, folder 6, box 68, Kaufman Papers; Michael Deutsch and Flint Taylor, "Victory at Marion Penitentiary," *Guild Notes* 3, no. 2 (February 1974): 4–5, 27, folder 2, box 73, Kaufman Papers. For a broader contextualization of the case, see Gómez, "Resisting Living Death."

65. Pam Britton, "Bedford Prisoners: 'A More Determined Breed of Women,'" *Blind Justice* 5, no. 1 (January 1975): 3, 14, folder "Blind Justice" 1970s, carton 57, NLG Records, Bancroft. On gender-specific discrimination in prison, see Haft, "Women in Prison."

66. Michael Deutsch and Flint Taylor, "The Marion Experience: Experiment in Control," *Up Against the Bench* 3, no. 1 (February 1974): 8–10, folder Chapter Newsletters Chicago, carton 57, NLG Records, Bancroft.

67. See Goffman, *Asylum*, notably 3–124, and, among others, the classic Kesey, *One Flew over the Cuckoo's Nest*.

68. See Chicago Peoples Law Office, "Check Out Your Mind," *Up Against the Bench* 2, no. 2 (February 1973): 9–15, folder Chapter Newsletters Chicago, carton 57,

NLG Records, Bancroft. On the coeval debate, see Peter R. Breggin, "The Return of Lobotomy and Psycho-surgery," 118 Cong. Rec. 5567–77 (1972).

69. As Dan Berger pointed out, in 1966 there were 218 civil rights claims filed by prisoners; in 1980 there were 12,718. After Attica, many inmates' requests had been implemented in New York State, from visiting privileges to new programs for education and diversity in the recruitment of personnel. Moreover, in 1977 California reformed its indeterminate sentence law and abolished Adult Authority. See Berger, *Captive Nation*, 222; "Attica Prisoners Have Gained Most Points Made in Rebellion," *New York Times*, September 12, 1972. For a longitudinal analysis of civil rights injunctive practice with regard to prisons, see Schlanger, "Civil Rights Injunctions over Time."

70. See the untitled article in *Bar None*, April 1972, 2, folder 652, box M-21, pt. 2, Hall and Hoag Collection.

71. "'Brooklyn House': New Approach to Prison Work," *Guild Notes* 2, no. 4 (August 1973): 10–11, box 42-14, pt. 1, Hall and Hoag Collection. Retrospectively, legal scholar Amanda Bell Hughett demonstrated that the efforts to address the complaints of incarcerated people in the 1970s ultimately provided judicial authorities with tools to undermine prisoners' organizing efforts, such as prison grievance procedures. In other words, as radical lawyers foresaw, civil liberties struggle on behalf of inmates sometimes hampered substantive change and shielded prison administrators from liability. See Bell Hughett, "'Safe Outlet' for Prisoner Discontent."

72. "In Tribute," *Up Against the Bench* 2, no. 8 (November–December 1973): 8–9, folder 7, box 68, Kaufman Papers; Benner and Eder, "Jailed Revolution."

73. Hiestand and Smith, "Of Panthers and Prisons," particularly 61–62.

74. NLG Prisoner Rights Committee, Los Angeles, "NLG Prison Position Paper," June 1972, folder NLG 1972, carton 26, NLG Records, Bancroft.

75. Jo Durden-Smith, "Last One Home: Requiem for a Mass Movement," *California*, January 1985, 84–96, folder Prison Reform, box 1, Roberts Papers.

76. A forty-two-year-old white deputy superintendent was also seriously wounded.

77. A broad discussion ensued about whether Hearst willingly joined the SLA or was a helpless victim of mental and physical manipulation whose only aim was to survive. See Graebner, *Patty's Got a Gun*.

78. U.S. House of Representatives, *Symbionese Liberation Army*. For a journalistic account, see McLellan and Avery, *Voices of Guns*.

79. The debate is summarized in Jelinek, *No Lawyers for the SLA*.

80. NLG SF Chapter, "Proposal to the Executive Board from the Prison Task Force" [defeated by the Executive Board], October 1975, folder NLG Memos and Announcements, carton 58, NLG Records, Bancroft.

81. "Berkeley Rally for SLA," *S.F. Sunday Examiner and Chronicle*, September 28, 1975; *Rally Support the SLA*, leaflet, September 27, 1975, folder NLG 1975, carton 26, NLG Records, Bancroft.

82. "SLA," *Conspiracy* 5, no. 10 (October 1975): 6, folder NLG–SF Chapter '75, carton 31, NLG Records, Bancroft.

83. Jelinek, *No Lawyers for the SLA*.

84. On the more recent SLA cases, see Serra, *Green, Yellow, and Purple Years*, 28; Jordan, "The SLA: A Recurring Nightmare."

85. For a couple of examples of the violent rhetoric on the paper, see Abdullah Aziz Ali, "Al' Aziz Jihad," and Assata Shakur, "To My People," *Midnight Special* 3, no. 9 (September 1973): respectively 12 and 13–14. On the legitimacy of a discussion on armed struggle, see Bay Area Prison Task Force, "On the Midnight Special," *Guild Notes* 4, no. 5 (July 1975): 25. On the necessity for lawyers to avoid excessive involvement in militancy, see Karen Jo Koonan, "On the Midnight Special," *Guild Notes* 4, no. 5 (July 1975): 26, folder 3, box 73, Kaufman Papers. It is worth noting that Ed Mead, a member of the George Jackson Brigade (a guerrilla group founded in Seattle) and a Guild sympathizer, was also denied Guild assistance during this period. See "Seattle under Attack," *Dragon*, June 1976, 43–45.

86. The Black Guerrilla Family also targeted Huey Newton, who was by then into drug dealing and prostitution.

87. Collier and Horowitz, *Destructive Generation*, 40–56.

88. Stender, interview.

89. Ezra Hendon, quoted in Collier and Horowitz, *Destructive Generation*, 57–66. On Stender's last months, see Pearlman, *Call Me Phaedra*, 364–73.

Chapter 9

1. Cowie, "'Vigorously Left, Right, and Center.'"

2. Windham, *Knocking on Labor's Door*, particularly 2–9, 67–71.

3. Brenner, preface, xi–xiv.

4. Moody, "Understanding the Rank-and-File Rebellion in the Long 1970s," particularly 128.

5. NY Labor Project, "Economic Outlook," *Labor Newsletter*, no. 10 (April 1974): 17–23, box 42-14, pt. 1, Hall and Hoag Collection.

6. See, among others, Bay Area Labor Committee, "Labor and the Law," and Bay Area Labor Committee, "The Right to Organize," *Labor Newsletter*, no. 5 (June 1973): 10 and 12–13, respectively; Sandy Karp and Randy Padgett, "Story behind 'New Morning' Decision," *Labor Newsletter*, no. 9 (February 1974): 15, box 42-14, pt. 1, Hall and Hoag Collection.

7. Wini Leeds, "National Labor Program," *Labor Newsletter*, no. 4 (April 1973): 18–21, folder 13, box 67, Kaufman Papers; Michael Adelman, "National Labor Committee: A Political Perspective," *Labor Newsletter*, no. 9 (February 1974): 5–9, box 42-14, pt. 1, Hall and Hoag Collection.

8. Lance Compa, "Working for a Union . . . ," *Labor Newsletter*, no. 8 (December 1973): 21–22, 24, box 42-14, pt. 1, Hall and Hoag Collection.

9. For a summary of these activities, see National Labor Project of the National Lawyers Guild, "Funding Proposal," August 1976, folder Labor Center NLG, carton 23, NLG Records, Bancroft. See also National Labor Center, "Funding Proposal," December 1978, folder NLG Labor, carton 24, NLG Records, Bancroft.

10. For a contextualization, see La Botz, "Tumultuous Teamsters of the 1970s."

11. Siegel, interview.

12. David Scribner, Arthur Kinoy, and Michael Tigar worked on the suit. See Laura Uddenberg, "Steel," *Labor Newsletter*, no. 8 (December 1973): 1–4, 10; Laura Uddenberg, "Legal Setback for Steel Workers," *Labor Newsletter*, no. 10 (April 1974): 15, box 42-14, pt. 1, Hall and Hoag Collection. For background information, see Winslow, "Overview."

13. See "N.Y. Taxi Drivers Sue over Illegal Contract," *Labor Newsletter*, no. 5 (June 1973): 1–2, 18–21; Debbie Honig, "Our Struggle! Taxi Holding Action," *Labor Newsletter*, no. 9 (February 1974): 3, 17, box 42-14, pt. 1, Hall and Hoag Collection.

14. "Action Caucus: How Legal Tactics Were Used to Support Organizing," *Labor Newsletter*, no. 7 (October 1973): 14–18, folder 13, box 67, Kaufman Papers.

15. See "Woodcutters Charged under Anti-Trust Laws," *Labor Newsletter*, no. 7 (October 1973): 1–3, folder 13, box 67, Kaufman Papers; NLG, *Summer Projects*, booklet, 1974, 12, folder 718, box N-34, pt. 2, Hall and Hoag Collection. For further details on the case, see Gulfcoast Pulpwood Association, *Anger in the Southern Pines* (Louisville, KY: SCEF, n.d.), in Civil Rights Movement Archive, www.crmvet.org; "Woodcutters Strike Cripples Large Southern Paper Companies: Production Down 80%," *Liberation News Service*, no. 555 (September 22, 1973): 8, GI Press Collection, 1964–1977, Wisconsin Historical Society Online Collections. See also Roy Reed, "Violence and Bruising Labor Plague Cutters of Pulpwood," *New York Times*, June 30, 1974.

16. Stender, interview.

17. For an insightful sociological analysis, see Jenkins, *Politics of Insurgency*.

18. Muñoz, *Youth, Identity, Power*, 52–54, 63.

19. Jenkins, *Politics of Insurgency*, 142–72.

20. Haberfeld, interview. See also Pearlman, *Call Me Phaedra*, 104–9.

21. Haberfeld, interview.

22. "Boycott," *Up Against the Bench* 1, no. 7 (November 1972): 6, folder Chapter Newsletters Chicago, carton 57, NLG Records, Bancroft.

23. "UFW Summer," *Guild Notes* 2, no. 5 (September 1973): 7, folder 1, box 73, Kaufman Papers.

24. "UFW-NLG," *Labor Newsletter*, no. 6 (August 1973): 13, box 42-14, pt. 1, Hall and Hoag Collection.

25. Haberfeld, interview.

26. NLG, *Summer Projects*, booklet, 1974, 7, folder 718, box N-34, pt. 2, Hall and Hoag Collection.

27. Alberta Blumin, "Si Se Puede!," *Guild Notes* 2, no. 5 (October 1973): 1, 18–19, folder 1, box 73, Kaufman Papers.

28. "Farmworkers," *Guild Notes* 3, special issue (September 1974): 5, folder 2, box 73, Kaufman Papers.

29. "Farmworkers Win Right to Choose Union," *Guild Notes* 4, no. 4 (June 1975): 1, 18–19, folder 3, box 73, Kaufman Papers.

30. Bardacke, "United Farm Workers from the Ground Up," 161.

31. In the summer of 1969, Chavez had already stigmatized the role of both illegal and green card immigrants in breaking the strikes. Jerry Cohen had filed suits against Delano growers, the INS, and the Farm Labor Service for promoting illegal immigration. See Jenkins, *Politics of Insurgency*, 170–71.

32. Jeanie Rucci and Dick Eiden, "Undocumented Workers: Guild Summer Projects & UFWA," *Guild Notes* 4, no. 1 (January 1975): 15–17, folder 3, box 73, Kaufman.

33. Jeff Lewis, Bill Monning and Glenn Rothner, "Undocumented Workers: Guild Summer Projects & UFWA," *Guild Notes* 4, no. 1 (January 1975): 17–18, folder 3, box 73, Kaufman.

34. Fruitvale Law Collective, "Support the UFW, End Attacks on Undocumented Workers!," memo, February 5, 1975; Ann F. Ginger and Doris B. Walker, "The Guild's United Farm Workers Summer Project and Immigration Law Project—a Class Analysis and Proposals for the February, 1975 National Executive Board," folder NLG 1975, carton 26, NLG Records, Bancroft.

35. See "NLG and the UFW," *Guild Notes* 4, no. 3 (May 1975): 22, folder 3, box 73, Kaufman. For the pro-UFW position, see Dan Boone and Deborah Peyton to Doron Weinberg, May 16, 1975, folder NLG 1975, carton 26, NLG Records, Bancroft; Haberfeld, interview. On the reaction of the UFW, see Bardacke, *Trampling Out the Vintage*, 504–6.

36. Barbara Hanfling, "UFW Forges Ahead," *Labor Newsletter*, no. 14 (September 1975): 1–3, 21, folder 13C:52, box N-35, pt. 2, Hall and Hoag Collection.

37. Bardacke, "United Farm Workers from the Ground Up."

38. See Lyons, "When You Talk about Client Relationships"; Tullberg and Coulter, "Failure of Indian Rights Advocacy."

39. Detroit Chapter, "Native Americans and the U.S. Government: A Historical Overview," *Guild Notes* 2, no. 3 (May 1973): 12–14, 20, folder 1, box 73, Kaufman Papers.

40. For an overview of Indian policies, see Burnette and Koster, *Road to Wounded Knee*, 49–104.

41. S. L. Smith, *Hippies, Indians, and the Fight for Red Power*, 15.

42. Josephy, "American Indian and the Bureau of Indian Affairs."

43. Meranto, "Litigation as Rebellion," 218.

44. Smith and Warrior, *Like a Hurricane*, 1–14, 128–38.

45. Burnette and Koster, *Road to Wounded Knee*, 165–92. For a broader contextualization, see Deloria, *Behind the Trail of Broken Treaties*.

46. D. Brown, *Bury My Heart at Wounded Knee*.

47. Tilsen, "US Courts and Native Americans at Wounded Knee."

48. Smith and Warrior, *Like a Hurricane*, 196.

49. Burnette and Koster, *Road to Wounded Knee*, 224–27.

50. Anderson et al., *Voices from Wounded Knee*, 37–39.

51. Sayer, *Ghost Dancing the Law*, 42–43.

52. See, for instance, Denver Guild Chapter, "Wounded Knee . . . ," *Guild Notes* 2, no. 2 (March–April 1973): 3, folder 1, box 73, Kaufman Papers.

53. "Siege at Wounded Knee," *Guild Notes* 2, no. 3 (May 1973): 1, folder 1, box 73, Kaufman Papers.

54. Detroit Chapter, "Native Americans and the U.S. Government," *Guild Notes*.

55. Anderson et al., *Voices from Wounded Knee*, 184–85.

56. WKLD/OC, *Remember Wounded Knee* (n.p., n.d.), booklet, folder 1, box 33, Thorne Papers.

57. S. L. Smith, *Hippies, Indians, and the Fight for Red Power*, 188–201.

58. Smith and Warrior, *Like a Hurricane*, 231–36.

59. See WKLD/OC and North American Media, untitled memo, n.d., folder 5, box 40, Thorne Papers.

60. Kunstler, *My Life*, 238–39.

61. See, for instance, *Wounded Knee 1973*, supplement to *Venceremos*, April 9, 1973, folder 8, box 68, New Left Collection.

62. Burnette and Koster, *Road to Wounded Knee*, 228–36, 255.

63. "Siege at Wounded Knee," *Guild Notes*.

64. Tilsen, "US Courts and Native Americans at Wounded Knee"; Sayer, *Ghost Dancing the Law*, 45–48.

65. Lane, *Rush to Judgment*.

66. "Wounded Knee Trials Begin," *Up Against the Bench* 3, no. 1 (February 1974): 6–7, folder Chapter Newsletters Chicago, carton 57, NLG Records, Bancroft.

67. Detroit Chapter, "Native Americans and the U.S. Government," *Guild Notes*.

68. Terri Schultz, "Bamboozle Me Not at Wounded Knee," *Harper's Magazine* 246, no. 1477 (June 1973): 46–56. As an example of AIM's bombastic rhetoric, see the Wounded Knee Eight, "Only the Beginning," *Midnight Special* 3, no. 7 (July 1973): 14, box 42-14, pt. 1, Hall and Hoag Collection.

69. Burnette and Koster, *Road to Wounded Knee*, 262–63.

70. Tilsen, "US Courts and Native Americans at Wounded Knee," 64–65.

71. Sayer, *Ghost Dancing the Law*, 55–56, 68–78.

72. Burnette and Koster, *Road to Wounded Knee*, 278–79.

73. Banks, *Ojibwa Warrior*, 216.

74. Sayer, *Ghost Dancing the Law*, 86–98, 150–53; Kunstler, *My Life*, 244. See also Kunstler and Kunstler, *William Kunstler*.

75. "Government Misconduct at Trial of Tears," *Up Against the Bench* 3, no. 2 (April–May 1974): 1–19, folder 6, box 68, Kaufman Papers.

76. Banks, *Ojibwa Warrior*, 266–82.

77. On the FBI's alleged vindictiveness against AIM, see U.S. House of Representatives, *FBI Authorization*, 234–46.

78. Sayer, *Ghost Dancing the Law*, 178–81.

79. "Victory at Wounded Knee," *Guild Notes* 3, no. 6 (October 1974): 1, 14–15, folder 2, box 73, Kaufman Papers.

80. WKLD/OC, *1868 Treaty in Court*, booklet, n.d. [1974?], folder 4, box 40, Thorne Papers; John Thorne, "Wounded Knee—Treaty Defense," *Guild Notes* 4, no. 3 (May 1975): 6, folder 3, box 73, Kaufman Papers.

81. Sayer, *Ghost Dancing the Law*, 204.

82. Tilsen, "Fair and Equal Justice."

83. Sayer, *Ghost Dancing the Law*, 226. By contrast, compare Smith and Warrior, *Like a Hurricane*, 270–72; Weyler, *Blood of the Land*, 96.

84. The Supreme Court established a generous reparation, but the Sioux refused the money, reaffirming that the Black Hills' land was never for sale. See United States v. Sioux Nation of Indians, 448 U.S. 371 (1980).

85. S. L. Smith, *Hippies, Indians, and the Fight for Red Power*, 185, 211.

86. "American Indian Movement Leader Murdered," *Up Against the Bench* 2, no. 8 (November–December 1973): 14, folder 7, box 68, Kaufman Papers.

87. "Wounded Knee: Trials Continue," *Up Against the Bench* 4, no. 1 (March–April 1975): 9, 13, folder Chapter Newsletters Chicago, carton 57, NLG Records, Bancroft.

88. See Kunstler, *My Life*, 249–50. The tragic ordeal that began in 1975 is sympathetically chronicled in Matthiessen, *In the Spirit of Crazy Horse*.

89. See, respectively, Committee on Native American Struggles to Guild Executive Committee, April 28, 1978; "The Native American Solidarity Committee, What Is It?," *Committee on Native American Struggles Newsletter* 2, no. 1 (April 1978): 6–9, folder NLG CONAS, carton 24, NLG Records, Bancroft.

90. Ann F. Ginger to George Conk, September 11, 1975, folder NLG 1975, carton 26, NLG Records, Bancroft.

91. See, for instance, Barbara Dudley and Mary Morgan, "Guild Forum: On Socialist Feminism," *Women's Newsletter*, Winter 1977, 6–7, folder 188B:36, box N-35, pt. 2, Hall and Hoag Collection.

92. See Firestone, *Dialectic of Sex*; Millet, *Sexual Politics*.

93. For example, see Anne Flower Cummings to Guild Sisters, August 10, 1973, folder NLG—SF Chapter 1972-3, carton 58, NLG Records, Bancroft; *You Are Invited . . . to the First Potluck Meeting of Women in the Guild*, San Francisco, leaflet, n.d. [October 1975?], folder NLG 1975, carton 26, NLG Records, Bancroft; Koonan, interview.

94. See Massachusetts Lawyer's Guild Anti-Sexism Convention '74 Presentation Committee, "Women Hold Up Half the Sky," presentation sheet, folder 14B:56, box M-21, Part II, Hall and Hoag Collection.

95. Pamela Douglas, "Woman in Court," *Up Against the Bench* 1, no. 5 (September 1972): 6–7, folder Chapter Newsletters Chicago, carton 57, NLG Records, Bancroft.

96. C. Goodman, "On the Oppression of Women Lawyers and Legal Workers."

97. Marsha Love, "Women Workers on the Move," *Blind Justice* 3, no. 2 (December 1973): 1, 22, folder "Blind Justice" 1970s, carton 57, NLG Records, Bancroft.

98. For instance, see Garfinkle, Lefcourt, and Schulder, "Women's Servitude under Law"; Fasteau, "Law and Women"; Dudley, interview.

99. Joan Andersson and Beth Livezey, "Trials of a Woman Lawyer," in *Law for the People: An Alternative for Law Students*, ed. NLG (New York: NLG, n.d. [1974?]), 5–7, folder 49, carton 1, PCS and MLO Records.

100. As for the debate on rape trials, see "Rape Workshop," *Mass Dissent*, July 1973, 3, folder 14B:56, box M-21, pt. 2, Hall and Hoag Collection; Kathy Segal, "Rape: Feminist Analysis of Criminal Defense," *Guild Notes* 2, no. 4 (August 1973): 7, box 42-14, pt. 1, Hall and Hoag Collection.

101. Alice Price, "'I Am Somebody!': The Case of Joanne Little," *Guild Notes* 4, no. 1 (January 1975): 1, 14, folder 3, box 73, Kaufman Papers. For a political framing of the case, see Davis, "JoAnne Little: The Dialectics of Rape."

102. Mary Morgan, "'A Common Struggle . . .' Feminist Defendants and Lawyers Try Case Together," *Guild Notes* 3, no. 3 (March 1974): 7, 19, folder 2, box 73, Kaufman Papers.

103. "Introducing NCWO," presentation sheet, n.d., folder NLG Women & NCWO, carton 23, NLG Records, Bancroft.

104. Following the example of the civil rights movements, plaintiffs' lawyers wanted to take depositions (sworn out-of-court testimonies) during a public event at the Washington Square Methodist Church in New York. However, defense counsel forced them to find a more neutral venue and move to the nearby courthouse.

105. The whole case is detailed in Schulder and Kennedy, *Abortion Rap*. On the lack of confidence in the courts, see F. Kennedy, *Color Me Flo*, 64; Randolph, "'Not to Rely Completely on the Courts.'"

106. The other lawyers were Ann Hill, Barbara Milstein, Marilyn Seichter, Kathryn Emmett, and Nancy Stearns. See "Women v. Conn.," *Guild Notes* 1, no. 3 (September–October 1972): 6–7, folder 1, box 73, Kaufman Papers. See also *Women vs. Connecticut Organizing Pamphlet*, circa November 1970, www.historyisaweapon .com/defcon1/womenvsconnecticut.html.

107. Roe v. Wade, 410 U.S. 113 (1973). For a contextualization, see, among many others, Hull and Hoffer, *Roe v. Wade*.

108. "A Pessimistic Prognosis," *Up Against the Bench* 2, no. 3 (March 1973): 1, folder 7, box 68, Kaufman Papers. On the case and its logic, see Garrow, *Liberty and Sexuality*.

109. See, for instance, Karen Slaney and Lory Rosenberg, "Abortion: The Right You Have to Buy," *Women's Newsletter*, Summer 1977, 3–4, folder NLG Women & NCWO, carton 23, NLG Records, Bancroft. See also NLG NYC to members and friends, October 1, 1979, folder 23, box 246, NLG Records, Tamiment.

110. Rhonda Copelon and Beth Bochnak, "Abortion Rights & Wrongs," *Women's Newsletter*, February 1978, 1–4, folder NLG Women & NCWO, carton 23. See also McRae v. Califano, 491 F. Supp. 630 (E.D.N.Y. 1980); Harris v. McRae, 448 U.S. 297 (1980).

111. Anne Kaufman, Anne Braudy, and Susan Thal, "Women and Shelters," and Patti Roberts, "Battered Women: Who Will Define the Solution?," *Women's Newsletter*, Summer 1977, respectively, 1–4 and 12–14, folder NLG Women & NCWO, carton 23, NLG Records, Bancroft.

112. Peggy Wiesenberg, "The Fight for Shelters: The Harriet Tubman Women's Shelter, Minneapolis," *Women's Newsletter*, Summer 1977, 6–9, folder NLG Women & NCWO, carton 23, NLG Records, Bancroft.

113. Farber and Bailey, *Columbia Guide to America in the 1960s*, 73.

114. See, respectively, Patti Roberts' letter in *NLG Gay Task Force Newsletter*, February 1978, 2, folder NLG—Gay Task Force, carton 24, NLG Records, Bancroft, and "Gay Caucus Alive and Well at S.F. N.E.B.," *Gay Caucus Newsletter*, n.d. [1974?], 1–2, folder NLG—SF Chapter 1974, carton 58, NLG Records, Bancroft.

115. "Gay Liberation: A Reply to Our Inquiry," *Crossing the Bar* 1, no. 1 (March 1972): 3, 6, folder 208B:80, box M-21, pt. 2, Hall and Hoag Collection.

116. On the establishment of the task force and other antidiscrimination activities, see Gay Rights Task Force, "Gay Rights Resolution," 20 August 1977, folder NLG—Gay Task Force, carton 24, NLG Records, Bancroft; Joe Stewart, "The Fight for Gay Rights," in *Law for the People: An Alternative for Law Students*, ed. NLG (New York: NLG, 1978), 28, folder Law Student, carton 23, NLG Records, Bancroft; Tom

Steel, "Gay Rights Task Force," in *Law for the People*, ed. NLG (New York: NLG, 1979), 19, folder 348B:27, box N-35, pt. 2, Hall and Hoag Collection.

117. On the increasing attention to this issue, see Rivers, "'In the Best Interest of the Child.'"

118. The negative impact that gay parents could have on their children's psychosexual development was a crucial issue in most of the 1970s gay custody cases. Yet the nexus was hard to prove, and the lawyers for the gay parents consistently relied on expert testimony, winning the majority of their cases between the late 1970s and the early 1980s. See George, "Custody Crucible."

119. Mary Howell, "Gay Mothers Win Custody," *Guild Notes* 4, no. 1 (January 1975): 3, folder 3, box 73. Later, in *Schuster v. Schuster*, 90 Wn.2d 626, 585 P.2d 130 (1978), the Washington State Supreme Court conclusively stated that the two lesbian mothers could live together with their children.

120. See Stevye Knowles, "1977 Summer Project," *NLG Gay Task Force Newsletter*, February 1978, 4, folder NLG—Gay Task Force, carton 24, NLG Records, Bancroft. See Rivers, *Radical Relations*, 86–87.

121. See NLG Bay Area Chapter, Anti-Sexism Committee, *A Gay Parents' Legal Guide to Child Custody* (San Francisco: NLG, 1978). As an example of the teaching formats, see Lesbian and Gay Law Students (New York University School of Law) to friends, invitation letter, February 1, 1979, and the leaflet NLG, *Gay Rights Skills Seminar*, San Francisco, February 14, 1979, folder NLG—Gay Task Force, carton 24, NLG Records, Bancroft.

Chapter 10

1. Nixon is quoted in McMahon, *Nixon's Court*, 169–70.

2. See Hinton, *From the War on Poverty to the War on Crime*, particularly chaps. 1–5. Data on the LEAA's allocation are on page 94.

3. Donner, *Protectors of Privilege*, 162, 346. It is worth remembering that the Supreme Court had recently backed the rights of police, and President Johnson had signed a divisive crime bill giving broad license to state and local law enforcement agencies. See Fred P. Graham, "High Court Backs Rights of Police to Stop and Frisk," *New York Times*, June 11, 1968; Max Frankel, "President Signs Broad Crime Bill, with Objections," *New York Times*, June 20, 1968. Regarding the crackdown on crime under Nixon, see Warren Weaver Jr., "Senate Approves Stiff Crime Bill for Washington," *New York Times*, July 24, 1970; Warren Weaver Jr., "Supreme Court Widens Power of Police to Search Individual without Warrant," *New York Times*, December 12, 1973.

4. Among the initiatives, the failed Huston Plan and the Cabinet Committee to Combat Terrorism featured prominently. The genealogy of counterterrorism in the context of Nixon's campaign against leftist guerrillas has been thoroughly examined by Daniel Chard. See Chard, *Nixon's War at Home*.

5. Goldstein, *Political Repression*, 465.

6. Naison, *White Boy*, 108.

7. Bloom and Martin, *Black against Empire*, particularly 299–302, 356–74.

8. Data are extrapolated from the Church Committee's investigation and are quoted in Chard, *Nixon's War at Home*, 54.

9. D. J. R. Bruckner, "Black Panther Repression Hit," *Los Angeles Times*, July 4, 1960.

10. Churchill, "'To Disrupt, Discredit and Destroy.'" Data are in Donner, *Protectors of Privilege*, 180.

11. Bloom and Martin, *Black against Empire*, 158.

12. The raid and the mounting repression in Los Angeles are examined in Davis and Wiener, *Set the Night on Fire*, particularly 461–71.

13. Regarding the contribution of the NLG, see "Legal First Aid," *Berkeley Barb* 10, no. 24 (June 19–June 25, 1970): 4.

14. Harris, interview; Hilliard and Cole, *This Side of Glory*, 219, 277, 289.

15. After graduating from UC Berkeley, Serra became a fixture on San Francisco's Haight Ashbury. Being a successful criminal lawyer and an unrepentant radical, he represented a number of political defendants, such as Huey Newton, Jacques Rogiers of the New World Liberation Front, Tom Stevens of the White Panthers, Russell Little and Joe Remiro of the SLA, and environmentalist leader Judi Bari. During an LSD session, he took a vow of poverty and pledged never to capitalize on the practice of law. See Serra, interview; Serra, *Green, Yellow, and Purple Years*; Frankl, *Lust for Justice*.

16. Cunningham, *There's Something Happening Here*, 49–51, 153–80.

17. Handschu, interview. In New York City, the Guild also provided volunteers for the city corps of civilian observers created by Mayor Lindsay to monitor police crowd control. See M. Johnson, *Street Justice*, 273.

18. See, among many others, "San Francisco Regional Office," *NLG Newsletter* 15, no. 1 (May–June 1969): 1–2, folder 25, box 6, Goldring Papers; "On Call Marches On," *Conspiracy* 1, no. 2 (October 1970): 8, folder NLG Internal Struggles and Speeches, carton 26, NLG Records, Bancroft.

19. "Pork Chops," *Up Against the Bench* 1, no. 4 (July 1972): 10, folder Chapter Newsletters Chicago, carton 57, NLG Records, Bancroft.

20. On the training of observers, see NLG Columbia Law Chapter, *Legal Observers Training Program*, flyer, n.d., folder 8, box 71, Kaufman Papers. On the information resources, see NLG, Regional Office Staff, *Legal Street Sheet*, no. 1–6, folder NLG Internal Struggles and Speeches, carton 26, NLG Records, Bancroft. As proof of the circulation of this legal self-help, see "When the Man Is at the Door," *Berkeley Tribe* 4, no. 56 (July 31–August 7, 1970): 8, GI Press Collection, 1964–1977, Wisconsin Historical Society Online Collections.

21. Boudin et al., *Bust Book*. On the background story, see Koonan, interview; E. Goodman, interview.

22. Jose Yglesias, "Right On with the Young Lords," *New York Times Magazine*, June 7, 1970.

23. Fernández, *Young Lords*, 184; see also 1–7, 178–9.

24. With regard to the de-escalating effect generated by lawyers' presence, see Gene Cerruti to NY NLG members, January 12, 1970; *NLG NYC News Letter* 3, no. 1 (January 1970), folder 38, box 7, Unger Papers; Handschu, interview.

25. "The Mass Defense Office of the National Lawyers Guild," n.d. [1970?], folder 1970 NLG Convention Reports, carton 57, NLG Records, Bancroft; Cerruti to NY NLG members, January 12, 1970.

26. Among others, Richard Asch, Daniel Meyers, Lewis Steel, Paul Chevigny, and Henry di Suvero worked on these cases. See *Defense Notes*, February 1970, 3, folder 5, box 25, New Left Collection.

27. "The Second Eviction of the Young Lords," *Guild News* 1, no. 2 (March 9, 1971): 3–4, folder 2, box 68, Kaufman Papers. See also Fernández, *The Young Lords*, 315–30. Rivera, whose real name was Jerry Rivers and would later become a popular television host, was the primary link between the YL and the Guild. See Melendez, *We Took the Streets*, 114.

28. Donner, *Protectors of Privilege*, 5.

29. See, for instance, the leaflets NLG, *Police Misconduct Seminar*, Santa Clara University Law School, Santa Clara, CA, May 20, 1978, and NLG, *Police Misconduct Litigation Seminar*, Eastern Kentucky University, Richmond, KY, August 10, 1978, folder NLG—Police Crimes Task Force, carton 23, NLG Records, Bancroft. On the LEAA, see Parenti, *Lockdown America*, 14–18; Hinton, *From the War on Poverty to the War on Crime*, 141–50.

30. Judy Mead to Senator Charles H. Percy, January 10, 1979, with enclosed Judy Mead, "The Grand Juries: An American Inquisition," in *The Lawless State: The Crimes of the U.S. Intelligence Agencies*, ed. Morton H. Halperin et al. (New York: Penguin Books, 1976), 209–36, folder Grand Jury, carton 24, NLG Records, Bancroft. On the polemics regarding the "use immunity," see also Paul Cowan, "A Kind of Immunity That Leads to Jail: The New Grand Jury," *New York Times Magazine*, April 29, 1973.

31. Reif, interview.

32. Jim Reif, "Current Use of Grand Juries," memo, n.d. [1971?], folder NLG-NEB 1971, carton 57, NLG Records, Bancroft.

33. NLG NYC chapter to Brothers and Sisters, June 16, 1972, folder 38, box 7, Unger Papers.

34. "Grand Juries," *Blind Justice* 3, no. 1 (October 1973): 13, folder "Blind Justice" 1970s, carton 57, NLG Records, Bancroft. See also NLG, Grand Jury Defense Office, *Representation of Witnesses Before Federal Grand Juries*; Coalition to End Grand Jury Abuse, *So You're Going to Be a Grand Juror?*

35. See the internal memos "How Do We Talk with the Enemy? A Discussion of Testifying and Grants of Immunity before Federal Grand Juries," n.d., and "Some Thoughts on Grand Juries," n.d., folder NLG-NEB 1971, carton 57, NLG Records, Bancroft.

36. In Re Kinoy, 326 F. Supp. 407 (S.D.N.Y. 1971). See also Kinoy, *Rights on Trial*, 322–23; Ratner, *Moving the Bar*, 120–24.

37. For a couple of examples of victorious outcomes, see "Lawyers Hobble Grand Juries," *Detroit Struggle* 2, no. 3 (November 1971): 3; "Grand Jury Loses Ground," *Detroit Struggle* 3, no. 1 (January 1972): 10–12, folder 21, box 18, Cockrel Collection; Reif and Fassler interviews.

38. Weather Underground, "This Is Being Sent to Movement Groups, Papers, and Individuals," Los Angeles, 1971, Beinecke Library.

39. Berger, *Outlaws of America*, 161–62.

40. Lexington Grand Jury Defense Fund Committee, "Will the Circle Be Unbroken?," *Guild Notes* 4, no. 4 (June 1975): 4–5, 24, folder 3, box 73, Kaufman Papers. See also Deming, *Remembering Who We Are*, 201–4. It is worth noting that a women lawyers' team that included Catherine Roraback and Nancy Gertner was able to successfully defend Susan Saxe on trial. A hung jury closed the case. See Norgren, *Stories from Trailblazing Women Lawyers*, 228–30.

41. Goodell, *Political Prisoners*, 263.

42. Goldstein, *Political Repression*, 454–58.

43. Goodell, *Political Prisoners*, 267.

44. Various versions of the essay were published in different outlets. See, for instance, Lewis F. Powell, "America Is Not a Repressive Society," *New York Times*, November 3, 1971.

45. Handschu v. Special Services Div., 605 F. Supp. 1384 (S.D.N.Y. 1985); Handschu and Stolar interviews.

46. See Title III of the Omnibus Crime Control and Safe Streets Act of 1968. On the widespread use of wiretap powers under Nixon, see Fred P. Graham, "Mitchell to Use Wiretap Powers in Fight on Crime," *New York Times*, January 15, 1969; Fred P. Graham, "Mitchell Reports Wiretapping Rise," *New York Times*, October 6, 1970; Fred P. Graham, "Wiretaps in U.S. Up 37% in Year; State Has Most," *New York Times*, May 6, 1972.

47. The Department of Justice officially authorized the record and transcript of defendants' and lawyers' public statements, but evidence proves that intelligence agents also monitored attorneys' movements and closed-door conversations. See, for example, Chicago Police Department, Intelligence Division, "Interview Report subject Democratic NC," March 27, 1969; Chicago Police Department, Intelligence Division, "Interview Report [subject removed]," April 7, 1969; SAC Chicago to FBI Director and all SACs, April 15, 1969; Newark to Chicago and FBI Director, March 6, 1971; FBI Director to SAC Chicago, April 2, 1974, folder United States v. David T. Dellinger, et al., 1969–1987, box 33, Hayden Papers.

48. Tigar, *Fighting Injustice*, 193–203. See also Alderman v. United States, 394 U.S. 165 (1969).

49. See In re Grand Jury Proceedings, Harrisburg, Penn, 450 F.2d 199 (3d Cir. 1971); Reif, interview.

50. See, for instance, the case of Melvin C. Smith in Tigar, *Fighting Injustice*, 203–5.

51. On the case, see Committee to Free John Sinclair, *The 10 Year Sentence of John Sinclair*, leaflet, n.d. [1971?], folder 8, box 67, New Left Collection; "John Free!," *Detroit Struggle* 3, no. 1 (January 1972): 10–11, folder 21, box 18, Cockrel Collection.

52. Arthur Kinoy, "U.S. v. U.S. Dist. Ct.," *Guild Notes* 1, no. 3 (September–October 1972): 1, 10–11, folder 1, box 73, Kaufman Papers. See also Kunstler, *My Life*, 205–9.

53. United States v. United States Dist. Ct., 407 U.S. 297 (1972), also known as the Keith case because of Judge Damon Keith of the U.S. District Court for the Eastern District of Michigan, who first ordered the government to disclose the illegally intercepted conversations. See also Kinoy, *Rights on Trial*, 3–40.

54. The project worked in cooperation with the ACLU, the Rutgers Constitutional Litigation Clinic, and the Center for Constitutional Rights, among others. See Judy Joshel et al., "Guild Initiates Electronic Surveillance Project," *Guild Notes* 3, no. 3 (March 1974): 8, 12 and Bill Bender, "The Elusive Search for the Primary Taint," *Guild Notes* 3, no. 3 (March 1974): 9–11, folder 2, box 73, Kaufman Papers. See also Fassler interview.

55. See NLG, "Committee to Set Aside the 1972 Election to Plaintiffs and Supporters," memo, December 24, 1973, folder 9, box 72, Kaufman Papers; National Office Staff, "Sue the Bastards," *Guild Notes* 2, no. 5 (September 1973): 1, 9, folder 1, box 73, Kaufman Papers; Adam Bennion, "Guild Files Peoples Lawsuit," *Guild Notes* 3, no. 5 (July 1974): 1, 25, folder 2, box 73, Kaufman Papers.

56. See Michael Sweeney, "Seattle Law Limits Police in Intelligence Gathering," *Washington Post*, July 3, 1979; Donner, *Protectors of Privilege*, 350–53.

57. NLG, "An Appeal to Reason: The Proposal of the Attorney General to List the National Lawyers Guild as 'Subversive'—Its Implications for the Democratic Process and the Bar," n.d., folder 8C:10, box N-34, pt. 2, Hall and Hoag Collection. It is worth remembering that in 1948, the ABA had resolved that any lawyer providing assistance to the communist movement was "unworthy" of its membership. See Auerbach, *Unequal Justice*, 234–39.

58. For an analysis of the effects of McCarthyism on lawyers, see Schrecker, *Many Are the Crimes*, particularly 301–4. See also Wark and Galliher, *Progressive Lawyers under Siege*.

59. "U.S. Indicts Ex-Aide of Lawyers Guild," *New York Times*, November 25, 1959.

60. Braverman admitted his communist ties but denied advocating the overthrow of the government. He was disbarred and won reinstatement only in the mid-1970s. See Jacques Kelly, "Maurice L. Braverman, 86, Lawyer Convicted of Being a Communist," *Baltimore Sun*, March 27, 2002.

61. U.S. House of Representatives, *Communist Legal Subversion*, 16.

62. See, for instance, the appendix on the NLG in the report SF FBI, "Charles R. Garry," March 9, 1966, folder 7, box 10, Series 4, Newton Collection.

63. See Victor Rabinowitz to NLG members, April 13, 1968, and enclosed amicus curiae brief in the case *Arthur Kinoy v. District of Columbia*, folder 16, box 8, Rabinowitz Papers; Kinoy to Rabinowitz, August 28, 1968, folder 16, box 8, Rabinowitz Papers.

64. "National Lawyers Guild Supports Judge George Crockett Jr.," press release, April 10, 1969, and "Statement by Judge George C. Crockett," April 3, 1969, folder 37, box 5, NLG Records, Tamiment.

65. Patti Roberts, "Attacks on Attornies [*sic*]," memo, n.d. [1971?], folder Prison Reform, box 1, Roberts Papers.

66. FBI SF, "New Left Activities concerning Prison Situation, San Francisco, California—1971," memo, October 12, 1971, folder 5, box 5, Thorne Papers.

67. See the report of Carl A. Gosting to FBI SF, February 17, 1971, folder 5, box 5, Thorne Papers.

68. State of California, Board of Corrections, *Report to Governor Ronald Reagan*, 1–24.

69. Roberts, "Attacks on Attornies [*sic*]."

70. "Terence Hallinan Asks Court for Bar Membership," *Independent Journal*, April 5, 1966, folder B. Dreyfus Papers, carton 10, NLG Records, Bancroft. See also Benjamin Dreyfus to the signers of the amici curiae brief, March 24, 1966, folder 1, box 3, Treuhaft Papers.

71. Siegel, interview.

72. Stolar, interview.

73. George Conk, "Forty Years of Struggle," in *Law for the People: An Alternative for Law Students*, ed. NLG (New York: NLG, 1978), 20–27, folder Law Student, carton 23, NLG Records, Bancroft. See also Ginger and Tobin, *National Lawyers Guild*, 124–28.

74. "Don't Let It Bring You Down," *Up Against the Bench* 1, no. 2 (April 1972): 3, folder Chapter Newsletters Chicago, carton 57, NLG Records, Bancroft.

75. On the controversy, see Georgakas and Surkin, *Detroit*, 162–63. Note that Cockrel's statement had been reported with inconsistent wordings.

76. Guild lawyer Sheldon Otis headed the defense team. See Jonathan Lubell to NLG Board members, July 16, 1969, with enclosed amicus curiae brief in the case *Mayer v. Cockrel*, folder 24, box 20, NLG Records, Tamiment. See also "Contempt Charges Dismissed Against Kenneth Cockrel," *NLG Newsletter* 15, no. 3 (September–October 1969): 1, folder 25, box 6, Goldring Papers.

77. Jonathan Lubell to NLG NYC members, August 25, 1970, folder 38, box 7, Unger Papers.

78. See "Lawyers under Attack," *Guild Notes* 1, no. 1 (April–May 1972): 1, 14–15; "Trying Times," *Guild Notes* 2, no. 3 (May 1973): 22, folder 1, box 73, Kaufman Papers; Andrew Wolfson, "'Crazy Dan' Taylor, Attorney Who Championed the Underdog, Has Died," *Courier-Journal*, November 26, 2018. See also Taylor v. Hayes, 418 U.S. 488 (1974).

79. "Treuhaft Arrested; Threatens to Sue," *Oakland Tribune*, December 3, 1964. See also Benjamin Dreyfus to the President and the Board of Governors of the State Bar of California, January 15, 1965, folder 19, box 3, Treuhaft Papers.

80. See SF FBI, report, July 28, 1965, folder 7, box 1, Treuhaft Papers; Treuhaft to Benjamin Dreyfus, November 26, 1965, folder 1, box 3, Treuhaft Papers; Dreyfus to Treuhaft, April 15, 1968, folder 19, box 3, Treuhaft Papers.

81. Jay et al., "Cops Try to Frame Lawyer," *Mass Dissent* 2, no. 11 (September 1972): 5, folder 164A:12G, box M-21, pt. 2, Hall and Hoag Collection.

82. See MLO, "Annual Report 1972–3," October 10, 1973; MLO, "Semi-Annual Report, September 1973–February 1974," folder 3, carton 2, PCS and MLO Records.

83. Yoder, *Breach of Privilege*, 8.

84. Turco v. Allen, 334 F. Supp. 209 (D. Md. 1971). See also Jean Marbella and Justin Fenton, "Release of Black Panther Leader Renews Decades-Old Debate, *Baltimore Sun*, March 8, 2014.

85. See the press communiqué, "For Immediate Release," n.d., folder 4, box 7, Goldring Papers.

86. Cloke, interview.

87. For a review of some of these cases, see "Don't let It Bring You Down," *Up Against the Bench*.

88. Judy Mead to Hank [Henry] di Suvero et al., August 16, 1978, with enclosed Testimony Before the Senate Subcommittee on Administrative Practice and Procedure, August 17, 1978, folder Grand Jury, carton 24, NLG Records, Bancroft.

89. See R. L. Shackelford (FBI, Section Chief) to W. Raymond Wannall (FBI, Assistant Director), February 27, 1975, and enclosed memo (prepared at the request of James B. Adams, FBI Associate Director), subject National Lawyers Guild, folder 1, box 293, NLG Records, Tamiment.

90. Yoder, *Breach of Privilege*, 6–7.

91. Ernest Goodman, "The Guild and the Civil Rights Movement, Part II," *Guild Notes* (May–June 1981): 3–9, folder 16, box 9, Rabinowitz Papers.

92. Donner, *Protectors of Privilege*, 137–38.

93. Cunningham, *There's Something Happening Here*, 281.

94. SAC SF to Director FBI, memo, subject National Lawyers Guild, November 20, 1970, folder 3, box 69, Thorne Papers.

95. See the cover page of the report FBI SA Charles S. Milliken, "National Lawyers Guild," October 28, 1971, folder 1, box 293, NLG Records, Tamiment.

96. FBI SA to SAC Detroit, memo, subject National Lawyers Guild IS—C, July 31, 1973, folder 1, box 293, NLG Records, Tamiment.

97. Shackelford to Wannall, February 27, 1975, and enclosed memo, subject National Lawyers Guild, folder 1, box 293, NLG Records, Tamiment.

98. James B. Adams to [Richard L. Thornburgh] Assistant Attorney General, Criminal Division, and [Clarence M. Kelley] Director, FBI, March 13, 1975, folder 2, box 293, NLG Records, Tamiment.

99. SAC Chicago to FBI Director, airtel with enclosed document "The Relationship between the Weather Underground Organization (WUO) and the National Lawyers Guild (NLG), Internal Security," September 16, 1975. On the chronology of the investigation, see SA William F. Dyson to SAC Chicago, April 5, 1976, memo, subject Weather Underground Organization (WUO) Legal Support, folder 4, box 235, NLG Records, Tamiment.

100. Richard L. Thornburgh to Director FBI, memo, subject National Lawyers Guild, March 15, 1976, folder 2, box 293, NLG Records, Tamiment.

101. Considering only the New York City chapter, Victor Rabinowitz, Kenneth Cloke, Ralph Shapiro, Stanley Faulkner, and Robert Silverstein were all listed in the Security Index in 1967. See FBI, "National Lawyers Guild," report, June 6, 1967, folder 1, box 293, NLG Records, Tamiment. In a later document, Dana Biberman, David Freedman, Mary Kaufman, Arthur Kinoy, William Kunstler, Eric Seitz, and Ralph Shapiro also appeared in the Security Index. See FBI, "National Lawyers Guild," report, October 28, 1971, folder 1, box 293, NLG Records, Tamiment.

102. SAC, Chicago to FBI Director, airtel, subject Weatherman (Legal Support), September 16, 1975, folder 5, box 235, NLG Records, Tamiment. Guild sources estimate that at least 1,221 informers were deployed to report on Guild activities over the years, but the evidence supporting such a claim is unknown. See Emerson, Krinsky, Moore, and Buitrago, "National Lawyers Guild v. Attorney General."

103. SF FBI, "Charles R. Garry," report, January 27, 1949, folder 4, box 11, Series 4, Newton Collection.

104. SF FBI, "Charles R. Garry," report, March 9, 1966, folder 7, box 10, Series 4, Newton Collection.

105. SAC SF to Director FBI, memo, subject Charles R. Garry, March 29, 1968; Director FBI to SAC SF, April 22, 1968, folder 7, box 10, Series 4, Newton Collection.

106. SF FBI to Director FBI, memo, subject Charles R. Garry, May 17, 1968, folder 7, box 10, Series 4, Newton Collection.

107. See, for instance, SF FBI, "Charles R. Garry," report, October 16, 1968, folder 7, box 10, Series 4, Newton Collection.

108. FBI Director to SAC SF, January 28, 1970, folder 7, box 10, Series 4, Newton Collection.

109. See, among many others, SF FBI, "Charles R. Garry," report, February 13, 1970, folder 8, box 10, Series 4, Newton Collection; SAC Seattle to FBI Director, airmail, "Appearance of David Hilliard . . . ," April 7, 1970; SF FBI, "Charles R. Garry," report, April 13, 1970, folder 9, box 10, Series 4, Newton Collection. See also SAC NYC to FBI Director, memo, subject Charles R. Garry, May 19, 1970; SF FBI, "Charles R. Garry," report, June 17, 1970, folder 10, box 10, Series 4, Newton Collection.

110. Earlier, he was priority III. See Director FBI to SAC SF, February 25, 1970, folder 7, box 10, Series 4, Newton Collection.

111. Director FBI to SAC SF, airtel, subject Charles R. Garry, March 11, 1970, folder 8, box 10, Series 4, Newton Collection.

112. On Garry's perceived fanaticism, see Director FBI to SAC SF, teletype, subject Charles R. Garry, April 29, 1971, folder 18, box 10, Series 4, Newton Collection. On the requests of strict surveillance, see Director FBI to SAC SF, May 10, 1971, folder 1, box 11, Series 4, Newton Collection.

113. SAC New Haven to Director FBI, memo, subject Charles R. Garry, May 26, 1971, folder 18, box 10, Series 4, Newton Collection.

114. For instance, see SF FBI, "Charles R. Garry," report, January 3, 1972, folder 2, box 11, Series 4, Newton Collection.

115. See, among many others, NY FBI, "Mary Metlay Kaufman," report, May 4, 1964; NY FBI, "Mary Metlay Kaufman," report, January 29, 1965; NY FBI, "Mary Metlay Kaufman," report, February 27, 1969; Legat Bonn (Germany) to Director FBI, memo, subject Mary Metlay Kaufman, November 26, 1971; Ohio FBI, "Mary Metlay Kaufman," investigative summary, March 24, 1975, box 1b, Kaufman Papers.

116. See, for example, SF FBI, "John Ebson Thorne," report, April 5, 1965; SF FBI, "John Ebson Thorne," report, May 31, 1968; SF FBI, "John Ebson Thorne," report, March 24, 1972, folder 3, box 69, Thorne Papers. See also SAC SF to LA ADIC, "Santa Barbara Legal Collective," report, October 23, 1973; SA Bertram Worthington to SAC (100-68932), memo, subject Venceremos Organization, October 13, 1971, folder 5, box 5, Thorne Papers.

117. *NLG v. FBI, CIA et al.*, Complaint-Class Action, March 1, 1977, folder NLG v. FBI, CIA et al., complaint 1977, carton 58, NLG Records, Bancroft.

118. Founded in 1958, the John Birch Society was (and still is) a right-wing organization dedicated to fighting against Communist influence over America and to preaching small government.

119. The New York State Assembly investigation on the Red Squad officially confirmed that the NLG was infiltrated by Sheila O'Connor. See Guild Investigative Group, "Report to Conference on Government Spying," January 22, 1977, and the sworn testimony of Patricia J. Richartz, November 5, 1976. Richartz was a leftist activist who allegedly discovered the espionage scheme of the Rees and was beaten by Sheila. All documents are in folder 13, box 264, NLG Records, Tamiment. The life of the Rees has also been chronicled in Rosenfeld, *Subversives*, 400–403.

120. As an example of the (modest) intelligence she provided, see SA Garry G. Lash to SAC (100-21623), November 23, 1973, and SA Garry G. Lash to SAC (100-21623), April 18, 1974, folder 13, box 124, NLG Records, Tamiment.

121. See the draft chapter by Beth Bonora and Eric Swanson, "Finding Twelve Fair Jurors," in Goodman's unpublished book on the Shango trial, folder 67, Microfilm, NLG Records, Bancroft.

122. "Doug Durham: FBI Operative," *Up Against the Bench* 4, no. 1 (March–April 1975): 8–9, folder Chapter Newsletters Chicago, carton 57, NLG Records, Bancroft.

123. See *NLG v. FBI, CIA et al.*

124. Pearlman, *Call Me Phaedra*, 218, 224.

125. Cloke, interview.

126. Doron Weinberg to Friends, November 1975, folder NLG 1975, carton 26, NLG Records, Bancroft. The publication denouncing the Guild's wrongdoings was Research Department of the Church League of America, *Attorneys for Treason: The True Story of the National Lawyers Guild* (Wheaton, IL: Church League of America, 1975), folder 12, box 263, NLG Records, Tamiment.

127. Emerson, Krinsky, Moore, and Buitrago, "National Lawyers Guild v. Attorney General."

128. Harris, interview.

129. See *NLG v. FBI, CIA et al.* and Michael Krinsky, "COINTELPRO Lingers On," *Rights*, n.d., 3–5, folder FBI, box 84, NLG Records, Bancroft.

130. Gladstein, interview. For similar points of view, see Gespass, interview; W. Goodman interview; Meyer interview. Archival evidence shows that while Guild lawyers were sometimes suspicious of affiliates, they were not too concerned about them. See Joel Graber to Frank Siegel, September 16, 1976, and Siegel to Michael Krinsky, October 25, 1977, folder 11, box 266, NLG Records, Tamiment.

131. Ratner Kunstler, interview.

132. Frank, interview.

133. Haberfeld, for example, remembers that neither an arrest in Mississippi nor the FBI's surveillance bothered him too much, due to his white privilege. Haberfeld, interview.

134. Siegel, interview.

Conclusion

1. Barbara Dudley, for example, ceased to be a lawyer for the movements and shifted to political organizing under the presidency of Ronald Reagan when she realized that the only way to be a radical lawyer was "defensive." See Dudley, interview.

2. Tigar, interview.

3. See the testimony of Philip Kurland in Vanderwicken, "Angry Young Lawyers," 74.

4. As an example of self-criticism, see "National Office Report," *Guild Notes* 3, no. 7 (December 1974): 2, folder 14B:93, box N-35, pt. 2, Hall and Hoag Collection. It must be noted that Black radical lawyers usually joined their own National Conference of Black Lawyers; thus, the NLG opted for teaming up with that organization. See Mayer, interview.

5. Given the common Marxist background, radical lawyers' analysis was most immediately reflected in the debate on critical legal studies. For an overview of the main theoretical positions of critical legal studies, see Kairys, introduction; Kelman, "Origins of Crime and Criminal Violence"; Chambliss, "Toward a Radical Criminology"; Gordon, "New Developments in Legal Theory." The foundational texts of critical race theory, with a compelling introduction outlining the genealogy of this intellectual movement and its differences from critical legal studies, are in Krenshaw et al., *Critical Race Theory*, particularly xiii–xxxii.

6. The dialectic "margin and mainstream" in the U.S. radical experience is fully explored in Brick and Phelps, *Radicals in America*, particularly 7–10.

7. Foner, *Story of American Freedom*, 301–3.

8. Harris, interview; Haberfeld, interview. See also Bloom and Martin, *Black against Empire*, 160.

9. Bingham, interview.

10. See, for instance, P. Harris, *Black Rage*, 60; Greenberg and Stender, "Prison as a Lawless Agency," 832–33. On radical lawyers' persistent hesitation between critique of law and mobilization of law, which has given rise to a "paradoxical legalism," see Israël, *À la gauche du droit*, particularly 90, 285–88, 338.

11. Lichtenstein, *Ghosts of Attica*.

Bibliography

Archival Primary Sources

Archives

Brown University
    John Hay Library Special Collections
        Gordon Hall and Grace Hoag Collection of Dissenting and Extremist
            Printed Propaganda
Columbia University
    Rare Books & Manuscript Library
        Individual Interviews Oral History Collection
Harvard University
    Schlesinger Library
        Papers of Angela Y. Davis, 1937–2017, MC 940
        Papers of Florynce Kennedy, 1915–2004, MC555
New York University
    Tamiment Library—Robert F. Wagner Labor Archives
        Center for Constitutional Rights Records, TAM 589
        Benjamin and Muriel Goldring Papers and Photographs, TAM 347
        National Lawyers Guild Records, TAM 191
        Martin Popper Papers, TAM 680
        Victor Rabinowitz Papers, TAM 123
        Robert E. Treuhaft Papers, TAM 664
        Abraham Unger Papers, TAM 157
San Francisco Public Library
    James C. Hormel LGBTQIA+ Center
    Patti Roberts Papers, 1968–2009, GLC 111
Smith College, Northampton, Mass.
    Sophia Smith Collection of Women's History
        Mary Metlay Kaufman Papers, SSC-MS-00300
Stanford University
    Hoover Institution Library & Archives
        New Left Collection, 69001
    Special Collections
        Dr. Huey P. Newton Foundation Inc. Collection, M0864
University of California, Berkeley
    Bancroft Library
        Eldridge Cleaver Papers, 1963–1988, BANC MSS 91/213c

Eldridge Cleaver Photograph Collection, 1966–circa 1982, BANC PIC
1991.078
Gregory Armstrong Papers Relating to the Publication of *Soledad Brother,
The Prison Letters of George Jackson*: ca. 1970–1971, BANC MSS 84/27c
Malcolm Burnstein Papers, 1963–1994, BANC MSS99/294c
Meiklejohn Civil Liberties Institute Collections, BANC MSS99/281c
National Lawyers Guild Records, BANC MSS99/280cz
Pacific Counseling Service and Military Law Office Records, 1969–1977,
BANC MSS86/89c
Regional Oral History Office
Oral Histories
University of California, Santa Cruz
University Library, Special Collections and Archives
John E. Thorne Papers, MS.423
University of Michigan, Ann Arbor
University of Michigan Library, Special Collections Research Center
Tom Hayden Papers
Wayne State University, Detroit
Walter P. Reuther Library
Kenneth V. and Sheila M. Cockrel Collection, UP001379
Yale University
Beinecke Rare Book & Manuscript Library

Interviews by the Author

Stephen Bingham, February 22, 2017
Richard M. Buxbaum, August 28, 2021
Kenneth Cloke, March 20, 2017
Barbara Dudley, November 17, 2017
Martin Fassler, February 27, 2017
Peter Franck, February 24, 2017
David Gespass, May 30, 2018
Amy Gladstein, September 15, 2017
Emily J. Goodman, September 13, 2017
William Goodman, December 3, 2020
Peter Haberfeld, March 24, 2017
Barbara Handschu, October 24, 2017
Paul Harris, February 20, 2017
Abdeen Jabara, December 21, 2017
Dennis James, December 20, 2017
Karen Jo Koonan, February 20, 2017

Gerald B. Lefcourt, May 11, 2017
Joseph Lipofsky, October 24, 2017
Carlin Meyer, September 14, 2017
Deborah Rand, October 9, 2017
Margaret Ratner Kunstler, May 8, 2018
James Reif, September 25, 2017
Eric Seitz, September 30, 2017
J. Tony Serra, February 16, 2017
Dan Siegel, March 5, 2020
Carol R. Silver, February 16, 2017
Michael S. Smith, October 24, 2017
Eleanor Stein, September 19, 2017
Marvin Stender, February 28, 2020
Martin Stolar, May 8, 2017
Michael E. Tigar, June 6, 2018
Melvin L. Wulf, November 13, 2017

Periodicals

Baltimore Sun
Berkeley Barb
Courier-Journal

Detroit Free Press
Detroit News
Guardian

Harper's Magazine
Los Angeles Times
Newsweek
New York Magazine
New York Review of Books
New York Times
New York Times Book Review

New York Times Magazine
Oakland Tribune
Ramparts
San Francisco Chronicle
Time
Village Voice
Washington Post

Non-archival Primary and Secondary Sources

Abt, John J., and Michael Myerson. *Advocate and Activist: Memoirs of an American Communist Lawyer.* Urbana: University of Illinois Press, 1993.

"The American College of Trial Lawyers: Its Principles." *Trial* 7, no. 1 (1971): 28–31.

Anderson, Robert, Joanna Brown, Jonny Lerner, and Barbara Lou Shafer, eds. *Voices from Wounded Knee, 1973: In the Words of the Participants.* Rooseveltown, NY: Akwesasne Notes, 1976.

Anderson, Terry H. *The Movement and the Sixties.* New York: Oxford University Press, 1995.

Anthony, Earl. *Picking Up the Gun.* New York: Dial Press, 1970.

Aptheker, Bettina. *The Morning Breaks: The Trial of Angela Davis.* New York: International, 1975.

——. "Statements and Appeals." In *If They Come in the Morning*, edited by Angela Y. Davis, 254–81. New York: Third Press, 1971.

Aptheker, Bettina, and Dayo F. Gore, eds. *Free Angela Davis, and All Political Prisoners! A Transnational Campaign for Liberation.* Alexandria, VA: Alexander Street Press, 2014.

Armstrong, Gregory. *"The Dragon Has Come."* New York: Harper & Row, 1974.

Aronson, Henry. "Getting Punched by Sheriff Clark and Other Misadventures." In *Voices of Civil Rights Lawyers: Reflections from the Deep South, 1964–1980*, edited by Kent Spriggs, 196–99. Gainesville: University Press of Florida, 2017.

——. "The Politics of Civil Rights Lawyering." In *Voices of Civil Rights Lawyers: Reflections from the Deep South, 1964–1980*, edited by Kent Spriggs, 148–54. Gainesville: University Press of Florida, 2017.

Atkins, Burton M., and Henry R. Glick, eds. *Prisons, Protest, and Politics.* Englewood Cliffs, NJ: Prentice-Hall, 1972.

Attica Defense Committee. *We Are Attica: Interviews with Prisoners from Attica.* New York: Attica Defense Committee, n.d. [1971?].

Auerbach, Jerold S. *Unequal Justice: Lawyers and Social Change in Modern America.* New York: Oxford University Press, 1976.

Avedon, Richard, and Doon Arbus. *The Sixties.* New York: Random House, 1999.

Avorn, Jerry L. *Up Against the Ivy Wall: A History of the Columbia Crisis.* New York: Atheneum, 1969.

Avrich, Paul. *The Haymarket Tragedy.* Princeton, NJ: Princeton University Press, 1984.

Axelrod, Beverly. "The Radical Lawyer." In *Radical Lawyers*, edited by Jonathan Black, 69–74. New York: Avon, 1971.

Ayers, Bill. *Fugitive Days*. Boston: Beacon, 2001.

Babson, Steve, Dave Riddle, and David Elsila. *The Color of Law: Ernie Goodman, Detroit, and the Struggle for Labor and Civil Rights*. Detroit: Wayne State University Press, 2010.

Baker, Michael A., Bradley R. Brewer, Raymond DeBuse, Sally T. Hillsman, Murray Milner, and David V. Soeiro. *Police on Campus: The Mass Police Action at Columbia University, Spring, 1968*. New York: New York Civil Liberties Union, 1969.

Bakke, Kit. *Protest on Trial: The Seattle 7 Conspiracy*. Pullman, WA: Washington State University Press, 2018.

Balagoon, Kuwasi, Joan Bird, Cetewayo, Robert Collier, Dhoruba, Richard Harris, Ali Bey Hassan, et al. *Look for Me in the Whirlwind: The Collective Autobiography of the New York 21*. New York: Random House, 1971.

Ball, Howard. *The* Bakke *Case: Race, Education, and Affirmative Action*. Lawrence: University Press of Kansas, 2000.

Banks, Dennis J. *Ojibwa Warrior: Dennis Banks and the Rise of the American Indian Movement*. Norman: University of Oklahoma Press, 2004.

Bannan, John F., and Rosemary S. Bannan. *Law, Morality and Vietnam: The Peace Militants and the Courts*. Bloomington: Indiana University Press, 1974.

Bardacke, Frank. *Trampling Out the Vintage: Cesar Chavez and the Two Souls of the United Farm Workers*. London: Verso, 2011.

——. "The United Farm Workers from the Ground Up." In *Rebel Rank and File: Labor Militancy and Revolt from Below during the Long 1970s*, edited by Aaron Brenner, Robert Brenner, and Cal Winslow, 149–70. London: Verso, 2010.

Barkan, Steven E. *Protesters on Trial: Criminal Justice in the Southern Civil Rights and Vietnam Antiwar Movements*. New Brunswick, NJ: Rutgers University Press, 1985.

Bass, Paul, and Douglas W. Rae. *Murder in the Model City: The Black Panthers, Yale, and the Redemption of a Killer*. New York: Basic Books, 2006.

Bates, Tom. *Rads: The 1970 Bombing of the Army Math Research Center at the University of Wisconsin and Its Aftermath*. New York: HarperCollins, 1992.

Batlan, Felice. *Women and Justice for the Poor: A History of Legal Aid, 1863–1945*. Cambridge: Cambridge University Press, 2015.

Belknap, Michal R. "Cold War in the Courtroom: The Foley Square Communist Trial." In *American Political Trials*, edited by Michal R. Belknap. 207–32. Westport, CT: Greenwood Press, 1994.

——. Introduction to *American Political Trials*, edited by Michal R. Belknap, xiii–xxviii. Westport, CT: Greenwood Press, 1994.

Bell Hughett, Amanda. "A 'Safe Outlet' for Prisoner Discontent: How Prison Grievance Procedures Helped Stymie Prison Organizing during the 1970s." *Law & Social Inquiry* 44, no. 4 (2019): 893–921.

Benner, L. Wayne and Philip Eder. "Jailed Revolution." *Guild Practitioner* 29, no. 3–4 (1972): 66–68.

Berger, Dan. *Captive Nation: Black Prison Organizing in the Civil Rights Era*. Chapel Hill: University of North Carolina Press, 2015.

——. *Outlaws of America: The Weather Underground and the Politics of Solidarity.* Oakland, CA: AK Press, 2006.

Berger, Dan, and Toussaint Losier. *Rethinking the American Prison Movement.* London: Routledge, 2017.

Berkman, Ronald. *Opening the Gates: The Rise of the Prisoners' Movement.* Lexington, MA: Lexington Books, 1979.

Berman, Jesse. "The Cuban Popular Tribunals." *Columbia Law Review* 69, no. 8 (1969): 1317–54.

Berrigan, Daniel. *The Trial of the Catonsville Nine.* Boston: Beacon, 1970.

Biderman, Paul. "The Birth of Communal Law Firms." In *Radical Lawyers*, edited by Jonathan Black, 280–88. New York: Avon, 1971.

Black, Jonathan. "An Interview with Gerald Lefcourt." In *Radical Lawyers*, edited by Jonathan Black, 307–13. New York: Avon, 1971.

——. "An Interview with William Kunstler." In *Radical Lawyers*, edited by Jonathan Black, 301–7. New York: Avon, 1971.

——, ed. *Radical Lawyers: Their Role in the Movement and in the Courts.* New York: Avon, 1971.

Blauner, Robert. "Sociology in the Courtroom: The Search for White Racism in the Voir Dire." In *Minimizing Racism in Jury Trials: The Voir Dire Conducted by Charles R. Garry in People of California v. Huey P. Newton*, edited by Ann F. Ginger, 43–73. Berkeley: National Lawyers Guild, 1969.

Bloom, Joshua, and Waldo E. Martin Jr. *Black against Empire: The History and Politics of the Black Panther Party.* Berkeley: University of California Press, 2013.

Bond, Julian. Preface to *The Summer That Didn't End: The Story of the Mississippi Civil Rights Project of 1964*, by Len Holt, 3–9. New York: Da Capo Press, 1992.

Boudin, Kathy, Brian Glick, Eleanor Raskin, and Gustin Reichbach. *The Bust Book: What to Do Till the Lawyer Comes.* New York: Grove Press, 1969.

Boudin, Leonard B. "Reflections on Violence in the United States." *Guild Practitioner* 32, no. 4 (1975): 105–9.

Bourg, Julian. *From Revolution to Ethics: May 1968 and Contemporary French Thought.* Montreal-Kingston: McGill-Queen's University Press, 2007.

Braudy, Susan. *Family Circle: The Boudins and the Aristocracy of the New Left.* New York: Alfred A. Knopf, 2003.

Brenner, Aaron. Preface to *Rebel Rank and File: Labor Militancy and Revolt from Below during the Long 1970s*, edited by Aaron Brenner, Robert Brenner, and Cal Winslow, xi–xix. London: Verso, 2010.

Brick, Howard, and Cristopher Phelps. *Radicals in America: The U.S. Left Since the Second World War.* New York: Cambridge University Press, 2015.

Brown, Dee. *Bury My Heart at Wounded Knee: An Indian History of the American West.* New York: Holt, Rinehart and Winston, 1970.

Brown, Sarah Hart. *Standing against Dragons: Three Southern Lawyers in an Era of Fear.* Baton Rouge: Louisiana State University Press, 1998.

Burnette, Robert, and John Koster. *The Road to Wounded Knee.* New York: Bantam Books, 1974.

Burnham, Margaret. Foreword to *Advocate and Activist: Memoirs of an American Communist Lawyer*, by John J. Abt and Michael Myerson, vii–x. Urbana: University of Illinois Press, 1993.

——. "Ruchell and Angela Want to Represent Themselves." In *If They Come in the Morning*, edited by Angela Y. Davis, 211–30. New York: Third Press, 1971.

Burns, Haywood. "The Federal Government and Civil Rights." In *Southern Justice*, edited by Leon Friedman, 228–54. New York: Pantheon Books, 1965.

Burnstein, Malcolm. "From Arrest to Verdict." In *The Relevant Lawyers: Conversations Out of Court on Their Clients, Their Practice, Their Politics, Their Life Style*, edited by Ann F. Ginger, 41–67. New York: Simon and Schuster, 1972.

——. "The FSM: A Movement Lawyer's Perspective." In *The Free Speech Movement: Reflections on Berkeley in the 1960s*, edited by Robert Cohen and Reginald E. Zelnik, 434–45. Berkeley: University of California Press, 2002.

Burrough, Bryan. *Days of Rage: America's Radical Underground, the FBI, and the Forgotten Age of Revolutionary Violence.* New York: Penguin, 2015.

Burton, Orisanmi. "Organized Disorder: The New York City Jail Rebellion of 1970." *Black Scholar* 48, no. 4 (2018): 28–42.

Carson, Clayborne. *In Struggle: SNCC and the Black Awakening of the 1960s.* Cambridge, MA: Harvard University Press, 1995.

Casper, Jonathan D. *Lawyers before the Warren Court: Civil Liberties and Civil Rights, 1957–1966.* Urbana: University of Illinois Press, 1972.

Castellucci, John. *The Big Dance: The Untold Story of Kathy Boudin and the Terrorist Family That Committed the Brink's Robbery Murders.* New York: Mead & Co, 1986.

Chambliss, William J. "Toward a Radical Criminology." In *The Politics of Law: A Progressive Critique*, edited by Kairys David, 230–241. New York: Pantheon, 1982.

Champy, Florent, and Liora Israël. "Professions et engagement public." *Sociétés Contemporaines* 73, no. 1 (2009): 7–19.

Chard, Daniel S. *Nixon's War at Home: The FBI, Leftist Guerrillas, and the Origins of Counterterrorism.* Chapel Hill: The University of North Carolina Press, 2021.

Churchill, Ward. "'To Disrupt, Discredit and Destroy': The FBI's Secret War against the Black Panther Party." In *Liberation, Imagination, and the Black Panther Party: A New Look at the Panthers and Their Legacy*, edited by Kathleen Cleaver and George Katsiaficas, 78–117. New York: Routledge, 2001.

Citizens Research and Investigation Committee and Louis E. Tackwood. *The Glass House Tapes.* New York: Avon Books, 1973.

Civil Liberties Docket, Leo Branton Jr., Seymour Mandel, and Ben Margolis. "The Watts Revolt and the Los Angeles Chapter Response." In *The National Lawyers Guild: From Roosevelt through Reagan*, edited by Ann F. Ginger and Eugene Tobin, 216–17. Philadelphia: Temple University Press, 1992.

Clark, Ramsey. *Crime in America: Observations on Its Nature, Causes, Prevention, and Control.* New York: Simon and Schuster, 1970.

Clark, Richard X. *The Brothers of Attica.* New York: Links, 1973.

Clavir, Judy, and John Spitzer, eds. *The Conspiracy Trial.* New York: Bobbs-Merrill, 1970.

Cleaver, Eldridge. Introduction to *Do It! Scenarios of the Revolution,* by Jerry Rubin, 6–11. New York: Simon and Schuster, 1970.

———. *Soul on Ice.* New York: McGraw-Hill, 1968.

Cloke, Kenneth. "The Economic Basis of Law and State." In *Law against the People,* edited by Robert Lefcourt, 65–80. New York: Vintage, 1971.

———. "Law Is Illegal." In *Radical Lawyers,* edited by Jonathan Black, 27–43. New York: Avon, 1971.

Coalition to End Grand Jury Abuse. *So You're Going to Be a Grand Juror?* Washington: CEGJA, 1977.

Collier, Peter, and David Horowitz. *Destructive Generation: Second Thoughts about the Sixties.* New York: Summit Books, 1989.

Collins, Hugh. *Marxism and Law.* Oxford: Oxford University Press, 1984.

Columbia University School of Law, *Opinion of the Disciplinary Tribunal of the School of Law of Columbia University in the Matter of Gustin L. Reichbach.* New York: Columbia University, 1968.

Condon, Gene A. "Comments on You Don't Have to Love the Law to Be a Lawyer." *Guild Practitioner* 29, no. 1 (1970): 19–21.

Cortright, David. *Soldiers in Revolt: GI Resistance during the Vietnam War.* Chicago: Haymarket Books, 2005.

Cowie, Jefferson. "'Vigorously Left, Right, and Center.' The Crosscurrents of Working-Class America in the 1970s." In *America in the Seventies,* edited by Beth Bailey and David Farber, 75–106. Lawrence: University Press of Kansas, 2004.

Crockett, George W., Jr. "Racism in American Law." *Guild Practitioner* 27, no. 4 (1968): 176–84.

Crowley, Walt. *Rites of Passage: A Memoir of the Sixties in Seattle.* Seattle: University of Washington Press, 1995.

Cummins, Eric. *The Rise and the Fall of California's Radical Prison Movement.* Stanford: Stanford University Press, 1994.

Cunningham, David. *There's Something Happening Here: The New Left, the Klan, and FBI Counterintelligence.* Berkeley: University of California Press, 2004.

Davis, Angela Y. *Angela Davis: An Autobiography.* New York: Random House, 1974.

———. "Angela Davis: Notes for Arguments in Court on the Issue of Self-Representation." In *If They Come in the Morning,* edited by Angela Y. Davis, 237–46. New York: Third Press, 1971.

———, ed. *If They Come in the Morning: Voices of Resistance.* New York: Third Press, 1971.

———. "JoAnne Little: The Dialectics of Rape." In *The Angela Y. Davis Reader,* edited by Joy James, 149–160. Malden, MA: Blackwell, 1998.

———. "Political Prisoners, Prisons and Black Liberation." In *If They Come in the Morning,* edited by Angela Y. Davis, 19–36. New York: Third Press, 1971.

———. "Prison Interviews." In *If They Come in the Morning,* edited by Angela Y. Davis, 177–88. New York: Third Press, 1971.

Davis, Mike, and Jon Wiener. *Set the Night on Fire: L.A. in the Sixties.* London: Verso, 2020.

Davis Jordan, Fania, Kendra Alexander, and Franklin Alexander. "The Political Campaign." In *If They Come in the Morning*, edited by Angela Y. Davis, 249–54. New York: Third Press, 1971.

DeBenedetti Charles. *An American Ordeal: The Antiwar Movement of the Vietnam Era.* With the assistance of Charles Chatfield. Syracuse, NY: Syracuse University Press, 1990.

Debouzy, Marianne. "Le procès des Huit de Chicago (1969–1970) : déconstruire l'image des ennemis publics." *Le Mouvement Social* 3, no. 240 (2012): 29–47.

de Graaf, Beatrice, and Alex P. Schmid, eds. *Terrorists on Trial: A Performative Perspective.* Leiden: Leiden University Press, 2016.

Dellinger, David T., ed. *Contempt: Transcript of the Contempt Citations, Sentences, and Responses of the Chicago Conspiracy 10.* Chicago: Swallow Press, 1970.

Deloria, Vine, Jr. *Behind the Trail of Broken Treaties: An Indian Declaration of Independence.* New York: Delacorte Press, 1974.

Deming, Barbara. *Remembering Who We Are.* Tallahassee, FL: Naiad, 1981.

Dershowitz, Alan M. *Taking the Stand: My Life in the Law.* New York: Broadway Books, 2019.

di Suvero, Henry. "The Movement and the Legal System." In *Radical Lawyers*, edited by Jonathan Black, 51–69. New York: Avon, 1971.

Dittmer, John. *Local People: The Struggle for Civil Rights in Mississippi.* Urbana: University of Illinois Press, 1994.

Dohrn, Bernardine. "When Hope and History Rhyme." In *Sing a Battle Song: The Revolutionary Poetry, Statements, and Communiqués of the Weather Underground, 1970–1974*, edited by Bernardine Dohrn, Bill Ayers, and Jeff Jones, 1–20. New York: Seven Stories Press, 2006.

Donner, Frank J. *Protectors of Privilege: Red Squads and Police Repression in Urban America.* Berkeley: University of California Press, 1990.

Dorsen, Norman, and Leon Friedman, eds. *Disorder in the Court: Report of the Association of the Bar of the City of New York, Special Committee on Courtroom Conduct.* New York: Pantheon Books, 1973.

Douglas, James. "Organization, Ego, and the Practice of Alternative Law." *Yale Review of Law and Social Action* 2, no. 1 (1971): 88–92.

Durden-Smith, Jo. *Who Killed George Jackson?* New York: Knopf, 1976.

Ebert, Justus. *The Trial of a New Society: Being a Review of the Celebrated Ettor-Giovannitti-Caruso Case, Beginning with the Lawrence Textile Strike That Caused It and Including the General Strike That Grew out of It.* Cleveland: I. W. W. Publishing Bureau, 1913.

Eckstein, Arthur M. *Bad Moon Rising: How the Weather Underground Beat the FBI and Lost the Revolution.* New Haven, CT: Yale University Press, 2016.

Ely, James W., Jr. "The Chicago Conspiracy Case." In *American Political Trials*, edited by Michal R. Belknap, 233–53. Westport, CT: Greenwood Press, 1994.

Emerson, Thomas I., Michael Krinsky, Jonathan C. Moore, and Ann Mari Buitrago. "National Lawyers Guild v. Attorney General." *Guild Practitioner* 42, no. 2 (1985): 33–45.

Epstein, Sandra P. *Law at Berkeley: The History of Boalt Hall.* Berkeley: University of California Press, 1997.

Fairclough, Adam. *To Redeem the Soul of America: The Southern Christian Leadership Conference and Martin Luther King Jr.* Athens, GA: University of Georgia Press, 1987.

Falciola, Luca. "A Bloodless Guerrilla Warfare: Why U.S. White Leftists Renounced Violence against People during the 1970s." *Terrorism and Political Violence* 28, no. 5 (2016): 928–49.

Farber, David. *Chicago '68.* Chicago: University of Chicago Press, 1994.

Farber, David, and Beth L. Bailey, eds. *The Columbia Guide to America in the 1960s.* New York: Columbia University Press, 2001.

Farber, Jerry. *The Student as Nigger: Essays and Stories.* New York: Pocket Books, 1970.

Fasteau, Brenda. "Law and Women." In *Radical Lawyers*, edited by Jonathan Black, 239–48. New York: Avon, 1971.

Felber, Garrett. *Those Who Know Don't Say: The Nation of Islam, the Black Freedom Movement, and the Carceral State.* Chapel Hill: University of North Carolina Press, 2020.

Fernández, Johanna. *The Young Lords: A Radical History.* Chapel Hill: University of North Carolina Press, 2020.

Finkel, Stuart. "The 'Political Red Cross' and the Genealogy of Rights Discourse in Revolutionary Russia." *Journal of Modern History* 89, no. 1 (2017): 79–118.

Firestone, Shulamith. *The Dialectic of Sex: The Case for Feminist Revolution.* New York: Morrow, 1970.

Flynn, George. *Draft, 1940–1973.* Lawrence: University Press of Kansas, 1993.

Foley, Michael S. *Confronting the War Machine: Draft Resistance during the Vietnam War.* Chapel Hill: University of North Carolina Press, 2003.

Foner, Eric. Foreword to *For the Hell of It: The Life and Times of Abbie Hoffman*, by Jonah Raskin, xiii–xv. Berkeley: University of California Press, 1998.

——. *Reconstruction: America's Unfinished Revolution, 1863–1877.* New York: Harper & Row, 1988.

——. *The Story of American Freedom.* New York: W. W. Norton, 1998.

Forbes, Flores A. *Will You Die with Me? My Life and the Black Panther Party.* New York: Atria Books, 2006.

Forman, James. *The Making of Black Revolutionaries: A Personal Account.* New York: Macmillan, 1972.

Frankl, Paulette. *Lust for Justice: The Radical Life & Law of J. Tony Serra.* Santa Fe, NM: Lightning Rod, 2010.

Franklin, Bruce H. *Vietnam and Other American Fantasies.* Amherst: University of Massachusetts Press, 2000.

Freed, Donald. *Agony in New Haven: The Trial of Bobby Seale, Erica Huggins and the Black Panther Party.* New York: Simon and Schuster, 1973.

Freire, Paulo. *Pedagogy of the Oppressed.* New York: Herder & Herder, 1970.

Friedman, Lawrence M. *A History of American Law.* New York: Simon and Schuster, 1973.

———. *Law in America: A Short History.* New York: Modern Library, 2002.

Fuchs Epstein, Cynthia. *Women in Law.* Urbana: University of Illinois Press, 1993.

Fuld, Stanley H. "The Right to Dissent: Protest in the Courtroom." *St. John's Law Review* 44, no. 4 (1970): 591–96.

Gardner, Fred. *The Unlawful Concert: An Account of the Presidio Mutiny Case.* New York: Viking Press, 1970.

Gardner, Lloyd C., and Ted Gittinger, eds. *Vietnam: The Early Decisions.* Austin: University of Texas Press, 1997.

Garfinkle, Ann M., Carol Lefcourt, and Diane B. Schulder. "Women's Servitude under Law." In *Law against the People,* edited by Robert Lefcourt, 105–22. New York: Vintage, 1971.

Garrow, David J. *Liberty and Sexuality: The Right to Privacy and the Making of* Roe v. Wade. New York: Macmillan, 1994.

Garry, Charles R. "Attacking Racism in Court before Trial." In *Minimizing Racism in Jury Trials: The Voir Dire Conducted by Charles R. Garry in People of California v. Huey P. Newton,* edited by Ann F. Ginger, xv–xxv. Berkeley: National Lawyers Guild, 1969.

———. Introduction to *Free Huey!,* by Edward M. Keating, xi–xviii. Berkeley: Ramparts Press, 1971.

———. "Political Lawyers and Their Clients." In *The Relevant Lawyers: Conversations Out of Court on Their Clients, Their Practice, Their Politics, Their Life Style,* edited by Ann F. Ginger, 68–97. New York: Simon and Schuster, 1972.

Garry, Charles R., and Art Goldberg. *Streetfighter in the Courtroom: The People's Advocate.* New York: E. P. Dutton, 1977.

Georgakas, Dan, and Marvin Surkin. *Detroit, I Do Mind Dying: A Study in Urban Revolution.* Chicago: Haymarket Books, 2012.

George, Marie-Amélie. "The Custody Crucible: The Development of Scientific Authority About Gay and Lesbian Parents." *Law and History Review* 34, no. 2 (2016): 487–529.

Gershman, Bennet. "In the Spirit of Reconciliation." In *A Time to Stir: Columbia '68,* edited by Paul Cronin, 78–82. New York: Columbia University Press, 2018.

Gilbert, David. *Love and Struggle: My Life in SDS, the Weather Underground, and Beyond.* Oakland, CA: PM Press, 2012.

Gildea, Robert, and James Mark. Introduction to *Europe's 1968: Voices of Revolt,* edited by Robert Gildea, James Mark, and Anette Warring, 1–18. Oxford: Oxford University Press, 2013.

Ginger, Ann F. *Angela Davis Case Collection: Annotated Procedural Guide and Index.* Berkeley: Meiklejohn Civil Liberties Institute, 1974.

———. *Carol Weiss King: Human Rights Lawyer, 1895–1952.* Niwot, CO: University Press of Colorado, 1993.

———, ed. *Civil Rights & Liberties Handbook: Pleadings & Practice.* Berkeley, NLG-CASL, 1963.

———. *The Law, the Supreme Court, and the People's Rights.* Woodbury, NY: Barron's, 1977.

———. *The New Draft Law: A Manual for Lawyers and Counselors.* Berkeley: National Lawyers Guild, 1968.

———. "Part of the Answer." In *Minimizing Racism in Jury Trials: The Voir Dire Conducted by Charles R. Garry in People of California v. Huey P. Newton*, edited by Ann F. Ginger, iii–v. Berkeley: National Lawyers Guild, 1969.

———. *The Relevant Lawyers: Conversations Out of Court on Their Clients, Their Practice, Their Politics, Their Life Style.* New York: Simon and Schuster, 1972.

Ginger, Ann F., and Eugene Tobin, eds. *The National Lawyers Guild: From Roosevelt through Reagan.* Philadelphia: Temple University Press, 1992.

Gitlin, Todd. *The Sixties: Years of Hope, Days of Rage.* New York: Bantam Books, 1987.

———. *The Whole World Is Watching: Mass Media in the Making and Unmaking of the New Left.* Berkeley: University of California Press, 2003.

Godfrey, Mark, and Zoé Whitley, eds. *Soul of a Nation: Art in the Age of Black Power.* London: Tate, 2017.

Goffman, Erving. *Asylums: Essays on the Social Situation of Mental Patients and Other Inmates.* New York: Doubleday, 1961.

Goldstein, Robert J. *Political Repression in Modern America from 1870 to the Present.* Urbana: University of Illinois Press, 2001.

Goluboff, Risa L. *The Lost Promise of Civil Rights.* Cambridge, MA: Harvard University Press, 2007.

Gómez, Alan E. "Resisting Living Death at Marion Federal Penitentiary, 1972." *Radical History Review*, no. 96 (2006): 58–86.

Goodell, Charles E. *Political Prisoners in America.* New York: Random House, 1973.

Goodman, Carol. "On the Oppression of Women Lawyers and Legal Workers." In *Radical Lawyers*, edited by Jonathan Black, 248–61. New York: Avon, 1971.

Goodman, Ernest. "The Shango Trial: The Lawyer, the Client, and the Jury." In *The National Lawyers Guild: From Roosevelt Through Reagan*, edited by Ann F. Ginger and Eugene Tobin, 293–98. Philadelphia: Temple University Press, 1992.

Gordon, Robert W. "New Developments in Legal Theory." In *The Politics of Law: A Progressive Critique*, edited by David Kairys, 281–93. New York: Pantheon, 1982.

Gorz, André. "On the Class Character of Science and Scientists." In *The Political Economy of Science: Ideology of/in the Natural Sciences*, edited by Hilary Rose and Steven Rose, 59–71. New York: Holmes & Meier, 1976.

Gosse, Van. *Rethinking the New Left: An Interpretative History.* New York: Palgrave Macmillan, 2005.

Graebner, William. *Patty's Got a Gun: Patricia Hearst in 1970s America.* Chicago: University of Chicago Press, 2008.

Grathwohl, Larry. *Bringing Down America: An FBI Informer with the Weathermen.* New Rochelle, NY: Arlington House, 1976.

Greenberg, David F., and Fay Stender. "The Prison as a Lawless Agency." *Buffalo Law Review* 21, no. 3 (1972): 799–838.

Greenberg, Jack. *Crusaders in the Courts: How a Dedicated Band of Lawyers Fought for the Civil Rights Revolution.* New York: Basic Books, 1994.

Grier, William H., and Price M. Cobbs. *Black Rage.* New York: Basic Books, 1968.

Grossmann, Atina. "Shadows of War and Holocaust: Jews, German Jews, and the Sixties in the United States, Reflections and Memories." *Journal of Modern Jewish Studies* 13, no. 1 (2014): 99–114.

Haas, Jeffrey. *The Assassination of Fred Hampton: How the FBI and the Chicago Police Murdered a Black Panther.* Chicago: Lawrence Hill Books, 2010.

Haft, Marilyn G. "Women in Prison: Discriminatory Practices and Some Legal Solutions." *Clearinghouse Review* 8, no. 1 (1974): 1–6.

Hakman, Nathan. "Old and New Left Activity in the Legal Order: An Interpretation." *Social Forces* 27, no. 1 (1971): 105–21.

Hall, Kermit L. *A Nation of States: Federalism at the Bar of the Supreme Court.* New York: Garland, 2000.

Hall, Simon. "Protest Movements in the 1970s: The Long 1960s." *Journal of Contemporary History* 43, no. 4 (2008): 655–72.

Halstead, Fred. *GIs Speak Out against the War: The Case of the Ft. Jackson 8.* New York: Pathfinder Press, 1970.

Handler, Joel F. *Social Movements and the Legal System: A Theory of Law Reform and Social Change.* New York: Academic Press, 1978.

Harris, Paul. *Black Rage Confronts the Law.* New York: New York University Press, 1997.

———. "You Don't Have to Love the Law to Be a Lawyer." *Guild Practitioner* 28, no. 4 (1969): 97–100.

Harris, Rutha Mae. "I Love to Sing." In *Hands on the Freedom Plow: Personal Accounts by Women in SNCC,* edited by Faith S. Holsaert, Martha Prescod Norman Noonan, Judy Richardson, Betty Garman Robinson, Jean Smith Young, and Dorothy M. Zellner, 144–46. Urbana: University of Illinois Press, 2012.

Hayden, Tom. *Reunion: A Memoir.* New York: Random House, 1988.

———. *Trial.* New York: Holt, Rinehart and Winston, 1970.

Heins, Marjorie. *Strictly Ghetto Property: The Story of Los Siete de la Raza.* Berkeley: Ramparts Press, 1972.

Henry, Milton. "Black Separation: New Africa." *Guild Practitioner* 27, no. 4 (1968): 169–75.

Hesse, Siegfried. "On Women Lawyers and Legal Secretaries." *Guild Practitioner* 28, no. 3 (1969): 73–77.

Hiestand, Fred, and Jim Smith, "Of Panthers and Prisons: An Interview with Huey P. Newton." *Guild Practitioner* 29, no. 3–4 (1972): 57–66.

Hilbink, Thomas M. "Constructing Cause Lawyering: Professionalism, Politics, and Social Change in 1960s America." PhD diss., New York University, 2006.

———. "Filling the Void: The Lawyers Constitutional Defense Committee and the 1964 Freedom Summer." Master's thesis, Columbia University, 1993.

———. "The Profession, the Grassroots and the Elite: Cause Lawyering for Civil Rights and Freedom in the Direct Action Era." In *Cause Lawyers and Social Movements*, edited by Austin Sarat and Stuart A. Scheingold, 60–83. Stanford: Stanford University Press, 2006.

Hill, Rebecca N. *Men, Mobs, and Law: Anti-Lynching and Labor Defense in U.S. Radical History.* Durham, NC: Duke University Press, 2008.

Hilliard, David, and Lewis Cole, *This Side of Glory: The Autobiography of David Hilliard and the Story of the Black Panther Party.* Boston: Little, Brown, 1993.

Hinton, Elizabeth. *From the War on Poverty to the War on Crime: The Making of Mass Incarceration in America.* Cambridge, MA: Harvard University Press, 2016.

Hoffman, Abbie. *The Autobiography of Abbie Hoffman.* New York: Four Walls Eight Windows, 2000.

Hoffman, Abbie, Bobby Seale, Rennie Davis, David Dellinger, John Froines, Tom Hayden, Jerry Rubin, and Lee Weiner. *The Conspiracy.* New York: Dell, 1969.

Hogan, Wesley C. *Many Minds, One Heart: SNCC's Dream for a New America.* Chapel Hill: University of North Carolina Press, 2007.

Holt, Len. *An Act of Conscience.* Boston: Beacon, 1965.

———. *The Summer That Didn't End: The Story of the Mississippi Civil Rights Project of 1964.* New York: Da Capo Press, 1992.

Horn, Gerd-Rainer. *The Spirit of '68: Rebellion in Western Europe and North America, 1956–1976.* New York: Oxford University Press, 2007.

Horwitz, Allan V. *PTSD: A Short History.* Baltimore: Johns Hopkins University Press, 2018.

Hull, Natalie E. H., and Peter C. Hoffer. *Roe v. Wade: The Abortion Rights Controversy in American History.* Lawrence: University Press of Kansas, 2001.

IRA Executive Committee. *Ten Years of International Red Aid in Resolutions and Documents, 1922–1932.* Moscow: IRA Executive Committee, 1932.

Israël, Liora. *À la gauche du droit. Mobilisations politiques du droit et de la justice en France (1968–1981).* Paris: Éditions EHESS, 2020.

———. *L'arme du droit.* Paris: Presses de Sciences Po, 2009.

Jackson, George. *Blood in My Eye.* New York: Random House, 1972.

———. *Soledad Brother: The Prison Letters of George Jackson.* Chicago: Lawrence Hill Books, 1994.

James, Marlise. *The People's Lawyers.* New York: Holt, Rinehart and Winston, 1973.

Jeffries, Judson L. *Huey P. Newton: Radical Theorist.* Jackson: University Press of Mississippi, 2002.

Jelinek, Donald A. *Attica Justice: The Cruel 30-Year Legacy of the Nation's Bloodiest Prison Rebellion, Which Transformed the American Prison System.* Berkeley: Jelinek, 2011.

———. "Evolution of a Radical Lawyer." *Guild Practitioner* 28, no. 1 (1969): 16–20.

———. *No Lawyers for the SLA.* n.p., n.d. but 1974.

Jenkins, J. Craig. *The Politics of Insurgency: The Farm Worker Movement in the 1960s.* New York: Columbia University Press, 1985.

Johnson, Earl, Jr. *Justice and Reform: The Formative Years of the American Legal Services Program.* London: Routledge, 2019.

Johnson, Marilynn. *Street Justice: A History of Police Violence in New York City.* Boston: Beacon, 2003.

Jones, Thai. *A Radical Line: From the Labor Movement to the Weather Underground, One Family's Century of Conscience.* New York: Free Press, 2004.

Jordan, Susan B. "The SLA: A Recurring Nightmare." *Guild Practitioner* 59, no. 2 (2002): 102–15.

Josephy, Alvin M., Jr. "The American Indian and the Bureau of Indian Affairs." In *Red Power: The American Indians' Fight for Freedom*, edited by Alvin M. Josephy Jr., Joane Nagel, and Troy Johnson, 105–40. Lincoln: University of Nebraska Press, 1971.

Kairys, David. Introduction to *The Politics of Law: A Progressive Critique*, edited by David Kairys, 1–8. New York: Pantheon, 1982.

——. *Philadelphia Freedom: Memoir of a Civil Rights Lawyer.* Ann Arbor: University of Michigan Press, 2008.

Kairys, David, Jay Schulman, and Sid Harring, eds. *The Jury System: New Methods for Reducing Prejudice. A Manual for Lawyers, Legal Workers, and Social Scientists.* Philadelphia: Philadelphia Resistance Print, 1975.

Kalba, Kas, and Jay Beste. "Lawyers and Revolutionaries: Notes from the National Conference on Political Justice." *Yale Review of Law and Social Action* 1, no. 1 (1970): 49–54.

Kalman, Laura. *The Strange Career of Legal Liberalism.* New Haven, CT: Yale University Press, 1998.

Karlen, Delmar. "Disorder in the Courtroom." *Southern California Law Review* 44, no. 4 (1971): 996–1035.

Kask, Melanie M. "Soul Mates: The Prison Letters of Eldridge Cleaver and Beverly Axelrod." PhD diss., University of California, Berkeley, 2003.

Kaufman, Mary M. "War Crimes and Cold-War 'Conspiracies.'" In *The Relevant Lawyers: Conversations Out of Court on Their Clients, Their Practice, Their Politics, Their Life Style*, edited by Ann F. Ginger, 184–215. New York: Simon and Schuster, 1972.

Kaufman, Robert. "Ruchell Magee." In *If They Come in the Morning*, edited by Angela Y. Davis, 155–60. New York: Third Press, 1971.

Keating, Edward M. *Free Huey!* Berkeley: Ramparts Press, 1971.

Kelman, Mark. *A Guide to Critical Legal Studies.* Cambridge, MA: Harvard University Press, 1987.

——. "The Origins of Crime and Criminal Violence." In *The Politics of Law: A Progressive Critique*, edited by David Kairys, 214–29. New York: Pantheon, 1982.

Kempton Murray. *The Briar Patch: The Trial of the Panther 21.* New York: De Capo Press, 1991.

Kennedy, Florynce. *Color Me Flo: My Hard Life and Good Times.* Englewood Cliffs, NJ: Prentice-Hall, 1976.

——. "The Whorehouse Theory of Law." In *Law against the People*, edited by Robert Lefcourt, 81–89. New York: Vintage, 1971.

Kennedy, Michael J. "The Civil Liberties Lie." In *Law against the People*, edited by Robert Lefcourt, 140–49. New York: Vintage, 1971.

Kesey, Ken. *One Flew over the Cuckoo's Nest.* New York: New American Library, 1962.

King, Martin Luther, Jr. *A Testament of Hope: The Essential Writings of Martin Luther King, Jr.* San Francisco: Harper & Row, 1986.

Kinoy, Arthur. "Brief Remarks on *Dombrowski v. Pfister*—a New Path in Constitutional Litigation?" *Guild Practitioner* 26, no. 1 (1967): 7–11.

——. *Rights on Trial: The Odyssey of a People's Lawyer.* Cambridge, MA: Harvard University Press, 1983.

——. "The Role of the Radical Lawyer and Teacher of Law." In *Law against the People*, edited by Robert Lefcourt, 276–99. New York: Vintage, 1971.

Kirchheimer, Otto. *Political Justice: The Use of Legal Procedure for Political Ends.* Princeton, NJ: Princeton University Press, 1961.

Klebanow, Diana, and Franklin L. Jonas. *People's Lawyers: Crusaders for Justice in American History.* Armonk, NY: M.E. Sharpe, 2003.

Kluger, Richard. *Simple Justice: The History of* Brown v. Board of Education *and Black America's Struggle for Equality.* New York: Knopf, 2004.

Kohn, Stephen M. *Jailed for Peace: The History of American Draft Law Violators, 1658–1985.* Westport, CT: Greenwood Press, 1986.

Kraft, Sandra. "Contention in the Courtroom: The Legal Dimension of the 1960s Protests in the German and US Student Movements." *Journal of Contemporary History* 50, no. 4 (2015): 805–32.

Krenshaw, Kimberlé, Neil Gotanda, Gary Peller, and Kendall Thomas, eds. *Critical Race Theory: The Key Writings that Formed the Movement.* New York: New Press, 1995.

Kunstler, William M. *Deep in My Heart.* New York: William Morrow, 1966.

——. *My Life as a Radical Lawyer.* With Sheila Isenberg. New York: Birch Lane Press, 1994.

——. "Open Resistance: In Defense of the Movement." In *Law against the People*, edited by Robert Lefcourt, 267–75. New York: Vintage, 1971.

——. "Some Thoughts about the Berrigans et al." In *Witness of the Berrigans*, edited by Stephen Halpert and Tom Murray, 166–72. Garden City, NY: Doubleday, 1972.

La Botz, Dan. "The Tumultuous Teamsters of the 1970s." In *Rebel Rank and File: Labor Militancy and Revolt from Below during the Long 1970s*, edited by Aaron Brenner, Robert Brenner, and Cal Winslow, 199–226. London: Verso, 2010.

Lahav, Pnina. "The Chicago Conspiracy Trial: Character and Judicial Discretion." *University of Colorado Law Review* 71, no. 5 (2000): 1327–64.

Lane, Mark. *Rush to Judgment: A Critique of the Warren Commission's Inquiry into the Murders of President John F. Kennedy, Officer J. D. Tippit and Lee Harvey Oswald.* New York: Holt, Rinehart and Winston, 1966.

Langum, David J. *William M. Kunstler: The Most Hated Lawyer in America.* New York: New York University Press, 1999.

Latner, Teishan A. *Cuban Revolution in America: Havana and the Making of a United States Left, 1968–1992.* Chapel Hill: University of North Carolina Press, 2017.

"A Lawyer for Hire." *American Bar Association Journal* 56, no. 6 (1970): 552.

Lefcourt, Carol H. *Women and the Law.* New York: Clark Boardman, 1984.

Lefcourt, Gerald B. "The Radical Lawyer under Attack." In *Law against the People*, edited by Robert Lefcourt, 253–66. New York: Vintage, 1971.

Lefcourt, Robert. "The First Law Commune." In *Law against the People*, edited by Robert Lefcourt, 310–26. New York: Vintage, 1971.

——. "Law against the People." In *Law against the People*, edited by Robert Lefcourt, 21–37. New York: Vintage, 1971.

——, ed. *Law against the People: Essays to Demystify Law, Order and the Courts.* New York: Vintage, 1971.

Lenin [Vladimir Ilyich Ulyanov]. *Collected Works.* Moscow: Progress, 1977.

Leonard, Norman. "The Movement Lawyer as Seen by One over Fifty." *Guild Practitioner* 28, no. 1 (1969): 14–16.

Levy, Peter B. *The Great Uprising: Race Riots in Urban America during the 1960s.* Cambridge: Cambridge University Press, 2018.

Lewis, John. *Walking with the Wind: A Memoir of the Movement.* With Mike D'Orso. New York: Simon and Schuster, 1998.

Liberatore, Paul. *The Road to Hell: The True Story of George Jackson, Stephen Bingham, and the San Quentin Massacre.* New York: Atlantic Monthly Press, 1996.

Lieberman, Robbie, and Clarence Lang, eds. *Anticommunism and the African American Freedom Movement: Another Side of the Story.* New York: Palgrave Macmillan, 2009.

Littlejohn, Bruce. "Legal Vandalism." *Trial* 7, no. 1 (1971): 15–16.

Losier, Toussaint. "Against 'Law and Order' Lockup: The 1970 NYC Jail Rebellions." *Race & Class* 59, no. 1 (2017): 3–35.

Lukas, Anthony J. *The Barnyard Epithet and Other Obscenities: Notes on the Chicago Conspiracy Trial.* New York: Harper & Row, 1970.

Lyons, Oren. "When You Talk about Client Relationships, You Are Talking about the Future of Nations." In *Rethinking Indian Law*, edited by National Lawyers Guild Committee on Native American Struggles, iv–vii. New York: NLG, 1982.

Macdonald, Dwight. Introduction to *The Tales of Hoffman*, edited by Mark L. Levine, George C. McNamee, and Daniel Greenberg, xi–xxiv. New York: Bantam Books, 1970.

Malatesta, Maria. "Défenses militantes. Avocats et violence politique dans l'Italie des années 1970 et 1980." *Le Mouvement Social* 3, no. 240 (2012): 85–104.

Marcuse, Herbert. *An Essay on Liberation.* Boston: Beacon, 1969.

Marwick, Arthur. *The Sixties: Cultural Revolution in Britain, France, Italy, and the United States, c. 1958–c. 1974.* Oxford: Oxford University Press, 1998.

Marx, Karl. *The Class Struggles in France (1848–1850).* London: Martin Lawrence, 1895.

———. "Debates on the Law on Thefts of Wood." In *The Sociology of Law: Classical and Contemporary Perspectives*, edited by A. Javier Treviño, 128–39. New York: Routledge, 2007.

Matthiessen, Peter. *In the Spirit of Crazy Horse*. New York: Viking Press, 1983.

Matusow, Allen J. *The Unraveling of America: A History of Liberalism in the 1960s*. New York: Harper & Row, 1986.

McCann, Michael W. "Law and Social Movements." In *The Blackwell Companion to Law and Society*, edited by Austin Sarat, 506–22. London: Blackwell, 2004.

McCann, Michael W., and Jeffrey Dudas. "Retrenchment . . . and Resurgence? Mapping the Changing Context of Movement Lawyering in the United States." In *Cause Lawyers and Social Movements*, edited by Austin Sarat and Stuart A. Scheingold, 37–59. Stanford: Stanford University Press, 2006.

McLean, Nancy. *Freedom Is Not Enough: The Opening of the American Workplace*. Cambridge, MA: Harvard University Press, 2006.

McLellan, Vin, and Paul Avery. *The Voices of Guns: The Definitive and Dramatic Story of the Twenty-Two-Month Career of the Symbionese Liberation Army, One of the Most Bizarre Chapters in the History of the American Left*. New York: Putnam, 1977.

McMahon, Kevin J. *Nixon's Court: His Challenge to Judicial Liberalism and Its Political Consequences*. Chicago: University of Chicago Press, 2011.

Meconis, Charles. *With Clumsy Grace: The American Catholic Left, 1961–1975*. New York: Seabury Press, 1979.

Medsger, Betty. *The Burglary: The Discovery of J. Edgar Hoover's Secret FBI*. New York: Knopf, 2014.

Melendez, Miguel. *We Took the Streets: Fighting for Latino Rights with the Young Lords*. New York: St. Martin's Press, 2003.

Melville, Samuel. *Letters from Attica*. New York: Morrow, 1972.

Meranto, Oneida. "Litigation as Rebellion." In *Social Movements and American Political Institutions*, edited by Anne N. Costain and Andrew S. McFarland, 216–30. Lanham, MD: Rowman & Littlefield, 1998.

Millet, Kate. *Sexual Politics*. Garden City, NY: Doubleday, 1970.

Minow, Martha. "Political Lawyering: An Introduction." *Harvard Civil Rights-Civil Liberties Law Review* 31, no. 2 (1996): 287–96.

Mitford, Jessica. *Kind and Usual Punishment: The Prison Business*. New York: Knopf, 1973.

———. *The Trial of Dr. Spock: The Rev. William Sloane Coffin, Jr., Michael Ferber, Mitchell Goodman, and Marcus Raskin*. New York: Knopf, 1969.

Moody, Kim. "Understanding the Rank-and-File Rebellion in the Long 1970s." In *Rebel Rank and File: Labor Militancy and Revolt from Below during the Long 1970s*, edited by Aaron Brenner, Robert Brenner, and Cal Winslow, 105–46. London: Verso, 2010.

"The Movement and the Lawyer." Pt. I. *Guild Practitioner* 28, no. 1 (1969): 1–10.

"The Movement and the Lawyer." Pt. II. *Guild Practitioner* 28, no. 1 (1969): 10–13.

Muñoz, Carlos, Jr. *Youth, Identity, Power: The Chicano Movement*. London: Verso, 1989.

Nadasen, Premilla. *Welfare Warriors: The Welfare Rights Movement in the United States.* New York: Routledge, 2004.

Naison, Mark D. *White Boy: A Memoir.* Philadelphia: Temple University Press, 2002.

National Advisory Committee on Criminal Justice Standards and Goals. *Disorders and Terrorism: Report of the Task Force on Disorders and Terrorism.* Washington, DC: U.S. Government Printing Office, 1977.

Navasky, Victor S. *Kennedy Justice.* New York: Atheneum, 1971.

"The New Public Interest Lawyers." *Yale Law Journal* 79, no. 6 (1970): 1069–1152.

New York Special Commission on Attica. *Attica: The Official Report of the New York State Special Commission on Attica.* New York: Bantam Books, 1972.

Nixon, Richard M. *No More Vietnams.* New York: Arbor House, 1985.

NLG. "Convention Resolutions." *Guild Practitioner* 24, no. 4 (1965): 137–48.

NLG, Grand Jury Defense Office. *Representation of Witnesses before Federal Grand Juries: A Manual for Attorneys.* San Francisco: NLG, 1974.

NLG, Middle East Delegation, 1977. *Treatment of Palestinians in Israeli-Occupied West Bank and Gaza*, New York: NLG, 1978.

NLG, National Conference of Black Lawyers, Minority Admission Summer Project. *Affirmative Action in Crisis: A Handbook for Activists*, Detroit: NLG, 1977.

Nordmann, Joë, and Anne Brunel. *Aux vents de l'histoire.* Arles: Actes Sud, 1996.

Norgren, Jill. *Stories from Trailblazing Women Lawyers: Lives in the Law.* New York: New York University Press, 2018.

Onaci, Edward. *Free the Land: The Republic of New Afrika and the Pursuit of a Black Nation-State.* Chapel Hill: University of North Carolina Press, 2020.

Organizer's Manual Collective. *The Organizer's Manual.* New York: Bantam Books, 1971.

Orrick, William H., Jr. *Shut It Down! A College in Crisis: San Francisco State College, October, 1968 to April, 1969: A Staff Report to the National Commission on the Causes and Prevention of Violence.* Washington, DC: U.S. Government Printing Office, 1969.

Parenti, Christian. *Lockdown America: Police and Prisons in the Age of Crisis.* London: Verso, 1999.

Parsons, David L. *Dangerous Grounds: Antiwar Coffeehouses and Military Dissent in the Vietnam Era.* Chapel Hill: University of North Carolina Press, 2017.

Pashukanis, Evgeny B. *The General Theory of Law and Marxism.* London-New York: Routledge, 2002

Pearlman, Lise. *Call Me Phaedra: The Life and Times of Movement Lawyer Fay Stender.* Berkeley: Regent Press, 2018.

———. *The Sky's the Limit: People v. Newton. The Real Trial of the 20th Century?* Berkeley: Regent Press, 2012.

Pell, Eve, and Prison Law Project, eds. *Maximum Security: Letters from California's Prisons.* New York: Dutton, 1972.

Peters, Shawn F. *The Catonsville Nine: An American Story.* New York: Oxford University Press, 2012.

Peterson, Richard E., and John A. Bilorusky. *May 1970: The Campus Aftermath of Cambodia and Kent State.* Berkeley: Carnegie Foundation for the Advancement of Teaching, 1971.

Pizzolato, Nicola. "Transnational Radicals: Labour Dissent and Political Activism in Detroit and Turin (1950–1970)." *International Review of Social History* 56, no. 1 (2011): 1–30.

Platt, Anthony. *The Politics of Riot Commissions, 1917–1970: A Collection of Official Reports and Critical Essays.* New York: Macmillan, 1971.

Poka, John. "Impressions of a Rookie Cop." In *A Time to Stir: Columbia '68,* edited by Paul Cronin, 263–68. New York: Columbia University Press, 2018.

Popper, Martin. "The Goodmans and Schwerners Go to the Oval Office." In *The National Lawyers Guild: From Roosevelt through Reagan,* edited by Ann F. Ginger and Eugene Tobin, 207–9. Philadelphia: Temple University Press, 1992.

President's Commission on Campus Unrest. *The Report of the President's Commission on Campus Unrest.* Washington, DC: U.S. Government Printing Office, 1970.

Rabinowitz, Victor. *Unrepentant Leftist: A Lawyer's Memoir.* Urbana: University of Illinois Press, 1996.

Rabinowitz, Victor, and Tim Ledwith, eds. *A History of the National Lawyers Guild, 1937–1987.* New York: National Lawyers Guild Foundation, 1987.

Randolph, Sherie M. *Florynce "Flo" Kennedy: The Life of a Black Feminist Radical.* Chapel Hill: University of North Carolina Press, 2015.

———. "'Not to Rely Completely on the Courts': Florynce 'Flo' Kennedy and Black Feminist Leadership in the Reproductive Rights Battle, 1969–1971." *Journal of Women's History* 27, no. 1 (2015): 136–60.

Raskin, Jonah. *For the Hell of It: The Life and Times of Abbie Hoffman.* Berkeley: University of California Press, 1998.

Ratner, Michael. *Moving the Bar: My Life as a Radical Lawyer.* New York: OR Books, 2021.

Redish, Martin H. *The Logic of Persecution: Free Expression and the McCarthy Era.* Stanford: Stanford University Press, 2005.

Reverby, Susan M. *Co-conspirator for Justice: The Revolutionary Life of Dr. Alan Berkman.* Chapel Hill: University of North Carolina Press, 2020.

Reynolds, Mike. "Hats and Bats." In *A Time to Stir: Columbia '68,* edited by Paul Cronin, 274–76. New York: Columbia University Press, 2018.

Rivers, Daniel W. "'In the Best Interest of the Child': Lesbian and Gay Parenting Custody Cases, 1967–1985." *Journal of Social History* 43, no. 4 (2010): 917–43.

———. *Radical Relations: Lesbian Mothers, Gay Fathers, and Their Children in the United States since World War II.* Chapel Hill: University of North Carolina Press, 2013.

Robb, Matthew Z. *Dean Robb: An Unlikely Radical.* Suttons Bay, MI: Lost Prairie Press, 2010.

Rockwell, David N. "The Education of the Capitalist Lawyer: The Law School." In *Law against the People: Essays to Demystify Law, Order and the Courts,* edited by Robert Lefcourt, 90–104. New York: Vintage, 1971.

Rogers, Kim L. *Righteous Lives: Narratives of the New Orleans Civil Rights Movement.* New York: New York University Press, 1993.

Rorabaugh, William J. *Berkeley at War: The 1960s.* New York: Oxford University Press, 1989.

Rosenberg, Gerald N. *The Hollow Hope: Can Courts Bring about Social Change?* Chicago: University of Chicago Press, 2008.

Rosenfeld, Seth. *Subversives: The FBI's War on Student Radicals, and Reagan's Rise to Power.* New York: Picador, 2013.

Rostow, Eugene V., ed. *Is Law Dead?* New York: Simon and Schuster, 1971.

Rowland, Hal H. "The Crucial Code." *Trial* 7, no. 1 (1971): 17.

Ruben, Albert. *The People's Lawyer: The Center for Constitutional Rights and the Fight for Social Justice, from Civil Rights to Guantánamo.* New York: Monthly Review Press, 2011.

Rubin, Jerry. *Do It! Scenarios of the Revolution.* New York: Simon and Schuster, 1970.

Rudd, Mark, *Underground: My Life with SDS and the Weathermen.* New York: HarperCollins, 2009.

Sale, Kirkpatrick. *SDS.* New York: Vintage Books, 1973.

Sánchez-Cuenca, Ignacio. *The Historical Roots of Political Violence: Revolutionary Terrorism in Affluent Countries.* Cambridge: Cambridge University Press, 2019.

Sandarg, Robert. "Jean Genet and the Black Panther Party." *Journal of Black Studies* 16, no. 3 (1986): 269–82.

Sarat, Austin, and Stuart A. Scheingold. "What Cause Lawyers Do *for*, and *to*, Social Movements: An Introduction." In *Cause Lawyers and Social Movements*, edited by Austin Sarat and Stuart A. Scheingold, 1–34. Stanford: Stanford University Press, 2006.

Sartre, Jean-Paul. *Saint Genet: Actor and Martyr.* Minneapolis: University of Minnesota Press, 2012.

Savoy, Paul N. "Toward a New Politics of Legal Education." *Yale Law Journal* 79, no. 3 (1970): 444–504.

Sayer, John W. *Ghost Dancing the Law: The Wounded Knee Trials.* Cambridge, MA: Harvard University Press, 1997.

Scheingold, Stuart A. *The Politics of Rights: Lawyers, Public Policy, and Political Change.* Ann Arbor: University of Michigan Press, 2010.

Schlanger, Margo. "Civil Rights Injunctions over Time: A Case Study of Jail and Prison Court Orders." *New York University Law Review* 81, no. 2 (2006): 550–630.

Schmalzer, Sigrid, Daniel S. Chard, and Alyssa Botelhox, eds. *Science for the People: Documents from America's Movement of Radical Scientists.* Amherst: University of Massachusetts Press, 2018.

Schornhorst, F. Thomas. "The Lawyer and the Terrorist: Another Ethical Dilemma." *Indiana Law Journal* 55, no. 4 (1978): 679–702.

Schrecker, Ellen. *Many Are the Crimes: McCarthyism in America.* Princeton, NJ: Princeton University Press, 1998.

Schulman, Jay, Phillip Shaver, Robert Colman, Barbara Emrich, and Richard Christie. "Recipe for a Jury." *Psychology Today* 6, no. 12 (1973): 33–84.

Schultz, John. *The Chicago Conspiracy Trial.* Chicago: University of Chicago Press, 2009.

Seale, Bobby. *A Lonely Rage: The Autobiography of Bobby Seale.* New York: Times Books, 1978.

Serra, J. Tony. *The Green, Yellow, and Purple Years in the Life of a Radical Lawyer.* Kensington, CA: Grizzly Peak Press, 2014.

Shames, Stephen, and Bobby Seale. *Power to the People: The World of the Black Panthers.* New York: Abrams, 2016.

Sherrill, Robert. *Military Justice Is to Justice as Military Music Is to Music.* New York: Harper & Row, 1970.

Shklar, Judith N. *Legalism.* Cambridge, MA: Harvard University Press, 1964.

Smith, Michael S. *Lawyers You'll Like: Putting Human Rights First.* New York: Smyrna Press, 1999.

———. *Notebook of a Sixties Lawyer: An Unrepentant Memoir and Selected Writings.* Brooklyn, NY: Smyrna Press, 1992.

Smith, Paul C., and Robert A. Warrior. *Like a Hurricane: The Indian Movement from Alcatraz to Wounded Knee.* New York: New Press, 1996.

Smith, Sherry L. *Hippies, Indians, and the Fight for Red Power.* Oxford: Oxford University Press, 2012.

SNCC. *The Story of SNCC.* New York: SNCC, 1966.

Sobieski, John L., Jr. "Civil Rights Act of 1871." In *Encyclopedia of American Civil Rights and Liberties: Revised and Expanded Edition*, edited by Kara E. Stooksbury, John M. Scheb II, and Otis H. Stephens Jr., 152–53. Santa Barbara, CA: ABC-Clio, 2017.

Spriggs, Kent. "'Summer Vacation' in Mississippi." In *Voices of Civil Rights Lawyers: Reflections from the Deep South, 1964–1980*, edited by Kent Sprigg, 141–46. Gainesville: University Press of Florida, 2017.

Stanton, Shelby. *The Rise and the Fall of an American Army: U.S. Ground Forces in Vietnam, 1965–1973.* Novato, CA: Presidio, 1985.

Starr, Meg. "'Hit Them Harder': Leadership, Solidarity, and the Puerto Rican Independence Movement." In *The Hidden 1970s: Histories of Radicalism*, edited by Dan Berger, 135–54. London: Rutgers, 2010.

State of California, Board of Corrections. *Report to Governor Ronald Reagan on Violence in California Prisons.* Sacramento, CA: The Board of Corrections, 1971.

Stavis, Morton. "The Mississippi Freedom Democratic Party Challenge." In *The National Lawyers Guild: From Roosevelt through Reagan*, edited by Ann F. Ginger and Eugene Tobin, 212–14. Philadelphia: Temple University Press, 1992.

Steel, Lewis M. *The Butler's Child: An Autobiography.* New York: Thomas Dunne Books, 2016.

Stender, Fay. Introduction to *Maximum Security: Letters from California's Prisons*, edited by Eve Pell and Prison Law Project, 9–13. New York: Dutton, 1972.

———. "Prisoners' Rights and Community Concern." In *The Relevant Lawyers: Conversations Out of Court on Their Clients, Their Practice, Their Politics, Their*

Life Style, edited by Ann F. Ginger, 275–88. New York: Simon and Schuster, 1972.

Stern, Susan. *With the Weathermen: The Personal Journal of a Revolutionary Woman*. New Brunswick, NJ: Rutgers University Press, 2007.

Stevens, Robert. *Law School: Legal Education in America from the 1850s to the 1980s*. Chapel Hill: The University of North Carolina Press, 1987.

"Summer Project: Mississippi, 1964; An Account of the National Lawyers Guild Program of Legal Assistance to Civil Rights Workers in Mississippi: Summer, 1964." *Guild Practitioner* 24, no. 2 (1965): 32–43.

Thomas, Tom. "The Second Battle of Chicago." In *Weatherman*, edited by Harold Jacobs, 196–226. New York: Ramparts Press, 1970.

Thompson, Heather A. *Blood in the Water: The Attica Prison Uprising of 1971 and Its Legacy*. New York: Pantheon Books, 2016.

———. *Whose Detroit? Politics, Labor, and Race in a Modern American City*. Ithaca, NY: Cornell University Press, 2017.

Tigar, Michael E. *Fighting Injustice*. Chicago: American Bar Association, 2002.

———. *Law and the Rise of Capitalism*. New York: Monthly Review Press, 1977.

———. "Lawyer's Role in Resistance." *Guild Practitioner* 27, no. 4 (1968): 196–200.

Tilsen, Kenneth E. "Fair and Equal Justice: The FBI, Wounded Knee and Politics." *Quaere* 3, no. 1 (1976): 1–9.

———. "US Courts and Native Americans at Wounded Knee." *Guild Practitioner* 31, no. 2 (1974): 61–69.

Tocqueville, Alexis de. *Democracy in America*. Vol. 1. New York: Vintage, 1990.

Tractenberg, Paul. *A Centennial History of Rutgers Law School in Newark: Opening a Thousand Doors*. Charleston, SC: History Press, 2010.

Tullberg, Steven, and Robert T. Coulter. "The Failure of Indian Rights Advocacy: Are Lawyers to Blame?" In *Rethinking Indian Law*, edited by National Lawyers Guild Committee on Native American Struggles, 51–56. New York: NLG, 1982.

U.S. Department of Justice. *Disruption in the Courtroom and the Publicly Controversial Defendant*. Washington, DC: U.S. Department of Justice, 1975.

U.S. House of Representatives. *Investigation of Attempts to Subvert the United States Armed Services: Hearings before the Committee on Internal Security*. Pt. 2, 92nd Cong. 2nd Sess. (1972–72). Washington, DC: U.S. Government Printing Office, 1972.

Useem, Bert, and Peter Kimball. *States of Siege: U.S. Prison Riots, 1971–1986*. New York: Oxford University Press, 1991.

U.S. House of Representatives. *Communist Legal Subversion: The Role of the Communist Lawyer: Hearings before House Committee on Un-American Activities*. 86th Cong. 1st Sess. (1959). Washington, DC: U.S. Government Printing Office, 1959.

———. *FBI Authorization: Hearings before the Subcommittee on Civil and Constitutional Rights of the Committee on the Judiciary*. 97th Cong. 1st Sess. (1981). Washington, DC: U.S. Government Printing Office, 1981.

———. *Investigation of Attempts to Subvert the United States Armed Services: Hearings before the Committee on Internal Security.* Pt. 1, 92nd Cong. 1st Sess. (1971). Washington, DC: U.S. Government Printing Office, 1971.

———. *Investigation of Attempts to Subvert the United States Armed Services: Hearings before the Committee on Internal Security.* Pt. 3, 92nd Cong. 2nd Sess. (1972). Washington, DC: U.S. Government Printing Office, 1972.

———. *Report on the National Lawyers Guild: Legal Bulwark of the Communist Party: Hearings before House Committee on Un-American Activities.* 81st Cong. 2d Sess. (1950). Washington, DC: U.S. Government Printing Office, 1950.

———. *The Symbionese Liberation Army: A Study Prepared for the Use of the Committee on Internal Security.* 93rd Cong. 2d Sess. (1974). Washington, DC: U.S. Government Printing Office, 1974.

———. *Terrorism: A Staff Study Prepared by the Committee on Internal Security.* 93rd Cong. 2nd Sess. (1974). Washington, DC: U.S. Government Printing Office, 1974.

U.S. National Advisory Commission on Civil Disorders. *Report of the National Advisory Commission on Civil Disorders.* Washington, DC: U.S. Government Printing Office, 1968.

U.S. Senate. *Riots, Civil and Criminal Disorders: Hearings before the Permanent Subcommittee on Investigations of the Committee on Government Operations.* 91st Cong. 2nd Sess. (1970). Washington, DC: U.S. Government Printing Office, 1970.

Vanderwicken, Peter. "The Angry Young Lawyers." *Fortune* 84, no. 3 (1971): 74–77, 125–27.

Varon, Jeremy. *Bringing the War Home: The Weather Underground, the Red Army Faction and Revolutionary Violence in the Sixties and Seventies.* Berkeley: University of California Press, 2004.

Vergès, Jacques. *De la stratégie judiciaire.* Paris: Éditions de Minuit, 1968.

Wald, Karen. "The San Quentin Six Case: Perspective and Analysis." *Crime and Social Justice* no. 6 (1976): 58–68.

Walker, Daniel. *Rights in Conflict: The Violent Confrontation of Demonstrators and Police in the Parks and Streets of Chicago during the Week of the Democratic National Convention of 1968.* New York: Bantam Books, 1968.

Walker, Doris B. "The Class Role of US Courts." *Guild Practitioner* 31, no. 2 (1974): 41–51.

Walker, Samuel. *In Defense of American Liberties: A History of the ACLU.* New York: Oxford University Press, 1990.

Wark, Colin, and John F. Galliher. *Progressive Lawyers under Siege: Moral Panic during the McCarthy Years.* London: Lexington Books, 2015.

Weather Underground. *Prairie Fire: The Politics of Revolutionary Anti-Imperialism: Political Statement of the Weather Underground.* Brooklyn: Prairie Fire Distributing Committee, 1974.

Weinrib, Laura. *The Taming of Free Speech: America's Civil Liberties Compromise.* Cambridge, MA: Harvard University Press, 2016.

Wells, Tom. *The War Within: America's Battle over Vietnam.* Berkeley: University of California Press, 1994.

Weyler, Rex. *Blood of the Land: The Government and Corporate War against the American Indian Movement.* New York: Everest House, 1982.

Wicker, Tom. *A Time to Die: The Attica Prison Revolt.* Lincoln: University of Nebraska Press, 1994.

Wiener, Jon, ed. *Conspiracy in the Streets: The Extraordinary Trial of the Chicago Eight.* New York: New Press, 2006.

Wilkerson, Cathy. *Flying Close to the Sun: My Life and Times as a Weatherman.* New York: Seven Stories Press, 2007.

Willard, Marcel. *La défense accuse . . . de Babeuf à Dimitrov.* Paris: Éditions Sociales Internationales, 1938.

Windham, Lane. *Knocking on Labor's Door: Union Organizing in the 1970s and the Roots of a New Economic Divide.* Chapel Hill: University of North Carolina Press, 2017.

Winslow, Cal. "Overview: The Rebellion from Below, 1965–81." In *Rebel Rank and File: Labor Militancy and Revolt from Below during the Long 1970s*, edited by Aaron Brenner, Robert Brenner, and Cal Winslow, 1–35. London: Verso, 2010.

Yoder, Traci. *Breach of Privilege: Spying on Lawyers in the United States.* New York: NLG, 2014.

Zimroth, Peter L. *Perversions of Justice: The Prosecution and Acquittal of the Panther 21.* New York: Viking Press, 1974.

Zinn, Howard. *SNCC: The New Abolitionists.* Boston: Beacon, 1965.

Video Recordings

Alk, Howard, and Mike Gray, dir. *The Murder of Fred Hampton*, 1971.

Bezjian, Roxanne, dir. *Charles Garry: Streetfighter in the Courtroom*, 1991.

Kitchell, Mark, dir. *Berkeley in the Sixties*, 1990.

Kunstler, Emily, and Sarah Kunstler, dirs. *William Kunstler: Disturbing the Universe*, 2009.

Lichtenstein, Brad, dir. *Ghosts of Attica*, 2001.

McCray, Judith, dir. *Mississippi, America*, 1995.

Payne, Roz B., dir. *What We Want, What We Believe: The Black Panther Party Library*, 2006.

Sachs, Lynne, dir. *Investigation of a Flame*, 2001.

Index

134, 188, 201, 257, 355n4; legal system
and structural racism against, 93–94,
104–6, 107–8, 178–79; mass defense
for protestors, 44–45; of Muslim
faith, 90, 168–69, 193, 194, 210;
Newark riots and student protests by,
131; underrepresentation in legal
profession, 10, 127, 132, 133, 319n72;
voter registration campaigns for,
19–20. *See also* racism; *names of
specific organizations and persons*
Black Cultural Association, 213
Black Guerrilla Family (BGF), 216–17
Black jurors, 10
Black Liberation Army (BLA), 166
blacklisting, 264
Black Muslims, 90, 168–69, 193, 194,
210
Black nationalism, 168, 170, 213
Black Panther (publication), 82
Black Panther Party (BPP): arrests and
bail of, 60; Attica prison revolt and,
197, 198; Axelrod and, 81–82; establishment of, 54–55; FBI surveillance of,
249; Garry as lawyer for, 80, 82,
92–94, 176, 250, 252–53, 273–74; New
York branch of, 113; Panther 6 case,
124; Panther 21 case, 110, 111–13; PLO
and, 123–24; policing and armed
self-defense of, 249–51; prisoner
affiliation with, 193; raid on, and
murders of, 123–24, 250, 316n21,
332n61; sexism in, 82, 105; Stender and,
82–83; ten-point program of, 94, 104;
Turco and, 269–70; on Weatherman/
Weather Underground actions, 112–13,
161. *See also names of specific persons*
Black People in Defense of Angela Davis
(organization), 186
Black Rage (Cobbs), 150
black rage, as legal defense strategy,
102, 150, 313n75. *See also* legal
defense strategies
Black Studies, as academic department,
58

Blauner, Robert, 94
Bloch, Ernst S., 187
Blood in My Eye (Jackson), 182
Boalt Law School (UC Berkeley), 132,
303n34
Böll, Heinrich T., 187
Bolshevik Revolution, 146
Bond, H. Julian, 178
Bonora, Beth, 206
Borus, Linda, 338n56
Boston Five trial, 90
Boudin, Kathy, 161, 166, 167, 327n94
Boudin, Leonard B., 68, 90–91, 150, 158,
267, 302n27, 310n10, 326n82, 327n94,
327n103
Boudin, Louis B., 68
BPP. *See* Black Panther Party
Brake, Robert, 153–54
Branch Queens House of Detention, 173
Brando, Marlon, 232, 236
Branton, Leo, Jr., 188, 189
Braverman, Maurice L., 264, 350n60
Brennan, William J., Jr., 16
Brewster, Kingman, Jr., 105
Broege, E. Carl, 159
Brooklyn Community Law Office,
124–25, 131
Brooklyn Draft Resistance Union, 141
Brooks, Edward G., 216
Brotherhood of Eternal Love, 85
Brotsky, Allan, 188
Brown, Dorris A. "Dee," 230, 236
Brown, E. Gerald "Jerry," Jr., 226
Brown, H. Rap, 93, 252, 310n12
Brown, John, 17
Brown, R. Jess, 10
Brownell, Herbert, Jr., 6
Brown v. Board of Education, 12, 75
Buckley, Gail Lumet, 112
BUILD (organization), 206, 337n51
Bureau of Indian Affairs (BIA), 228,
229, 230–31
Burger, Warren E., 116
Burnette, Robert, 234
Burnham, Margaret A., 188

Kunstler, William "Bill": as AIM lawyer, 233, 234–36, 239; as Attica prisoners lawyer, 193, 195–99, 202–3, 207; as BPP lawyer, 110, 166; as Catonsville Nine lawyer, 157; as CCR founder, 65; as Chicago Eight lawyer, 96, 98, 99, 100, 107–8; civil rights movement and, 12, 17, 23, 30, 32–33, 34–35; courthouse protest by, 87; legal purpose of, 30; on role of radical lawyers, 77, 80; on SLA defense, 215; on Soledad Brothers case, 178; student protests and, 61; surveillance of, 353n101; Weather Underground and, 85, 162–63, 164

Kurland, Philip B., 73–74, 281

labor lawyers, 4, 219–22
labor union movement, 218–27, 342n31
Lafferty, James "Jim," 140
Lamont, Corliss, 302n27
Lane, Mark, 234–36
La Raza National Law Students Association, 130
La Raza Studies, as academic department, 58
Law Center for Constitutional Rights (LCCR), 65
law communes, 110–11, 118–22. *See also* alternative law practices
Law Day, 87, 88
Law Enforcement Assistance Act (1965), 248
Law Enforcement Assistance Administration (LEAA), 248, 254
Law Students Civil Rights Research Council (LSCRRC), 27, 65–66
lawyers. *See* radical lawyers
Lawyers Alliance for New York, 336n31
Lawyers' Committee for Civil Rights Under Law, 26
Lawyers Constitutional Defense Committee (LCDC), 26–27
Lawyers Military Defense Committee, 152

lawyers' protest, 87–88, 100
Lawyers Selective Service Panel, 143
Leary, Timothy F., 85
Lefcourt, Carol, 111, 118, 119, 243
Lefcourt, Gerald B.: as BPP lawyer, 110–12; charges against, 98; on legal profession, 66, 101; New York Law Commune by, 110–11, 118–19; prisoner defense by, 173–74; as Rudd's lawyer 328n113
Lefkowitz, Louis J., 243
leftist internationalism, 134–38
leftist lawyers. *See* radical lawyers
Legal Aid Society, 66, 201, 202
legal conferences, 15, 16, 20, 275
Legal Defense Fund (LDF), 12, 17, 19, 21, 188, 201
legal defense strategies: battlefield trauma, 154; black rage, 102, 150, 313n75; civil disobedience as, 159–60; cultural heritage in, 207–8; mental insanity, 103; morality, 90, 92, 104, 157, 159; political trials, 89–101, 114–17, 309n3; racism, 102–3, 110, 122–23, 188–89; revolutionary history, 104, 113; self-defense, 98, 108, 153, 189–90, 328n117, 330n24. *See also* jurors and jury selection process; mass defense; militant litigation; radical lawyers
legal education: criticisms of, 125–28; NLG student chapters, 47, 63, 133; people's law schools, 128–34; sexism in, 241. *See also* legal system
legalism, 2–3, 281, 288n6
legal militancy, 4. *See also* militant litigation
Legal Rights Center, 235
Legal Services Program, U.S. Office of Economic Opportunity, 66
legal system: as function of power, 73–78; homophobia within, 245–47; for incarcerated prisoners, 168–70; racism in, 10, 93–94, 104–6, 107–8, 267. *See also* legal education

May Day, 87, 88

McAlister, Elizabeth, 158

McCarthyism, 14, 32, 264, 282. *See also* anti-communist campaigns; House Un-American Activities Committee; red baiting

McClain, James, 181

McDonald, Lawrence Patton "Larry," 275

McKay, Robert B., 209

McKinney, Charles T., 111

McLuhan, H. Marshall, 97

McRae v. Califano, 244

McTernan, John T., 184

Mead, Edward A. "Ed," 340n85

Means, Russell C., 229, 234–39

Medina, Harold R., 90

Meiklejohn Civil Liberties Institute, 127

Meisenbach, Robert J., 38, 39

Melville, Samuel J. "Sam," 193–94, 270

mental insanity, as legal defense, 103, 154. *See also* legal defense strategies

Meredith, James H., 127

Metropolitan Defense Committee, 45

Meyer, Carlin, 65, 99, 124, 131, 132

Michigan Bar Association, 140

Midnight Special (publication), 203–4, 215

militant litigation, 4; defense strategies and jury selection in, 101–14, 188; defined, 89; disorderly trials, 89–101, 114–17. *See also* alternative law practices; legal defense strategies; mass defense; radical lawyers

military draft, 45–48, 90, 144, 323n31. *See also* draft resisters; Vietnam War

Military Law Project (MLP; NLG), 147–48

military lawyers, 146–56

military racism, 150, 152, 153–55

Miller, Edward S., 165–66

Miller, John J., 179

Minimizing Racism in Jury Trials (NLG), 105

Mische, George, 157, 326n79

Mississippi, 10, 19–24

Mississippi Democratic Party, 23–24

Mississippi Emergency Bail Fund, 23

Mississippi Freedom Democratic Party (MFDP), 23–24

Mitchell, John N., 165

Mobe (National Mobilization Committee to End the War in Vietnam), 55, 69

Monroe v. Pape, 292n37

Moore, Howard, Jr., 188

Moore, Richard E., 112

MOPR/IRA (International Red Aid), 4–5, 289n15

morality, as legal defense strategy, 90, 92, 104, 157, 159. *See also* legal defense strategies

Morey, R. Hunter, 20

Morgan, Mary C., 242

Moses, Robert Parris "Bob," 29

Mount Rushmore occupation attempt, 229

Movement for a Democratic Military (MDM), 145–46, 148

Moylan, Mary, 157, 326n79

Murray, George M., 58

Murtagh, John M., 110

Muslim community. *See* Black Muslims; Nation of Islam

NAACP (National Association for the Advancement of Colored People), 290n8; COFO and, 19; in Kennedy's LCDC, 26; Legal Defense Fund, 12, 173, 188, 201; on Mississippi violence, 28; offices of, 21; trial support by, 90

Naison, Mark D., 249

National Advisory Commission on Civil Disorders, 94

National Alliance against Racist and Political Repression, 189

National Association for the Advancement of Colored People. *See* NAACP

National Association of Criminal Defense Lawyers, 232

National Bar Association (NBA), 25
National Behavioral Research Center, 212
National Commission on Women's Oppression (NLG), 242
National Committee on Prisoners' Rights (ACLU), 173
National Conference of Black Lawyers (NCBL), 130, 134, 188, 201, 257, 318n63, 355n4
National Council of Churches, 22, 27
National Emergency Civil Liberties Committee (NECLC), 67, 143, 257, 302n27
National Farm Workers Association. *See* United Farm Workers
National Indian Youth Council, 229
National Labor Committee, 219, 220
National Lawyers Guild (NLG), 279–84; alternative legal education by, 128–29; on the Bakke case, 134; Black caucus of, 70; career liability by association to, 63, 68, 264–65, 277; Chicago chapter, 56–58; of the civil rights era, 12–30; COGS and, 263; in defense of antiwar movement, 46–48, 139–44, 151–54; in defense of Attica prisoners, 193, 195–99, 200–210; in defense of BPP, 250–52; in defense of Chicago DNC protestors, 55–58; in defense of Davis, 184–85, 188; in defense of labor unions, 4, 219–22; in defense of Native American activism, 228, 231–39; in defense of prisoners, 172–75, 177, 182, 183–84; in defense of racial justice protestors, 44–45, 94–97, 100–101; in defense of student protestors, 39–43, 49–54, 59, 60; in defense of Weatherman/Weather Underground, 160–62; in defense of White Panthers, 261–62; establishment and early years of, 5–8, 134, 289n16; on farmworkers' movement, 224, 225; FBI and, 271–78; federal

repression of, 264–71; gay caucus of, 246; on gay rights, 245; on grand juries, 256–27, 270; Grand Jury Defense Office, 256–57, 262, 350n54; individual political expression and membership of, 63–65, 67–69, 132; internationalism of, 134–38; lawyers' demonstrations and, 87–88; Los Angeles chapter, 135, 246; Massachusetts chapter, 240; Mass Defense Office, 60–62, 253; on militant litigation, 101–2; Military Law Project (MLP), 147–48; National Task Force on Police Crimes, 254; New York City chapter, 49–54, 77, 129, 142, 166, 215–16; organizational expansion of, 63–64; organizational transition from Old Left to New Left of, 69–73, 78; PLO and, 124; on police surveillance, 260; Prison Task Force, 215; Puerto Rico Legal Project, 137; San Francisco chapter, 173, 191, 266; Seattle chapter, 263; sexism within, 239, 240; on SLA defense, 214; student chapters of, 47, 63, 133; on undocumented workers, 226–27; Weather Underground and, 308n133; Wisconsin chapter, 129; women's caucus of, 72, 240. *See also* mass defense; radical lawyers; *names of specific lawyers*
National Mobilization Committee to End the War in Vietnam. *See* Mobe
National Organization for Women, 241
National Prison Project (ACLU), 174
National Task Force on Police Crimes (NLG), 254
National United Committee to Free Angela Davis (NUCFAD), 108, 185–86
Nation of Islam (NOI), 90, 168, 193, 329n4. *See also* Black Muslims
Native American rights and activism, 228–39, 344n84
Native American Solidarity Committee, 239
Navasky, Victor S., 11

Nazism, 67, 89, 112
Neufeld, Russell T., 204
Newark Law Collective, 221
Newark riots (1967), 131
New Bethel Baptist Church, 109, 265
New Bethel trials, 109, 267
New College, San Francisco, 131
New Deal programs, 5
The New Draft Law: A Manual for Lawyers and Counselors (NLG), 142
New Left: formation of, 37–38; on law as function of power, 74–78; policing of, 251; transition from NLG's Old Left to, 69–71. *See also* Marxism; Old Left; radical lawyers
Newton, Huey P.: on armed self-defense, 249; BPP establishment by, 54; Garry and, 80; legal defense and trials of, 81–82, 92–95, 103–4, 176, 347n15; on revolution, 213
New World Liberation Front, 214
New Year's Gang, 163–64
New York City NLG, 49–54, 77, 129, 142, 166, 215–16. *See also* National Lawyers Guild
New York City Police Department, 260
New York City Taxi Drivers Union, 221
New York Draft and Military Law Panel (NYDMLP), 143
New York Law Commune, 110–11, 118–19
New York Police Department, 250
New York University School of Law, 61, 125, 133
Nichol, Fred J., 235
Nixon, Richard M.: antiwar movement and, 153, 323n31; on conflict in Cambodia and Vietnam, 60, 144, 145; on federal grand juries, 255; Native American activism and, 230; police and counterterrorism policies of, 165, 248–49, 256, 259, 347n4. *See also* Watergate scandal
NLG. *See* National Lawyers Guild
Nolen, W. L., 176

nonviolent principles and practices, 18, 38. *See also* civil disobedience; pacifism
Nordmann, Joë, 135
North Carolina, 10
North Vietnam, 137
Novak, Robert D. S., 28
Nuremberg principles, 47, 91, 134, 139, 164

Oakland Seven trial, 91–92, 95, 156
Ochs, Phil, 98
O'Connor, Sheila, 275, 354n119
October League, 125, 245
Office of Law Enforcement Association (OLEA), 248
Oglala Sioux Civil Rights Organization, 230–31
Oglesby, Carl P., 70
Old Left, 38, 67–69, 280. *See also* Marxism; New Left; radical lawyers
Omnibus Crime Act (1968), 259, 260
Ondiga, Sekou, 328n117
Ono, Yoko, 262
"Open Letter to My Sister, Miss Angela Davis" (Baldwin), 186
Operation Abolition (film), 38
Operation CHAOS, 269
oral history, 238
Organized Crime Control Act (1970), 255
Oswald, Russell G., 194, 195, 199, 201, 335n4
Otis, Sheldon, 188, 351n76

Pacific Counseling Service (PCS), 153, 156
pacifism, 18, 46, 95, 289n10. *See also* antiwar movement; civil disobedience; nonviolent principles and practices
Palestine Liberation Organization, 138
Panther 21 case, 110, 111–13. *See also* Black Panther Party

Panther Six case, 124. *See also* Black Panther Party

parenting cases, 246–47, 346n118

Park, James W., 265

Parks, Rosa L. McCauley, 160

passive resistance, 38. *See also* civil disobedience; nonviolent principles and practices

Patterson, William L., 176

peace activism. *See* antiwar movement; civil disobedience

Peace and Freedom Party, 93, 310n21

Pearlman, Lise, 82, 190

Peck, E. Gregory, 158

Pecora, Ferdinand, 289n17

Peltier, Leonard, 239

Penn, William, 113

People's Church occupation (1969), 252–53

Peoples College of Law, 130–31

People's Law Office (PLO), 114, 123–24, 165, 211, 271, 273

people's law schools, 128–34. *See also* legal system

Pernasalice, Charles J., 207, 208

Peterman, Sidney, 153

Philippines, 152, 153, 156

Phillips, George W., 92

Picasso, Pablo, 178, 187

Pinell, Hugo, 217

Pine Ridge Reservation, South Dakota, 230–31, 232, 344n84

Plamondon, Lawrence "Pun," 261

Planned Parenthood, 244

Pochoda, Daniel "Dan," 203

police brutality: at Attica prison, 199–200; against Black Americans, 44, 49; disorderly trial on, 90; policing the police in prevention of, 251; radical lawyers on, 254; against student protestors, 38–39, 59, 61, 62, 65. *See also* racism

police surveillance. *See* surveillance

policing: of BPP, 249–51; Johnson on, 248; of mass demonstrations, 47; in Mississippi, 20; Nixon on, 165, 248–49, 256, 259, 347n4; of student protests, 51–52, 59

political trials, 89–101, 114–17, 309n3. *See also* legal defense strategies

Pomerantz, Abraham L., 134

Popper, Martin, 29, 135, 295n108

Port Huron Statement, 45

post-traumatic stress disorder, 154

Potter, Paul, 45

Powell, Lewis F., Jr., 260

Power, Katherine A., 258

Prairie Fire (publication), 165

Prairie Fire Distribution Committee, 165

Presidio, San Francisco military jail, 149–50

prisoner defense, 169, 172–84. *See also* incarceration; *names of specific prisoners*

prisoner rights and conditions, 168–70, 174, 179–80, 191–92, 193, 329n19. *See also* incarceration

prisoner segregation, 210–12. *See also* prisoner rights and conditions

Prisoners' Rights Committee (Brooklyn Law School), 174

Prison Law Collective, 191

Prison Law Project, 190–91

prison protests and revolts, 168–72, 193–94, 213. *See also* Attica prison rebellion; Jackson, George L.

prison reform, 212–13, 339n69

Prison Task Force (NLG), 215

Procunier, Raymond K., 265

Progressive Party, 72

Project on Political Surveillance (ACLU), 159

Puerto Rican Socialist Party (PRSP), 137

Puerto Rico, 137

Puerto Rico Legal Project (NLG), 137

pulpwood industry, 221–22

Quinn, William E., 194, 197

United Prisoners Union, 171

United States of America, Plaintiff, v. David T. Dellinger et al. Defendants No. 69 Crim. 180. See Chicago Eight trial

United Steelworkers of America (USWA), 220–21

Universal Declaration of Human Rights, 135

University of Michigan Law School, 127

U.S. Constitution: First Amendment, 16, 67, 90, 150, 151, 244, 260, 277; Fourth Amendment, 165, 261, 277; Fifth Amendment, 244, 255, 261, 267; Sixth Amendment, 104, 271; Fourteenth Amendment, 34, 104, 292n37

U.S. Department of Justice, 11, 29, 101, 107, 255, 349n47

U.S. Department of the Interior, 231

U.S. District Court for the Southern District of Mississippi, 22

U.S. Servicemen's Fund, 146

USS *Midway*, 155

USSR. *See* Soviet Union

U.S. Supreme Court, 33–34, 116. *See also* names of specific cases

U.S. v. U.S. District Court, 131, 261, 262

Utt, James B., 28

Valdez, Luis M., 223

Vanzetti, Bartolomeo, 4, 67, 307n114, 309n3

Venceremos Brigade, 135, 213, 275

Vergès, Jacques, 309n8

Vietnam Day Committee (VDC), 45–46, 156

Vietnam Summer West Side Project, 141

Vietnam War, 44, 45–48, 60, 137, 162. *See also* antiwar movement

Virginia, 10, 17

VISTA (Volunteers in Service to America), 66

voir dire, 104, 107, 235. *See also* jurors and jury selection process

voter intimidation and suppression, 24

voter registration, 10, 19–20, 29

Walker, Daniel, 57

Walker, Doris B., 41, 72, 78, 188, 297n14

Walker, Wyatt T., 195

Wallace, George C., 218

Walsh, Frank P., 5

Waltzer, Bruce C., 15–17

War Resisters League, 141

Watergate scandal, 159, 233, 236, 255, 256. *See also* Nixon, Richard M.

Watts riots (1965), 44

Weather Underground (formerly Weatherman): domestic terrorism by, 112–13, 171, 327n101; FBI on, 165, 308n133; formation of, 68; grand juries and, 257–58; legal defense and trials of, 84–85, 124, 160–66, 256; names of, 303n35. *See also* Students for a Democratic Society

Weinberg, Doron, 121

Weinberg, Jack, 40, 93

Weiner, Lee, 95, 96

Weinglass, Leonard I., 96, 99, 104, 130, 178, 184, 328n119

Weinrib, Laura M., 66

Weinstein, Hannah, 112

White Panthers, 261

white privilege, 278

Wicker, Thomas Grey "Tom," 156, 195

Wiesenberg, Peggy A., 245

Wilkerson, Cathlyn Platt "Cathy," 161, 328n113

Willard, Marcel, 309n6

Williams, Evelyn, 166

Wilson, Richard A., 230, 238

Wisconsin NLG, 129. *See also* National Lawyers Guild

Wobblies (IWW), 4, 175, 323n30

Wolfe, Thomas Kennerly, Jr., "Tom," 112

CPSIA information can be obtained
at www.ICGtesting.com
Printed in the USA
LVHW041912021222
734473LV00004B/542